Introduction to
ASP.NET®,
Second Edition

Kathleen Kalata

THOMSON
COURSE TECHNOLOGY

Australia • Canada • Mexico • Singapore • Spain • United Kingdom • United States

Introduction to
ASP.NET®,
Second Edition

Kathleen Kalata

THOMSON
™
COURSE TECHNOLOGY

Australia • Canada • Mexico • Singapore • Spain • United Kingdom • United States

Introduction to ASP.NET®, Second Edition

is published by Thomson Course Technology

Executive Editor:
Mac Mendelsohn

Senior Acquisitions Editor:
Maureen Martin

Senior Product Manager:
Tricia Boyle

Production Editor:
Philippa Lehar

Development Editor:
Jill Batistick

Marketing Manager:
Brian Berkeley

Manufacturing Coordinator:
Laura Burns

Associate Product Manager:
Sarah Santoro

Editorial Assistant:
Jennifer Smith

Composition House:
GEX Publishing Services

Quality Assurance Testers:
Shawn Day, Chris Scriver

Cover Designers:
Jeanne Wilcox, Steve Deschene

Proofreader:
Harold Johnson

Indexer:
Alexandra Nickerson

ISBN: 0-619-21685-9 [Student Edition]

ISBN: 0-619-21774-X [Instructor Edition]

BRIEF Contents

TABLE OF
Contents

Preface

Introduction to ASP.NET, Second Edition will familiarize you with ways to create dynamic Web applications using server-side programming technologies. A well-rounded Internet programmer needs to be able to integrate server technologies to produce Web applications that not only interact with visitors, but also integrate other computer applications.

Web sites today need to validate form data, as well as provide ways of interacting with visitors. In the past, you might have used JavaScript to create client-side scripts. You may have worried about which browser application and browser version would support your Web site. Today, with the wide range of Internet-enabled devices, Internet applications must support devices such as mobile phones and hand-held devices that do not support JavaScript. Your challenge is to create applications that can be used in a variety of settings and on a variety of devices. With Visual Studio .NET you can create ASP.NET Web applications that are portable. These applications can be displayed on a simple hand-held device, or in the latest browser.

In the early days of the World Wide Web, a company might have created a Web presence consisting of a few Web pages that contained general information about the company. Today, companies are building Web applications to manage and deliver information to their customers and business partners. They are using databases to store, retrieve, and display data on the Web. Although the need for business-to-business applications was recognized early, Internet programmers did not have the tools or skills to develop these types of Web sites. Large companies could afford to build custom applications, while small to medium size businesses lacked the resources to develop Internet business applications. Visual Studio .NET and ASP.NET are Microsoft's solution to building e-business applications with a new type of Internet application known as a Web Service. Web Services are built on Internet standards and allow companies to share data and build applications that communicate over the Internet. Microsoft provides tools within Visual Studio .NET and ASP.NET to build Web Services.

In this book, you will learn how to use ASP.NET to process form data from the client, and to send out e-mail from a Web page. You will also learn how ASP.NET can be used to interact with other computer applications on the server. You will learn how to use ASP.NET to read and write information to a file on the server, and how ASP.NET can also be used to build Web applications that interact with a database. Finally, you will learn how to develop Web Services and mobile Web applications.

THE INTENDED AUDIENCE

Introduction to ASP.NET, Second Edition is intended for the individual who wants to create dynamic Web applications. You should be familiar with the Windows operating system and know how to use Internet Explorer to view Web pages. A basic understanding of the Internet and HTML is recommended. No prior knowledge of programming is required. This book has been successfully used in a variety of settings including online. Students will get the most out of this book when it is used in conjunction with an instructor-led course.

This book provides background chapters on beginning programming concepts, including object-oriented programming and Visual Basic .NET, as well as the .NET Framework and the ASP.NET model. No prior knowledge of server programming is required. In later chapters, the book describes how to create Web pages that interact with a Microsoft Access database and a SQL Server database. These chapters explain relational database concepts, and use the Access database environment to upsize your database to SQL Server. No prior knowledge of database programming is required.

It is recommended that instructors structure the class presentations, course objectives, and class assignments to the level of experience of the students. Students who have a stronger background in Web programming concepts, client-side programming, Visual Basic .NET, networking, and database programming will be able to develop more complex ASP.NET Web applications than a beginner. However, students who do not have prior knowledge of these topics will be able to accomplish all of the chapter objectives and successfully perform all of the in-chapter and hands-on project exercises.

WHAT'S NEW

Introduction to ASP.NET, Second Edition updates the book for use with Visual Studio .NET Professional 2003 running on Windows XP Professional. To aid instructors, difficult topics such as software installation and database connectivity have been included in Appendix A and Appendix B. Instructors will want to refer to Appendix C to get ideas on how to organize student projects and solutions on their Web server. No major reorganization occurred within this edition, so instructors can continue to provide continuity within their course across semesters. To clarify some of the more complex topics, such as ADO.NET, security, and Web server configuration, the text has been expanded with additional samples, graphics, and screenshots. The Teaching Tools have been updated to reflect the new edition. All of the databases that the students create are included within the solution files. We have also provided text files for the stored procedures and SQL scripts to build the SQL Server Tara Store database. Instructions on how to use these files are included within the Instructor's Manual. A project assignment sheet in an HTML page is provided in the Teaching Tools. It includes hyperlinks to all of the solutions to the exercises in the book. Instructors can have students use this page to keep track of their activities or can customize this page for their own course requirements.

Students will be importing the data files only once for each chapter, saving them time and decreasing the likelihood of input errors. We have included a swooping arrow as the line continuation character to indicate to students when to continue typing on the subsequent line. We have decreased the amount of typing required in many of the exercises. In addition, all of the hyperlinks to the Microsoft-related help files use the Internet address so that students who choose not to install the MSDN documentation will still have access to the help files. Students not using Visual Studio .NET Professional 2003 may want to use one of the editors listed in Appendix E.

THE APPROACH

To facilitate the learning process, this book presents content and theory integrated with sample exercises. Each chapter includes references to additional Internet resources, as well as a summary and review questions that highlight and reinforce major concepts that were presented. The Hands-On Projects are guided activities that let you practice and reinforce the techniques presented in the chapter. They also enhance your learning experience by providing additional ways to apply your knowledge in new situations. At the end of each chapter, there are several Case Projects that allow you to use the skills that you have learned in the chapter to solve real world problems.

The examples provided in each chapter were developed to provide you with the opportunity to practice the skills discussed within the chapter. They are not dependent upon successful completion of the previous chapter. Therefore, you can always move ahead to another chapter, while still reviewing content presented in a previous chapter.

The approach and sequence of topics was chosen based upon experience teaching ASP.NET in the classroom. Beginning ASP.NET developers need to have a strong grasp of the basic concepts. They need to see a variety of techniques that are used in real-world applications. In this book, a layering approach is integrated within the chapters. Instead of jumping into Web databases, this book begins with form processing and validation. Then, it moves to binding data using controls and data structures such as ArrayLists and HashTables. In later chapters students take another step to bind to data objects such as the DataReader and DataSet. Then, they extract this knowledge to build a data component in Visual Basic .NET. Finally, they expose their Web database application as a Web Service. By using this layered approach, students build upon the knowledge that they learned in previous chapters. This helps them review the information as well as focusing on learning new concepts and skills.

There are several ways to accomplish the same task within Visual Studio .NET. This book uses several different methods to import data files, create connection strings, insert Web controls, configure Web applications, and preview Web pages. Students are presented with different techniques so that they can select the ones that they prefer.

Too much variety in a complex course tends to be difficult for students because they cannot focus on the learning objectives, and instead spend more time on assessment of the case study. Therefore, the majority of this book uses a sample fictional store called Tara Store as the focus of the hands-on activities. This is not a running case study. It provides a conceptual framework for students, so that they can focus on learning the material, but are not reading about a new company in each chapter.

OVERVIEW OF THIS BOOK

The examples, hands-on exercises, projects, and cases in this book will help you achieve the following objectives:

- Describe the architecture of the .NET Framework and the ASP.NET object model
- Create basic Web pages using ASP.NET using Visual Studio .NET
- Use Server controls to create dynamic Web applications
- Validate form data using server-side Validation controls
- Locate Internet resources that include information ASP.NET and Visual Studio .NET
- Create XML documents and transform them into XHTML using XSLT style sheets
- Become familiar with object-oriented programming and Visual Basic .NET programming techniques
- Become familiar with relational database concepts and learn how to create queries using SQL
- Create and manage databases using Microsoft Access and SQL Server
- Create dynamic Web applications that interact with a database using server-side programming
- Create reusable server components to retrieve data from SQL Server using stored procedures and Visual Basic .NET
- Configure your Web applications to optimize Web performance and minimize security risks
- Become familiar with methods to debug and troubleshoot your Web application.
- Create Web Services that allow your Web application interact with other server based applications

- Use server-side programming to process forms, send e-mail from a Web page, and read and write to files on the server

- Create Web applications that can be displayed on mobile devices

In **Chapter 1**, you will learn about the ASP.NET object model. You will also learn about the new HTML and ASP.NET Server controls, and about how Visual Basic .NET programs are integrated with ASP.NET pages. You will locate Internet resources that provide additional information on ASP.NET, and you will learn about the architecture of the .NET Framework. In **Chapter 2**, you will use the Visual Studio .NET tools to create a Web application. You will learn to create User controls to store reusable content and code. You will create ASP.NET pages using HTML Server controls. You will build cascading style sheets using the Style Builder tool. You will learn how to customize the toolbox. In **Chapter 3**, you will create ASP.NET pages with Web Server controls. You will create, validate, and process forms. You will use ASP.NET controls to bind to data lists such as ArrayLists and HashTables. In **Chapter 4**, you will learn how to enhance your Web application using additional Web Server controls. You will create XML data files, XSLT style sheets, and transform them into an XHTML page using the XML control. You will create an XML file to store your Web site banner ads, and use an AdRotator control to manage your banner ads. You will use the File Upload control to upload files to the Web Server without requiring a file transfer program. Appendix D provides additional content on Web Server controls, control hierarchy, custom controls and third party controls. **Chapter 5** explains how to program using Visual Basic .NET. You will learn basic object-oriented-programming concepts such as how to create classes, functions, and procedures. You will learn how to create code to handle server events and store data. You will use decision control structures to alter the execution order of a program and looping control structures to repeat blocks of code.

There are three chapters that focus specifically on Web databases. **Chapter 6** provides database basics. In this chapter, you will learn about the ADO.NET Framework. This chapter contains step-by-step instructions for installing the a developer version of SQL Server (MSDE) and the QuickStart sample databases and Web site. You will learn how to create database connections, create SQL Server databases, and build SQL scripts and stored procedures. You will use Access to upsize your database to SQL Server. You will also learn to use the database tools within Visual Studio .NET to create your table structures, insert data, and build SQL queries. **Chapter 7** shows you how to create data-driven Web pages. This chapter explains how to bind a Data object to various Data controls which are located within the Web page. You will also learn to work with a variety of new Data controls such as a DataGrid and Repeater. **Chapter 8** describes how to build more complex Web database applications. You will learn how to use different Data objects such as the DataReader and DataSet to retrieve data. You will learn to customize the DataGrid control to sort and filter data. You will use SQL commands to insert, modify, and delete data. You will also build reusable Visual Basic .NET components using

Visual Studio .NET to store your database logic. You will learn how to secure your SQL Server databases.

In **Chapter 9**, you will learn how to maintain state between the client and the server using the Global Application File, application variables, session variables, and cookies. You will learn to read and write cookies using the Response object. You will learn how to maintain state without cookies. You will also learn about the methods used to build secure Web sites. In **Chapter 10**, you will learn how to handle errors within your applications. You will learn to interpret error messages, and create custom error messages. You will learn how to use structured exception handling to help you capture and identify your errors. In **Chapter 11**, you will learn to create Web Services. You will describe the standards and protocols used to create Web Services. You will locate and consume third party Web Services from a Web page. In **Chapter 12**, you will learn to integrate your Web application with the file system. You will learn how to manage files and directories on the server and to store and retrieve data from a file on the server. You will learn how to send e-mail from a Web page. Finally, you will create Web pages that can be viewed on mobile devices using Mobile Server controls.

Appendix A details the software and hardware requirements, provides guidelines for installing Windows XP Professional and the Web server, and provides step-by-step instructions for installing Visual Studio .NET 2003 Professional. While Chapter 6 covers installation of the database server, Appendix B covers troubleshooting installation, configuration, and data connectivity issues. Appendix C provides detailed information working with projects and solution files, using the data and solution files, and alternative ways to configure the classroom servers. Appendix D discusses control hierarchy, Server controls, third-party controls, and custom controls. Appendix E provides information on additional applications that can be used to create ASP.NET applications, including ASP.NET WebMatrix.

FEATURES

- **Chapter Objectives:** Each chapter in this book begins with a list of the important concepts to be mastered within the chapter. This list provides you with a quick reference to the contents of the chapter as well as a useful study aid.

- **Step-By-Step Methodology:** As new concepts are presented in each chapter, tutorials are used to provide step-by-step instructions that allow you to actively apply the concepts you are learning. Many of the Hands-On Projects at the end of the chapter also provide step-by-step instruction. Students often need additional cases to apply the concepts learned in the chapter. These hands-on activities provide a great way to reinforce the material.

- **Modular Approach:** Each chapter contains exercises, Hands-On Projects, and Case Projects that are self-contained. Many of the chapters can be taught in a different scope and sequence. For example, a course in Web databases may only need to cover Chapters 1, 2, 3, 6, 7, and 8. A course in Visual Basic .NET may want to use this book to teach about Web programming and include only a subset of chapters, such as Chapters 1, 2, 3, 5, and 11. This book can be used to teach two separate courses in ASP.NET using Chapters 1 – 5 in the first course and 6 – 12 in the second course.

- **Figures and Tables:** Figures help you visualize Web-architecture components and relationships, and other basic concepts. Tables list examples of code components and their variations in a visual and readable format.

- **Tips:** Chapters contain Tips designed to provide you with practical advice and proven strategies related to the concept that being discussed. Tips also provide suggestions for resolving problems you might encounter while proceeding through the chapters.

- **Chapter Summaries:** Each chapter's text is followed by a summary of chapter concepts. These summaries provide a helpful way to recap and revisit the ideas covered in each chapter.

- **Review Questions:** End-of-chapter assessment begins with a set of approximately twenty Review Questions that reinforce the main ideas introduced in each chapter. These questions ensure that you have mastered the concepts and understand the information you have learned.

- **Hands-On Projects:** Along with conceptual explanations and step-by-step tutorials, each chapter provides Hands-On Projects related to each major topic aimed at providing you with practical experience. Some of the Hands-On Projects provide detailed instructions, while others provide less detailed instructions that require you to apply the materials presented in the current chapter with less guidance. As a result, the Hands-On Projects provide you with practice implementing Web programming in real-world situations.

- **Case Projects:** Approximately four cases are presented at the end of each chapter. These cases are designed to help you apply what you have learned in each chapter to real-world situations. They give you the opportunity to independently synthesize and evaluate information, examine potential solutions, and make recommendations, much as you would in an actual business situation.

TEACHING TOOLS

The following supplemental materials are available when this book is used in a classroom setting. All of the Teaching Tools available with this book are provided to the instructor on a single CD-ROM.

Electronic Instructor's Manual. The Instructor's Manual that accompanies this textbook includes additional instructional material to assist in class preparation, including items such as Sample Syllabi, Chapter Outlines, Technical Notes, Lecture Notes, Quick Quizzes, Teaching Tips, Discussion Topics, and Key Terms.

ExamView®. This textbook is accompanied by ExamView, a powerful testing software package that allows instructors to create and administer printed, computer (LAN-based), and Internet exams. ExamView includes hundreds of questions that correspond to the topics covered in this text, enabling students to generate detailed study guides that include page references for further review. The computer-based and Internet testing components allow students to take exams at their computers, and also save the instructor time by grading each exam automatically.

PowerPoint presentations. This book comes with Microsoft PowerPoint slides for each chapter. These are included as a teaching aid for classroom presentation, to make available to students on the network for chapter review, or to be printed for classroom distribution. Instructors can add their own slides for additional topics they introduce to the class.

Solution Files. Solutions to steps within a chapter and end-of chapter exercises are provided on the Teaching Tools CD-ROM and may also be found on the Course Technology Web site at *www.course.com*. The solutions are password protected.

Distance Learning. Thomson Course Technology is proud to present online test banks in WebCT and Blackboard to provide the most complete and dynamic learning experience possible. Instructors are encouraged to make the most of the course, both online and offline. For more information on how to access the online test bank, contact your local Thomson Course Technology sales representative.

ACKNOWLEDGMENTS

No book is written on an island. So, I would like to thank Jill Batistick, Developmental Editor, who did a phenomenal job managing the day-to-day project tasks. I would also like to thank Tricia Boyle, who had the great task of keeping us focused and on schedule! Thanks to Mac Mendelsohn, Maureen Martin, Philippa Lehar, Mirella Misiaszek, and the entire Course Technology team for making this book happen. Thank you to the

QA team: Shawn Day and Chris Scriver. They had the huge task of reading and testing every line of code in this book! Their effort has greatly improved the quality of this book. Thanks also to the reviewers who provided invaluable comments and suggestions during the development of this book: Jason Blazzard, Lewis-Clark State College; Sanjay Gosain, University of Maryland; Dan Hagen, South Seattle Community College; Patrick Paulson, Winona State University; Bonnie Ryan-Gauthier, New Brunswick Community College, Moncton; and Jamey Weare, Santa Fe Community College.

The Tara Store case study is modeled after Joy of Ireland (www.JoyOfIreland.com), which was a real brick and mortar store well known for their customer service, quality products, and vast product line. I'd like to thank the owner Mike Joy for allowing me to use the photographs of his store and products in the fictitious Tara Store. Slainte!

Thank you to my children, Christy, Vincent, and Molly, and to my other "mom", Mary Ann Kalata. Thank you to my husband John. To the whole world you may be one person but to me you are my whole world. – All my love.

I'd like to dedicate this book to my father-in-law, John Joseph Kalata, a truly inspiring man whose wisdom, courage, support, and encouragement has always been greatly appreciated. You will always be warmly remembered.

Read This Before You Begin

TO THE USER

You can use your own computer to complete the exercises, Hands-on Projects, and Case Projects in this book. To use your own computer, you will need the following:

- **Microsoft Windows XP Professional.** Your computer must be configured so that you can connect to the Internet. You must have TCP/IP software loaded on your computer. You cannot use Windows XP Home Edition because that version does not support an ASP.NET compatible Web server. You can learn more about these operating systems at *www.microsoft.com/windows*. Your login user account will need to be able to modify NTFS security permissions to folders and files and have access to administrative tools that are installed with Windows XP.

- **Internet Information Server (IIS).** The IIS Web Server is packaged with the Windows XP Professional disks. The Web server must have the FrontPage 2000 server extensions installed and configured. Appendix A discusses IIS installation, and Web server configuration is discussed throughout the book. On Windows XP Professional, the Web server can be used to host only one Web site, but it can host many subwebs and projects. To perform some of the exercises, you will need access to the IIS configuration utility called the Microsoft Management Console. You can also view additional information at *www.microsoft.com/windows2000/technologies/web/default.asp*.

- **Microsoft Visual Studio .NET Professional, Visual Studio .NET Developer, or Visual Studio .NET Enterprise Architect.** You can select the default installation. It is recommended that you install all of the documentation locally so that you do not need the CD each time you view a Help file. You should read the ReadMe file that comes with the installation disks. The entire installation requires at least three gigabytes of free disk space on your hard drive. It is important that you install Visual Studio .NET correctly; otherwise, some of the features of ASP.NET may not be available. Appendix A provides a step-by-step guide for installing Visual Studio .NET Professional 2003. You can learn more about the features of Visual Studio .NET at *http://msdn.microsoft.com/vstudio*. If you purchased your copy of the text, then you also received a 60-day trial version of Microsoft Visual Studio .NET 2003 Professional on DVD.

- **Microsoft Access XP.** You will need Access XP to create the database tables and queries and upsize your database to SQL Server. You will learn how to upsize an Access database in Chapter 6. You can learn more about the features in Access at *www.microsoft.com/office/access*.

- **Microsoft SQL Server Desktop Engine (MSDE).** MSDE is needed to create the database tables, queries, and stored procedure in SQL Server. You will learn how to install the MSDE and the database samples in Chapter 6. The MSDE 2000 is soon to be replaced with SQL Server 2005 Express, which is compatible with the exercises in this book. Alternately, you can use the full version of SQL Server. However, Visual Studio .NET Professional does not allow you to create databases, tables, or stored procedures with the full-version of SQL Server or other database server. You can perform these activities only with the MSDE. If you want to use the full version, you can create these objects within Enterprise Manager or Query Analyzer, which is installed with the full version of SQL Server. You can learn more about the features of SQL Server at *www.microsoft.com/sql/default.asp*. Instructions on installing and configuring the MSDE database server are located in the Chapter 6 data files directory. You can learn more about the features of the MSDE at *http://www.microsoft.com/sql/msde/default.asp*. Appendix B contains useful information on troubleshooting database connectivity problems with the MSDE. Your instructor may want to install the free SQL Server Web Data Administrator from *www.microsoft.com/downloads/details.aspx?FamilyID=C039A798-C57A-419E-ACBC-2A332CB7F959&displaylang=en*, which allows you to import the solution databases.

- **Student Data Files.** To complete the steps and projects in the chapters, you will need data files that have been created specifically for this book. You may obtain these files from your instructor. You may also download them from the Course Technology Web site by going to *www.course.com*, and then searching by title or ISBN. You will need a place to store your data files. The data files are named after the chapter, for example Chapter01Data, Chapter02Data, etc. Appendix C contains additional information about how to manage projects, solutions, data files, and solution files.

- **Web folder on a Web Server.** In each chapter, you will create a single project named after the chapter, for example, Chapter1, Chapter2, and Chapter3. You will be creating many files as you proceed through the tutorials, Hands-on Projects, and Case Projects within this single project. This way you will be able to manage all of your files for the chapter within a single location. Appendix C contains additional setup information for organizing Web applications on the Web server.

- **The QuickStart Web Site and .NET Framework Samples.** These samples are used to help you learn how to build Web Forms. You will learn how to install these samples in Chapter 6. If you would like to preview these samples, you can view them online at *http://samples.gotdotnet.com/quickstart/*.

A NOTE ON SYNTAX

The exercises in this book often contain code statements that the user must type in the Web page. These statements are sometimes too long to fit on one line in a book, and must be split over two lines. A swooping arrow character is used to identify when the code statement is split across two or more lines. It is important that the student type the code statement on a single line. An example of using the swooping arrow is as follows:

```
<%@ Page Language="vb" AutoEventWireup="false" ↵
Codebehind="WebForm1.aspx.vb" ↵
Inherits="TaraStore.WebForm1"%>
```

TO THE INSTRUCTOR

To complete all the exercises and chapters in this book, your users must work with a set of files, called a Data Disk, and download software from Web sites. The data files are included on the Instructor's Resource CD. They may also be obtained electronically through the Course Technology Web site at *www.course.com*. Follow the instructions in the Help file to copy the user files to your server or standalone computer. You can view the Help file using a text editor, such as WordPad or Notepad.

After the files are copied, you can make Data Disks for the users, yourself, or tell your students where to find the files so they can make their own Data Disks. Make sure the files are set up correctly by having students follow the instructions in the "To the User" section of Read This Before you Begin.

Students will require access to a Web server that supports ASP.NET Web applications. The book uses the local Web server to publish the chapter Web projects. If students use a remote Web server, they will need to either FTP their projects or use FrontPage extensions to upload their projects to the remote Web server. You should work with your network system administrator to setup permissions to your Web server and to configure Visual Studio .NET.

For example, in order for Visual Studio .NET Professional 2003 to create the Web project, the VS Developers group needs to be assigned Windows NTFS "Change" permissions to the Web folders. You can protect the Web folders by creating a student group, such as ASPStudent, and assigning that group Windows NTFS "Change" permissions to the Web folders. Another issue that you will need to address is where Visual Studio .NET will store the projects and solutions files. These files are required by Visual Studio .NET to manage your Web application. If a student works remotely, he or she will need access to these files.

These are some of the software issues that you will need to consider when setting up your course. You should thoroughly read Appendices A, B, and C before you plan your course. These appendices will provide additional information required to create remote Web projects and configure Visual Studio .NET.

COURSE TECHNOLOGY DATA FILES

You are granted a license to copy the data files to any computer or computer network used by individuals who have purchased this book.

VISIT OUR WORLD WIDE WEB SITE

Additional materials for your course may be available at the Course Technology Web site. Go to *www.course.com* and search for this book by title, author, or ISBN for more information and materials to accompany this text.

1

INTRODUCTION TO ASP.NET

In this chapter, you will:

♦ Learn about the differences between static and dynamic Web pages
♦ Identify the controls used in ASP.NET pages
♦ Describe how server-side processing occurs with ASP.NET pages
♦ Learn about the ASP.NET object programming model
♦ Identify Internet resources about ASP.NET and Visual Studio .NET
♦ Import a namespace
♦ Describe the common language runtime
♦ View an assembly

Businesses use the Internet to promote their companies or to allow customers to purchase their products online. The cost of developing and maintaining a custom e-commerce solution, such as an online store, can vary from a few thousand to millions of dollars per year. Research predicts that the majority of Internet activities in the future will be business-to-business transactions, which are often referred to as e-business. Microsoft has redesigned ASP.NET and Microsoft Visual Studio .NET to support developers who need to build both e-commerce solutions and e-business applications.

ASP.NET is a language-independent technology that is used to develop Web applications. ASP.NET enables Web developers to create a new type of business application for the Web called Web Services. Throughout this book you will learn how to use Visual Studio .NET to generate ASP.NET applications and Web Services. In this chapter, you will learn how ASP.NET processing allows you to create dynamic Web applications.

STATIC AND DYNAMIC WEB APPLICATIONS

In the first years of the World Wide Web, the Hypertext Markup Language (HTML) was the primary tool for developing Web pages. HTML generates static content that can be viewed via a browser over the Internet. Browser software interprets HTML tags and formats the output. Every time a **static** Web page is loaded in a browser, the browser displays the same content. As the Internet expanded from governments and universities to businesses and individuals, Web applications needed to become more dynamic. A **dynamic** Web application enables the user to interact with the Web application in ways that change the appearance or the content of the Web page. Examples of dynamic Web applications include shopping carts, membership databases, online catalogs, and personalized Web sites.

You cannot create dynamic Web applications using HTML alone. However, you can use many other different technologies along with HTML, including client- and server-side scripting and server-side programming. A major limitation of client-side scripting is browser dependency, because client-side scripts are executed via the browsers' scripting engines and not all browsers support all scripting languages. Another major limitation of client-side scripting is security. The client can easily view the scripts within the Web page. Server-side programs allow you to create dynamic Web applications that can process a form or manage a database. With server-based applications, you can create a secure Web site because the programs are run on the Web server. The Web server sends static HTML to the client's browser. Because the processing of the program occurs on the server, you can hide code from the client. There are several types of server-side programming technologies, including Perl CGI programming and Java programming.

Recall that Microsoft's implementation of Web server programming technology is referred to as Active Server Pages .NET (ASP.NET), which makes it easier for Web developers to create dynamic Web applications. An **Active Server Page (ASP)** is a Web page that contains server-side programming. Figure 1-1 shows how HTML Web pages are processed on the Web server.

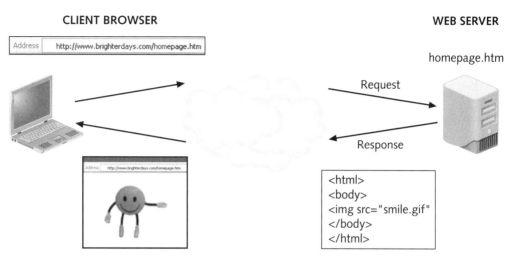

Figure 1-1   Processing a request for a Web page

The most recent version of ASP is called ASP.NET, and the two main types of Web resources created with ASP.NET applications are Web Forms and Web Services. **Web Forms** allow you to quickly develop and process forms on Web pages and develop cross-browser Web applications. Web Forms are Web pages identified with the file extension `.aspx`. Any page ending in `.aspx` is directed to the ASP.NET engine, which is located in a file named `aspnet_isapi.dll`. An example of an ASP.NET application is a shopping cart. Web Forms can be used to target any browser or device without requiring you to write a separate application for each.

Web Services are ASP.NET Web pages that contain publicly exposed code so that other applications can interact with them. Web Services are identified with the file extension `.asmx`. A company could, for example, expose the product-ordering functionality of its Web site in order to allow other Web sites to connect to this function. For each sale that originated from other Web sites, the company could pay a referral fee. You will learn how to create Web Services later in this book.

Both types of ASP.NET applications support several new features, including support for a variety of programming languages, enhanced performance, improved session management, enhanced scalability, improved error handling, tracing capability, debugging capability, simpler deployment, and multiple platforms.

WEB FORMS

Web Forms are ASP.NET pages within an ASP.NET application. The ASP.NET Web Form is separated into two logical areas, the HTML template and a collection of code behind the Web Form.

The **HTML template** usually contains the design layout, content, and controls. (*Note*: Most HTML books refer to controls as tags or elements. Within ASP.NET these are known as HTML controls.) The HTML template creates the user interface, or **presentation layer**. These controls tell the browser how to format the Web page. Although there are many controls available in ASP.NET, Web Forms can also use any of the traditional HTML controls. The HTML template is created by using a combination of HTML controls, HTML Server controls, Mobile controls, and ASP.NET controls.

HTML Server Controls

HTML Server controls are similar to HTML controls, except that they are processed by the server. In a traditional HTML page the developer creates a text box by writing `<input type="text">`. Using HTML Server controls, you only need to write `runat ="server"` to transform the HTML control into an HTML Server control. In this case, you would write `<input type="text" runat="server"/>`. When the runat property is set to server, the control is processed by the server. By transforming HTML controls to HTML Server controls, you can create server-side programs that interact with the control before it is rendered as a plain HTML control and sent to the browser. The following is a sample of an HTML Server control:

```
<input type="radio" runat="server" value="Yes"/> Yes
```

Notice in the sample that the HTML Server control ends with `/>`. In previous versions of HTML, HTML elements such as the line break required only the opening tag. However, the most recent version of HTML, known as XHTML, requires that all HTML elements be compliant with XML standards. XML is another type of markup language that can be used to build applications. One of the rules of XML is that all controls must have a closing tag, or end with `/>`. Thus, all controls that do not have a closing tag are closed in the initial tag with `/>`. The XML, HTML, and XHTML standards are maintained by the World Wide Web Consortium. For more information on XHTML, visit the World Wide Web Consortium at *www.w3c.org*.

 A common error is forgetting to specify the runat attribute for the Server control. When you refer to the control in your code behind the page, the compiler displays an error message with the message ID BC30451, and text that specifies that the control is not declared.

There are a variety of new ASP.NET Server controls, including ASP.NET Form controls, Data Validation controls, User controls, and Mobile controls. ASP.NET controls are usually identified with the prefix asp: followed by the name of the control. ASP.NET Form controls are similar to HTML Server controls. For example, the control for an ASP.NET button is written like this: `<asp:Button id="ShowBtn" runat="server" Text="Show the message." />`. Notice that the forward slash is also used with ASP.NET Form controls to indicate that there is no closing tag.

ASP.NET Form controls also have different properties than their HTML Server control counterparts. ASP.NET Form controls allow you to create controls that render HTML output and that provide more flexibility when you are creating your programs. ASP.NET Form controls can interact with client-side events such as the user clicking a button. When the event occurs, ASP.NET can trigger a script to run on the server. ASP.NET Form controls will create the HTML code.

HTML Server controls and ASP.NET Server controls use different properties to generate output. In the sample code following this paragraph, the HTML Server Label control named Message1 contains an InnerHTML property that is used to assign the value to an HTML tag. However, the ASP Server Label control named Message2 uses the Text property to assign the value to the HTML tag.

```
Message1.InnerHTML = "Product 1"
Message2.Text = "Product 2"
```

 It is very important that you look at the browser source code of each ASP.NET page that you create in order to understand what the Web server is sending to the browser. ASP.NET code is never sent to the browser. Only HTML tags, along with client-side scripts, are sent to the browser. Many errors are related to the syntax of the HTML code, such as a missing closing tag or a missing quotation mark, that is sent to the browser. By viewing the source code in the browser, you can more quickly locate the HTML syntax errors. Sometimes it's also useful to paste the code into an editor such as FrontPage XP, which can help you locate and identify HTML errors quickly.

Data Validation controls are a series of controls that validate form data without extensive JavaScript programming; they are supported in both Internet Explorer and Netscape Navigator. Data Validation controls also have some unique properties and methods.

User controls are external files that can be included within other Web Forms. User controls allow you to reuse code across multiple files. For example, you can create a User control that displays the top ten music selections this week. You can use this control on the home page and on the product category pages. User controls are often used to create self-contained code, headers, menus, and footers. User controls replace the functionality of ASP server-side include pages. They are identified with the file extension `.ascx`. When the User control is inserted into the Web page, the control must be assigned a custom prefix instead of ASP.

Mobile controls are a series of controls that provide form functionality within wireless and mobile devices. The rendering of the user interface occurs automatically, depending upon which device is used.

Literal controls are page content that is not assigned to a specific HTML control. For example, any text sent to the browser is a Literal control. Literal controls can be used to send a combination of HTML tags and text to the browser.

The Web developer uses these new controls to build Web pages. Figure 1-2 shows some of the Server controls in the Visual Studio .NET Toolbox. You will learn how to use each of these types of controls in this book.

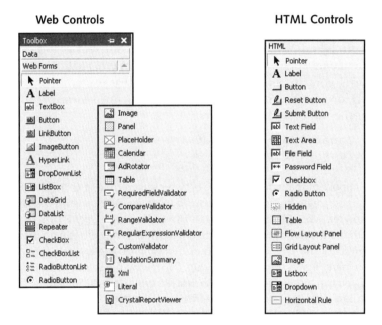

Figure 1-2 Server controls within Visual Studio .NET

The Code Behind the Page

The Web Form contains the HTML controls, client-side scripts, and Server controls. In previous versions of ASP, the server scripts were written within the Web page. With Web Forms, the server programs are written in a separate file known as the code behind the page. The **code behind the page** contains programming routines that are directly related to the various Server controls on the Web Form. Only Server controls can interact with the code behind the page.

The code behind the page may be written in any ASP.NET-compatible language, including Visual Basic .NET, C#, Perl, and J#. The code behind the page has the same filename as the Web Form. However, the file extension varies with the programming language used. The filename for the code behind the page has the extension `.vb` if the code is written in Visual Basic .NET. (In this book, you will use Visual Basic .NET to create the code behind the page.) If the page is written in C#, the file has the extension `.cs`.

The location of the code behind the page is determined by a property that is set on the first line in the page, using the @Page directive. The **@Page** directive allows you to set the default properties for the entire page. There are many properties that can be set using the @Page directive, as you will learn later in this book. In the sample code following this paragraph, the default Language property is set to vb to indicate that the code behind the page is written in Visual Basic .NET. The **CodeBehind** property indicates that the code behind the page is located in a file named WebForm1.vb. The **Inherits** property indicates that the code behind the page inherits the page class named TaraStore.WebForm1. This class contains the compiled code for the entire page.

```
<%@Page Language="vb" Codebehind="WebForm1.vb"  ↵
Inherits="TaraStore.WebForm1"%>
```

 The preceding code should be displayed on one line as indicated by the symbol ↵. This symbol is used throughout this book to identify lines of code that are longer than one line of printed text.

The compiled code behind the page is the class definition for the page. A **class** is a named logical grouping of code. The **class definition** contains the functions, methods, and properties that belong to that class. In Visual Studio .NET, the process of compiling a class is called **building**. When you build the application, you compile the code into an executable file.

When you use Visual Studio .NET to create your application, Visual Studio .NET compiles the code behind the page into an executable file and places the file in the `bin` directory. As you can see in Figure 1-3, the code behind the page is compiled into a class and cached on the Web server. When there is a change in the page class file, the page class is recompiled, and cached again.

There are several reasons for separating the server code and the page. For example, assume that you place an HTML Server control button on a page. When the user clicks the button, an event signals the server that the event occurred. An event handler named OnServerClick is called. The code for the OnServerClick event handler is located in the code behind the page. The OnServerClick event handler could display a message in the Web page. By separating the programming logic and the presentation layer, the application becomes easier to maintain. When the message changes, you need only change it within the logic code behind the page. You don't need to modify the page itself.

 In this book, you will use Visual Studio .NET to create all of your ASP.NET applications. However, some programmers prefer to create their ASP.NET templates and the code behind the page in a single file and not use Visual Studio .NET. In this situation, there is only one ASP.NET file, and the entire page is compiled at runtime. If you do not use Visual Studio .NET to manage your projects, and instead create the ASP.NET template and the code behind the page in a text editor, then you must compile your components using a command-line compiler. You must also set the Web server permissions of your `bin` directory to execute and the ASP.NET directories to read and script.

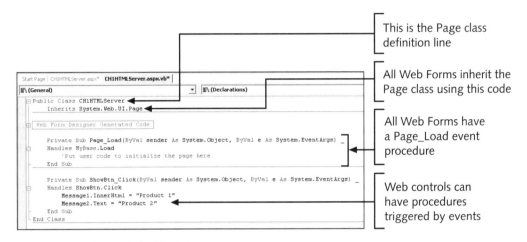

Figure 1-3 labels (right side):
- This is the Page class definition line
- All Web Forms inherit the Page class using this code
- All Web Forms have a Page_Load event procedure
- Web controls can have procedures triggered by events

Figure 1-3   The code behind the page

Postback

When a user fills out a form and clicks the Submit button, the data is sent to the Web server for processing. If the user enters an invalid value, the form is redisplayed to the client. It is helpful to redisplay the values that the user entered. Maintaining this information across browser requests is known as **maintaining state**. The server code must retrieve the values from the initial page and merge them with the code for the subsequent page.

Server controls allow you to send data to the browser without writing the data-gathering and data-rendering code. By default, the Server control automatically supports the posting of data back into the form, a process known as **postback**. When the user enters the data into a text box on a form, the server collects the value and rerenders the text box with the data.

A hidden form field named **_ViewState** is a very long string that contains information required to maintain the form data across multiple page requests. The Web server decodes this encoded string. Therefore, the value of _ViewState changes each time the form is reposted back to the server. Then, the values that are stored with the page remain with the page, even if it is redirected to a different Web server. In an enterprise network, it is common to have a group of Web servers called a WebFarm. In a WebFarm, when one server stops, the clients are redirected to another server. By storing the information on the client and not on the server, you enable the information to travel with the client across page requests and across servers. In Figure 1-4, the _ViewState hidden field demonstrates how postback maintains state. You will learn more about how state management works later in this book.

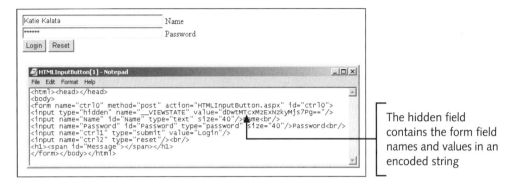

The hidden field contains the form field names and values in an encoded string

Figure 1-4   Postback data using the _ViewState hidden field

The Web page does not have to support the postback feature. You can turn the property on or off by setting the EnableViewState property to true or false within the @Page directive. You can also turn the EnableViewState property on or off by setting the property for any individual Server control. You can also do it for the entire application by setting the property in the application configuration files. In the following sample code, the property is turned off for the entire page for all Server controls:

```
<%@ Page EnableViewState="false" %>
```

Page Class Events

All Web pages created with ASP.NET are objects based upon the Page class in the .NET environment. The **Page class** consists of a variety of methods, functions, and properties that can be accessed within the code behind the page. The first time a page is requested by a client, a series of page events occurs. As shown in Figure 1-5, the first page event is the **Page_Init** event, which initializes the page control hierarchy.

After the page control hierarchy is initialized, the Page_Load event loads any Server controls. You can access the Page_Load event handler within code behind the page. When the Page_Load event occurs, all controls on the page are loaded into memory. You can place code that you want to execute when the page opens in the Page_Load event handler. The Page_Load event occurs every time the page is executed.

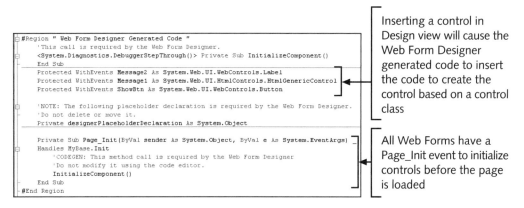

```
#Region " Web Form Designer Generated Code "
    'This call is required by the Web Form Designer.
    <System.Diagnostics.DebuggerStepThrough()> Private Sub InitializeComponent()
    End Sub
    Protected WithEvents Message2 As System.Web.UI.WebControls.Label
    Protected WithEvents Message1 As System.Web.UI.HtmlControls.HtmlGenericControl
    Protected WithEvents ShowBtn As System.Web.UI.WebControls.Button

    'NOTE: The following placeholder declaration is required by the Web Form Designer.
    'Do not delete or move it.
    Private designerPlaceholderDeclaration As System.Object

    Private Sub Page_Init(ByVal sender As System.Object, ByVal e As System.EventArgs)
    Handles MyBase.Init
        'CODEGEN: This method call is required by the Web Form Designer
        'Do not modify it using the code editor.
        InitializeComponent()
    End Sub
#End Region
```

Inserting a control in Design view will cause the Web Form Designer generated code to insert the code to create the control based on a control class

All Web Forms have a Page_Init event to initialize controls before the page is loaded

Figure 1-5   Page class event cycle

In the sample code following this paragraph, a message is displayed when the Page_Load event occurs. In Visual Basic .NET, the event handler is known as a **procedure**. When you create a procedure, you must identify the beginning of the procedure with the keyword **Sub**, and the ending with the keywords **End Sub**. You also need to indicate if any values, known as **parameters**, are passed to the procedures. (*Note*: You will learn how to create procedures and pass parameters in Chapter 2.)

```
Sub Page_Load(sender As Object, e As EventArgs)
    Message.InnerHtml = "Welcome!"
End Sub
```

Within the Page class you can define specific **Server control events**, which occur when the page is posted back to the server. Control events can be **action events**, such as the click event for a Server Button control, or **change events**, such as when the value of a server Text control changes. For example, if a user clicks an HTML Server Button control, then you can execute code in the OnServerClick event handler. Server control events are executed only when the event related to the Server control occurs. In the following sample code, the page contains an HTML Server Button control named MyBtn and a span tag named Message:

```
<input type="button" value="Click me!" id="MyBtn"
runat="server" OnServerClick="MyBtn_Click">
<h1><span id="Message" runat=server/></h1>
```

When the page first opens, no message would be displayed. However, when the user clicks the button, an OnServerClick event handler is called. The event handler calls a procedure named MyBtn_Click. In the code behind the page, the OnServerClick event handler can send a message back to the browser. Figure 1-6 shows the results of the server code. Notice that the message in the span tag has changed. Also notice how the client page contains client-side code written in JavaScript. The client-side JavaScript is created by the server to trigger the event that returns a server click event, which is processed on the server. That is how the server knows that the click event has occurred in the browser. (*Note*: If there are client- and server-side OnClick event handlers, the server-side OnClick event handler takes precedence.)

```
Sub MyBtn_Click(sender As Object, E as EventArgs)
    Message.InnerHtml = "You clicked me!"
End Sub
```

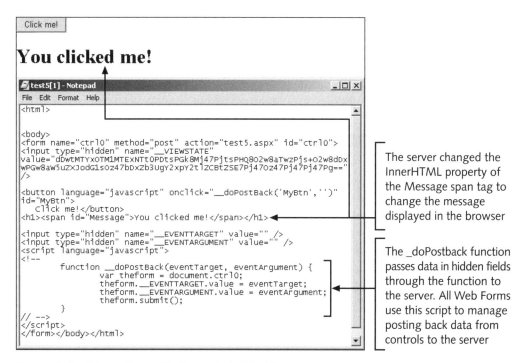

Figure 1-6   Interacting with the code behind the page

You will most likely add your server code to the Page_Load event handler, event procedures, and functions. However, there are additional page events, such as Page_CommittTransaction and Page_AbortTransaction. These events are used in combination to define a sequential series of events that together are called a **transaction**. In a transaction, all events must occur; otherwise, all events are rolled back to their original state.

The **Page_PreRender** event occurs immediately before the control hierarchy is rendered and sent to the browser. Although the page contains Server controls, the client sees only the rendered Client controls, such as HTML and client script. Not all controls need to be rendered to the client. For example, you may not want to render a control to the browser until the user completes the login form correctly.

If you want to view the order in which the Server controls are rendered to the Web page, turn on the Trace feature. The **Trace** feature allows you to view the page controls, the order in which they are loaded, and the time it takes to load the control. To turn on the Trace feature, set the Trace property for the page to true, as shown in this sample code:

```
<%@ Page trace = "true" %>
```

When the trace feature has been turned on, the page is displayed along with the Page class Control Tree. Figure 1-7 shows the Page class Control Tree. Notice how the type of control is listed, along with the time it takes to load each control. The ID is a property that is assigned to the Server control in the Web page. If no ID is provided for the Server control, a generic ID value is assigned. The Control Tree uses indentation to illustrate how the objects are organized within the page class hierarchy.

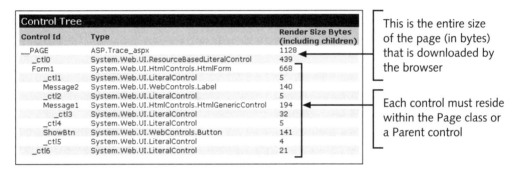

Figure 1-7   The Page class Control Tree

When the page unloads, the **Page_Unload** event occurs, and the page is removed from the server's memory. You can use the Page_Unload event handler to close database connections, close files, and release any programming variables or objects. In the following sample code, the database connection is closed when the page is unloaded:

```
Sub Page_UnLoad(sender As Object, e As EventArgs)
   objCn.Close
End Sub
```

It is a common programming practice to release programming variables or objects after they have been used. However, in the .NET framework, the server collects any unused memory assigned to objects that are no longer referenced in your program. It then reconfigures the memory storage to free the memory. Although you do not have to release your variables and objects, it is still a recommended programming practice.

Using ASP.NET to Access Built-In Web Server Objects

ASP.NET pages have access to objects that are built into the Web server, along with their properties and methods. You can access built-in ASP.NET objects in the code behind the page. The following is a list of some of those built-in objects:

- *HTTPRequest*—Used to access information that is passed from the client's browser to the Web server. For example, the Request object retrieves information that a user entered into a form. The names and values are stored within a collection that can be accessed from the code behind the page. The HTTPRequest object is mapped directly to the Request property of the Page object. Although you can access this data in other ways, it is much easier to access the Request object directly using the Page object.

- *HTTPResponse*—Used to send information from the Web server to the client's browser. For example, the Response object redirects the user to another Web page. The HTTPResponse object is mapped directly to the Response property of the Page object. Although you can access this data in other ways, it is much easier to access the Response object directly using the Page object.

- *Session*—Used to share information between a single client and the Web server. The Session object stores data during the course of a session. For example, the name of the visitor can be shared as a session variable. When the user closes the browser, the session doesn't end, and the session variables are no longer referencable. The session can also end when the default session timeout is reached.

- *Application*—Allows developers to treat a folder of Web pages as a single application, which means that information, such as the name of the application or the total number of visitors on the Web site, can be shared among all the users of an ASP application. The capacity to treat a collection of pages as a single application greatly broadens the possibilities for application development.

The Page.Request Property

The Page object contains a Request property. When a browser sends a request for a Web page to the Web server, the Web server receives the request and some additional information in the header. The **header** is a portion of the data packet that includes information that determines how and where to send the file. The header includes the date and time, the type of request (Get or Post), the page requested, and the HTTP version. Additional information includes the default language, the referring page, the IP address of the client, the cookies associated with that domain, and the user agent. The **user agent** can be used to identify the client software. If the client has a certificate, the values from the certificate are also sent with the request. This information can be retrieved from the header as server variables or with the Request property. The Request property allows you to retrieve any information sent by the browser, including the names and values of form fields and the server variables. Because the Request property belongs to the Page class, you can refer to the Request property using `Page.Request.PropertyName` or `Request.PropertyName`.

In the sample code following this paragraph, three server variables are written to the browser. Server variables are variables that are passed in the header. This example displays the physical path to the file using Request.PhysicalPath. The page also displays the IP address of the client, and the domain name of the previous page that contained the link to the current page. Notice that the **Response.Write** method is used to write out the content to the browser. In the next section, you will learn more about the Response property.

```
Response.Write(Request.PhysicalPath)
Response.Write(Request.UserHostAddress)
Response.Write(Request.UrlReferrer.Host)
```

The Request property can also provide you access to additional properties. For example, the user agent provides a string that can be used to detect the browser version. However, the string must be parsed to locate the browser application name and version. With the Browser property, you can directly access the browser application's name and version without the user agent. The following sample code uses the Browser property to display the client browser's version and then writes out the short name of the browser application, the version number, and the platform:

```
Response.Write(Request.Browser.Browser)
Response.Write(Request.Browser.Version)
Response.Write(Request.Browser.Platform)
```

The Request property provides access to the form field names and values. If there is a form on the page, the form field name and value pairs are sent to the Web server. If the form method is GET, then the form is sent appended to the URL requested as a single string called the **QueryString**. If the form method is POST, it is sent as part of the HTTP request body. The Request property contains a Form collection and QueryString collection that allow you to collect form information from both methods. In the sample code following this paragraph, a QueryString containing the values of two form fields, name and topic, is attached to the URL. The QueryString is separated from the URL by a question mark.

```
http://www.tarastore.com/index.aspx?name=katie&topic=asp
```

The following code creates a text box named password and a button named MyBtn:

```
<span id="Message" runat="server">    ↵
Please enter your password</span>
<input id="PWD" type="password"
size="8" runat="server"><br />
<input id="MyBtn" type="submit" value="Login"
OnServerClick="MyBtn_Click" runat="server"/>
```

This page uses the Request property to retrieve information from the form field and displays the value, as follows:

```
Response.Write(Request.Form("PWD"))
```

A simpler method for retrieving the value from a form field is to access the value properties of the form field directly. The property name that you use to access the value is different for each type of Server control. However, this method works only with Server controls. If you use a simple HTML control, you must request the form or QueryString collection to retrieve the form field values. For the exercises in this book, you will work primarily with Server controls and can, therefore, use the Value property to access the value of a particular form field directly.

To retrieve the value of the form field, you can create an event handler that processes the form, as shown in the code example following this paragraph and as further illustrated in Figure 1-8. For example, the event handler could be the event handler for the Submit button. When the user clicks the Submit button, the event handler is called. Then, in the code behind the page, you retrieve the value of the text box in the event handler. If the value of the submitted password is correct, the page displays a welcome message. (*Note*: To detect if the value matches a string, such as Course, you need to put the string in quotation marks. You can use an If-Then-Else statement to structure your code. The Then keyword must be on the same line as the If keyword. The code following the keyword Then is executed only if the password matches. The code following the keyword Else is executed if the password does not match.) Otherwise, if the password does not match, the page displays a message instructing the user to try again.

```
Private Sub MyBtn_ServerClick(ByVal sender As System.Object,
ByVal e As System.EventArgs) Handles MyBtn.ServerClick
   If (PWD.Value = "Course") Then
      Message.InnerHtml = "Welcome!"
   Else
      Message.InnerHtml = "Try again!"
   End If
End Sub
```

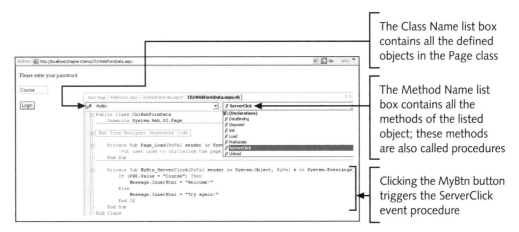

The Class Name list box contains all the defined objects in the Page class

The Method Name list box contains all the methods of the listed object; these methods are also called procedures

Clicking the MyBtn button triggers the ServerClick event procedure

Figure 1-8   Retrieving form values and server variables

You can obtain information about the members of the Request property by going to the Visual Studio .NET documentation at *http://msdn.microsoft.com/ library/en-us/cpref/html/frlrfsystemwebuipageclassrequesttopic.asp*.

The Page.Response Property

The Page object also contains a Response property. The Response object is used to send information to the browser. Some of this information identifies the server and server properties. For example, the IP address of the server and the name and version number of the Web server software are sent to the client. The Cookies collection is used to send cookies to the browser. A status code is sent to indicate whether the browser request was successful or encountered an error.

The Response object has several methods, such as Write and WriteFile. The **Write method** allows you to send a string to the browser. You can send text, HTML, and client script to the browser using the Write method. You can use a variable or expression to store the string. Then, you can write out the contents of the variable with the Write method. The **WriteFile method** allows you to send the entire contents of a text file to the Web page. In the code example following this paragraph, the Write method is used to write out a string and a variable that contains a string. The WriteFile method is used to write the entire contents of a file named copyright.txt to the Web page.

```
Response.Write("Copyright by TaraStore<br/>")
Dim strMessage as String = "Copyright by TaraStore<br/>"
Response.Write(strMessage)
Response.WriteFile("c:\copyright.txt")
```

The Response object allows you to redirect the browser to another page. The Response object also allows you to hold the contents of the page in an area of memory called the **buffer** until you send the page. The methods and properties of the Response object allow you to control the caching of content from the ASP page. **Caching** is the process by which a page is generated and stored on the server. This copy of the page is known as a cached page. If you enable caching on the Web server, the next time the user requests the page, the cached copy is sent. All data sent to the browser is sent using the Response object either via the HTTPResponse object or via the Response property. The sample code following this paragraph shows how to redirect the visitor to another page. Because this redirection occurs on the server, the visitor never knows that he or she has been been redirected to a new page.

```
Response.Redirect("http://www.course.com/")
```

LOCATING YOUR ASP.NET APPLICATION

You can only view ASP.NET Web pages on a Web server that supports ASP.NET. A local Web server allows you to preview ASP applications on the desktop without connecting to the Internet. In this book, you use the Microsoft Internet Information Server (IIS), which comes with Windows 2000 Professional, Windows 2000 Server, and Windows XP Professional. When you install the Web server software, it creates a default directory for

1

the root Web site at `C:\Inetpub\wwwroot`. The root Web site is mapped as **localhost**. Therefore, you can reach the Web site with a browser by typing in *http://localhost/*. If you enter this URL in the browser, the IIS help and documentation windows appear. (*Note*: You can stop this by renaming the default.aspx page in the wwwroot folder default_old.aspx.)

When you create your ASP.NET Web applications in Visual Studio .NET, the program places a folder in the root directory, named after your application. (*Note*: Don't put blank spaces in the names of the projects you create. The name is used in the URL for the application. Some browsers do not recognize blank spaces in URLs.) When you have finished creating your applications, you can deploy them to a production Web server on the Internet. To **deploy** a Web application, you copy all of the Web application files to a live Web server on the Internet. You will learn how to deploy your application in a later chapter.

If you do not have your own Web server, you can use a third-party Web server. There are several hosting service providers that are currently supporting ASP.NET applications. Brinkster (*www.brinkster.com*), EraServer (*www.eraserver.com*), and Media3 (*www.media3.com*) all support ASP.NET applications. If you choose to set up an account with an ISP, you may have to write your ASP.NET pages with the ASP.NET code and the code behind the page all within the same file. Some providers may not allow you access to a bin directory either. Some providers require you to use their file transfer software, while others require you to use your own File Transfer Protocol (FTP) software to upload your Web pages to the Web site. WS_FTP by Ipswitch (*www.ipswitch.com*) is a commonly used file transfer program. You can also locate other FTP programs through Tucows (*www.tucows.com*). Currently, if you use Media3, you can use the deployment features within Visual Studio .NET to deploy your application directly to the Media3 Web server.

WEB SERVICES

Web Services allow you to expose part or all of your programs over the Internet. For example, if your business partner is Course Technology and you want to query that company's product catalog from your Web site, you could post a link with the query that sends the user to Course Technology's Search Page. A controversial method is to screen scrape the site. **Screen scraping** a Web site is the process of using a program to view a Web site and capture the source code. To do this, the programmer has to create an application that parses the HTML from the data and a program that integrates the new data into the Web site.

A better solution is for Course Technology to provide a Web Service to its catalog application. Then you can use the Catalog Web Service within your own Web applications. Course Technology could limit access to the Catalog Web Service; it could expose the entire program as a Web Service or only certain parts of the catalog application. Once the catalog application is public, you can use Visual Studio .NET tools such as Server Explorer to view the Web Services available from Course Technology. Currently, there is a public registry known as UDDI that contains registered public Web Services. You can learn more about UDDI at *www.microsoft.com/uddi*. You can also locate more Web Services at *www.xmethods.com*.

In Visual Studio .NET, the Web Services source file is contained in a file that has the extension **.asmx**. When a Web Service is created in Visual Studio .NET, a discovery file containing information on how to interact with the Web Service, and how to format and send data to the Web Service, is created. Because Web Services are built using open standards, Web Services are supported across applications and platforms. For example, a Web Service could be accessed from a Windows application, a Web application, or a mobile application. The client accessing the Web Service might be on a Windows system, a UNIX system, or a mobile device.

Web Services are used to create business-to-business applications. For example, in Figure 1-9 Tara Store has a Web Service that exposes the product-ordering functions within its inventory application to its business partners and distributors. With it, visitors can view the product catalog, determine which products are in stock, and order products directly from Tara Store, or from one of its partners or distributors. You will learn more about Web Services in a later chapter.

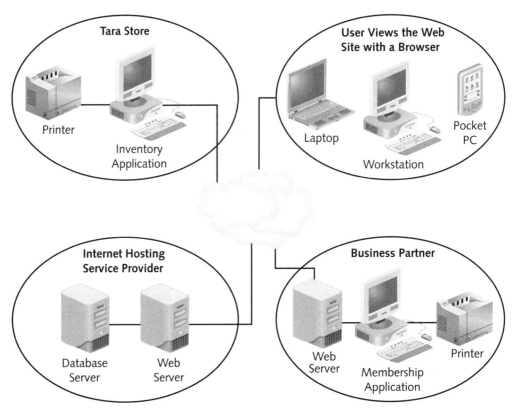

Figure 1-9   The Tara Store Web Service

THE .NET FRAMEWORK

ASP.NET is used to develop dynamic Web applications within the .NET Framework. In ASP.NET, the Page class is a class in the .NET Framework. This means that the page code must conform to the .NET Framework standards. Therefore, it is important to understand the basics of the Page class hierarchy and the .NET Framework. The .NET Framework consists of a common language runtime (CLR) and a hierarchical set of Base Class Libraries (BCL). As shown in Figure 1-10, the **.NET Framework** is the architectural model for creating programs that interface with the operating system and the base class libraries.

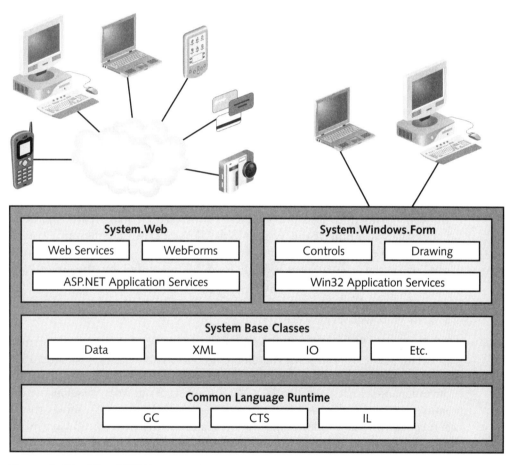

Figure 1-10   The .NET Framework

The Base Class Libraries

The **base class libraries** are commonly used code that provide general functions that can be accessed from any application. The base class libraries are organized into logical groupings of code called **namespaces**. These compiled .NET programs and base class libraries are called **assemblies**.

Microsoft has created a large group of these code libraries known as the .NET base class libraries. These libraries contain fundamental code structures and methods that allow you to communicate with the operating system software and other applications. The actual library of code is located in one or more dynamic link library files. For example, the code for accessing a database object is stored in the database class library, which is located in the file called System.Data.dll. By storing commonly used code in libraries, the code can be reused across applications.

Namespace

A namespace is a hierarchical way to identify types in .NET. The System namespace is at the top of the namespace hierarchy, and all classes inherit from it. Because all classes inherit the System class, you can refer to any object within the System namespace as System.[ObjectName]. All ASP.NET applications must inherit the System.Web namespace.

Web Forms comprise a visual HTML template and the code behind the page. The code behind the page is compiled as a class within the .NET Framework. Thus, all Web Forms must also inherit the System.Web.UI namespace. All ASP.NET Web Form pages also inherit the System.Web.UI.Page class. The System Base Class known as System.Web.UI.Page is required to create the Page class. The ability to store information in the _ViewState hidden field is controlled by the StateBag class. The StateBag class is known as System.Web.UI.StateBag. Web Services is the class that is used to create Web Service applications. So, all Web Services must also inherit the System.Web.WebService class.

When you use Server controls, you must see that they inherit the appropriate Server control class. (*Note*: As you learn the different controls and classes, you should read the documentation for the corresponding namespace from the help files. You can read the documentation that describes the .NET namespaces at *http://msdn.microsoft.com/library/ en-us/cpref/html/frlrfsystemwebuipagememberstopic.asp*.) Figure 1-11 shows that the HTML Server controls that you learned about belong to the System.Web.UI.Control.HtmlControl class. In the next chapter, you will learn to add these HTML Server controls to your Web Form.

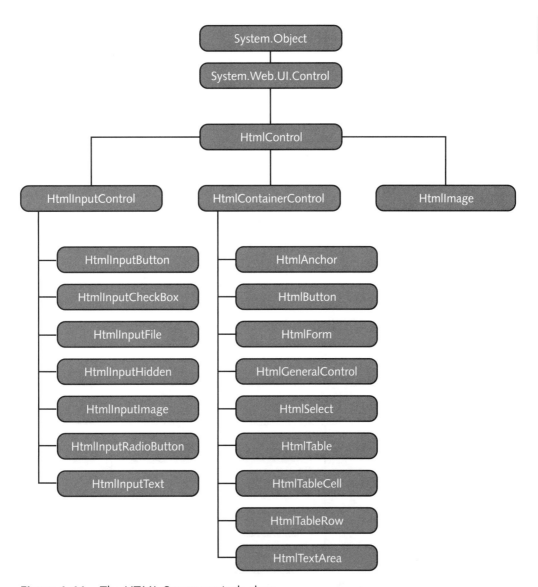

Figure 1-11   The HTML Server controls class

Figure 1-12 shows that the ASP.NET Server controls that you already learned about belong to the System.Web.UI.Control.WebControl class. As you can see, there are many other ASP.NET Server controls. Later in this book, you will learn to add these ASP.NET Server controls to your Web Form.

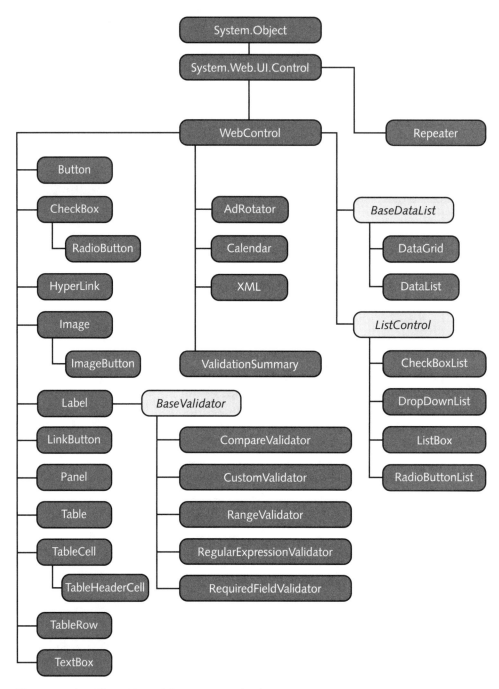

Figure 1-12   The ASP.NET Server controls class

Visual Studio .NET adds references to your projects' commonly used classes by default. (*Note*: You must ensure that any code library you use in your application inherits the appropriate namespace. You can import a class more than once without causing any errors or diminished performance.) You can import the namespaces into your page. The following is the syntax for importing a .NET namespace:

```
Imports NamespaceName
```

The following is a sample of how you would import the ASP.NET Page class:

```
Imports System.Web.UI.Page
```

It is possible to extend the .NET Framework and create your own set of code in a user-defined namespace. You can import a .NET namespace, or a user-defined namespace. You must import each namespace individually. When you compile your application, the .dll file contains a namespace with all of your compiled code. The namespace is named after your application. (*Note*: You can create additional namespaces within your application.) The following is the syntax used to import a user-defined namespace in the code behind the page:

```
Imports NamespaceName = "MyNamespaceName"
```

Common Language Runtime

Out of the box, Visual Studio .NET supports Visual Basic, scripting languages such as JavaScript and VBScript, Java, and C# (pronounced C Sharp). Many third-party code providers of languages such as PERL, COBOL, Fortran, and Eiffel will also support .NET. This open language model allows companies to leverage their existing skills, because they don't need to retrain their programmers to use a new language in order to improve application performance. Language independence is achieved via the use of the Common Language Runtime (CLR). The CLR supports new features such as a Common Type System (CTS), garbage collection (GC), and an Intermediate Language (IL).

Each .NET language provides a compiler that supports the CLR. Therefore, each language must support the Common Type System. The **Common Type System (CTS)** requires that all applications built within .NET, including ASP.NET applications, support the same basic data types. Examples of data types are strings and integers. These common data types are found from the System namespace. Each of these languages stores data in different formats on the computer and uses a different syntax. **Syntax** is the rules that are applied when the code is written so that the compiler can correctly transform the program code into compiled code. Each of the languages continues to maintain its own syntax.

When the program code is compiled, the code is transformed into an intermediate language called the **Microsoft Intermediate Language (IL)**. At that time, an integer in Visual Basic .NET or an int in C# is converted to the same .NET data type, which is Int32. No matter what language is used to create the program, the IL created may be the same. (*Note*: This also means that you can create applications using multiple languages at the same time.)

The **assembly** is the compiled .NET program. The assembly contains the intermediate language along with additional information called **metadata**. Metadata contains information about the assembly. Web Services uses this metadata to describe the contents of the IL in a discovery file so that developers can find out how to create an application that can communicate with the Web Service.

When the application is requested, the Loader program (also called Verifier) loads the program into a compiler called **JIT** (also called **JITter** or **Just in Time compiler**). The compiler converts the IL code to **managed code** and then executes the code.

In Figure 1-13, you can see how the developer will work in Visual Studio .NET 2003, create the files for the project, and then build the project. The Web developer will use the build command to build the projects. This creates the project assembly that contains the MSIL. The assembly is a file in the bin directory of the Web site, and it is named the same as the project, but with the file extension .dll.

When the client requests the Web page, the Web server will use the JIT compiler to compile the page to machine code. This occurs only the first time the page is requested. After that, the page is stored in memory and can be recalled very quickly from a browser.

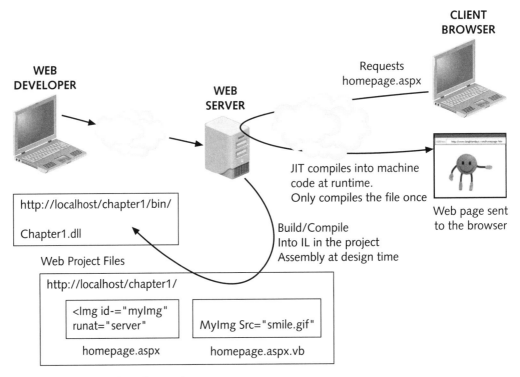

Figure 1-13   Building the application

You can use the IL Disassembler (ildasm.exe) to view the IL within an assembly. There is a tutorial on using the IL Disassembler at *ms-help://MS.NETFrameworkSDK/cptutorials/html/il_dasm_tutorial.htm*.

In the following exercise, you will create a simple class in Visual Basic .NET, compile the class into an assembly, and then view the class using the IL Disassembler. The Visual Basic file will be saved as hello.vb and compiled using the Visual Basic command-line compiler named vbc. You can then run the program from the executable file.

1. Make a directory named **Chapter1** in the C:\Inetpub\wwwroot directory. Click **Start**, and then click **Run**. In the Run dialog box, type **cmd /c md c:\Inetpub\wwwroot\Chapter1** in the Open text box and click **OK**.

2. Open a new document in Notepad and type in the following code:

```
' hello.vb - displays hello world
' Created 06/01/2005
Imports System
Public Module Hello
   Sub Main()
```

In this code, the Imports System statement imports the System namespace into the application. You use the single apostrophe to identify inline comments. You create a public module named hello. Modules declared with the Public keyword have public access. You call the Main method as a sub procedure. (*Note*: Sub procedures are public by default, so the keyword Public is not required.)

3. Type in the code after this paragraph to create the string. The .NET Framework requires that you declare the data type for all variables. In the next line of code, you will create a variable that contains a string, so you have to declare the variable as a string data type. Notice that the Dim keyword is used to declare the variable. The variable can be declared and then assigned a value in the same statement.

```
Dim s1 As String = "Hello World"
Console.WriteLine(s1)
```

4. Add the closing End statements, which are used to end the code blocks. Additional comments are added at the end of the file.

```
   End Sub
End Module
' Run this at the command line
' vbc hello.vb
```

5. Save the file as **hello.vb** in your c:\Inetpub\wwwroot\Chapter1 directory.

6. Exit Notepad.

7. Click **Start**, point to **All Programs**, point to **Microsoft Visual Studio .NET 2003**, point to **Visual Studio .NET Tools**, and then click **Visual Studio .NET 2003 Command Prompt**. (*Note*: You cannot go to the run command and get to the Visual Studio .NET Command Prompt. The path to the SDK tools is not installed into the default command prompt.)

8. Change to your c:\Inetpub\wwwroot\Chapter1 directory by typing **cd c:\Inetpub\wwwroot\Chapter1** and then pressing **Enter**.

9. Type **vbc hello.vb** and press **Enter**. This compiles your program into an executable file named hello.exe in the same folder.

10. Type **hello** at the command prompt and press **Enter**. The program runs and displays the Hello World string.

11. You can view the compiled assembly using the IL Disassembler. At the command prompt, type **ILDASM hello.exe**, and then press **Enter**. The IL DASM window opens, as shown in Figure 1-14. (*Note*: The name of your assembly is hello, which is the name of your executable. You can compare where the class appears in your program and in the assembly.)

12. Close the IL DASM window by clicking **File** and then clicking **Exit**.

13. Close the command prompt window by clicking the **Close** button.

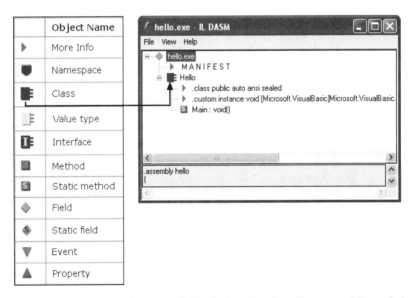

Figure 1-14   Using the IL DASM window to view the assembly and classes

Garbage Collection

Programs that don't release references to objects cause memory leaks. **Memory leaks** occur when memory is no longer being used by the application, but cannot be reassigned to another object. In .NET, the common language runtime uses the garbage collector to manage memory. **Garbage collection (GC)** is the process of allocating and managing the reserved memory known as the managed heap. The **managed heap** is a reserved address space in memory that can be subdivided into and allocated in smaller pieces. All .NET objects are allocated memory at the top of the heap when the object is created. The garbage collector is an object that runs periodically within a background thread. Starting from the root, it removes the objects from the heap that are no longer referenced by the application and moves objects to lower areas in the heap. This process is known as **compaction**. Because of the garbage collection process, .NET applications have less problems with memory leaks and circular references than do current Windows applications. (*Note*: Although you can also explicitly call the garbage collector using the Finalize method of the object that you are removing, it is not recommended.)

OTHER RESOURCES

There are numerous Web sites that provide help, documentation, support, sample code, and sample applications. One sample ASP.NET application is an online catalog and shopping cart application for the fictitious company I Buy Spy. I Buy Spy was created to help developers learn about using Web Forms, accessing a database from the Web, and creating a simple Web Service. I Buy Spy sells spy products. The online catalog allows you to view and place orders for one or more products. Products placed within the shopping cart are temporary and are deleted when the customer leaves the Web site, unless he or she has registered and logged in. In order to place an order, the customer must register with the site and provide his or her contact and shipping information. If he or she has logged into the site, the shopping cart information is recorded directly within the database. Then, if the customer exits the browser, he or she can retrieve the shopping cart by simply logging into the Web site.

The Web site also allows for other companies to place orders and check the status of an order using a Web Service. The Web Service allows these business partners to integrate their Web site with I Buy Spy. The I Buy Spy Store can be found at *http://www.IBuySpy.com/IBS_Store*. You can download the files to recreate the store at *http://www.ibuyspy.com/ibuyspy/download.aspx?tabindex=5*.

The following is a list of some useful Web sites that cover Visual Studio .NET, Visual Basic .NET, ASP.NET, ASP, Web Services, and the .NET Framework.

- *msdn.microsoft.com/net/aspnet*

- *msdn.microsoft.com/net*

- *msdn.microsoft.com/vstudio*

- *www.microsoft.net*

- *www.asp.net*
- *www.gotdotnet.com*
- *www.microsoft.com/trainingandservices*
- *uddi.microsoft.com/default.aspx*
- *xmethods.com*
- *www.asp101.com*
- *www.ibuyspy.com*
- *www.scottgu.com*
- *www.brinkster.com*
- *www.fmstocks.com*

Some of the applications created by Microsoft and third-party developers are located in the QuickStart Web site that is installed with the Visual Studio .NET Framework SDK. Information on how to install the QuickStart Web site is located in Hands-on Project 1–3. If you install the .NET SDK that comes with Visual Studio .NET, you also have access to additional local Web sites to help you become familiar with .NET. The local Web site known as **QuickStart** provides tutorials and walkthroughs. All of the tutorials and sample code can be accessed from *http://localhost/quickstart/*. You can access these samples via a browser at *http://localhost/quickstart*. If you do not have access to the local version of the QuickStart Web site, you can view it remotely at *http://samples.gotdotnet.com/quickstart/*.

CHAPTER SUMMARY

- ASP.NET pages can contain programs written in a variety of programming languages. The default language for ASP.NET pages is Visual Basic .NET. ASP.NET pages end in a variety of file extensions. Web Forms end in .aspx. Web Services end in .asmx. User-defined controls end in .ascx. The terms "ASP.NET pages" and "Web Forms" are synonymous.

- The entire ASP.NET Web page is a class called the Page class. Therefore all items on an ASP.NET page and the page itself are objects.

- The .NET framework is the architectural framework in which ASP.NET applications are created. ASP.NET applications interface with the .NET Framework, instead of interfacing directly with the operating system. .NET applications are compiled to an Intermediate Language (IL) that contains metadata. These compiled programs are called assemblies. Namespaces are a hierarchical way to organize objects. All objects are found in the System.Objects class. .NET applications import the namespaces so that they can refer to the .NET base class objects without using their fully qualified names.

1

❑ .NET requires strict data typing. You must identify the type of data stored in the variable. At compile time, all languages must support the same common .NET data types.

❑ The Page class hierarchy loads all the controls into the Web page. The Page class renders the HTML and Server code to the browser. The Page class contains the HTML and the code behind the page, which is located in a separate file.

❑ Web Services allow you to expose processes publicly to other businesses and applications.

❑ When you create a Web Form in Visual Studio .NET, you do not have to compile the code behind the form manually. Visual Studio .NET places the Page class file into the BIN directory. The BIN directory must have execute permissions.

❑ You do not need to have Visual Studio .NET installed to create or run ASP.NET pages. However, you do need a Web server to post your pages and a platform that supports the .NET Framework. There are a variety of help resources within Visual Studio .NET and on the Internet.

REVIEW QUESTIONS

1. Which of the following is the file extension for an ASP.NET page?
   a. .asp
   b. .html
   c. .aspx
   d. .apx
2. Which of the following is *not* an ASP.NET object?
   a. Session
   b. Application
   c. Client
   d. Response
3. What Web server can be used to view ASP.NET Web pages on Windows 2000?
   a. O'Reilly Web Server
   b. Apache
   c. Internet Information Server
   d. Personal Web Server
4. Which of the following sends output to the browser?
   a. Response.File
   b. Document.Write
   c. Document.Writeln
   d. Response.Write

5. Which concept provides a universal type format for types in the .NET Framework?

   a. Universal type system

   b. garbage collector

   c. Page class

   d. Common Type System

6. What is the name of the feature that ensures that data types, such as integers and strings, are consistent within each language within the .NET Framework?

   a. common language runtime

   b. Common Type System

   c. garbage collection

   d. Web Service

7. What object do all other objects inherit in ASP.NET?

   a. system.variant

   b. system.variable

   c. system.object

   d. system.new

8. What is as the name for the hierarchical treelike structure used to categorize the base class types within the .NET Framework?

   a. namespace

   b. common language runtime

   c. Command-line compiler

   d. portable executable

9. What tool is used to view the managed IL code?

   a. Command-line compiler

   b. IL Disassembler

   c. Just in Time compiler

   d. Command-line Interpreter

10. Which technique allows you to send back data on a Web page automatically?

    a. Postback

    b. Data Validation controls

    c. Response.write

    d. Flush

11. Which technology is used to create e-business applications that can be exposed over the Internet?

    a. Web Forms

    b. WinForms

    c. WebServices

    d. ASPServices

12. Where is the Web site that contains the local support documentation files for ASP.NET?

    a. www.asp.net

    b. http://quickstart

    c. http://localhost/quickstart

    d. http://localhost/help

13. What type of application is a shopping cart?

    a. static

    b. dynamic

    c. local

    d. none of the above

14. What technique is used to retrieve data from other Web sites?

    a. screen scraping

    b. garbage collecting

    c. redirecting

    d. integrating

15. Where is Visual Basic code usually located?

    a. with the HTML Server controls

    b. with the ASP.NET Server controls

    c. with the HTML body tag

    d. with the code behind the page

16. What property transforms an HTML control to an HTML Server control?

    a. runat= "server"

    b. id= "mybtn"

    c. value= "onserverclick"

    d. onclick= "onerverclick"

17. Which of the following ASP.NET controls does not require the prefix ASP?

    a. Data Validation controls

    b. User controls

    c. Mobile controls

    d. Web controls

18. What property of the @Page directive is used to set the location of the code behind the page?

    a. inherits

    b. language

    c. codebehind

    d. href

19. Which phase of the Page class event cycle is responsible for initializing the controls?

    a. Page_Init

    b. Page_Load

    c. Page_Prerender

    d. Page_Unload

20. What is the correct way to import the WEB FORM page class in Visual Basic .NET?

    a. Imports System.Web.Ui.Page

    b. System.Web.Ui.Page

    c. Import MyNamespaceName= System.Web.Ui.Page

    d. Imports Web.Ui.Page

HANDS-ON PROJECTS

Project 1-1

In this project you create a simple Visual Basic program in Notepad and view the IL with the IL Disassembler.

1. Open a new document in Notepad.

2. Type in comments to identify the file, the purpose of the program, and the date the file was created, as follows. (*Note*: It is also common to include the name of the programmer in the comment section in your code.)

```
' Ch1Proj1.vb
' Displays hello world
' Created 06/01/2005
```

3. Type in the code that imports the System namespace. The Imports System statement imports the System namespace into the application. A public module named hello is created. Modules declared with the Public keyword have public access. The Main method is called as a sub procedure.

```
Imports System
```

4. Type in the code to create a public module named **hello**. Modules declared with the Public keyword have public access.

```
Public Module Hello
```

5. Type in the code that creates the Main method. It is the first procedure called when the application is started.

```
    Sub Main()
```

6. Create the string. Use the keyword *Dim* to declare the variable. The variables can be declared on one line when they are both of the same data type. A variable can be declared and then assigned a value in the same statement.

```
Dim s1, s2 As String
s1 = "Hello"
s2 = " World"
```

7. Add the code to write out the contents of the variables to the window using the Write and WriteLine methods. (*Note*: Because the window is the command prompt window, you must use the Console object to access the command prompt window.)

```
Console.Write(s1)
Console.WriteLine(s2)
```

8. Write the closing End statements to end the code blocks.

```
    End Sub
End Module
```

9. Add comments to the end of the file. Comments at the end of the file often include information about how the file was processed. This comment indicates that the code is compiled using the vbc command-line compiler.

```
' Run this at the command line
' vbc Ch1Proj1.vb
```

10. Save the file as **Ch1Proj1.vb** in your c:\Inetpub\wwwroot\Chapter1 directory. Make sure to save the file using quotation marks.

11. Exit Notepad.

12. Click **Start**, point to **All Programs**, point to **Microsoft Visual Studio .NET 2003**, point to **Visual Studio .NET Tools**, and then click **Visual Studio .NET 2003 Command Prompt**.

13. Change to **c:\Inetpub\wwwroot** using the cd c:\Inetpub\wwwroot\Chapter1 command.

14. Type **vbc Ch1Proj1.vb** and press **Enter**. This compiles your program into an executable file named Ch1Proj1.exe in the same folder.

15. Type **Ch1Proj1** at the command prompt and press **Enter**. The program runs and displays the Hello World string.

16. View the compiled assembly using the IL Disassembler. At the command prompt, type **ILDASM Ch1Proj1.exe**, and then press **Enter**. The IL DASM window opens.

17. Click **File** on the menu bar, then click **Dump Tree View**.

18. In the Filename text box type **Ch1Proj1.txt**. You should save the file within quotation marks in order to save the information as a text file. Save the file in the directory c:\Inetpub\wwwroot\Chapter1.

19. Close the IL DASM window by clicking **File** on the menu bar, then click **Exit**.

20. Close the command prompt window by clicking the **Close** button.

21. Open the Ch1Proj1.txt file, which is located in c:\Inetpub\wwwroot\Chapter1, in Notepad. Click **File** on the menu bar, then click **Print**. Then, exit Notepad.

Project 1-2

In this project you create a simple Visual Basic program in Notepad and view the IL with the IL Disassembler.

1. Open a new document in Notepad.

2. Type in comments to identify the file, the purpose of the program, and the date the file was created.

```
' Ch1Proj2.vb
' Displays hello world
' Created 06/01/2005
```

3. Add the code to import the System namespace into the application, create a public module named hello, and create the Main method. Modules declared with the Public keyword have public access. The Main method is called as a sub procedure. It is the first procedure called when the application is started.

```
Imports System
Public Module Hello
   Sub Main()
```

4. Create the string to declare three variables using the keyword *Dim*. A variable can be declared in the same statement. Then, assign values to each variable. Use the Visual Basic .NET concatenation operator (&) to display both s1 and s2 in the s3 variable.

```
Dim s1, s2, s3 As String
s1 = "Hello"
s2 = " World"
s3 = s1 & s2
```

5. Add the code to write out the s3 variable to the console window.

```
Console.WriteLine(s3)
```

6. Write the closing End statements to end the code blocks. Additional comments are added at the end of the file.

```
    End Sub
End Module
' Run this at the command line
' vbc Ch1Proj2.vb
```

7. Save the file as **Ch1Proj2.vb** in your c:\Inetpub\wwwroot\Chapter1 directory. Make sure to save the file using quotation marks.

8. Exit Notepad.

9. Click **Start**, point to **All Programs**, point to **Microsoft Visual Studio .NET 2003**, point to **Visual Studio .NET Tools**, then click **Visual Studio .NET 2003 Command Prompt**.

10. Change to your c:\Inetpub\wwwroot\Chapter1 directory using the cd **c:\Inetpub\wwwroot\Chapter1** command.

11. Type **vbc Ch1Proj2.vb** then press **Enter**. This compiles your program into an executable file named Ch1Proj2.vb in the same folder.

12. Type **Ch1Proj2** at the command prompt and press **Enter**. The program runs and display the Hello World string.

13. At the command prompt type **ILDASM Ch1Proj2.exe**. The IL DASM window opens, and displays the compiled assembly.

14. Click **File** on the menu bar, then click **Dump Tree View**.

15. In the Filename text box type **Ch1Proj2.txt** and save the file to c:\Inetpub\wwwroot\Chapter1. This allows you to save the information as a text file.

16. Close the IL DASM window by clicking **File** on the menu bar, then clicking **Exit**.

17. Close the command prompt window by clicking the **Close** button.

18. Open the file c:\Inetpub\wwwroot\Chapter1\Ch1Proj2.txt. Click **File** on the menu bar, then click **Print**. Click **File** on the menu bar, then click **Exit**.

Project 1-3

In this project you will install the samples from the Framework SDK. These samples are not installed by default, and require installation of the Microsoft SQL Server 2000 Desktop Engine SP3 (MSDE). The basic steps for installing the QuickStart samples are provided. You can obtain more detailed information on installation and use of the MSDE at *www.microsoft.com/sql/msde/* and in the appendix.

1. Go to the Microsoft .NET Framework SDK QuickStarts, Tutorials and Samples page. To get to this page click **Start**, point to **All Programs**, point to **Microsoft .NET Framework SDK v1.1**, then click **Samples and QuickStart Tutorials**. (*Note*: If you have already installed the samples, the page has been modified. You can reopen the page at C:\Program Files\Microsoft Visual Studio .NET 2003\SDK\v1.1\Samples\Setups\html\Start.htm.)

2. Click the **Set up the Quickstarts** link to configure the samples for your computer.

3. This configures the QuickStart virtual directory and creates the sample SQL Server database files and some registry keys. When the samples are installed, you see a window that says Congratulations. Click the **Launch** button. (*Note*: If you get any other message, view and save the log file. It will indicate where the installation was halted.)

4. You will know when the samples are installed correctly when you are redirected to the QuickStart Web site. If you are not redirected, visit the page at *http://localhost/ quickstart/*. If the page exists, then it's installed correctly.

5. Exit Internet Explorer.

Project 1-4

In this project, you view the samples that come with the Framework SDK. (*Note*: You must complete Hands-on Project 1-3 before completing this project, or you can visit an online version of the QuickStart samples at *http://samples.gotdotnet.com/quickstart/Default.aspx*.)

1. Start **Internet Explorer**.

2. Go to the SDK Tutorials and Samples page at *http://localhost/quickstart/*.

3. Click the link **Start the ASP.NET QuickStart Tutorial**.

4. Click the **list arrow** in the upper-right corner of the page labeled I want my samples in, then click **VB**, if it is not already selected. All samples are given in Visual Basic .NET by default. (*Note*: You can change this for individual samples by clicking on the language box below the sample code.)

5. Click the **Language Support** hyperlink in the left menu. Read the sample code for the statements listed after this paragraph. (*Note*: You will learn more about how to implement these Visual Basic .NET statements later in this book.)

   ▫ Declare a variable

   ▫ Comment my code

   ▫ Declare a simple property

   ▫ Declare and use a method

   ▫ Statically initialize a variable

   ▫ Write an if statement

   ▫ Write a case statement

   ▫ Write a for loop

   ▫ Write a while loop

   ▫ Concatenate a string

   ▫ Declare an event

1

❑ Declare an event handler

❑ Add an event handler

❑ Declare a class or interface

❑ Write a standard module

6. Print the page for your reference.

7. Click the **Back** button on the browser.

8. Click the **Introducing Web Forms** link in the menu.

9. Read the following sections:

❑ What is ASP.NET Web Forms?

❑ Writing Your First Web Forms Page

❑ Code-Behind Web Forms

❑ Introduction to Server Controls

10. Click the **Run Sample** link under the Introduction to Server Controls topic.

11. Click **View** on the browser's menu bar, then click **Source**. The client's view is displayed in Notepad. (*Note*: The square brackets [ ] indicate that you are opening a temporary file that contains the client's view of the code, not the actual server-side source code for the page.) Close the sample's window.

12. Under the Introduction to Server Controls topic, click **View Source**. Print the page. Close the browser. Click **View**, click **Source**, then print this page and close Notepad.

13. Compare the two printouts. Write a one-page paper describing how the ASP.NET form works and posts back data into the form fields. Provide specific details based on the examples you printed out. Save the paper as a Web page named **Ch1Proj4.aspx** in your c:\InetPub\wwwroot\Chapter1 directory.

14. Open your browser and enter the path to your Web page to view your Web page. The default path would be *http://localhost/chapter1/Ch1Proj4.aspx*. Print the page and exit your browser.

Project 1-5

In this project you view more Framework SDK samples. Make sure you have installed the Framework SDK samples before doing this exercise, or you can visit an online version of the QuickStart samples at *http://samples.gotdotnet.com/quickstart/Default.aspx*.

1. Start **Internet Explorer**.

2. Go to the SDK Tutorials and Samples page at *http://localhost/quickstart/*.

3. Click the link **Start the ASP.NET QuickStart Tutorial**.

4. Click the link **A Personalized Portal** in the lower-left corner to open a new window displaying the Portal Application. Click the **Run sample** hyperlink.

5. Click the link **Create New Account**.

6. Click **View** on the menu bar, then click **Source**. The source code is displayed in Notepad.

7. Click **File** on the menu bar, then click **Print** to print the source code. Locate the _ViewState hidden field. Underline the value of the _ViewState field. Close the Notepad window.

8. Fill out the entire form without entering a User ID.

9. Click the **Create Account** button. A red asterisk (*) appears after each field that is required. Your data for the other fields is posted back to the page.

10. Click **View** on the menu bar, then click **Source**. The source code is displayed in Notepad.

11. Click **File** on the menu bar, then click **Print** to print the source code. Find where the _ViewState hidden field is located. Underline the value of the _ViewState field. Close the Notepad window.

12. Write a one-page paper that compares the two values of the _ViewState field, and that explains why they are different or not different in each version of the page. Save the paper as a Web page named **Ch1Proj5.aspx** in your c:\InetPub\wwwroot\Chapter1 directory.

13. Open your browser and enter the path to your Web page to view your Web page. The default path would be *http://localhost/chapter1/Ch1Proj5.aspx*. Print the page and exit your browser.

Project 1-6

In this project you view more Framework SDK samples. Make sure you have installed the Framework SDK samples before doing this exercise, or you can visit an online version of the QuickStart samples at *http://samples.gotdotnet.com/QuickStart/Default.aspx*.

1. Start **Internet Explorer**

2. Go to the SDK Tutorials and Samples page at *http://localhost/quickstart/*.

3. Click the link **Start the ASP.NET QuickStart Tutorial**.

4. Click the link **Web Forms Controls Reference** in the left-hand corner. This contains links to documentation for HTML Server controls and Web Server controls. Pick three server controls to read about.

5. Click on each link for the control you selected, then read about the control.

6. For each control you selected, run the sample. Print the client's view of the source code by clicking **View** on the menu bar, then clicking **Source**. In the new window that opens, click **File** on the menu bar, then click **Print**.

7. For each control you selected, view and print the server source code.

8. Write a one-page paper describing the differences between the server source code and the client's view of the source code. Save the paper as a Web page named **Ch1Proj6.aspx** in your c:\InetPub\wwwroot\Chapter1 directory.

9. Open your browser and enter the path to your Web page to view your Web page. The default path would be *http://localhost/chapter1/Ch1Proj6.aspx*. Print the page and exit your browser.

Project 1-7

In this project you view more Framework SDK samples. Make sure you have installed the Framework SDK samples before doing this exercise, or you can visit an online version of the QuickStart samples at *http://samples.gotdotnet.com/QuickStart/Default.aspx*.

1. Start **Internet Explorer**.

2. Go to the SDK Tutorials and Samples page at *http://localhost/quickstart/*.

3. Click the link **Start the ASP.NET QuickStart Tutorial**.

4. Click the link **Web Forms Controls Reference** in the left-hand corner. This contains links to documentation for HTML Server controls and Web Server controls. Pick one HTML Server control and the corresponding ASP.NET Server control.

5. Click each link for the control you selected, then read about the control.

6. For each control you selected, run the sample. Print the client's view of the source code by clicking **View** on the menu bar, then clicking **Source**. In the new window that opens, click **File** on the menu bar, then click **Print**.

7. For each control you selected, view and print the server source code.

8. Write a one page paper describing the differences between the server source code and the client's view of the source code. Compare the differences between the HTML Server control and the ASP.NET Server control. Save the paper as a Web page named **Ch1Proj7.aspx** in your c:\InetPub\wwwroot\Chapter1 directory.

9. Open your browser and enter the path to your Web page to view your Web page. The default path would be *http://localhost/chapter1/Ch1Proj7.aspx*. Print the page and exit your browser.

CASE PROJECTS

Microsoft Support Sites for .NET Programming

Your project manager would like to know what new events are occurring that relate to the .NET technologies. Visit at least one of the following Microsoft Web sites that frequently discusses the .NET technologies:

- ❏ *www.microsoft.net*

- ❏ *msdn.microsoft.com/vstudio*

- ❏ *www.asp.net*

Read the documentation that appears on the Web site. After you have read the documentation, pick a topic that relates to ASP.NET or Visual Studio .NET. Create a one-page report that summarizes your findings. The one-page report should contain the answers to the following information:

- ❏ What topic did you read about? Provide a 5–6 paragraph summary of the topic.

- ❏ At which URL did you find your information?

- ❏ Can you provide one sample of code you found during your research?

Create your report in a Web page format. Use Notepad and HTML to create the Web page. Then save the page as Ch1Case1.htm. Add graphics, fonts, and color to enhance the page.

Open your browser and enter the path to your Web page to view your Web page. The default path would be *http://localhost/chapter1/Ch1Case1.htm*. Print the page and exit your browser.

Sample Business ASP.NET Web Sites — I Buy Spy

Visit the IBuySpy Web site listed in the first section of the chapter at *www.IBuySpy.com/IBS_Store*. After you have read the documentation, create your report in a Web page format. The one-page report should contain the answers to the following questions:

- ❏ Who built the store?

- ❏ How many files were required to create the store?

- ❏ What programming languages were used to create the Web site?

- ❏ What was required to build and run the store?

Use Notepad and HTML to create the Web page. Then save the page as Ch1Case2.aspx. Add graphics, fonts, and color to enhance the page. Then save the page as Ch1Case2.htm.

Open your browser and enter the path to your Web page to view your Web page. The default path would be *http://localhost/chapter1/Ch1Case2.htm*. Print the page and exit your browser.

ASP.NET and Visual Studio .NET Web Resources

Your project manager wants to know where she can learn more about ASP.NET, because your company cannot send her for off-site training. You know that there are many Web sites that discuss ASP.NET and Visual Studio .NET. Visit five of the links listed in this chapter. Within each site, visit at least five Web pages. Create your report in a Web page format. Use Notepad and HTML to create the Web page. Add links to at least five sites, and the five pages you visited. Add a short paragraph about why the site is valuable to ASP Web programmers, and summarize the contents of each page. Use your knowledge of HTML to format the page. Add graphics, fonts, and color to enhance the page. You may add additional links to other resources if you think that might be useful to your project manager. Then save the page as Ch1Case3.aspx. Open your browser and enter the path to your Web page to view your Web page. The default path would be *http://localhost/chapter1/Ch1Case3.aspx*. Print the page and exit your browser. Print out the Web page and the source code.

2

INTRODUCTION TO VISUAL STUDIO .NET

In this chapter, you will:

♦ Familiarize yourself with the Visual Studio .NET user interface

♦ Create Web pages using the Visual Studio .NET HTML editor

♦ Use Visual Studio .NET to create reusable User controls

♦ Create Cascading Style Sheets with the Style Builder

♦ Customize the Toolbox

♦ Locate Help resources within Visual Studio .NET

One of the challenges companies face is adapting to the ever-changing software industry. Software applications are usually created with a single programming language. However, to take advantage of newer techniques, software developers often must learn programming languages as they are created. Learning to program in a new language is as difficult as learning to speak a new language, and there are hundreds of different programming languages and versions. Visual Studio .NET allows programmers to learn one interface for many languages. More importantly, you can use Visual Studio .NET to build programs using a combination of languages.

In this chapter, you will learn how to use Visual Studio .NET to generate ASP.NET Web applications. You will learn how to manage project files and create basic Web pages. You will create cascading style sheets with the Style Builder to format your Web pages. You will also create User controls that can be reused across multiple ASP.NET pages.

VISUAL STUDIO .NET USER INTERFACE

Where applications were once hand-coded by developers, rapid application development (RAD) tools now allow developers to build higher-quality applications more quickly. RAD tools allow developers to create prototypes, develop reusable software components, and facilitate communication and file management. Visual Studio .NET is a RAD tool geared to the creation of Web applications and Web Services.

Visual Studio .NET provides a new user interface called the **Integrated Development Environment (IDE)**, which is shown in Figure 2-1. All of Microsoft's major programming languages, such as C++, C#, J#, JScript, Visual Basic, Transact-SQL, and Visual FoxPro, share this single IDE. For example, the IDE provides a better interface between the .NET Framework and Visual Basic .NET. For a Visual Basic developer, the most important benefit of the .NET Framework is direct and easy access to the underlying .NET platform, using a consistent programming model. As a Visual Basic .NET developer, you have access to the same features and capabilities of the .NET Framework as you do with other platform languages. The IDE is consistent across languages and applications. You can manage your Windows applications, Web applications, and Web Services all within the same development environment using **Solution Explorer** to manage all of the files and resources.

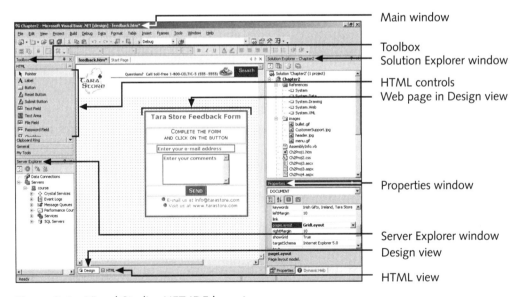

Figure 2-1   Visual Studio .NET IDE layout

There are many other windows, controls, and toolbars within the Visual Studio .NET user interface. The **main window** is used to view your project files. When you open multiple documents in the main window at the same time, a **document tab** appears in the main window of the IDE to allow you to easily switch between documents. If you open a large

2

number of documents, you can use the next and previous buttons to navigate through the other tabs. (*Note:* These buttons appear to the right of the document tabs.)

When you create a project, Visual Studio .NET includes the appropriate references to the base class libraries in the Solution Explorer window. Visual Studio .NET also imports the namespaces required when you use the templates to create your files. In addition, when you build Windows applications, Web applications, or Web Services, Visual Studio .NET creates all of the other ancillary files and folders, including the bin directory.

As you learned in the previous chapter, the code behind the ASP.NET page is compiled by Visual Studio .NET. When you call the Build command, Visual Studio .NET compiles the ASP.NET code into a file with the extension .dll and places this file within the bin directory of the project. Visual Studio .NET assigns the bin directory execute permissions so that the code can be executed at runtime. Therefore, you can build and deploy your application from within Visual Studio .NET.

Some developers have chosen to create ASP.NET applications with other editors, such as Notepad. If you do not use Visual Studio .NET to create, build, and deploy your application, you have to manually compile your application with a command-line compiler. You also need to use other various XCOPY methods, such as FTP, to deploy your application.

Each Visual Studio .NET project template contains several default files. Figure 2-2 shows all of the default Web application files in the Solution Explorer window, including the hidden project files. You can click the Show All Files icon to toggle between showing files and hiding files. The Web application contains Web Forms, global configuration files, and different built-in references to the .NET base classes, such as System.Web. In the Solution Explorer window, you can click the Show All button to view all of the files in the Web project. A Windows application contains different types of files, such as a Visual Basic Windows Form, and references to .NET base classes, such as Windows.Forms.

Visual Studio .NET provides many more features to help developers be more productive. For example, Visual Studio .NET supports Add Item, Application, and Solution Wizards that you can use to quickly create .NET applications. You can access these wizards via the menu or by right-clicking on the project or solution in the Project Explorer window.

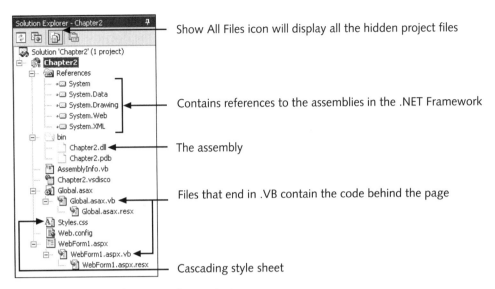

Figure 2-2 The Solution Explorer window

Server Explorer provides access to public components on your network servers. Server Explorer also provides you with wizards to create Data Connections to databases. Data Connections are required when you want your application to access data from a database. Server Explorer provides access to the server event logs, performance counters, and services without requiring you to have physical access to the server. You can record macros that perform activities, such as adding a form to the Web page, that can be shared with other developers. You can manage your macros in the **Macros Explorer**. The **Task window** allows you to manage a to do list. You can mark code so that you can locate it quickly. You can use a common debugging tool to debug an entire application at once and do so across physical servers. You can control the source code within Visual Studio .NET by checking out files. These are only a few of the basic features that Visual Studio .NET supports.

Creating a Web Application

A Web application consists of many projects. When you create a Web application, you need to create a solution to maintain the projects. A **solution** contains several solution files, which are used to maintain information about each of the projects within the application. Each **project** maintains its own set of **project files**. The types of files within each project vary with the type of project. For example, in a Web project, you find Web related files such as Web Forms.

By default, Visual Studio .NET creates the project files and places them in a folder named after the project and located in the Visual Studio projects folder within My Documents. The Web files are published to the default Web directory in a folder named after the project. The default Web directory is located at c:\Inetpub\wwwroot. (*Note*: Your system

2

administrators may change the default location of the Visual Studio projects folder and the default location of the Web server.) You can preview your Web page on a Web server such as Internet Information Server.

When you create the Web application, you need to specify the name of the Web server and the name of the project. The project name is also the name of the folder on the server that stores the project Web pages. When you create a Web application, the Name text box in the New Project window is dimmed. You must enter the name of the project in the Location text box. Therefore, you must have access to a Web server when you create Web applications with Visual Studio .NET. However, you can change the folder that stores your solution files by clicking the Browse button in the New Project dialog box. Many of the Web pages are not viewable until the Web pages are stored on a Web server.

The name of the local Web server is usually the name of your computer. If your machine name is Course, then your Web address would be *http://Course/Chapter2*. You can also use the IP address of the computer. In addition, you can use the keyword **localhost** or the loopback address 127.0.0.1 to refer to the local Web site. The loopback address is a reserved IP address that works only while you are logged in at the local computer. In this case, the Web address would be *http://localhost/Chapter2* or *http://127.0.0.1/Chapter2*. If you want to create your Web application on a remote Web server, you must type in a valid URL to the Web server, and you must be connected to the Internet while you are creating and editing the Web application.

In the following exercise, you will create a Web application. You will create a new solution named Chapter2 and a project named Chapter2. You will use this solution and project for the rest of the examples in the chapter.

1. Start **Visual Studio .NET**. (On most computers, you click **Start**, point to **All Programs**, point to **Microsoft Visual Studio .NET 2003**, and then click **Microsoft Visual Studio .NET 2003**.)

2. Click **File** on the menu bar, point to **New**, and then click **Project** to open the New Project window. (*Note*: The New Project window displays the various types of project templates available.)

3. If necessary, click **Visual Basic Projects** in the Project Types pane. (*Note*: Your default project type will vary. Make sure you are selecting the correct project type.) Click the **ASP.NET Web Application** icon in the Templates pane.

4. Click the **Location** text box, and then type **http://localhost/Chapter2** to name the project Chapter2. The new project is created on your default Web server. The Web address of the project is *http://localhost/Chapter2*.

5. Click **OK** to create the solution, project, and default files. Look at the files that were created in the Solution Explorer window. A Web Form named Web Form1.aspx is created in the project file by default. This Web Form is opened by default in the main window.

6. If necessary, click the **plus sign** next to the References folder to expand the references. You can see the references that are included with the project. These are references to the assemblies within the .NET Framework.

7. Click the **minus sign** next to the References folder to hide the references.

When you start Visual Studio .NET, a **Start Page** provides access to your recently created applications, and Help Resources opens. After you have created an application, you can click the application name on the Start Page to reopen the solution and related project files.

While you are working with the project, you have access to the .NET Framework. The .NET Framework is the foundation on which you build and run applications. For example, you can access the .NET data class, which provides you with objects to connect your Web application to a database. Visual Studio .NET also provides you with graphical tools that represent these data objects. Having such a foundation makes it easier to build applications using a consistent, simplified programming model.

NAVIGATING THE WINDOWS

Visual Studio .NET has a variety of productivity tools that you can access from the various windows. Each window has four common properties that determine where the window is positioned on the desktop. You set these properties by right-clicking the window. The first window property is the **Dockable** property. Windows that are dockable can be moved to other locations on the desktop. The Dockable feature is checked by default. Docked windows can also be placed on top of one another. When one window is docked on top of another window, the user interface creates several tabs that you can use to move back and forth between each window. Any time windows are docked on top of each other, you can click a named tab to place the corresponding window on the top layer. A second common feature of windows is the Hide property. Setting the **Hide** property hides, or closes, the window. You can reopen a hidden window via the View menu. The third window property is the Floating property. The **Floating** property allows you to select the window and drag and drop it to any location on the desktop. It is different from the Dockable property in that the floating window does not have to be placed on top of another window. The **Auto Hide** property is a new feature that allows you to store the window on the desktop as a tab. The tab is labeled with the name of the window. When you click the tab, its associated window slides open. To turn this feature off and make the window stick to the desktop, click the pushpin icon on the window's menu bar.

By default, the Server Explorer and the Toolbox windows are set to Auto Hide. When there are multiple windows that are set to Auto Hide, some of the names of the windows may not appear on the tab. Only the icon that represents the window appears on the tab. This feature allows you to have quick access to many windows at the same time. When Visual Studio .NET first opens, the Solution Explorer window and the Properties window are both open. They split half of the window on the right side of the monitor. You can expand either window by placing the pointer over the top of the Properties window. When the cursor changes to a double-headed arrow, click and drag the cursor up or down. When you move the cursor up, the Properties window is enlarged. When you move the cursor down, the Solution Explorer window is enlarged. You can also resize the other windows in the same way.

The Solution Explorer Window

You use the **Solution Explorer** window to manage your files and projects. For example, Solution Explorer offers a means to manage and publish a solution without requiring that you use a file transfer program such as FTP. In the following exercise, you will add files to the Chapter2 project using the Solution Explorer window. You will also learn how to work with the sliding windows.

1. Right-click **Chapter2** in the Solution Explorer window to display the shortcut menu. (*Note:* The shortcut menus that are displayed when you right-click an object are also called pop-up menus. Just as in other Microsoft applications, any task listed in the pop-up menus can also be accessed via the standard menus or a keyboard shortcut.) Point to **Add**, and then click **New Folder**.

2. Type **images** to name the folder, and then press **Enter**. You will store the application images in this folder.

3. Right-click the **images** folder, point to **Add**, and then click **Add Existing Item**.

4. Navigate to the **Images** folder inside the **Chapter02Data** folder. (*Note:* The Chapter02Data directory contains the data files required for this chapter. If you do not have the data files for this chapter, you can download them from the Course Technology Web site at *www.course.com*. In the front of this book, you will find directions for downloading the data files.) In the Files of type drop-down list box, change the selection from VB Code Files to **Image Files**.

5. Select all of the files. Click the **Open** button. This imports the images into the images directory of your Chapter2 project. You can click the **minus** sign next to the Images folder to collapse the folder.

6. Right-click **Chapter2** in the Solution Explorer window, point to **Add**, and then click **Add New Item**. The Add New Item-Chapter2 dialog box displays typical Web Project and Windows Project files.

7. In the Categories pane, click **Web Project Items** if necessary, and in the Templates pane, click **Web Form**. (*Note:* Although you can use the pop-up menu to add a Web Form, use the templates for this step.) See Figure 2-3.

8. In the Name text box, highlight the existing content, type **home.aspx**, and then click **Open**. (*Note:* The default file extension for Web Forms is aspx.) The Web Form is added to the project and opens in the main code window.

9. Click **File** on the menu bar, and then click **Save All**.

10. Click the **Close** button to close the home.aspx page.

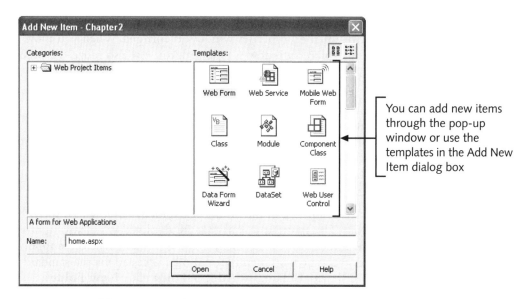

You can add new items through the pop-up window or use the templates in the Add New Item dialog box

Figure 2-3   Adding items to the project

The Toolbox

The Visual Studio .NET **Toolbox** contains a set of commonly used controls, including HTML controls and Web Form controls, which are organized using tabs. The HTML tab provides access to the HTML controls. The Web Forms tab contains the ASP.NET Server controls. The Toolbox is a window and can be hidden. The Toolbox slides out when you drag the pointer over the Toolbox tab.

The Properties Window

You use the **Properties window** to set properties for objects, controls, and classes. The object can be a Windows Form, a Web Form, an image, a form field, or even a label on the page. Figure 2-4 shows what the Properties window looks like. When you click an object, such as the document window, the properties for that object are displayed in the Properties window.

Many properties can be set through the Properties window during the design of the Web pages. However, some properties of Web pages and controls can only be set programmatically in the code behind the page. In later chapters, you will learn to set properties of the server controls and the Web page using the Properties window and the code behind the page.

HTML Controls

Hypertext Markup Language (HTML) is a markup language that consists of a predefined group of tags that identify and format content on a Web page. The World Wide Web

Consortium (*www.w3c.org*) maintains HTML standards. The current HTML standards allow you to enter HTML tags in uppercase, lowercase, or a mixture of uppercase and lowercase. The case in the beginning tag does not have to match the case in the closing tag. Most HTML tags contain a beginning and an ending tag. However, some tags, such as the horizontal rule, do not require a closing tag. The HTML standards allow HTML tags to contain minimized attributes. **Minimized attributes** can be specified by a keyword, instead of the name of the attribute and the keyword. For example, you specify the property of the check box by using the minimized attribute "checked". No value has to be provided with the checked attribute.

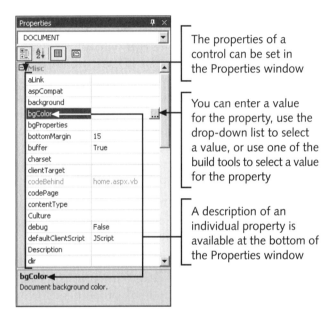

Figure 2-4   The Properties window

The newest version of HTML is known as **Extensible Hypertext Markup Language (XHTML)**. XHTML is an updated version of HTML that applies the syntax from Extensible Markup Language (XML). XML represents a new standard. It was created to provide a universal format for structured documents and data. XHTML is a version of HTML that is compliant with XML standards. HTML was updated to XHTML because Web content is being ported to an increasing variety of browsers and devices, such as cell phones and PDAs. XML requires that all tags consist of a beginning and closing tag. Tags that do not use a closing tag can be closed using a forward slash at the end of the beginning tag. Minimized attributes must be written using a name and a value. When you create Web applications using Visual Studio .NET, the HTML controls create HTML that is XHTML compliant. For example, instead of `<hr noshade>`, the HTML editor writes `<hr noshade="noshade"/>`.

You can learn more about HTML, XML, and XHTML by visiting the W3C Web site at www.w3c.org.

In Visual Studio .NET, you can create pages with HTML using the HTML editor. The HTML editor is also known as the **HTML Designer**. There are several views within the HTML Designer. The view can be identified by the tabs at the bottom of the Web page. Design view allows you to add HTML controls to the page via the Toolbox. HTML view allows you to view and edit the HTML code. When you create a page, the page opens in Design view by default. You can click the HTML tab to change to HTML view.

When you are editing a page in HTML view, you must choose how you want to position the HTML controls on the Web page. There are two types of page layout settings, maintained by the **MS_POSITIONING** property. In HTML view, the body tag has the property **MS_POSITIONING** set to GridLayout by default. **GridLayout** allows the page to use absolute positioning to place objects. **FlowLayout** positions elements on the page in top-down format. Controls are displayed in the page in the order in which they appear in HTML view. You can use a grid to assist you when you are placing controls on the page. When the showGrid property is set to True, the grid is displayed in Design view. The grid is not shown when the Web page is viewed in the browser. The showGrid property is set to True by default.

You should also determine which browsers your Web site will support. You can target any level of browser by configuring the targetSchema property for the page. The **targetSchema** property is Internet Explorer 5.0 by default.

There are several document properties that correspond to the attributes of the HTML body tag. The alink, vlink, link, text, bgColor, and background properties are all configurable via the Properties window. The alink, vlink, and link properties allow you to configure the color of the active hyperlinks, visited hyperlinks, and default hyperlinks, respectively. The Text property allows you to configure the color of the default text. The bgColor property allows you to configure the color of the page background. The Background property allows you to configure the URL of a graphic as the page background. If you insert a background image, the image will tile across and down the page by default. bgProperties is a property that allows you to set the background image to a fixed position. So, if the user scrolls down the page, the background image will not scroll. It will remain in place while the content of the page changes. The rightMargin, leftMargin, topMargin, and bottomMargin properties allow you to set the margin properties for the page. Not all browsers support the setting of Web page margins.

The HTML Designer supports a new feature called IntelliSense. **IntelliSense** detects what you have typed and tries to predict what you will type next. IntelliSense detects built-in keywords and properties, as well as third-party controls installed with your application. Drag-and-drop controls and IntelliSense are available for all languages within .NET. You can jump to the listings that begin with "b" by pressing the B key. Because you can select the keyword from a predefined list, IntelliSense helps prevent syntax errors in your HTML code.

CREATING AN HTML PAGE

The Web page can be created using the menu commands or Toolbox controls or edited directly in HTML view. In the following exercise, you will use all three techniques to create a basic Web page. In the first steps, you will use HTML view to add code to the page. You will learn how to use the IntelliSense feature. You will verify the page properties using the Properties window. You will also modify the code in HTML view using the Properties window.

1. Right-click **Chapter2** in the Solution Explorer window (you may have to scroll up to see it), point to **Add**, and then click **Add HTML Page**.

2. In the Name text box, type **feedback.htm**, and then click **Open**.

3. The Properties window shows the DOCUMENT properties by default. Verify the DOCUMENT properties in the Properties window. Verify that the value of the pageLayout property is GridLayout. Verify that the targetSchema property is Internet Explorer 5.0. Verify that the showGrid property is set to True.

4. In the title property field, change the value from feedback to **Tara Store**. The title property corresponds to the HTML title tag.

5. In the keywords property field, type **Irish Gifts, Ireland, Tara Store**.

6. Expand the **images** folder in the Solution Explorer window. Drag the **header.jpg** image from the Solution Explorer window to the page and:

    a. Position the image in the upper-left corner of the page.

    b. In the Properties window of the header.jpg image, type **Tara Store Banner** in the alt field.

7. Click the **HTML** tab in the bottom-left corner of your screen to change to HTML view. Notice that the keywords were placed inside a meta tag, and the title was added using a title tag.

8. Insert a blank line below the image tag, and then type **<**. The IntelliSense feature detects that you have started to enter a beginning tag. The choice of tags is presented in a drop-down list.

9. Click the **br** tag to select it, as shown in Figure 2-5, and then press **Enter**.

10. Close the tag by typing **>**. Add three more **
** tags, pressing **Enter** after each insertion.

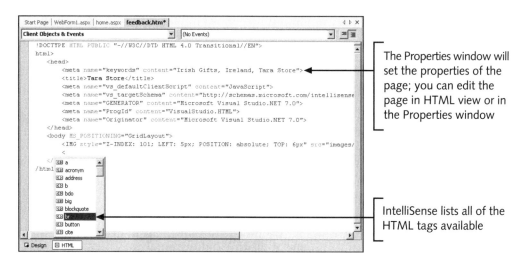

The Properties window will set the properties of the page; you can edit the page in HTML view or in the Properties window

IntelliSense lists all of the HTML tags available

Figure 2-5   Selecting an HTML tag

11. Add a horizontal rule tag by typing **<hr>**.

12. Click inside the <hr> tag. The Properties window displays the property page for the hr tag. Change the noshade property to **True** using the drop-down list box to its right. Notice that the keyword noshade is added to the HTML tag.

13. Click **File** on the menu bar, and then click **Save All**.

In the following steps, you will add a table to the page you just created, using the Table menu. You will use the Properties window to set the properties of individual HTML controls. You will also use the HTML controls to add a form.

1. Click the **Design** tab in the lower-left corner of your screen to switch to Design view. Click the **Tara Store** form.

2. Make sure the form, not the image on the form, is selected. Click **Table** on the menu bar, point to **Insert**, and then click **Table**. Your screen should resemble Figure 2-6. Change the number of rows to **6** and columns to **1**. Click **OK**.

3. Change the properties of the table using the Properties window, as follows:

   a. Change the border property from 1 to **0**.

   b. Change the style property to **Z-INDEX: 106; LEFT: 244px; POSITION: absolute; TOP: 132px**. (*Note*: Depending on your screen resolution, you may have to resize the Properties window to edit the style property. Place the cursor over the edge of the window and drag the edge to the left until you can see the entire style property value text box.) Press the **Enter** key, which will move the table to the center of the page. Then, click somewhere on the page (other than on the table).

2

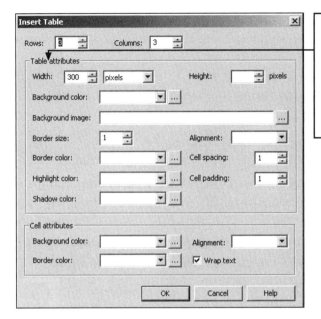

You can configure the table properties and the cell properties when you create the table; you can also configure the properties using the Properties window after you create the table

Figure 2-6   The Insert Table dialog box

4. Click in the first table cell, then type **Tara Store Feedback Form**.

   a. Select the entire phrase **Tara Store Feedback Form**.

   b. In the Formatting toolbar, change the format from Normal to **Heading 2** in the Style drop-down list box.

   c. In the Formatting toolbar, change the font to **Verdana** and the size to **4**.

5. Place the pointer over the **Toolbox** tab to slide out the Toolbox. (The tab should be on the left margin of your screen.) Click the **pushpin** icon to make the Toolbox remain open.

6. In the Toolbox, click the **HTML** tab, if necessary, to show the HTML controls.

7. Drag the HTML **Label** control to the page and position the control inside the second table cell.

   a. Click inside the new Label control, and then delete the text **Label**.

   b. Type **Complete the form**. Press **Shift+Enter** to insert a single line break.

   c. Then type **and click on the submit button**.

   d. Drag the handles on the Label control to make the text fit the table cell.

   e. In the Properties window, in the class property field, type **TSHeading**.

8. Drag a **Text Field** control to the page and position it inside the third table cell.

   a. In the Properties window, change the value property to **Enter your e-mail address**.

   b. Set both the (id) property and the name property of the text box to **Email**.

   c. Set the size property of the text box to **30**.

   d. Set the class property to **txtBox**.

In the following steps, you will use the HTML controls to add a form. You will use the Properties window and HTML view to set the properties of individual HTML controls.

1. Drag a **Text Area** control from the HTML tab and drop it in the fourth cell.

   a. In the Properties window, set the cols property to **25** and the rows property to **5**.

   b. Set the name property of the Text Area control to **comments**.

   c. Set the (id) property of the Text Area control to **comments**.

   d. Set the class property to **txtBox**.

2. Right-click the **Text Area** control on the form, and then click **View HTML Source**. HTML view is displayed in the code window.

   a. Place the cursor after the opening textarea tag, which looks like <TEXTAREA ... cols="25">. Type **Enter your comments**. (*Note:* If you type this on the next line, you will be adding white space to the textarea box.)

3. Click the **Design** tab to return back to Design view.

4. Drag a **Submit Button** control from the HTML tab to the page and position the button inside the fifth cell.

   a. In the Properties window, change the value property to **Send**.

   b. Change the name and (id) properties to **btnSubmit**.

   c. Make the Class property **TSButton**.

5. Click **File** on the menu bar, and then click **Save All**.

In the following steps, you will insert a hyperlink. You can set the properties of hyperlinks in the Properties window or in HTML Code view. If you insert the hyperlink in Design view, the IDE will recognize the link as a Web address or mailto hyperlink and insert the appropriate hyperlink code.

1. In the last table cell, type **E-mail us at info@tarastore.com**. Press **Enter**, type **Visit us at www.tarastore.com**, and press the **spacebar**.

2

2. Click the **info@tarastore.com** mailto hyperlink.

   a. Verify that the href property is set to mailto:info@tarastore.com.

   b. Set the class property to **TSLinks**.

3. Click the text **www.tarastore.com**.

   a. Verify that the href property is set to http://www.tarastore.com.

   b. Set the class property to **TSLinks**.

4. Highlight all the text in the sixth cell, and then click the **Bullets** icon on the Formatting toolbar. This creates an unordered list.

5. Click **File** on the menu bar, and then click **Save All**.

6. Click the **Build** menu, and then click **Build Solution**. This will compile the ASP.NET Web application.

Previewing Your HTML Page

You can preview your page within Visual Studio .NET or in a Web browser by typing in the URL of your project, the path, and the name of the Web page. Visual Studio .NET also allows you to start the application by clicking the Start button on the Standard toolbar. The Start button is a blue arrowhead located to the left of the debug drop-down list. This method always opens the starting page, which is not necessarily the page you want to preview. You can change the start page by right-clicking the desired page in the Solution Explorer window and selecting Set Start Page. If you use the Start button, Visual Studio .NET indicates that your application is running. As a result, you must close the browser window before Visual Studio .NET allows you to make further changes to your Web application.

In the following steps, you will preview your Web page using a browser and from the browser within Visual Studio .NET. You will also set the page as the start page of the project and view the page.

1. Start Internet Explorer.

2. Enter **localhost/Chapter2/feedback.htm** in the Address box and then press **Enter** to view the page.

3. Close the browser window.

4. In Visual Studio .NET, verify that you are in Design view.

5. Right-click the Web page, and then click **View in Browser**. Your results should look like the page shown in Figure 2-7. The name of the window is Browse – Tara Store. You can see the name in the blue title bar at the top of your screen.

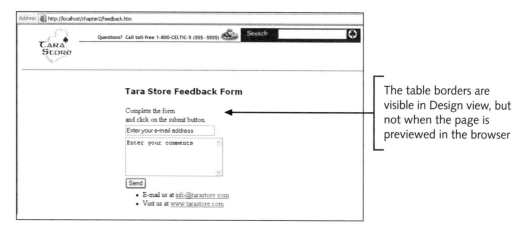

The table borders are visible in Design view, but not when the page is previewed in the browser

Figure 2-7   An HTML page created with Visual Studio .NET

6. Click the **Close** button to close the window.

You can open additional tab groups that allow you to work with more than one Web Form at a time. This feature makes it possible to view a form in both Design and Code view at the same time. To reorganize your Web Forms in the main code window into groups, right-click the Web Form tab and select New Vertical Tab Group or New Horizontal Tab Group. You can return the Web Form to the original tab group by right-clicking the tab, and then clicking Move to Previous Tab Group.

User Controls

User controls allow you to separate content and programming code that can be reused in other pages. User controls make it easier to maintain Web pages. For example, you might use a User control to display a header image throughout the hundreds of pages on your Web site. The User control contains an image tag with the name of the file that contains the image. If the filename changes, you need only modify the name of the image in the User control and not in the hundreds of pages on the Web site.

It is important to plan your Web application before you start to develop the code. After planning the desired outcome of your Web site, you can try to identify areas where code can be reused. Then, you can create User controls to replace this code.

User controls are compiled by Visual Studio .NET and must be registered with each ASP.NET page. You cannot include the <html>, <head>, or <body> elements in the User control. The User control must have the file extension **.ascx**. The first line of the User control must identify the file as a User control with the keyword Control. All User controls are identified with this keyword. Because the User control can contain code, it also contains a reference to the code behind the page. You can place the server code within the code behind the page, or you can include the code within HTML view.

The following sample code creates a User control that displays a list of months and could be saved in a file named Ch2_months.ascx:

```
<%@ Control %>
<select id=months>
<option>January</option>
<option>February</option>
<option>March</option>
<option>April</option>
<option>May</option>
<option>June</option>
<option>July</option>
<option>August</option>
<option>September</option>
<option>October</option>
<option>November</option>
<option>December</option>
</select>
```

Because ASP.NET pages place a form tag within the ASP.NET page, you should not include an additional <form> control in the Web page. If the <form> element is used in the User control and the User control is nested within a <form> element, your code will not work.

Within each ASP.NET page that contains the User control, you must register the User control. To register the control, the first line of the page must contain the **@Register** directive. The @Register directive allows you to include the file as a custom control. The **TagPrefix** property is used to identify the User control's namespace, just like the ASP prefix is used with ASP controls. The following sample code shows how you would register the User control from the previous sample:

```
<%@ Register TagPrefix="Months" TagName=⤵
"ListMonths" src="Ch2_months.ascx" %>
```

You can also add the code to register and insert the User control by dragging the User control from the Solution Explorer window to the Web page in Design view. This adds the Register code and the User control tags to the new Web page. You can still edit this code manually in HTML view.

Once the TagPrefix has been registered, you can add an ASP.NET tag with the TagPrefix. You can use the new tag anywhere in the Web page. You can reuse any User control many times within the same page. However, you must provide a unique ID name for each user control instance. The following is a sample of how you would add a User control to the Web page by inserting the new ASP.NET tag:

```
<Months:ListMonths id = "ListMonths1" runat= "server" />
```

User controls can contain HTML code or ASP.NET code. The User control may be as simple as a heading image or as complicated as a list of records returned from a database. Because the page is compiled, you can include code within the User control or in the code behind the page for the User control. The User control can be reused in other Web pages within the same application and across projects.

User controls are set up to use the flow layout mode as the default. You can change the layout to grid layout so that you can use absolute positioning of controls. To do this, you open the HTML tab on the Toolbox and add a Grid Layout Panel control. Then, you can position the elements within the Panel. This places the items within a <DIV> tag in the resulting Web page.

Creating and Registering a User Control

The following exercise illustrates how to create and register a User control. The User control contains an image and some basic ASP.NET code. In the Web page, you will register the User control and add the new tag to the Web page.

1. Right-click **Chapter2** in the Solution Explorer window, point to **Add**, and then click **Add Web User Control**.

2. In the Name text box, type **header.ascx**. Click the **Open** button.

3. Click the **HTML** tab at the bottom of your screen. Notice that the first line includes the keyword Control. The first line also identifies the default language, "vb" for Visual Basic .NET, and other properties, which will be covered in the next chapter.

4. Click the **Design** tab to return to Design view.

5. Drag the file **header.jpg** from the images folder in the Solution Explorer window to the page, and position the image in the upper-left corner.

6. Drag a **Label** control from the Web Forms tab in the Toolbox to the Web page and position it beneath the header image. (*Note:* You may need to place the cursor at the end of the header image and press **Enter** to position the label below the image.)

7. Click the **HTML** tab. Insert a blank line under the image tag, and then enter the code following this paragraph. (*Note:* You must type this code all on a single line. The Visual Studio .NET editor will place this code on the line below the @Control directive.)

```
<% Response.Write("<h1 align='center'>↵
Welcome to Tara Store</h1>") %>
```

8. Click the **Design** tab to return to Design view.

9. Right-click on the page, and then click **View Code**. The code behind the page located in header.ascx.vb opens.

10. Locate the Page_Load event procedure. As you learned in the first chapter, the Page_Load event procedure is run when the page is loaded in memory on the Web server. Below the comment in the code, enter the code that follows this paragraph, which sets the Text property of the Label control named Label1 to the current date. The Now class provides you with access to the date and time. The Date class returns the Date object for the current date. The date is formatted as *mm/dd/yy* by using the ToShortDateString method. (*Note*: The comment is colored green.)

```
Label1.Text = Now.Date.ToShortDateString
```

11. Click **File** on the menu bar, and then click **Save All**.

12. Close the header.ascx.vb page and the header.ascx page.

In the following steps, you will open the home page you created earlier, register the User control, and add the new tag to the Web page. When you register your User control, it is useful to use the name of the application or project as the TagPrefix. If you use the same name as the TagPrefix, it will be easier for you to recognize and maintain your User controls. The User control must be compiled before you can view the page. The Build command instructs Visual Studio .NET to compile your application.

1. Double-click **home.aspx** in the Solution Explorer window to open the Web page.

2. Right-click the Web page, and then click **View HTML Source**.

3. Insert a blank line below the @Page directive, which is the first line of text on the screen.

4. On the blank line, type the following code to register the User control:

```
<%@ Register TagPrefix = "Chapter2" ↵
TagName = "MyHeading" src = "header.ascx" %>
```

5. Scroll down the page to the opening body tag. The next tag is the form tag. Below the opening form tag, insert a blank line, if necessary. Then, on the blank line, type the code following this paragraph, which inserts the User control. (*Note*: Notice that an ID is used to identify the control. The naming convention for the User controls is to use the tag name and add a number.)

```
<Chapter2:MyHeading id="MyHeading1" runat="server"> ↵
</Chapter2:MyHeading>
```

6. Click the **Design** tab to return to Design view. The User control appears as a graphical control in the page. This helps you plan where to insert your User controls in the Web page.

7. Click the **File** menu, and then click **Save All**. Click **Build** on the menu bar, and then click **Build Solution**.

8. Right-click on the page, and then click **View in Browser**. Your results should look like the page in Figure 2-8.

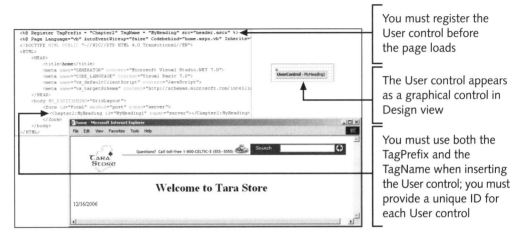

You must register the User control before the page loads

The User control appears as a graphical control in Design view

You must use both the TagPrefix and the TagName when inserting the User control; you must provide a unique ID for each User control

Figure 2-8 Inserting User controls in an ASP.NET page

9. Close the browser window.

Remember that the User control has its own page events and can contain its own code behind the page. You can implement User controls to contain code only in this code behind the page and with no visual presentation.

CREATING CASCADING STYLE SHEETS

Most Web applications use cascading style sheets to store information about how to present the Web site. **Cascading style sheets (CSS)** can be used to separate page content from presentation. The World Wide Web Consortium (*www.w3c.org*) is responsible for developing and maintaining the CSS standards, of which there are now several versions. A browser must support HTML 4.0 to support CSS. Older browsers simply ignore the CSS. Cascading style sheets can be used with Web pages created using HTML, XML, and ASP.NET. Web sites that use cascading style sheets are easier to maintain. For example, when you need to make a change to the font color of the H1 tag, you can simply change the Color property within the style sheet. The change is reflected immediately across the entire Web site. Because style sheets can be used to help manage the presentation of the Web site, it is important to plan and create your style sheets before you start developing your application.

Visual Studio .NET supports the ability to create and maintain cascading style sheets. You can create your cascading style sheet manually or use a Style Builder graphical user interface to create your style sheet. The Style Builder allows you to quickly build and preview complicated style sheets.

CSS Overview

A **style rule** is the information that is applied to a single HTML tag. There are different style formats that are used to create style rules. The syntax for the style rules varies depending upon where the style rule is located. The inline style rules add the style information within the HTML tag. The inline style rule would be applied only to the single tag. In an embedded style sheet, the style rules are located in the heading section of the Web page. A single pair of style tags, <style></style>, is used to identify the embedded style rules. Embedded style rules can apply to all tags within the same page. For example, a paragraph tag that is formatted in the embedded style sheet is reflected in all the paragraph tags within the Web page.

External style sheets are used to apply style rules across multiple Web pages. Each Web page must include a reference to the external style sheet using a <LINK> tag. When a paragraph tag is formatted in an external style sheet rule, all of the paragraphs within the Web pages will apply the new style rule.

Inline Style Sheets

Inline style sheets format a single HTML tag. Inline style sheet rules are also called internal style sheet rules. When referring to an HTML tag within a style sheet, the tag is referred to as an **element**. The style information is stored with the HTML tag using the keyword style. In the style rule, you separate the name of the property and the value that is assigned to that property with a colon. You can format multiple style rules by separating each name and value pair with a semicolon. The following is the syntax for using an inline style rule. (*Note*: Not all tags contain content.)

```
<tagname "style=property1:value;property2:value2;">
    Content goes here
</tagname>
```

In the following sample code, HTML used the Color property of the <FONT> tag to format the color of the text:

```
<FONT COLOR="green">
    <H1>Welcome to Tara Store!</H1>
</FONT>
```

Using cascading style sheets, you can format a heading using an inline style rule. The Color property is formatted using the color style rule. There is no need to include the <FONT> tag.

```
<H1 style="color:green;">Welcome to Tara Store!
</H1>
```

Embedded Style Sheets

Embedded style sheets are style rules that are placed in the heading section of the HTML page. Because embedded style sheet rules are placed in the heading section, they can be applied to more than one tag within the HTML page. Following this paragraph is the syntax for inserting an embedded style sheet. All style sheet rules are contained within a pair of style tags. In this example, the ElementName represents any valid XML or HTML control. Examples of HTML controls are <H1>, <P>, and <DIV>. The entire listing of property names and values are enclosed within a single pair of curly braces. The PropertyName represents any property that is valid for that control. For example, you can format the font color with the Color property. The value represents any value that is valid for that property. You can learn about the valid controls, property names, and values on the W3C cascading style sheet Web site at *www.w3c.org/Style/CSS*.

```
ElementName {
    PropertyName: value;
    PropertyName: value;
}
```

Although some programmers prefer to write the CSS rules on a single line, it is a good idea to enter only one style rule per line. Then, you can easily detect if there is a colon or semicolon missing from the style rule. You can also easily detect if there is a missing curly brace.

Embedded styles are useful when you need to create custom style rules that apply to all elements within the same page. The code following this paragraph is a sample of an embedded style sheet. All of the <H1> tags on the page format the text as 12 point, green.

```
<HTML><HEAD><TITLE>Sample Embedded Style
Sheet</TITLE>
<STYLE>
H1{
     color:green;
     font-size:12pt;
}
</STYLE>
</HEAD>
<BODY>
<H1>Welcome to Tara Store!</H1>
</BODY></HTML>
```

External Style Sheets

The third type of cascading style sheets is the external style sheet, which is also known as a linked style sheet. The **external style sheet** contains style rules that can be used by many files at the same time. The link tag (<LINK>) is used to attach a style sheet to the Web page. Because the style sheet is external to the Web page, the style rules can be reused. The benefit of using an external style sheet is that if you need to make a change to a style rule, you have to make the change in only one location. All of the Web pages that use that style sheet would instantly display the new style rule. Because this is an efficient way to manage style rules, external style sheets are commonly used in business Web sites. External style sheets provide the greatest flexibility.

Following this paragraph is a sample of the code that would be inserted in the external style sheet. The style sheet format for external style sheet rules is the same as the format for embedded style sheet rules. However, you do not need to include the style (<STYLE>) tags within the external style sheet. The name of the file of the external style sheet ends with .css. In the last code example in this section, the name of the style sheet is MyStyle.css.

```
H1{
      color:green;
      font-size:12pt;
}
```

The <LINK> tag is an HTML tag that is used to identify the location of the external style sheet. The **REL** property indicates that the linked document contains a style sheet. In an external style sheet, the style tags are omitted because the REL property indicates that the linked file is a style sheet. The **TYPE** property is used to indicate the MIME type of the linked file. The MIME type is used to indicate which types of programs can open the files. The MIME type, text/css, indicates that the file is a text file and contains cascading style information. The **HREF** property is used to indicate the location of the external style sheet. The URL can be the absolute URL, such as http://www.domain.com/path/StyleSheetName.CSS, or a relative URL, such as /includes/StyleSheetName.CSS. The URL should be placed within quotation marks. The following is the syntax for adding the external style sheet to the Web page using the <LINK> tag:

<link rel=stylesheet type="text/css" href="URL">

The following sample code uses the <LINK> tag to insert the external style sheet into the Web page. (*Note*: The code for the <LINK> tag is entered on one line within the heading section.)

```
<HTML><HEAD><TITLE>Sample Embedded Style Sheet</TITLE>
<LINK REL="stylesheet" TYPE="text/css" HREF="MyStyle.css">
</HEAD>
<BODY>
<H1>Welcome to Tara Store!</H1>
</BODY></HTML>
```

Comments Within Cascading Style Sheets

You can add a multiline comment by adding the symbol /* before the comment and adding */ after the comment. You can add comments to external style sheets or embedded style sheets. The sample code following this paragraph uses comments to document the external cascading style sheet. A multiline comment is used to document the style sheet. An inline comment is used to indicate the purpose of the style information.

```
/* Styles.CSS
Created By: Katie Kalata
Date Created: 9/5/2005
This style sheet is used to format the main menu
*/
```

```
/* Corporate logo */
H1 {color:green}
/* Red heading */
H2 {color:red}
/* Blue heading */
H3 {color:blue}
```

Cascading Style Sheet Rules

These three types of cascading style sheets can contain conflicting style rules. These conflicts are resolved through a series of **cascading rules**. In most cases, inline style rules take precedence over embedded style rules, and embedded style rules take precedence over external style rules. In other words, if the external style sheet indicates that the heading tag is to be formatted in blue, the embedded style sheet indicates that the heading tag is to be formatted in green, and the inline style sheet indicates that the heading tag is to be formatted in red, the heading tag is formatted in red.

Classes

Style sheets are often used to create a class. A **class** can be used to format a group of different tags or a subgroup of a specific tag. For example, you can use a class named MyHeader to format the heading1 tags. The sample code following this paragraph changes the color of all heading 1 tags in the document to green. The class named BlueHead is used to change the color of any element with a class of BlueHead to blue.

```
H1 {color:green}
.SelCat {color:red}
.BlueHead {color:blue}
```

Then, in the Web page, you could format any element with the class. In the sample code following this paragraph, the first message would appear in green. The SelCat class is used only with one item to indicate that the category was selected by formatting the text as red. The <H2> and <H3> headings are formatted with the BlueHead class. Both of these headings would appear in blue.

```
<h1>Welcome to Tara Store!</h1>
<h2 class="BlueHead">Product Listing:</h2>
   <ul>
   <li>Gifts</li>
   <li class="SelCat">Jewelry</li>
   <li>China & Crystal</li>
   <li>Food</li>
   <li>Clothing</li>
   <li>Books, Music, & Videos</li>
   </ul>
```

```
<h3 class="BlueHead">About Tara Store</h3>
   <ul>
   <li>What's New</li>
   <li>Current Sales</li>
   <li>Location</li>
   <li>Contact Us</li>
   <li>Members Only</li>
   </ul>
```

You can set the element's Class property in HTML view or in Design view by selecting the control and changing the Class property in the Properties window.

There are several books that cover cascading style sheets, including *Designing Web Pages with Cascading Style Sheets* by J. Sklar (Course Technology, © 2001), which can be located at *www.course.com/webwarrior*.

In some cases a Web designer may develop the external style sheet. The Web designer is a computer graphic arts specialist who has Web page layout and design skills. He or she can assist you with selecting the appropriate colors, fonts, and images for your Web site.

Using the CSS Editor

Although you can create style sheets in a text editor, it is useful to use a CSS editor to create your style sheets. A **CSS editor** uses a graphical user interface to represent the Web page elements and properties. Although many programs, such as Visual Studio .NET, integrate a Web page editor and a CSS editor into their development environment, CSS editors are available independently of Web page editors. However, having the CSS editor integrated with the development environment makes it easier for you to design and create cascading style sheets. For example, as you make changes to your cascading style sheets, you can see the resulting effects within Visual Studio .NET. CSS editors help ensure that you use only valid tags, properties, and values. Most CSS errors are caused by incorrect syntax.

Visual Studio .NET comes with a complete CSS editor called the **Style Builder**. You can use the dialog boxes to build your style rules, or you can type them in manually. You can create the style sheets, view the CSS code, and preview the output within the Style Builder. Visual Studio .NET also helps you build style rules with the Add Style Rule dialog box and IntelliSense. When you create an ASP.NET application, a default style sheet named styles.css is created.

Visual Studio .NET includes the IntelliSense feature within the CSS editor, which is useful when you choose to enter your style rules manually. For example, when you type font-family:, the IntelliSense feature displays a list of font faces from which to choose. You can use the arrow keys to navigate through the list, or type the first few letters to go directly to the entry in the list. When you have selected the font you want to use, press Enter to make the selection. After you add the semicolon, the IntelliSense feature provides a list of other PropertyNames from which to choose. You can quickly build style sheets using the IntelliSense features.

The Style Builder recognizes any style properties you enter manually. All of the properties are organized using the tabs located on the left of the Style Builder. The Style Builder lets you select the property names and values for fonts, background, text, position, layout, edges, lists, and other properties. You can navigate across these style properties by using the menu located on the left side of the Style Builder window.

The Style Builder includes a **Color Picker** feature, which can be used to help you select a color. The Color Picker is useful because you can select your colors from a predefined palette based on your design and business objectives. Some Web sites prefer to use only the Web colors. The Web colors are 216 colors that are supported by the majority of computers and browsers. Therefore, if you select a color from the Web Colors palette, you can be confident that the end users see the same color on their monitors.

There are four tabs in the Color Picker. They identify how the colors are commonly used. The **Web Palette** tab provides the 216 basic Web colors. Clicking a color selects the color, and displays the hexadecimal equivalent at the bottom of the table. The **Named Colors** tab provides the 16 Windows colors and the 122 other named colors. Although some browsers support only the name feature for the 16 Windows colors, it is useful to refer to the colors by name because the colors are commonly used in daily life. The **System Colors** tab allows you to select a color that matches the colors used to create system graphical user interfaces such as windows, menus, scroll bars, and buttons. This is usually a more useful feature for intranets and Windows applications where you can be certain of the users' color schemes. The **Custom Color** tab allows you to use three slider controls to select the red, green, and blue (RGB) values for the color. In addition to displaying the hexadecimal equivalent of the RGB value, a preview of the color is displayed. The Custom Color palette allows you to select any one of millions of possible colors. However, some computers and browsers may not display all of these colors properly. It is useful to test your Web application to ensure that the colors applied in your Web site are acceptable on different browsers and platforms.

Creating a Cascading Style Sheet

When you create an ASP.NET Web application in Visual Studio .NET, a default cascading style sheet is created. The default style sheet is named Styles.css. The default style sheet already contains many commonly used style rules. You can edit these style rules or remove them in Code view or in the Style Builder. In the following example, you will modify the default style sheet using the Add Style Rule dialog box, IntelliSense, and the Style Builder.

1. Double-click the **Styles.css** file in the Solution Explorer window.

2. The style sheet opens. Locate the BODY tag in the style sheet.

  a. Locate the style rule for the default FONT-FAMILY.

  b. Type **Arial,** before the Verdana font name, as shown in Figure 2-9. This formats all of the fonts in the page with the Arial typeface. (*Note*: Make sure to include the comma between Arial and Verdana.)

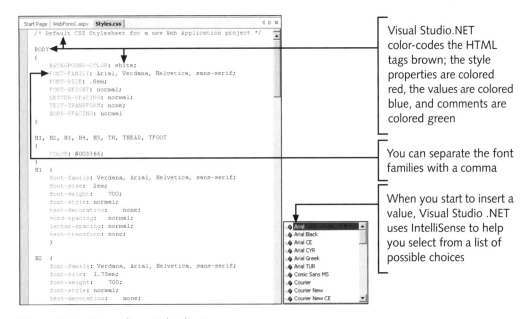

Figure 2-9 Cascading style sheet

  c. To change the background color of the page, right-click the word **BODY**, and then click **Build Style**. Notice that the first value in the Font Family property is Arial.

  d. Click the **Background** tab in the Style Builder dialog box.

  e. Click the **Color** list arrow. Notice that the 16 Windows named colors are listed. Do not select a color.

  f. Click the **Build** button next to the Color list box to open the Color Picker dialog box. The Build button's icon is a series of three dots, and it is used to provide additional tools to assist with selecting a value.

  g. Click the **Web Palette** tab, as shown in Figure 2-10. Do not select a color. Click **Cancel** twice. (*Note*: The preview box in the Style Builder dialog box displays the color selected with sample text.)

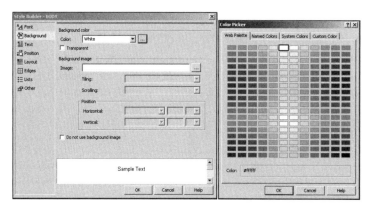

Figure 2-10   Changing style properties in the Style Builder

The Background property is often used to add a color or image to the background of an object. In browsers, the background applies to the entire line, not just the text. By specifying margins, you can specify where the background color is implemented.

3. To insert another style rule, right-click the CSS page above the BODY tag, and then click **Add Style Rule**. HTML elements, class names, and element IDs are provided in three drop-down lists.

4. In the Element drop-down list box, select **TABLE**, as shown in Figure 2-11. Click the **>** button to place the element in the Style rule hierarchy list, and then click **OK**.

5. Use the process described in Steps 3 and 4 to insert the **HR** and **TD** tags. The style rules are added to the bottom of the style sheet. You must click **OK** after each element has been selected. Do not select both the HR and TD tags at the same time.

6. Right-click within the curly braces of the H2 tag, and then click **Build Style**. The Style Builder dialog box opens. Click the **Color** drop-down list arrow. Select **Green** from the 16 Windows named colors list, and then click **OK** to close the dialog box.

7. Right-click the **HR** style rule at the bottom of the page, and then click **Build Style**. In the Color drop-down list box, select **Green**. Click the **OK** button.

2

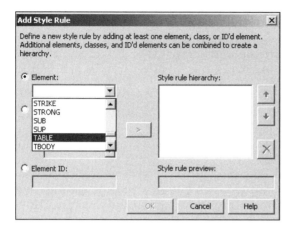

Figure 2-11   The Add Style Rule dialog box

8. Right-click in the **UL LI** style rule, then click **Build Style**.

   a. In the Color drop-down list, select **Green**. Click the **Build** button in the top-right corner of the dialog box, select **Verdana** from the Installed fonts list, and then click **OK**. Click the **Specific** text box, and type **10** (**pt** will be filled in for you automatically).

   b. Click the **Lists** tab and then check the **Custom bullet** check box.

   c. Click the **Build** button next to the Image text box. In the Projects pane, click the **images** folder. In the Contents of 'images' pane, click **bullet.gif**. (*Note*: You can browse the directory tree on your computer to insert images or select images from within the project files.) Click the **OK** button. Click the **OK** button in the Style Builder dialog box.

9. Right-click the **TABLE** element, and then click **Build Style**.

   a. Click the **Edges** tab.

   b. Select **Solid Line** in the Style setting drop-down list box.

   c. Click **Green** in the Color drop-down list box. Click the **OK** button.

10. Right-click the **TD** element, and then click **Build Style**.

   a. Click the **Text** tab.

   b. Click **Centered** in the Horizontal drop-down list box. Click the **OK** button.

11. Add a class by right-clicking the style sheet, and then clicking **Add Style Rule**.

   a. Click the **Class name** option button. Click the accompanying text box and type **TSHeading**. Click the > button and then click the **OK** button.

   b. Right-click in the **TSHeading** class style rule, and then click **Build Style**.

   c. Set the Small caps property to **Small caps**.

   d. Click the Specific option button, if necessary, and enter **12** and **pt** for the size of the text font (note that "pt" may be filled in for you automatically here and in subsequent similar steps). Click **OK**.

12. Add a class by right-clicking the style sheet and then clicking **Add Style Rule**.

    a. Click the **Class name** option button. Click the accompanying text box, and then type **TSLinks**. Click the **>** button and the **OK** button.

    b. Right-click in the **TSLinks** class style rule, then click **Build Style**.

    c. In the Font tab, select **Green** in the Color drop-down list box.

    d. Click the **Specific** option button, if necessary, and enter **10** and **pt** for the size of the text font. Click **OK**.

13. Add a class by right-clicking the style sheet and then clicking **Add Style Rule**. Click the **Class name** option button. Click the accompanying text box, and then type **txtBox**. Click the **>** button and then the **OK** button.

14. Right-click in the **txtBox** class style rule, and then click **Build Style**.

    a. In the Color drop-down list box, select **Green**.

    b. In the Bold section, the Absolute option button is selected. Select **Bold** from the accompanying drop-down list.

    c. Click the **Specific** option button, if necessary, and enter **10** and **pt** for the size.

    d. In the Family text box, use the Build button to select **Verdana**, click the **>** button, and then click **OK**.

    e. On the Edges tab, select **Solid Line** as the style and **Green** as the color. Click **OK**.

15. Add a class by right-clicking the style sheet and then clicking **Add Style Rule**. Click the **Class Name** option button. Click the accompanying text box, and then type **TSButton**. Click the **>** button and then click the **OK** button.

16. Right-click in the **TSButton** class style rule, and then click **Build Style**.

    a. On the Font tab, set the Family text box entry to **Verdana**.

    b. Set the Small caps property to **Small caps**.

    c. In the Color drop-down list box, select **White**.

    d. Click the **Specific** option button, if necessary, and enter **10** and **pt** as the size.

    e. In the Bold section, the Absolute option button is selected. Click **Bold** from the accompanying drop-down list.

    f. On the Background tab, set the Color drop-down list box to **Green**.

    g. On the Edges tab, set the Style drop-down list box to **Ridge** and the Color drop-down list box to **Yellow**. Click **OK**.

17. Click **File** on the menu bar, and then click **Save All**.

In the following steps, you will apply the style sheet to the feedback.htm page you created earlier. You can simply drag the cascading style sheet from the Solution Explorer window to the Web page. Visual Studio .NET will insert and configure the <LINK> tag for you. (*Note:* You can also enter the link information manually in HTML view.)

1. Preview the style sheet by right-clicking it and then clicking **View in Browser**. The CSS Editor Preview Page opens with a preview of what the style sheet looks like when applied to a sample Web page.

2. Close the CSS Editor Preview Page.

3. Open the **feedback.htm** page if it is not already open.

4. Click the **Design** tab, if necessary, to view the Web page in Design view.

5. Drag the **Styles.css** file from the Solution Explorer window to the feedback.htm page. This adds the link tag into the HTML code.

6. Click **File** on the menu bar, and then click **Save All**.

7. Right-click the page, and then click **View in Browser**. Your page should look like the one on the left side in Figure 2-12.

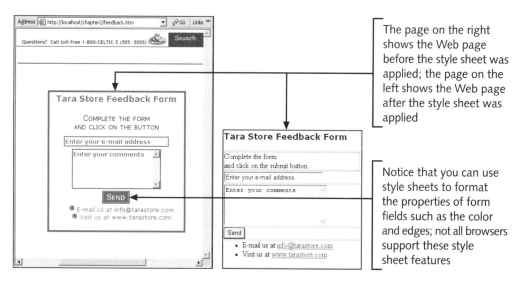

Figure 2-12   Linking a style sheet to a Web page

8. Close the feedback.htm page and the style sheet.

Customizing the Toolbox

The Clipboard Ring is a Toolbox tool that stores the list of items that have previously been copied to the Clipboard. The **Clipboard** is the area in memory that Windows uses to copy information that can be used in another part of a document or even in another program. The Clipboard is also found in Windows Office applications. If you do not create a custom control for a piece of code, and you happen to have recently copied it somewhere, the code might appear in the Clipboard Ring. However, if you create code that you plan to reuse, it is best to customize the Toolbox and add the code to the General tab. You can add additional tabs to the Toolbox to help organize your frequently used code. You can add third-party customized controls, including code fragments, to any of the tabs in the Toolbox.

In the following exercise, you will create a new tab and add a code fragment to this new tab.

1. Right-click in the Toolbox area, click **Add Tab**, type **My Tools**, and then press **Enter**.

2. Open the **feedback.htm** page.

3. Click the **My Tools** tab, which is at the very bottom of the Toolbox area.

4. Click and drag the **header.jpg** image to the My Tools tab. The code is represented as MarkUp Fragment on the toolbar.

5. Right-click **MarkUp Fragment**, and then click **Rename Item**. Type **HeaderImage**, and then press **Enter**.

6. Right-click **Chapter2** in the Solution Explorer window, point to **Add**, and then click **Add Web Form**.

7. In the Name text box, type **Contact.aspx**, and then click the **Open** button.

8. Click the **My Tools** tab. Drag the new custom **HeaderImage** code from the My Tools tab to the top-left corner of the Contact page. This places the control on the Web page.

9. Click **File** on the menu bar, and then click **Save All**.

10. Close the Contact page.

USING VISUAL STUDIO .NET HELP RESOURCES

In the exercise following this paragraph, you learn how to locate Help resources within Visual Studio .NET. **Dynamic Help** provides help for the currently selected item. **Search Help** provides a text box to enter a search phrase. **Index Help** provides a dictionary index that lets you search for a term alphabetically. **Contents Help** allows you navigate the Help documentation using a table of contents. All Help methods provide results in a ranked list. You can double-click on the items in the list to view the documentation from within the user interface. You do not have to leave the Visual Studio .NET application to locate Help or documentation. You can view the actual URL of the Help files in the URL drop-down list box on the Web toolbar.

1. With the file feedback.htm open in Visual Studio .NET, right-click the page, and then click **View HTML Source**. Highlight the word **HTML** in the

first line of code. Click **Help** on the menu bar, and then click **Dynamic Help**. In the Dynamic Help window click the **HTML View, HTML Designer** link to open a Web page within the main window that contains information about the HTML editor.

2. Read the documentation on the Object Selector and Event Selector. By default the HTML Designer shows you the HTML and any scripts. They are both drop-down list boxes that appear at the top of the HTML page. The Object Selector is a list of all scriptable objects in the current document. The Event Selector is a list of all events sent to the selected object for which you can write handlers. Close the Dynamic Help window.

3. Click **Help** on the menu bar, and then click **Search**. In the Look for text box, type **Style Builder**. In the Filtered by drop-down list box, click **Internet Development**. Click the **Search** button. The Search Results window opens with your results. (You may have to resize windows on your screen to see the Search Results window.)

4. In the Search Results window, double-click **Introduction to Cascading Style Sheets**. The documentation appears in a new window. Read the documentation for creating cascading style sheets. When you are finished, close the page.

5. Click Help on the menu bar, and then click **Index**. The Filtered by text box should still say Internet Development. In the Look for text box, type **STYLE tag**. The list changes as you type the characters. Click **HTML markup** underneath the STYLE tag selection. In the Results window, the Style Builder Dialog Box text is displayed. Scrolling as necessary, read the paragraphs under the heading "Creating Inline CSS Styles in Design View." Close the page.

6. Click **Help** on the menu bar, and then click **Contents**. Expand the following: **Visual Studio .NET**; **Developing with Visual Studio .NET**; **Working with Code, HTML, and Resource Files**; **Editing Code, HTML, and Text**; and **HTML**. Expand **Working with CSS Styles**. Click **Introduction to Cascading Style Sheets**, as shown in Figure 2-13. (*Note*: Although this method requires more clicks to locate what you're looking for, you might stumble upon other useful information as you browse through the documentation. You can search the MSDN & the Visual Studio .NET SDK documentation and Help files all from within the same user interface.)

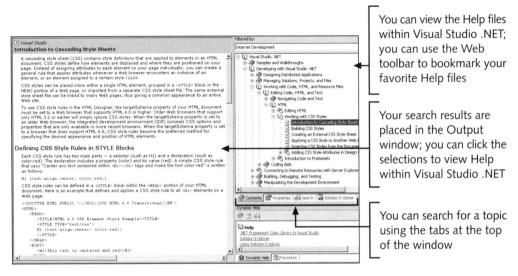

You can view the Help files within Visual Studio .NET; you can use the Web toolbar to bookmark your favorite Help files

Your search results are placed in the Output window; you can click the selections to view Help within Visual Studio .NET

You can search for a topic using the tabs at the top of the window

Figure 2-13   Help search results

CHAPTER SUMMARY

❑ Visual Studio .NET provides many options for configuring the Visual Studio .NET desktop. Auto-hiding allows you to shelve windows until they are needed. Floating windows allow you to drag windows anywhere on the desktop.

❑ The Solution Explorer window allows you to manage all of your project files from one location.

❑ The Properties window allows you to set properties for objects.

❑ The Toolbox contains a set of commonly used controls, which are organized into tabs. You can customize the Toolbox to include your own custom controls.

❑ The HTML editor can be used to create HTML pages. You can write the HTML code directly in HTML view, or use Design view and drag-and-drop controls from the HTML tab in the Toolbox. HTML tags can be formatted using the Formatting toolbar, the menus, or the Properties window.

❑ You can create your own custom controls called User controls. User controls can contain HTML code and programming code. User controls must be registered within an ASP.NET page before they can be used. Once a tag has been registered as a User control, you can use the tag throughout the Web page. User controls are compiled, and can be reused across multiple pages within the same application.

❑ There are three types of cascading style sheets. The inline style sheet rules apply only to a single element. The embedded style sheet rules can be applied to multiple elements within the same page. A linked style sheet contains rules that can be applied to multiple pages. Cascading style sheets can be created manually or with the Style Builder.

❑ Additional features such as IntelliSense and Dynamic Help help programmers learn how to use Visual Studio .NET.

2

REVIEW QUESTIONS

1. If you want the window to be hidden, but want the ability to click on the name of the window on the desktop and show the window, which selection should you choose?

   a. Hide

   b. Auto Hide

   c. Floating

   d. Sliding

2. What is the file extension for a Web Form?

   a. .asp

   b. .aspx

   c. .asx

   d. .asxp

3. What is the name of the style property that allows you to position elements on a page using absolute positioning from the Properties window?

   a. pageLayout

   b. pageView

   c. gridlock

   d. position

4. What character(s) is/are used to comment out code in a style sheet?

   a. /* */

   b. *

   c. &

   d. #

5. You have just created a page named Spooks.htm. If your project name is ghost, and you created your project using the default settings, where can you view your page in a browser?

   a. *http://www.ghost.com/spooks.htm*

   b. *http://localhost/ghost.htm*

   c. *http://255.255.255.0/ghost.htm*

   d. *http://localhost/ghosts/spooks.htm*

6. Which tab in the Toolbox is most commonly used to insert custom code fragments?

   a. HTML

   b. General

   c. Web Form

   d. WinForm

7. Which property is used to set the target browser for the Web page from the Properties window?

   a. targetPage

   b. targetSchema

   c. targetBrowser

   d. none of the above

8. Which toolbar provides access to text format tools?

   a. Design toolbar

   b. Image editor

   c. Format toolbar

   d. Paint toolbar

9. The Start window has been closed. What menu allows you to reopen the Start window? (*Hint:* Go to each menu and look for "Show Start Page.")

   a. File

   b. Window

   c. Help

   d. Edit

10. What feature supplies context-sensitive help?

    a. Index

    b. Start Page

    c. Dynamic Help

    d. Contents

11. Which type of style sheet takes precedence over all other style rules?

    a. inline

    b. external

    c. linked

    d. embedded

12. What tag is used to attach an external style sheet to a Web page?

    a. Link

    b. MIME

    c. Rel

    d. Href

13. What is the character that separates the name and values within a style rule?

    a. :

    b. *

    c. { }

    d. ,

14. Which style element can be applied to more than one element?

    a. Class

    b. ID

    c. H2

    d. none of the above

15. What is the file extension of a cascading style sheet?

    a. .css

    b. .ccs

    c. .html

    d. .ascx

16. Which keyword is used to define a User control?

    a. control

    b. pagelets

    c. fragments

    d. register

17. Which tag(s) cannot be included within a User control?

    a. HTML

    b. head

    c. body

    d. all of the above

HANDS-ON PROJECTS

Project 2-1

In this project you will import additional samples from the Chapter02Data folder into your Chapter2 project. This project requires that you have already created a Chapter2 project and imported all of the images from your Chapter02Data\images folder into the Chapter2 project images directory. A chapter samples home page named Ch2Proj1Demo.aspx will be imported. This page contains the links to these samples and additional resources. In this project you will view the sample home page and one of the sample Web pages.

1. Right-click **Chapter2** to display the shortcut icon. Point to **Add**, and then click **Add Existing Item**.

2. Navigate to your Chapter02Data folder. In the Files of type drop-down list, change the selection to **All Files**.

3. Select all of the files except the Images directory, and click **Open**. (*Note*: You can press and hold the Control key and click once on each file to select all of the files.)

4. Click **File** on the menu bar, and then click **Save All**.

5. Click the **Build** menu and click **Build Solution**.

6. In the Solution Explorer window, double-click **Ch2Proj1.css**. Heading 1 is formatted green, the SelCat class is formatted red, and the BlueHead class if formatted blue. Close the file.

7. In the Solution Explorer window, double-click **Ch2Proj1.aspx**. Click the **HTML** tab. Note that the Link tag points to the Ch2Proj1.css style sheet. Close the file.

8. Open a browser and type **http://localhost/Chapter2/Ch2Proj1Demo.aspx** in the Address box.

9. Under Additional Samples, click **Ch2_Class.aspx**. Note that the page was formatted using the style properties in the external style sheet.

10. Visit at least one of the Web sites listed under the links to Web sites listed at the bottom of the Ch2Proj1Demo.aspx page.

Project 2-2

In this project you will use Visual Basic .NET to create a feedback form.

1. Start **Visual Studio .NET** and open your **Chapter2 solution** if necessary.

2. Create a new HTML page named **Ch2Proj2.htm**.

3. Add a title to the page using the title tag that says **Feedback Form**.

4. Add the **header.jpg**, **menu.gif**, and **CustomerSupport.jpg** images to the Web page.

5. Add a heading that says **Feedback Form** using the Label control on the HTML tab of the Toolbox. Format the text as Heading2. Drag the handles of the control to show the text on one line.

6. Add HTML Text controls to collect the user's name and e-mail address. Add labels for each of the Text controls.

7. Add a Label control that says **How did you hear about our Web site?** Add a drop-down list box containing five choices such as "Magazine, Radio, E-mail, Friend, Television". Right-click on the drop-down list box and then click **Properties** to display the Select Property Pages dialog box. Enter the options. The options should

be the same value as the text displayed, as shown in Figure 2-14. You must click the Insert button after each Text and Value pair you enter. Leave the **Allow multiple selections** check box unchecked. Change the Size property to **1**. Click **OK**.

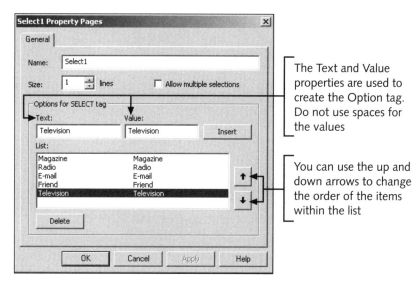

The Text and Value properties are used to create the Option tag. Do not use spaces for the values

You can use the up and down arrows to change the order of the items within the list

Figure 2-14   Using the Select Property Pages dialog box to enter the options list

8. Add a Label control that says **What products are you interested in?** Add three check boxes and corresponding Label controls that say **Jewelry**, **Clothing**, and **China**. (*Note*: You may add additional check boxes and option buttons to enhance the form.)

9. Add a Submit button that says **Send Your Comments**.

10. You can make it look presentable and professional by adding color and by changing the text fonts, graphics, and style sheets.

11. Go to the **File** menu and select **Save All** to save all of your solution files.

12. Click **Build** on the menu bar, then click **Build Solution**.

13. View your page in a browser. Go to *http://localhost/chapter2/Ch2Proj2.htm*. From the browser, print the page and the source code view. Your page should look like the one in Figure 2-15.

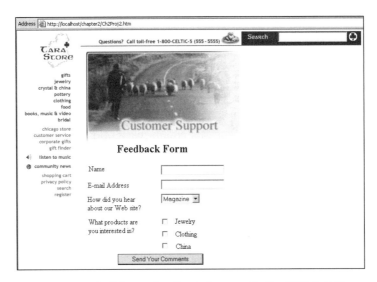

Figure 2-15 Building a feedback form with the HTML Editor

14. Close the page.

Project 2-3

In this project you will create an external Cascading Style Sheet using the Style Builder.

1. Start **Visual Studio .NET** and open your **Chapter2 solution** if necessary.

2. Create a new style sheet named **Ch2Proj3.css**.

3. Add the following elements to the style sheet: **TABLE**, **UL**, **H1**, **H2**, and **HR**.

4. Modify the BODY, TABLE, UL, H1, H2, and HR elements using the Style Builder. Choose at least three properties to modify with each element.

5. Create a class named **Ch2Proj3**. Format the class with the Style Builder. Choose at least three properties to modify.

6. Go to the File menu and select **Save All** to save all of your solution files.

7. Preview the style sheet using the **CSS Editor Preview Page**. Print the page and the style sheet.

Project 2-4

In this project you will create a custom user control. You will register the User control in an ASP.NET page, and use the control in the Web page.

1. Start **Visual Studio .NET** and open your **Chapter2 solution** if necessary.

2. Create a new Web User control named **Ch2Proj4UC.ascx**.

3. Go to the HTML tab in the Toolbox and drag the **Grid Layout Panel** to the page.

2

4. Place the **header.jpg**, **menu.gif**, and **CustomerSupport.jpg** image files inside the panel on the User control page.

5. Add a label that says **Welcome to Tara Store Customer Support** and format the label with the Heading3 tag.

6. Create an ASP.NET Web page named **Ch2Proj4.aspx**. Make sure to select **Add Web Form** when you create the page. The page opens in Design view.

7. Drag the **Ch2Proj4UC.ascx** file from the Solution Explorer window, and place it on the Ch2Proj4.aspx Web page.

8. Click the **HTML** tag to view the code that registered and inserted the User control.

9. Make the page look presentable and professional by adding content and color and by changing the text fonts, graphics, and style sheets.

10. Click the **Save All** button on the Toolbar to save all of your solution files. Click **Build** on the menu bar, and then click **Build Solution**.

11. View your page in a browser. Go to *http://localhost/chapter2/Ch2Proj4.aspx*. From the browser, print the page and the source code view. Your Web page should appear like the one in Figure 2-16.

Figure 2-16   Inserting a User control

Project 2-5

In this project you will create a custom User control that contains a menu.

1. Start **Visual Studio .NET** and open your **Chapter2 solution** if necessary.

2. Create a new Web User control named **Ch2Proj5Header.ascx**.

3. Add the **header.jpg** file to the User control.

4. Create a new Web User control named **Ch2Proj5Menu.ascx**.

5. Add the **menu.gif** image to the User control.

6. Create an ASP.NET Web page named **Ch2Proj5.aspx**. Make sure to select **Add Web Form** when you create the page.

7. Create a table using the Table menu that contains two rows and two columns. Change the Border size property to **0**.

8. To merge the first two cells, click inside the first cell in the first row. Change the colspan property in the Properties window to **2**. Click inside the second cell in the first row. Right-click in the cell, point to **Delete**, then click **Cells**.

9. Drag the **Ch2Proj5Header.ascx** User control from the Solution Explorer window to the first cell in the first row. The User control graphic is placed in the cell.

10. Drag the **Ch2Proj5Menu.ascx** User control from the Solution Explorer window to the first cell of the second row. The User control graphic is placed in the cell.

11. Click the **HTML** tab to view the code that registered and inserted the User control into the Web page.

12. Make the page look presentable and professional by adding content and color and by changing the text fonts, graphics, and style sheets.

13. Click the **Save All** button to save all of your solution files.

14. Click **Build** on the menu bar, then click **Build Solution**.

15. View your page in a browser. Go to *http://localhost/chapter2/Ch2Proj5.aspx*. From the browser, print the page and the source code view.

Project 2-6

In this project you will locate additional Help topics within Visual Studio .NET. You will use the Help windows within Visual Studio .NET to learn more about ASP.NET. You will create a Web page that summarizes your findings.

1. Start **Visual Studio .NET** and open your **Chapter2 solution** if necessary.

2. Open the **Search** Help window. Make sure to select **Internet Development** as the filter from the drop-down list.

3. Select a topic and enter the topic in the text box. Topics you can select from include:

   ◻ Introduction to ASP.NET

   ◻ Introduction to Web Forms

   ◻ Creating an ASP.NET Application

   ◻ Web Server Controls

   ◻ Other ASP.NET related topics

4. Create a page named **Ch2Proj6.aspx**. Summarize your findings in this page. Format the page using the HTML editor.

5. Visit the Microsoft Office Clip Art and Media Home Page at *http://office.microsoft.com/clipart/default.aspx*. Select three graphics. Right-click each graphic and select **Copy**. Save the graphics to your Chapter02Data directory. Import the three graphics from your Chapter02Data directory to your images folder in your Chapter2 project. Add the three graphics to your Web page.

6. Make the page look presentable and professional by adding content and color and by changing the text fonts, graphics, and style sheets.

7. Click the **Save All** button to save all of your solution files.

8. View your page in a browser. Go to *http://localhost/chapter2/Ch2Proj6.aspx*. From the browser, print the page and the source code view. (*Note:* Your Web page will vary depending upon which topic you selected, which content you added, and which graphics you added.)

CASE PROJECTS

Creating Web Pages with Visual Studio .NET

You are hired as the Web developer for a new Web site called MyStore. You are responsible for creating the home page for the Web site. Use Visual Studio .NET to create a home page. Add at least three graphics, three hyperlinks, a bulleted list, and a table. Use the Properties window to modify the appearance of the controls and the Web page. Format the page using additional graphics, content, fonts, and color to enhance the appearance of the page. You may change the name of the store. Save the home page as Ch2Case1.htm. View your Web page in your browser. Print your Web page and the source code from the browser.

Creating Style Sheets with Visual Studio .NET

You are hired as the Web developer for a new Web site called MyStore. Your store manager has requested that you make several product category pages. Choose at least five product categories such as shirts, accessories, china, jewelry, or books. Create a Web page for each product category named Ch2Case2Cat1.aspx, Ch2Case2Cat2.aspx, Ch2Case2Cat3.aspx, Ch2Case2Cat4.aspx, and Ch2Case2Cat5.aspx. On each Web page, include a menu that lists all product categories. Each category listed contains a hyperlink to the specific category page.

Create a style sheet that formats the category menu. There should be two classes defined in the style sheet. The first class, named Unselected, is used for the categories that are not selected. The Selected class is used to format the current hyperlink. The current hyperlink is the hyperlink that would take you to the current page. The Selected class changes the format of the link to a different color and font size using a style sheet rule. For example, each of the categories may be formatted blue with a font size of 10 pt. When the user is on the books page, the books hyperlink is red, with a font size of 12 pt. Save the style sheet at Ch2Case2.css. Add a link from the external style sheet to each of the Web pages using the link tag. Format each page using additional graphics, content, fonts, and color to enhance the appearance of the page. You may change the name of the store. View your Web pages in your browser. Print each Web page and the source code from the browser.

Creating User Controls with Visual Studio .NET

Your store manager has requested that you make several product category pages. However, you don't have the budget to create custom pages and to maintain individual pages. Create a Web page for each product category. The product category pages should be named Ch2Case3Cat1.aspx, Ch2Case3Cat2.aspx, Ch2Case3Cat3.aspx, Ch2Case3Cat4.aspx, and Ch2Case3Cat5.aspx. Create three User controls, named Ch2Case3Header.ascx, Ch2Case3Menu.ascx, and Ch2Case3Footer.ascx. In the Ch2Case3Header.ascx control, add a banner graphic. Create a menu in the Ch2Case3Menu.ascx User control that lists at least five product categories. Each category listing should contain a hyperlink to the category home page. In the Ch2Case3Footer.ascx control, add the store address, and a hyperlink to the store home page. Within each page, register the three controls, and insert them into the page. Format each page using additional graphics, content, fonts, and color to enhance the appearance of the page. You may change the name of the store. View each Web page in your browser. Print each Web page and the source code from the browser.

Customizing the Visual Studio .NET Desktop

You need to customize your desktop within Visual Studio .NET so that you will be able to more efficiently locate resources that you will commonly use. Create an HTML page named Ch2Case4.htm. Create a form on the page with at least five form fields. Set a default value for the name and ID properties for each field. You can select which additional properties you would like to modify. For example, the default property for a text box name might be txtName. Customize the toolbar. Add a new tab with your name. Create an HTML fragment on the General tab in the Toolbox that contains one of the form fields from the Web Form. Rename the HTML fragment according to the name of the form field. With the custom tab displayed, capture a screen shot of your desktop by using the Print Screen key. Open WordPad. Paste the screen shot into WordPad. (Press Ctrl+V to paste the screen shot, or go to the Edit menu in WordPad and select Paste.) Print the screen shot and the Ch2Case4.htm page.

Locate Help Using the Built-In Resources

As project manager you need to customize Visual Studio .NET for all the programmers. Your Web pages will be used by the other programmers to learn how to customize Visual Studio .NET. You also have to provide training for your programmers so that they know how they can customize the development environment. To do this, you need more information about customizing the user interface. Use Dynamic Help, Contents, Index, Search, and the Start Page to locate information on three of the following topics:

- Customizing the Toolbox
- Setting Properties Using the Properties Window
- Customizing the Toolbox
- Docking Windows
- Modifying the Start Page
- Customizing the User Interface
- The Clipboard Ring

Create three Web pages, named Ch2Case5Topic1.aspx, Ch2Case5Topic2.aspx, and Ch2Case5Topic3.aspx. Provide a summary of the information you learned about the topics you researched. In your Web page, provide step-by-step instructions how to customize the development environment. Modify the presentation of the pages using the toolbars, Toolbox, and Properties window. View each Web page in your browser. Print each Web page and the source code from the browser.

Creating a Form with Visual Studio .NET

You are responsible for developing a survey for your Web site. Develop a survey Web page that uses multiple choice, true and false, short answer, and open-ended questions. Use Visual Studio .NET to create the form in an ASP.NET page named Ch2Case6.aspx. The form should consist of questions that use text boxes, option buttons, check boxes, drop-down lists, and command buttons. Add hyperlinks and images to the Web page. Modify the presentation of the page using the toolbars, Toolbox, and Properties window. View the Web page in your browser. Print the Web page and the source code from the browser.

3

USING SERVER CONTROLS

In this chapter, you will:

♦ Create Web pages using HTML Server controls and ASP.NET Web controls

♦ Examine the difference between HTML Server controls and ASP.NET Web controls

♦ Create and process a form using HTML Server controls

♦ Create and process a form using ASP.NET Web controls

♦ Populate form field controls dynamically using ArrayLists and HashTables

♦ Populate a list control dynamically using ArrayLists and HashTables

♦ Validate a form using Validation controls

One of the responsibilities of a Web developer is to create and process Web Forms. In the past, Web Forms were created using HTML, and processed and validated using client-side JavaScript. However, forms processed using client-side JavaScript are not secure because they can be easily altered before the form is submitted by the user. Also, client-side JavaScript is browser dependent. Today, most Web Forms are validated on the Web server, which is both more secure and browser independent.

In this chapter, you will learn to use HTML Server controls and ASP.NET Web controls to create, process, and validate Web Forms. You will then create form fields that can be changed dynamically by using data structures such as ArrayLists and HashTables.

USING HTML SERVER CONTROLS

As you learned in Chapter 1, the two types of server controls are HTML Server controls and ASP.NET Server controls. (ASP.NET Server controls are also known as ASP.NET Web Server controls, Web Server controls, or simply Web controls.) HTML Server controls are HTML controls that are converted to Server controls by setting the runat attribute to "server". HTML Server controls generate the HTML Server and Web Server controls that are sent to the browser. In Visual Studio .NET, all of the Web page HTML Server controls and ASP.NET Web controls (also called Web controls) are objects on the Web server. **Object-oriented programming** allows you to use objects, which can be accessed by other programs, including Web pages. An **object** is a set of related methods and properties that are compartmentalized. **Properties** are used to set the value of a variable defined within an object. You change the values of the properties of the Web server objects by using the Properties window in Visual Studio .NET.

All HTML Server controls inherit from the same HTMLControl class, which is known as `System.Web.UI.HTMLControl`. So, all HTML Server controls inherit the same properties and methods from the HTMLControl class. For example, all HTML Server controls inherit a property called ID. The ID property is used to identify the control within server programs. The ID property is also used to generate the ID for the HTML control on the client. All HTML Server controls also inherit a property called Visible. All HTML Server controls are visible by default because the Visible property is True by default. The **Visible property** is a Boolean value that indicates whether a Server control is rendered as an HTML control on the page. Another commonly used property is the Style property. The Style property retrieves a collection of all cascading style sheet (CSS) rules applied to a specified HTML Server control. The Style property can be configured by using a cascading style sheet, or by using the Style Builder. You can access the Style Builder for a specific control by using the pop-up menu or the Properties window. The ToString method returns the name of the class in the form of a string. If, for example, a text box contains a class name, you can use the ToString method to write out that value in a browser. Although each HTML Server control inherits these properties, each type of HTML Server control has additional properties specific to that control.

The properties and methods common to all HTML Server controls can be found in the Visual Studio .NET online documentation for the HTMLControl class.

All that's required to turn any HTML element into a Server control is the addition of the extra attribute runat="server". This attribute enables the server to recognize the control as a Server control. One of the most cumbersome tasks when creating interactive Web sites and applications is managing the values passed to the server from HTML Form controls, and maintaining the values in these controls between page requests. So one of the core aims of ASP.NET is to simplify this programming task. This involves no extra effort on the part of the programmer, and works on all browsers that support basic HTML and above. You can access the properties of Server controls by using server programs. In plain HTML, it is difficult for the server to retain the values and properties of the HTML control across page requests. With HTML Server controls, the state of the control can be maintained using ASP.NET.

The four main groups of HTML Server controls are the HTMLImage, HTMLContainer, HTMLGeneric, and HTMLInput controls. The **HTMLImage control** is used to represent simple images and returns an image tag. The **HTMLContainer control** group is a base class for elements that can contain other elements and that must have a closing tag. HTMLContainer controls create HTML controls such as the italic, bold, and div tags. The **HTMLGeneric control** is used for other HTML elements not listed in the HTMLControls such as the div and span tags. The **HTMLInput control** group retrieves information from the user. For example, HTMLInputText generates a text box in a form. Table 3-1 lists the HTML controls and the HTMLControl class that each inherits.

Table 3-1   HTMLControls generate client HTML controls

Control Class	Inherits from this Class	HTML Generated by Visual Studio .NET
HtmlAnchor	HTMLContainerControl	`<a href="page.aspx" runat="server">`
HtmlButton	HTMLContainerControl	`<button runat="server">`
HtmlSelect	HTMLContainerControl	`<select runat="server">`
HtmlTextArea	HTMLContainerControl	`<textarea runat="server">`
HtmlInputButton	HTMLInputControl	`<input type="button" runat="server">`
HtmlInputCheckBox	HTMLInputControl	`<input type="check" runat="server">`
HtmlInputRadioButton	HTMLInputControl	`<input type="radio" runat="server">`
HtmlInputText	HTMLInputControl	`<input type="text" runat="server">` and `<input type="password" runat="server">`
HtmlInputHidden	HTMLInputControl	`<input type="hidden" runat="server">`
HtmlInputImage	HTMLInputControl	`<input type="image" runat="server">`
HtmlInputFile	HTMLInputControl	`<input type="file" runat="server">`
HtmlForm	HTMLContainerControl	`<form runat="server">`
HtmlImage	HTMLImage	`<img src="page.jpg" runat="server">`
HtmlTable	HTMLContainerControl	`<table runat="server">`
HtmlTableRow	HTMLContainerControl	`<tr runat="server">`
HtmlTableCell	HTMLContainerControl	`<td runat="server">`
HtmlGenericControl	HTMLContainerControl	Any other unmapped tag, such as `<span runat="server">`, `<div runat="server">`, etc.

3

HTML Server Control Event Handlers

Web developers have used client-side scripting to interact with the user. JavaScript and cascading style sheets are used in combination to create Dynamic HTML (DHTML). DHTML allows you to interact with the user when he or she completes a form or clicks a hyperlink. There are various levels of browser support for JavaScript. There are many different types of platforms that are now Web enabled. With Server controls, you do not have to write the client-side script. Rather, you write the code to configure the properties and events of the Server controls. By using a server-side control, you generate output that is supported by the client. If the client's browser supports JavaScript and DHTML, the output is generated using JavaScript and DHTML. Events such as the form validation could be performed on the client. If not, then the output is HTML, and events such as form field validation are performed on the server.

When the control in the browser detects an event, such as a mouse click, the browser can respond to the event by using an event handler, which executes code statements when the event occurs. HTML Server control events include OnServerChange and OnServerClick. The **OnServerChange event** occurs when an HTML Server control value has changed. The HTML Server controls that support the OnServerChange event are HTMLInputCheckBox, HTMLInputRadio, HTMLInputHidden, HTMLInputText, HTMLTextArea, and HTMLSelect. The **OnServerClick event** occurs when the visitor clicks an HTML Server control. The HTML controls that support the OnServerClick event include HTMLInputImage, HTMLAnchor, and HTMLButton.

The names of the controls are not always the same as the class. For example, the HTML Hyperlink Server control is created by the HTMLAnchor class and the HTML DropDown List Server control is created by the HTMLSelect class. You can refer to the control by its name or by its class name. The rest of this book will refer to the HTML Server controls by the generic control name. For example, you can refer to the Label control as the HTML Label Server control. The online and local MSDN help files contain the class, properties, members, and events for each HTML Server control and each Web control.

Client- and server-side event handlers can sometimes occur with each other. For example, if you create a hyperlink tag using an HTML Server control, the output created is a simple anchor tag. If there is a client script such as a mouseover, and the user points at the hyperlink, the mouseover event occurs. If the user clicks the hyperlink, the server click event handler is executed. However, if the anchor tag contains both a server-side click event handler and a client-side click event handler, an autogenerated client-side script intercepts the click event and directs the handler to the server-side click event handler. The client-side click event handler runs before the server-side click event handler.

The HTML Server controls generate the HTML control, as well as JavaScript to capture the events on the client, including the onchange and onclick events. In the sample code that follows this paragraph, the input text box captures the onchange event and calls the JavaScript function __doPostBack. A **function** is a named grouping of one or more programming statements. This JavaScript function only occurs once in the page, no matter how many controls are used. This function is used to pass information to the server. The Web page contains two hidden fields, named __EVENTTARGET and __EVENTARGUMENT, that are used to determine which control called the function and what parameters were passed with the control. Then, the client-side script calls the submit method to submit the form to the server. Note that, although these events are called HTML Server control events, they do require the client to capture the initial event and call the function. They are called HTML Server control events because the event is processed, or handled, by the server event handler, and not by the client event handler.

```
<input name="WebAddress" type="text" id="WebAddress"
    onchange="__doPostBack('WebAddress','')"
    language="javascript" />
<input type="submit" name="GoBtn" value="Go" id="GoBtn" />
<input type="hidden" name="__EVENTTARGET" value="" />
<input type="hidden" name="__EVENTARGUMENT" value="" />
<script language="javascript">
<!--
function __doPostBack(eventTarget, eventArgument) {
    var theform = document.ctrl0;
    theform.__EVENTTARGET.value = eventTarget;
    theform.__EVENTARGUMENT.value = eventArgument;
    theform.submit();
}
// -->
</script>
```

Creating an ASP.NET Page

In the following exercise, you will create an ASP.NET page that uses HTML Server controls to dynamically change the contents of the page. You will add Image controls and HTML Button and Label Server controls to the Web page. Because the Layout property is already set to Grid Layout, you will be able to position your controls absolutely, by dragging and dropping the controls onto the Web page. The HTML Button Server control creates the HTML code equivalent to the input tag with the Type property set to button. The Label control creates a DIV tag within the Web page. You will use Visual Basic .NET code to change the properties of the Label controls. In the following steps, you will create the Web page and add the HTML Server controls. At the end of the exercise, Figure 3-3 shows the Web Form with the HTML controls in the browser.

1. Start **Visual Studio .NET**. Note that on most computers, this can be accomplished by clicking **Start**, pointing to **Programs**, pointing to **Microsoft Visual Studio .NET 2003**, and then clicking **Microsoft Visual Studio .NET 2003**.

2. Click **File** on the menu bar, point to **New**, and then click **Project** to open the New Project window.

3. In the Project Types pane, click **Visual Basic Projects**. In the Templates pane, click the **ASP.NET Web Application** icon. Change the text in the location text box to **http://localhost/Chapter3**. Click **OK** to create the solution, project, and default files.

4. To add a folder, right-click the project name, point to **Add**, and then click **New Folder**. Type **images** as the folder name, and then press **Enter**.

5. Right-click the **images** folder, point to **Add**, and then click **Add Existing Item**. Browse to locate the Chapter03Data\images folder. (*Note*: In the Files of type drop-down list box, you must change the selection from VB Code Files to **Image Files**.)

6. Select all of the files in the Chapter03Data\images folder. (*Note*: In some versions of Windows, you can use the Ctrl+A key combination to select all of the files.) Click the **Open** button to import the images into the images directory of the Chapter3 project. (*Note*: You can collapse the list of files in your Solution Explorer window by clicking the minus sign in front of the images folder.)

7. Right-click the project, point to **Add**, and then click **Add Web Form**. Type **HTMLButton.aspx** to name the Web Form, and then click the **Open** button.

8. To add the header graphic, drag the **header.jpg** graphic in the images folder and drop the image at the top of the HTMLButton.aspx page. Click the **Style** property in the Properties window. Click the **Style Builder** button, which is a button with three dots. The Style Builder window opens. Click the **Position** tab. Figure 3-1 shows the Style Builder button, also known as the Build button, and the Style Builder window. Make sure that the Top and Left properties are both set to **0**. Click **OK**.

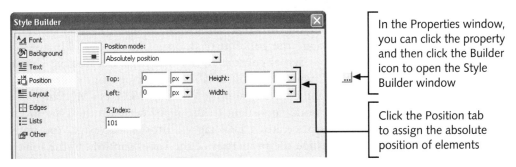

In the Properties window, you can click the property and then click the Builder icon to open the Style Builder window

Click the Position tab to assign the absolute position of elements

Figure 3-1 Setting the absolute position of elements in the Style Builder

9. To add the menu graphic, drag and drop the **menu.gif** graphic from the images folder to the left side of the page. Click the **Style** property in the Properties window. Click the **Style Builder** button. Click the **Position** tab. Make sure that the Top and Left properties are set to **85** and **17** respectively. Click **OK**.

10. To add the main graphic, drag and drop the **waterfordgifts.jpg** graphic from the images folder to the left side of the page. Click the **Style** property in the Properties window. Click the **Style Builder** button. Click the **Position** tab. Make sure that the Top and Left properties are set to **38** and **134** respectively. (*Note:* The Z-Index order value may vary. You do not need to change this number.) Click **OK**.

11. Click the **HTML** tab in the Toolbox. Drag and drop the **Label** from the Toolbox to the page. Right-click the control, and then select **Run As Server Control**. In the Properties window, change the Label (ID) property to **lblTitle**. Click the **Style** property and the **Style Builder** button. Figure 3-2 shows the Style Builder Window Font property sheet with the settings for the lblTitle label control. (*Note:* You can type the font name within single quotation marks inside the font name Family text box or click the Build button and use the Font Picker dialog box, as you learned in Chapter 2.) Change the Font Family to **'Trebuchet MS'** and the Font Size to **15 pt**. Select the Position tab and change the position to top: **243**, left: **139**, height: **26**, and width: **365**. Click **OK**. Click inside the Label control and delete the word **Label**. Type **Select the gender of the gift recipient.** in the label control.

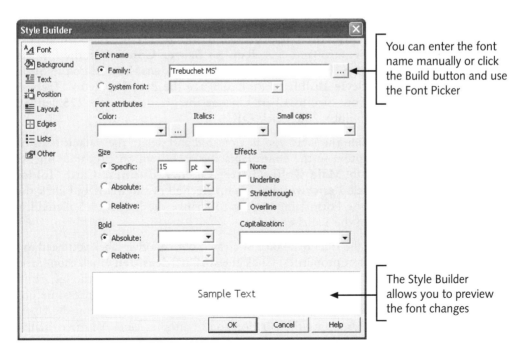

Figure 3-2   Setting the font type and size in the Style Builder

12. Drag and drop the **Button** control from the HTML tab to the page. Right-click the control, and then select **Run As Server Control**. In the Properties window, change the (ID) property to **btnMale** and the value to **Male**. Open the **Style Builder** and change the position to top: **274**, left: **138**, height: **27**, and width: **89**. Click **OK**.

13. From the Toolbox, drag and drop the **Button** control from the HTML tab to the page. Right-click the control, and then click **Run As Server Control**. In the Properties window, change the Label (ID) property to **btnFemale** and the value to **Female**. Open the **Style Builder** and change the position to top: **310**, left: **138**, height: **27**, and width: **89**. Click **OK**.

14. Drag and drop the **Label** control from the HTML tab to the page. Right-click the control, and then click **Run As Server Control**. In the Properties window, change the (ID) property to **lblGiftIdeasWomen**. Click the **Style** property and the **Style Builder** button. Change the Font Family to **'Trebuchet MS'** and the Font Size to **12 pt**. Change the position to top: **275**, left: **235**, height: **210**, and width: **250**. Click **OK**.

15. Click inside the label you just created, which will put an I-beam into the box. Delete the default text within the Label control. Add the following text in the control, placing each item on a separate line: **Make–Up Brush**, **Tyrone Bell**, **Butterfly**, **Balmoral Vase**, **Abbey Clock**, **Heart Shaped Ring Holder**, **Wellsley Picture**. Then, select all of the items and click the **Bullets** icon on the Formatting toolbar to change the list into a bulleted list. Click outside the Label control.

16. Drag and drop the **Label** control from the HTML tab to the page. Right-click the control and click **Run As Server Control**. In the Properties window, change the (ID) property to **lblGiftIdeasMen**. Click the **Style** property and the **Style Builder** button. Change the Font Family to **'Trebuchet MS'** and the Font Size to **12 pt**. Change the position to top: **275**, left: **500**, height: **210**, and width: **250**. Click **OK**.

17. Click inside the label you just created and delete the default text. Add the following text in the control, placing each item on a separate line: **Golf Ball**, **Golf Club**, **Male Golfer**, **Letter Opener**, **Business Card Holder**, **Shamrock Paperweight**. Then, select all of the items and click the **Bullets** icon on the Formatting toolbar to change the list into a bulleted list. Click outside of the Label control.

18. To move the label that you just created onto another label, you need to change the Position properties. Click the **lblGiftIdeasMen** label, then click the **Style** property and the **Style Builder** button. Change the left position to **235**. Click the **OK** button. The two labels will occupy the same position, so the contents will not be readable. (*Note*: Do not reposition the label by dragging and dropping the label on top of another label. You may inadvertently place the label within the other label.)

19. Click the **Save All** button. (*Note*: You should save your files often by clicking the **Save All** button.)

You have created the Web Form and added the HTML controls. In the following steps, you will add the code that will hide the two Label controls when the page loads. Then, you will add code to create two buttons. When you click one button, one of the labels will be visible. When you click the second button, the second label will be visible.

1. Double-click on the whitespace on the page, other than on a control. The file containing the code behind the page, called HTMLButton.aspx.vb, opens. Add the code that follows this paragraph within the Page_Load event handler. This code changes the Visible property for the two Label controls to false. When the page loads, these controls will not be seen by the visitor.

```
lblGiftIdeasMen.Visible = False
lblGiftIdeasWomen.Visible = False
```

2. Click the **HTMLButton.aspx** page tab to return to the Design page. Double-click the **Male** button to return to the code behind the page. This action also inserts a server click event handler for the Male button. Add the code that follows this paragraph to this new event handler. This code changes the message within the title label and shows the lblMale Label control, which contains the list of recommended products for male customers. (*Note*: Do note break the string across two lines. All strings must be typed on a single line.)

```
lblTitle.InnerHtml = _
"<b>We have lots of gift ideas for men.</b>"
lblGiftIdeasWomen.Visible = False
lblGiftIdeasMen.Visible = True
```

3. Click the **HTMLButton.aspx** page tab to return to the Design page. Double-click the **Female** button to return you to the code behind the page. This action also inserts a server click event handler for the Female button. Add the code that follows this paragraph to this new event handler. This code changes the message within the title label and shows the lblFemale Label control, which contains the list of recommended products for female customers.

```
lblTitle.InnerHtml = _
"<b>We have lots of gift ideas for women.</b>"
lblGiftIdeasWomen.Visible = True
lblGiftIdeasMen.Visible = False
```

4. Click the **Save All** button. Click **Build** on the menu bar, and then click **Build Solution**. If you have an error, a message will appear in the Task List window indicating the line of the error. Recheck your code to see if it matches the line in the steps. Then, resave your page and rebuild your solution.

5. Click the **HTMLButton.aspx** page tab to return to the Design page. Right-click the page, and then click **View in Browser**. Click the **Male** and **Female** buttons to see the contents of the labels change. Figure 3-3 shows how the page looks after you click the Male button. The Image control in this example is an HTML control, not an HTML Server control. You can mix and match HTML and HTML Server controls within the same page.

6. Close the Browser page, the HTMLButton page, and the code behind the page (HTMLButton.aspx.vb).

Figure 3-3   HTML Image, Button, and Label Server controls on a Web Form

HTML Image Button and Label Server Controls

There are many kinds of HTML controls that can be added to a Web page. Some controls, such as text boxes and check boxes, are used to obtain information from the user. Some controls, such as buttons, are used to provide a means for the visitor to interact with the Web page. When the user clicks a button, you can capture the button click event and create a response. The response may be to change the properties of the button, such as hiding the button, or to change the message on the button. You can also change the properties of another control.

The properties of individual controls can be changed via the Properties window. You can also change the properties of individual controls by adding code to the code behind the page. You can change the property when the page loads, or when an event occurs, such as a button click. In order to access the HTML controls, you must set the runat attribute to server. Then, the code behind the page will be aware of the HTML control. You can set the property in HTML view or by selecting Run As Server Control in the controls pop-up menu.

You can add new pages to a Web site. You can also import an existing Web page into a project. Visual Studio .NET will create the code behind the page that is associated with the Web page. Visual Studio .NET refers to the code behind the page as a class file. The page is an object that is derived from the class code within the code behind the page. Therefore, after you import a Web page, you will have to build your solution before you can view the Web page in the browser.

The properties are not always the same for HTML Server controls and ASP.NET Server controls. You can change the values of the Label controls by using the Properties window. Two properties often used to assign the value of an HTML Server Label control are **InnerHTML** and **InnerText**. However, in ASP.NET controls, the property that changes the value of the Server Label controls is **text**.

In the following exercise, you will create an ASP.NET page that uses HTML Server controls to create and process a registration form. You will insert several buttons that change the properties of a control when the button is clicked. The Image button creates the HTML code that uses the button tag. The button tag is not supported in all browsers. You will also use the Input Button control to create an image input.

3

1. Right-click **Chapter3** in the Solution Explorer window, point to **Add**, and then click **Add Existing Item**. Navigate to the Chapter03Data folder. Select **All Files** in the Files of type drop-down list box. Select all of the files except the Images directory, and click **Open**. Messages will appear that ask you to create a class for several of the .aspx files. Click **Yes** in each instance.

2. Double-click the **HTMLImageButton.aspx** file to open it.

3. Drag and drop the **Button** control from the HTML tab to the left of the lblGiftIdeasMen label.

4. Right-click on the control, and then select **Run As Server Control**. In the Properties window, change the Label (ID) and Name properties to **btnMale**.

5. Note that the property sheet does not allow you to change the type of the button, and that there is no Image Button control on the HTML tab in the Toolbox. Click the **HTML** tab to view the HTML code. Change the code for the control from type = "button" to **type = "image"**. Click the **Design** tab to return to Design view. Select the **btnMale** image placeholder icon. Additional properties appear in the Properties window for the Image Button control. Change the btnMale src property to **images/Male.gif**.

6. Click the **Style Builder** in the Properties window, and change the position to top: **280**, left: **150**. Click the **OK** button.

7. Drag and drop the **Button** control from the HTML tab to below the Male Image Input button. Right-click the control, and then click **Run As Server Control**. In the Properties window, change the (ID) and Name properties to **btnFemale**.

8. Click the **HTML** tab to view the HTML code. Change the code for the control from type = "button" to **type = "image"**. Click the **Design** tab to return to Design view. Select the **btnFemale** image placeholder icon. Additional properties appear in the Properties window for the Image Button control. Change the btnFemale src property to **images/Female.gif**.

9. Click the **Style Builder** in the Properties window, and change the position to top: **315**, left: **150**. Click **OK**.

10. Drag and drop the **Image** control from the HTML tab to below the Menu.gif image. Right-click the control and click **Run As Server Control**. In the Properties window, change the (ID) and Name properties to **imgLogo**. Change the src property to **images/logo.gif**.

11. Click the **Style Builder** in the Properties window, and change the position to top: **390**, left: **40**. Click **OK**.

12. Double-click the **Male** button to open the code behind the page. In the click event handler, type the following code to change the title label contents and show the label with the gift ideas for men:

```
lblTitle.InnerHtml = _
"<b>We have lots of gift ideas for men.</b>"
lblGiftIdeasWomen.Visible = False
lblGiftIdeasMen.Visible = True
```

13. Click the **HTMLImageButton.aspx** tab to return to the Web page. Double-click the **Female** button. In the click event handler, type the following code to change the title label contents and show the label with the gift ideas for women:

```
lblTitle.InnerHtml = _
"<b>We have lots of gift ideas for women.</b>"
lblGiftIdeasWomen.Visible = True
lblGiftIdeasMen.Visible = False
```

14. Within the Page_Load event procedure, you need to insert the code to hide the labels when the page is first loaded. Type the following code under the comment indicated by a green font on your screen:

```
If Not IsPostBack Then
        lblGiftIdeasMen.Visible = False
        lblGiftIdeasWomen.Visible = False
End If
```

15. Click the **Save All** button. Click the **HTMLImageButton.aspx** tab. Go to the **Build** menu and click **Build Solution**. Right-click the page, and then click **View in Browser**. Click the **Male** and **Female** buttons. Close each of the pages you created.

Creating a Form with HTML Server Controls

You can add Form controls such as text boxes and radio buttons within a Web Form. The Form controls can be added from the HTML tab or the Web Forms tab. However, the Form controls from the HTML tab are generic HTML controls. Web Form controls (which are also called ASP.NET Server controls or simply Web controls) on the Web Forms tab have additional properties that are not available with HTML controls. You can create server code that will interact with HTML control events—for example, when the user clicks on a button. You must configure the form field to be a Server control in order for you to create server code that will interact with the HTML Form control. You can modify the properties of the form fields. In the next activity in this chapter, you can hide the Help button if the help text field is visible. You can also get the values of form fields, and perform calculations, or evaluate their contents. For example, the code can detect if the username and password match a predefined string. The strings are always case sensitive, which means that you must type the values as they are shown. If the user is not authenticated, a message instructing him or her to click on the Help button is displayed in the label, and the Help button is made visible.

When you have code that is very long, you can use an underscore to split the code across multiple lines. It is important not to break the contents of a string across multiple lines, unless each string is contained within its own pair of quotation marks and the string is concatenated. Concatenation is the process of putting together two or more expressions. The ampersand (&) is used to separate the concatenated expressions.

In the following exercise, you will add HTML Form controls to a Web page. You will add input and password text boxes, and Submit, Reset, and Help buttons as shown in Figure 3-4. When the Help button is displayed, a label appears with a helpful message. When the user is authenticated, the title label displays a message to the user.

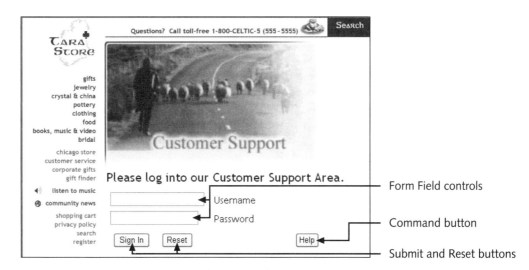

Figure 3-4   HTML Server Controls on a Web Form

1. In the Solution Explorer window, locate the HTMLInputButton.aspx file. This is one of the files that was imported into your solution in the previous exercise. If you have not imported the data files, you need to follow the directions in Step 1 of the previous exercise.

2. Double-click the file **HTMLInputButton.aspx** to open it.

3. Drag and drop the **Text Field** control from the HTML tab in the Toolbox to the left of the Username label. Right-click the control, and then click

Run As Server Control. In the Properties window, change the (ID) and Name properties to **txtUsername**. Click the **Style** property and the **Style Builder** button. In the Position tab, change the position to top: **280**, left: **145**. Click **OK**.

4. Drag and drop the **Password Field** control from the HTML tab to the left of the Password label. Right-click the control, and then click **Run As Server Control**. In the Properties window, change the Label (ID) and Name properties to **txtPassword**. Click the **Style** property and the **Style Builder** button. In the Position tab, change the position to top: **310**, left: **145**. Click the **OK** button.

5. Drag and drop the **Submit Button** control from the HTML tab to below the Password control. Right-click the control, and then select **Run As Server Control**. In the Properties window, change the Label (ID) and Name properties to **btnSubmit**. Change the Value property to **Sign In**. Click the **Style** property and the **Style Builder** button. In the Position tab, change the position to top: **345**, left: **150**. Click the **OK** button.

6. Drag and drop the **Reset Button** control from the HTML tab to below the Password control. Right-click the control, and then click **Run As Server Control**. In the Properties window, change the (ID) and Name properties to **btnReset**. Click the **Style** property and the **Style Builder** button. In the Position tab, change the position to top: **345**, left: **230**. Click **OK**.

7. Drag and drop the **Button** control from the HTML tab to below the Password control. Right-click the control, and then select **Run As Server Control**. In the Properties window, change the (ID) and Name properties to **btnHelp**. Change the Value property to **Help**. Click the **Style** property and the **Style Builder** button. In the Position tab, change the position to top: **345**, left: **450**. Click **OK**.

8. Right-click on the whitespace of the page, and then select **View Code**. In the Page_Load event handler, type the code following this paragraph where the comment stipulates. This code assigns the default message using the InnerHTML property, and hides the Help button and the Help label.

```
lblTitle.InnerHtml = _
"Please log into our Customer Support Area."
lblHelp.Visible = False
btnHelp.Visible = True
```

9. Click the **HTMLInputButton.aspx** page to return to Design view. Double-click the **Sign In** submit button. In the btnSubmit_ServerClick event handler, type the code following this paragraph. This code hides the Help button if it's visible. If the user is not authenticated, a message instructing him or her to click on the Help button is displayed in the label, and the Help button is made visible.

3

```
lblHelp.Visible = False
If ((txtUsername.Value = "Course") And _
(txtPassword.Value = "Technology")) Then
    lblTitle.InnerHtml = "You are authenticated!"
Else
    lblTitle.InnerHtml = _
    "Please click on the Help button for help!"
    txtUsername.Value = ""
    txtPassword.Value = ""
    btnHelp.Visible = True
End If
```

10. Click the **HTMLInputButton.aspx** tab to return to the page. Double-click the **Reset** button. Do not enter any code in this click event handler.

11. Click the **HTMLInputButton.aspx** tab to return to the page. Double-click the **Help** button. Enter the following code, which displays the Help label:

```
lblTitle.InnerHtml = _
"Please log into our Customer Support Area."
lblHelp.Visible = True
btnHelp.Visible = False
```

12. Click the **HTMLInputButton.aspx** tab to return to the Web page. Click the **Save All** button. Go to the **Build** menu and select **Build Solution**. Right-click the page, and then select **View in Browser**. Click the **Help** button. A helpful message is displayed. Then try to sign in with different usernames and passwords. Only the correct username and password will allow the user to be authenticated. Close each of the pages you created.

HTML Radio Button, Dropdown List, and Hyperlink Server Controls

Hyperlinks allow you to create links to other pages or to internal targets within the same page. Check boxes, radio buttons, and drop-down lists are form fields that allow you to select from lists of options. The difference between check boxes and radio buttons is that you can select only one option from a group of radio buttons. You can select none, one, many, or all options from a group of check boxes. Therefore, the radio button group must all be identified with a single name. (*Note*: You will learn how to process check boxes with ASP.NET controls later in this chapter.)

Creating a Web Page with Radio Button Controls

1. In the Solution Explorer window, locate the HTMLRadioButton.aspx file. This is one of the files that was imported into your solution.

2. Double-click the file **HTMLRadioButton.aspx** to open it.

3. Drag and drop the **Radio Button** control from the HTML tab to below the existing radio buttons. Right-click the control, and then select **Run As Server Control**. In the Properties window, change the Label (ID) property to **rdBridal** and the Name property to **category**. The Checked property should be **False**. Click the **Style** property and the **Style Builder** button. In the Position tab change the position to top: **383**, left: **310**. Click **OK**.

4. Double-click the **Search** button. Select the entire comment area in the btnSearch_ServerClick event handler. Click the **Edit** menu, point to **Advanced**, and click **Uncomment Selection**.

On the first line within the btnSearch_ServerClick event handler, insert the code that follows this paragraph. The code determines if the rdBridal button was checked. (*Note:* The code uses the Checked property to determine which radio button was checked. If the radio button has been checked, the code will change the message and picture displayed using the InnerHtml and Src properties.) The code to check the other radio buttons has already been inserted for you.

```
If (rdBridal.Checked = True) Then
        lblTitle.InnerHtml = "Celebrate your Wedding!"
        imgTop.Src = "images/28.jpg"
```

5. Click the **HTMLRadioButton.aspx** tab to return to the Web page. Click the **Save All** button. Go to the Build menu and select **Build Solution**. Right-click the page and select **View in Browser**. Click the **btnBridal** radio button, which is labeled bridal, and click the **Search** button. The lblTitle message and the imgTop image change. The page should look like the one shown in Figure 3-5. Close each of the pages you created.

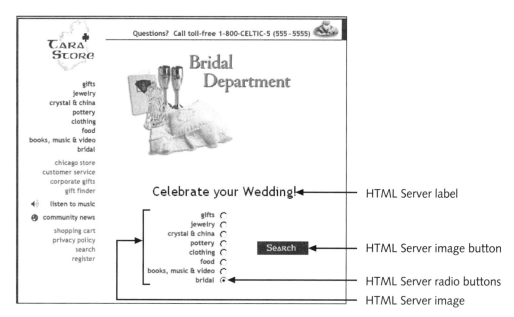

Figure 3-5   HTML Radio Button Server controls

Creating a Page with a Dropdown Server Control

In the following exercise, you will create a drop-down list box using the HTML Server controls. You will also populate the control using HTML code, and dynamically add items to the list using server-side programming. Drop-down lists and list boxes can be created using HTML Server controls named Dropdown and Listbox Server controls. They both are created using the <SELECT> tag, so they are classified together as HTMLSelect controls. The Dropdown Server control creates a drop-down list in the browser, and a Listbox Server control creates a list box. The drop-down list displays one item at a time, and a list box displays multiple items at a time.

Dropdown Server controls are created with the HTML Select tag. Option tags are used to create each individual item in the list. A value can be associated with each item in the list. The value of the item does not have to match the displayed text of the item. For example, sometimes your username is displayed, but not your ID number. The ID number is used as the value, and would be passed to the server when the form was submitted. You can obtain information about the option selected by using the SelectedIndex property of the Dropdown server control. When nothing has been selected the SelectedIndex property returns the value -1.

With Dropdown Server controls, you can add items dynamically to the Dropdown Server control at runtime using code, or you can add them at design time through the Properties window. The **Add method** allows you to add items to the list dynamically when the page loads, or when an event occurs. Each Dropdown Server control and Listbox Server control contains an Items collection with properties and methods. The Add method adds an item to the **Items collection**. You might use the ServerChange event to detect a change in the Dropdown Server control. If the user chooses the first option on the list, which is checked by default, there is no change, and the page is redisplayed. Otherwise, the new list is displayed along with a graphic, and the old list is removed. The contents of the Dropdown Server control are cleared before new items are added, because the user may repeat the exercise and select the other option. In some cases this results in the items being appended to the list instead of replacing the items in the list. It's useful to clear the items from the list anytime you are beginning a list. You can do this with the **Clear method**.

In this example, you will use the **isPostBack page property** to determine if the user has visited the page before. This is the Boolean value that has a value of true when the user has visited the page. The_doPostBack function is created by ASP.NET to handle events that must be returned to the Web server. For example, if the user clicks a button, the server click event is handled on the server. But, you need to pass the object that called the event and any parameters to the server. The isPostBack property will be able to recognize the visitor based upon the _ViewState and the information obtained from the _doPostBack function.

1. In the Solution Explorer window, locate the HTMLSelect.aspx file. This is one of the files that was imported into your solution.

2. Double-click the file **HTMLSelect.aspx** to open it.

3. Drag and drop the **Dropdown** Server control from the HTML tab to the left of the picture frame. Right-click the control, and then click **Run As Server Control**. In the Properties window, change the (ID) and Name to **CatList**. Click the **Style** property and the **Style Builder** button. In the Position tab change the position to top: **320**, left: **150**. Click **OK**.

4. Click the **HTML** tab and find the default pair of Option tags (<OPTION selected></OPTION>) associated with the CatList control. Enter **Select a Main Category** as the text displayed for the option. Click the **Design** tab to return to Design view. (*Note:* The Dropdown List control is displayed on top of the picture frame image. When you view the page in a browser, the picture frame image is not displayed while the Dropdown List control is displayed.)

5. Drag and drop the **Dropdown** Server control from the HTML tab to the left of the Submit button. Right-click on the control, and then click **Run As Server Control**. In the Properties window, change the (ID) and Name to **ProductList**. Click the **Style** property and the **Style Builder** button. In the Position tab change the position to top: **320**, left: **350**. Click **OK**.

6. Double-click in the whitespace area on the page. In the Page_Load event handler type the code that follows this paragraph to display the Dropdown Server control. Notice that the Add method allows you to add items to the list dynamically. Each Dropdown Server control and Listbox Server control contains an Items collection with properties and methods. The Add method adds an item to the Items collection.

```
If (Not IsPostBack) Then
    lblTitle.InnerHtml = _
    "Select the gender of the gift recipient."
    imgProduct.Visible = False
    ProductList.Visible = False
    CatList.Items.Add("Gifts for Men")
    CatList.Items.Add("Gifts for Women")
End If
```

7. Locate the CatList_ServerChange procedure, which is triggered when the user makes a selection. Select the entire CatList_ServerChange procedure. Click the **Edit** menu, point to **Advanced**, and click **Uncomment Selection**.

(*Note:* This code will hide the CatList controls, display the ProductList controls, and determine which selection the user makes from the CatList Dropdown Server control using the CatList.Value method. The label is changed with the InnerHTML property. Any previous items in the ProductList Dropdown Server control are removed with the Clear method, and new items are inserted with the Add method.)

8. Click the **HTMLSelect.aspx** tab to return to the Web page. Click the **Save All** button. Click **Build** on the menu bar, and then click **Build Solution**. Right-click the page, and then select **View in Browser**. Select **Gifts for Women** from the CatList Dropdown Server control, as shown in Figure 3-6,

and click the Submit button. The ProductList control displays gift ideas for women and changes the lblTitle message. Close each of the pages you created.

Figure 3-6   HTML Dropdown List Server controls

Creating a Page with a Hyperlink Control

In this final HTML Server control exercise, you will add several hyperlinks to a Web page. The hyperlinks can act as anchor tags and redirect the visitor to a new page, using the URL property. You can use a relative or absolute URL. You can set the URL property of the hyperlink dynamically when the page loads, or in one of your functions or procedures. You can also capture the click from the hyperlink and initiate the click event handler for the hyperlink.

1. In the Solution Explorer window, locate the GiftsForWomen.aspx, GiftsforMen.aspx, and HTMLAnchor.aspx files. These are some of the files that were imported into your solution.

2. Double-click the file **HTMLAnchor.aspx** to open it. Note that there is no Hyperlink control in the HTML Toolbox. You need to insert the link for each piece of text.

3. Click the **HTML** tab to view the HTML code. Locate the word "Men" and replace it with the following code:

```
<A href="http://www.tarastore.com" id="AMale"
name="AMale" runat="server">Men</A>
```

4. Click the **Design** tab. Double-click the page. In the Page_Load event handler, type the code that follows this paragraph to change the href properties of the hyperlinks and hides the label that displays the sale items:

```
AMale.HRef = "GiftsForMen.aspx"
AFemale.HRef = "GiftsForWomen.aspx"
AHome.HRef = "http://www.tarastore.com"
```

 If IntelliSense displays the URL in blue and underlined, along with a message indicating that href is not a member of the control group, ignore it. Href is a valid property of the anchor tag.

5. Click the **HTMLAnchor.aspx** tab to return to the Web page. Click the **Save All** button. Click **Build** on the menu bar, and then click **Build Solution**. Right-click the page, and then select **View in Browser**. Click the **Women** hyperlink. The GiftsForWomen.aspx page appears in the browser. The page should appear as shown in Figure 3-7. Click the **Women** hyperlink. The GiftsForWomen.aspx page appears in the browser. Close each of the pages you created.

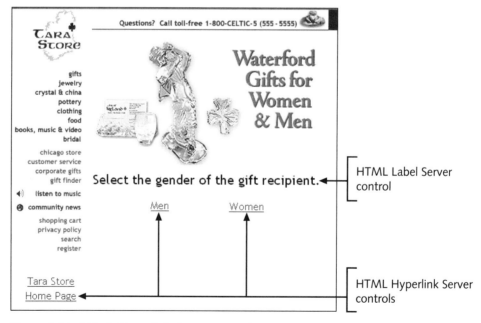

Figure 3-7   HTML Hyperlink Server controls

USING ASP.NET WEB FORM CONTROLS

ASP.NET Server controls, also known as Web controls, are located on the Web Forms tab in the Toolbox. The ASP.NET Web Forms inherit from the **Web Control class** which is found in the `System.Web.UI.WebControls` namespace. ASP.NET controls are similar to HTML Server controls, but they support additional properties, methods, and events. ASP.NET controls generate the necessary HTML and DHTML, which is supported by the client. ASP.NET controls can be grouped into Web Form controls, Rich controls, Data controls, Validation controls, and Mobile controls. In this section you will learn about Web Form controls. ASP.NET controls are known as Web controls.

Dynamically assigning properties and calling methods to Web Form controls is different from calling HTML Server control properties. For example, to change the text displayed in an HTML Server Label control, you set the InnerHTML property. To change the text value for the Web Label control, you set the Text property. If you assign a property to the Label control you can simply assign the value using a string. However, if you assign the value dynamically, using programming code, you must be careful how you assign the value to the property. For example, the Color properties must be assigned using a different syntax. Color is a class that inherits its properties from the System.Drawing assembly. So, to retrieve a color, you have to directly or indirectly inherit from the Color namespace. You can assign the value by the known color name, a 32-bit value, a hexadecimal value, or a property of an object. In the following sample code, the BorderColor property is assigned Green. Green is one of the known colors that you can refer to by name:

```
MyControl.BorderColor = System.Drawing.Color.Green
```

You can select the property using the known color name, such as Green, or from a value from another object. The following sample code shows how to assign the color value from the text box or form:

```
MyControl.BackColor = Color.FromName(txtBackColor.Value)
```

Some of the properties of ASP.NET controls require a numeric value. You cannot simply assign the numeric value dynamically; ASP.NET requires that you use a new object, known as a unit. The unit class represents numeric values for the properties of other objects. You need to use the keyword New to create the Unit object, and then pass the numeric value to the class. In the following example, you can assign the BorderWidth property using the Unit object:

```
MyBtn.BorderWidth = New Unit(4)
```

DropDownList and Image Controls

In the following Web Form Server control exercise, you will add a DropDownList to a Web page, and dynamically add the options to the list when the page first loads. You will also add the code to retrieve the value of the item the user clicked.

In this exercise, you will change the property of an Image control. The Web Form Image Control class produces an <img> tag to display an image on the Web page. This control only displays an image. If you need to capture mouse clicks on the image, you use the ImageButton control. The **ImageURL property** provides the path to the image by creating the **SRC property** for the IMG tag. The **AlternateText property** provides the text that is displayed when the image is not available, or when the user places the pointer over the image. The AlternateText property generates the ALT property in the HTML tag. (*Note*: You should make your Web site accessibility-compliant. There are many Web sites that contain information about Web site accessibility. One such site is *http://bobby.watchfire.com/bobby/html/en/index.jsp*.) The **ImageAlign property** provides for aligning the image.

1. In the Solution Explorer window, locate the ASPSelect.aspx file. This file is one of the files that was imported into your solution.

2. Double-click the file **ASPSelect.aspx** to open it.

3. Drag and drop the **DropDownList** control from the Web Forms tab in the Toolbox to the left of the Select a Category button. Change the (ID) property to **dlCategory**. Change the Height property to **25** and Width property to **155**. Reposition the dlCategory control, if necessary.

4. Double-click in the whitespace on the page. In the Page_Load event handler, enter the code that follows this paragraph to add the items to the DropDownList. The code checks whether the user has visited the page before by using the IsPostback property. In this example, you only add the items to the control the first time the control is created.

```
If (Not IsPostBack) Then
   dlCategory.Items.Add("Gifts")
   dlCategory.Items.Add("Jewelry")
   dlCategory.Items.Add("China and Crystal")
   dlCategory.Items.Add("Pottery")
   dlCategory.Items.Add("Clothing")
   dlCategory.Items.Add("Food")
   dlCategory.Items.Add("Books, Music, and Video")
   dlCategory.Items.Add("Bridal")
End If
```

5. Locate the btnSubmit_Click procedure. Select the entire **btnSubmit_Click** procedure. Click the **Edit** menu, point to **Advanced**, and click **Uncomment Selection**.

On the first line in the btnSubmit_Click procedure, type the code that follows this paragraph. (*Note*: The btnSubmit_Click procedure will retrieve the index number of the selected item using the SelectedIndex property. The position of each item in a drop-down list is represented by the index number. The index number of the first element in the list is 0. The btnSubmit_Click procedure changes the text of the lblTitle label control and the ImageURL property of the imgTop image control based on which item was selected.)

```
Select Case dlCategory.SelectedIndex
    Case 0
            lblTitle.Text = _
            "Let us help you find the best gift!"
            imgTop.ImageUrl = "images/21.jpg"
```

6. Click the **ASPSelect.aspx** tab to return to the Web page. Click the **Save All** button. Click **Build** on the menu bar, then click **Build Solution**. Right-click the page, and then click **View in Browser**. Select **Jewelry** from the DropDownList control, as shown in Figure 3-8, and click the **Select a Category** button. Close each of the pages you created.

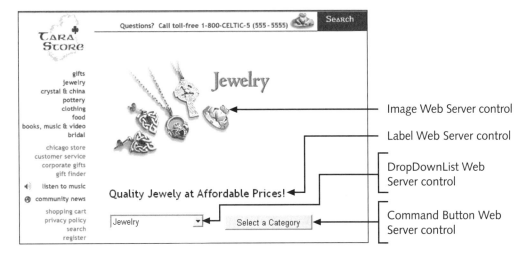

Figure 3-8 DropDownList Web controls

Panel and Literal Web Controls

There are many similarities between HTML Server and ASP.NET controls. However, there are new ASP.NET controls that are not available as HTML Server controls. This section discusses some of these new controls, specifically the Panel and Literal controls.

The **Panel control** can contain other controls and creates a DIV tag to enclose the contents. You can set properties such as wrapping, absolute positioning, font type, and scroll bars. For example, if you want to add some text to a panel, simply add a Label control within the panel tags or enter the text directly into the panel. The Label control creates contents within a Panel control using the SPAN tag. You use the Text property to display text in a Label control. You can also use a **Literal control** to write content directly to the page. Literal controls are often used to add client-side HTML and text to the page. Any non-server code, such as HTML tags or tags without an ID property assigned, is placed within Literal controls when the page is rendered.

1. In the Solution Explorer window, locate the ASPPanel.aspx file. This file is one of the files that was imported into your solution.

2. Double-click the file **ASPPanel.aspx** to open it.

3. Drag and drop the **Panel** control from the Web Forms tab in the Toolbox to the right of the Current Articles list. Change the (ID) property to **PanelAboutNews**. Change the Height property to **180** and Width property to **235**. Change the

ForeColor property to **Teal**. You can click the drop-down list arrow and select the color. It is the fifth color in the sixth column in the Custom tab. Click on the **plus sign** next to the Font property to expand the Font properties. Change the Name to **Trebuchet MS**. Change the Size to **Small**.

4. Click inside the panel, delete the word **Panel**, type **Editorial Contributors Wanted**, and press **Enter**. Then type **Do you have a passion for Irish culture? We are currently seeking individuals with experience in journalism to contribute to our Community News section.** Reposition the panel control, if necessary.

5. Click the **Save All** button. Click **Build** on the menu bar, then click **Build Solution**. Right-click on the page, and then click **View in Browser**. Your page should appear as shown in Figure 3-9. Close each of the pages you created.

Figure 3-9   Panel Web control

Placeholder and HyperLink Web Controls

The Placeholder control inherits from the Control class. The **Placeholder control** is used as a container to store dynamically added Web controls. The Placeholder control does not produce any visible output without the use of other controls. To add, insert, or remove a control from the Placeholder control, you can use the Control class of the control namespace. To do this, you must know how to use the constructor to create a control dynamically. For example, say you create and initialize a new instance of the Button class. This won't display anything. You have to add it to the Controls Property collection of the Placeholder class. Then, it will display the control in its place, and format the Button properties.

In the next step sequence in this chapter, you will dynamically create a HyperLink control. The HyperLink control is used to create an anchor tag that can link to another page or a target by using the ImageURL property. The displayed text is configured using the Text property. The Text property also becomes the ToolTip by default. The **ToolTip** is a new property that is used to display a message when the user places the pointer over the object. Notice that the image hyperlink does not have to be any specific size, color, or font. You can change the Target property of the hyperlink. The **target** is the window or frame used to load the Web page linked to when the HyperLink control is clicked. The default value for the target is String.Empty. You can change the target to any named window, or one of the reserved window names. The named window must begin with a letter in the range of a through z and is case sensitive. The reserved windows are as follows:

- _blank_—renders the content in a new window without frames
- _parent_—renders the content in the immediate frameset parent
- _self_—renders the content in the frame with focus
- _top_—renders the content in the full window without frames

In the following step sequence, you will dynamically create a HyperLink control using the Placeholder control.

1. In the Solution Explorer window, locate the ASPPlaceholder.aspx file. This file is one of the files that was imported into your solution.

2. Double-click the file **ASPPlaceholder.aspx** to open it.

3. Drag and drop the **Placeholder** control from the Web Forms tab in the Toolbox directly onto the empty Panel control. Change the (ID) property to **placeholder**.

4. Double-click in the whitespace area on the page to open the code behind the page. Locate the comments in the Page_Load procedure. Select all of the comments, except the first comment. Click the **Edit** menu, point to **Advanced**, and click **Uncomment Selection**.

   On the first line after the comment 'Create a hyperlink,' type the following code, which will dynamically create and configure a hyperlink and add it to the placeholder controls collection:

```
Dim MyLink As New HyperLink
placeholder.Controls.Add(MyLink)
MyLink.Text = _
"Click here to see a larger image"
MyLink.ForeColor = _
System.Drawing.Color.FromName("#004040")
MyLink.Font.Name = "Trebuchet MS"
MyLink.Font.Size = MyLabel.Font.Size.Smaller
```

```
MyLink.ID = "HLHome"
MyLink.NavigateUrl = "images/LgButterfly.jpg"
MyLink.Target = "_new"
```

5. Click the **ASPPlaceholder.aspx** tab to return to the Web page. Click the **Save All** button. Click **Build** on the menu bar, then click **Build Solution**. Right-click the page, and then click **View in Browser**. Your page should appear as shown in Figure 3-10. Click the hyperlink to view the larger graphic. Close each of the pages you created.

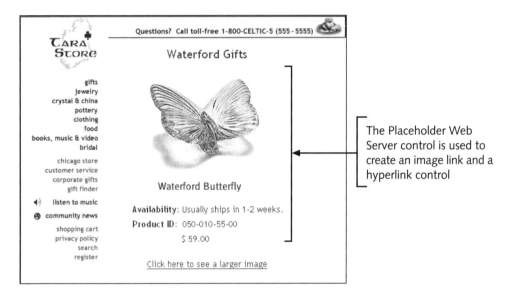

Figure 3-10   The Placeholder Web control

Working with CheckBoxes

You previously learned how to process a form using HTML Server control radio buttons. In this exercise, you will learn how to work with check boxes using the ASP.NET CheckBox control. The control has some additional properties to help you format the check boxes and retrieve the values.

1. In the Solution Explorer window, locate the ASPCheckbox.aspx file. This file is one of the files that was imported into your solution.

2. Double-click the file **ASPCheckbox.aspx** to open it.

3. Drag and drop the **CheckBox** control from the Web Forms tab in the Toolbox to directly beneath the Hiking in Ireland CheckBox control. Change the (ID) property to **CB8**. Change the Text property to **Sports in Ireland**. Change the ForeColor property to **#004040**. You can enter the value in the drop-down list box. Click the **plus sign** next to the Font property to expand the Font properties. Change the name to **Trebuchet MS**. Change the Size to **X-Small**. To align the CheckBox control with the other

controls, press the **Shift** key, and select the last two **CheckBox** controls. Click the **Format** menu, point to **Align**, and then select **Lefts**.

4. Double-click on the whitespace on the page. Locate the comments in the btnSubmit_Click procedure. Select all of the comments. Click the **Edit** menu, point to **Advanced**, and click **Uncomment Selection**.

On the first blank line inside the btnSubmit_Click procedure, type the code following this paragraph. (*Note:* This code will determine if the first check box was clicked, and then it will write the text value of the CheckBox control to the MyMessage string. A line break tag is used to separate lines. The code has been entered for the rest of the check boxes. At the end of the event handler, the MyMessage string is assigned to the Text property of the lblTopics label. This will display all of the clicked check boxes in one label control.)

```
Dim MyMessage As String
        MyMessage = "<b>You selected:</b><br/><br/>"
        If CB1.Checked Then
            MyMessage += CB1.Text & "<br/>"
        End If
```

5. Click the **ASPCheckbox.aspx** tab to return to the Web page. Click the **Save All** button. Click **Build** on the menu bar, then click **Build Solution**. Right-click the page, and then click **View in Browser**. Select **Irish History**, **Fishing in Ireland**, and **Sports in Ireland**, as shown in Figure 3-11, and then click the **Submit** button. Your page will display your selections. Close each of the pages you created.

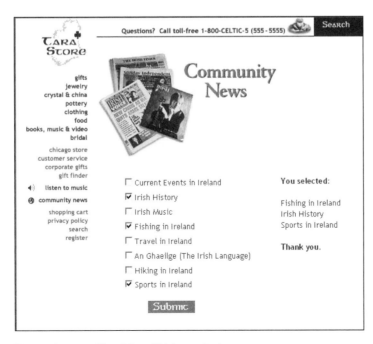

Figure 3-11   CheckBox Web controls

USING VALIDATION CONTROLS

You have learned that form fields contain values that can be retrieved as strings in the code behind the page. Although you can use Visual Basic .NET string functions to validate form field contents, a more efficient method to manage validation of form contents is the use of Validation Web controls (also called Validation controls).

Validation controls are used to compare your form field controls to a rule. Validation controls are also used to configure the rules to validate the contents of form fields. The rule may require that the control contain any value or a specific form of data such as alphabetical or numeric. The rule may also specify what data must be contained within a range of two values. The rule may be general, or it may be very specific and require formatting, such as uppercase letters and periods.

There are five built-in ASP.NET Validation controls. All five controls can be added to your ASP.NET page using the Web Forms tab on the Toolbox. The five validation controls are:

- *RequiredFieldValidator*—Makes sure a form field is not left blank
- *RangeValidator*—Makes sure a field's value falls within a given range
- *CompareValidator*—Compares a field's value with other values or other fields' values
- *RegularExpressionValidator*—Evaluates data against a regular expression
- *CustomValidator*—Evaluates data against custom criteria

The Validation controls inherit from the BaseValidator class, which inherits from the Label class. Therefore, Validation controls can display custom error messages using labels. They all support common properties and methods such as ForeColor. The **ForeColor property** sets the color of the error message. The default ForeColor property is red. Validation controls that perform comparisons also inherit from the BaseCompareValidator base class, and therefore inherit additional properties.

One of the common properties of all Validation controls is Display. When the Display property is set to dynamic, space for the validation message is dynamically added to the page if validation fails. The Validation control is inserted into the page and assigned to a hidden field. The error message takes up space in the page, which can offset your HTML elements. If the Display property is set to static, then space for the validation message is allocated in the page layout. If the validation does not fail, then no message is sent to the browser. However, the space for the message is still reserved on the page. If the Display property is set to none, then the validation message is never displayed in the browser.

Each of the controls inherits the validate method, which performs validation on the associated Input control and updates the IsValid property. The IsValid property indicates whether the control that is being validated is valid. The code sample following this paragraph shows how you can check if the entire page is valid at the same time by calling the `Page.Validate` method and then using the `Page.IsValid` property:

```
Page.Validate()
If Page.IsValid Then
    Message.Text = "Result: Valid!"
Else
    Message.Text = "Result: Not valid!"
End If
End Sub
```

The **RequiredFieldValidator control** is used to determine if any value is entered or selected. The **ControlToValidate property** specifies the Input control to validate. This control can be combined with other controls, for further validation. For example, this control can detect whether you typed in a number for your credit card, but would not apply any rules to see if the number is valid.

The **RangeValidator control** checks whether the value of an Input control is within a specified range of values. In addition to the ControlToValidate property, you must assign the **MinimumValue** and **MaximumValue properties** to specify the minimum and maximum values of the valid range. Then, the value entered in the field is compared against these two values. The values may be any valid data type. The Type property is used to specify the data type of the values to compare. The values to compare are converted to this data type before the validation operation is performed. Data types that can be compared are strings, integers, doubles, dates, and currency.

The **CompareValidator control** inherits from the BaseCompareValidator class. This Validation control compares the value entered by the user into an Input control, such as a text box, with the value entered into another Input control, or with a constant value. You must specify the Input control to validate by setting the ControlToValidate property. If you want to compare a specific Input control with another Input control, set the **ControlToCompare property** to specify the comparison control. If you want to compare the Input control with a constant value, you can specify the constant value with the **ValueToCompare property**. You must use the Operator property to specify the type of comparison to perform between the Input control and the CompareToControl or ValueToControl.

You can create your own validation rules by building a Regular Expression. A Regular Expression is a rule that describes a value. The Regular Expression isn't a programming language, but it is a language that describes one or more groups of characters. These characters can be alphanumerics or symbols, such as the comma. In this chapter, you will learn to use the validation controls within Visual Studio .NET and to use the built-in regular expressions to validate a form.

The **RegularExpressionValidator control** inherits from the BaseCompareValidator class. This control checks whether the value of an Input control matches a pattern defined by a regular expression. A regular expression can be used to check for predictable sequences of characters, such as those in Social Security numbers, e-mail addresses, telephone numbers, and postal codes.

Make sure the clientTarget property is set to downlevel. Also, it's important to note that the validation will succeed if the Input control is empty. Therefore, you should use the RequiredFieldValidator in conjunction with this control.

You can set the validation to occur on the client, if the client supports JScript, or on the server. If the validation occurs on the client, then JScript regular expression syntax is used. If the validation occurs on the server, then the `System.Text.RegularExpressions.Regex` syntax is used. Since the JScript regular expression syntax is a subset of the `System.Text.RegularExpressions.Regex` syntax, it is recommended that you use the JScript regular expression syntax in order to obtain the same results on both the client and the server.

You must provide the ValidationExpression property to compare the Input control to the regular expression. There are several basic regular expressions already built in to Visual Studio .NET. A global RegExp object is used for creating pattern-matching expressions called regular expressions. The regular expression pattern is stored in the Pattern property of the RegExp object. You can construct a regular expression by putting the various components of the expression pattern between a pair of delimiters. In JScript, the delimiters are a pair of forward slash (/) characters. The components of a regular expression can be individual characters, sets of characters, ranges of characters, choices between characters, or any combination. The following is a listing of some common regular expressions that are included with Visual Studio .NET:

- *Social Security Number*—/\d{3}-\{2}-d{4}/
- *Internet E-Mail Address*—\w+([-+.]\w+)*@\w+([-.]\w+)*\.\w+([-.]\w+)*
- *Internet URL*—http://([\w-]+\.)+[\w-]+(/[\w- ./?%&=]*)?
- *U.S. Phone*—((\(\d{3}\) ?)|(\d{3}-))?\d{3}-\d{4}
- *U.S. Zip Code*—\d{5}(-\d{4})?
- *Phone Number*—\d{3}-\d{2}-\d{4}

The **ValidationSummary control** is used to summarize the error messages from all validators on a Web page, in one location. Like other Validation controls, the ValidationSummary class inherits properties and methods from the WebControl class. The ValidationSummary control has additional properties such as DisplayMode, ShowSummary, ShowMessageBox, and HeaderText. You can display the summary as a list, a bulleted list, or a single paragraph by setting the **DisplayMode property** to

BulletList, List, or SingleParagraph. The **ShowSummary property** shows the entire list of error messages from invalid controls. You can display an additional message in an alert box by setting the **ShowMessageBox property**. The **HeaderText property** allows you to display a heading message. The other validation properties, such as the ForeColor property, still apply to the ValidationSummary control. You can format the validation summary list and the error messages.

If none of these Validation controls is applicable to your form field, you can create your own validation functions on the client or server using the **CustomValidator control**. When you use Visual Studio .NET to validate your forms, you don't have to write the client-side scripts. The benefit of using the Validation controls is that the single control works for multiple browsers. Even if you select client-side validation, the data is still validated on the server.

Validating Form Data

The following exercise demonstrates how to add required field and regular expression Validation controls to a Web page.

1. In the Solution Explorer window, locate the ASPValidateForm.aspx file. This file is one of the files that was imported into your solution.

2. Double-click the file **ASPValidateForm.aspx** to open it.

3. Drag and drop the **RequiredFieldValidator** control from the Web Forms tab in the Toolbox to the left of the lblFirstName label. Change the (ID) property to **ValRFirstName**. Change the ControlToValidate property to **txtFirstName**. Verify that the Display property is **static** and that the ForeColor property is **Red**. Change the ErrorMessage property to *.

4. Drag and drop the **RegularExpressionValidator** control from the Web Forms tab in the Toolbox to a spot above the e-mail address error message. Change the (ID) property to **ValREPhone**. Change the ControlToValidate property to **txtPhone**. Change the Font Name property to **Trebuchet MS** and the Size property to **X-Small**. Verify that the Display property is **static** and the ForeColor property is **Red**. Change the ErrorMessage property to **Please submit the phone number as (999) 999-9999**. Click the **ValidationExpression Build** icon in the Properties window, and from the Regular Expression Editor select **U.S. Phone Number**, and then click **OK**. Change the Height property to **34px** and the Width property to **166px**.

5. Click the **Save All** button. Click **Build** on the menu bar, then click **Build Solution**. Right-click the page, and then click **View in Browser**. Leave the FirstName and LastName text boxes empty. Enter an invalid phone number and an invalid e-mail address, and then click the **Submit** button. The form will display the error messages. Your page should appear similar to the one in Figure 3-12. Close each of the pages you created.

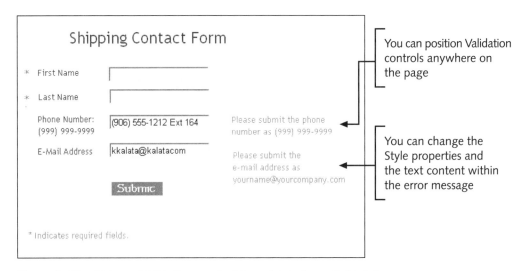

Figure 3-12 Using a Validation control to validate form field data

The following exercise demonstrates how to add a Validation Summary control to a Web page. The individual error messages are not displayed, because the individual Validation controls have the Display property set to none. The ShowMessageBox property is set to true, which displays an alert box with the error messages in the newer browsers.

1. In the Solution Explorer window, locate the ASPValidationSummary.aspx file. This file is one of the files that was imported into your solution.

2. Double-click the file **ASPValidationSummary.aspx** to open it.

3. Drag and drop the **ValidationSummary** control from the Web Forms tab in the Toolbox to below the Submit button (below the label that says * Indicates required field). Change the (ID) property to **ValSummary**. Change the DisplayMode property to **List** and verify that ShowSummary is **True**. Change the ShowMessageBox property to **True** and the HeaderText property to **"You have one or more errors that must be corrected. Please resubmit the form."** Change the Height to **40px** and Width to **480px**. Change the Font Name to **Trebuchet MS** and the Size to **X-Small**.

4. Click the **Save All** button. Click **Build** on the menu bar, then click **Build Solution**. Right-click the page, and then click **View in Browser**. Enter a valid first name, a valid last name, an invalid phone number, and an invalid e-mail address in the form. Click the **Submit** button. A message box will appear with the error messages, and the page will display the error message, as shown in Figure 3-13. Close each of the pages you created.

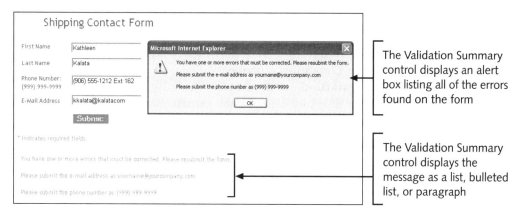

Figure 3-13   The Validation Summary Web control

BINDING TO SIMPLE DATA

Visual Studio .NET makes it easy to bind Form controls to data sources. In a later chapter, you will learn how to bind controls to databases such as Access, SQL Server, and Oracle. In this section, you will learn how to bind data from ArrayLists and HashTables.

Binding RadioButtonLists to ArrayLists

In the next step sequence in this chapter, you will bind the data from an ArrayList to an ASP.NET RadioButtonList control. **RadioButtonList controls** allow you to group a series of one or more radio buttons. You can easily bind the RadioButtonList to several types of data sources such as ArrayLists, HashTables, and databases. By grouping them together in a single control, you can set the properties for the entire group. For example, you can set the **RepeatDirection property** so that the group is displayed horizontally or vertically. You can specify the **RepeatLayout property**, which will group the list using a table or using paragraph tags.

The ArrayList allows you to store a list of data in a structure, which can later be assigned to a Web control. The System.Array class is the base class of all array types. The **ArrayList** is a type of array whose size dynamically increases as required. The ArrayList is declared using the keyword Dim, the name of the array, and the keyword New. The Capacity property is the number of items the list can hold. As items are added to an ArrayList, the capacity is automatically increased as required through reallocation. You must pass the number of items in the array as a parameter when the array is first created. The ArrayList is **zero-based**, which means that the counting of items in the ArrayList starts at 0 and not 1. If the **Capacity property** is explicitly set to zero, the CLR sets the Capacity property to a default capacity of 16. The **Count property** determines the number of items that are actually in the ArrayList. You can add items to the ArrayList by using the Add method of the Items collection, which is the collection that belongs to the ArrayList object for storing the items.

In the following step sequence, you will create a simple ArrayList that will populate a RadioButtonList control, as shown in Figure 3-14. After creating the RadioButtonList control and the ArrayList object, you must assign the ArrayList object to the RadioButtonList control by using the **DataSource property**. Then, you need to bind the data to the control by using the **DataBind method** of the RadioButtonList control. You can also bind all the controls on a Web page by using the DataBind method of the Page object.

1. In the Solution Explorer window, locate the ASPDBRadioButtonList.aspx file. This file is one of the files that was imported into your solution.

2. Double-click the file **ASPDBRadioButtonList.aspx** to open it.

3. Drag and drop the **RadioButtonList** control from the Web Forms tab in the Toolbox to the inside of the empty Panel control. Change the (ID) property to **RBL**. Verify that the AutoPostback property is **False**. Change the Font Name to **Trebuchet MS**, the Size to **X-Small**, and the ForeColor to **#004040**. Verify that the RepeatDirection property is set to **Vertical** and the RepeatLayout property is set to **Table**.

4. Double-click in the whitespace area on the page to open the code behind the page. Locate the comments in the Page_Load procedure. Select all of the comments, except the first comment. Click the **Edit** menu, point to **Advanced**, and click **Uncomment Selection**. This code will create the ArrayList named AR1 and add several items to the list. Type the following code below the comment 'insert the code snippet here,' which will insert another item, assign the ArrayList to the DataSource property, and bind the data to the control:

```
AR1.Add("Sports in Ireland")
RBL.DataSource = AR1
RBL.DataBind()
```

5. Click the **ASPDBRadioButtonList.aspx** tab to return to the Web page.

6. Double-click the **Submit** button to view the btnSubmit_Click procedure in the code behind the page. Add the code that follows this paragraph. The code determines which element is selected with the SelectedItem object. The SelectedItem object contains a value and Text property. Assign the Text property to a variable, which is used to change the Text property of the Label control.

```
Dim strResult As String
strResult = "<b>You selected: </b><br /><br />"
If RBL.SelectedIndex > -1 Then
    strResult += RBL.SelectedItem.Text
End If
lblTopics.Text = strResult
```

7. Click the **ASPDBRadioButtonList.aspx** tab to return to the Web page. Click the **Save All** button. Click **Build** on the menu bar, then click **Build Solution**. Right-click on the page, and then click **View in Browser**. Select **Hiking in Ireland**, as shown in Figure 3-14, and click the **Submit** button. Close each of the pages you created.

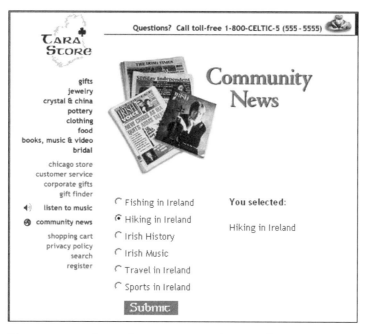

Figure 3-14   The RadioButtonList Web control

Binding CheckBoxLists to HashTables

In the following example, you will bind the data from a HashTable to an ASP.NET CheckBoxList control. **CheckBoxList controls** allow you to group a series of one or more CheckBox controls. You can easily bind the CheckBoxList to several types of data sources such as ArrayLists, HashTables, and databases. By grouping them together in a single control, you can set the properties for the entire group. For example, you can set the **RepeatDirection property** so that the group is displayed horizontally or vertically. You can specify the **RepeatLayout property**, which will group the list using a table or using paragraph tags.

In the steps below, you create a simple HashTable that populates a CheckBoxList control. You can create a HashTable by declaring the object using the keyword Dim, the name of the HashTable, and the keyword New. You do not need to identify the number of items in the HashTable. You can add items to the HashTable by using the Add method of the HashTable object to store the items. The items are added using a key and value pair. You can use the key in your programming to retrieve the value for a particular item. Because you have a key and value pair, you must specify the key and value using the **DataTextField** and **DataValueField properties**. The DataValueField is used to create the value for the control, and the DataTextField is used to create the text displayed for the control.

1. In the Solution Explorer window, locate the ASPDBCheckboxList.aspx file. This file is one of the files that was imported into your solution.

2. Double-click the file **ASPDBCheckboxList.aspx** to open it.

3. Drag and drop the **CheckBoxList** control from the Web Forms tab to the inside of the empty Panel control. Change the (ID) property to **CBL**. Verify that the AutoPostback property is **False**. Change the Font Name to **Trebuchet MS**, the Size to **X-Small**, and the ForeColor to **#004040**. Verify that the RepeatDirection property is set to **Vertical** and the RepeatLayout property is set to **Table**.

4. Double-click in the whitespace area on the page to open the code behind the page. Locate the comments in the Page_Load procedure. Select all of the comments, except the first comment. Click the **Edit** menu, point to **Advanced**, and click **Uncomment Selection**. This code will create the HashTable named HS1 and add several items to the list. Type the following code below the comment 'insert the code snippet here,' which will insert another item, assign the HashTable to the DataSource property, and bind the data to the control:

```
HS1.Add(5, "Sports in Ireland")
CBL.DataSource = HS1
CBL.DataTextField = "Value"
CBL.DataValueField = "Key"
CBL.DataBind()
```

5. Click the **ASPDBCheckboxList.aspx** tab to return to the Web page.

6. Double-click the **Submit** button to view the btnSubmit_Click procedure in the code behind the page. Add the code following this paragraph. The code determines which items are selected by using the Selected property. The Selected property indicates if the item was selected. However, because you can have multiple items selected, you must loop through each control in the list and read the Selected property for each control. Then, you can assign the Text property of that control to a variable, which will be used to change the Text property of the Label control. The code to determine if any item was selected is CBL.SelectedIndex > -1. To retrieve the number of items in the list, use the property CBL.Items.Count.

```
Dim strResult As String
If CBL.SelectedIndex > -1 Then
   strResult = _
   "You selected the following categories:<br /><br />"
   Dim i As Integer
   For i = 0 To CBL.Items.Count - 1
      If CBL.Items(i).Selected Then
      strResult += CBL.Items(i).Text + "<br />"
   End If
 Next
Else
```

```
strResult = "You did not select a category."
End If
lblTopics.Text = strResult
```

7. Click the **ASPDBCheckboxList.aspx** tab to return to the Web page. Click the **Save All** button. Click **Build** on the menu bar, then click **Build Solution**. Right-click the page, and then click **View in Browser**. Select **Hiking in Ireland**, **Fishing in Ireland**, and **Sports in Ireland**, as shown in Figure 3-15, and click the **Submit** button. Close each of the pages you created.

8. Exit Visual Studio .NET by clicking **File** on the menu bar, and then clicking **Exit**.

Figure 3-15   The CheckBoxList Web control

CHAPTER SUMMARY

❑ Visual Studio .NET allows you to create Web pages using HTML controls, HTML Server controls, and ASP.NET controls. In order to use HTML Server controls or ASP.NET controls, you must save your page as an ASP.NET page. You can only use HTML controls when creating a basic HTML page.

❑ HTML Server controls are HTML controls where the runat attribute has been set to server. Because the server is aware of the control, you can create server code to manipulate the control's properties and values. ASP.NET controls are Server controls by default. The server will generate the output required by the browser to view and interact with the ASP.NET control. ASP.NET controls are also known as Web controls.

❐ Both HTML Server controls and ASP.NET controls are used to build forms. Forms are used to collect information from the user, and to increase interactivity with the user. Both HTML Server controls and ASP.NET controls support text boxes, radio buttons, and check boxes. However, ASP.NET controls include collections of radio buttons and check boxes called RadioButtonLists and CheckBoxLists.

❐ There are many other types of controls such as HyperLink, Panel, and Placeholder controls. You can modify the contents and properties of these controls by using the Properties window, or dynamically through the code behind the page.

❐ Validation controls are a form of ASP.NET controls that allow you to assign validation rules to other controls. You can build custom validation rules to validate your form fields, or use one of the prepackaged form field Validation controls.

❐ Server controls can be modified programmatically. Some controls, such as simple lists and drop-down lists, can be populated programmatically using ArrayLists and HashTables.

REVIEW QUESTIONS

1. A(n) _____ is a set of related procedures and properties that are compartmentalized.

   a. object

   b. control

   c. method

   d. function

2. What is the full namespace for the HTMLControl class?

   a. System.Web.UI.HTMLControl

   b. System.Web.HTMLControl

   c. System.UI.WebControl

   d. System.HTML.UI.Control

3. Which property is used to uniquely identify the Server controls?

   a. ID

   b. Name

   c. GUID

   d. Style

4. What is/are the possible values of the Visible property?

   a. True

   b. False

   c. Visible

   d. a and b

5. Which HTMLControl is used to create hyperlink?

   a. HTMLAnchor

   b. HTMLTarget

   c. HTMLHyperlink

   d. HTMLImageLink

6. Which events do the HTML Server controls intercept?

   a. ServerChange

   b. ServerClick

   c. MouseClick

   d. a and b

7. What is the name of the function that is created by the server event handlers?

   a. __PostBack

   b. __doPostBack

   c. __EVENTTARGET

   d. __EVENTARGUMENT

8. What property is used to change the text displayed by an HTML Label control?

   a. Text

   b. InnerHTML

   c. DisplayMode

   d. OuterText

9. What must you do to change an HTML control into an HTML Server control?

   a. Add runat = "server" in the control tag.

   b. Right-click the control and select Run As Server Control.

   c. Type "server" in the runat property in the Properties window.

   d. a and b

10. What does the Build Solution command do?

   a. opens the debugger

   b. compiles the code behind the page

   c. executes the code

   d. opens the page in a browser

11. What is the name of the event handler that activates when the page is visited?

   a. IsPostback

   b. IsValid

    c. Page_Load

    d. Page_OnLoad

12. What property is used to retrieve the value of a TextBox control?

    a. Value

    b. Label

    c. ID

    d. InnerText

13. What method is used to remove all the items in a Dropdown List control?

    a. Remove

    b. Delete

    c. Clear

    d. none of the above

14. Which Server controls inherit from the System.Web.UI.WebControls class?

    a. Web Form controls

    b. Rich controls

    c. Validation controls

    d. all of the above

15. Which method(s) is/are used to assign a color to a control?

    a. MyControl.BackColor = Color.FromName(txtBackColor.Value)

    b. MyControl.BorderColor = System.Drawing.Color.Green

    c. MyControl.BorderColor = Green

    d. a and b

16. Which type of control is assigned to HTML controls that do not have the runat=server property configured?

    a. Label control

    b. Panel control

    c. Placeholder control

    d. Literal control

17. What type of ASP.NET control is used as a container to store dynamically added Server controls to the Web page?

    a. Label control

    b. Panel control

    c. Placeholder control

    d. Literal control

18. Which is a valid value for the Target property of a hyperlink?

    a. New

    b. _blank

    c. parent

    d. href

19. Which value is used to turn off the display of a Validation control error message?

    a. dynamic

    b. none

    c. static

    d. off

20. Which Validation control is the best choice to ensure that Zip code values entered in a form are all numeric?

    a. RequiredFieldValidator

    b. RangeValidator

    c. CompareValidator

    d. RegularExpressionValidator

HANDS-ON PROJECTS

Project 3-1

You work for an office supply store that currently has Web pages that display the company's products. Your boss wants you to convert the pages to work with the company's new ASP.NET application. In this project you create a Web page that uses HTML Server controls to change the Source property of an image. This page will change the image when you click on the buttons.

1. Start **Visual Studio .NET** and open your **Chapter3** solution.

2. Start the browser. Open the page named **CaseProducts.htm** in your browser. The butterfly.gif image used in this example was imported into the images folder when you created the solution.

3. In Visual Studio .NET create a Web Form named **Ch3Proj1.aspx**. Add HTML Server controls that replicate the same features as the CaseProducts.htm page without using client-side JavaScript. Use the example you created in the chapter and the sample code following this paragraph to help you change the Source property of the image in the code behind the page. (*Hint:* You will need to intercept each button ServerClick event and then assign a new image name as the source of the switcher graphic control.)

```
Private Sub Button1_ServerClick(ByVal _
sender As System.Object, _
ByVal As System.EventArgs) Handles _
Button1.ServerClick
    switcher.Src = "images/yellowNotepad1.gif"
End Sub
```

4. Save the file. Build the solution. Open the page in your browser. Print the Web page and the ASP.NET source code and code behind the page within Visual Studio .NET.

Project 3-2

You are to recreate one of the features of the Online Dictionary of Internet Terms. The page currently has a list of terms that open to a new window when the term is clicked. Your job is to recreate the page for the ASP.NET application. In this project you create a Web page that uses HTML Server controls to open new windows using server-side hyperlinks. To enable you to manipulate the window dimensions and toolbars, you will use a client-side script.

1. Start **Visual Studio .NET** and open your **Chapter3** solution.

2. Open the browser. Open the page named **CaseTerm.htm** in your browser.

3. In Visual Studio .NET, create a Web Form named **Ch3Proj2.aspx**. Add HTML or ASP.NET Server controls that replicate the same features as the CaseTerm.htm page without using client-side JavaScript. Use the example you created in the chapter to help you change the hyperlink to open the page in a new window. You can use link buttons for the hyperlinks. In the code behind the page, you can create a function that will write out the client-side script, like so:

```
Function newWin(ByVal varWindow As String)
Dim WinCode As String
WinCode = "<script>" & _
"window.open(" & varWindow & ",'newWin'," & _
"'height = 465,width = 450, status = no, " &_
"toolbar = no, menubar = no, location = no');" & _
"</script>"
Response.write(WinCode)
```

4. Then, you can call the client-script and pass the URL to the function, as shown in the code following this paragraph. You will have to call the function and pass the new URL for each button click event.

```
Private Sub LinkButton1_Click(ByVal ↵
sender As System.Object, ↵
ByVal e As System.EventArgs) Handles ↵
LinkButton1.Click
    newWin("'DocumentObjectModel.htm'")
End Sub
```

5. Save the file. Build the solution. Open the page in your browser. Print the Web page, the ASP.NET source code, and code behind the page within Visual Studio .NET.

Project 3-3

The Northfield Children's Zoo has a Web page with a simple question game that they would like you to rewrite for their ASP.NET application. In this project you create a Web page that uses server events to change the Source property of an image.

1. Start **Visual Studio .NET** and open your **Chapter3** solution.

2. In your browser open the page named **Zoo.htm**. The page contains questions and images. When the visitor clicks the image, a new image appears, showing the answer to the question. The images used in this example were imported into the images folder when you created the solution. These images are named turtle.gif, farm.gif, zebra.gif, ladybug.gif, and swan.gif.

3. In Visual Studio .NET create a Web Form named **Ch3Proj3.aspx**. Create an ASP.NET page using HTML or ASP.NET Server controls that replicates the same features as the Zoo.htm page without using client-side JavaScript. (*Hint:* You can use the ImageButton to create the Image controls.) You can change the code so that the user must click on the image to change the image and view the answer, as follows:

```
Private Sub ImageButton1_Click(ByVal _
sender As System.Object, _
ByVal e As System.EventArgs) _
Handles ImageButton1.Click
    ImageButton1.ImageUrl = "images/farm.gif"
End Sub
```

4. Save the file. Build the solution. Open the page in your browser. Print the Web page, the ASP.NET source code, and code behind the page within Visual Studio .NET.

Project 3-4

Growlite Marketing has a member preferences page written in client-side scripting that they would like you to rewrite for their ASP.NET application. In this project you create a Web page that uses Server controls to change the page properties dynamically when the form is submitted.

1. Start **Visual Studio .NET** and open your **Chapter3** solution.

2. In your browser open the page named **MemberPrefs.htm**. This page retrieves user information, then that information is used to redisplay the page according to the member's preferences.

3. In Visual Studio .NET create a Web Form named **Ch3Proj4.aspx**. Add HTML or ASP.NET Server controls that replicate the same features as the MemberPrefs.htm page without using client-side JavaScript. (*Hint:* You should assign default values to the fields.)

4. You should refer to the example code provided in the chapter to change the color of a property dynamically. The following code is a sample of what you will need to do to the <body> tag to change the property of the page text color and the background color:

```
<body text="<% = txtFgColor.text %>"
    bgColor="<% = txtBgColor.text %>"
    MS_POSITIONING="GridLayout">
```

5. Then, you can display the Welcome message, change the Source property of the logo image, and change the background color of the table, as shown in the following code:

```
Private Sub Button1_Click(ByVal sender As System.Object, ↵
ByVal e As System.EventArgs) Handles Button1.Click
    msg.Text = "Welcome " & txtUser.Text
    logoImage.Src = _
    animal.SelectedItem.Value.ToString
    Table1.BgColor = _
    txtTableColor.Text
End Sub
```

6. Save the file. Build the solution. Open the page in your browser. Print the Web page, the ASP.NET source code, and code behind the page within Visual Studio .NET.

Project 3-5

The IT Department at Night Crawlers has a login page that they would like you to rewrite for their ASP.NET application. In this project you create a Web page that retrieves user login information, authenticates the user, and then redirects the user to the appropriate member or administration home page.

1. Start **Visual Studio .NET** and open your **Chapter3** solution.

2. In your browser open the page named **AdminLogin.htm**. The page retrieves the user login information, then uses that information to redirect the user to his or her home page. You can create the additional member and administrative home pages in Visual Studio .NET.

3. In Visual Studio .NET create a Web Form named **Ch3Proj5.aspx**. Add HTML or ASP.NET Server controls that replicate the same features as the AdminLogin.htm page without using client side JavaScript.

4. Retrieve the values of the form fields when the user clicks on the button as shown in the following code:

```
Private Sub Submit1_ServerClick _
(ByVal sender As System.Object, ByVal e As _
System.EventArgs) _
Handles Submit1.ServerClick
    Dim strUserName, strPassword
    strUserName = txtUsername.Value
    strPassword = txtPassword.Value
```

5. Use the code following this paragraph to determine if the username is the manager. Then, determine if the password field matches "pwd". If yes, then redirect the user to the Admin.htm page. If the password does not match, redirect them to the login page. (*Note*: The Redirect method of the Response object will cause the Web page request to be changed to a new URL. You can pass a fully qualified

Web address, such as *http://www.tarastore.com*, or a relative Web address, such as *admin.asp*.)

```
Select Case StrUserName
Case "manager"
    If (strPassword = "pwd") Then
        Response.Redirect("admin.htm")
    Else
        Response.Redirect("Ch3Proj5.aspx")
    End If
```

6. You will need to repeat the Case-Select and If-Then-Else control structures for each user that you allow in the site. You should include at least one administrator, named admin, with a password named pass, to log in to the Web page.

7. Save the file. Build the solution. Open the page in your browser. Print the Web page, the ASP.NET source code, and code behind the page within Visual Studio .NET.

Project 3-6

Red River Boats has a list of names and addresses written in client-side JavaScript with arrays and a buttonlist that they would like you to rewrite for their ASP.NET application. In this exercise you create an ASP.NET page that displays data in a list.

1. Start **Visual Studio .NET** and open your **Chapter3** solution.

2. In your browser open the page named **RedRiverBoats.htm**. The page displays employee information dynamically.

3. In Visual Studio .NET create a Web Form named **Ch3Proj6.aspx**. Add an ASP.NET RadioButtonList control that is populated with the employee data without using client-side JavaScript. You should refer to the sample code provided in the chapter to add items to the list dynamically when the page loads. (*Hint:* You can use an ArrayList to populate the list, then bind the ArrayList to the RadioButtonList.)

4. Save the file. Open the page in your browser. Print the Web page, the ASP.NET source code and code, behind the page within Visual Studio .NET.

Project 3-7

In this exercise you create an ASP.NET page that processes and validates form data.

1. Start **Visual Studio .NET** and open your **Chapter3** solution.

2. In your browser open the page named **ApplebeeBooks.htm.** This page processes and validates form data.

3. In Visual Studio .NET create a Web Form named **Ch3Proj7.aspx**. Add at least four ASP.NET Validation controls that validate the form fields. If the form is valid, display a message in the browser. (*Hint:* The code following this paragraph is a sample of how you can detect if the entire page is valid by using the IsValid property.)

```
Private Sub Submit1_ServerClick(ByVal _
sender As System.Object, _
```

```
          ByVal e As System.EventArgs) _
          Handles Submit1.ServerClick
              If Page.IsValid = True Then
                  Label1.Text = _
                  "Thank you for completing the form."
              End If
          End Sub
```

4. Save the file. Build the solution. Open the page in your browser. Print the Web page, the ASP.NET source code and code, behind the page within Visual Studio .NET.

CASE PROJECTS

World Culture Foundation — Using HTML Server Controls

The World Culture Foundation has hired your company to create a Web site to promote cultural awareness and diversity. The project manager has asked you to create a sample Web site using Visual Studio .NET. Select a culture that you are interested in. Visit Web sites that discuss your topic. Create a Web site containing at least two Web pages that present the information you researched. Use the HTML Server controls to create the Web pages. At least one of the pages must contain a form. Save the Web pages as Ch3Case1_1.aspx and Ch3Case1_2.aspx. Print out your Web pages and the source code for the ASP.NET page and the code behind the page.

See Figure 3-16 for a sample page. You can locate sample images in the Chapter03Data folder. You can also locate graphics from Microsoft Clipart and Media at *http://office.microsoft.com/clipart/default.aspx*.

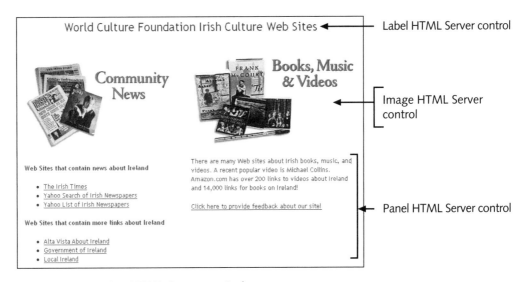

Figure 3-16   Using HTML Server controls

Tara Store Product List Page — Passing Form Field Data to a Web Page

The project manager has asked you to create a sample Web site that displays Tara Store's products. Create a form that displays five product images, along with their product name, price, and product number, as shown in Figure 3-17. Add a Submit button that is labeled "Add to My Cart" below each of the products. Display the quantity ordered as a single text box. You can add additional form fields and ASP.NET controls as needed.

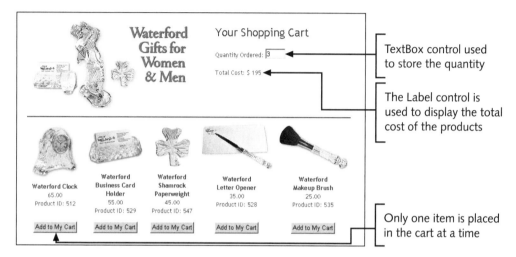

Figure 3-17   Form controls

When the visitor clicks the Submit button, calculate the price by using the quantity times the cost of the item. Display the total cost to the user. Save the Web page as Ch3Case2.aspx. Print out your Web pages and the source code for the ASP.NET page and the code behind the page. (*Hint*: On each button click, you will calculate the total cost and change the Text property of a Label control to the total cost, as shown in the following code.)

```
Private Sub Button1_Click(ByVal _
sender As System.Object, _
ByVal e As System.EventArgs) _
Handles Button1.Click
    Dim Cost As Integer
    Cost = quantity.Text * txt512.Text
    lblOrder.Text = "Total Cost: $ " & Cost.ToString
End Sub
```

Tara Store Product Shipping Form — Form Field Validation

Your project manager has asked you to create the shipping form for the Tara Store Shopping Cart. Create a form for the visitor's name, address, phone, and e-mail address. Use the ASP.NET Validation controls to validate the form. Modify the error messages to indicate the error to the visitor. Once the page is validated, display a thank you message to the visitor. (*Hint:* You can use the IsValid property to detect if all of the Validation controls have been used successfully.) Save the Web page as Ch3Case3.aspx. Print out your Web pages and the source code for the ASP.NET page and the code behind the page.

Tara Store Product Main Category List — Displaying the Main Categories Using Dynamic Lists

Your project manager has asked you to create the main category list for the Tara Store Online Catalog. Create a Web page that displays the category list as a RadioButtonList control, as shown in Figure 3-18. When the visitor clicks a Submit button, its associated category page should open. Save the Web page as Ch3Case4.aspx. You can use an ImageButton for the Submit button. You will need to create each of the associated category pages. (*Hint:* You can add the items directly using the Collections property, or use an ArrayList and programmatically add the items when the page loads.) Place a menu on each category page, so the user can jump to any of the category pages from any Web page. Print out your Web page and the source code for the ASP.NET page and the code behind the page.

Figure 3-18   The RadioButtonList Web controls

Tara Store Product List — Displaying the Product List Using Dynamic Lists

Your project manager has asked you to create the product list page for the Tara Store Online Catalog. Create a Web page that displays the product list as a CheckBoxList control. Display a default graphic when the page loads. When the visitor clicks the Submit button, the related product image should be displayed in place of the default graphic. (*Hint:* You should review the ASPPlaceholder.aspx page before attempting this assignment.) Because the user can select more than one item, you must retrieve the value for each check box checked and create an image for each check box checked. For each item checked in the check box list, you will create an image control, such as MyImage, and a Literal control, such as MyLiteralBR. The image control will be assigned to the value of the check box control. You can do this by assigning the MyImage.ImageUrl property to "images/" & CBL.Items(i).Value. If nothing is selected, then show the default image. You can use any of the product images in the Chapter3\images directory in your project or use your own product images. Save the page as Ch3Case5.aspx. Print out your Web page and the source code for the ASP.NET page and the code behind the page. A sample of a product listing is shown in Figure 3-19.

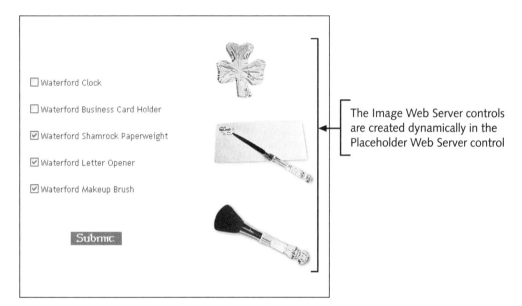

The Image Web Server controls are created dynamically in the Placeholder Web Server control

Figure 3-19 Displaying data with a CheckBoxList Web control

4

USING ASP.NET CONTROLS

Today businesses need to be able to enhance the appearance of their Web pages, as well as to manage the data within the Web site. In this chapter, you will learn about the ASP.NET controls that will enhance your Web pages, not only in appearance, but also by providing the user with more information and interactivity. XML is the glue that allows applications to share information. By using XML files and data sources, you can share data across networks and firewalls to any application that supports the XML standards. Companies can use XML-based data to create data-driven Web applications that are not database dependent. Once the data has been provided to your Web site, you will want to format the data so that the output will appeal to your visitors. You will learn to edit the XML data file by using the XML editor built into Visual Studio .NET. You will learn to use the ASP.NET XML control to read and format XML data. You will use the ASP.NET Web controls to create XML-based rotating banner ads and display an interactive calendar. You will also learn to upload files using the HTMLInputFile control. These ASP.NET controls, also known as Web controls, enhance the interactivity within a Web site. In this chapter, you will learn how to use these controls, and other advanced Web controls, to enhance your Web site. These controls will not necessarily be implemented on all Web sites. However, they provide a sample of how ASP.NET can be used to enhance ASP.NET applications.

ASP.NET Controls

As you learned in Chapter 1, you use ASP.NET controls to enhance your Web applications. There are several ASP.NET controls that are installed with Visual Studio .NET. The File Upload control allows you to upload a file to the Web server. The XML control allows you to read and display XML document data in a Web page. The AdRotator control allows you to display rotating banner advertisements based upon the data stored in an XML data file. The Calendar control allows you to insert a customized calendar into the Web page. ASP.NET controls are Web controls that inherit the Web control class from the `System.Web.UI.WebControl` namespace. Microsoft and third-party software companies also provide additional ASP.NET controls. In this chapter, you will learn how to work with each of several ASP.NET controls to enhance your Web site.

Introduction to XML Technologies

Extensible Markup Language (XML), like HTML, is a markup language that provides access to structured content. But, unlike HTML, XML is not limited to a set of tags or to being displayed in a browser. XML allows you to define your own elements. XML documents can be shared across applications, file systems, and operating systems. Because XML enables cross-platform interoperability, XML is a powerful tool for developing Internet applications. The exercises in this section of this chapter focus on a small segment of XML technologies. These technologies include creating XML and XSL stylesheet documents, using the XML editor, and implementing the XML control in a Web Form. In a later chapter, you will learn additional XML-related content while working with Web databases and Web services. (*Note*: As XML grew, the standards and technologies expanded. It's useful to keep a list of terms and definitions of these technologies as you proceed through the chapter.)

The XML standards are maintained by the World Wide Web Consortium (*www.w3c.org*). The XML standards allow you to add content, referred to as data, to an XML document. However, an XML document can also include information that describes the data, which is known as the data structure or schema. The XML standards contain the **XML Document Object Model (DOM)**, which is a standard language-neutral interface for manipulating XML documents from a script or program. With a DOM, a program or script can access and update the content, structure, and style of an XML document.

There are many technologies that work with XML documents. You can add a hyperlink to an XML document using the **Xlink** standard. You can point to parts of an XML document using the **XPointer** and **XFragments** standards. The XML document can be formatted using a stylesheet known as **XSLT stylesheets**. **XSL Transformations (XSLT)** is a language for transforming XML documents. XSLT stylesheets use XSLT to interact with an XML document. XSLT stylesheets can format individual elements or groups of elements within the XML document.

You can view the XML document using a simple text editor, such as Notepad. You can view XML files also by using the Microsoft Internet Explorer browser, because built into the browser is software named Microsoft XML Core Services. Note that the Microsoft XML Developer Center at *http://msdn.microsoft.com/xml* contains information on XML technologies and software.

 XML documents can be used by other types of applications, such as Window Forms. These applications access the data in the XML document using the XML Document Object Model (DOM) and the Simple API for XML (SAX).

You can insert an XSLT stylesheet directly into the XML document and view the formatted output using an XML parser. However, if you do this, the stylesheet is hardcoded into the XML document. If you want to switch to a new XSLT stylesheet, you would have to manually change the code in the XML document. With the XML control, you can create a Web page that formats the XML document using an external XSLT stylesheet.

The benefit of using the XML control is that you can programmatically change the XML document source or the XSLT stylesheet without directly altering the XML document. To use the XML control, you use an XML document, an XSLT stylesheet, and an ASP.NET Web page. You can use ASP.NET to take an XML data source and format it appropriately for the different types of output devices shown in Figure 4-1.

 This chapter will provide introductory information about XML, XSLT, and the XML control. You can learn more about the standards for creating a well-formed XML document at *www.w3c.org/XML*.

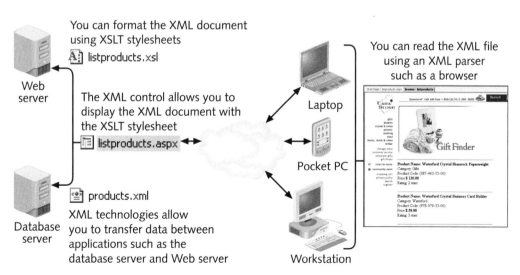

Figure 4-1 XML technologies

Although you can integrate your ASP.NET applications with XML documents and XSLT stylesheets, you do not need to use ASP.NET to build XML applications. However, Visual Studio .NET contains many tools that will help you create and modify your XML documents, and integrate them within your existing ASP.NET applications. The benefit of using XML technologies is that the technology is platform independent and language neutral. You can share your XML document with an application that was created with Java on a UNIX platform. Web Services, which is built on XML technologies, helps call applications remotely across the Internet and share data. You will learn more about how to use XML documents to integrate your databases and Web Services in later chapters.

XML Editing Tools

To create XML documents, you can use a variety of tools, including Notepad, Microsoft XML Notepad, and Visual Studio .NET. Visual Studio .NET provides an HTML/XML editor that you can use to create and edit HTML or XML files. Microsoft XML Notepad provides a graphical view of the XML hierarchical document object model. (*Note*: The Microsoft XML Notepad executable file is called xmlpad.exe, and you can download it from Snapfiles for free at *www.snapfire.com/get/xmlnotepad.html*. You can locate information on how to use this software at *http://support.microsoft.com/default.aspx?scid=kb;en-us;296560*.)

Because all XML documents self-describe their contents, it is not necessary to use the application that created the XML document in order to modify it. XML documents are generally saved with the file extension .xml. Some applications, including Visual Studio .NET, Access XP, and SQL Server 2000, allow you to save a set of data from a database as an XML document. These XML documents are saved with the file extension .XSD. Visual Studio .NET comes with many XML templates and tools to help you create XSLT and other XML documents. In this chapter, you will use Visual Studio .NET to create and edit XML documents.

Well-Formed XML Documents

The XML standards contain rules regarding how to create and format XML documents. The most important rule is that the XML document must be well formed. A **well-formed document** follows XML standards and can therefore be read by any XML parser. All XML documents must comply with these rules. In a well-formed document, there can be only one root element, within which all other elements are nested. You cannot mix nesting elements. For example, in HTML, you can write `<b>Welcome to <i>Tara Store</b></i>`. In the new, XML-compliant version of HTML, known as **XHTML**, this statement is illegal. You must rewrite the statement as `<b>Welcome to <i>Tara Store</i></b>`. In a well-formed document, you must enclose the values of properties within double quotation marks. XML is case sensitive. The case for the opening and closing tags of an element must match. (*Note*: It is recommended that you use lowercase letters when naming elements.) So, in a well-formed document the tag `<b>` does not correspond to the closing tag `</B>`. In a well-formed document, all tags must be closed.

You should read through the XML standards on the W3C Web site. Some of the tags, such as the <br> tag, have been changed. If you have an empty element, such as the line break tag <br>, that does not usually have a closing tag, you can add a forward slash (/) before the closing bracket to close the tag. The resulting tag would then be <br />. To support older browsers that implement previous versions of HTML, you need to add a space after the br characters. By leaving a space the browser will read <br and recognize that this tag is a line break tag. When the browser sees a space and a slash it interprets the code as an unrecognized attribute. The browser ignores the slash while still using the <BR> tag correctly. However, if you do not leave a space before the slash, some browsers will not recognize <br/> as a valid tag, and ignore it. For more information, you can read the XHTML standards located at *www.w3.org/TR/xhtml1/#guidelines*.

It is useful to validate your XML code to ensure that it is well formed. Microsoft has a free validation tool located at *http://msdn.microsoft.com/ archive/default.asp?url=/archive/en-us/samples/internet/xml/xml_ validator/default.asp*. Visual Studio .NET comes with several XML tools, including a validation tool that will indicate your XML documents. You will learn how to use the validation tool later in this chapter.

The Prologue

When you create an XML document, you must first select which version of XML standards you will be working with. The first section, known as the **prologue**, contains global information such as the XML version, formatting information, and schema definitions.

XML Version

The first line in an XML document specifies the version of XML, using the **Version property**, as shown in the code following this paragraph. The question mark indicates that this tag, xml, is a processing instruction and therefore does not contain data. The version property identifies the XML standards version to be used to read the document. You can also indicate the Character-encoding property used such as UTF-8 or UTF-16. The Character-encoding property is optional and describes any coding algorithms that are used within the page. (*Note*: In 2004, the World Wide Web Consortium approved version 1.1 of the XML Recommendations. All XML documents will follow these standards. Visual Studio .NET 2003 will insert version 1.0 as the standard XML version.)

```
<?xml version="1.0" encoding="utf-8" ?>
```

Formatting XML Documents

The prologue of the XML document can contain a reference to an external cascading stylesheet (CSS) or an XSL file. CSS files are often used to format HTML documents or XML documents. Unlike HTML, elements contained within XML documents do not contain any formatting instructions. You must include the formatting instructions within the processing instructions inside the XML document, or use an external file such as a CSS or XSL stylesheet. The sample code following this paragraph shows how to add a reference to a CSS stylesheet in an XML document. This code would appear in the prologue below the XML version.

```
<?xml-stylesheet type="text/css" href="taragifts.css"?>
```

You can also use XSL stylesheets to process and format XML documents. XSL is Extensible Style Language. XSLT is a form of XSL that transforms the XML data by using processing rules in the XSLT stylesheet. There are two types of XSL stylesheets. XSLT is responsible for transforming an XML document. The XSLT stylesheet can analyze the XML document, process instructions, and produce output such as HTML. The other type of XSL stylesheet, called XSL-FO, contains formatting objects, and is used to format the XML document. In this chapter, you will work with XSLT stylesheets.

The XML Body

The XML document complies with the **XML Document Object Model (XML DOM)** standards. (*Note:*You can locate the DOM specifications at *www.w3c.org/TR/REC-DOM-Level-1/.*) The two parts of the XML DOM are the DOM Core and DOM HTML. The **DOM Core** is used to represent XML documents, and also serves as the basis for DOM HTML. The **DOM HTML** is used to represent XML/HTML documents. (*Note:* you can read more about the DOM HTML at *www.w3c.org/TR/REC-DOM-Level-1/level-one-html.html.*) The XML DOM was influenced by the document object models that were used by browsers. The document object model within a browser is used to enable JavaScript to interact with objects and events within the browser. This application of JavaScript to manipulate the document object model in the browser is called Dynamic HTML (DHTML). However, the objects, properties, and methods within the XML DOM are very different from the DHTML document object models.

The XML DOM states that XML documents must have a logical structure. The **XML body** of the XML file contains the elements, attributes, and data in the XML document. In an XML document, you must define a root container element to carry all the elements and data in the file. All tags must be nested within the **root tag**. The root tag in an XML document is also known as the **root node** or **root element**.

A **container element** is an element in which other elements can nest. The root node is a container element because all elements must be nested within the root element in an XML document. In an HTML page, the HTML tag is the root element. The HTML element is a container element because it contains child elements such as <head></head> and <body></body>. In this case, the element is also the **parent element** for the head and body tags. The head and body tags are referred to as the **child elements**.

In the sample code following this paragraph, productlist is the root node. The root node can contain many other elements. In this sample, the productlist root node contains two product nodes.

```
<productlist>
 <product>
 </product>
 <product>
```

4

```
  </product>
 </productlist>
```

You can create elements that are containers for other elements. In an HTML page, the <title> tag is nested within the <head> tag. The <head> tag is a container element, and the parent element for the <title> tag. In the sample code following this paragraph, the productlist element is the root element. The product element contains data about a single product. There are multiple product elements contained within the productlist root element. The product element is a container element because it contains the code, name, price, category, image, and rating elements. Notice that each element has an opening and a closing tag.

```
<productlist>
 <product>
  <code>387-463-55-00</code>
  <name>Waterford Crystal Shamrock Paperweight</name>
  <price>99.00</price>
  <category>Waterford</category>
  <image>547.gif</image>
  <rating>4</rating>
 </product>
 <product>
  <code>978-979-53-00</code>
  <name>Waterford Crystal Business Card Holder</name>
  <price>59.00</price>
  <category>Waterford</category>
  <image>529.gif</image>
  <rating>3</rating>
 </product>
</productlist>
```

Modifying an XML Document

In the previous chapter, when you edited an ASP.NET page, you were able to edit the page manually in HTML view, or you could have used the visual editor in Design view. You clicked the HTML and Design tabs to switch back and forth between the two views. When you edit an XML document in Visual Studio .NET, you can edit the data manually in XML view, or in Data view. **Data view** is the visual tool that you use to enter or modify data in an XML file. Data view allows you to enter the data using a table structure. You can use the XML and Data tabs to switch between XML view and Data view. **XML view** allows you to edit the raw XML document manually.

In the products.xml document the root node is named productlist, as shown in the sample code following this paragraph. The productlist node contains one or more product elements. Each product element contains six child elements.

```
<?xml version="1.0" ?>
<productlist>
    <product>
```

```
          <code></code>
          <name></name>
          <price></price>
          <category></category>
          <image></image>
          <rating></rating>
      </product>
<productlist>
```

 XML view supports IntelliSense and color coding to help you create your XML code. If you type the < character, the list of elements is displayed. You can use the arrow keys to move up and down the list of elements. You can use the Enter key to select the element. If you press the spacebar, a list of attributes associated with the element will be available to you in a list. When you insert an element using IntelliSense, the closing tag will also be inserted for you.

Modifying an XML File with the XML Designer

In the following exercise, you will modify the products.xml file. You will use the **XML Designer** in Visual Studio .NET to add a product to the XML document. The XML Designer allows you to edit the document in XML view or Data view. You will add the product using XML view. Then, you will modify some data in the XML file using Data view. You will display the XML document structure using the Document Outline window. The **Document Outline window** opens and displays the structure of the XML document. Later in this chapter you will use the XML control to display the XML data.

1. Start **Visual Studio .NET**. (In most computers, you can go to the **Start** menu, select **All Programs**, **Microsoft Visual Studio .NET 2003**, and then **Microsoft Visual Studio .NET 2003**.)

2. Click **File** on the menu bar, point to **New**, then click **Project** to open the New Project window.

3. Under Project types, click **Visual Basic Projects**, and under Templates, click **ASP.NET Web Application**. The location of your project should be http://localhost/WebApplication1. Change WebApplication1 to **Chapter4** in the Location text box, then click **OK** to create the solution, project, and default files.

4. To add a folder, right-click **Chapter4** in the Solution Explorer window, point to **Add**, then click **New Folder**. Type **images**, then press **Enter**.

5. Right-click the **images** folder, point to **Add**, then click **Add Existing Item**. Browse to locate your data files for this chapter. (*Note*: In the Files of type drop-down list, change the selection from VB Code Files to **Image Files**.)

6. Select all of the images from the images directory within the Chapter04Data folder. (*Note*: You can use the Ctrl+A key combination to select all of the files.) Click the **Open** button to import the images into the images directory

of the Chapter4 project. (*Note:* You can collapse the list of files in the Solution Explorer window by clicking the minus sign in front of the images folder.)

7. Right-click **Chapter4** in the Solution Explorer window, point to **Add**, then click **Add Existing Item**. Browse to locate your data files for this chapter in the Chapter04Data folder. (*Note:* In the Files of type drop-down list, change the selection from Image Files to **All Files**.) Select all of the files except the Images directory, and click **Open**. Messages will appear that ask you to create a class for several of the .aspx files. Click **Yes** in each instance. (*Note:* You can close the Start Page and the default WebForm1.aspx file in the main code window. You will not be modifying these pages in this chapter.)

8. Double-click the file **products.xml** in the Solution Explorer window. Your document opens in XML view. Scroll down the page and look at the structure of the XML document. Verify that the first line contains the version of the XML document, that the productlist element is the root node, and that there are eight product nodes, one for each product.

9. Below the opening productlist node, type the code following this paragraph to create another product record. Your page should look like the XML document in Figure 4-2.

```
<product>
  <code>387-463-55-00</code>
  <name>Waterford Crystal Shamrock Paperweight</name>
  <price>120.00</price>
  <category>Gifts</category>
  <image>547.gif</image>
  <rating>2</rating>
</product>
```

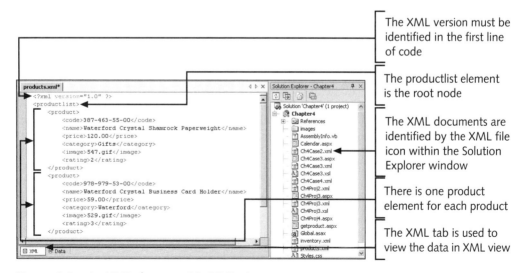

Figure 4-2   An XML document in XML view

10. Click the **Data** tab to open the file in Data view using the XML editor. Place the cursor over the divider line between the code and name cells in the header row. When you move the cursor over the divider lines between the columns, the cursor changes from a single arrow to a double-headed arrow. Click and drag the divider to the right until you can see all of the codes.

11. Place the cursor over the divider line between the name and price cells in the header row. Click and drag the divider to the right until you can see all of the product names.

You can set the column width to **autosize**, which means the column will conform to the contents of the column. To autosize the column, move the mouse cursor over the right border of the column, and when the cursor changes to a double-headed arrow, double-click the mouse.

12. Change the price of the Waterford Crystal Shamrock Paperweight to **99.00**. Change the rating from 2 to **4**. Change the category from Gifts to **Waterford**, as shown in Figure 4-3.

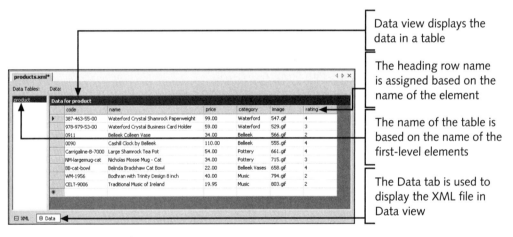

Data view displays the data in a table

The heading row name is assigned based on the name of the element

The name of the table is based on the name of the first-level elements

The Data tab is used to display the XML file in Data view

Figure 4-3 An XML document in Data view

13. Click the **XML** tab. Right-click on the XML document, and then click **Synchronize Document Outline**. Note that in the Document Outline window the productlist element is the root node, and that the product elements are all nested under the productlist element.

The Document Outline window provides a nested outline view of the elements in the current document. This provides an easy way to find and select elements on the page and helps you gain a better understanding of the logical structure of the document. You can expand entities as you scroll through the outline. In addition, you can double-click any element listed to find and select it in the editor.

14. View the XML file in the browser at *http://localhost/chapter4/products.xml*. The browser displays the raw contents of the XML file. It does not contain any formatting information. Close the browser. (*Note:* You can collapse and expand each node by clicking the minus and plus signs next to the node.)

15. Click the **Save All** button. Click **Build** on the menu bar, and then click **Build Solution**. Close the Output window and the Document window. Close the page.

4

Using Special Characters in an XML Document

In early versions of HTML, special characters had to be entered using their markup code. For example, the blank space was represented by ` `. In XML, certain characters are not supported within the tags because they are used to separate XML elements. You must replace these characters with the equivalent element markup codes. Table 4-1 lists common XML characters and their markup codes.

Table 4-1   XML character entity references

Character	XML Character Markup Code
'	&apos;
"	&quot;
&	&amp;
<	&lt;
>	&gt;

You can find additional information on commonly used characters at *http://msdn.microsoft.com/workshop/author/dhtml/reference/charsets/charset1.asp*. This is the ISO Latin-1 character set that represents the first 256 values of the Unicode character set. In HTML, you can use the decimal code or named entity to represent the character. You can find additional information on escape characters at *http://msdn.microsoft.com/library/en-us/dncnt/html/sdkquickref_specialcharacters.asp*. You will find links to single-character escapes such as the ampersand and other types of escape characters.

XSLT Stylesheets

In Chapter 2, you learned to create a Web page using HTML and Visual Studio and modify the appearance of a Web page with a cascading stylesheet (CSS). XHTML documents are Web pages with HTML tags that follow the XML standards. The XHTML documents can be formatted using CSS or an XSLT stylesheet. XSLT can be used to format any XML document, not just XHTML documents. The XSLT stylesheet is an XML document that contains information about how to format a different XML document. The XSLT stylesheet can contain HTML, style rules, and XSLT commands.

The XSLT stylesheet must be formatted according to the XML standards, and therefore the first line identifies the version of XML. A root node is used to indicate that the document is an XSLT stylesheet. The sample code following this paragraph shows the basic code required to create an XSLT stylesheet. The usual file extension for a cascading stylesheet is .css. However, the file extension for the XSLT stylesheet can be .xsl or .xslt. Because the XSLT file is an XML document, the first line will contain the XML version statement. If you save the file as .xsl, <xsl:stylesheet> is the root node. You must include the xmlns:xsl property, which identifies the xsl tags that you will use in the stylesheet. These xsl tags are used to manipulate the contents within the XML file. If you save the file as .xslt, <stylesheet> is the root node. The xmlns:xsl attribute indicates the schema to be supported for the stylesheet. The schema or rules are the XSL Transform standards which are maintained by the W3C. These standards describe how XSLT stylesheets are used to format XML documents. Like other XML documents, you can include comments within the stylesheet using the <! - - and - - > tags. You must close the root element at the bottom of the XSLT stylesheet.

```
<xsl:stylesheet version="1.0"
  xmlns:xsl="http://www.w3.org/1999/XSL/Transform">
<!- - Put your formatting code here - - >
</xsl:stylesheet>
```

 Within the comment tag, do not use any blank spaces between the exclamation point and the hyphen, between the two hyphens, or between the hyphen and the closing bracket.

For XSLT files with the .xslt file extension, the opening tags would appear as follows:

```
<?xml version="1.0" encoding="UTF-8" ?>
<stylesheet version="1.0"
xmlns="http://www.w3.org/1999/XSL/Transform">
</stylesheet>
```

Formatting the Main Template

XSLT stylesheets use templates to group together formatting rules. You can create a generic template, or you can create custom templates that can be used to format specific elements. You can format all the elements at the same time by using the generic template, or you can specify how you want to format each element within the document with the custom template. The following sample code formats several of the elements within the XML document. In this example, the product element is the root node. Notice that the images element is missing from the XSLT document. You do not have to use all of the elements that are contained within the XML document. You can specify which fields to retrieve and which fields to display. In this first segment of code, the default template is defined. This is the main template, as indicated by the match attribute with a forward slash, and is used to format the XML document. You must match the root node of the existing XML document. This is used by the XSLT processor to read the document and to know where to start formatting the document.

Notice that the main template, **xsl:template**, is also used to send basic HTML output to the browser. You can nest basic HTML tags within the templates. The first template, which is shown in the code following this paragraph, will start applying the template, using the root node in the XML document. (*Note:*You do not have to use the entire XML document when formatting the page.) In the HTML code, an embedded stylesheet is used to format the heading. You can mix stylesheets across traditional Web pages, and XSL stylesheets. You can still use embedded and external stylesheets. The **xsl:for-each** statement is a processing instruction that is applied to the node provided in the selected attribute. In this example, for each product node, the product name element, a colon, and the product category element would be written, followed by a line break tag.

```
<xsl:template match="/">
  <html><head><title>Tara Store Product List</title>
  <style type="text/css">
  H1 {color:#003366; font-size:16pt;}
  </style>
  </head>
  <body>
    <H1>Products and their categories.</H1>
    <xsl:for-each select="//product">
          <xsl:apply-templates select="name" />:
          <xsl:apply-templates select="category" /> <br />
    </xsl:for-each>
  </body></html>
</xsl:template>
```

Applying the Main Template with Element Templates In the sample code following this paragraph, processing is applied to the product elements. Different formatting can then be applied to each child element within the product element. Classes are defined within the embedded stylesheet and applied to the product elements. For example, the `<xsl:apply-templates select="name"/>` code means that there is a template in the page that is outside of the main template, that contains the formatting instruction for the name element. In the preceding example, there was no template created for the elements. The XML templates can use the stylesheets defined here to format the XML output to a browser. Although the output is the value of the element, no formatting is applied yet. You will need to create the element template and the formatting within the element template. The following sample code shows only the main template, which corresponds to the root node of the XML document:

```
<xsl:template match="/">
  <html><head><title>Tara Store Product List</title>
  <style type="text/css">
  .heading {font-family: trebuchet ms;
      color:#003366; font-size:16pt;}
```

```
.product {font-family: Verdana;
    color:#003366; font-size:10pt;}
</style>
</head>
<body>
<div class="heading">
 <br /><img src="logo.gif" align="left" hspace="10" />
 <p>Tara Store <br /> Product List</p>
 <br /><br />
</div>
<hr size="1" width="550" align="left" color="#003366"/>
<xsl:for-each select="//product">
        <xsl:apply-templates select="name" />
        <xsl:apply-templates select="category" />
        <xsl:apply-templates select="code" />
        <xsl:apply-templates select="price" />
        <xsl:apply-templates select="rating" />
</xsl:for-each>
<hr size="1" width="550" align="left" color="#003366"/>
</body></html>
</xsl:template>
```

Formatting the Elements Using Element Templates

After using the main template, you can define individual templates for individual elements. In the following sample code, a template is defined for each element. The match attribute indicates the name of the element to apply the template. When the name element template is called, a string is displayed, along with the value of the contents within the name element. The xsl:value-of attribute indicates that the value of the element is retrieved and displayed. So, to display the contents of any node, just use `<xsl:value-of select="." />`. The period means that everything within the node is selected.

```
<xsl:template match="value">
    <b><xsl:value-of select="." /> </b>
</xsl:template>
```

If you want a template to apply to all the other elements, you can use an asterisk as the value for the Match property, as follows:

```
<xsl:template match="*">
    <div class="product"><xsl:value-of select="."/></div>
</xsl:template>
```

The div tag uses the class defined in the embedded stylesheet to determine how to format the output. In addition, the bold tag is applied locally to format the output. You can use a mixture of inline, embedded, and linked styles to format the output. You can add other HTML tags such as the line break tag to format the output for a Web page, as follows:

```
<xsl:template match="name">
  <div class="product">
    <b>Product Name: <xsl:value-of select="." /> </b><br />
  </div>
</xsl:template>
```

Element templates are applied to the category, code, price, and rating elements. Each of the elements defined in the for-each code in the main template references the style template shown in the code following this paragraph. This technique allows you to create very custom XSLT stylesheets.

```
<xsl:template match="name">
  <div class="product">
    <b>Product Name: <xsl:value-of select="." /> </b><br />
  </div>
</xsl:template>
<xsl:template match="category">
  Category: <xsl:value-of select="." /><br />
</xsl:template>
<xsl:template match="code">
  Product Code: (<xsl:value-of select="." />)<br />
</xsl:template>
<xsl:template match="price">
  Price: <b>$ <xsl:value-of select="." /></b> <br />
</xsl:template>
<xsl:template match="rating">
  Rating: <xsl:value-of select="." /> stars<p />
</xsl:template>
```

Creating an XSLT Stylesheet

In the following exercise, you will create a simple XSLT stylesheet named listproducts.xsl that will be used to display the data in the products.xml file. The XSLT stylesheet merely displays the data in a list. The style information is located in the ASP.NET page and in the stylesheet.

1. In Visual Studio .NET, open the **Chapter4** project if it is not already open.

2. Right-click **Chapter4** in the Solution Explorer window, point to **Add**, and then click **Add New Item**. Under Templates click **Style Sheet**, type **listproducts.xsl** in the name text box, and then click **Open**.

3. Notice that the body { } style element has been inserted, but you cannot use the style builder. Delete **body { }**.

4. Type the following code, which will insert the opening and closing stylesheet tags and indicate the XSL stylesheet version:

```
<xsl:stylesheet ↵
xmlns:xsl="http://www.w3.org/1999/XSL/Transform" ↵
version="1.0">
```

5. In between the xsl:stylesheet tags, add the code to create the main template, as shown in the code following this paragraph. (*Note:* You must include a closing stylesheet tag, </xsl: stylesheet>, at the bottom of the page. All of the code must be nested within the stylesheet tags. It's a good idea to add it when you create the opening tag.) The main template will retrieve the name, category, code, price, and rating elements.

```
<xsl:template match="/">
</xsl:template>
```

6. In between the main template tags, add the for-each processing instruction as shown in the code following this paragraph. The **product** is the name of the node that you want to retrieve. The for-each statement should look like this:

```
<xsl:for-each select="//product">
    <xsl:apply-templates select="name" />
    <xsl:apply-templates select="category" />
    <xsl:apply-templates select="code" />
    <xsl:apply-templates select="price" />
    <xsl:apply-templates select="rating" />
</xsl:for-each>
```

7. Enter the code following this paragraph to display and format the data from the name element in the XML file. Add a horizontal ruler, which will divide each product listing.

```
<xsl:template match="name">
    <hr size="1" width="400" align="left" ↵
    color="#003366" />
    <b>Product Name: <xsl:value-of select="."/></b><br />
</xsl:template>
```

8. Enter the code to display and format the data from the other four elements in the XML file, like so:

```
<xsl:template match="category">
  Category: <xsl:value-of select="."/><br />
</xsl:template>
<xsl:template match="code">
  Product Code: (<xsl:value-of select="."/>)<br />
</xsl:template>
<xsl:template match="price">
  Price <b>$ <xsl:value-of select="."/></b><br />
</xsl:template>
<xsl:template match="rating">
```

```
Rating: <xsl:value-of select="."/> stars<p/>
</xsl:template>
```

9. Click the **Save All** button. Click **Build** on the menu bar, then click **Build Solution**. Your page should look like the one in Figure 4-4.

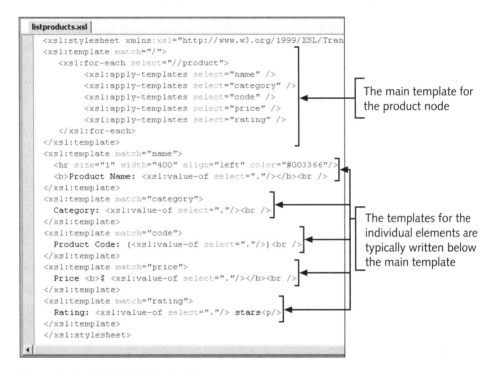

Figure 4-4 An XSLT stylesheet

10. View the XSLT file in the browser at *http://localhost/chapter4/listproducts.xsl*. View the XML file at *http://localhost/chapter4/products.xml*. The browser will show only the XML file. No additional formatting is applied.

11. If necessary, open the products.xml file in the XML Designer. After the first line, insert a blank line. Type the following code, which will link the XML file to the XSLT file:

```
<?xml:Stylesheet type="text/xsl" href="listproducts.xsl" ?>
```

12. Click the **Save All** icon, click the **Build** menu, and select **Build Solution**. View the XML file at *http://localhost/chapter4/products.xml*. The browser will show the formatted XML data.

13. Return to the XML file in Visual Studio .NET. Delete line 2. Click the **Save All** icon, click the **Build** menu, and select **Build Solution**.

Using the XML Control

In the previous exercise, the stylesheet location was hard coded into the XML document. The XML control allows you to programmatically set the XML document and XSLT stylesheet by changing the XML control properties. You can set these properties at design time in the Properties window, or you can create code in the code behind the page that will set the properties at runtime. Creating the XML control in a Web page involves three steps. First, you must determine how to locate the source document. There are three attributes that can be configured to locate the XML data. The **Document property** indicates that the XML data is located in an object called **XMLDocument**. The **DocumentContent property** indicates that the XML data is a string containing the entire text of the XML document. The **DocumentSource** property allows you to identify a physical or virtual path to the XML document. You can also set the DocumentSource property in code to System.XML.XMLDocument, which is an XML string object. Then, you would have an XML input stream as the DocumentSource property instead of a physical file. The XML input stream could be a string that contains the entire XML file, which is read into the DocumentSource property.

In the XML control, you also have to specify where the style information is located. The **Transform attribute** allows you to use an object called **XSLTransform**, which contains the XSL or XSLT stylesheet. This stylesheet is then used to transform the document before displaying it. You can also use the **TransformArgumentList**, which contains a reference to an object called **XsltArgumentList** that contains the arguments to be passed to the stylesheet. Finally, you can use the **TransformSource** attribute to identify the physical or virtual path to the XSL or XSLT stylesheet. You can also set the TransformSource property programmatically to an object from System.XML. XSLTransformObject. This would allow you to use a stream that contained the XSL style information without having a physical file. The XSLT input stream could be a string that contains the entire XSLT file, which is read into the TransformSource property.

Recall that because this is an ASP.NET control, the control is identified with the prefix asp and a colon. In the XML control, you must set the run at property to server to indicate that the control is a Server control. The code following this paragraph is an example of how you insert an XML control in a Web page. You can close the tag with /> or </asp:Xml>. You do not need to type this code in the Web page, because Visual Studio .NET provides a graphical tool in the Toolbox to insert the XML control.

```
<asp:Xml runat="server" id="Xml1"
TransformSource="listproducts.xsl"
DocumentSource="products.xml" />
```

Inserting an XML Control in a Web Page

In the exercise following this paragraph, you will create a Web page that displays an XML document named products.xml using an XSLT stylesheet. The XML control allows you to read, process, and display XML data using an XSLT stylesheet. This process is known as transformation. You will use the DocumentSource and TransformSource properties of the XML control to identify the physical path to the XML document and the XSLT stylesheets.

1. In Visual Studio .NET, open the **Chapter4** project if it is not already open.

2. Double-click **listproducts.aspx** in the Solution Explorer window to open the file.

3. In the Toolbox, drag the **XML** control from the Web Forms tab onto the Panel control. The XML control is labeled Xml.

4. In the Properties window change the DocumentSource property to **products.xml**. Change the TransformSource property to **listproducts.xsl**. (*Note:* You can type in the names of the files, or you can use the Build button to open the dialog box and browse to locate the file.)

5. Click the **Save All** button. Click **Build** on the menu bar, then click **Build Solution**. Your Web Form will look like the one in Figure 4-5.

6. Right-click on the page, and then click **View in Browser**. Close all of the pages you have created. Your Web page will look like Figure 4-6.

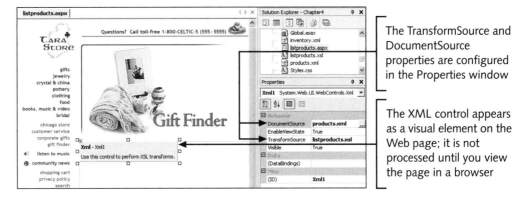

Figure 4-5   XML control

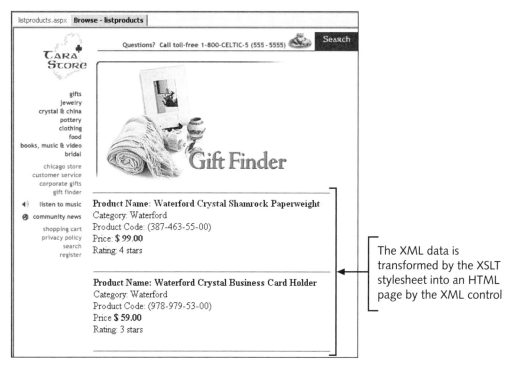

The XML data is transformed by the XSLT stylesheet into an HTML page by the XML control

Figure 4-6   Displaying the XML control in an ASP.NET Web page

Modifying XSLT Stylesheets

There are many ways to format XSLT stylesheets. You can insert HTML, embedded stylesheets, and XSLT commands. This means that all of the HTML tags are available for use within an XSLT stylesheet. As shown in the sample code following this paragraph, you can insert images, tables, and hyperlinks within an XSLT stylesheet. You can specify the attributes for any of the HTML properties in the template by using the **xsl:attribute** command. You can insert the value using the data retrieved from an XML file.

```
<xsl:template match="image">
  <a>
    <xsl:attribute name="href">
      <xsl:value-of select="." />
    </xsl:attribute>
     Click here to go to the Web site.
  </a>
</xsl:template>
```

Inserting a Table with an XSLT Stylesheet

The following sample code shows how you can change the preceding code to format the contents as a table. Instead of using line breaks, the cell tag is used to separate individual elements. The heading of the table is separated outside of the for-each loop so that the heading only appears once. The closing table tag is also located outside of the for-each loop.

```
<xsl:template match="/">
<table border="0" cellspacing="10">
   <tr><th>Image</th><th>Name</th><th>Category</th>
      <th>Code</th><th>Price</th></tr>
   <xsl:for-each select="//product">
      <tr><td><xsl:apply-templates select="image"/></td>
      <td><xsl:apply-templates select="name"/></td>
      <td><xsl:apply-templates select="category"/></td>
      <td><xsl:apply-templates select="code"/></td>
      <td><xsl:apply-templates select="price"/></td></tr>
   </xsl:for-each>
   </table>
</xsl:template>
<xsl:template match="*">
      <div class="product">
            <xsl:value-of select="."/>
      </div>
</xsl:template>
```

Inserting an Image with an XSLT Stylesheet

To output an image to a Web page, you simply modify the image element template. In the previous version the name was simply displayed. In the sample code following this paragraph, the image is displayed using an <img> tag. Recall that the template is processed by the XML parser built into the browser. The browser uses the image tag to create an <img> tag, but you must retrieve the properties for the image tag, such as the Source property. In this example, you define the src property of the image tag. The value is assigned from the contents of the image element in the product node in the XML document. The Align attribute is used to define the Align property for the image tag. In this sample, the value was hard-coded as left-aligned. (*Note:* The align value can also come from the XML document, if the data is available there.)

```
<xsl:template match="image">
   <img>
     <xsl:attribute name="src">
        <xsl:value-of select="." />
     </xsl:attribute>
     <xsl:attribute name="align">left</xsl:attribute>
   </img>
</xsl:template>
```

One of the common things people want to do is to create a link to another document using the XML data. When you want to combine the values, it is simpler to create the hyperlink within the main template. The sample code following this paragraph creates a hyperlink to a URL, and passes the name of the image in a querystring. The **xsl:text** instruction is used to write out the value of the text. You can use this instruction to write out literal text, as well as special control characters, which are listed in Table 4-1. The disable-output-escaping attribute is used to generate characters without escaping, such as the single < character. (*Note:* You need to be careful not to split the xsl:text instruction across multiple lines because the XML parser will process the carriage return and blank spaces. In this example, the text is wrapped to illustrate how the code is spliced across XSLT instructions.) You create an anchor tag that creates a basic hyperlink such as `<a href = "ProcessingPage.aspx?ImageUrl=15.jpg">Belleek Frames & Clocks</a>`. Then, in the processing page, you can retrieve the image name. You can use this technique to create and process more complex querystrings based on values in the XML document.

```
<xsl:template match="/">
  <xsl:for-each select="//Category">
    <xsl:text disable-output-escaping="yes">
        &lt;a href="ProcessingPage.aspx
    </xsl:text>
    <xsl:text disable-output-escaping="yes">
        ?ImageUrl=
    </xsl:text>
    <xsl:value-of select="ImageUrl" />
    <xsl:text disable-output-escaping="yes">
        "&gt;
    </xsl:text>
    <xsl:value-of select="CategoryName" />
    <xsl:text disable-output-escaping="yes">
        &lt;/a&gt;
    </xsl:text>
    <br />
  </xsl:for-each>
</xsl:template>
```

You can alter this code slightly to create simple links to the images. In the sample following this paragraph, a simple hyperlink is used to display the image when the hyperlink is clicked. The link is created using the anchor tag, and the href property is set to the ImageUrl value from the XML document.

```
<xsl:template match="/">
  <xsl:for-each select="//Category">
    <xsl:apply-templates select="ImageUrl" />
    <xsl:apply-templates select="CategoryName" />
  </xsl:for-each>
</xsl:template>
<xsl:template match="ImageUrl">
    <a>
        <xsl:attribute name="href">images/
            <xsl:for-each select=".">
```

```
      </xsl:attribute>
      Click here to see the image.
    </a>
</xsl:template>
<xsl:template match="CategoryName">
    <b><xsl:for-each select="."></b>
</xsl:template>
```

Processing XML Data with an XSLT Stylesheet

In addition to retrieving the data and formatting the output, the XSLT stylesheet can analyze the contents of the element and perform actions. This sample code looks at the contents of the XML document and displays the product name and rating. If the product rating is equal to or greater than 4, then it displays a clover image and the message "Excellent!". The text is formatted using a class called over, which is defined in the embedded stylesheet. If the product rating is 3, then only the message "This is within current projections" is displayed. No special formatting is applied to the message. If the product rating is equal to or less than 2, then a message is displayed that says "WARNING: this is below our target." This message is formatted using the over class, which is defined in the embedded stylesheet. The following is the stylesheet code that must be added to define the over and under classes:

```
.over {font-family:Verdana; font-size:11pt;
    color:green; font-weight:bold}
.under {font-family:Verdana; font-size:10pt;
    color:red; font-weight:bold}
```

In the XSLT stylesheet, you can use the xsl:for-each statement to select which elements to retrieve. Again, this does not mean that you must display them, only that they are retrieved. You can use the template listed in the select attribute to format the output, which may contain the value of the element, as follows:

```
<xsl:for-each select="//product">
    <xsl:apply-templates select="name"/>
    <xsl:apply-templates select="rating"/>
</xsl:for-each>
```

In the name template, the name is displayed and formatted with the product class defined in the embedded stylesheet and the inline bold tag, as follows:

```
<xsl:template match="name">
  <div class="product">
    <b><xsl:value-of select="." /></b>
  </div>
</xsl:template>
```

In the rating template, the rating is displayed with some additional text. Then, **xsl:choose** is used to allow you to analyze the value of the rating. The **xsl:when** statement is used if the condition listed in the test attribute is met. Notice that the greater than sign is written as >. As you saw earlier, this is necessary because otherwise the XML parser may interpret the sign as part of an XML tag. If the first condition is met, then the formatting within the statement occurs. Otherwise, the parser moves to the next condition. The **xsl:otherwise** statement is used to format any data that may not apply to the other choices listed. (*Note*: Don't forget to always include the closing HTML tags.)

```
<xsl:template match="rating">
  <blockquote>Average Customer Rating:
    <b><xsl:value-of select="."/></b> stars.
    <xsl:choose>
      <xsl:when test=". &gt; 3">
        <span class="over">
          <img src="clover.gif" align="bottom" ⤶
              hspace="5"/>
          Excellent!
        </span>
      </xsl:when>
      <xsl:when test=". &lt; 3">
        <span class="under">
          WARNING: this is below our target.
        </span><br />
      </xsl:when>
      <xsl:otherwise>
        This is within current projections.
        <br />
      </xsl:otherwise>
    </xsl:choose>
  </blockquote>
  <hr size="1" width="550" align="left" ⤶
      color="#003366"/>
</xsl:template>
```

You can locate more information on the XSL attributes within the Visual Studio .NET Help files at *http://msdn.microsoft.com/library/en-us/ xmlsdk/html/xmrefxslattributesetelement.asp*.

There are many other processing instructions that can be used with XSLT stylesheets. You can sort the data by using the **xsl:sort** command. You can create and use variables and parameters with XSLT instructions. You can use the test instruction to determine if a condition has been met—for example, to determine the length of the element. The following sample code tests to see if the length of the element named ProductImage is greater than zero. You can use the period (.) to represent the element data or the element name. You can also use > to represent the greater than symbol. The **xsl:if** statement is similar to the xsl:if-else-end if control statement, but does not run unless the conditional statement resolves to true, as follows:

```
<xsl:template match="ProductImage">
<xsl:if test="string-length(ProductImage)>0">
```

```
<img><xsl:attribute name="src">
        <xsl:value-of select="." />
    </xsl:attribute></img>
</xsl:if>
</xsl:template>
```

XML Schemas

One of the benefits of XML is that it allows you to define your own markup language. You can create a document that contains a set of rules, and share them with other programmers. You have to be careful when you are using XML documents to follow the same set of rules. For example, one XML document may use the <p> tag to mean a paragraph, and another XML document may use <p> to represent a person. To eliminate confusion when working with multiple XML documents, XML documents can identify a namespace associated with the document. This set of rules, or namespace, is called a **schema**. Schemas are used to define the structure, content, and semantics of XML documents.

The schema can be written in a Document Type Definition (DTD) document or an XML schema document. **Document Type Definition (DTD)** is an older method used to identify the rules used to structure a document. Different types of documents implement different DTDs. The code following this paragraph is the DTD that is used with Web pages that comply with the strict HTML 4.0 standards. This statement must be the first line in the Web page, before the beginning <html> tag. You can read more about how to use the DTD within a Web page at *www.w3.org/TR/html401/sgml/dtd.html*.

```
<!DOCTYPE HTML PUBLIC "-//W3C//DTD HTML 4.01//EN" ↵
    "http://www.w3.org/TR/html4/strict.dtd">
```

Again, the ↵ character is not part of the code. It is used where a single line of code is split over multiple lines to fit it on the book page.

The W3C is upgrading DTD to a newer format called **XML schemas**. XML schemas will eventually replace DTD. An XML schema is like a DTD document in that they both are ways to structure elements. Both data and schema are transportable through HTTP and can be used on any platform that understands XML.

The two models of XML schemas are available from the W3C and Microsoft. The Microsoft XML schema is extensible because you can add elements to a document without invalidating the document. This is not possible within the W3C XML schemas. You can learn more about XML schemas at *http://msdn.microsoft.com/xml*, and *www.w3c.org/XML/Schema*.

When you create your XML document, you can point to the schema to identify the rules that the document will follow. To do this, you place a reference to a DTD or XML schema in the prologue of the XML document. Then, the XML parser uses that schema to validate the structure of the XML document. When you create an ASP.NET page with Visual Studio .NET, the property used to identify the schema is called **TargetSchema**. Parsers use the schema to determine the rules to validate the XML data.

When you edited the product.xml file, you used the XML Designer. You inserted the new element using XML view and modified the element using Data view. Any XML document can be created or edited in XML view. However, only XML documents that end in .xml can be edited in Data view. The XML Designer supports another view, called Schema view. Schema view is used to edit schema documents. Schema view can display the schema using DataSet view or XML view. DataSet view displays the schema using tables, while XML view displays the schema using XML code. Visual Studio .NET can create a schema for you based on an existing XML document within the XML Designer. The schema document file extension is .xsd. The XML Designer will create the schema document and name it after the XML document, except that it will change the file extension to .xsd. The xmlns attribute is added to the inventory element to identify the XML schema document associated with the XML document, as shown in the following sample code:

```
<elementname xmlns="http://tempuri.org/schemaname.xsd">
```

Validating an XML Document with a Schema

In the following exercise, you will create a schema, using Visual Studio .NET, based on an existing XML document named inventory.xml. You will then modify the schema. The inventory document contains information about the products, the number of items currently in inventory, the reorder level, and the number of items on order. When the number of items in stock reaches the number of items in the reorder level, the manager must place an order for the product. The current values in the inventory document are all strings. In the schema, you will change the types from strings to integers.

1. In Visual Studio .NET, open the **Chapter4** project if it is not already open.

2. Double-click the file **inventory.xml** in the Solution Explorer window. Your document opens in XML view.

3. Click the **Data** tab to open the file in Data view using the XML editor.

4. Right-click on the page, and then click **Create Schema**. A new document named inventory.xsd appears in the Solution Explorer window.

5. Click the **XML** tab to return to XML view. Notice that the inventory node has been changed. The attribute xmlns="http://tempuri.org/ inventory.xsd" has been added to the inventory element. This identifies the XML schema document associated with the inventory.xml document. Select the **XML** menu and then select **Validate XML Data**. A message appears on the

status bar at the bottom-left corner of the IDE, "No validation errors were found." This means that the XML document conforms to the XML schema that was created.

6. Double-click the **inventory.xsd** document to open the document in the XML Designer. Notice that the values in the first column are all E, which identifies the entry as an element. The second column contains the name of the element. The third column contains the description of the type. In the inventory.xsd file all of the element types are defined as string.

7. Click the word **string** for the instock element. Click the arrow that appears in the string cell. A list of data types appears. Scroll up the list and click **integer**, as shown in Figure 4-7.

8. Click the **Save All** button.

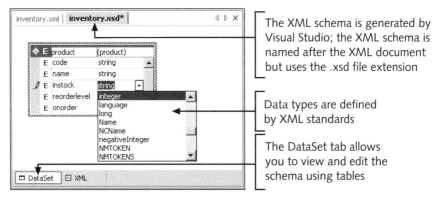

The XML schema is generated by Visual Studio; the XML schema is named after the XML document but uses the .xsd file extension

Data types are defined by XML standards

The DataSet tab allows you to view and edit the schema using tables

Figure 4-7   The DataSet view of the inventory XML schema

10. Go back to the inventory.xml page by clicking the **inventory.xml** tab.

11. Change the instock value for the Waterford Crystal Business Card Holder from 5 to **5abc**.

12. Click the **Data** tab. Notice that the value displayed in Data view for the instock value is listed as (null). Because a schema is used with the XML document, the values must conform to the rules in the schema document.

13. Click the **XML** tab and change the instock value to **–5**. Click the **Data** tab. Notice that the value is displayed in Data view. Because you do not use negative numbers for inventory, you can change the data type in the schema to only accept positive integers.

14. Click the **XML** tab and change the value back to **5**.

15. Go back to the XML schema by clicking the **inventory.xsd** tab. Change the instock data type from integer to **positiveInteger**. Click the **Save All** button.

16. Go back to the inventory.xml page by clicking the **inventory.xml** tab.

17. Click the **XML** tab and change the instock value to **-5**. Click the **Data** tab. Notice that the value displayed is (null).

18. Click the **XML** tab and change the value to **5**. Click the **Save All** button.

19. Go back to the XML schema by clicking the **inventory.xsd** tab. Change the type for the reorderlevel and onorder elements to **positiveInteger**. Go back to the inventory.xml page by clicking the **inventory.xml** tab. Click the **Save All** button. Select the **XML** menu and then select **Validate XML Data**. The Task List window opens with five errors listed. This means that the XML document does not conform to the XML schema that was created. In this case, the error messages indicate that the onorder element has an invalid value according to its data type. The values for the onorder element are 0, and the schema is expecting a positiveInterger data type. (*Note:* You can double-click any of the error messages, which places the cursor at the element.)

20. Click the **inventory.xsd** tab. Click the **XML** tab. The XML schema is displayed using XML code. Notice that the elements are identified using the name attribute and the data type using the type attribute. The type for the code and name elements is string, and the type for the other elements is positiveInteger. The XML schema should look like the XML schema in Figure 4-8. (*Note:* The layout of the xs:schema element was modified so that you can view the entire file.)

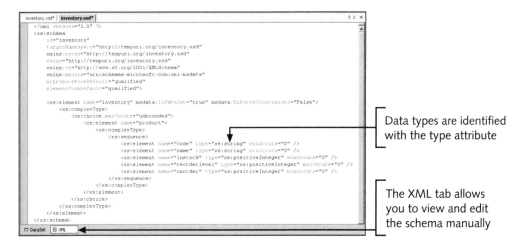

Figure 4-8   XML view of the inventory XML schema

21. Click the **Save All** button. Click **Build** on the menu bar, then click **Build Solution**.

Visual Studio .NET, the MSDN Library, the World Wide Web Consortium, the Microsoft XML Developer Center, and the QuickStart Web sites contain a vast amount of documentation on XML. You can use XML techniques in a business environment. For example, a business partner might maintain a database of parts that you order on a regular basis. They can send you the XML data. With that data, you can create a Web page using your own XSLT stylesheet that lists the parts within your own company intranet. Then your workers can use the same data to order parts. You can use schemas to validate their data each time the XML data file is updated. In a later chapter, you will also learn how to save data from a database into XML using methods built into ASP.NET so that you can send your data to other business partners using XML. You can create an AdvertisementFile using the Ad Rotator Schedule File template in the XML designer. Create an XML file from the Templates window, and in the TargetSchema property in the Properties window, select Ad Rotator Schedule File. The Advertisements root node is inserted for you.

THE ADROTATOR CONTROL

The **AdRotator control** allows you to display a banner ad on a Web page. When you refresh the page, the banner ad is changed to another image. The AdRotator control is created from the `System.Web.UI.WebControl.AdRotator`. The two parts to the AdRotator are the Advertisement File and the Web page. The **Advertisement File** is an XML document that stores the ad information. This file is also known as the rotation file because it includes the information about the rotating ads. You will see each ad for the proportion of time that you indicate in the Advertisement File. The Web page is an ASP.NET page that contains a Web Form, which displays the ads.

The banner ad is a hyperlinked image. So, you need to obtain your graphics and import them into your Web application. You can create your own image using a graphics software package, such as PhotoShop or Paint Shop Pro, or use an existing graphic. You don't have to use the dimensions in a traditional banner ad. You can use any type of rectangular graphic.

You can find several books on Web graphics and Photoshop at *www.course.com*.

The information used to create the banner ad is stored in an external file called the Advertisement File. The Advertisement File is an example of an XML document. The Advertisement File contains information that creates the HTML image tag, which inserts the image in the Web page. The file also contains information that creates the hyperlink using an anchor tag. When you click the banner ad, you are redirected to the URL defined within the hyperlink. The image source and the URL for the hyperlink are defined within the Advertisement File. Each time the page is displayed, the AdRotator class retrieves a different image and hyperlink from the Advertisement File.

The XML document can be edited with a basic text editor such as Notepad, or an XML editor. Visual Studio .NET contains an editor that can create and edit XML documents such as the Advertisement File. Because the Advertisement File is an XML document, the filename has the file extension .xml.

The first line of the Advertisement File indicates the version of the XML document. The following is the syntax for defining the XML version that is used in the XML document. It follows the same format as all XML documents.

```
<?xml version="1.0" encoding="utf-8" ?>
```

The rest of the file is contained within a root node named advertisements. In an XML document, all tags must be nested within the root node. The root tag in an XML document is also known as the **root node**. Contained within the advertisement tag are one or more repeating groups of tags named ad. The **ad tag** is an element that contains the individual properties for the ad.

Each ad contains several properties that are used to create the image and hyperlink tags within the Web page. The **ImageUrl property** identifies the absolute or relative location of the image. Only images in the JPEG, GIF, or PNG formats are currently supported on most Web browsers. The ImageUrl is used to create the SRC property in the image tag. The ImageUrl is the only required property for the AdRotator control. The **NavigateUrl property** identifies the URL to which the browser will be directed when the user clicks on the image. The NavigateUrl is used to create the href property in the hyperlink. The NavigateUrl page is also known as the ad response page, the target page, or the destination page. The **AlternateText property** identifies the text that is displayed when the user places the mouse icon over the image. AlternateText is used to create the ALT property of the image tag. If the user's browser does not support images, the text is displayed instead of the image.

Remember that the NavigateURL corresponds to the href property in the hyperlink created by the anchor (<a>) control. You may want to redirect the user to a Web site outside of your Web site, or to another page within your Web site. You can also pass additional information with the hyperlink in a hard-coded querystring. For example, you could use the value getproduct.aspx?id=529.jpg. The querystring is separated by the URL with a question mark. When the user clicks on the image, the hyperlink takes them to the getproduct.aspx page and passes the querystring to the next page. The next page can retrieve the name and value pairs in the querystring using the Page.Request.Querystring collection.

There are two properties that do not have a corresponding HTML function. The **Impressions property** is used to indicate the frequency with which the banner ad is displayed. The Ad Scheduler File may contain data for thousands of banner ads. You can indicate how often you would like each banner ad to be displayed. Then, when the banner ad is created, the AdRotator class selects a banner ad from the XML file based upon the Impressions property. The Impressions property identifies the relative frequency with which the ad should be displayed. So, if there are three banner ads defined in the file, the first banner ad Impressions property is 20, and the other banner ads' Impressions properties are 35 and 45, then the first banner ad would appear in the Web page 20 times out of 100 page views. The higher the number, the more often the banner ad will be displayed. (*Note*: The total of all of the ad impressions does not have to add up to 100. This is a relative weight value, not a percentage.) This property is important because you can specify to a customer the number of times that their banner ads are displayed within the Web page. You can also refer to your log files to determine the exact number of times that the ad was displayed.

The AdRotator control can be configured to only display images from a group of banner ads. The **Keyword property** is used to indicate one or more words that categorize the banner ad. The AdRotator class uses the keyword to group the banner ads. For example, a newspaper Web site may contain one area that is for adults and another area for children. The adult Web site can display all of the banner ads. However, not all of the banner ads may be appropriate for children. Therefore, the newspaper can configure the AdRotator control using the KeywordFilter property. In the children's area on the Web site, the banner AdRotator would screen the banner ads in the XML file for those where the Keyword property matched the KeywordFilter property. Children would only be able to see age-appropriate content. Thus, one Advertisement File can be used to create the banner ads in multiple pages. If you want a banner ad to belong to multiple categories, you can create an additional entry with the other keywords. The following is a sample of the code used to display two banner ads:

```
<Advertisements>
  <Ad>
    <ImageUrl>banner1.gif</ImageUrl>
    <NavigateUrl>http://www.course.com/ </NavigateUrl>
    <AlternateText>Course Technology</AlternateText>
    <Impressions>60</Impressions>
    <Keyword>Books</Keyword>
  </Ad>
  <Ad>
    <ImageUrl>banner2.gif</ImageUrl>
    <NavigateUrl>http://www.microsoft.com/ </NavigateUrl>
    <AlternateText>Microsoft</AlternateText>
    <Impressions>40</Impressions>
    <Keyword>Software</Keyword>
  </Ad>
</Advertisements>
```

Creating the AdvertisementFile File

In the following example, you will import an AdvertisementFile file. Then, you will use the XML editor to add a new banner ad. You will insert a banner ad in Code view and in Data view.

1. In Visual Studio .NET, open the **Chapter4** project if it is not already open.

2. Double-click the **ads.xml** file in the Solution Explorer window. Notice that you can edit the XML code manually. Under the opening Advertisements tag, add the following code to create a new banner ad element. (*Note*: Remember that the ↵ symbol means that the line of code should be written on one continuous line. Do not type the ↵ character in the code.) The document should appear as shown in Figure 4-9.

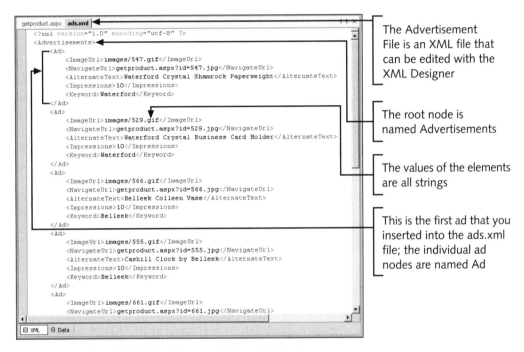

Figure 4-9   The XML Advertisement File in XML view

```
<Ad>
    <ImageUrl>images/547.gif</ImageUrl>
    <NavigateUrl>getproduct.aspx?id=547.jpg ↵
    </NavigateUrl>
    <AlternateText>Waterford Crystal Shamrock ↵
        Paperweight</AlternateText>
    <Impressions>10</Impressions>
    <Keyword>Waterford</Keyword>
</Ad>
```

3. Click the **Data** tab to edit the XML file in Data view.

4. Place the cursor over the divider line between the ImageUrl and NavigateUrl cells in the header row. Click and drag the divider to the right until you can see all of the names of the graphic images.

5. Place the cursor over the divider line between the NavigateUrl and AlternateText cells in the header row. Click and drag the divider to the right until you can see all of the URLs.

6. Place the cursor over the divider line between the AlternateText and Impressions cells in the header row. Click and drag the divider to the right until you can see all of the alternate text.

7. Click the column heading **ImageUrl** to sort the rows based on the ImageUrl.

8. In the last row, enter the data for a new record as shown in Figure 4-10. (*Note*: When you first click in the last row, all of the values will be null.) The ImageUrl value is **images/803.gif**. The NavigateUrl value is **getproduct.aspx?id=803.jpg**. The AlternateText value is **Traditional Music of Ireland**. The Impressions value is **10**. The Keyword value is **Music**.

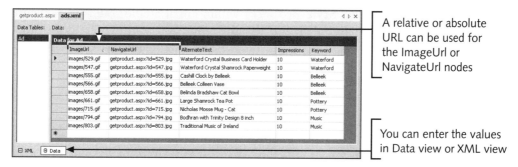

A relative or absolute URL can be used for the ImageUrl or NavigateUrl nodes

You can enter the values in Data view or XML view

Figure 4-10   XML Advertisement File in Data view

9. Click the **Save All** button. Click **Build** on the menu bar, then click **Build Solution**. Close the ads.xml file and the Output window.

Inserting the AdRotator Control

When you insert the banner ad in the Web page, you must insert the banner ad control, which is called **AdRotator**. Recall that because this is an ASP.NET control, the control is identified with the prefix asp and a colon. In the AdRotator control, you must set the run at property to server to indicate that the control is a Server control. Also, you must configure the **AdvertisementFile** property to point to the location of the Advertisement File. The code following this paragraph is an example of how you insert an AdRotator control in a Web page. You can close the tag with /> or </asp:AdRotator>. You do not need to type this code in the Web page because Visual Studio .NET provides a graphical tool in the Toolbox to insert the AdRotator control.

```
<asp:AdRotator runat="server" id="AdRotator1"
AdvertisementFile="ads.xml"
KeywordFilter="Waterford" />
```

 The ID property should be explicitly assigned to each Server control. If you do not assign an ID, the code behind the page still recognizes the object, and the Web server assigns an ID to the control. If you do not assign an ID to the control, you cannot create programs to interact with the control.

There are several additional properties that can be set in the AdRotator control. The **Height** and **Width properties** define the height and width of the image that will be displayed. If you want to display images that have different Height and Width properties, then you should not set the Height and Width property of the AdRotator control. However, if you use the AdRotator control from the Toolbox within Visual Studio .NET, the default Height and Width are 468px and 60px.

You can also use the **Style property** within Visual Studio .NET to configure the styles for the AdRotator control. Recall that the AdRotator control inherits the properties from the Web control class. Therefore, you can configure many of the basic Web control Style properties that you learned in the previous chapter, such as BorderColor, BorderWidth, BorderStyle, Visible, TabIndex, and Absolute Positioning.

By default, when you click a hyperlink, the browser opens the new URL in the current window. You can force the browser to open the new URL in a different window or frame by using the **Target property**. The Target property is set to _top by default. When the target is set to _top, the URL is displayed in the current, unframed window. If the target is set to _blank, the URL is displayed in a new unframed window. If the hyperlink is within a frame, you can set the target to display the URL in the current frame, or in the parent frameset. The _self value displays the URL in the current frame, and the _parent value displays the URL in the parent frameset. The Target property also can place the URL in the Search window by changing the value to _search.

The **KeywordFilter property** retrieves only those banner ads from the XML document whose keyword matches exactly. Because the Keyword property can contain one or more words, the keyword value should be contained within quotation marks. The ToolTip property is used to provide more information about the banner ad. The ToolTip property stores a message as a string. The browsers display the message in the ToolTip when the user mouses over the banner image.

There are several help resources within Visual Studio .NET that document the AdRotator control and the AdRotator class. Documentation about the AdRotator class can be found at *http://msdn.microsoft.com/library/en-us/cpref/html/frlrfSystemWebUIWebControlsAdRotatorClassTopic.asp*. Documentation about the members of the class can be found at *http://msdn.microsoft.com/library/en-us/cpref/html/frlrfsystemwebuiwebcontrolsadrotatormemberstopic.asp*. You can learn more about the AdRotator control at *http://msdn.microsoft.com/library/en-us/vbcon/html/vbconAdRotatorWebControl.asp*.

Creating the Web Page to Display the AdRotator

In Visual Studio .NET you can insert the AdRotator control directly in the HTML code, or drag and drop the control from the Web Forms tab in the Toolbox. In the following exercise you create a banner advertisement in a Web page using the AdRotator control from the Toolbox. This page will contain two banner ads. One of the ads will display only Waterford products, and one will display only Belleek products, by using the KeywordFilter property. They both use the same Advertisement file. When the user clicks the banner ad, he or she is redirected to a new page that retrieves the product ID and displays the large product image. In an actual application, this page would also display product information, such as price.

4

1. In Visual Studio .NET, open the **Chapter4** project if it is not already open.

2. Double-click the **AdRotator.aspx** file to open the page in the main window.

3. In the Toolbox, click the **Web Forms** tab, if necessary, and then drag the **AdRotator** control to the page, placing it to the right of the AdRotator1 control. In the Properties window, change the KeywordFilter property to **Belleek**. Change the AdvertisementFile property to **ads.xml**. Delete the values listed for the height and width properties. Click the **Save All** button.

4. Double-click the **getproduct.aspx** file in the Solution Explorer window.

5. Double-click the **getproduct.aspx** page to open the code behind the page. In the Page_Load handler, type the code that follows this paragraph. This code retrieves the value from the URL and displays the image.

```
Dim imagename As String
imagename = Page.Request.QueryString("ID")
Image1.ImageUrl = "images/" & imagename
```

6. Click the **Save All** button. Click **Build** on the menu bar, then click **Build Solution**.

7. Click the **AdRotator.aspx** tab to return to Design view.

8. Right-click on the page, and then click **View in Browser**. Click **View** on the menu bar, and then click **Refresh** to reload the page. Note which image is displayed.

9. Repeat the previous step 10 times, noting each time which image is displayed for each AdRotator control. Figure 4-11 shows how the banner advertisement appears in the Web page.

10. Click the image. The getproduct.aspx page should open, displaying a larger picture of the product.

11. Double-click the **ads2.xml** file in the Solution Explorer window. (*Note:* The Advertisement File is a basic XML file. You can customize the file by adding custom elements defined within the XML document. This might be used to pass information such as the product ID or caption for the image. You can

pass this information from the custom elements in the querystring to the next page instead of building the querystring in the NavigateUrl property as you did in the previous exercise.) Locate the two additional elements, <Price> and <PriceRange>.

12. Close all of the pages.

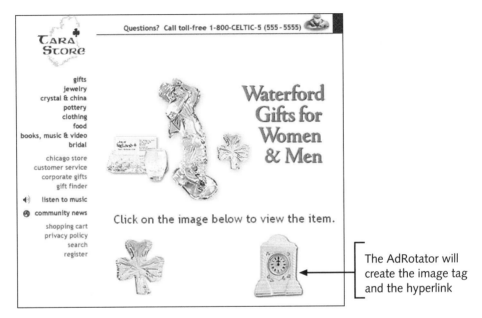

Figure 4-11   Creating a rotating banner advertisement in a Web page

THE CALENDAR CONTROL

You can use the **Calendar control** to insert and configure an interactive calendar within the Web page. The Calendar control is created by the calendar class. The calendar class is `System.Web.UI.WebControls.Calendar`. The calendar displays a single calendar month. By default, the current month is displayed. You can configure the appearance of the calendar by setting the properties of the Calendar control. You can create programs that interact with the calendar using methods and event handlers. Each date is displayed as a hyperlink. You can retrieve the current date or a date that the user selects by clicking on the hyperlink. (*Note:* The Date data type is equivalent to the .NET Framework DateTime data type.)

In Visual Studio .NET, you can insert the Calendar control directly in the HTML code, or drag and drop the control from the Web Forms tab in the Toolbox. The code following this paragraph is the code to insert the Calendar control. Because the control is an ASP.NET control, the name of the control includes the prefix asp followed by the word calendar. The run at property must be assigned to server, and you should assign a value to the ID property. You can close the tag with /> or </asp:calendar>. You do not need to type this code in the Web page because Visual Studio .NET provides a graphical tool in the Toolbox to insert the Calendar control.

```
<asp:calendar id="MyCal" runat="server" />
```

The Calendar control supports several properties that you can configure when you insert the control. You can also change these properties dynamically in the code behind the page. There are several styles that can be configured to change the appearance of the calendar. Most of the Style properties can modify the background color; text color; font face, size, and style; alignment; width and height; wrapping; and border style. You can also assign a CSS class to the property, which can be used to configure the styles from an external stylesheet. The various Calendar control Style properties that can be configured are as follows:

- *DayHeaderStyle*—sets the style for the days of the week
- *DayStyle*—sets the style for the individual dates
- *NextPrevStyle*—sets the style for the navigation controls in the heading
- *OtherMonthDayStyle*—sets the style for dates that are not in the current month
- *SelectedDayStyle*—sets the style for the dates that are selected
- *SelectorStyle*—sets the style for the month date selection column
- *TitleStyle*—sets the style for the title in the heading
- *TodayDayStyle*—sets the style for the current date
- *WeekendDayStyle*—sets the style for weekend dates

There are several properties that allow you to modify the Calendar control's appearance. The ShowDayHeader property is used to show or hide the days of the week heading row. The ShowGridLines property is used to show or hide the gridlines that divide the days of the month. The ShowNextPrev property is used to show or hide the navigation controls. The Navigation controls are used to navigate to the next or previous month. The ShowTitle property is used to show or hide the title in the heading.

There are several methods exposed by the Calendar control. The SelectionChanged event occurs when the user clicks a new date. This event changes the selected date to a new selected date. The SelectedDate property is the new selected date. The Calendar control visually indicates to the user which date is selected.

There are several events that can be intercepted by the code behind the page. You can write event handlers to intercept the event and execute your own custom code. The VisibleMonthChanged event occurs when the user clicks on the next or previous month hyperlinks. If you create an event handler for the VisibleMonthChanged event, you also pass the MonthChangedEventHandler object as a parameter to the event handler. The MonthChanged event handler object contains several properties. For example, when you click on the next or previous month, a new month appears in the calendar. The NewDate property is the current date in the new month. The property is the selected date in the previously selected month.

There are several Help documents within Visual Studio .NET that document the Calendar control and the Calendar class. Documentation about the calendar class can be found at *http://msdn.microsoft.com/library/en-us/cpref/html/frlrfsystemwebuiwebcontrolscalendarclasstopic.asp*. Documentation of the members of the class can be found at *http://msdn.microsoft.com/library/en-us/cpref/html/frlrfsystemwebuiwebcontrolscalendarmemberstopic.asp*.

The calendar output on the client may support new features such as altering the month name without page reloading. You can configure the target client browser using the **ClientTarget property**.

Creating a Program to Interact with the Calendar Control

You can build code within the code behind that page to interact with Calendar controls. The following activity has two parts. In the first part you will create a Calendar control and modify the properties of the Calendar control. In the second part, you will modify the code behind the page to interact with the Calendar control. You can assign a default selected date using the SelectedDate property. When the user clicks a date, you can create an event handler to capture the selected date. Then, you can retrieve the value that was clicked using the SelectedDate property. You can use the **ToShortDateString property** of the SelectedDate to display the selected date using the short date format. (*Note*: The short date format is mm/dd/yyyy). You can refer to each date selected by its position within the **SelectedDates** object. An example is `MyCalendar.SelectedDates()`. You can also refer to each date selected by using `MyCalendar.SelectedDate()`.

```
Label1.Text = _
Calendar1.SelectedDate.ToShortDateString()
```

Setting the Calendar Control Properties

In the following exercise, you will create a calendar in a Web page using the Calendar control located in the Web Forms tab in the Toolbox. You will also set the properties of the Calendar control. The calendar you create is shown in Figure 4-12.

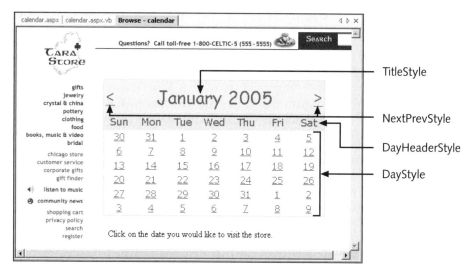

TitleStyle

NextPrevStyle

4

DayHeaderStyle

DayStyle

Figure 4-12   Creating an interactive calendar in a Web page

1. Open the **Chapter4** project in Visual Studio .NET, if it is not already open.

2. Double-click the **calendar.aspx** file to open the page in the main code window.

3. Click the **Web Forms** tab in the Toolbox if necessary, then drag the **Calendar** control to the page, placing it below the heading graphics.

4. In the Properties window, change the Height property to **240px** and the Width property to **400px**.

5. In the Properties window, click the **plus sign** in front of DayHeaderStyle to expand the properties. Change the BackColor property to **#E0E0E0**. This turns the background color a light shade of gray. Click the **ForeColor** property drop-down list arrow, click the **Web** tab, then click **Firebrick** to change the ForeColor property to **Firebrick**. Click the **plus sign** next to the Font property to expand the Font properties. Change the Name property to **Verdana**. Change the Size property to **Medium**. Click the **minus sign** in front of DayHeaderStyle to collapse the properties.

6. Click the **plus sign** in front of DayStyle, then click the **ForeColor** property drop-down list arrow. Click the **Web** tab, then click **Maroon**, which changes the ForeColor property to Maroon. Change the HorizontalAlign property to **Center**. Click the **plus sign** in front of the Font property to expand the Font properties. Change the Name property to **Verdana**. Change the Size property to **Small**. Click the **minus sign** in front of DayStyle to collapse the properties.

7. Click the **plus sign** in front of NextPrevStyle, then click the **plus sign** in front of Font. Change the Font Name property to **Trebuchet MS**. Click the **ForeColor** property drop-down list arrow, click the **Web** tab, then click **Firebrick** to change the ForeColor property to FireBrick. Click the **minus sign** in front of NextPrevStyle to collapse the properties.

8. Click the **plus sign** in front of TitleStyle, then click the **plus sign** in front of Font. Change the Font Name property to **Comic Sans MS** and the Font Size property to **X-Large**. Change the BackColor property to **#FFE0C0**. Change the ForeColor property to **Firebrick**. Click the **minus sign** in front of TitleStyle to collapse the properties.

9. From the Web Forms tab in the Toolbox, drag a **Label** control to the Web page below the Calendar control. Change the Text property of the label to **Click on the date you would like to visit the store.**

10. Click the **Save All** button.

11. From the Web Forms tab in the Toolbox, drag a **Label** control to the Web page below the Label1 control. Delete the word **Label** from the Text property value box. The Text property will be empty and will not display a message by default.

Creating a Page to Interact with the Calendar Control

In the exercise that follows, you will add the code behind the page to the calendar.aspx page. You will create an event handler to detect when the user clicks a new date, and display a message in the Web page indicating the value of the new date. You will use an If-Then control structure to determine if the date selected is the current date. If the date selected is the current date, you will display a different message in the Label control.

1. Double-click the **Calendar** control. This opens the code behind the page and places the cursor in the Calendar1_SelectionChanged procedure.

2. Type the code following this paragraph within the Calendar1_SelectionChanged procedure. This code executes when the user clicks a new date. The code changes the Text property of a Label control named Label1. The message displayed includes a string message.

```
Label1.Text= "You selected: " & _
Calendar1.SelectedDate.ToShortDateString()
```

3. Below the preceding code, add an If-Then control structure to determine if the selected date is equal to today's date. You need to use the ToShortDateString property for both Date objects when comparing the dates.

```
If Calendar1.SelectedDate.ToShortDateString _
 = Date.Now.ToShortDateString Then
 Label2.Text = _
 "Today all Waterford products are 30% off."
Else
 Label2.Text = _
 "All products are 10% off during this month"
End If
```

4. Click the **Save All** button. Click **Build** on the menu bar, then click **Build Solution**.

5. Click the **calendar.aspx** tab, then click the **Design** tab to return to Design view. Right-click the page, and then click **View in Browser**. Click the link for next Monday.

6. Click the link for today. The message should appear as shown in Figure 4-13.

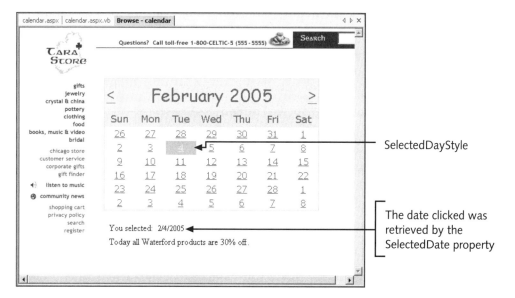

Figure 4-13   Creating an interactive calendar in a Web page

7. Close all of the pages.

Working with Multiple Dates

When the visitor clicks multiple dates, such as when he or she selects the entire week, you can retrieve the values selected with the SelectedDates object. You will use a **For-Next loop** to iterate through each date that was selected. The **Count property** provides the number of dates that were selected. You can refer to each date selected by its position within the SelectedDates object such as `MyCalendar.SelectedDates(i)`. The position within the object is often called the **index position**. The first index position in all arrays and collections in Visual Basic .NET is 0. The value of the last index position in the SelectedDates object is equal to the value of Count property minus 1. You can use a **loop counter** to keep track of how many times the looping structure repeats.

For example, you can loop through the list of dates that were selected by the user by looping through the SelectedDates collection. The loop counter is declared as an integer outside of the loop. The counter is initialized at a beginning value such as 0. Because the loop counter started with the number 0, the loop should repeat until the counter reaches the value of the Count property minus 1. If there are three dates selected, the Count property equals 3. Because the first element in the array is at index position 0, the loop counter begins at 0. The loop displays the first date. During the second loop, the loop counter is 1, and the second date is displayed. During the third loop, the loop counter is 2, and the third date is displayed. During each loop, the loop counter is also used to retrieve the ToShortDateString property of the SelectedDate. The loop ends when the loop counter reaches the value of the Count property minus 1. You need to include the minus 1 so that the loop will continue to run the code for the last iteration.

The sample code following this paragraph shows you how you can iterate through the list of selected dates. This code could be placed within the SelectionChanged event procedure for the Calendar control. The dates selected are displayed in the Label2 control.

```
Label1.Text= "You selected: <br><br>"
Dim i as Integer
For i = 0 to Calendar1.SelectedDates.Count - 1
  Label2.Text &= _
  Calendar1.SelectedDates(i).ToShortDateString() _
  & "<br>"
Next i
```

USING THE FILE UPLOAD CONTROL

The **File Upload control** allows you to upload a file to a Web server. There are many uses for a File Upload control. For example, in an online store, the store manager is often required to complete an online form when adding a product to the store database. You can use a File Upload control to allow the manager to upload a graphic image of the product. Community and volunteer organizations often have several people who submit materials such as monthly newsletters and event flyers to be placed on the Web site. By using a File Upload control, the members can upload the documents to the Web site without having to learn how to use a Web editing tool or a file transfer program. (*Note*: File transfer programs are also known as an FTP programs because they use the File Transfer Protocol.) Business Web sites will also find many uses for the File Upload component. Businesses often share documents with other businesses. These documents can be delivered through e-mail as attachments. However, some types of files such as graphics are very large. If the document is delivered to a large number of employees or a mailing list, the mail server could have difficulty storing the files and could crash. Because of this, businesses have limited the size of the files that can be sent through e-mail attachments to their company mailing lists. In order to make these documents accessible, you can use the File Upload control to upload the file to the Web server. Then, you can create a Web page that will provide employees with the ability to view or to download the document.

In recent versions of HTML, the **File Field control** allows you to browse your network and locate a file. The File Field control consists of a browse button that allows you to search your network and locate the file, and a text box that stores the URL of the file. This control allows you to select and store the URL of the file. However, it does not allow you to upload the file to the Web server.

To actually upload the file, you have to use an external COM component to handle the file upload. You could use third-party file upload components such as SA-FileUp by Software Artisans (*www.softwareartisans.com*), or Posting Acceptor from Microsoft. Both of the components must be installed on the Web server. The file upload capability is completely built into ASP.NET, and is available to all ASP.NET applications. The upload services are built into the ASP.NET runtime. Once you start building your ASP.NET applications, you won't need a third-party file upload component anymore. You can now use the File Upload control to upload files such as Web pages, PDF documents created with Adobe Acrobat, word-processing documents, spreadsheets, and databases.

The key to building an upload feature into your Web site is the InputFile HTML server control. The File Upload control is an HTML Server control. The File Upload control class is the `System.Web.UI.HTMLInputControl`. Therefore, you cannot only browse your file system and select a file, you can also upload the file to the Web server.

Uploading a File

When you create the file upload page, you must modify the attributes of the Form tag. You can then use an object on the Web server to upload the file. You can use an object on the Web server to obtain information about the uploaded file. For example, you can obtain information about the file size and type. This section will describe the processes for modifying the Form tag, uploading the file, and obtaining information about an uploaded file.

When you create the page that uploads the file, you must include the File Upload control within a form. The form tag must contain an **Enctype** attribute named enctype that is set to multipart/form-data. This property indicates that there is a file attached to the URL request.

You must insert a file field tag to upload the file. However, you can also insert other tags, such as input tags, to obtain a user's login information. In the code behind the page, you can verify the user's credentials before allowing them to upload the file. You can allow the user to select a name from a drop-down list, allow them to enter the name in an input textbox control, or not allow them to change the filename, programmatically. The following sample code shows the File Upload control named uploadFilePath and the Form control. The form field named txtFileName is used to retrieve a different filename for the file. There is also a button named btnUpload. The OnServerClick server event handler detects when the user clicks the button. Then, the server handler specifies the file parameters and uploads the file. This code appears in HTML view of the ASP.NET Web page.

```
<form enctype="multipart/form-data" runat="server">
  <INPUT id="uploadFilePath" type="file"
  size="40" name="txtFileName" runat="server">
  <input id="FileName" type="text" runat="server">
  <br /><br />
```

```
      <input type=button id="btnUpload"
      value="Upload a File" runat="server"
      OnServerClick="btnUpload_Click">
</form>
```

In addition to the type attribute, the file field accepts the **Accept attribute**. The Accept attribute allows you to specify the MIME formats that can be uploaded. To upload only JPEG images, you would set the Accept attribute to image/jpg. If you want to upload any image, you can set the attribute to image/*. The asterisk represents any image type. You can enter multiple MIME formats if they are delimited with a comma. You can set the **MaxLength attribute** in the file field to limit the length of the filename that can be entered in the text box. The **Size attribute** allows you to set the width of the file field text box as shown in the sample code that follows this paragraph. In your HTML code, you don't see the attributes listed in the Properties window. You can set the attributes in the code behind the page in a procedure such as the Page_Load event procedure just as you can set the properties of other HTML and ASP.NET Server controls.

```
<INPUT id="uploadFilePath" type="file" MaxLength="50"
    size="40" name="txtFileName" runat="server"
Accept = "images/*, text/css, text/htm">
```

Uploading the File in the Code Behind the Page

In the btnUpload_ServerClick event procedure in the code behind the page, you can include the code to set the File Upload properties, then upload the file. In the code sample that follows this paragraph, the path is hard-coded in the event handler. The name of the file is retrieved from a form field named txtFileName. This code appears in the code behind the ASP.NET Web page. The file is uploaded using the **HTTPPostedFile** class. To save the file, you must call the **PostedFile.SaveAs** command from the HTTPPostedFile class and pass the path to the file on the client's computer. **PostedFile** allows you to upload the file, manipulate the file, and retrieve information about the file.

```
    Private Sub btnUpload_ServerClick(ByVal ↵
    sender As System.Object, ByVal e As System.EventArgs)↵
    Handles btnUpload.ServerClick
        strFilePath = "c:\upload\images\" & txtFileName.Value
        uploadFilePath.PostedFile.SaveAs(strFilePath)
    End Sub
```

Obtaining Information About the File Uploaded

Once you have selected the file, the PostedFile object handles the file. You can obtain the size of the file using the **ContentLength property**. You can use this information to determine if the user has not selected a file to upload as shown in the sample code following this paragraph. You can also detect the MIME type of the file using the **ContentType property**. A file contains a file extension. The operating system maintains a listing of the file extensions and the applications that can open the files. The **MIME** type is a reference to the contents and format of a file. For example, a file with extension .GIF contains an image. So the MIME type would be images/GIF. You can retrieve the path, filename, and file extension using the FileName property. The **InputStream property** of the PostedFile is used to create a **Stream object**, which will be used to place a binary image file within a database.

```
Dim UploadedFile as HttpPostedFile = _
UploadedFile.PostedFile
If UploadedFile.ContentLength = nothing then
    "No file was selected. Pick a file to upload."
Else
    "The file has been uploaded."
End if
```

The Server control contains a **MapPath method** to map the path to a file. This code is written as Server.MapPath(filename). Once you get the filename, you can retrieve the file extension using the **GetExtension method** of the **Path object**. The Path object is derived from the `System.IO` namespace. The **FileName property** retrieves the complete filename on the client's computer. The following sample code shows how to retrieve the path and filename from the uploaded file and the Path object:

```
Dim UploadedFile as HttpPostedFile = _
UploadedFile.PostedFile
Dim FilePath As String = UploadedFile.FilePath
Dim FileName As String  Path.GetFileName(FilePath)
Dim FileExtension As String = Path.GetExtension(FileName)
Dim ContentType As String = UploadedFile.ContentType
```

You must determine where you want to store your images. If you store them in the server's file system, it's more difficult to manage the files. If you store the images within the database, the images are stored in a central location, and are therefore easier to maintain. However, when you store images in a database, they are stored as BLOB objects (Binary Large Objects). Not all databases support BLOBs. When you store binary files in a database, the physical size of the database may become very large, requiring more hard drive space and memory on the database server.

Creating the File Upload Page

You may want to enable only authenticated users to upload a file. In the following exercise, you will create a login form. After the user is authenticated, you will show the file upload control. Then, you will allow the user to upload the file to the Web server. Figure 4-14 shows the screen when the user logs in and after the user selects a file to upload.

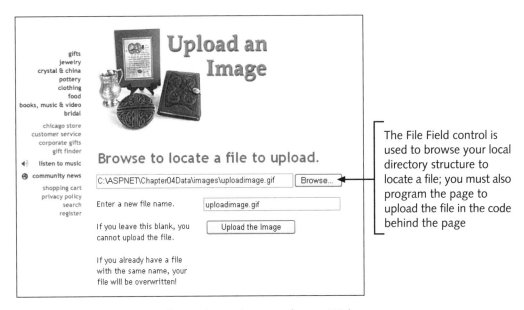

Figure 4-14   Uploading a file to the Web server from a Web page

1. In Visual Studio .NET, open the **Chapter4** project if necessary.

2. Right-click **Chapter4** in the Solution Explorer window, point to **Add**, and then click **New Folder**. Type **Uploads**, and then press **Enter**. Double-click the **uploadfile.aspx** file in the Solution Explorer window to open the file in the main code window.

3. Click the **HTML** tab in the Toolbox to open it, if necessary. Then drag the **File Field** control, which is the File Upload control, from the HTML tab to the page. Position the control below the Label1 control. Right-click the control, and then click **Run As Server Control**. In the Properties window, change both the Label (ID) and Name properties to **uploadFilePath**. Change the size property to **50**.

4. Click the **HTML** tab. In the opening Form tag, enter the following code to indicate that a file is attached. Then, click the **Design** tab to return to Design view.

   ```
   encType="multipart/form-data"
   ```

5. Double-click the **Upload the Image** button, which will open the code behind the page. Insert into the btnUpload_ServerClick event procedure the code snippet that follows this paragraph. This code declares the path variable, retrieves the path from the path of the current file, and uploads the file that was received from the form. It will also display a hyperlink to the new file and a file upload message. The entire code is placed within a structure called Try-Catch-Finally. This structure is used to capture errors that may occur. You will learn more about this structure in a later chapter.

```
If Not (uploadFilePath.PostedFile Is Nothing) Then
Try
    Dim strFilePath As String
    strFilePath = System.IO.Path.GetDirectoryName ↵
    (Server.MapPath("uploadfile.aspx"))
    uploadFilePath.PostedFile.SaveAs ↵
    ((strFilePath & "\Uploads\" & txtFileName.Value))
    lblDirections.InnerHtml = _
    "Your file was uploaded successfully" & _
    "<br> to the Web server at<br>" & _
    "<b>" & strFilePath & "\Uploads\" & _
    txtFileName.Value & "</b>"
    HyperLink1.NavigateUrl = _
    "http://localhost/chapter4/Uploads/" _
    & txtFileName.Value
    HyperLink1.Visible = True
Catch exc As Exception
    lblDirections.InnerHtml = _
    "Error saving file. <br>" & exc.Message
End Try
End If
```

6. Click the **Save All** button. Click **Build** on the menu bar, then click **Build Solution**.

7. Click the **uploadfile.aspx** file tab in the main window. Click the **Design** tab to change to Design view, if necessary. Right-click on the page and click **View in Browser**. (*Note*: You can also view the page in your browser at *http://localhost/chapter4/uploadfile.aspx*.)

8. Click the **Browse** button to locate a file in your Chapter04Data\images folder named uploadimage.gif. Enter **uploadimage.gif** in the File Name text box. Click the **Open** button. The filename and path appear in the text box. Click the **Upload the Image** button.

9. A message is displayed, indicating the image was not uploaded. The message says "Error saving file. Access to the path 'c:\inetpub\wwwroot\chapter4\ Uploads\uploadimage.gif' is denied". This means that you do not have permission set to upload a file. In the next exercise, you will learn to set the security permissions to upload a file. (*Note*: In a real situation, you would also include a button to return to the login screen. Although this example is used to upload images, you can also use this code to upload other file types. You can practice uploading a file with this sample using a file named uploadtest.txt located in your Chapter04Data folder.)

10. Close any open pages.

Security Issues with the File Upload Control

Security is a complex topic because there are several types of security that can be implemented with Web applications. You can layer page security and application level security by programming login methods within the application. Page level security affects only a single page. Application level security applies to an entire Web application, such as the Chapter4 project. There are two steps that you will have to accomplish to allow the ASP.NET Machine user account to upload files from a browser. First, you will need to make sure your files support displaying the NTFS information in the Windows Explorer application. To do this, complete the following steps:

1. Click the **Start** menu, and then click **Run**.

2. Type **%SystemRoot%\explorer.exe** in the Open text box, and then click **OK**. (The variable %SystemRoot% is the location of your windows files. For most users, this is C:\windows, so you would enter C:\windows\explorer.exe.)

3. The Windows Explorer application opens. Click the **Tools** menu, and then click **Folder Options**. Click the **View** tab.

4. Scroll down to and uncheck the **Use Simple File Sharing (Recommended)** check box.

5. Click the **OK** button.

You can set security at the Web server using the Internet Information Server administration tools. (*Note:* You can learn more about the IIS Server administration tools in the Appendix D.) You can also set the security level within Windows using NFTS. NTFS is the Windows NT file system that allows you to assign permissions to individual files and folders based on the user account. The default user account for the Web browser is the **anonymous** user, which is **IUSR_MACHINENAME**. If your machine was named KALATA, then your anonymous user account is IUSR_KALATA. You do not need to change permissions for this account with ASP.NET. However, you do need to modify permissions to allow the ASP.NET Machine user account to access the files and folders. The **ASP.NET Machine** user account is the account that ASP.NET Web applications use to communicate with the operating system.

By default, the user cannot upload pages because the user does not have NTFS permissions to write to the uploads directory. The following steps will allow you to set the permissions for the ASP.NET Machine user account.

1. Open **Windows Explorer**, if necessary. Navigate through Windows Explorer in the folders pane until you find the Uploads directory. (*Note:* By default, it's located at C:\Inetpub\wwwroot\Chapter4\Uploads.)

2. Right-click the **Uploads** folder and select **Properties**.

3. Click the **Security** tab. This tab allows you to add Windows user accounts and set the NTFS permissions for each user. A message may appear that says

the following: "The permissions on Uploads are incorrectly ordered, which may cause some entries to be ineffective. Press OK to continue and sort the permissions correctly, or Cancel to reset the permissions." Click **OK**. (*Note*: If you click Cancel, the permissions will be reset to allow the Everyone account to have full access to the folder, which is a security risk.)

4. Click the **Add** button. In the lower text box, enter the full name for the ASP.NET Machine user account called MACHINENAME\ASPNET. The full name consists of the "ASPNET\" and the name of your machine. For instance, if the name of the machine were KALATA, then the full name would be KALATA\ASPNET.

5. After you enter the full name for the ASP.NET Machine user account, click the **OK** button.

6. In the Properties window, verify that the ASP.NET Machine user account is selected. If not, select it in the top list box.

7. Then, click the Allow check boxes labeled **Modify**, **Read & Execute**, **List Folder Contents**, **Read**, and **Write** in the Permissions panel. (See Figure 4-15.)

8. Click the **OK** button and close Windows Explorer.

9. View the uploadfile.aspx page in the browser at *http://localhost/chapter4/uploadfile.aspx*. Upload the uploadimage.gif file again as instructed in the previous exercise. A new message will appear stating that the file has been uploaded successfully. Click the hyperlink to view the image in the browser. Close the browser window. (*Note*: If you receive an error message, you should contact your system administrator or Web administrator to request the NTFS permissions to be set for the Uploads folder.)

You should always check with your system administrator or Web administrator for the company policy on uploading files before implementing the ability for users to upload files. If you include a login page, make sure to inform your users that login names and passwords on Web Forms are case sensitive.

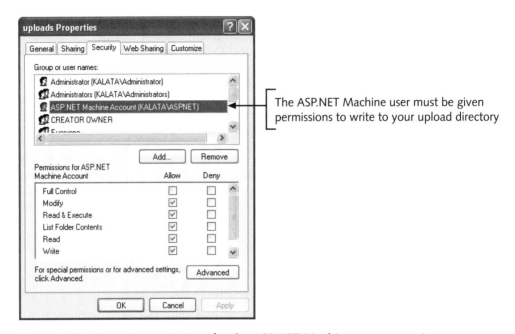

The ASP.NET Machine user must be given permissions to write to your upload directory

Figure 4-15   Security permissions for the ASP.NET Machine user account

CHAPTER SUMMARY

◻ ASP.NET controls enhance the user interface and increase interactivity within Web pages. Examples of ASP.NET controls are the XML control, the AdRotator control, and the Calendar control. Third-party providers are likely to create additional ASP.NET controls, which can be added to your application.

◻ XML standards are maintained by the World Wide Web Consortium. XHTML is a version of HTML that is XML compliant. An XML parser is an application that can read the file and process the instructions in the file. A Web browser such as Internet Explorer can read XML files. XML files can be formatted with cascading stylesheets or XSLT stylesheets. XML files must be well formed. They must follow the rules defined by the W3C. An XML schema is a set of rules used to define document format and structure. Industries can create their own schemas and define their own sets of tags. The XML control allows you to read, process, and display XML data using an XSLT stylesheet. This process is known as transformation.

❏ The AdRotator control allows you to display rotating banner ads. The banner contains a hyperlink, alternate text, and an image. If you do not specify the height and width, you can display images of varying sizes. The Advertisement File is an XML file that is used to store the ad information. The Advertisement File can be edited with a text editor, such as Notepad, or an XML editor. The root node is named advertisements. The Impressions property determines the ad's relative display frequency. The Keywords property is used to group banner ads. You can apply a filter and only show some of the banner ads using the KeywordFilter property.

❏ The Calendar control displays an interactive calendar. There are many properties that you can use to format the calendar. The SelectionChanged event allows you to detect when the user clicks on a new date. The SelectedDate property indicates the value of the currently selected date. You can retrieve the value of the date that users click, or execute code when they click a particular date.

❏ The File Upload control is an HTML Server control that allows you to upload files to a Web server. The Form enctype property must be set to multipart/form-data. The upload file field type must be set to file. On the server, you must retrieve the filename. You can change the filename or path on the server in the code behind the page. The SaveAs method saves the file to the Web server.

Review Questions

1. Which of the following is not an ASP.NET control, but still enhances the Web application?

   a. FileUpload control

   b. AdRotator control

   c. Calendar control

   d. XML control

2. Which class is inherited by the FileUpload class?

   a. System.Web.UI.HTMLControl

   b. System.Web.HTMLControl

   c. System.UI.WebControl

   d. System.Web.UI.HTMLInputControl

3. Which value is used to identify a file that is attached to the form?

   a. multipart/form-data

   b. type=form-data

   c. attachedFile

   d. type=form/file

4. What is the value of the Type property for the upload file field?

   a. Upload

   b. File

   c. Text

   d. Attached

5. What method is used to upload the file to the server?

   a. Upload

   b. FileUpload

   c. Save

   d. SaveAs

6. Where is the banner ad information stored?

   a. in memory

   b. in the Advertisement File

   c. in the AdRotator File

   d. in the Windows Registry

7. Who is responsible for the maintenance of the XML standards?

   a. Microsoft

   b. Sun Microsystems

   c. IBM

   d. W3C

8. In the ads.xml file, what is the name of the root node?

   a. Advertisements

   b. AdSchedule

   c. AdRotator

   d. Products

9. What is the name of the tag used to insert the Calendar control?

   a. calendar

   b. asp:calendar

   c. xml:calendar

   d. asp/calendar

10. Which property is used to create the hyperlink tag in the banner AdRotator control?

    a. ImageURL

    b. NavigateURL

   c. NavigateHREF

   d. HREF

11. Assume that you have four banner ads, and all four banner ad Impression properties are set to 25. You visit your page 100 times. How many times would you expect to see each banner?

   a. 4

   b. 10

   c. 20

   d. 25

12. What property is used to search for a subset of the banner ads in the Advertisement File?

   a. Keyword

   b. KeywordFilter

   c. Advertisement

   d. Impressions

13. What property of the Calendar control is used to capture the date that the user clicked on?

   a. VisibleMonthChanged

   b. SelectedDate

   c. DayChanged

   d. SelectionChanged

14. Which word describes the position of an item in a collection?

   a. index position

   b. counter

   c. loop index

   d. counter

15. Which of the following rules is not part of the XML standards?

   a. Element names must not be more than 32 characters long.

   b. All container elements must be closed.

   c. The opening and closing element tags must have the same case.

   d. A child container element can be nested within a parent container element.

16. Which prefix is used to indicate that the XML document should use a cascading stylesheet?

   a. xml:css

   b. xml-stylesheet

   c. asp:stylesheet

   d. type = css

4

17. What character code is not part of the XML markup code by default?

    a. '

    b. "

    c. &

    d. @

18. Which of the following is used to add a comment to an XML document?

    a. <! - - comment - - >

    b. /* comment /*

    c. ' comment

    d. # comment

19. Which XML processing instruction retrieves the contents of any element within the node?

    a. <xsl:value-of∫select="."∫/>

    b. <xsl:apply-templates∫select="*"∫/>

    c. <xsl:template∫match="/*">

    d. <xsl:apply-templates∫select="."∫/>

20. Which property is used to identify the XSL stylesheet in an XML control?

    a. DocumentContent

    b. TransformSource

    c. HREF

    d. XML:CSS

HANDS-ON PROJECTS

Project 4-1

In this project, you create an XML data file using Visual Studio .NET.

1. Open your **Chapter4** solution in Visual Studio .NET, if it is not already open.

2. Right-click **Chapter4** in the Solution Explorer window, point to **Add**, then click **Add New Item**. Click the **XML File** button, type **Ch4Proj1.xml** in the name text box, and then click **Open**. The prologue with the version and encoding attributes has already been entered for you.

3. On the second line, create a root node named **ProductCategories**.

4. Create a child node named **Category** for each of the eight product categories.

5. Create elements named **ImageURL**, **CategoryID**, and **CategoryName** for each product category.

6. Add the data to each of the category nodes using the information in Table 4-2. (*Hint:* You will have to replace each of the ampersands (&) with the character code **&**.)

Table 4-2   Data for the category nodes

ImageURL	CategoryID	CategoryName
21.jpg	1	Irish & Celtic Gifts
22.jpg	2	Jewelry
23.jpg	3	Crystal & China
24.jpg	4	Pottery & Handblown Glass
25.jpg	5	Foods from Ireland & England
26.jpg	6	Irish Clothing
27.jpg	7	Books, Music & Video
28.jpg	8	Bridal Department

4

7. Save the file. Open the page in your browser using the following URL: *http://localhost/chapter4/Ch4Proj1.xml.*

8. Print the page from the browser.

9. In Visual Studio .NET, create a schema based on the XML document. (*Hint:* You can right-click on the XML document in XML view or Data view and select **Create Schema**.)

10. Print the schema. You can then open the Ch4Proj1.xsd document and print the schema within XML view. Validate your XML data file. Select the **XML** menu, and then select **Validate XML Data**. (*Note:* If you have an error appearing in the Task window, go back and review the XML file for typos and syntax errors. Make sure you have included the XML prologue and only one root node, which includes an opening and closing tag. All elements must be well formed.)

11. Click the **Save All** button. Click **Build** on the menu bar, then click **Build Solution**. Close all files.

Project 4-2

In this project, you create an XSLT stylesheet to format an XML file. The XML file named Ch4Proj2.xml contains a listing of product categories.

1. Open your **Chapter4** solution in Visual Studio .NET, if it is not already open.

2. Double-click the **Ch4Proj2.xml** file in the Solution Explorer window to view the listing of product categories.

3. Right-click **Chapter4** in the Solution Explorer window, point to **Add**, then click **Add New Item**. Click the stylesheet button, type **Ch4Proj2.xsl** in the Name text box, then click **Open**.

4. Delete the Body style rule, **body { }**.

5. On the second line, add the main template using the code following this paragraph. Add the horizontal line, which inserts a line in between each row of data.

```
<xsl:stylesheet xmlns:xsl=
"http://www.w3.org/1999/XSL/Transform"
version="1.0">
<xsl:template match="/">
  <xsl:for-each select="//Category">
    <xsl:apply-templates select="ImageUrl" />
    <xsl:apply-templates select="CategoryName" />
    <xsl:apply-templates select="CategoryID" />
    <hr size="1" width="550" align="left"
    color="#003366" />
  </xsl:for-each>
</xsl:template>
```

6. Add the code following this paragraph to display the image and create a hyperlink to the image. Set the Border property to 0.

```
<xsl:template match="ImageUrl">
  <a>
    <xsl:attribute name="href">
      images/<xsl:value-of select="." />
    </xsl:attribute>
    <img>
      <xsl:attribute name="src">
        images/<xsl:value-of select="." />
      </xsl:attribute>
      <xsl:attribute name="border">0
      </xsl:attribute>
    </img>
  </a>
</xsl:template>
```

7. Add the code to display and format the Category ID and Category Name, like so:

```
<xsl:template match="CategoryName">
  <div class="cat">Category Name:
    <b><xsl:value-of select="." /></b>
  </div><br />
</xsl:template>
<xsl:template match="CategoryID">
  <div class="cat">Category ID:
  (<xsl:value-of select="." />)
  </div><br />
</xsl:template>
</xsl:stylesheet>
```

8. If necessary, open the **Ch4Proj2.xml** file in the XML Designer. After the first line, insert a blank line. Type the following code, which will link the XML file to the XSLT file:

```
<?xml:Stylesheet type="text/xsl" href="Ch4Proj2.xsl" ?>
```

9. Click the **Save All** icon, click the **Build** menu, and then click **Build Solution**. View the XML file at *http://localhost/chapter4/Ch4Proj2.xml*. The browser will show the formatted XML data. The page will look like the one in Figure 4-16.

Figure 4-16   Using XSLT to display images

10. Save the file. Print the page within Visual Studio .NET. Close all of the pages.

Project 4-3

In this project, you create an ASP.NET page that displays the data in the Ch4Proj3.xml file using the XML control. The XML file named Ch4Proj3.xml contains a listing of product categories. The XSLT stylesheet named Ch4Proj3.xsl contains the style rules to format and display the XML document.

1. Open your **Chapter4** solution in Visual Studio .NET, if it is not already open.

2. Double-click the **Ch4Proj3.xml** and **Ch4Proj3.xsl** files in the Solution Explorer window to open them in the main code window. Verify that the files contain XML data and XSLT stylesheet information.

3. Double-click **Ch4Proj3.aspx** in the Solution Explorer window to open the page, then double-click on the page to open the code behind the page. In the Page_Load handler, type the code following this paragraph. This code retrieves the value from the URL and displays the image.

```
Dim ImageUrl As String
If Request.QueryString.Count > 0 Then
  ImageUrl = Page.Request.QueryString("ImageUrl").ToString
  If ImageUrl.Length > 0 Then
    Image1.ImageUrl = "images/" & ImageUrl
  Else
    Image1.ImageUrl = "images/giftfinder.jpg"
  End If
End If
```

(*Note*: The editor places the End If statement when you create an If-Then statement. There should only be one End If statement for each If-Then statement.)

4. Click the **Ch4Proj3.aspx** tab to return to Design view. Drag an ASP.NET **XML** control from the Toolbox and place the control inside the Panel control. Set the DocumentSource property to **Ch4Proj3.xml**. Set the TransformSource property to **Ch4Proj3.xsl**.

5. Click the **Save All** button. Click **Build** on the menu bar, then click **Build Solution**.

6. Right-click on the page, and then click **View in Browser**. The page should appear as shown in Figure 4-17. Click a hyperlink to see the main image change to a new category image.

7. Print the Web page, the ASP.NET source code, and the code behind the page. Close all of the pages.

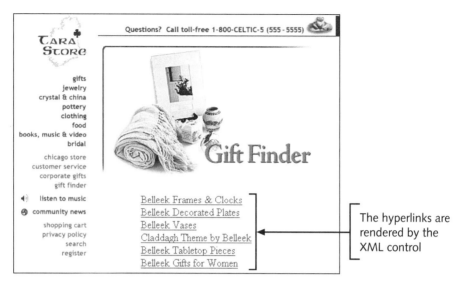

Figure 4-17   Using XSLT to transform an XML document into a Web page

Project 4-4

In this project, you create a Web page that displays a rotating banner ad using the AdRotator control.

1. Open your **Chapter4** solution in Visual Studio .NET, if it is not already open.
2. Create the Advertisement File named **Ch4Proj4.xml** using the data in Table 4-3. (*Note*: If you imported the entire folder of images in the chapter, then you do not have to import them again. However, if you did not import these images, then you need to import them into your images directory in your project.)

Table 4-3   Image information

ImageUrl	NavigateUrl	AlternateText	Keyword	Impressions
images/15.jpg	images/15.jpg	Frames & Clocks	Belleek	10
images/16.jpg	images/16.jpg	Decorated Plates	Belleek	15
images/17.jpg	images/17.jpg	Vases	Belleek	20
images/18.jpg	images/18.jpg	Claddagh Theme	Belleek	25
images/19.jpg	images/19.jpg	Tabletop Pieces	Belleek	30
images/20.jpg	images/20.jpg	Gifts for Women	Belleek	35

3. Double-click the **Ch4Proj4.aspx** file in the Solution Explorer window.
4. Drag and drop the **AdRotator** control from the Web Forms tab in the Toolbox to the Web page, placing it below the header.jpg image.

5. Change the AdvertisementFile property in the Properties window to **Ch4Proj4.xml**.

6. Delete the Height and Width properties in the Properties window.

7. Click the **Save All** button. Click **Build** on the menu bar, then click **Build Solution**.

8. Right-click on the page, and then click **View in Browser**. Click **View** on the menu bar, then click **Refresh** to reload the page.

9. Repeat the previous step 10 times, noting which image is displayed each time.

10. Print the ASP.NET source code within Visual Studio .NET. In Browser view, print the Web page and the source code. Close all of the pages.

Project 4-5

In this project, you create a Web page that uses File Upload Server controls to upload a file. You should always have some way for end users to view that their file has been uploaded. After the file is uploaded, you are redirected to the newly created file. You can redirect the user to a new page using Response.Redirect(URL). You can specify a relative or fully qualified URL. (*Note*: You can specify the absolute path including the filename or a relative path and filename. A relative path is where you use symbols such as two dots (..), which means the file is placed one level above the current file.)

1. Start **Visual Studio .NET** and open your **Chapter4** solution.

2. In Visual Studio .NET create a Web Form named **Ch4Proj5.aspx**.

3. Click the **HTML** tab to edit the HTML code.

4. Type the following code snippet within the opening form tag:

```
enctype="multipart/form-data"
```

5. Click the **Design** tab to return to Design view.

6. Drag the file **header.jpg** from the images folder in the Solution Explorer window to the top of the page. Drag the **menu.gif** file from the images folder in the Solution Explorer window to the left of the page below the header.jpg image. Drag the **uploadheader.jpg** image from the images folder in the Solution Explorer window to below the header.jpg image and just to the right of the menu.gif file.

7. Add the File Upload Server control to the Web page. The File Upload control is located on the HTML tab and is named File Field. Right-click the control, and then click **Run As Server Control**.

8. Drag and drop a **TextBox** control from the Web Forms tab in the Toolbox to the Web page, placing it below the File Upload control. Change the ID property of the TextBox control to **txtFileName**.

9. Drag and drop a **Label** control from the Web Forms tab in the Toolbox to the Web page, placing it next to the TextBox control. Change the Text property of the Label control to **File Name**.

10. Drag and drop an **ImageButton** from the Web Forms tab in the Toolbox to the Web page, placing it below the text box. Change the ImageUrl property to **images/upload.gif**.

11. Double-click the **Upload** button. Add the code that follows this paragraph. The code allows you to upload the file in the ImageButton1_Click procedure:

```
Dim Path As String
Path = System.IO.Path.GetDirectoryName ↵
    (Server.MapPath("Ch4Proj5.aspx"))
File1.PostedFile.SaveAs((Path & "\Uploads\" ↵
    & txtFileName.Text))
Response.Redirect(Path & "\Uploads\" & txtFileName.Text)
```

12. Click the **Save All** button. Click **Build** on the menu bar, then click **Build Solution**.

13. Switch to Design view. Right-click on the page, and then click **View in Browser**.

14. Print the source code of this page from the browser.

15. Click the **Browse** button. From your data directory select the file **uploadtest.txt**. In the text box, enter **uploadtest.txt**. Click the **Upload** button.

16. The file should be uploaded to the Uploads directory. You can use a different name for the upload files. View the **Ch4Proj5.aspx** page in a browser. Click the **Browse** button. From your data directory, select the file **uploadtest.txt**. In the text box, type **test.txt**. Click the **Upload** button. The newly uploaded page is displayed, and it is named test.txt.

17. Print the ASP.NET source code and the code behind the page within Visual Studio .NET. Close all of the pages.

Project 4-6

In this project, you create a Web page that uses server events to display a Calendar control.

1. Open your **Chapter4** solution in Visual Studio .NET, if it is not already open.

2. Create an ASP.NET page named **Ch4Proj6.aspx**.

3. Drag the file **header.jpg** from the images folder in the Solution Explorer window to the top of the page. Drag the **menu.gif** file from the images folder in the Solution Explorer window to the left of the page, below the header.jpg image.

4. Drag and drop the **Calendar** control from the Web Forms tab in the Toolbox to the Web page. Place the calendar below the header.jpg image.

5. In the Properties window, change the Height property to **240px** and the Width property to **400px**.

6. Click the **plus sign** in front of DayHeaderStyle to expand the properties. Change the BackColor property to **#C0C0FF**. Change the ForeColor property to **MidnightBlue**. Change the Font property to **Trebuchet MS**. Change the Size property to **Medium**.

7. Click the **plus sign** in front of DayStyle. Change the ForeColor property to **MidnightBlue**. Change the HorizontalAlign property to **Center**. Change the Font Name property to **Verdana** and the Size property to **Small**.

8. Click the **plus sign** in front of NextPrevStyle. Change the Font Name property to **Trebuchet MS**. Change the ForeColor property to **MidnightBlue**.

9. Click the **plus sign** in front of TitleStyle. Change the Font Name property to **Trebuchet MS** and the Font Size property to **X-Large**. Change the BackColor property to **#C0C0FF**. Change the ForeColor property to **MidnightBlue**.

10. Add a Label control from the Web Forms tab to the Web page and position the control below the Calendar control. Change the Text property from Label to **Select your birthday.**

11. Right-click on the page, and then click **View Code** to open the code behind the page.

12. Type the code following this paragraph below the Page_Load procedure. This code executes when the user clicks a new date. The code displays a message and the selected date.

```
Private Sub Calendar1_SelectionChanged(ByVal sender As
System.Object, ByVal e As System.EventArgs) Handles
Calendar1.SelectionChanged
   Dim Msg As String
   Msg = Calendar1.SelectedDate.ToShortDateString()
   Label1.Text= "You selected: " & Msg
End Sub
```

13. Add an If-Then control structure to determine if the selected date is equal to today's date, as shown in the code following this paragraph. You need to use the ToShortDateString property for both date objects when comparing the dates. If the user's birthday is today, display a Happy Birthday message.

```
If Calendar1.SelectedDate.ToShortDateString = _
   Date.Now.ToShortDateString() Then
   Label1.Text &= _
   "<br /><br /><b>Happy Birthday!</b>"
Else
End If
```

14. Click the **Save All** button. Click **Build** on the menu bar, then click **Build Solution**.

15. Click the **Ch4Proj6.aspx** tab. Click the **Design** tab to return to Design view. Right-click on the page, and then click **View in Browser**. Click the link for next Monday. Click the link for today. Note what messages are displayed on each date.

16. Print the Web page and the source code from the browser. Print the ASP.NET source code and code behind the page within Visual Studio .NET. Close all of the pages.

CASE PROJECTS

Tara Store — Data Storage with XML

Your store provides products from a distributor named Shea's Superstore, in Ireland. Shea's would like you to provide an XML file of your Belleek product inventory. In Visual Studio .NET, you will use the information in Table 4-4 to create an XML file named Ch4Case1.xml in your Chapter4 solution. The root node should be ProductNode. The elements should be named ProductID, SubCatID, ModelName, ProductImage, UnitCost, and Thumbnail. Create a schema for your XML file. Validate your XML file using the schema. When you are finished, go to your browser and view the XML file at *http://localhost/chapter4/Ch4Case1.xml*. Print out the view from the browser. View the schema in the browser at *http://localhost/chapter4/Ch4Case1.xsd*. Print the schema from the browser.

Table 4-4   Product information

ProductID	SubCatID	ModelName	Product Image	Unit Cost	Thumbnail
550	16	Marriage Blessing Plate	550.jpg	75.00	550.gif
551	16	Claddagh Plate	551.jpg	45.00	551.gif
552	16	Irish Blessing Plate	552.jpg	75.00	552.gif
554	15	Shamrock Picture Frame	554.jpg	70.00	554.gif
555	15	Cashill Clock	555.jpg	110.00	555.gif
557	15	Killarney Clock	557.jpg	70.00	557.gif
559	15	Child's Picture Frame - Boy	559.jpg	50.00	559.gif
561	17	Glendalough Vase	561.jpg	45.00	561.gif
564	17	Tall Daisy Vase	564.jpg	65.00	564.gif
568	19	Shamrock Creamer	568.jpg	50.00	568.gif
570	19	Cup	570.jpg	48.00	570.gif
571	19	Saucer	571.jpg	35.00	571.gif
573	18	Claddagh Bud Vase	573.jpg	30.00	573.gif
556	15	Oval Shamrock Picture Frame	556.jpg	50.00	556.gif
560	15	Child's Picture Frame - Girl	560.jpg	50.00	560.gif
563	17	Claddagh Bud Vase	563.jpg	30.00	563.gif
565	17	Galway Vase	565.jpg	25.00	565.gif
566	17	Colleen Vase	566.jpg	34.00	566.gif

Table 4-4   Product information (continued)

ProductID	SubCatID	ModelName	Product Image	Unit Cost	Thumbnail
567	19	Shamrock Sugar	567.jpg	50.00	567.gif
572	19	Dinner Plate	572.jpg	80.00	572.gif
574	18	Claddagh Plate	574.jpg	45.00	574.gif
575	18	Claddagh Makeup Bell	575.jpg	25.00	575.gif
576	18	Heart-Shaped Trinket Box	576.jpg	30.00	576.gif
578	18	Heart-Shaped Claddagh Dish	578.jpg	40.00	578.gif
579	20	Kylemore Trinket Box	579.jpg	35.00	579.gif
580	20	Shamrock Ring Holder	580.jpg	35.00	580.gif
581	20	Kylemore Bowl	581.jpg	100.00	581.gif
582	20	Claddagh Makeup Bell	582.jpg	25.00	582.gif
583	20	Daisy Candle Holder	583.jpg	45.00	583.gif
584	20	Child's Cup for a Girl	584.jpg	25.00	584.gif
585	20	Child's Cup for Boy	585.jpg	25.00	585.gif
553	16	Mother's Blessing Plate	553.gif	65.00	553.gif
569	19	Shamrock Teapot	569.jpg	250.00	569.gif

Case Project

Tara Store — Data Transformation with the XML Control

Shea's Superstore has asked you to create a Web page to view the data. Use an XSLT stylesheet to transform the data in the Ch4Case2.xml document into a Web page. First, create an XSLT stylesheet to read and format the data. You should use the Thumbnail data to create an image that is displayed in the Web page. You should format the price of the products with a dollar sign. You should format the data using a table. Save this stylesheet as Ch4Case2.xsl in your Chapter4 solution.

Create a Web page named Ch4Case2.aspx. Add the XML control to the Web page. Change the DocumentSource property to Ch4Case2.xml. Change the TransformSource property to Ch4Case2.xsl. Your page should appear as shown in Figure 4-18. Add your company logo, graphics, color, and content to enhance the appearance of the page. Print out your Web page and the source code. Print out the XSLT stylesheet.

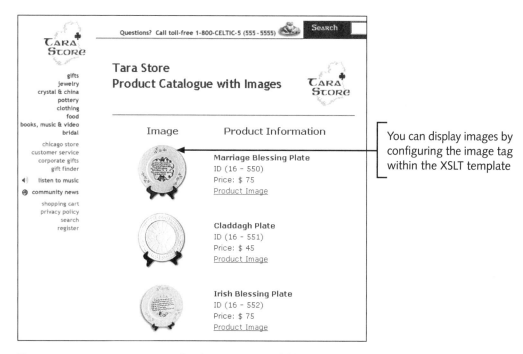

Figure 4-18   Using XSLT to display images and filter data

Tara Store — Data Transformation with the XML Control

Your manager would like you to create a report that will display graphic images for the product ratings. Your manager created an XML file named Ch4Case3.xml and XSLT stylesheets named Ch4Case3.xsl and Ch4Case3_XSL2.xsl to display and format the report. He would like to know which XSLT stylesheet provides better information for the management team. He also created a third file, named Ch4Case3.aspx, that contains the page layout. These files were added to your solution when you imported the Chapter04Data files. The report applies a different format style based upon the number of stars awarded to the product. Your boss would like to add the product data from the XML document. Use the XML control to add the data to the Web page. You will need to set the XML control ID to MyXML and the properties to point to the XML document and XSLT stylesheet. First set the XMLDocument property to Ch4Case3.xml and set the TransformSource to Ch4Case3.xsl, and then save the ASP.NET page and view it in a browser. Then change the TransformSource in the XML control to a modified version of the XSLT file named Ch4Case3_XSL2.xsl. Save the ASP.NET page and view it in a browser. (See Figure 4-19.) Write a short paragraph stating which XSLT stylesheet provided better information for the management team, and provide reasons why you selected that stylesheet. Modify the XSLT stylesheet and the ASP.NET page to enhance the appearance of the page. Add your company logo, graphics, color, and content to enhance the appearance of the page. Print out the Web page and the ASP.NET source code. Print out the XSLT stylesheet and the XML document.

Figure 4-19   Using XSLT to process data and format

Tara Store — Filtering Data with XSLT

Your boss only wants to display the Belleek products for Shea's department store. Use an XSLT stylesheet to transform the data in the Ch4Case3.xml document into a Web page. First, create an XSLT stylesheet to read and format the data. Only display Belleek products, where the subcategory ID is 20. You may format the stylesheet using tables and display the product images. Save this stylesheet as Ch4Case4.xsl in your Chapter4 solution.

Create a Web page named Ch4Case4.aspx. Add the XML control to the Web page. Change the DocumentSource property to Ch4Case4.xml. Change the TransformSource property to Ch4Case4.xsl. Add your company logo, graphics, color, and content to enhance the appearance of the page. Print out your Web page and the source code. Print out the XSLT stylesheet. A screenshot of a possible sample solution is shown in Figure 4-20.

Tara Store — Creating a Rotating Banner Ad

The marketing manager at Tara Store has sold contracts to several other Irish Web sites to allow them to display their banner on the Tara Store Web site. Create a page named Ch4Case5.xml that contains the ads, using data from Table 4-5.

4

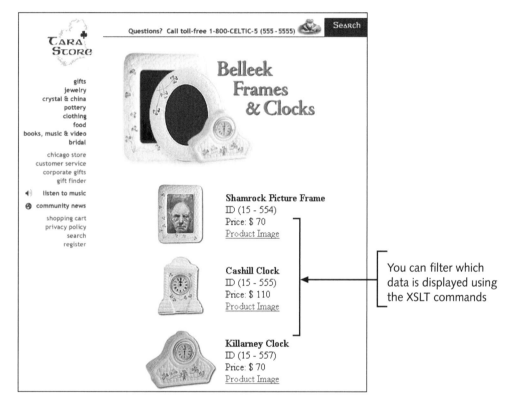

Figure 4-20   Using XSLT to filter data

Table 4-5   Ad information

ImageURL	NavigateURL	AlternateText	Keyword	Impressions
Images/4a.jpg	http://www.joyofireland.com	Joy of Ireland	Store	10
Images/4b.jpg	http://www.rootsweb.com/~irish	The Irish Genealogical Society-International	Culture	15
Images/4c.jpg	http://www.aoh.com	Ancient Order of Hibernians	Culture	20

Table 4-5 Ad information (continued)

ImageURL	NavigateURL	AlternateText	Keyword	Impressions
Images/4d.jpg	*http://www.ireland.com*	The Irish Times	News	25
Images/4e.jpg	*http://home.iol.ie*	Ireland On-Line	News	30
Images/4f.jpg	*http://www.irelandseye.com*	Ireland's Eye	Culture	35
Images/4g.jpg	*http://www.irishamhc.com*	Irish American Heritage Center	Culture	25

Create a page named Ch4Case5.aspx. Add an AdRotator control to the page. Filter the ads to only show culture-related links. Enhance the page with text, color, and graphics. View the page and print out the Web pages and the ASP.NET source code. View the page 10 times. Tally the number of times each culture-related link is displayed.

Tara Store — Creating an Interactive Calendar Control

The store manager needs a method to display a calendar to his employees in order to schedule employee vacation time. Create a Web page with the Calendar control, named Ch4Case6.aspx. Create two buttons labeled Start Date and End Date. When the user clicks on a date, then clicks the Start Date button, display a message confirming the start date of the vacation. When the user clicks on a date, then clicks the End Date button, display a message confirming the end date of the vacation. Display the start and end dates to the user using Label controls. Add your company logo, graphics, color, and content to enhance the appearance of the page. Use Figure 4-21 to guide you work. Print out your Web page, the source code for the ASP.NET page, and the code behind the page.

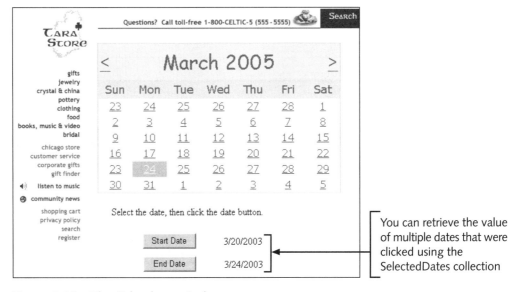

Figure 4-21 The Calendar control

Tara Store — Creating an Administration File Upload Tool

You have been asked to create an administration tool for the shopping cart on the Tara Store Web site. Open the Chapter4 solution in Visual Studio .NET. Create a login form that authenticates the user. Save the page as Ch4Case7Login.aspx. If the user is validated, allow the user to the upload the file. If the user is not authenticated, redisplay the form. Add the File Upload control to the page. Allow the user to enter a new filename in a text box. (*Note*: The user must enter a valid filename and extension.) Create a new folder in your project, named Ch4Case7, in your c:\InetPub\ wwwroot\Chapter4 directory. Allow only the store manager to upload only image files to the Ch4Case7 directory. (*Note*: Using the Accept property feature may only work in some browsers.) His username is StoreMan and his password is GalwayBay. Enhance the page with text, color, and graphics. Provide a link to the Ch4Case7 folder so that users can browse the folder and view their uploaded image. Print your Web pages and the source code for each ASP.NET page and the code behind the page. Figure 4-22 shows the login form authentication page. If the user is authenticated, the upload form is displayed as shown in Figure 4-23. After the file is uploaded, a message is displayed, as shown in Figure 4-24.

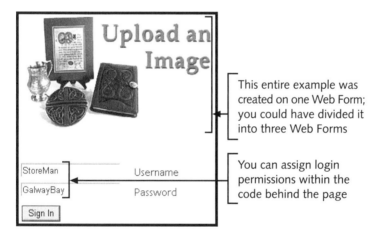

Figure 4-22   The login form

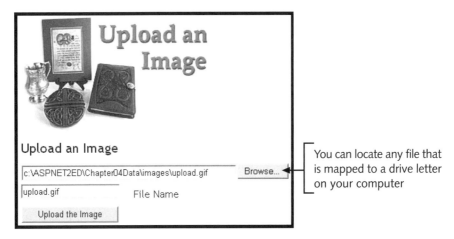

You can locate any file that is mapped to a drive letter on your computer

Figure 4-23   The upload form

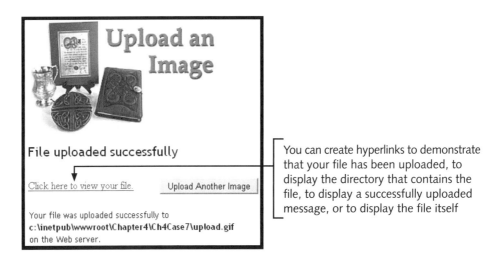

You can create hyperlinks to demonstrate that your file has been uploaded, to display the directory that contains the file, to display a successfully uploaded message, or to display the file itself

Figure 4-24   Displaying the uploaded file

5

USING VISUAL BASIC .NET
WITHIN AN ASP.NET PAGE

In this chapter, you will:

♦ Define object-oriented programming

♦ Use Visual Basic .NET to manipulate the code behind the page

♦ Create classes using Visual Basic .NET

♦ Use variables to store data

♦ Learn how data types are stored in the .NET Framework

♦ Use collections to store groups of data elements

♦ Create and use procedures in Visual Basic .NET

♦ Learn how to use Visual C# .NET instead of Visual Basic .NET to create ASP.NET pages

Today, companies want programs that can be easily maintained and integrated with other applications. Companies need to build reusable programs with different data sources. To accomplish this, programmers use object-oriented programming techniques to encapsulate the business logic. Then, they create applications that can access the business logic, regardless of how the program was written. ASP.NET code can be written using a variety of programming languages. In this chapter, you will learn how to use object-oriented programming techniques and Visual Basic .NET within an ASP.NET page.

The entire ASP.NET application is compiled into one or more logical groupings known as namespaces. Within the namespace, you can build reusable code from classes. Within the .NET Framework, the Base Class Library provides access to many built-in classes. You can also create your own class, which in turn enables you to create objects. These objects can be used in your program to store reusable code. You can store data in a variety of data structures—variables, constants, collections, and databases—and retrieve it at a later time. In this chapter, you will learn to create classes, store data using several data structures, and access the data using functions and methods.

OBJECT-ORIENTED PROGRAMMING

In the very early days of BASIC (the precursor to Visual Basic), each line of code was given a number, and the statements were executed sequentially in a single file. Commands such as GOTO allowed you to divert the code to another line in the program. Later, decision control structures were used to control the execution order of the program. **Decision control structures** use conditional expressions to determine which block of code to execute. The code is a group of one or more programming statements. If a condition is met, then a block of code is executed, otherwise, an alternate block of code is executed. Visual Basic allows you to create decision control structures, as well as functions and procedures, which are used to control the order that the programming statements are executed. This type of programming is often referred to as procedural programming, and the programming statements are known as **procedural code**.

Today an ASP.NET application organizes code into several physical files called **modules**. When the application is written in Visual Basic .NET, each module ends in the file extension .vb. Modules consist of one or more classes. Within each module are programming statements. Some of these programming statements are grouped as event handlers and procedures. These programming statements are stored in a class definition. An **object** is a set of related code that is compartmentalized. In **object-oriented programming**, you create objects based upon a class, and then you can access the procedures and properties of the object across multiple Web pages.

Within a Web application, classes may be defined in several module files. If the Web Form is named WebForm1.aspx, the Page class is defined within the WebForm1.aspx.vb page. In addition to the code behind the page, you can create a class for a User control, as you learned in Chapter 2. The code behind the page for the User Control object contains the class definition. If the User control is named UC.ascx, the Page class is defined within the UC.ascx.vb page. You can also create a class with no visual component. In such a case, you would define the class in a single file. For example, the name of the class that contains the global variables and procedures for the TaraStore application might be named TaraStoreClass.vb.

The creation of an object consists of two separate tasks. The first task is to create the object definition, called the **class**. The class is not an object that you can access directly; it is the code that contains the procedures and properties of the object. Once you create the class, you can create objects based upon the class definition. In other words, the class is the template for the new object. When you create an object, you are really creating an instance of the class. **Instantiation** is the process of declaring and initializing an object from a class. You can create many objects from the same object definition. This process is analogous to making cookies. If you have a recipe to make cookies, you know what the ingredients are, and you know how to combine the ingredients to make the cookies. But a recipe is not a cookie. First you make the cookie dough, then you bake it, and only then have you made cookies. The class is like the cookie recipe, since it contains the directions to create a cookie. Instantiation is like the process of mixing and baking the dough.

The ability to create many cookies based on a single recipe is useful, because then all of the cookies have the same properties (for example, they all taste the same). Each object you create from the class inherits the properties and procedures from the class definition. However, there may be times when you want to make oatmeal cookies instead of chocolate chip cookies. If the cookie recipe contains general information about making cookies, you can reuse the recipe to make an oatmeal cookie by changing some of the ingredients and measurements. Similarly, you can create multiple objects from the same class, and also assign different values to each object's properties.

The code following this paragraph is a sample of how to create a class named TaraStoreClass. The line `Public Class TaraStoreClass` means that the class is available to other applications, and that the name of the class is TaraStoreClass. The line `End Class` identifies the end of the code within the class definition. This class contains one variable named StoreName. Later in this chapter, you will learn to create a class, instantiate an object, and reuse the code stored within the object.

```
Public Class TaraStoreClass
   Private StoreName As String = "Tara Store"
End Class
```

In the class definition, you can restrict which applications have access to the class. Only procedures and properties that are declared **Public** can interact with other objects outside of the base class. Procedures and properties that are declared as **Private** can only be called within the base class. Protected procedures and properties can be called from within the base class, and within subclasses. **Subclasses** are used to create a class that inherits from a base class. Procedures and properties that are declared as **Friend** can be called from anywhere within the same application.

After you have created the class definition, you can instantiate an object based on the class definition. You must use the keyword Dim to declare a variable in which to store the object, and the keyword New to identify that this is an object based on a class definition. The class in the sample code that follows this paragraph is named TaraStoreClass. The object is stored in the variable named Ch5Class. The class is contained within the Chapter5 namespace. Therefore, the class is referred to as `Chapter5.TaraStoreClass`.

```
Dim Ch5Class As New Chapter5.TaraStoreClass()
```

Both procedures and event handlers can also contain one or more programming statements. Some of these statements are action statements, for example, changing the value of a text box. Some of the statements are decision control structures, which allow you to organize the order in which the code is executed. As you learned previously, when an action occurs, such as the button being clicked, the click event triggers the OnClick event handler. The **event handler** executes code when the event occurs. Procedures are executed only when they are called by another procedure or event handler.

There are two types of procedures: **subprocedures** and **functions**. Both contain one or more programming statements, and both are a named grouping of one or more programming statements. You can pass values, called **parameters**, to subprocedures and functions in the class. Parameters can be passed to the method in a comma delimited list within a pair of parentheses. The parentheses are required even if no parameters are passed. Built-in functions include mathematical, date and time, string, and formatting functions, among others. However, functions can return a value to the program that called the function. When the function ends, a value can be returned to the main program by using the **Return** keyword. The code following this paragraph is an example of a function named GetStoreName that returns the name of the store. The keyword Return is used to identify a value that is returned to the code that called the function. You will learn more about functions later in this chapter.

```
Public Function GetStoreName() As String
    Return "Tara Store"
End Function
```

Properties are used to set the value of a variable defined within an object. You can call any of the object's methods and properties that are defined in the class. You can also assign values to properties that are declared in the class after the object is created, and you can assign values to the properties when you create the object from the class. Then, when you create the object, you use the class to create a new instance of the object, which contains different values for the properties. The sample code that follows this paragraph shows how a property is defined within a class. You will learn more about defining properties later in this chapter.

```
Public ReadOnly Property StoreName() As String
    Get
        Return StoreName
    End Get
End Property
```

Properties are identified by the name of the object, followed by a period, followed by the name of the property. Some properties are assigned to the object by default within the object definition. Then, all new objects inherit the same properties as the original object definition. However, if an object does not assign a value to a property, and a new object is created without assigning a value to the property, the property is assigned the default value "undefined." (*Note:* In the next section, you will learn to use property methods to expose private variables that are defined within the class.)

```
lblContact.Text = Ch5Class.StoreName.ToString()
```

Object-oriented programming languages support concepts such as inheritance, encapsulation, abstraction, and polymorphism. **Inheritance** allows you to derive the interface and behaviors from another class. The keyword **Inherits** allows you to inherit from another .NET class. With the Common Language Runtime, all objects are inherited from the System namespace, and these objects are referred to as types. Each object inherits properties and procedures from the System.Object, including Equals, GetHashCode, GetType, and ToString. Therefore, because all objects are inherited from the System.Object, some of the properties such as ToString apply to most objects. For example, all of the form fields are objects within the System.UI.Web class, and so they all can use the ToString function to display their class names as a string. The ToString function is inherited from the System class. It is also possible to override the interface and behaviors that were inherited from another class.

Polymorphism is a variable that can reference two different objects that share a common interface and call members on that interface. **Encapsulation** means that the inner workings of the object, such as the procedures and properties, are maintained within the object. Encapsulation enables you to create objects or programs that are self-contained. You can create multiple objects based on the same class, as long as the names are unique. For example, your inventory application needs to interact with the shopping cart application to provide the number of items in stock. Both applications contain objects that interact with each other. If the Purchasing Department changes the database server application that stores the inventory data, the inventory application needs to be changed to reflect the new database software. However, the shopping cart application does not have to be altered because the interface between the two applications remains consistent. The business logic within the inventory application is isolated from the business logic within the shopping cart application. Therefore, encapsulation makes it easier to upgrade applications that interact with other applications.

Abstraction is the ability to create a concept using code. For example, a customer is a person who makes purchases from a company. A customer object is the programming code that represents the customer. The customer object may contain information about the customer, such as the shipping address and purchases. The objects interact with each other via a public **interface** that is defined in the class. You can use the functions, properties, events, and attributes to interact with the interface.

Polymorphism is the ability to create code that can be applied to objects that are derived from different classes. If you have an application that contains a student object and a faculty object, you can write an application that retrieves the name property from both objects. Polymorphism allows you to apply programs across different classes.

INTRODUCTION TO VISUAL BASIC .NET

It's important to have an understanding of where Visual Basic .NET fits within ASP.NET and Visual Studio .NET. Visual Basic .NET code can be created using simple text editors such as Notepad. This code must be compiled manually using the command-line compiler that is provided with the .NET Framework. The code is compiled into the MSIL, Microsoft Intermediate Language. In Chapter 1, you used the compiler to create a simple Visual Basic .NET program. When you create an ASP.NET application using Notepad instead of Visual Studio .NET, you may include your Visual Basic .NET code within the Web page. Typically the code is inserted at the top of the Web page. Logically, this code represents the code behind the Web page that you created in the previous chapter. You lose the developer tools, such as the debugging tools, that are part of Visual Studio .NET.

A typical Visual Basic .NET application contains a graphical user interface called a **form** through which the program interacts with the user. The form is an object that is created from the `System.Windows.Forms` namespace. The Visual Studio .NET Toolbox contains a tab called **Windows Forms**, which provides controls that are typically added to a Windows Form. The form contains code behind the graphical interface, which is used to interact with any of the objects contained on the form. When you build the application, Visual Studio .NET compiles the code and stores the .dll file that contains the namespace in the project's bin directory. The bin directory has execute permission, which allows the code to be executed at runtime.

In this book, you use Visual Studio .NET to create the code behind the ASP.NET page, and not behind the Windows Form. Because you are working on a Web page and not a Windows Form, you do not have the same type of controls available. However, you do have the same access to the Visual Basic .NET programming language. You can create classes using an external file, or create the class in the code behind the page. If you want to use a class that is located in a different file, you need to import the class into the Web page, and then create a new object using the class. Then, all of the properties and procedures of the class will be available to the new object.

In the .NET Framework, the ASP.NET page is a class within the application that inherits from the class that is inherited from the ASP.NET page class. The ASP.NET page inherits the code behind the page. By default, when you create an ASP.NET Web page in Visual Studio .NET, a class that represents that page is created. The name of the class is the same as the name of the Web page. On the first line of the Web page, Visual Studio .NET inserts the keyword Inherits and identifies the name of the class that is created in the code behind the Web page.

Within your ASP.NET page, you have access to the same System namespace as Windows Forms. Therefore, your application can inherit the same value and reference types as Visual Basic .NET. You can also define your own classes, and the properties and procedures within those classes. When the build method is called, the code behind the page is compiled into the same .dll file that contains the namespace for the application.

Most of the documentation on ASP.NET contains code samples created in Notepad. In these examples, the Visual Basic .NET code is contained within the ASP.NET page. However, it is better to use Visual Studio .NET to create your Visual Basic .NET code in the code behind the page. The code is split between two files, which makes your code easier to maintain. Not only do you have the benefits of Visual Studio .NET development and debugging tools, but you also have the ability to work in a multiuser environment, and all of the project files can be managed within Visual Studio .NET. The Visual Studio .NET Enterprise Edition comes with an additional application called Visual Safe Source, which provides additional resources to help teams of developers who want to work on the same project files, but don't want the problems of having multiple versions of documents and developers deleting other developers' work.

Creating a Class

In the following exercise, you will create a new project and define a class. Because you have only created the class definition, and have not created an instance of the object yet, you cannot refer to the object by its name within the class definition. Therefore, the keyword **Me** can be used in place of the object name within the class definition. (*Note*: In C# the keyword Me is replaced with the keyword **This**.) Procedures are identified by the name of the object followed by a period, followed by the name of the procedure. After you define the class and create the object, you will modify the value of the variables defined within the object.

1. Start **Visual Studio .NET**.

2. Click **File** on the menu bar, point to **New**, and then click **Project**. This opens the New Project window.

3. Under Project Types, click **Visual Basic Projects**, and under Templates click **ASP.NET Web Application**. Type **Chapter5** in the Location text box in place of WebApplication1. Click **OK** to create the solution, project, and default files.

4. Right-click **Chapter5** in the Solution Explorer window, point to **Add**, and then click **New Folder**. Type **images** for the folder name, and then press **Enter**.

5. Right-click the **images** folder, point to **Add**, and then click **Add Existing Item**. Browse to locate your data files for this chapter. (*Note*: In the Files of type drop-down list, you need to change the selection from VB Code Files to **Image Files**.)

6. Select all of the files in the Chapter05Data\images directory. (*Note*: You can use the Ctrl+A key combination to select all of the files.) Click the **Open** button to import the images into your project within the images directory.

7. Right-click **Chapter5** in the Solution Explorer window, point to **Add**, and click **Add Existing Item**. Navigate to your Chapter05Data folder. In the Files of type drop-down list box, change the selection to **All Files**. Select all of the files except the images directory, and click **Open**. Messages will appear that ask you to create a class for several of the .aspx files. Click **Yes** in each instance.

8. Right-click **Chapter5** in the Solution Explorer window, point to **Add**, and then click **Add New Item**. In the dialog box, under Templates, click the **Class** icon. In the Name text box replace the default name by typing **TaraStoreClass.vb**, and then click **Open**. The page opens in Code view. The class declaration is already inserted for you.

9. Within the TaraStoreClass definition, add the code that follows this paragraph. This code creates two variables that can be called from your Web pages. The keyword Dim is not used here, because then each variable would be made private to the class by default. The keyword Public is required to ensure that

the class in the Web page can retrieve the variables. The StoreName and StoreEmail variables are instance variables that are private to the TaraStoreClass class. They are not available outside of the TaraStoreClass class. Refer to Figure 5-2 to see where the code is placed within the TaraStoreClass definition.

```
Public StoreName As String = "Tara Store"
Public StoreEmail As String = "info@TaraStore.com"
```

10. Click Edit on the menu bar, point to **Outlining**, and then click **Start Automatic Outlining**. This allows you to visually see the code using a graphical outline. (*Note*: If this option is already running, it is not displayed on the Outlining menu.)

11. Click **Tools** on the menu bar, then click **Options**. The Options window opens. Click the folder labeled **Text Editor**, click the folder labeled **Basic**, then click the **Line numbers** check box to select it. See Figure 5-1. Click the **OK** button to close the window.

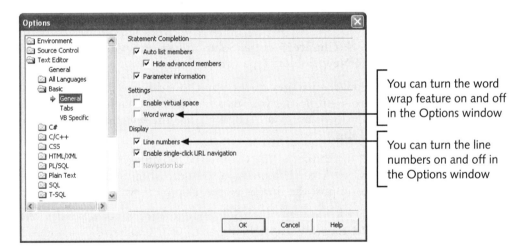

Figure 5-1   Configuring the Code view options

12. Click the **Save All** button. The code to create the class should look like the code in Figure 5-2.

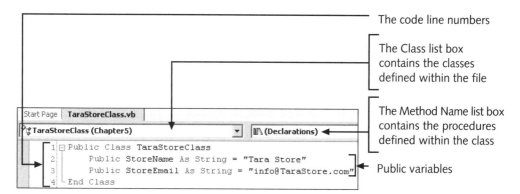

The code line numbers

The Class list box contains the classes defined within the file

The Method Name list box contains the procedures defined within the class

Public variables

Figure 5-2   Creating a class in an external Visual Basic .NET file

13. Double-click the **ClassVariables.aspx** file in the Solution Explorer Window to open it.

14. Double-click on the whitespace on the page to open the code behind the page. In the Page_Load procedure, add the code that follows this paragraph to create a new object named **Ch5Class** based on TaraStoreClass. Because the variable contains an object, you must use the keyword **New** to instantiate the object from a class. As you type each period, notice that the IntelliSense list box appears. Your Chapter5 namespace contains a class named TaraStoreClass. As you type the name of the assembly, Chapter5 and the period, a list of objects defined is displayed in a drop-down list box. You can use the arrow keys or the pointer to make your selection, as shown in Figure 5-3.

```
Dim Ch5Class As New Chapter5.TaraStoreClass
```

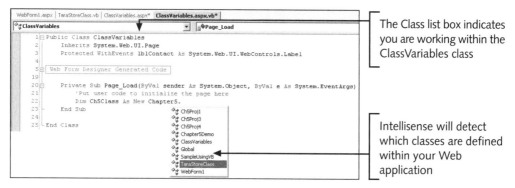

The Class list box indicates you are working within the ClassVariables class

Intellisense will detect which classes are defined within your Web application

Figure 5-3   Instantiating an object in a Web page from a class

15. On the next line, add the code that follows this paragraph to retrieve the values from the new class. By default, this new object inherits the properties and methods of the TaraStoreClass. You can assign the properties to the Text property of the Label control that is located on the Web Form. The ToString method is used to retrieve the value of the two variables from the string objects. The values are inherited when the object was created from the initial class. The code should appear as shown in Figure 5-4.

```
lblContact.Text = Ch5Class.StoreName.ToString() _
& "<br />" & Ch5Class.StoreEmail.ToString()
```

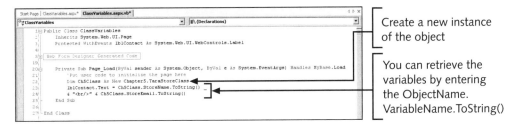

Create a new instance of the object

You can retrieve the variables by entering the ObjectName. VariableName.ToString()

Figure 5-4   Retrieving the values of variables defined within an object

16. Click the **Save All** button. Click **Build** on the menu bar, then click **Build Solution**.

17. Click the **ClassVariables.aspx** tab in the main window. Click the **Design** tab to change to Design view if necessary. Right-click on the page and click **View in Browser**. (*Note:* You can also view the page in your browser at *http://localhost/chapter5/ClassVariables.aspx*.) The page should appear as shown in Figure 5-5.

Variables retrieved from the object

Figure 5-5   Viewing the ClassVariables page

You can use the IL Disassembler (ILDASM) tool to view the namespace and locate any of the classes created within your Windows or Web application. The ILDASM is the graphical tool used to visually look at the objects within the application. In the following steps you will view the Chapter5 assembly using the ILDASM.

1. Go to the Visual Studio .NET command prompt. In most computers, to access this command click the **Start** menu, point to **All Programs**, point to **Microsoft Visual Studio .NET 2003**, point to **Visual Studio .NET Tools**, and then click **Visual Studio .NET 2003 Command Prompt**.

2. At the command prompt enter **cd \Inetpub\wwwroot\Chapter5\bin**. By default your assembly is compiled and placed within this directory.

3. At the command prompt enter **ILDASM Chapter5.dll** to open the ILDASM window. (*Note:* The name of your assembly and the namespace is Chapter5, which is also the name of your .dll file.)

4. Click the **plus sign** next to the Chapter5 icon to expand the Chapter5 namespace.

5. Click the **plus sign** next to the TaraStoreClass icon to expand the class information. Double-click **StoreEmail:public string**. This opens a window that tells you that the StoreEmail is a field within the TaraStoreClass type, and is a public variable of type string. Notice in Figure 5-6 that ClassVariables.aspx and WebForm1.aspx are also shown as classes because all Web pages are now classes within the application namespace.

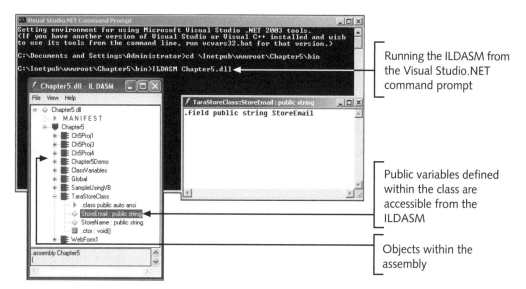

Figure 5-6   Viewing the new object properties in the ILDASM tool

6. Close all of the ILDASM windows and the command prompt window by clicking the **Close** button in each window.

7. Close any open pages.

Variables

In the previous example you created a variable and retrieved the value. In this section, you will learn more about how to use variables within your application. **Variables** are used to store data that can be retrieved at a later time. For example, a variable might be used to store a value that is to be used during a calculation. If you need to calculate several values, compare values, or perform multiple operations on a value, then it is worthwhile to use variables to store them, in lieu of using the values themselves. The program can then refer to the variable instead of the value. In the previous exercise, you created a class that contained two variables. You declared each variable as a string, and assigned it a value. Because the variable is defined within a class definition, you are able to retrieve the values from within the Web page by creating an object based upon that class definition.

A **variable declaration** consists of three parts: the **declaration keywords**, a **variable name**, and a **data type**. The variable name refers to the name of the variable as well as a section of memory in the computer. The exact location of the variable in the computer's memory is unimportant because you can refer to the location by using the name of the variable.

The data type identifies what kind of data the variable can store. For example, a variable might be an **integer** used in a calculation, or it might be a **string** of characters that is used to store the name of the company.

Although Visual Basic .NET and Visual C# .NET support different data types, when the application is compiled, the managed code converts the data types to the same data type across all languages.

Variable Declaration

Some programming languages, including Visual Basic .NET, require that you declare variables before using them in scripts or programs. When you declare a variable, the computer reserves the memory required to store the variable. **Declaring** a variable is the process of reserving the memory space for the variable before it is used in the program. Variables that are declared in the class are referred to as **members, member variables,** or **instance variables**.

The Web Form module is simply a class module with a visual interface. Both types of modules may contain variables and procedures. Figure 5-7 shows a sample of a Web Form module and a class module with several variables and procedures. The variable is defined within a class or a procedure. The **scope** of the variable indicates where the variable can be accessed. (*Note:* Variable scope is also known as variable accessibility). The **lifetime** of a variable indicates how long the variable and its value persist in memory.

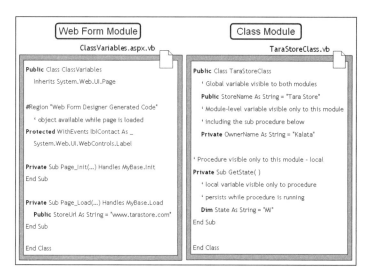

Figure 5-7   Declaring local and module-level variables within Web Form and class modules

Variables that are defined within a procedure are called **local** variables because they can be used only by the procedure in which they were declared. Local variables persist in memory only while the procedure in which they were declared is being executed. For example, in the button_click event procedure, a local variable named strCourseNumber is declared and assigned to the value WWW499. When the page loads, no memory resources are used related to this variable. When the user clicks the button, the memory is allocated to the variable and the contents are assigned to the memory location. After the button_click event procedure has completed, the memory can be reallocated to other resources.

Local variables are declared with the **Dim** keyword. You can also use the keyword **Public** to declare a variable. However, if the button_click event procedure was declared with the keyword **Private** and a local variable named strCourseNumber is declared using the word **Public**, only the button_click event procedure would be allowed to access the strCourseNumber variable.

Variables defined after the Web Form Designer Generated Code and before the Page_Load event procedure can be used by any of the procedures within the page, and they are called **module-level** variables. Module-level variables are declared with the **Private** keyword. These module-level variables are defined within a class, such as the Page class. Module-level variables are not available to other Web Forms or other classes within the application. When the page loads, the memory is allocated to the variable and the contents are assigned to the memory location. Any procedure within the Web Form can read or change the value of the variable. After the page has been unloaded and discarded, the memory can be reallocated to other resources.

Local variables are more readable, easier to maintain, and require less server memory resources than module-level variables. Therefore, you should choose local variables unless multiple procedures require the same variable.

> There are other types of declarations that you will use with more complex applications. When you create classes and objects, you will use declaration keywords to define their scope. **Global** or public variables are defined with the **Public** keyword and can be accessed from outside the class or the Web Form. **Friend** variables are public variables that are used only within the current application or project. **Protected** variables can be called from within the base class, such as the Web Page class, and from within subclasses. You can learn more about the Dim statement, variable scope, and declaring variables at *http://msdn.microsoft.com/library/en-us/vblr7/html/vastmdim.asp* and *http://msdn.microsoft.com/library/en-us/vbcn7/html/vaconDeclaringVariables.asp*.

In Visual Basic .NET, you declare a variable using the keyword Dim and the name of the variable, as shown in the code that follows this paragraph. Variables declared exist as long as the procedure or function in which they are declared exists.

```
dim intQuantity as Integer
dim intPrice as Integer
dim strName as String
dim strEmail as String
```

If you have multiple variables to declare, you can declare each one on a separate line, or use a single line. To declare several variables on a single line, use the declaration keyword once, followed by the list of variables separated by a comma. The following examples illustrate how to declare multiple variables in Visual Basic .NET:

```
dim intQuantity, intPrice as Integer
dim strName, strEmail as String
dim decPrice, decCost as Decimal
```

You can force a program written in Visual Basic .NET to declare all variables before the variables can be used. Declaring variables before they are used makes it easier to debug your code. For example, it helps you catch spelling and syntax errors. If you type in the wrong name for a variable, the program will not run until you declare the variable with the correct name. The **Option Explicit** mode is used to require the page to declare all variables before they can be used. Use the phrase `<%@ Page Explicit = true %>` in the first line within HTML Code view to force all variables to be declared before they can be used. This statement must be placed at the top of the Web page before any other HTML or scripts. You can also place this code in the Web.config configuration file. Then, all pages inherit this property. Although by default you are required to declare all variables before they can be used, you can turn off this feature using `<%@ Page Explicit = false %>` at the top of the Web page.

Naming Variables

When naming variables, your options are almost infinite, but there are certain naming rules in Visual Basic .NET that you must adhere to. Violations of these conventions result in errors in your programs.

- You cannot use any of the Visual Basic .NET commands or keywords as your variable name.

- Variable names must begin with a letter.

- You cannot use a period or space within a variable name.

- Avoid using any special characters in a variable name except for the underscore.

Variables are more useful if you name them with a standardized naming convention. This makes them easier to identify, and also makes spelling and syntax errors less likely. One important convention is case sensitivity. Visual Basic .NET commands and variables are not case sensitive. Therefore, Visual Basic .NET interprets intPrice and INTPRICE and IntPrice the same way. However, it is useful to be consistent in the naming of variables because other programming languages, such as C#, would interpret those variable names as two separate variables. Variables often consist of two or more combined words. The first letter of each word is often capitalized, for example, as in the variable names LastName and IntPrice.

It is also useful to provide your variables with a descriptive name, one that has some meaning or association with the contents or purpose of the variable. Using the data type prefix and a descriptive variable name makes your code much more readable. The naming convention does not affect how the memory space is reserved for the variable. For example, the variable that holds the price of a product can be named IntPrice to indicate that the variable contains an integer that describes the price of a product. This technique, known as Hungarian notation, uses the first three characters to identify the datatype. Table 5-1 contains a list of common prefixes used in Visual Basic .NET.

Table 5-1   Common prefixes used in Visual Basic .NET

Data Type	Prefix	Sample Variable Name
Boolean	Bln	BlnMember
Byte	Byt	BytZero
Char	Chr	ChrLetter
Date	Dat	DatBirthDate
Double	Dbl	DblWeight
Decimal	Dec	DecProductPrice
Integer	Int	IntNumberProducts
Long	Lng	LngSalary
Single	Sng	SngAverage
Short	Sho	ShoYears
String	Str	StrLastName

Assigning Values to Variables

You can store values in variables using the assignment operator. The **assignment operator** is the equals sign (=). To assign a value to a variable, enter the name of the variable on the left side of the assignment operator, and enter the new value on the right side of the assignment operator. You can assign the value to the variable when you declare the variable, or after the variable has been created. The following sample code shows you how to declare multiple variables at the same time, and how to assign a value to a variable when the variable is declared:

```
Dim LastName, FirstName as String
Dim StoreName As String = "Tara Store"
```

Note that the equals sign is an assignment operator, and not an arithmetic operator.

Constants

You can use a **constant** instead of a variable when you want to assign a value to a variable that does not change. For example, you can use constants for tax rates, shipping fees, and values used in mathematical equations. The keyword **Const** is used to declare a constant. The naming rules for variables also apply to constants. However, the names of constants are usually all uppercase, as shown in the code that follows this paragraph. In addition, when you declare a constant, you need to assign the value to the constant.

```
Const TAXRATE As Integer = 8
```

Concatenation

In Visual Basic .NET, strings can be manipulated using several techniques. **Concatenation** is the process of joining together one or more strings. The string can be a literal string, the result returned from an expression, or a variable that contains a string data type. You can also use built-in methods to determine the length of the string, locate characters within the string, and truncate the spaces at the beginning or end of the string. In the sample code that follows this paragraph, the variable is used to store the result of an expression. The expression is built using the values from the properties, and a line break tag. The ampersand is used to concatenate the expression to one single string. (*Note*: Because the code is long, the underscore character is used to continue the code to the next line.) Then, the variable is assigned to the Text property of the Label control.

```
Dim lblControlContent = Ch5Class.StoreName.ToString() _
& "<br />" & Ch5Class.StoreEmail.ToString()
lblContact.Text = lblControlContent
```

You can also use the plus sign (+) for concatenation of strings. However, because the plus sign also represents the addition operator for mathematical equations and because it can be used with non-strings, it's recommended to use the ampersand as the concatenation operator.

Data Types

There are several data types built into the .NET Framework. All of the variables are declared as a data type, or type. The two categories of types are reference types and value types. Examples of **reference types** are strings, classes, arrays, collections, and objects. Value types are also referred to as **primitive types** or **structures**. Examples of some of the **value types** built into the .NET Framework are as follows:

- Boolean and Char: These have been discussed earlier in the book.

- DateTime: Within Visual Basic .NET, DateTime is represented as the Date data type.

- All numeric data types: Within Visual Basic .NET, these data types include Byte, Decimal, Double, Long, Integer, and Short.

Value types and reference types are stored in different locations in memory. Value types store their data in an area called the **stack**, because they contain numeric data that can be stored using a fixed number of bytes. Searching for variables that contain value types is more efficient if they are stored in the stack than in the managed heap. Reference types are stored in the managed heap because the amount of memory required to store them may vary.

The **managed heap** contains memory addresses that are used to store variables that are reference types. All newly created objects are allocated at the top of the managed heap. When an object is no longer being used, the memory that was required to create the object can be collected and reallocated to other objects. The garbage collector from the common Language Runtime allocates and manages the managed heap. The main purpose of the garbage collector is to manage memory and to free up memory that is no longer being used by the application. Periodically, the garbage collector removes objects that are no longer referenced from the heap.

String

The **String data type** is used to store text, which can consist of numbers, characters, and date information. Number values not used in mathematical expressions are more efficiently stored as strings. Social Security numbers, Zip codes, and phone numbers are typically stored as strings. However, strings are stored as basic text, and must be explicitly converted to a numerical data type before a string value can be used in an arithmetic expression. When you assign a string a value, the value must be within quotation marks. All strings are stored as Unicode. Unicode allows you to have more letters than the 26 letters of the American alphabet. Strings are variable in length. Therefore, you don't have to specify the number of characters in the string when you create the string object.

There are several methods built into the string object.

- The **Ltrim**, **Rtrim**, and **Trim methods** remove the blank spaces from the preceding, ending, and both ends of the string, respectively.

- The **Asc method** provides the string's ANSI (American National Standards Institute) character equivalent.

- The **Chr method** provides the ASCII (American Standard Code for Information Interchange) character equivalent. Chr is a useful method when you want to create control characters such as carriage returns.

- The **Replace method** replaces one string with another.

- The **Split method** returns a string that has been split, using a delimiter to identify where to split the string.

- The **Concat method** allows you to join strings together without using the concatenation operator.

- The **Compare method** allows you to compare two strings. If they are equal, the method returns 0. If the value on the left side is less than the value on the right side, then a negative integer is returned; otherwise a positive integer is returned.

- The **LCase** and **UCase methods** convert the case to lowercase and uppercase, respectively.

- The **Format method** allows you to format numeric output.

The following sample code retrieves the value from a text box and stores the value in a variable as all lowercase:

```
Dim Password As String
Password = LCase(txtPassword.Value)
lblPassword.Text = Password
```

The Format method allows you to format the string using currency, percent, and other format properties. The sample code that follows this paragraph illustrates how to format the number as currency, decimal, number, hexadecimal, and percentage. The Number property is used to format the number using commas.

```
System.Console.WriteLine({"0:c"}, 1441.33)
System.Console.WriteLine({"0:D"}, 1441.33)
System.Console.WriteLine({"0:N"}, 1441.33)
System.Console.WriteLine({"0:x"}, 255)
System.Console.WriteLine({"0:00%"}, 255.25)
```

Char

The **Char** data type allows you to store a single text value as a number between 0 and 65,535. The Char data type can be used to create new character sets for other types of languages that use Unicode standards.

Numeric

The numeric data types include Byte, Short, Long, and Integer. Real number data types are represented by the types Single, Double, and Decimal.

- A **Byte data type** stores an integer between 0 and 255. A byte data type is stored in a single byte on the computer. (*Note:* A byte is composed of 8 bits. Each bit is represented by 0 or 1.)

- A **Short data type** is a 16-bit number. Therefore, a short data type can only store values from −32,768 to 32,767.

- The **Integer data type** is a 32-bit whole number and is the preferred data type for representing a 32-bit number on a 32-bit operating system.

- The **Long data type** is a 64-bit number and is the preferred data type for representing a 64-bit number on a 64-bit operating system.

- The **Single data type** represents a single-precision floating point number.

- The **Double data type** supports larger numbers than the Single data type.

- The **Decimal data type** can store numbers up to 28 decimal places and is often used to store currency data. Variables that store monetary values have a subtype called Decimal. (*Note:* In previous versions of Visual Basic .NET this data type was known as **currency**. You can use formatting methods to change the appearance of the Decimal data type to currency.)

When you convert a long number to an integer, you may lose some data. Visual Studio .NET sets the option strict on by default so that any conversion that would result in data loss is halted. Only widening conversions are allowed, because there is no data loss. If you place `Option Strict Off` in the Visual Basic .NET code, you enable your code to implicitly convert Long data types to integers.

DateTime

The **DateTime data type** is used to store dates. The date and time values are stored in the formats mm/dd/yyyy and hh:mm:ss. The date value is enclosed within a pair of pound signs. Visual Basic .NET can store any date between 01/01/0001 and 12/31/9999. Use the DateTime class to declare a date object. You can retrieve or assign a value to the date using the pound sign before and after the date, as shown in the following sample code:

```
Dim MyBirthday As DateTime
MyBirthday = #3/22/2002#
```

The Object Browser

The **Object Browser** can be used to display the classes, properties, and methods built into the namespaces within the .NET Framework. In addition to the System classes, the Object Browser will also show the classes for other namespaces including the Microsoft.VisualBasic namespace. (*Note*: To open the Object Browser window, open your solution, go to the View menu, and select Object Browser. To view classes within a namespace, you can expand the list by clicking the plus sign next to the namespace.)

Figure 5-8 shows the Object Browser with the DateAndTime Class. This is a specific class within Visual Basic .NET and is not the same DateTime object within the .NET System namespace. When the project is compiled into the Intermediate Language within an assembly, these data types will be modified to their equivalent .NET Framework data types.

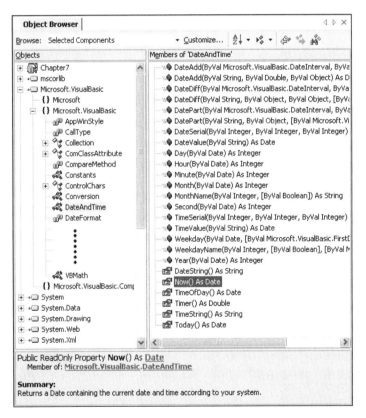

Figure 5-8   Using the Object Browser to view namespaces and classes

The DateTime data type is part of the .NET Framework classes. Visual Basic .NET uses the Date data type, which is equivalent to the DateTime data type. The preceding example would be `Dim MyBirthday as Date`. When you declare a DateTime object, the object is not blue, indicating that it's not a Visual Basic .NET keyword. However, either method may be used to declare dates. If you have installed the QuickStart tutorials, you can view a listing of the namespaces and the .NET classes at *http://localhost/quickstart/aspplus/samples/classbrowser/vb/classbrowser.aspx*. You can locate instructions to install the QuickStart tutorials in Chapter 1, Project 1-3. You can download a poster of the Visual Basic .NET classes at *http://msdn.microsoft.com/vstudio/productinfo/posters/posterfiles/ Visual_Basic_Net_X0849461pst_b_OL.pdf*. To view this poster, you must have Adobe Acrobat Reader installed on your system.

Boolean

A **Boolean data type** only has two possible values: either a True value or False value. (*Note*: George Boole developed the branch of mathematics related to outcomes of true or false.) Typically, in binary math, 1 represents true and 0 represents false. However, when a Boolean value is used within a mathematical expression, the value of the Boolean variable is converted to a number. When these values are converted to an integer, the True value is converted to -1, and the False value is converted to 0. (*Note*: In the previous version of Visual Basic, the True value was converted to 1.)

Using a Property to Retrieve and Set the Value of a Variable

To use an instance variable from a different class, you need to use the Property function, or to declare the variable public. A property is not the same thing as a variable. A **property** is a method that is used to get and set values. These values may be stored within a variable within the class. You can use the Property method to make the instance variable available to code outside of the class. In the code that follows this paragraph, the Property method is used to retrieve the value of the internal instance variable named StoreName. By having the property store the value of the variable, the internal variable is not exposed outside of the class. Property methods are used to keep private the variables internal to your code.

```
Public Class TaraStoreClass
  Private StoreName As String = "Tara Store"
  Private StoreEmail As String = "info@TaraStore.com"
  Public ReadOnly Property StoreName() As String
    Get
      Return StoreName
    End Get
  End Property
End Class
```

You should not declare the variable public or friend, because that directly exposes the variable outside of the class. Rather, you can use the property to retrieve the variable within the class. Then, only the property is exposed outside of the class.

You can set the value of the variable directly, or by using the Property method. The code that follows this paragraph passes the NewValue string to the SetName method. Then, the value assigns a new value to the NewStoreName variable. The GetName method retrieves the value of the variable named NewStoreName. No value is passed to the GetName method. Therefore, you can simply return the value as a String data type using the Return keyword. You must identify the data type of the variable that is returned to your main code.

```
Public Class TaraStoreClass
  Public Sub SetName(ByVal NewValue As String)
    NewStoreName = NewValue
  End Sub
  Public Sub GetName() As String
    Return NewStoreName
  End Sub
End Class
```

The preceding technique offers direct access to your variables. You can use the property method to retrieve and set the value of the variables. In the sample code that follows this paragraph, the value of the variable is set using the property. Although it may appear that you are still using the Get and Set keywords, the values are set and retrieved indirectly.

```
Public Class TaraStoreClass
  Private StoreName As String = "Tara Store"
  Public Property NewStoreName() As String
    Get
      Return StoreName
    End Get
    Set(ByVal NewValue As String)
      NewStoreName = NewValue
    End Set
  End Property
End Class
```

 You can set the property to read-only by using the keyword ReadOnly. This prevents you from writing to the property. You can also set the property to write-only with the keyword WriteOnly. This allows the value to be changed, but not retrieved from the property. The ReadOnly and WriteOnly keywords are placed before the Property keyword.

Collections

Data can be stored in structures called collections. A **collection** is an object that can store other elements. A collection is like an egg carton. The collection and the egg carton are both containers. You can refer to the carton as a whole, or to an individual egg in that carton. In the same way, you can refer to the collection as a whole, or to each element within the collection.

These elements can be any valid data type such as a string or an integer, an object, or even another collection. Sometimes collections are used to group items you intend to treat in a similar manner. For example, a list of employee names, a list of states, or a list of tax rates would all be used for similar purposes, and so could easily be stored within a collection. This data could also be stored in other types of structures such as a database. However, some data such as the names of the states would require significant processing every time the Web application had to retrieve the list, because it would need to return to the database to get the values. By storing some types of data in a collection, you would not need to use a database.

The `System.Collections` namespace provides access to classes that manage data. The `System.Collections` namespace defines five types of collections. These five collections are the ArrayList, HashTable, SortedList, Queue, and Stack. All collections can store objects such as integers, strings, dates, other objects, and other collections.

There are differences between the collections. The Queue and Stack collections need to rotate through the collection sequentially in order to locate an element. Because each collection is created within the `System.Collections` namespace, they share several properties and methods. The ArrayList, HashTable, and SortedList collections can provide access to any element without having to rotate through the other elements. In the previous chapter you learned to use the ArrayList to store related data. ArrayLists, SortedLists, and HashTables are all collections used to store data. You can use the collection to refer to the group of items, or to refer to an individual item within the collection. Each item in the collection is also referred to as an **element**.

The ArrayList

An **ArrayList** is a series of related data items. The ArrayList object is created from the `System.Array` class. Arrays are objects that are also reference values, which means that they are stored in the memory heap. The ArrayList stores each item in sequential order, and each item is indexed with a number. Therefore, you do not have to worry about defining the size of the ArrayList when you create the array, add items, or remove items. These items are grouped together using a group variable name. Each item in the ArrayList is identified using an index number that indicates its position within the ArrayList. All of the items within the ArrayList are not required to be of the same data type. When you declare the ArrayList, you specify the name of the ArrayList, but you do not need to specify the size of the ArrayList. You must specify that the collection is an ArrayList. The ArrayLists are **zero-based**, which means the first item in the ArrayList is at position 0. So, an ArrayList size of three means that the ArrayList has four items.

Assigning values to elements in an ArrayList is called **populating the ArrayList**. You can populate the ArrayList when you declare it, or you can obtain values from the user with which to populate the ArrayList. To populate the ArrayList, specify the index number, and then specify the value for each element. You populate an element by using the Add method. As with all variables, the value of each element within the ArrayList is undefined until you assign it a value. The sample code that follows this paragraph illustrates how to create an ArrayList named StateAbbrev. The ArrayList is populated with three elements.

```
Dim StateAbbrev As New ArrayList
StateAbbrev.Add("IL")
StateAbbrev.Add("MI")
StateAbbrev.Add("IN")
```

 The **Clear method** can be used to clear the values of all of the elements in the array. The IsArray function returns a Boolean value that indicates whether a variable is an ArrayList. If the variable is an ArrayList, the function returns True, otherwise it returns False.

After the ArrayList is populated, the program can retrieve the value of any element in the array. To retrieve the value of an ArrayList element in the ArrayList, you use the ArrayList name and the index number of the element. You can then use this value in an expression, display it in a Web page, or assign it to a variable. When the array element is used in an expression or assigned to a variable, it must appear on the right side of the assignment operator (=). To write out the first element of an ArrayList to the Web page using Visual Basic .NET, you can write `Response.Write(StateAbbrev(0))`. In the preceding example, you added elements using the Add method. You can create an ArrayList and rotate through the list using the For-Next loop. The following is a list of methods that apply to the ArrayList collection:

- The **Add** and **Remove methods** add or delete a single element.

- The **Insert** and **RemoveAt methods** add and remove elements at a specific location preceding the ArrayList. You can insert or remove an element at a specific index position within the ArrayList by specifying the element's index position number.

- The **AddRange** and **RemoveRange methods** allow you to add or remove a group of elements. When you remove a range, you must specify the index number of the first element you want to delete, and then the number of elements you want to delete.

- The **IndexOf property** returns an integer which represents the index position of the element in the list. A value of –1 means that the element was not found in the list.

- The **Count property** identifies the number of items in the array, which will be the largest index number plus 1.

- The **Clear method** allows you to remove all of the elements within the ArrayList.

In the following sample code, an ArrayList is inserted into the first position, and then removed:

```
StateAbbrev.Insert(0, "OK")
StateAbbrev.Remove("OK")
```

ArrayList elements can be directly manipulated, or the values of the ArrayList elements can be assigned to variables and the variables can be manipulated. In the sample code that follows this paragraph, the index position of the OK element is retrieved and all of the values are written to a TextBox control:

```
Dim iPos as Integer
iPos = StateAbbrev.IndexOf("OK")
Dim MyCount As Integer
MyCount = StateAbbrev.Count
For I = 0 to MyCount -1
    MyStates.Text = StateAbbrev(I) & "<br />"
Next
```

The HashTable

In a previous chapter you used a HashTable to populate a CheckBoxList control in a Web page. The HashTable collection is different from an ArrayList—it creates the index of elements using an alphanumeric key. In other words, each item is referenced by an alphanumeric key, like an encyclopedia. The order in which the elements are stored is based upon a built-in set of rules known as the **hashing algorithm**. The keys are a collection of alphanumeric values, and the values are a collection of elements. When you call the Add method, the key is the first parameter and is passed using quotation marks. The second parameter is the value. The value parameter is separated from the key parameter with a comma.

You can also create a HashTable within a class by declaring the object using the keyword Dim, the name of the HashTable, and the keyword New. You do not need to identify the number of items in the HashTable. You can add items to the HashTable using the **Add method** of the HashTable object to store the items. The items are added using the key and value pair. You can use the key in your programming to retrieve the value for a particular item. Because you have a key and value pair, you must specify the key and value. The **DataValueField** is used to create the value for the control, and the **DataTextField** is used to create the text displayed for the control. You can add and remove items using the Add and **Remove methods**. The sample code following this paragraph would create a HashTable within a class. The code to add a value to the HashTable is HashTableName.Add(key, value).

```
Public Shared Sub Main()
  ' Create & initialize a new Hashtable.
  Dim HS1 As New HashTable()
  HS1.Add("1", "Current Events in Ireland")
  HS1.Add("2", "Fishing in Ireland")
  HS1.Add("3", "An Ghaeilge (The Irish Language)")
  HS1.Add("4", "Hiking in Ireland")
  HS1.Add("5", "Irish History")
  HS1.Add("6", "Irish Music")
  HS1.Add("7", "Irish Step and Set Dancing")
  HS1.Add("8", "Travel in Ireland")
  HS1.Add("9", "Sports in Ireland")
End Sub
```

The **Clear method** of the HashTable class lets you delete all of the elements in the HashTable. The **ContainsKey** and **ContainsValue methods** can help you determine if a key or value exists. These methods are often used before adding or removing an item. For example, you might only want unique values in the HashTable. You could use the ContainsKey method to verify that the element does not already exist before calling the Add method. If the key or value exists, the method returns True.

The SortedList

The SortedList class collection also uses a key, but the collection is indexed by both the key and the item. Because the sorting of the list is based on the key, the index position of the element changes frequently. Therefore, you cannot insert the element based on its index position. You can iterate through the list with a For-Next loop. The Add method allows you to add an element to the SortedList. You can remove the element using the **Remove** or **RemoveAt method**. The **GetKeyList method** is used to provide the collection of keys within the list.

The Queue

The Queue class can only be used to provide sequential access to the elements. This is similar to a roller coaster ride. Typically, the people in the first car are let out first. This sequential ordering system is known as first in, first out (FIFO). There are two parts to the list: the tail, called the enqueue, and the head, called the dequeue. When you add an element to the list, they are added using the enqueue and dequeue methods. You can iterate through the list with a For-Next loop. The following are some methods used to add and remove items from the queue:

- **Enqueue** is used to retrieve an element from the tail of the class.

- **Dequeue** returns each element from the head of the queue. You can remove elements from the head of the queue.

- **Clear** removes all elements.

- **Peek** is a method that returns the element at the head of the queue without removing the element from the queue. If you try to look at an empty queue with the Peek method, the InvalidOperationException is thrown.

- **Contains** is a method that can be used to determine if an element is a member of the queue. If the element exists within the queue, the method returns True.

The Stack

The Stack class provides sequential access but stores the elements in last in, first out (LIFO) order. The stack is similar to the line in a theatre, church, or crowded elevator. The first one to enter the room is the last one to leave the room. The following are some methods used to add and remove items from the stack:

- Add an element in the stack using the **Push method**.

- Remove an element from the stack using the **Pop method**.

- The **Peek** method is used to look at the top of the stack without removing the element from the stack.

Procedures

There are two types of procedures in Visual Basic .NET. Using functions in Visual Basic .NET, you can create a block of code, assign a name to it, and call it from another location. You can also create another kind of code block, called a subprocedure. A **subprocedure** is similar to a function in that it is a block of code that can be called from other locations. This allows you to create blocks of code that can be reused within your Web application rather than writing the same code over and over again. (*Note*: Subprocedures are also called subroutines or methods.)

Subprocedures

Like a function, a subprocedure can accept zero or more arguments. Variables declared within the subprocedure are local and are only available to the subprocedure. When you create the subprocedure, you declare it public or private. The keyword Public is used to explicitly declare the subprocedure public. Public subprocedures are available to all other methods in all the applications, while private subprocedures are only available to other subprocedures in the context in which they are declared.

The main differences between functions and subprocedures are that subprocedures do not return values, and cannot be used in an expression value. Subprocedures are declared using the keyword **Sub**. You can use the `Exit Sub` statement to exit the subprocedure.

Subprocedures are often used to respond to an event such as a button click. The syntax for a subprocedure is shown in the code that follows this paragraph. The keyword Sub indicates that the subprocedure is being created. The name of the subprocedure and the parameters are identified in the Sub statement. The subprocedure can issue action and control statements. The end of the subprocedure is identified with the keywords `End Sub`. It is important to note that the order in which procedures are declared does not affect the order of their execution. Subprocedures always execute in the order in which they are called, not the order in which they are created. You can call multiple subprocedures in the same function.

```
Sub SubprocedureName (parameters)

        Action and Control Statements

End Sub
```

Subprocedures can be used more than once and anywhere within your application, including within other subprocedures, functions, or control structures. Once your method has been declared, it is executed by specifying the name of the subprocedure. The keyword **Call** can be used to call a function or subprocedure and is optional. If you use the Call keyword, then the parameters passed to the subprocedure must be enclosed in parentheses. Multiple arguments are passed in a comma-delimited list. The code following this paragraph is the syntax for calling a method in Visual Basic .NET. Using the **Call** keyword makes your code easier to read.

```
[Call] SubprocedureName (arguments)
```

Functions cannot define other functions, but they can call other functions and subprocedures. You can call multiple subprocedures in the same function. This allows for a program to be segmented. Segments can be reused in other scripts, which can help you produce more efficient code. The subprocedures are executed in the order they are called. Each step can be called separately from the program. One benefit of using multiple methods is that if one of the steps changes, then only that step needs to be modified. By using multiple subprocedures instead of combining them into one, each subprocedure can be reused without having to rewrite entire sections of code. If multiple variables are to be used across functions and procedures, they need to be global to the application and defined before the functions and procedures that reference them.

You previously learned that subprocedures do not return values. However, there are ways to access values from a subprocedure. The subprocedures can assign their value to the value property of one of the Web Form controls. This way, the values can be made available to multiple subprocedures.

Event Procedure

As you previously learned, when you call an event handler from within the ASP.NET controls, the event handler is identified with the prefix "on" and the event name. Events such as Click are intercepted by event handlers such as onServerClick. You can intercept the event using an event handler. The **event procedure** is the code which will execute when the event handler intercepts the event. When you open the code behind the page, the

Page_Load event procedure is created by default. An **event procedure** is a procedure that is attached to an object. An event procedure is not executed until an event triggers the event procedure. The Page_Load event procedure is triggered when the page is loaded into the browser. An event procedure does not return a value. When an object recognizes an event, it immediately calls the event procedure. The event procedure provides a connection between the object and the code.

Event procedure names are based upon the name of the object and the event name. An underscore (_) is used to separate the object name and the event name. For example, if you create a button named btnExit that calls an event procedure when it is clicked, you name the event procedure btnExit_onServerClick. You must assign the name of the object in the page code before you define an event procedure. If you change the name of an object after defining an event procedure for that object, you must change the name of the procedure to match the new name of the object. Note that the event procedure is not called, but rather is triggered when the event occurs for that specific object. The object calls the event procedure when it detects that the event has occurred. The following is the syntax for creating event procedures:

```
Sub objectName_eventHandler(sender as Object, e as EventArgs)

      action and control statements

End Sub
```

Functions

A **function** is a block of code that is grouped into a named unit. Functions are also procedures and are implemented with the keyword Function. Visual Basic .NET supports built-in and user-defined functions. Built-in functions are inherited from a class within the .NET Framework. There are hundreds of built-in functions available within the .NET Framework. For example, you can locate more information on string functions at *http://msdn.microsoft.com/library/en-us/vbcn7/html/vaconmanipulatingstrings.asp.*

You use the keyword **Function** to identify the start of a user-defined function. The function is identified by a unique name. You can declare a function as public, private, protected, or friend. The public, private, protected, or friend status is identified before the Function keyword, as shown in the following code:

```
Public Function GetStoreName() As Integer
'This function returns an integer
    Return 23422
End Function
```

Passing an Argument to a Function

A pair of parentheses follows the name of the function. Within the parentheses you include zero or more **arguments**, also known as **parameters**, which are passed to the function when it is called. If no arguments are passed, you use an empty pair of parentheses. If multiple arguments are used, you use a comma to separate each argument. You can call the function several times, passing different arguments each time. The result of the function is different each time, because the argument that was passed was different each time.

Returning a Value from a Function

The block of code can contain any number of action statements or control statements. A function can return a value—one value only—to the script that called it, but it does not necessarily return a value. The keyword **Return** is used to identify the value that is returned to the function call. Usually the code assigns the value returned by the function to a variable. If no return value is explicitly identified by the function, the return value is the default value of the function's definition. When the Return statement executes, control of the program passes back to the calling procedure. No statements are executed following the Return statement. The functionality of the Return statement is similar to the Exit Function statement described in the following section.

Exiting a Function

In Visual Basic .NET the keywords Exit Function are used to exit a function. **Exit Function** is a jumping control; jumping controls allow you to temporarily halt the execution of a code block and move to another section of code outside the function. Unlike the End Function statement that appears at the end of a function, the Exit Function statement can appear as an action statement in the middle of the function code, as shown in the following code:

```
Public Function GetStoreName() As String
    Dim UserName as String
    UserName = txtUserName.text.ToString
    If UserName = "Admin" then
        Return "Welcome Administrator!"
        Exit Function
    Else
        Return "Welcome!"
        Exit Function
    End If
End Function
```

Creating a Function

You can create a function within the class of the Web page, or within the Visual Basic .NET file. In the sample code that follows this paragraph, the function GetStoreName returns a string to the code that called the function. The function is public, so it can be accessed from outside of the class. (*Note*: If you want to make the methods and functions public, you can also put them into a Visual Basic .NET module. The module is not contained within any one class, so it is available to all classes.)

```
Public Class TaraStoreClass
  Public Function GetStoreName() As String
    Return "Tara Store"
  End Function
End Class
```

You can call the function from within the code behind the page, or from within another section of code within the class. The following sample instantiates a new object and calls the GetStoreName function from the new object:

```
GetTheFunction(New TaraStoreClass().GetStoreName)
```

Using Visual Basic .NET in a Web Page

In the following exercise, you will use Visual Studio .NET to create an ASP.NET page, and you will insert your business logic in the code behind the page using Visual Basic .NET.

1. Double-click the **SampleUsingVB.aspx** file in the Solution Explorer window to open it.

2. Double-click in the whitespace on the page to open the code behind the page. Insert a blank line after the End Class statement located at the bottom of the page. Create a new class named **TSClass1**. Add the code to create a function named **GetStoreName** that returns a string that contains the name of the store in Chicago, as shown in the code that follows this paragraph. Add another function named **GetStoreImage** that returns a string with the filename of the Chicago Store image. (*Note*: Don't forget to add the code to end the class.) You can refer to Figure 5-9 to see how the code appears within Visual Studio .NET.

```
Public Class TSClass1
  Public Function GetStoreName() As String
    Return "Tara Store - Chicago"
  End Function
  Public Function GetStoreImage() As String
    Return "ChicagoStore.jpg"
  End Function
End Class
```

3. With the code that follows this paragraph, create a new class named **TSClass2**. Add the code to create two private instance variables, named **StoreName** and **StoreImage**. Declare both as String and assign the values of the store name and image to the variables.

```
Public Class TSClass2
    Private StoreName As String = "Tara Store - New York"
    Private StoreImage As String = "NewYorkStore.jpg"
```

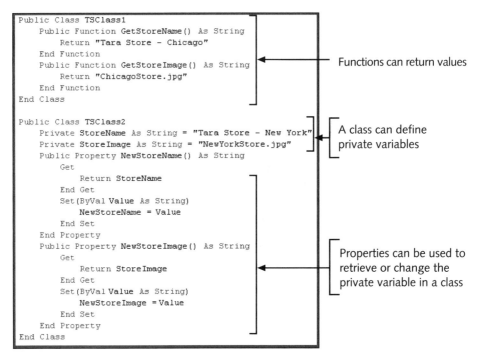

```
Public Class TSClass1
    Public Function GetStoreName() As String
        Return "Tara Store - Chicago"
    End Function
    Public Function GetStoreImage() As String          ◄─── Functions can return values
        Return "ChicagoStore.jpg"
    End Function
End Class

Public Class TSClass2
    Private StoreName As String = "Tara Store - New York"    A class can define
    Private StoreImage As String = "NewYorkStore.jpg"        private variables
    Public Property NewStoreName() As String
        Get
            Return StoreName
        End Get
        Set(ByVal Value As String)
            NewStoreName = Value
        End Set
    End Property
    Public Property NewStoreImage() As String          Properties can be used to
        Get                                            ◄─── retrieve or change the
            Return StoreImage                          private variable in a class
        End Get
        Set(ByVal Value As String)
            NewStoreImage = Value
        End Set
    End Property
End Class
```

Figure 5-9   Creating functions and properties within Visual Studio .NET

4. With the code that follows the Tip below, create a property called
   NewStoreName. Return the value of the private StoreName variable to the
   NewStoreName property when it is called. Create the code to allow the class
   to set the property of the variable as shown in the code that follows the Tip.

IntelliSense sets up the basic code structure after you enter the public property.
Be careful not to repeat this code:

```
Public Property NewStoreName() As String
    Get
        Return StoreName
    End Get
    Set(ByVal Value As String)
        NewStoreName = Value
    End Set
End Property
```

5. With the code that follows this paragraph, create a property named **NewStoreImage**. Return the value of the private StoreImage variable to the NewStoreImage property when it is called. Create the code that follows this paragraph to allow a class to set the property of the variable. (*Note*: Don't forget to add the code to end the class.)

```
Public Property NewStoreImage() As String
    Get
        Return StoreImage
    End Get
    Set(ByVal Value As String)
        NewStoreImage = Value
    End Set
End Property
End Class
```

6. Click the **Save All** button. Click **Build** on the menu bar, then click **Build Solution**.

7. Add the code that follows this paragraph in the Page_Load event handler to declare three string variables and to assign the default message in the topics and title Label controls. You can see the complete code as it appears in Visual Studio .NET in Figure 5-10.

```
Dim strClass, strStoreName, strStoreImage As String
lblTopics.Text = "Please select the Tara Store" & _
    " you would like to visit:"
lblTitle.Text = "Welcome to Tara Store"
```

8. Type the code that follows this paragraph to create an If-Then statement that determines if the user has visited the page before. If this is the first time, then set the properties of the RadioButtonList control and declare an array that contains two values. Bind these two values to the RadioButtonList control using the DataBind method.

```
If Not Page.IsPostBack Then
  RBL.RepeatLayout = RepeatLayout.Table
  RBL.RepeatDirection = RepeatDirection.Vertical
  Dim AR1 As New ArrayList(2)
  AR1.Add("Tara Store in Chicago.")
  AR1.Add("Tara Store in New York.")
  RBL.DataSource = AR1
  RBL.DataBind()
```

 Visual Studio .NET inserts the End statements when you insert a beginning statement such as If-Then or Select-Case. If you enter the End statement twice you will generate an error.

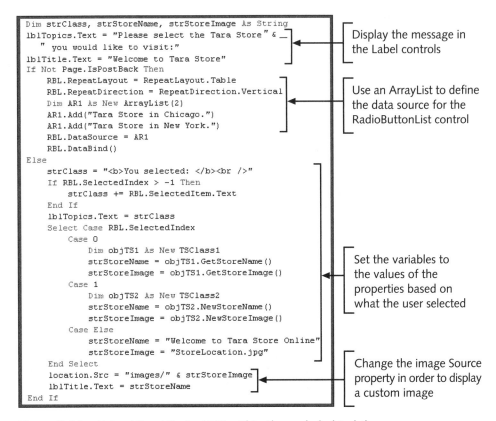

```
Dim strClass, strStoreName, strStoreImage As String
lblTopics.Text = "Please select the Tara Store" & _
    " you would like to visit:"
lblTitle.Text = "Welcome to Tara Store"
If Not Page.IsPostBack Then
    RBL.RepeatLayout = RepeatLayout.Table
    RBL.RepeatDirection = RepeatDirection.Vertical
    Dim AR1 As New ArrayList(2)
    AR1.Add("Tara Store in Chicago.")
    AR1.Add("Tara Store in New York.")
    RBL.DataSource = AR1
    RBL.DataBind()
Else
    strClass = "<b>You selected: </b><br />"
    If RBL.SelectedIndex > -1 Then
        strClass += RBL.SelectedItem.Text
    End If
    lblTopics.Text = strClass
    Select Case RBL.SelectedIndex
        Case 0
            Dim objTS1 As New TSClass1
            strStoreName = objTS1.GetStoreName()
            strStoreImage = objTS1.GetStoreImage()
        Case 1
            Dim objTS2 As New TSClass2
            strStoreName = objTS2.NewStoreName()
            strStoreImage = objTS2.NewStoreImage()
        Case Else
            strStoreName = "Welcome to Tara Store Online"
            strStoreImage = "StoreLocation.jpg"
    End Select
    location.Src = "images/" & strStoreImage
    lblTitle.Text = strStoreName
End If
```

Display the message in the Label controls

Use an ArrayList to define the data source for the RadioButtonList control

Set the variables to the values of the properties based on what the user selected

Change the image Source property in order to display a custom image

Figure 5-10   Using Visual Basic .NET within the code behind the page

9. Type the code that follows this paragraph. If the user has visited the page before, then IsPostback is True. In this case, assign a value to the strClass variable, which is a concatenated string. The string contains a bolded heading statement and the value of the Text property of the RadioButtonList control that the user selects.

```
Else
    strClass = "<b>You selected: </b><br />"
    If RBL.SelectedIndex > -1 Then
        strClass += RBL.SelectedItem.Text
    End If
    lblTopics.Text = strClass
```

10. Type the code that follows this paragraph to create a Select Case statement to determine which RadioButtonList control is selected using the SelectedIndex property. If the first item is selected, then create a new object named **objTS1** based upon TSClass1. TSClass1 contains two values, which can be accessed using the functions GetStoreName and GetStoreImage. Both functions return strings that can be assigned to the strStoreName and strStoreImage variables.

GetStoreName returns a message that identifies the store name as the Tara Store – Chicago. GetStoreImage returns a message that identifies the store image as ChicagoStore.jpg.

```
Select Case RBL.SelectedIndex
Case 0
  Dim objTS1 As New TSClass1
  strStoreName = objTS1.GetStoreName()
  strStoreImage = objTS1.GetStoreImage()
```

11. Add the code that follows this paragraph. This code runs if the second item is selected, and then creates a new object named **objTS2** based upon TSClass2. TSClass2 contains two values, which can be accessed using the properties NewStoreName and NewStoreImage. Both Property methods return a string that can be assigned to the strStoreName and strStoreImage variables. NewStoreName returns a message that identifies the store name as the Tara Store – New York. NewStoreImage returns a message that identifies the store image as NewYorkStore.jpg. These values are not stored in the properties, but within the private variables within the Property method. Therefore, you are accessing the values of these variables indirectly.

```
Case 1
  Dim objTS2 As New TSClass2
  strStoreName = objTS2.NewStoreName()
  strStoreImage = objTS2.NewStoreImage()
```

12. With the code that follows this paragraph, create a Select Case statement that runs if neither item is selected. Assign strings to the strStoreName and strStoreImage variables that contain the name of the store and the filename of the image to be displayed in the Web page. (*Note*: Don't forget to end the Select Case statement with the keywords End Select.)

```
Case Else
  strStoreName = "Welcome to Tara Store Online"
  strStoreImage = "StoreLocation.jpg"
End Select
```

13. Now you use the variables that have been retrieved from the classes to set the properties of the Web page controls. Type the code that follows this paragraph. The strStoreImage variable is concatenated with the path to the images directory and assigned to the Source property of the Image control named location. The strStoreName variable is assigned to the Text property of a Label control named lblTitle. (*Note*: Make sure not to delete the End Sub and End Class keywords at the bottom of the code.)

```
location.Src = "images/" & strStoreImage
lblTitle.Text = strStoreName
End If
```

14. Click the **Save All** button. Click **Build** on the menu bar, and then click **Build Solution**.

15. Click the **SampleUsingVB.aspx** tab in the main window. Click the **Design** tab to change to Design view if necessary. Right-click on the page, and then click **View in Browser**. When you click the radio buttons, the messages in both Label controls change, and the image changes as shown in Figure 5-11. (*Note:* You can also view the page in your browser at *http://localhost/ chapter5/SampleUsingVB.aspx.*)

16. Close any open pages.

Figure 5-11   Using Visual Basic .NET to display variables within a Web page

INTRODUCTION TO C#

C# is a new language created by Microsoft to allow non-Visual Basic .NET programmers to take advantage of the powerful features of Visual Studio .NET. The syntax of C# is similar to JavaScript and C++. However, it is important to remember that when the program is compiled by the C# compiler, the code is compiled into the same managed Intermediate Language code as that generated by the Visual Basic .NET compiler.

As you learned in Chapter 1, all of the .NET Framework, the .NET base classes, and the Visual Studio development environment are available across programming languages. So, you can include programs written with C# within your ASP.NET application. In addition, you have access to the same Windows Form tools and ASP.NET Web Form tools. Therefore, the user interface to your application is not language dependent. You can create your Web Form the same way for all .NET programming languages. In this book, you use Visual Basic .NET primarily because most beginning programming courses use Visual Basic. However, once you learn one programming language, the programming concepts are similar with other languages. It is useful to be aware of the differences between programming languages. In addition, some of the samples you may find on the Internet are written in C#. If you are familiar with some of the structure of the C# application, you can convert the C# code into Visual Basic .NET.

 When you open the QuickStart Web site at *http://localhost/quickstart/*, you can specify the samples to be displayed by default using C# by changing the drop-down list box located in the upper-right corner from VB to C# (C# is pronounced *C-Sharp*).

One of the first things that you will notice in a C# program is that each statement ends with a semicolon. The semicolon is called the line termination character because it indicates the end of the statement. Therefore, you can write statements that extend across multiple lines without using an underscore, because the program knows that the end of the statement occurs where the semicolon is located. C# uses the plus sign as the concatenation operator instead of the ampersand that is used in Visual Basic .NET. The following sample code shows how to concatenate strings in C#:

```
var s1 : String;
var s2 : String = "Welcome to ";
s2 += "Tara Store";
s1 = s2 + " !!!";
```

To improve performance, you can use the **StringBuilder class**. The StringBuilder class is available to both Visual Basic .NET and C#. The sample code that follows this paragraph shows how to concatenate strings in C# using the StringBuilder class. The Append method is used to concatenate two or more strings.

```
var s1:StringBuilder = new StringBuilder();
s1.Append("Welcome to ");
s1.Append("Tara Store");
s1.Append(" !!!");
```

One difference between the two programs is that C# is case sensitive. You must be careful about the names of variables, properties, namespaces, functions, and other programming keywords. In C# you often use lowercase for the names of programming elements within the C# language.

When you assign a value to a variable in C#, you do not have to use the keyword Dim to declare it. When you declare a string variable, you must indicate in both languages that the variable is a string data type. In Visual Basic .NET, you use the keywords As String after the variable name. In C# you specify the data type first, String, then you specify the variable name; don't forget that the data types are different and are transformed to the Common Language Runtime data types at compile time. When you create an object data type in Visual Basic .NET, you declare the object using the keyword Dim and the object name. Then, you assign the name using the keyword **As** to **New Object()**, where Object is the name of the class that is used to create the new object. In C#, you do not use Dim or As keywords. You specify the data type of the object first, then the name of the object. You use the assignment operator **new Object()**, where the keyword New is lowercase. If you declare the variable public in Visual Basic .NET, you capitalize the first letter in Public. If you declare the variable public in C#, you use all lowercase letters for the keyword Public. The following sample code shows how to declare a variable and assign it a value in C#:

```
String StoreName = "Tara Store";
int counter = 1;
```

Comments in C# are similar to comments in JavaScript. A single line comment is preceded by two forward slashes. A multiline comment begins with a forward slash and an asterisk. After the comment, an asterisk and forward slash mark the end of the comment. The following sample code illustrates how to create a comment in C#:

```
// This is a single line comment
/*
This is a multiline comment
Always document your code
*/
```

When you create an array using C# instead of using parentheses around the index position, use square brackets. Anytime you work with one or more statements, you enclose the code in curly braces. This nesting of code within curly braces is the same in JavaScript and C#. Certain types of control structures use the curly braces to indicate which blocks of code should be executed. In a Visual Basic .NET If-Then statement, the keyword Then is used to identify the first block of code. Because there are no curly braces, there is also an End If statement to indicate when the function ends. In C#, the If-Then statement does not require the Then or End If keywords because the curly braces indicate which blocks of code are executed when the statement is True or False.

CHAPTER SUMMARY

❐ Object-oriented programming languages support concepts such as abstraction, encapsulation, polymorphism, and inheritance. The process of creating an object from a class is called instantiation.

❐ The keyword Inherits identifies the name of the class that is created in the code behind the Web page. The keyword Imports is used to identify the namespaces used within the code behind the page.

❐ The IL Disassembler (ILDASM) can be used to view the assembly, namespaces, classes, functions, methods, and properties within your compiled .dll file. The compiled .dll file is located in the bin directory. You can create multiple classes within a single class file. The compiler places all the classes into a single namespace by default.

❐ Variables are used to store data. You must assign a data type to a variable when the variable is created. You can also assign a value to the variable when the variable is created. All data types are the same across languages after the application is compiled into managed code. Data types in Visual Basic .NET include String, Boolean, Date, Char, Byte, Short, Integer, Long, Decimal.

❐ Instance variables are variables defined within a class. Option explicit is used to force all variables to be declared before they can be used. You cannot start a variable with a number. You can start the name of a variable with an underscore or letter.

❐ Value types are stored in the stack and consist of primitive types such as Boolean, Integer, Decimal, Char, and DateTime. Reference types are stored on the managed heap and consist of strings, classes, arrays, collections, and objects. The garbage collector manages the memory addresses within the managed heap.

❐ Properties are used to set the value of a variable defined within an object. Public means that the properties, variables, and methods can interact with other objects outside of the base class. Private variables can only be called within the base class. Protected variables can be called from within the base class, and within subclasses. Friend variables can be called from anywhere within the same application or project.

❐ A property is a method that is used to get and set values. You can directly manipulate variables within a class, or you can use a property to indirectly read and change the variable.

❐ Constants are used to store values in variables that do not change within the application. The keyword Const is used to declare the constant. The value must be specified when the constant is declared.

❐ The concatenation operator in Visual Basic .NET is the ampersand. In C# the concatenation operator is the plus sign. In Visual Basic .NET there is no line termination character. If you write code that expands over multiple lines you must use the line continuation character, which is the underscore. In C# the line termination character, which is the semicolon, is used to identify the end of a statement.

❐ ArrayLists, HashTables, SortedLists, Queues, and Stacks are examples of collections. When you create a collection, you must declare the name of the collection first. Each item in the collection is referred to by its index position, which is in parentheses. In C# the index position is contained within square brackets. The Add method can be used with the HashTable or ArrayList to add items to the collection. Remove is used to remove items from the HashTable or ArrayList.

❐ Procedures are used to organize the order in which the code is executed. The event handlers are used to execute code when an event occurs. The two types of procedures are functions and subprocedures. Functions are used to return values. Subprocedures do not return a value to the code that called it. Functions use the keyword Return to return the value to the code that called the function. The values that are passed to the subprocedure or function are called parameters. Multiple parameters are separated by commas when they are passed to the procedure.

❑ C# is a new programming language that can be used to create ASP.NET applications. Although the syntax of C# code is different from that of Visual Basic .NET, they share the same development tools, .NET base classes, and .NET Framework.

REVIEW QUESTIONS

1. Which of the following is not a value type?

   a. Boolean

   b. Integer

   c. Char

   d. ArrayList

2. Where is the reference type stored in memory?

   a. in the garbage heap

   b. in the memory heap

   c. in the memory stack

   d. in the managed heap

3. Which object-oriented feature enables you to create code that can be applied to objects that are derived from different classes?

   a. abstraction

   b. encapsulation

   c. polymorphism

   d. inheritance

4. Which object-oriented feature is the ability to create a concept using code?

   a. instantiation

   b. abstraction

   c. polymorphism

   d. inheritance

5. What is the process for creating an object from a class?

   a. instantiation

   b. polymorphism

   c. inheritance

   d. abstraction

6. Which access modifier makes an element available anywhere within the application or project?

   a. public

   b. private

   c. friend

   d. dim

7. Which access modifier makes an element available anywhere to any class?

   a. public

   b. private

   c. friend

   d. protected

8. Which keyword identified the class that the aspx file will be compiled with?

   a. Instantiate

   b. Inherits

   c. Imports

   d. Integer

9. Which term when used in code requires you to declare all variables before they are used?

   a. instantiation

   b. instance

   c. option explicit

   d. option strict

10. Which of the following is the only variable name that is allowed in Visual Basic .NET?

   a. My_ImageName

   b. Public

   c. Image Name

   d. $NewImage

11. What is the concatenation operator in Visual Basic .NET?

   a. $ (dollar sign)

   b. ' (single quotation mark)

   c. '' (quotation marks)

   d. & (ampersand)

5

12. What is the line termination character in C#?

    a. _ (underscore)

    b. & (ampersand)

    c. ; (semicolon)

    d. + (plus sign)

13. Which collection is used to store the sort index and the key?

    a. HashTable

    b. Variables

    c. Properties

    d. Parameters

14. Which of the following returns a value?

    a. subprocedure

    b. procedure

    c. event procedure

    d. function

15. What is a subprocedure also known as?

    a. a function

    b. a subroutine

    c. an event procedure

    d. an event handler

16. What is used to separate multiple arguments passed to a function?

    a. ; (semicolon)

    b. : (colon)

    c. / (forward slash)

    d. , (comma)

17. Which keyword is used to stop a program from writing to a private variable within a property?

    a. Read Only

    b. WriteOnly

    c. ReadOnly

    d. Write Only

5

18. Which are possible values for a Boolean variable?

    a. 0 or 1

    b. T or F

    c. True or False

    d. On or Off

19. Which format method outputs the value 1441.33 with a dollar sign preceding the value?

    a. `System.Console.WriteLine({"0:c"}, 1441.33)`

    b. `System.Console.WriteLine({"0:N"}, 1441.33)`

    c. `System.Console.WriteLine({"0:D"}, 1441.33)`

    d. `System.Console.WriteLine({"0:x"}, 1441.33)`

20. Which numeric data type is a 32-bit number?

    a. Byte

    b. Short

    c. Long

    d. Integer

21. Which data type stores values between –32,768 and 32,767?

    a. Byte

    b. Short

    c. Long

    d. Integer

22. Which keyword is used to declare a constant variable?

    a. Var

    b. Dim

    c. Con

    d. Const

HANDS-ON PROJECTS

Project 5-1

In this project, you will create an ASP.NET page that creates a class using Visual Basic .NET.

1. Start **Visual Studio .NET** and open your **Chapter5** solution, if it is not already open.

2. In Visual Studio .NET create a class named **Ch5Proj1VBC** that is stored in a file named **Ch5Proj1VBC.vb**.

3. Create a public instance variable named **StoreAddress** that is a String data type. Assign the value **555 Michigan Avenue, Chicago, IL 60016** to the variable.

4. Click the **Save All** button to save the class file.

5. Double-click the **Ch5Proj1.aspx** file in the Solution Explorer window.

6. Double-click on the whitespace on the page to open the code behind the page. In the Page_Load procedure add the code that follows this paragraph to create a new object named **Ch5Proj1Class**, based on the Ch5Proj1VBC class. Because the variable contains an object, the keyword New must be used to instantiate the object from a class. As you type each period, notice that the IntelliSense list box appears. Your Chapter5 namespace contains a class named Ch5Proj1 and a class named Ch5Proj1VBC.

```
Dim Ch5Proj1Class As New Chapter5.Ch5Proj1VBC
```

7. Type the code that follows this paragraph to retrieve the values from the new class and assign the variable from the class to the Text property of the lblContact Label control in the Web page. (*Note:* You need to use the ToString method to retrieve the value from the string stored in the variable.)

```
lblContact.Text = Ch5Proj1Class.StoreAddress.ToString()
```

8. Click the **Save All** button. Click **Build** on the menu bar, then click **Build Solution**. Return to Design view of the file Ch5Proj1.aspx.

9. Right-click on the page, and then click **View in Browser**. (*Note:* You can go to a browser and try to view the page at *http://localhost/chapter5/Ch5Proj1.aspx*.)

10. Print the Web page, the ASP.NET source code, and the code behind the page within Visual Studio .NET. Close all your pages.

Project 5-2

In this project, you view the compiled assembly and class you created in the previous exercise using the ILDASM tool. You must complete Project 5-1 before you can complete this project.

1. Start **Visual Studio .NET** and open your **Chapter5** solution if necessary.

2. Go to the Visual Studio .NET command prompt. In most computers, to access this command prompt, click **Start**, point to **All Programs**, point to **Microsoft Visual Studio .NET**, point to **Visual Studio .NET Tools**, and then click **Visual Studio .NET Command Prompt**.

3. At the command prompt, enter **cd \Inetpub\wwwroot\Chapter5\bin**. By default, your assembly is compiled and placed within this directory.

4. Open the .dll file using the ILDASM. At the command prompt, type **ILDASM Chapter5.dll**. The ILDASM window opens. (*Note:* The name of your assembly and the namespace is Chapter5, which is also the name of your .dll file.)

5. Click the **plus sign** next to the Chapter5 icon to expand the Chapter5 namespace. The namespace is the blue shield icon.

6. Click **File** on the menu bar, and then click **Dump TreeView**. In the Save As dialog box type the filename **Ch5Proj2.txt**. Make sure to save the file in your C:\Inetpub\wwwroot\Chapter5\ directory. Then, click the **Save** button. Figure 5-12 shows the tree view of the Chapter5 assembly. (*Note:* When you create a Web Form page or a class file, the module is created and included within the assembly. Because you may have created different Web Form modules and class modules, you may have a different list of classes than the ones shown here.)

7. Start **Notepad**, click **File** on the menu bar, and then click **Open**. Browse to locate your C:\Inetpub\wwwroot\Chapter5\ directory. Select the file **Ch5Proj2.txt**, and then click **Open**. A text view of the assembly will be displayed in the file.

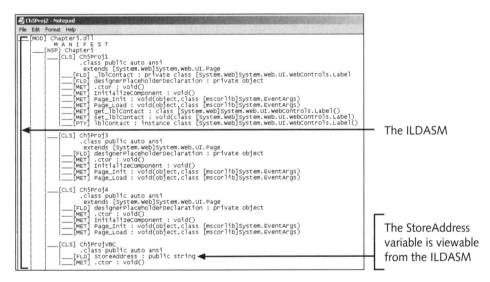

The ILDASM

The StoreAddress variable is viewable from the ILDASM

Figure 5-12   Retrieving the values of variables defined within an object

8. Print the file, and then exit Notepad.

9. Close the ILDASM windows and the command prompt window by clicking the **Close** button in each window.

10. Close any open pages.

Project 5-3

In this project, you create a Web page that uses a property to retrieve the values of private variables defined in a class.

1. Start **Visual Studio .NET** and open your **Chapter5** solution if necessary.

2. Double-click the **Ch5Proj3.aspx** file in the Solution Explorer window.

3. Double-click in the whitespace on the page to open the code behind the page. In the Page_Load procedure, add the code that follows this paragraph to create a new object named **objCh5Proj3Class**, based on the Ch5Proj3Class class. Because the variable contains an object, the keyword New must be used to instantiate the object from a class. You will create the Ch5Proj3Class class in Step 5.

```
Dim strClass As String
Dim objCh5Proj3Class As New Chapter5.Ch5Proj3Class
```

4. Type the code that follows this paragraph to retrieve the property named NewStoreAddress from the object you just created. Assign the value to the strClass varible. Assign the variable contents to the Text property of the Topics Label control. (*Note*: Don't delete the End Sub and End Class keywords that were put in by Visual Studio .NET.)

```
strClass = objCh5Proj3Class.NewStoreAddress()
lblTopics.Text = strClass
```

5. Type the code following this paragraph to create a public class named **Ch5Proj3Class**. The class declaration entered should be placed below the End Class statement of the Ch5Proj3 class.

```
Public Class Ch5Proj3Class
```

6. Type the code that follows this paragraph to assign the street address provided to the private variable named **StoreAddress**. The variable should be a String data type.

```
Private StoreAddress As String = _
    "555 Michigan Avenue, Chicago, IL 60016"
```

7. Type the code that follows this paragraph to create a read-only property named **NewStoreAddress**, which contains a string. Return the private StoreAddress variable when the NewStoreAddress property is called. (*Note*: Don't delete the End Class keywords that Visual Studio .NET adds to the page.)

```
Public ReadOnly Property NewStoreAddress() As String
    Get
        Return StoreAddress
    End Get
End Property
End Class
```

8. Click the **Save All** button. Click **Build** on the menu bar, and then click **Build Solution**. Return to the Ch5Proj3.aspx page.

9. Click the **Design** tab to return to Design view if necessary. Right-click the page, and then click **View in Browser**. The store's name and address are displayed under the graphic.

10. Print the Web page, the ASP.NET source code, and the code behind the page within Visual Studio .NET. Close any open pages.

Project 5-4

In this project, you create a class and create a custom message based on the user input from the ASP.NET page.

1. Start **Visual Studio .NET** and open your **Chapter5** solution if necessary.

2. Double-click the **Ch5Proj4.aspx** file in the Solution Explorer window.

3. Double-click in the whitespace on the page to open the code behind the page. In the Page_Load procedure, use the IsPostBack property to determine if the user has been to the page before. If the user has not been to the page before, display the default message and image. Add the following code to assign the Source property for the location image and Text property of the Title control:

```
If Not Page.IsPostBack Then
    location.Src = "images/" & "StoreLocation.jpg"
    lblTitle.Text = "Welcome to Tara Store"
```

4. Type the code that follows this paragraph, which determines if the user has visited the page before and declares a variable named strEntered to store the value the user types in the text box named txtLocation. Assign the value entered to the strEntered variable. Use this variable to change the Text property of the title Label control named lblTitle.

```
Else
    Dim strEntered As String
    strEntered = txtLocation.Text
    lblTitle.Text = strEntered
```

5. Add the code that follows this paragraph to create a new object named **objCh5Proj4Class** based on the Ch5Proj4Class class. Because the variable contains an object, the keyword New must be used to instantiate the object from a class. You will create the Ch5Proj4Class class in Step 8.

```
Dim objCh5Proj4Class As New Chapter5.Ch5Proj4Class
```

6. Add the code that follows this paragraph to call a function named **ChangeImage** within the class. Pass the strEntered variable as a parameter to the function. The variable contains the information that the user typed in the text box. The function uses this information to change a property that stores the image name.

```
objCh5Proj4Class.ChangeImage(strEntered)
```

7. Type the code that follows this paragraph to declare a string variable named **strNewImage** to store the name of the new image. Use the NewStoreImage property to retrieve a new image name and assign it to the variable you just created. Then, display the message and the image name in the topics Label control.

Change the source property of the location image object to the images directory and to the new image filename that is stored in the strNewImage variable.

```
Dim strNewImage As String
strNewImage = objCh5Proj4Class.NewStoreImage()
lblTopics.Text = "The image above is: " & strNewImage
location.Src = "images/" & strNewImage
End If
```

8. With the code that follows this paragraph, create a new file named **Ch5Proj4Class.vb**, which contains a public class named **Ch5Proj4Class**. Verify that the class definition is entered correctly by Visual Studio .NET.

```
Public Class Ch5Proj4Class
End Class
```

9. Within the class definition, type the code that follows this paragraph to assign the store image provided to the private variable named StoreImage. The variable should be a String data type. Assign StoreLocation.jpg as the default value in the StoreImage variable.

```
Private StoreImage As String = "StoreLocation.jpg"
```

10. Type the code that follows this paragraph to create a property named **NewStoreImage**, which contains a string. Return the private StoreImage variable when the NewStoreImage property is called.

```
Public Property NewStoreImage() As String
  Get
    Return StoreImage
  End Get
```

11. Type the code that follows this paragraph. The code uses the Set keyword to assign a new value to the StoreImage private variable.

```
Set(ByVal Value As String)
  StoreImage = Value
End Set
End Property
```

12. Type the code that follows this paragraph to create a function named **ChangeImage**. The function receives a string value when it is called. Use the Select Case control structure to determine which city the user entered in the text box. Provide a default selection for users who did not enter the correct text. This function assigns a new value to the private variable in the property method. (*Note*: Don't delete the End Class keywords that Visual Studio .NET adds to the page.)

```
Public Sub ChangeImage(ByVal StoreLocation As String)
    Select Case StoreLocation
      Case "Chicago Store"
        StoreImage = "ChicagoStore.jpg"
      Case "New York Store"
        StoreImage = "NewYorkStore.jpg"
      Case Else
```

```
                    StoreImage = "StoreLocation.jpg"
              End Select
        End Sub
```

13. Click the **Save All** button. Click **Build** on the menu bar, and then click **Build Solution**. Return to the Ch5Proj4.aspx page.

14. Click the **Design** tab to return to Design view if necessary. Right-click on the page, and then click **View in Browser**. Type **New York Store** in the text box and click the **Submit** button. The image and heading will change, and the Label control will be visible and indicate the name of the image. Figure 5-13 shows you what the page looks like before and after you submit the form.

The value selected will change the image Source property and the message in the Label control

Figure 5-13   Using properties to change variables with Visual Basic .NET

15. Print the Web page, the ASP.NET source code, and the code behind the page within Visual Studio .NET.

CASE PROJECTS

Tara Store — Using a Class to Store Global Variables

You have been assigned to create a class to store variables that will be reused throughout your Web site. Your manager would like you to create a class named Ch5Case1Class.vb, which will contain the properties for the Web site. The properties should be public so that they can be directly changed via the Web page. You must create a Web page to retrieve and display these values. Create a Web page named Ch5Case1.aspx that displays these properties. You need to create properties to store the name of the store (Tara Store), the address (555 Michigan Ave, Chicago IL 60016), e-mail address (info@tarastore.com), phone number (800-555-5555), store description (We provide a variety of Irish cultural products including china, crystal, pottery, food, clothing, books, music, jewelry, bridal, and gifts.), number of visitors per year (3,245,120), and tax rate (8%). Add graphics, color, content, and text to enhance the appearance of your Web page. Print out the Web page and the source code of the Web page and the code behind the page, and the Ch5Case1Class.vb page.

Tara Store — Using Properties to Store Global Variables

You have been assigned to create a method to store variables that will be reused throughout your Web site. Your manager would like you to create a class named Ch5Case2Class.vb, which will contain the properties for the Web site. The properties should be private so that they cannot be directly changed via the Web page. You must create a Web page to retrieve and display these values. Create a Web page named Ch5Case2.aspx that displays these properties. You need to create properties to store the name of the store (Tara Store), the address (555 Michigan Ave, Chicago IL 60016), e-mail address (info@tarastore.com), phone number (800-555-5555), store description (We provide a variety of Irish cultural products including china, crystal, pottery, food, clothing, books, music, jewelry, bridal, and gifts.), number of visitors per year (3,245,120), and tax rate (8%). Add graphics, color, content, and text to enhance the appearance of your Web page. Print out the Web page and the source code of the Web page, the code behind the page, and the Ch5Case2Class.vb page.

Tara Store — Object-Oriented Programming with Visual Basic .NET within an ASP.NET Application

The current Web site was created using ASP. Before you upgrade the site to ASP.NET, your manager would like you to explain what changes in programming would need to be performed during the upgrade process. Specifically, you are to focus on the changes within Visual Basic .NET. Visit the QuickStart Web site at *http://localhost/quickstart* and click the How Do I? hyperlink. In the left menu, click the hyperlink Languages. The Language Support documentation page opens in the browser. Read the documentation provided. List at least five techniques that are used within Visual Basic .NET. Provide an example of each. Create a Web page named Ch5Case3.aspx to display your research. Add graphics, color, content, and text to enhance the appearance of your Web page. Print out the Web page and the source code of the Web page.

Tara Store — Object-Oriented Programming with C# and Visual Basic .NET

Your manager would like you to explain what changes in programming would need to be performed if the company used C# or Visual Basic .NET. Visit the QuickStart Web site at http://localhost/quickstart/aspplus/. In the top menu, click the hyperlink How Do I...?. (*Note:* The same documentation can be found online at the GotDotNet Web site at *http://samples.gotdotnet.com/quickstart/howto/.*) The Common Tasks documentation page opens in the browser. Read the documentation provided in the Languages section. List at least five techniques that are used in Visual Basic .NET and C#. Provide an example of each technique in both languages. Create a Web page named Ch5Case4.aspx to display your research. Add graphics, color, content, and text to enhance the appearance of your Web page. Print out the Web page and the source code of the Web page.

Tara Store — Researching Web Programming Careers

Your coworker suggests that you learn Visual Basic .NET because the company plans to use Visual Studio .NET to create their Web applications. Your coworker doesn't know if other companies are planning to use Visual Basic .NET. Visit at least three of the Web sites in the following list to locate information on Web Programming careers:

5

- ❏ Chicago ComputerJobs.Com – *www.chicago.computerjobs.com*
- ❏ CNET Online Career Center – *www.cnet.com/techjobs/0-7067.html?tag=boxhl1*
- ❏ Dice.com – *www.dice.com*
- ❏ IT Headhunter.com – *www.itheadhunter.com*
- ❏ Techies.com – *www.techies.com*
- ❏ Monster – *www.monster.com*

After reading the information, create a Web page named Ch5Case5.aspx that discusses your findings. Discuss what positions are available, what programming skills and languages are required, and what educational requirements are required. Provide information about three specific jobs. Add graphics, color, content, and text to enhance the appearance of your Web page. Print out the Web page and the source code of the Web page.

6

MANAGING DATA SOURCES

In this chapter, you will:

♦ Learn about the ADO.NET model
♦ Build a database connection
♦ Create an SQL Server database using Visual Studio .NET
♦ Manage a database using the Visual Studio .NET database tools
♦ Create SQL scripts using Visual Studio .NET
♦ Create SQL stored procedures using Visual Studio .NET

In order to develop flexible and effective data-driven Web applications, you must use multiple tools to access data from a wide variety of sources. Internet applications integrate Web pages, style sheets, multimedia, Web servers, e-mail servers, e-commerce servers, certificate servers, and authentication servers in addition to databases and database servers. As the number of available Web development tools increases, the task becomes ever more complex. Visual Studio .NET integrates many of these Web development tools into one development environment. In this chapter, you will learn how to create, manage, and access Web data using the tools available in Visual Studio .NET.

261

OVERVIEW OF THE ADO.NET FRAMEWORK

In the past, database management systems were proprietary; stored data could be accessed only via the program that was used to create the database. Programs could not share data unless you built an interface to the database application. Today, business needs demand database management systems that are more flexible. This flexibility has been achieved by means of the **Universal Data Access (UDA) model**, which provides a method whereby data can be shared across different applications and platforms. The UDA model is implemented by means of standards called Open Database Connectivity (ODBC) and Object Linking and Embedding (OLE DB), as well as XML and the ActiveX Data Object Model (ADO.NET). The ODBC drivers and OLE DB providers provide the low-level interface to the database. The ActiveX Data Object Model (ADO) provides objects that allow you to interface with the database. With the .NET Framework, a new version of ADO called ADO.NET is installed. XML is a standard that allows you to describe and store data within text files. ADO.NET allows you to retrieve data from a variety of sources, including XML data. By using these technologies together, you can exchange data across products and platforms.

 The UDA model is now simply referred to as data access. To learn more about data access and data storage, refer to the Microsoft Data Access and Storage Web site at *http://msdn.microsoft.com/data/*.

There are many ways to connect your Web application to a database using this UDA model. First you must build your database tables and determine what information you want to retrieve from them. Then, you decide what technology you will use to connect to your database, and how the connection information will be stored on the server. The connection information identifies the location of the database (the data source) and the connection method (using providers to manage the underlying connection), along with any other connection settings such as username or password. Once all these elements are in place, you can create a Web page that connects to the database using technologies such as ADO.NET. You can use the built-in objects within ADO.NET to connect to the database, execute commands, and return data from the database. From there, you can interact with the data, display the data, perform calculations on the data, or upload changes to the database.

 There are many acronyms used in programming. ASP, ADO, ODBC, OLE DB, XML, .NET, IIS, PWS, and VB are all commonly used programming acronyms. The large number of acronyms can make programming seem more complicated than it really is. It is very useful to create a listing of these acronyms and their definitions as you read about them. You can search *http://msdn.microsoft.com* to find out more details about specific acronyms. Then, as you learn more about these acronyms, you will be able to differentiate them.

ADO.NET Model

The ADO.NET model separates the process of connecting to the data source from the manipulation of the data. For example, suppose your company uses a non-Microsoft database server. They then create a Web application using Visual Studio .NET that can access their products database and display their products on the Web. The Web application makes the connection using the .NET providers for OLE DB data sources. The Web pages use the ADO.NET data objects to retrieve the data from the products table and display the data using a DataGrid control. The following year, the company decides that they are going to support all future Web applications with SQL Server, a database server from Microsoft. After the database has been converted to the new database server, the only changes you must make are those to the connection methods. You do not have to modify the Web application itself because the data connection is separate from the application layer.

ODBC, OLE DB, and OLE DB .NET

In the United Nations, many members need to communicate with members from other countries. They use translators to translate their language into another language. A member who speaks American English would use a translator who could speak French. The French prime minister would receive the message in French, and respond with a return message in French. The translator would translate the message from French to American English. This kind of simultaneous translation, when applied to databases, allows you to interact with a database using its own proprietary interface. You can use a standard such as Open Database Connectivity (ODBC) or Object Linking and Embedding Database (OLE DB) to translate commands between your application and the database.

In 1992, the standard known as **Open Database Connectivity (ODBC)** was created to provide a common interface to relational database systems. ODBC drivers are used to provide access to an ODBC-compliant database. Using ODBC drivers, an application can access a database without an application- or database-specific interface. You do not need to know how the database application stores the data in order to access the data. The ODBC drivers provide the low-level interface to the database applications. ODBC drivers are available for most Database Management Systems (DBMSs), including Access, SQL Server, and Oracle. Therefore, if you want to create an application that accesses an Access database, you would use the ADO.NET Provider objects to create a connection to the database via the ODBC driver.

E-mail programs and server software such as Exchange Server store data in a different format than relational database applications. The UDA model provides a method for accessing relational database stores, as well as these nonrelational data stores, which is called **Object Linking and Embedding Database (OLE DB)**. Using OLE DB allows your application to access a database without an application- or database-specific interface. In other words, you do not need to know how the database application stores the data in order to access it. OLE DB providers are available for most common data stores, including Access, SQL Server, and Exchange Server. Microsoft provides an OLE DB provider that will interface with the ODBC driver in order to support legacy database applications. For example, if your database application does not have an OLE DB provider, but does have the ODBC driver, you can use the OLE DB provider for ODBC to access the database.

Relational databases store data in a collection of rows of data. Some types of programs store data in a different format than relational database applications. ADO.NET Data Providers were created to provide a common interface to not only relational database systems, but also to many types of data systems. You do not need to know how the database application stores the data in order to access the data. ADO.NET provides the software to access many types of data, including relational databases such as Access, SQL Server, and Oracle.

The ADO.NET model, ODBC drivers, and OLE DB providers reside on the server, not the client. The Web application interacts with objects built within the ADO.NET model, as shown in Figure 6-1. Then ADO.NET Data Providers interface with the database via the ODBC and OLE DB. Your Web application interfaces with the ADO.NET objects.

ADO.NET Data Providers are responsible for providing the connection to the data source, executing commands, and returning data results. The data returned can be processed directly by the Data Provider, placed into an ADO.NET object such as a DataSet, or sent to another tier of an application. It's important to note that the lower level communication is still maintained by the set of generic data access software, such as ODBC drivers and OLE DB Data Providers. The .NET Data Provider is used to create a more uniform way to access and manage the data within your applications. You don't need to be familiar with this lower level software, only with the .NET Data Providers themselves.

ADO.NET Data Providers are also referred to as .NET Data Providers or simply .NET Providers.

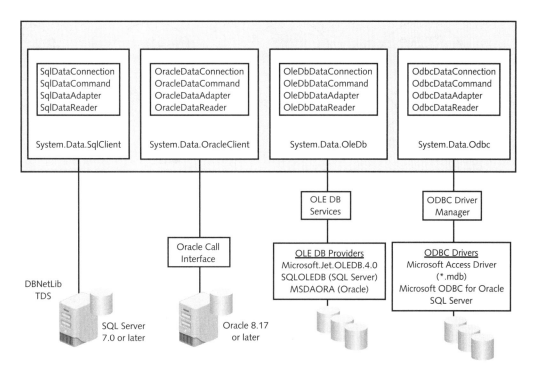

Figure 6-1   .NET Data Providers

Visual Studio .NET includes a new set of Data Providers, known as **Managed Providers** or .NET providers. There are four versions of the .NET managed providers available by default. The SQL Server .NET Data Provider is used to connect to an SQL Server database. The OLE DB .NET Data Provider is used to connect to any other data source that can be accessed via the OLE DB interface. The ODBC Data Provider is used to access data using the ODBC interface, and the Oracle Data Provider is used to access an Oracle database. As was shown in Figure 6-1, the .NET providers create a method to simplify your application development. The ASP.NET application interacts with ADO.NET objects built into the ADO.NET model. Then, ADO.NET uses the interface of the .NET Data Provider to access the database, as shown in Figure 6-2. If you create an application with an older version of Microsoft Access, you would use the ODBC .NET Data Provider. But, if you later upgrade your database to SQL Server, you won't have to change your entire application, only the .NET Data Providers to the SQL Server .NET Data Provider.

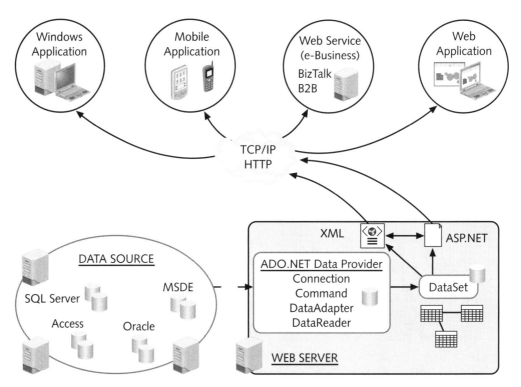

Figure 6-2   ODBC drivers, OLE DB Data Providers, and .NET Data Providers

There are some important differences between the SQL Server .NET Data Provider and the OLE DB .NET Data Provider. The SQL Server .NET Data Provider uses a native communication method to communicate with SQL Server. The SQL Server .NET Data Provider does not have to convert the COM datatypes from the OLE DB providers to the .NET datatypes in the SQL Server .NET Data Providers. Therefore, there is about a 70 percent performance improvement when you use the SQL Server .NET Data Provider.

ADO.NET Data Provider

The .NET Data Provider establishes a connection to a specific data source using the Connection Object. The .NET Data Provider contains a Command object that executes a command against a data source. The Command object exposes Parameter objects, which can be used to send information with the command. For example, the command might be to retrieve all of the employees within a particular state. A Parameter object can be used to send in a specific state, such as Michigan. Then, the command would only retrieve employees who live in Michigan. The .NET Data Provider contains a DataReader object, which reads a forward-only, read-only stream of data from a data source. The .NET Data Provider also contains a DataAdapter object that will populate an ADO.NET DataSet. Once the DataSet is populated, the data remains disconnected from the database. Changes can be made to the data within the DataSet. The DataAdapter will update the DataSet with the data source. The DataAdapter manages the changes between the DataSet and the original source of data. Therefore, the .NET Data Provider is often referred to as a Managed Provider.

.NET Data Providers are available for most common data stores, including Access, SQL Server, and Oracle. They all contain a Connection, Command, DataReader, and DataAdapter object. The names of the ADO.NET objects contain a prefix that identifies the type of data source that is managed by the .NET Data Provider. For example, SQL Server Data Provider objects contain the prefix "Sql". So SQL Server and .NET Data Provider objects include the SqlConnection, SqlCommand, SqlDataReader, and SqlDataAdapter objects. Oracle databases use the prefix "Oracle," such as OracleConnection, OracleCommand, OracleDataReader, and OracleDataAdapter objects. The underlying code between SQL Server and Oracle .NET Data Providers is different. Because the SQL Server .NET Data Provider has been optimized to take advantage of the .NET Framework and uses a native communication method to communicate with SQL Server databases, it has a performance gain over Oracle databases.

Other types of data sources, including legacy systems, use the OLE DB .NET Data Provider or ODBC .NET Data Provider. SQL Server databases before version 6.5 use the OLE DB .NET Data Provider. The OLE DB .NET Data Provider objects are prefixed with "OleDb", and the ODBC .NET Data Provider objects are prefixed with "Odbc". Older versions of Microsoft Access would use the ODBC .NET Data Provider.

ADO.NET Objects

When you use the ADO.NET Data Provider, you can access the data source using ADO.NET objects. When you use the SQL Server .NET Data Provider, these objects are known as the SqlConnection, SqlCommand, SqlDataReader, and SqlDataAdapter objects. When you use the OLE DB Data Provider, these objects are known as the OleDbConnection, OleDbCommand, OleDbDataReader, and OleDbDataAdapter objects. There is also a DataSet object that is used to retrieve data from the database. Within the Web page, the ASP.NET data controls are bound to the DataReaders or DataSets.

The ADO.NET Connection Object

The **Connection object** provides the connection to the database. Within the data connection, you must specify the location of the database, the access permissions, and any additional required parameters using a **connection string**. The connection string format is different for each .NET Data Provider because each provider has its own name. The provider is identified with the keyword **Provider**. The name of the server is identified as the **Data Source**. The User ID and Password identify the authentication data required to connect to the database. The following sample code shows how to create a connection string to an Oracle data source using OLE DB:

```
Dim CS
CS = "Provider=msdaora; Data Source=TheOracleDBName;
      User ID=MyUserID; PASSWORD=MyPassword;
```

 The connection string can be manually entered into the code. However, Visual Studio .NET comes with several wizards that will create the connection string for you. You will have to supply the same information to the wizards that you would have used if you typed the connection string manually. However, because typographical errors easily occur with connection strings, it is better to use the wizards. Later in the chapter, you will use a wizard to create the connection string.

In SQL Server, the name of the database is identified as the **Initial Catalog**. The code following this paragraph is a sample of an OLE DB connection string to an SQL Server database. (*Note*: The default user ID in SQL Server is sa and the password is blank.) The name of the SQL Server OLE DB provider is Provider=SQLOLEDB.1. You do not include the name of the SQL Server .NET Data Provider because it is selected by default. This string should be placed on one line.

```
Dim CS
CS = "Data Source=WindamereServer;
      User ID=sa; PASSWORD=;
      Initial Catalog=MyDatabase;"
```

When you use Visual Studio .NET to create a connection to a database, you will fill out the connection information using a dialog box, and the software will create the connection string for you. In this chapter, you will learn how to use Visual Studio .NET to make a connection to a database and create the connection string.

The Connection object provides access to the **Transaction object**, which allows you to group data commands together as a logical **transaction**. If any command within the transaction fails, the entire transaction fails, and all data is returned to the original values. Transactions are often used with credit card processing. The BeginTransaction method of the Connection object begins a transaction and returns a Transaction object, which is used to commit or abort transactions.

The ADO.NET Command Object

The ADO.NET **Command object** is used to identify an SQL command or a stored procedure. SQL is the **structured query language** that is used to identify what records to add, delete, or modify within the database. **Stored procedures** are SQL commands that are stored within the database. The Command object also exposes a **Parameters collection** that can be used to apply parameters, which are passed to stored procedures. The connection used by the Command object is defined in the **Connection property**. The command is defined in the **CommandText property**. The **CommandType**

property is used to indicate the type of command being executed. The CommandType property is **Text** by default, which indicates that the command is an SQL text string. The CommandType property can also be **TableDirect**, which specifies the name of a table to return, or **StoredProcedure**, which specifies the name of a stored procedure. The **Execute method** of the Command object executes the command and passes the results to the DataReader object. The **ExecuteNonQuery method** does not return rows because it's used to insert, modify, and delete data. Therefore, the method returns an integer representing the number of rows affected by the command.

The ADO.NET DataReader Object

The **DataReader object** is used to deliver a stream of data from the database. It is included in the ADO.NET model in order to provide a high-performance method of accessing read-only data, as shown in Figure 6-3. The DataReader provides a read-only, forward-only stream of data from the database. Therefore, you cannot make changes to the database using the DataReader. The DataReader requires continual access to the database, while the DataAdapter uses a disconnected dataset to access the data. You can access the DataReader using the Command object.

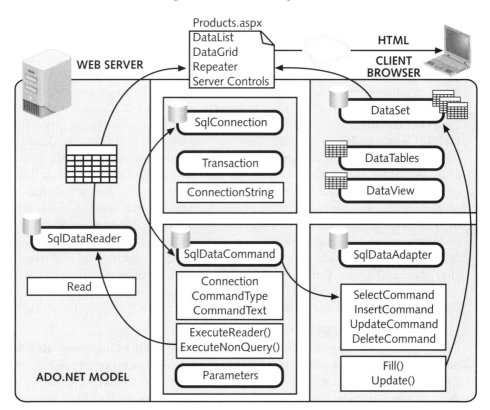

Figure 6-3   ADO.NET core objects

When you call the **ExecuteReader method** of the Command object, the DataReader opens a connection to the database and then retrieves rows of data as they are located in the database. The **Read method** of the DataReader returns a single row and caches each row in memory only once, then moves the current record pointer to the next record or row. You must remain connected until you have finished reading the stream of data. When you are finished, you need to close the connection using the **CommandBehavior property** of the Command object. If you set the CommandBehavior to **CloseConnection**, the connection closes automatically when the **Close method** of the DataReader object is called. You must call the Close method to close the DataReader object and release the references to the rowset. (*Note*: Some features of ASP.NET Data controls won't work with the DataReader. For example, automatic paging with the DataGrid control won't work with DataReader. Instead, you will have to use a DataView object, which is available through the DataSet object.)

The ADO.NET DataAdapter and DataSet Objects

The **DataAdapter object** is primarily used to populate a DataSet object, as shown in Figure 6-4. The DataAdapter object provides four commands that you can use to access the DataSet object. **SelectCommand** is used to retrieve data. When you use SelectCommand, the data must be inserted into the DataSet object. The **Fill method** of the DataAdapter inserts the data returned from the SelectCommand into the DataSet object. The DataSet object is effectively a private copy of the database, and does not necessarily reflect the current state of the database. If you want to see the latest changes made by other users, you can refresh the DataSet object by calling the appropriate Fill method of the DataAdapter object. **InsertCommand** is used to add a new record. **UpdateCommand** is used to modify the data within an existing record. **DeleteCommand** is used to permanently remove a record from the database. (*Note*: If no records are returned, then the command returns a count of records affected.) These four commands are used to manage the data within the DataSet object. The **DataSet object** is a disconnected collection of one or more tables that are stored in memory on the server. Because the DataSet object is disconnected, there must be methods used to maintain the original set of data, and the changes. When the code has completed making changes to the DataSet object, there must be a method to upload the changes to the database. The DataSet contains the methods required to maintain the list of changes made to the DataSet object. The DataAdapter connects to the database and reconciles changes made to the data in the DataSet object with the data source when the **Update method** is called.

One useful feature of Visual Studio .NET is that when you use the DataAdapter, the DataAdapter commands are automatically generated via the **CommandBuilder object**. So, the DataAdapter provides the bridge between the DataSet object and the data source. The DataSet object is a passive container for the data. The DataSet object is accessed through the `System.Data` namespace. To actually fetch data from the database and (optionally) write data to the database, you use the DataAdapter object.

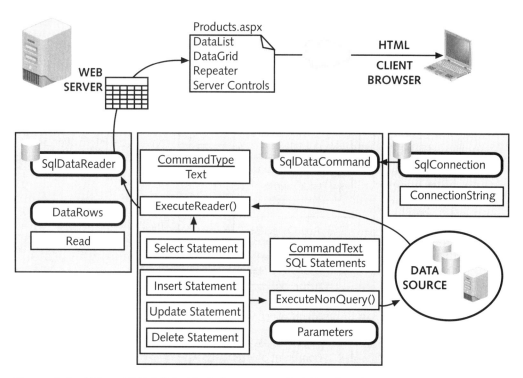

Figure 6-4 Using ADO.NET objects to access a DataReader object

The DataSet object consists of the DataTableCollection and the DataRelationCollection. As shown in Figure 6-5, the **DataTableCollection** is a collection of one or more **DataTable objects**. Each DataTable object consists of a DataRowCollection, a DataColumnCollection, and a ConstraintCollection. The DataRowCollection and DataColumnCollection store information about the rows and columns of data. (*Note*: The column is also referred to as the field.)

The **ConstraintCollection** includes information about the primary and foreign keys, and constraint rules. A **primary key** is used to ensure that no duplicate records appear in this column. Therefore, if one customer has a specific customer number, no other customer can have that number. The **constraint rules** are used to ensure that the field contains the correct datatype and values. The UniqueConstraint and ForeignKeyConstraint are used to create the relationships. The **DataRelationCollection** contains the data required to maintain relationships between the DataTable objects. Relational data can be exposed via ADO.NET because relationships can be made between DataTable objects. The tables are joined using the primary and foreign keys that are defined in the DataTable object. The **ExtendedProperties property** of the DataSet object allows you to specify information that can be stored with the DataSet object and later retrieved. The ExtendedProperties can be used to store the date the DataSet object was generated, the SQL statement, or any other data.

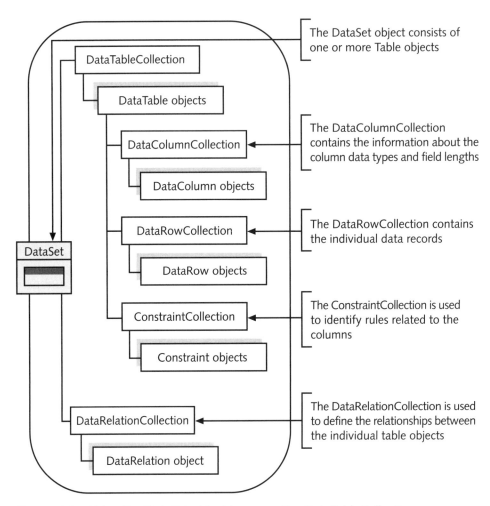

Figure 6-5   Using the DataSet object to access the DataTableCollection

The ADO.NET DataView Object

A **DataView object** contains the data from the DataSet object for a single DataTable or subset of records from a table. The DataTable object has a DefaultView property that returns all the records in the DataTable. However, you can select a subset of records from a table. You can add columns to the DataColumnCollection as well as filter and sort the data in a DataView object. The **RowFilter property** of the DataView object allows you to filter a subset of the DataView object. The **Sort property** of the DataView object also allows you to sort the data based upon a specific criterion in one or more of the columns.

ADO.NET and XML

If you have XML data, you can use it in the Web application by converting the XML data to a DataSet object. The XML data contains the data as well as the definitions (or schema) of the data. The DataSet object can also store the data as XML in memory, and store the schema as an XSD document. **XML Schema definition language (XSD)** is used to define the schema of a DataSet object. The **schema** defines the structure and datatypes for XML documents. Visual Studio .NET generates your XML data and the XSD document for you when you create a DataSet object and fill it with data.

In Visual Studio .NET you can generate a DataSet object and the XSD documents from your data source, whether it's a database or an XML document. However, if you don't have access to Visual Studio .NET, both SQL Server 2000 and Access XP are able to generate XML data. You can export a table or query from Access XP into XML. Thus, a component can transmit a data set to another component using XML. The receiving component receives the data set as a DataSet object within the .NET Framework. In the same way, the DataSet object can generate the XML and XSD documents, which can be used by applications that do not support DataSet objects.

Data Related Namespaces

The ADO.NET data objects are created using the classes within the System.Data namespace. You can access these objects via the data namespaces. These namespaces must be imported into your Web application. (*Note:* These namespaces are the same for both Web and Windows applications.) You can manage these namespaces within the Web.config global application file. The SQL Server .NET Data Provider has its own namespace, called SqlClient. The OLE DB .NET Data Providers use the OleDb namespace. (*Note:* The OLE DB .NET Data Provider works only with OLE DB versions 2.6 or higher.) Table 6-1 lists the common data related namespaces.

Table 6-1   Data related namespaces

ADO.NET Object	Namespace
Data objects (contains DataSet, DataTable, and DataRelation objects)	`System.Data`
ODBC .NET Data Provider (includes the Connection, Command, DataReader, and DataAdapter objects)	`System.Data.Odbc`
OLE DB .NET Data Provider (includes the Connection, Command, DataReader, and DataAdapter objects)	`System.Data.OleDb`
Oracle Data Provider (includes the Connection, Command, DataReader, and DataAdapter objects)	`System.Data.OracleClient`
SQL Server OLE DB .NET Data Provider (includes the Connection, Command, DataReader, and DataAdapter objects)	`System.Data.SqlClient`

6

BUILDING DATABASE CONNECTIONS

Visual Studio .NET provides a graphical user interface that you can use to create a connection to a database. The Server Explorer window provides you access to your local and network databases and data connections. The two nodes within the Server Explorer window are Servers and Data Connections. The **Servers node** provides you with access to the services running on the computer, such as a database server. The **Data Connections node** provides you with access to the data connection to a database and to the graphical tool used to create a database. Once a data connection is made, the information is stored in the data connection properties. The properties of the data connection include the ConnectString, Database, Driver, Server, State, Type, and User. The **ConnectString property** contains all of the values of the data connection properties in a single string. It also may contain additional properties required to connect to the database such as the username and password. The **Database property** is the name of the database, and the **Server property** is the name of the server. The **Type property** is the name of the database application such as Microsoft Access Database or SQL Server 2000 Database. The **Driver** is the name of the ODBC driver, OLE DB provider, or .NET Data Provider that is used to communicate with the database. The **State property** indicates if the database is currently connected. You can create data connections to remote databases. If the remote computer crashes, then the data connection will no longer work. The State property indicates if the connection to the database is still valid. The **User property** identifies the name of the user account that created the database. The creator of the database is known as the database owner, or dbo.

When you installed Visual Studio .NET, by default a version of SQL Server called the **Microsoft SQL Server Desktop Engine (MSDE)** may have been installed. The name of the SQL Server is *MachineName*\NetSDK, where *MachineName* is the name of your local computer and NetSDK is the name of the instance or SQL Server installed. The default name of the instance of SQL Server is NetSDK or NETSDK. The server can be referred to as (local)\NetSDK or localhost. (*Note:* There can be several versions of the SQL Server installed on the same computer. Your system administrator may have changed the default settings.)

 The MSDE server uses Windows authentication by default. The ASP.NET Windows account must have permission to access each database you create. You can find instructions on assigning database permissions in Appendix B.

The following exercise shows you how to install the samples that come with the .NET Framework and the data server. (If you have already installed the samples and QuickStart tutorials, then you can skip this exercise.)

You can complete most of the exercises in this chapter without installing the sample databases. However, you do need to have either the MSDE or SQL Server available. (*Note*: You can use Oracle, if you are familiar with creating a connection to an Oracle database.) You can use a local or remote version of the MSDE or SQL Server. You must have the fully qualified name of the SQL Server, or the IP address, and the authentication information, which can be obtained from your system administrator or ISP. The only difference is completing the form in the DataLink Properties window. You must use the login information for your remote database server.

The ASP.NET Web database samples installed with the QuickStart Web site are not available online from either the GotDotNet Web site or the DotNetJunkies Web site. You can modify the QuickStart configuration files to work with SQL Server, but that is recommended only for advanced Web programmers who are familiar with SQL Server installation scripts.

You must install the MSDE before you can install and configure the samples that come with the .NET Framework. The MSDE does not come with the Visual Studio .NET software, but it is available for download free from Microsoft. The directions say to click the Download and Install the Microsoft SQL Server 2000 Desktop Engine (MSDE) link. Do not click this link. If you have already installed the MSDE, you can install the QuickStart samples. If you have not, then you must install the MSDE before proceeding. Refer to the installation instructions in Appendix B for additional information on how to download, install, and configure the MSDE.

Downloading the MSDE Files

To download the MSDE files from the Microsoft Web site, do the following:

1. In Windows Explorer, create a directory named **c:\MSDETempDE**.

2. Open a browser and go to **http://go.microsoft.com/fwlink/?linkid=13962**.

3. Click the **Download** button located on the right side of the page. A window appears that asks if you would like to open or save a file named sql2kdesksp3.exe. Click **Save**. The Save As window appears. Navigate to your c:\MSDETempDE directory. Click **Save** to save the files to the c:\MSDETempDE directory.

4. In Windows Explorer, navigate to **c:\MSDETempDE** and double-click **sql2kdesksp3.exe** to extract all files required to install MSDE to your computer.

5. Click **Finish**. The files are extracted to c:\sql2ksp3 by default. (*Note*: Although you no longer need the sql2kdesksp3.exe file, you should keep it in case you need it when you upgrade to another version of the MSDE in the future. The files are extracted to the same location as the data components located in the SQL2KSP3.exe file.)

6. A dialog box appears and says the following: "The specified output folder does not exist. Create it?" Click **Yes**. The files are unpacked into your directory. When it's completed, a message box appears and says the following: "The package has been delivered successfully." Click **OK**.

To install the MSDE from the command prompt window, do the following:

1. Go to the **Start** menu, and then click **Run**. Type **cmd** in the text box and click **Open**.

2. In the command prompt window, type **cd C:\sql2ksp3\MSDE**. Press **Enter**.

3. Type **setup INSTANCENAME="NetSDK" SECURITYMODE=SQL SAPWD="password"**. Press **Enter**.

4. A dialog box may appear saying you must restart your system for the program configuration changes to take effect. Click **Yes** to restart your system.

5. When the computer has restarted and the installation is complete, close the window.

6. Verify that the files and folders were installed. Go to the Windows Explorer and navigate to **C:\Program Files\Microsoft SQL Server\MSSQL$NETSDK**.

7. Verify that there is a Binn, Data, Install, and Log folder. Close the Windows Explorer window.

Installing the .NET Framework SDK Samples Databases

To install the .NET Framework SDK samples databases, do the following:

1. Click **Start**, point to **All Programs**, point to **Microsoft .NET Framework SDK v1.1**, and then click **Samples and QuickStart Tutorials**. The browser opens to the samples Web page. If you have already installed the MSDE and QuickStart samples, skip to Step 4. Otherwise, continue with Step 2.

2. Click the **Set up the QuickStarts** hyperlink. In the download window, click the **Open** button. There will be a message in the File Download Window that ConfigSamples.exe can harm your computer. Click **Open**. The installation begins processing. The installation program will configure the IIS server to support the QuickStart site. It will configure the installation script, create SQL Server databases in the MSDE, create virtual directories, and register samples.

3. When the samples are installed, a window that says Congratulations! opens. Click the **Launch** button. Click the **Connect** button if you are given an opportunity to do so. The browser opens the Web page located at *http://localhost/quickstart*. If the page loads, then the samples and the data environment were installed correctly. (*Note*: If this page does not appear, then the QuickStart Web site or the Visual Studio .NET software was not installed correctly. You should click the View log hyperlink to view and save the setup and installation log file which may contain information as to why the samples could not be installed correctly. The documentation for the .NET Framework SDK can be found by clicking **Start**, pointing to **All Programs**, pointing to **Microsoft .NET Framework SDK v 1.1**, and clicking **Tools**.)

4. To test if the database server has been installed and configured correctly and started, click the **Start the ASP.NET QuickStart Tutorial** hyperlink.

5. Scroll down the page. On the left menu, near the bottom, click the **An E-Commerce Storefront** hyperlink.

6. On the right side of the page, click the **Run Sample** hyperlink. If you see four images of cartons of milk on the Web page, your database server, Web server, and sample Web sites are installed and configured correctly. The GrocerToGo Web site uses the GrocerToGo database installed with the sample MSDE databases. (*Note*: If this page does not appear, then the MSDE software was not installed or configured correctly. You should review the information located in Appendix B and the online documentation to locate possible reasons for the failure for the application to connect to the MSDE GrocerToGo database.)

7. Close all windows. You must click the **Exit** link to close the Visual Studio .NET Setup window.

It is important to have enough random access memory (RAM) on the computer to use Visual Studio .NET and the database server. Database processing requires a significant amount of memory. If you do not meet the minimum requirements for the installation of Visual Studio .NET, you should not attempt to create or maintain your databases using the Visual Studio .NET MSDE. You may, however, be able to use Visual Studio .NET in conjunction with a database server located on a different computer.

 You can find detailed information about the SQL Server installation process and the .NET Framework SDK samples in Appendix A. If you are working with Internet Information Server version 6.0, you should refer to this page for information on how to configure your application so that it will be authenticated by the SQL Server database.

Once the samples are installed, the server appears in the Visual Studio .NET Server Explorer window. The sample databases that are installed include GrocerToGo, Northwind, Portal, and pubs. GrocerToGo and Portal were created primarily to display the capabilities of data-driven ASP.NET applications. In the following exercise, you create a new Web application named Chapter6, view the list of databases installed on your server, and list the columns within the Products table in the GrocerToGo database.

1. Start **Visual Studio .NET**.

2. Click **File** on the menu bar, point to **New**, then click **Project**. This opens the New Project window.

3. Under Project Types, click the **Visual Basic Projects** folder icon, and then under Templates, click the **ASP.NET Web Application** icon. Type **Chapter6** in the Location text box in place of WebApplication1. Click **OK** to create the solution, project, and default files.

4. Click the **Server Explorer** tab to slide the window out. (*Note*: If the tab is not visible, click **View** on the menu bar, and then click **Server Explorer**. If the window is open, but you cannot see it, click the **Server** tab next to the Toolbox tab near the bottom left of the window.) Then, click the **pushpin** on the title bar of the Server Explorer window to make the window remain open.

5. Click the **plus sign** next to the Servers icon to expand the list of your local and network servers. (*Note*: This may already have been expanded on your system.) Click the **plus sign** next to the name of your computer (the *MachineName*). Click the **plus sign** next to the SQL Servers icon. Click the **plus sign** next to the database that is named *MachineName*\NETSDK, where *MachineName* is the name of your computer.

6. Click the **plus sign** next to the GrocerToGo icon. Click the **plus sign** next to the Tables icon. Click the **plus sign** next to the Products table icon to display the list of fields in the Products table.

7. Click the **ProductID** field. The list of properties of the ProductID field is displayed in the Properties window. The properties include the DataType and Length, as shown in Figure 6-6.

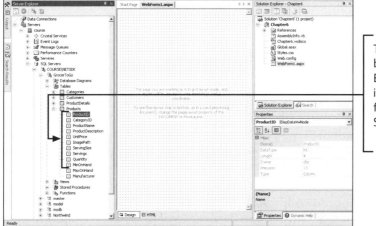

The tables and fields can be viewed from the Server Explorer window. You can insert, edit, and delete data from the tables within the Server Explorer window

6

Figure 6-6   Displaying fields within tables in the Server Explorer window

8. Click the **minus sign** next to the Servers icon to collapse the list of your local and network servers.

In the following exercise, you will make a connection to the GrocerToGo database. (*Note*: This does not create a Connection object, just the connection to the database. You will create the Connection objects in the next chapter.) The exercises in this chapter can be applied to both Web and Windows applications created with Visual Studio .NET.

1. In the Server Explorer window, right-click the **Data Connections** icon, which is located at the top of the window, and then click **Add Connection**. The Data Link Properties dialog box opens.

2. In the Server Name text box enter your database server name, which is **(local)\NETSDK**. (*Note*: You can also use the name for the local server, which is known as localhost or *MachineName*\NetSDK.)

3. Select the authentication mode for the SQL Server. There are radio buttons, which indicate the two possible methods to authenticate your connection with the SQL Server database.

   a. If you use the default installation, you can select the first radio button, which indicates that the connection should use integrated Windows NT security. With this option, you do not have to enter a user name or password.

   b. If you have installed your own version of SQL Server, then you should select the second radio button and enter the default user name and password. The default user name is sa with no password. In the **User name** text box, type **sa**, and type **password** in the Password text box. Check the **Allow saving password** check box. If you did not install the sa user, you must type the name of the user account that was configured during the installation of the SQL Server software. (*Note*: If you did not install the software, you should contact your system administrator to obtain the permission settings to connect to the SQL Server. The default installation of the current version of MSDE does not allow for the sa user to have no password assigned for security reasons. The sa is the system administrator account. You can locate more information on configuring the MSDE user accounts in Appendix B.)

4. In the drop-down list box, select **GrocerToGo**, as shown in Figure 6-7. (*Note*: You will only see the databases that you have permission to access.)

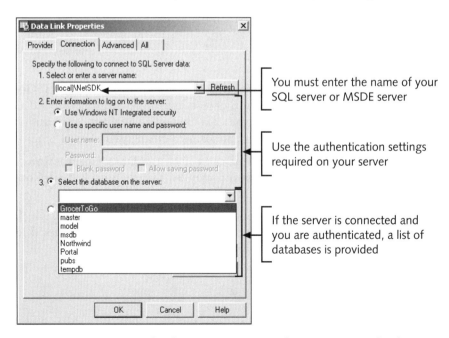

Figure 6-7   Creating a database connection to the GrocerToGo database

5. Click the **Test Connection** button. An alert box should appear that says Test connection succeeded. Click the **OK** button to close the alert box. (*Note*: If the connection does not occur, an alternate message is displayed, showing the type of error. If an error occurs, you should verify that the database and the settings are correct, and then create a new connection to the database.)

6. Click **OK**. The connection is named *MACHINENAME*\NETSDK. GrocerToGo.dbo and is placed in the list under Data Connections in the Server Explorer window. You can use this connection later, to create the Connection object. (*Note*: Remember that this is not a Connection object, just a reference to the database connection in the project. If you click the connection, the connection properties are displayed in the Properties window. The properties are dimmed because the values were set with the Visual Studio .NET program and are not meant to be edited manually.)

7. Click the **plus sign** next to the *MACHINENAME*\NETSDK. GrocerToGo.dbo icon. Click the **plus sign** next to the Tables icon. Click the **plus sign** next to the Products table icon to display the list of fields in the Products table. These are the same fields that you displayed earlier using the Servers node.

8. Click the **minus sign** next to the *MACHINENAME*\NETSDK. GrocerToGo.dbo icon to collapse the view.

You can use the Data Link Properties dialog box with nonlocal data sources. You have to provide the URL to the SQL Server database in the server name text box.

VISUAL STUDIO .NET BUILT-IN DATABASE TOOLS

There are a variety of Visual Studio .NET tools that allow you to create and manipulate a database. Once you have created your database in the Server Explorer, you will want to add tables and stored procedures. You can add a table using the Table Designer. There is also a Query and View Editor for creating database queries. (*Note*: In some databases, such as Access, you must use queries to create stored procedures and pass the parameter to the query.) The Visual Studio .NET SQL Editor is used to create and edit SQL scripts and stored procedures.

Creating an SQL Server Database in Visual Studio .NET

Visual Studio .NET provides a graphical user interface that you can use to create a connection to a database. When you create the database, you need to know which type of authentication is required for access to the SQL Server. You can use the authentication built within Windows NT, or SQL Server authentication.

You must have permission to create the database. Within SQL Server, a user ID identifies users, and controls which users can access the Database objects. Each user has roles that identify if they are able to create or modify a Data object. You can read more about the permissions and authentication modes in Appendix B. You can also read more about managing SQL Server security in the appendix.

In the following exercise, you will create a basic database named Chapter6.

1. In the Server Explorer window, right-click **Data Connections**, and then click **Create New SQL Server Database**.

2. In the Create Database dialog box, enter the name of your SQL Server in the Server text box, which is **(local)\NetSDK**. (*Note*: You can also enter *Machine*\NETSDK, where *Machine* is the name of your computer.)

3. In the New Database Name text box type **Chapter6**, as shown in Figure 6-8. The Use Windows NT Integrated Security option is selected by default. Click the **Use SQL Server Authentication** radio button. Type **sa** in the Login Name text box and **password** in the Password text box.

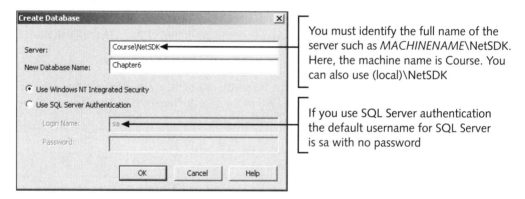

You must identify the full name of the server such as *MACHINENAME*\NetSDK. Here, the machine name is Course. You can also use (local)\NetSDK

If you use SQL Server authentication the default username for SQL Server is sa with no password

Figure 6-8   Creating a database

If you used the default MSDE installation according to the directions provided in the chapter, the Login Name entry is "sa" and the Password entry is "password". You should check with your database administrator to obtain the login values for your server. If you are provided with an additional login window, select the option for Windows Integrated Security.

4. Click **OK** to create the Chapter6 database. (*Note*: A dialog box may appear asking you to reenter your SQL Server user name of "sa" and your password of "password". Enter the requested information if you are prompted to do so.) The connection to the *MACHINENAME*\NETSDK.Chapter6.dbo database appears under the Data Connections in the Server Explorer window. The Chapter6 database also appears under *Machine*\NETSDK within the SQL Servers. (*Note*: You may need to right-click **Data Connections** in the Server Explorer, then click **Refresh** to view the data connection.)

While using Visual Studio .NET, if your database connection does not work, you should close Visual Studio .NET, then reopen Visual Studio .NET and your solution. If you still cannot create a database, you should consult the security documentation or your system administrator to verify your SQL Server authentication settings.

The Table Designer

The **Table Designer** allows you to create the schema for the table and enter the data. In **Table Design** view, you can create new columns, and modify the properties of the columns. In Table Data view, you can create a new row, modify an existing row, or delete a row. In Table Design view, the top half of the Table Designer allows you to create the structure of the columns within the table. You define the name of the column, and the datatype. Each column is defined within a row in the Table Designer. Each row contains a row selector box and the following fields: Column Name, Datatype, Length, and Allow Nulls. The currently selected row can be identified by the triangle in the row selector box. The **row selector** is the gray square located next to the column name. The row selector can also be used to select the current row. The lower half of the Table Designer allows you to modify the properties of the column. The properties within the second half of the Table Designer vary with the datatype selected. Most of the datatypes provide a description property and a default value for the column length property.

You must specify a name for the column and a datatype. Do not use any blank spaces or special characters in a column name other than an underscore. It is best to keep the column name short, but descriptive. For example, the column name LastName describes a field that might contain customer last names. However, if the column name is LN, it's not clear what information is stored in the column. You must select a datatype from a drop-down list. You must also provide the length of each column in bytes, and whether or not the column requires a value. If a column does not contain a value for a particular record, a null value is returned.

You must specify a datatype for each column when you create the column. The .NET providers convert the SQL Server data types to .NET data types when you retrieve your data using .NET. There are many datatypes defined within SQL Server. For example, the int datatype is used to identify an integer.

The possible datatypes for MSDE and SQL Server are as follows:

- bigint
- binary
- bit
- char
- datetime
- decimal
- float

- image
- int
- money
- nchar
- ntext
- numeric
- nvarchar

- real
- smalldatetime
- smallint
- smallmoney
- sql_variant
- text
- timestamp

- tinyint
- uniqueidentifier
- varbinary
- varchar

6

You can set the default column properties such as column length using the Visual Studio .NET Options window. You can access the Options window by clicking Tools on the menu bar, then clicking Options. In the left pane of the Options window, click Database Tools, click Database Designer, and then click SQL Server. The SQL Server column options are shown in Figure 6-9.

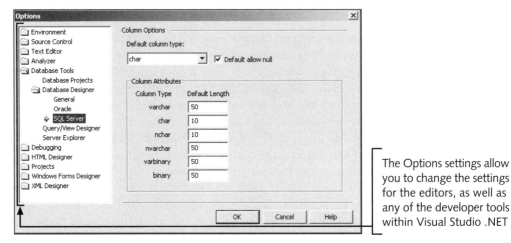

The Options settings allow you to change the settings for the editors, as well as any of the developer tools within Visual Studio .NET

Figure 6-9   The SQL Server column options

There are many properties that can be set in the Properties pane, as shown in Figure 6-10. The properties that you can set will depend upon the datatype you selected. For example, you can specify if a column with an int datatype is an **identity column** with the **Identity property**. The identity column is used to provide a unique value for each row. This value can be used to locate a specific row of data. To change a column to an identity column, change the Identity property from No to Yes. Then, you can set the Identity Seed and Identity Increment properties. The **Identity Seed property** shows the initial value of the column, which is used to create the value for the first row. The **Identity increment property** holds the value that is used to increment the seed when a new row is added. For example, you can increment the identify column by one, so that the value of the identity column increases by one for each new record.

The **primary key** is used to identify the column as a unique column. Each value for each row must be unique within this column. All rows must have a value for this column. No record will be allowed that contains a null value for this column. The primary key is configured for a specific column by using the row selector, the Table toolbar, or the Diagram menu.

In the following exercise, you will create a table named Products and create the columns using the Table Designer.

1. In the Server Explorer window, click the **plus sign** next to the Data Connection for the *MACHINENAME*\NETSDK.Chapter6.dbo database. Right-click the **Tables** icon, and then click **New Table** to open the Table Designer.

2. In the first row, type **ProductID** as the column name. Select **int** as the datatype from the drop-down list. The length should be **4**. Click the **Allow Nulls** check box to deselect it, since all products are required to have a ProductID. In the properties at the bottom half of the window, change the Identity from No to **Yes** using the drop-down list arrow. Identity Seed should be set to **1**, and Identity Increment should be set to **1**. This creates a new value for each new record entered in the database.

3. Right-click the **ProductID** row selector, and then click **Set Primary Key**. A yellow key appears at the side of the column name to indicate that this column is the Primary Key column.

4. Add the other columns as shown in Table 6-2 and in Figure 6-10. You can leave the default properties for each column.

6

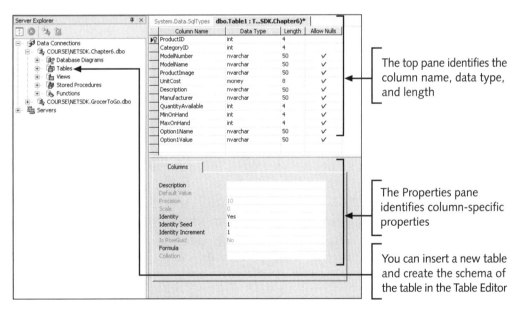

Figure 6-10   Creating a database table using the Table Editor

Table 6-2 The Products table for the Chapter6 database

Column Name	DataType	Length	Allow Nulls
ProductID	int	4	No
CategoryID	int	4	No
ModelNumber	nvarchar	50	Yes
ModelName	nvarchar	50	Yes
ProductImage	nvarchar	50	Yes
UnitCost	money	8	Yes
Description	nvarchar	50	Yes
Manufacturer	nvarchar	50	Yes
QuantityAvailable	int	4	Yes
MinOnHand	int	4	Yes
MaxOnHand	int	4	Yes
Option1Name	nvarchar	50	Yes
Option1Value	nvarchar	50	Yes

5. Click the **Save All** button. The Choose Name dialog box opens. Enter **Products** as the table name, and then click **OK**. Close the Table Designer window.

6. The Products table should appear under the Chapter6 Tables icon in the Server Explorer window. If it does not, then you may have to complete one or more of the following substeps:

   a. If you cannot see your Chapter6 database objects, click the **plus sign** next to the MACHINENAME\NETSDK.Chapter6.dbo connection icon to expand the database objects.

   b. If you cannot see your tables list, click the **plus sign** next to the Tables icon to expand the tables list.

   c. If the Products table is not shown, right-click the **MACHINENAME\ NETSDK.Chapter6.dbo** connection icon, and then click **Refresh**.

   d. If you still cannot see the Products table, it may not have been saved. Return to Step 1 and recreate the table.

7. Click the **plus sign** to expand the Products table and view the columns that you created in Step 4.

In the following exercise you will add data for four records into the table.

1. Right-click the **Products** table name, and then click **Retrieve Data from Table**. The table opens in Data view. You can enter data for each record in Data view. The cursor is placed in the ProductID column. Because SQL Server assigns this value, press the **Tab** key to move to the next column. Enter **1** for CategoryID. If prompted, enter your user name and password.

2. Add the values for the other fields using the information in Table 6-3. Leave the other fields empty and press **Enter**. Notice that the option1 and value1 columns are replaced with the keyword null in the first record.

3. Enter the other three records. The data for all of the records is shown in Table 6-3. The ProductID field has been assigned a value of 1, 2, 3, and 4 respectively as shown in Figure 6-11.

Table 6-3   The Products table data for the Chapter6 database

Column Name	Row 1 Data	Row 2 Data	Row 3 Data	Row 4 Data
ProductID	1 (to be filled in by the database)	2 (to be filled in by the database)	3 (to be filled in by the database)	4 (to be filled in by the database)
CategoryID	1	1	1	2
ModelNumber	756	387	978	979
ModelName	Letter Opener	Shamrock Paperweight	Business Card Holder	Cat Bowl
ProductImage	528.jpg	537.jpg	529.jpg	658.jpg
UnitCost	69	99	59	22
Description	Letter Opener by Waterford.	Shamrock Paperweight by Waterford	Business Card Holder by Waterford	Cat Bowl by Belinda Bradshaw
Manufacturer	Waterford	Waterford	Waterford	Bradshaw
QuantityAvailable	10	5	50	25
MinOnHand	5	10	25	10
MaxOnHand	20	30	100	75
Option1Name		Size		Color
Option1Value		S, L		Yellow, Blue

The row selector column indicates which is the current row

You can change the column width by clicking on the line between the columns and dragging the line to the right

You can display data from the table and edit the table data within the Table Designer

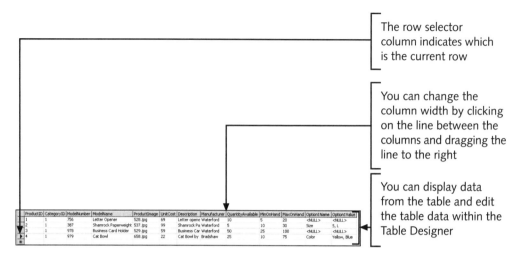

ProductID	CategoryID	ModelNumber	ModelName	ProductImage	UnitCost	Description	Manufacturer	QuantityAvailable	MinOnHand	MaxOnHand	Option1Name	Option1Value
1	1	756	Letter Opener	528.jpg	69	Letter opene	Waterford	10	5	20	<NULL>	<NULL>
2	1	387	Shamrock Paperweight	537.jpg	99	Shamrock Pa	Waterford	5	10	30	Size	S, L
3	1	978	Business Card Holder	529.jpg	59	Business Car	Waterford	50	25	100	<NULL>	<NULL>
4	1	979	Cat Bowl	658.jpg	22	Cat Bowl by	Bradshaw	25	10	75	Color	Yellow, Blue

Figure 6-11   Table values displayed

Tip
If you do not enter a value, the column will display <NULL>. If you make a mistake, you can delete the value you entered and configure the column to display <NULL>. When you press Ctrl key and 0 while inside the column, the contents of the column will be replaced with the <NULL> value.

4. Click the **Save All** button and close the window.

5. Create a second table by right-clicking **Tables** and clicking **New Table**. The table has two columns. The name of the first column in the new table is CategoryID. Type **CategoryID** in the Column Name column in the Table Designer window, and assign it as an integer (**int**) with a length of **4** bytes. Click the **Allow Nulls** check box to deselect it. A CategoryID is required for all categories. In the properties at the bottom half of the window, change the Identity from No to **Yes** using the drop-down list arrow. The Identity Seed should be set to **1**, and the identity increment should be set to **1**. This creates a new value for each new record entered in the database.

6. Right-click the **CategoryID** column name in the row selector, and then click **Set Primary Key**. A yellow key appears at the side of the column name to indicate that this column is the Primary Key column.

7. The name of the second column in the database is Category Name. Type **CategoryName** in the Column Name column in the Table Designer window. Enter **nvarchar** as the datatype and the length as **50** bytes. The CategoryName column is allowed to have null values, so leave the Allow Nulls check box checked.

8. Click the **Save All** button. The Choose Name dialog box opens. Enter **Categories** for the table name, then click **OK**, and then close the window.

9. Open the table and add two records. Right-click on the **Categories** table in the Server Explorer window and select **Retrieve Data from Table**. In the first row, press the **Tab** key to move to the CategoryName column. The database server adds the CategoryID for you. Type **Waterford** as the CategoryName. If prompted, enter your user name and password.

10. Press the **Tab** key twice to get the CategoryName for the second row. Type **Pottery**, and then press **Enter**.

11. Click the **Save All** button. Close the window.

Creating a View with the Query and View Editor

The Query and View Editor allows you to create a query in the database. There are four windows called **panes** displayed within the editor. The top pane is the Table pane. In the **Table pane**, you can add tables and select which columns to include in the query. The query is displayed visually with icons next to the columns. For example, if you sort the table based on a column, a sort icon is placed next to the column name in the Table pane. This provides a quick method for viewing the query. The second pane is the Grid pane. You use the **Grid pane** to select columns and criteria, just as you do when using Microsoft Access. The **column name** and **table** indicate where to retrieve the values for the column. The **Output property** indicates if the column should be visible in the results when the query is executed. (*Note:* The Output property is like the "show" check box in Access.) The **sort order** is used to specify one or more columns for sorting the results. You can number the sort order to specify which column should be sorted first. (*Note:* The sort order with the lowest number is sorted first.) You can specify the sort order as ascending or descending by using the **Sort Type property**. The **Alias property** is used to display an alternate name in the results. Because the field names do not contain spaces or special characters, it is sometimes useful to provide a more readable alias name for the end user. You use the **Criteria property** to create a conditional statement that must be met before the record can be retrieved. The **Or property** indicates an alternate condition that could be met for the record to be retrieved.

The third pane is the SQL pane. The **SQL pane** generates the SQL for you based upon the Table pane and Grid pane. However, you can edit the SQL directly within the SQL pane. The Grid pane and Table pane are updated automatically when you make a change to the SQL pane. The last pane is the Output pane. In the **Output pane**, the output from the query is displayed. Therefore, you can test your queries from within Visual Studio .NET before you place them in your Web pages.

In the following example, you will use the Query and View Editor to create a view that will display the products from the Waterford manufacturer.

1. In the Server Explorer window, under the *MACHINENAME*\NETSDK. Chapter6.dbo data connection, right-click **Views**, then click **New View**. The Query and View Editor opens along with the Add Table dialog box. You need to select which tables you would like to add to the query. Select the **Products** table, click the **Add** button, and then click the **Close** button. The Products table is added to the Table pane.

2. In the Table pane, click the **check box** next to the following column names to select them: **ProductID**, **CategoryID**, **ModelName**, and **Manufacturer**. This places the column names into the query in the Grid pane and the SQL pane. (*Note:* You may have to scroll down the table fields list in order to view and select some of the fields.)

3. In the Grid pane, go to the Sort Type property for the ModelName column, and select **Ascending** from the drop-down list. The sort order is entered as **1**, which indicates that this is the first column to be sorted.

4. In the Manufacturer column enter **= Waterford** in the Criteria property, as shown in Figure 6-12.

5. Right-click the Table pane, and then click **Run**. (*Note:* You can also click the **Run Query** icon in the SQL toolbar. The Run Query icon is the red exclamation point icon.) The three Waterford products are displayed, with the Business Card Holder displayed first. (*Note:* You can manipulate the size of the panes, windows, and columns as you would with other Windows software products. You can enlarge your field list window in the Table pane by clicking on the right lower corner and dragging the window until it reaches the desired size. You can increase the width of the columns in the Grid and Preview panes by placing the mouse over the line between the two columns. When the mouse arrow icon changes to a double headed arrow, click and drag the mouse until the desired column width is reached. If you perform a double mouse click while the double-headed arrow appears, the column width will be autosized.) If prompted, enter your user name and password.

6. Click the **Save All** button to save the view. In the Save New View dialog box, enter **DisplayWaterford** as the name of the view, and then click **OK**.

7. Close the Query and View Editor.

8. To rerun the query, first click the **plus sign** next to the Views icon under Data Connections to display the list of views.

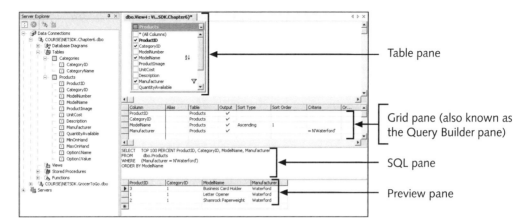

Table pane

Grid pane (also known as the Query Builder pane)

SQL pane

Preview pane

6

Figure 6-12   The Query and View Editor

9. Right-click the **DisplayWaterford** view, and then click **Retrieve Data from View**. The query runs and displays the results, but does not display the Query and View Editor. If prompted, enter your user name and password.

10. Close the window.

Creating a Relationship with the Data Diagram

The **Database Designer** allows you to define relationships between tables using columns. In the Database Designer, each table contains a **title bar**, which displays the name of the table. If the table has an owner, the owner's name is shown in parentheses in the title bar after the table name. By default the tables are displayed showing the table names in the title bar and the column names. This view of the table is called the **Column Names view**. You can change the view of the tables using the Table view property. When you right-click on a table, you can change the view from Column Names by selecting **Table View** and then selecting the view name. The **Standard view** displays the column names and the schema for the columns. The **Keys view** displays the names of the tables in the title bar and the names of the primary key columns. The **Name view** displays only the names of the tables in the title bar. The **Custom view** allows you to add any of the properties to the view.

A line is drawn from a field from one table to a field in another to indicate which fields are used to define the relationship between the tables. The endpoints of the line indicate whether the relationship is one-to-one or one-to-many. If a relationship has a key at one endpoint and a figure eight at the other, it is a one-to-many relationship. However, if the relationship has a key at each endpoint, then it is a one-to-one relationship.

It's important to note that these diagrams are useful before building the database and entering the data. Once the data has been entered, if you try to create a relationship that is not valid, the Database Designer will not let you create the relationship. For example, if you enter the records for the Products table but not the Categories table, then you cannot create a relationship between the two tables based on the CategoryID. (*Note:* This enforcement of referential integrity also applies to Microsoft Access and other relational databases.) In the following example, you will use the Database Designer to create a relationship between the Categories table and the Products table. The CategoryID is used to create a one-to-many relationship. The CategoryID is assigned as the primary key in the Categories table and as the foreign key in the Products table. The primary key means that each row of data must contain a unique value for that column. The **foreign key** means that any row of data can contain the same value for the CategoryID column as other rows, but the value must appear in the CategoryID column in the Categories table. You can configure the database to enforce this rule to maintain the integrity of the data relationships. Configuring the primary and foreign keys results in a one-to-many relationship between the two tables.

1. In the Server Explorer window, under the *MACHINENAME*\NETSDK. Chapter6.dbo data connection, right-click **Database Diagrams**, then click **New Diagram**. The Data Diagram Editor opens along with the Add Table dialog box. Select both the **Categories** table and the **Products** table by holding down the **Shift** key while you make the selections. Click the **Add** button and then the **Close** button. The tables are added to the Database Designer.

2. Click the **row selector** next to the CategoryID column in the Categories table and drag the row to the row selector next to the CategoryID column in the Products table. The Create Relationship window opens. The CategoryID is assigned as the primary key in the Categories table and as the foreign key in the Products table.

3. Click **OK**. The line now indicates a one-to-many relationship between the two tables, as shown in Figure 6-13. There is only one CategoryID value in the Categories table. There can be many products that have the same CategoryID value.

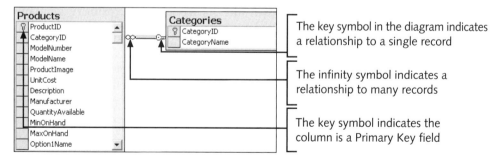

Figure 6-13 Database diagram

4. Click the **Save All** button to save the view. In the Save New Database Diagram dialog box, type **Category_Products** as the name of the view, and then click **OK**. A warning message may appear indicating that the tables will be saved to the database. Click **Yes**.

5. Close the window.

BUILDING SQL SCRIPTS AND STORED PROCEDURES

Stored procedures can be used to create an SQL command that is stored within the database. Because the command is stored with the database server, it has already been parsed and compiled by the server. Therefore, the stored procedure is more efficient than an SQL statement. Prior to Visual Studio .NET, you had to create the stored procedure from within an SQL Server tool such as Query Analyzer or Enterprise Manager. Today, you can create your stored procedure from within Visual Studio .NET.

You can use a stored procedure to run an SQL query. You can also create a stored procedure that uses input and output parameters. An **input parameter** is a value that is passed to the stored procedure when it is called. This value must match the datatype and length that is specified within the stored procedure. The name of the parameter within the stored procedure always begins with the @ symbol. Any of the values within the SQL statement can be replaced with the input parameters. Usually, the input parameter is compared to a value. Then, the subset of matching records is retrieved, modified, or deleted. The other type of parameter is the output parameter. **Output parameters** can send values back to the object that called the stored procedure. (*Note*: Text, ntext, and image parameters can be used as output parameters. However, in SQL Server 2000 the output parameter cannot have the datatype as Text.) You can also have a value that is passed to and returned from the stored procedure. This value is known as an **InputOutput parameter**. In addition, you can have a return value passed back to the stored procedure call. The return value is indicated with the keyword **Return** and is known as a **ReturnValue parameter**. It is often used for queries that don't return columns, such as an INSERT query. You can specify information such as the number of records affected in the return value. You can specify a default value for the parameter in the stored procedure. Therefore, if the user does not enter a parameter, the default is used. The default value must be a constant, or it can be null. You can return values of integer, money, and varchar but not text.

Visual Studio .NET provides an **SQL Editor** to create and edit SQL scripts and stored procedures. Although the SQL Editor does not have IntelliSense prompting, it does color-code SQL keywords, which helps minimize syntax and spelling errors. Comments in the SQL skeleton script are indicated with /* and */ characters. The comments are displayed in green text to differentiate the comments from SQL commands. The SQL Editor also inserts a skeletal stored procedure when you create a new stored procedure. You can change the editor's default behaviors such as tab size, word wrapping, and line numbers by selecting Options on the Tools menu.

6

Creating Stored Procedures with the SQL Editor

In the following exercises, you will create stored procedures using the SQL Editor. The first procedure will retrieve all of the records from the table where the QuantityAvailable column is less than MinOnHand. This creates a listing of products that must be reordered because there are not enough units available. The stored procedure will return the number of rows affected, and the @RETURN_VALUE. The @RETURN_VALUE is the value of the output parameter. If there is no value, then the value 0 is returned. The results are displayed as text in the Output window, which can be saved as a text file.

1. In the Server Explorer window, under the *MACHINENAME*\NETSDK. Chapter6.dbo data connection, right-click **Stored Procedures**, and then click **New Stored Procedure**. The stored procedure document opens with the default text for creating the stored procedure.

2. Replace the text dbo.StoredProcedure1 with **dbo.sp_ReorderProducts**.

3. Under the As keyword, insert a new line and type the code that follows this paragraph. The code retrieves all of the columns from the database where the QuantityAvailable column is less than the MinOnHand column. The asterisk is a wildcard character, which indicates that all columns are selected. Because this is SQL and not Visual Basic .NET, you do not have to add the underscore to continue onto the second line. A blue line will appear around the code, which indicates that the code can be edited manually or in the graphical user interface within the SQL Editor.

```
SELECT * FROM Products
WHERE QuantityAvailable < MinOnHand
```

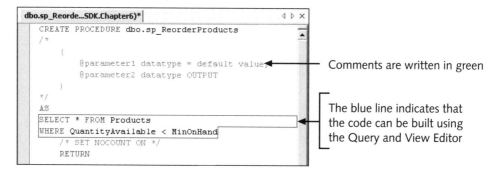

Figure 6-14   The SQL Editor

4. Click the **Save All** button. The stored procedure is saved. The first line of the SQL command changes from CREATE PROCEDURE to ALTER PROCE-DURE. This means that the procedure has been created. At this point, you can only change the procedure using the ALTER PROCEDURE command. Close the window.

5. Click the **plus sign** next to Stored Procedures in the Server Explorer window. Right-click the **sp_ReorderProducts** stored procedure, and then click **Run Stored Procedure**. The results are displayed in the **Output window**. There should be one row returned, which contains ProductID 2. The results will return the number of rows affected, which is 1, and the @RETURN_VALUE, which is 0. (*Note:* You can save the output as text. Click the **Output window**. Click the **File** menu, and click **Save Output As**.) Close the window. If prompted, enter your user name and password.

Now you will create a stored procedure that returns the products that match an input parameter value. Then you will create another stored procedure to display the product information for a single product, based upon the product name supplied by the end user.

1. In the Server Explorer window, under the *MACHINENAME* NETSDK.Chapter6.dbo data connection, right-click **Stored Procedures**, and then click **New Stored Procedure**. The stored procedure document opens with the default text for creating the stored procedure.

2. Replace the text dbo.StoredProcedure1 with **dbo.sp_DisplayProduct**.

3. Insert a blank line after the CREATE PROCEDURE line. Type the code listed after this paragraph to define a parameter named @param_ModelName. The column name that will be mapped to the parameter is **ModelName**. The datatype for the parameter and column is **nvarchar**, with a length of **50** bytes.

```
@param_ModelName nvarchar(50)
```

4. Under the As keyword create a new line and type the code that follows this paragraph. The code retrieves a subset of the columns from the database. You must supply the name of the product when the stored procedure is called. The stored procedure is also shown in Figure 6-15.

```
SELECT ProductID, ModelName,
UnitCost, ModelNumber, ProductImage
FROM Products
WHERE ModelName = @param_ModelName
```

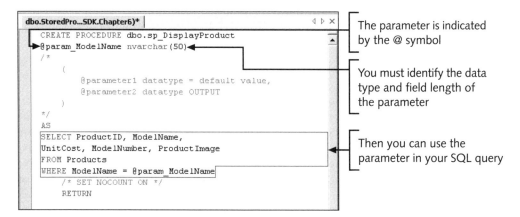

Figure 6-15   Creating stored procedures using the SQL Editor

5. Click the **Save All** button. The stored procedure is saved. The first line of the SQL command changes from CREATE PROCEDURE to ALTER PROCEDURE. This means that the procedure has been created. At this point, you can only alter the procedure, using the ALTER PROCEDURE command.

6. Right-click the **sp_DisplayProduct** stored procedure, and then select **Run Stored Procedure**. The Run stored procedure window appears. (*Note*: You can have multiple input parameters listed here.)   In the Value column for the @param_ModelName procedure, enter **Letter Opener**, as shown in Figure 6-16, and then click the **OK** button. Only one column matches the criteria. The columns listed for the first record are displayed in the Output window. If prompted, enter your user name and password.

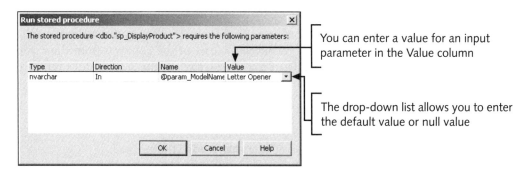

Figure 6-16   Running the stored procedure

7. Close the output window and the stored procedure.

In the following exercise, you use the SQL Editor to create a stored procedure that will insert a new record in the Categories table and return the value of the identity column.

1. In the Server Explorer window, under the *MACHINENAME\ NETSDK.Chapter6.dbo* data connection, right-click **Stored Procedures**, and then click **New Stored Procedure**. The stored procedure document opens with the default text for creating the stored procedure.

2. Replace the text dbo.StoredProcedure1 with **dbo.sp_InsertCat**.

3. Insert a blank line after the CREATE PROCEDURE line. Type the code that follows this paragraph. The code defines an input parameter named @param_CatName. The column name that will be mapped to the parameter is CategoryName. The datatype for the parameter and column is nvarchar, with a length of **50** bytes. All parameters are considered input parameters by default, so you don't have to indicate that the parameter is an input parameter.

```
@param_CatName nvarchar(50)
```

4. Under the As keyword, insert a new line and type the code that follows this paragraph. The code inserts the new row using the value passed from the parameter as the value for the CategoryName column. You can pass a list of column names separated by commas. You must pass the values for each of the columns in a comma-separated list if there is more than one column. The values that are passed must be in the same order as the column names.

```
INSERT INTO Categories (CategoryName)
VALUES (@param_CatName)
```

5. After the RETURN keyword, press the **spacebar** once and then type **@@Identity**, as shown in Figure 6-17 and in the code snippet following this paragraph. The @@Identity code will retrieve the identity column when the stored procedure is run.

```
RETURN @@Identity
```

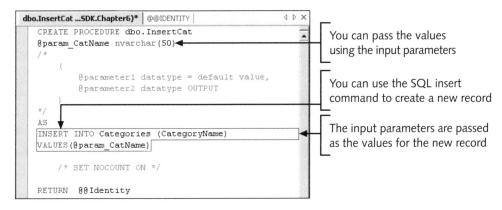

Figure 6-17 Creating a stored procedure to insert a row

6. Click the **Save All** button and close the window. The stored procedure is saved in the SQL Server database.

7. Right-click the **sp_InsertCat** stored procedure, and then click **Run Stored Procedure**. The Run stored procedure window opens. In the Value column for the @param_CatName procedure, type **Jewelry** as shown in Figure 6-18, and then click the **OK** button. If prompted, enter your user name and password.

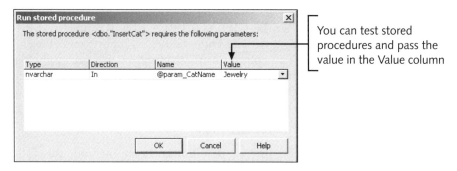

You can test stored procedures and pass the value in the Value column

Figure 6-18   Passing an input parameter

8. Right-click the **Categories** icon under the Tables list for the Chapter6 database in the Solution Explorer window, and then click **Retrieve Data from Table**. The Jewelry entry should be listed in a new record in the third row, as shown in Figure 6-19. If prompted, enter your user name and password.

9. Close all of the windows.

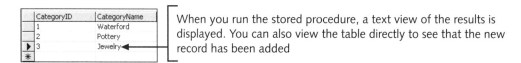

When you run the stored procedure, a text view of the results is displayed. You can also view the table directly to see that the new record has been added

Figure 6-19   Viewing the new record

In the following exercise, you will create a stored procedure that searches a field in the database for a matching value. You will search a text string under the ModelName field, then display the results.

1. In the Server Explorer window, under the Chapter6 data connection, right-click **Stored Procedures**, and then click **New Stored Procedure**. The stored procedure document opens with the default text for creating the stored procedure.

2. Replace the text dbo.StoredProcedure1 with **dbo.sp_SearchProducts**.

3. Insert a blank line after the CREATE PROCEDURE line. Enter the code that follows this paragraph. The code defines an input parameter named @param_SearchProducts. The column name that will be mapped to the

parameter is ModelName. The datatype for the parameter and column is nvarchar with a length of 50 bytes.

```
@param_SearchProducts nvarchar(50)
```

4. Under the As keyword, insert a new line and type the following code, which retrieves a subset of the columns from the database:

```
SELECT ProductID, ModelName,
ModelNumber, UnitCost, ProductImage,
Manufacturer
FROM Products
```

5. Type the code that follows this paragraph. The code uses the WHERE clause to search for a condition that contains the string that was passed with the parameter. It uses the wildcard character and the Like keyword to locate any text that contains the string passed, as shown in Figure 6-20.

```
WHERE
ModelNumber LIKE '%' + @param_SearchProducts + '%'
OR
ModelName LIKE '%' + @param_SearchProducts + '%'
OR
Description LIKE '%' + @param_SearchProducts + '%'
OR
Manufacturer LIKE '%' + @param_SearchProducts + '%'
```

6. Click the **Save All** button and close the window.

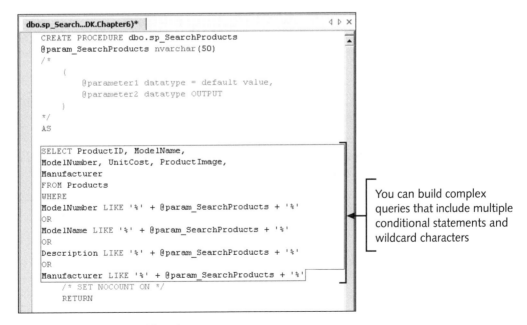

Figure 6-20   Using wildcards

7. Right-click the **sp_ SearchProducts** stored procedure, and then click **Run Stored Procedure**. The Run stored procedure window opens. In the Value column for the @param_SearchProducts procedure, type **Letter** and then click the **OK** button. Only one column matches the criteria. The columns listed for the first record are displayed. If prompted, enter your user name and password.

8. Run the stored procedure again with a different value entered for the input parameter. Right-click the **sp_ SearchProducts** stored procedure and click **Run Stored Procedure**. The Run stored procedure window opens. In the Value column for the @param_SearchProducts procedure, type **Waterford** and then click the **OK** button. Now all three columns match the criteria. If prompted, enter your user name and password.

9. Close the windows.

Modifying Stored Procedures with the SQL Query Builder

The SQL Query Builder has the same user interface as the Query and View Editor that you used earlier. However, the code to create the query is stored in the stored procedure. Within the stored procedure, you can edit the blocks of code that are enclosed within a blue line, via the SQL Query Builder. Simply right-click the block and select Design SQL Block. In the following exercise, you will modify a stored procedure using the SQL Query Builder.

1. In the Server Explorer window, under the Chapter6 data connection, right-click the **sp_ReorderProducts** stored procedure, and then click **Edit Stored Procedure**. The stored procedure script you created earlier opens.

2. Right-click the blue-outlined block of code, and then click **Design SQL Block**. This opens the block of code within the SQL Query Builder.

3. In the SQL pane change the QuantityAvailable criteria from < MinOnHand to **<=10**.

4. Click the **Save All** button.

5. Right-click the **sp_ReorderProducts** stored procedure, and then click **Run Stored Procedure**. There should be two records displayed in the Results pane. If prompted, enter your user name and password.

6. Close the window. If you are asked to save your changes, click **Yes**. Save your solution. Click the **Build** menu and then click **Build Solution**.

INTERNET RESOURCES

This chapter provides an introduction to the database tools contained within Visual Studio .NET. You can learn more about SQL from a variety of Internet resources. These Internet resources contain information about SQL, databases, and data-driven Web applications. While Microsoft supports ADO.NET technology, other vendors may not support it. For example, Java provides an alternate solution that involves using JDBC, the Java Database Connection. Because these technologies change frequently, the latest information about ADO.NET is located on the Internet through the Microsoft MSDN Library at *www.msdn.microsoft.com/library/*. You should try to review these Web sites frequently to keep current with the latest database technologies.

6

- Microsoft SQL Server—*www.microsoft.com/sql*

- MSDE 2000—*www.microsoft.com/sql/msde/default.asp*

- SQL Server 2005, the newest version of SQL Server— *www.microsoft.com/sql/2005/default.asp*

- SQL Server Web Data Administrator—*www.microsoft.com/downloads/ details.aspx?FamilyID=C039A798-C57A-419E-ACBC-2A332CB7F959& displaylang=en*

- SQL Server 2000 Security—*www.microsoft.com/sql/techinfo/administration/ 2000/security/default.asp*

- 10 steps to help secure SQL Server—*www.microsoft.com/sql/techinfo/ administration/2000/security/securingsqlserver.asp*

- Oracle—*www.oracle.com*

- SQL Server Magazine—*www.winnetmag.com/SQLServer*

- SQL Interpreter and Tutorial—*www.sqlcourse.com*

- Small & Medium Business—*www.microsoft.com/sql/smb/default.asp*

- Case Study of Mary Kay: Reducing costs with SQL Server 2000 Reporting Services—*www.microsoft.com/resources/casestudies/CaseStudy. asp?CaseStudyID=14592*

CHAPTER SUMMARY

❐ In the ADO.NET model, you connect to data sources using managed providers. The .NET Data Provider for SQL Server is located in the System.Data.SqlClient namespace. Each of the .NET Data Providers is located in its own namespace within the System.Data namespace. There are .NET Data Providers for SQL Server, Oracle, OLE DB, and ODBC data sources. These providers maintain the interface with the lower level providers and drivers that communicate directly with the data source. The .NET application interfaces only with the .NET Data Providers.

❐ The ADO.NET object model consists of four objects: Connection, Command, DataAdapter, and DataReader. Each of the .NET Data Providers contains its own version of these four ADO.NET objects. The DataAdapter serves as a bridge between the DataSet object and the data source. The DataReader object is a high-performance object that provides a stream of data. The data is read-only and forward-only.

❐ The DataSet object is a disconnected set of data that is stored in memory. Therefore, the DataSet is not the most current version of the data. The DataSet maintains the changes in the DataSet, and pushes the changes to the server. The DataSet consists of a DataTableCollection and DataRelationCollection. The DataTable can consist of many DataViews. A DataView is a subset of data from a single DataTable. A DataSet can be persisted as an XML document. You can import XML data into a DataSet object, or store the DataSet as an XML document.

❐ You can use the Visual Database Tools within Visual Studio .NET to create and maintain your databases. The Table Editor allows you to create tables and enter data. The Query and View Editor allows you to create queries called views. The SQL Editor allows you to create stored procedures. Stored procedures are SQL commands that are stored with the SQL Server, and compiled. Therefore, stored procedures run faster than SQL commands that are stored in a Web page. The SQL Query Builder allows you to use the visual tools to build your stored procedures.

❐ Database and Web technologies change frequently. There are a variety of Web sites that you can consult for up-to-date information about ADO.NET, SQL Server, SQL, queries, and stored procedures.

REVIEW QUESTIONS

1. Which of the following is not a datatype in SQL Server 2000?

   a. int

   b. nvarchar

   c. char

   d. array

2. What is required to connect a database to an ADO.NET Web application?

   a. an ODBC provider

   b. a Managed Provider

   c. a UDA database

   d. an OLE DB driver

3. Which object is used to connect the Web application to the database?

   a. connection

   b. command

   c. parameter

   d. transaction

4. What is the keyword used to identify the MSDE server within a connection string?

   a. database

   b. data source

   c. service

   d. data store

5. What is the name of property that is used to identify the values that are passed to the Command object?

   a. Connection

   b. ActiveConnection

   c. Parameter

   d. CommandText

6. Which is not a valid option for the CommandType property?

   a. Text

   b. SQL

   c. TableDirect

   d. StoredProcedure

7. Which object provides a read-only, forward-only stream of data from the database?

    a. DataReader

    b. Connection

    c. Recordset

    d. Command

8. What is the name of the parameter that is used to close the connection using the Command object?

    a. CommandClose

    b. Close

    c. CommandBehavior

    d. ConnectionClose

9. Which is not one of the ADO.NET objects?

    a. Connection

    b. Recordset

    c. DataReader

    d. DataAdapter

10. Which method is used to populate a DataSet object from a DataAdapter object?

    a. SelectCommand

    b. Select

    c. Fill

    d. InsertCommand

11. What is used to ensure that no duplicates can appear in a column?

    a. a foreign key

    b. a primary key

    c. a connection string

    d. a relationship

12. What property allows you to specify information that can be stored with the DataSet object and later retrieved?

    a. DataView

    b. DataSet

    c. CommandBuilder

    d. ExtendedProperties

13. Which property allows you to retrieve a subset of the DataView?

    a. RowFilter

    b. Sort

    c. Filter

    d. GetRows

14. What is the file extension for the DataSet generated from the database using Visual Studio .NET?

    a. .xml

    b. .xsl

    c. .xslt

    d. .xsd

15. What is the name of the namespace for the OLE DB .NET Data Provider?

    a. System.Data.SqlClient

    b. System.Data

    c. System.Data.OleDb

    d. System.Data.ODBC

16. What is the tool used to create a new table in Visual Studio .NET?

    a. Table Designer

    b. Database Designer

    c. SQL Builder

    d. Query and View Editor

17. Which pane in the SQL Editor shows the criteria as visual icons?

    a. Table pane

    b. Grid pane

    c. SQL pane

    d. Results pane

18. What is the value of a column within a row that has no value assigned?

    a. ()

    b. an empty string " "

    c. false

    d. null

6

19. If the relationship in the database diagram has a key at each endpoint, then what type of relationship is it?

   a. one-to-two

   b. many-to-one

   c. one-to-one

   d. many-to-many

20. What symbol is used to identify the parameter in a stored procedure?

   a. @

   b. $

   c. #

   d. *

HANDS-ON PROJECTS

Project 6-1

In this project, you will create a connection to the Pubs database. The Pubs database is one of the sample databases installed when you installed the MSDE samples.

1. Start **Visual Studio .NET** and open your **Chapter6** solution. Create a Web page named **Ch6Proj1.aspx** that will be used to display your answers to the questions in Steps 7-9

2. Right-click the **Data Connections** in the Server Explorer window, and click **Add Connection**.

3. Type **(local)\NetSDK** in the server name text box.

4. Click the radio button labeled **Use Windows NT Integrated security** to select it. (*Note*: If your server uses SQL Server authentication, in the User name text box type **sa**. Leave the password text box blank. Click the **Blank password** check box to select it.)

5. In the "Select the database on the server" drop-down list box, select **pubs**.

6. Click the **Test Connection** button. Click **OK** in the alert message. Click the **OK** button in the dialog box.

7. Look at the database contents within the Data Connections tool and answer the questions in the following list. Type your answers on the Ch6Proj1.aspx page.

   ❐ What are the names of the tables in the Pubs database?

   ❐ How many records are in the authors table?

   ❐ What is the primary key column for the authors table?

❏ Which datatypes are used in the authors table?

❏ Which columns are required to have a value?

❏ Which field(s) must contain unique values within the column?

8. Look at the **titleview** view and answer the questions in the following list. Type your answers on the Ch6Proj1.aspx page.

❏ What are the three tables that are joined together in the query?

❏ What is the relationship between the titleauthor table and the titles table?

❏ What field is used to establish a relationship between the authors table and the titleauthor table?

❏ How many records are displayed in the titleview table?

9. Look at the **byroyalty** stored procedure and answer the questions in the following list. Type your answers on the Ch6Proj1.aspx page.

❏ What is the name of the table being used?

❏ What is the name of the parameter?

❏ What symbol is used to identify the parameter?

❏ What is the datatype of the parameter?

❏ Is the parameter an input or output parameter?

❏ Why does the stored procedure say ALTER PROCEDURE instead of CREATE PROCEDURE?

10. Save the Ch6Proj1.aspx page in your Chapter6 solution. Print the Web page.

Project 6-2

In this project, you will create a connection to the Northwind database. The Northwind database is one of the sample databases that was installed when you installed the MSDE samples.

1. Start **Visual Studio .NET** and open your **Chapter6** solution if necessary. Create a Web page named **Ch6Proj2.aspx** that will be used to display your answers to the questions in Steps 7-10.

2. Right-click the **Data Connections** in Server Explorer, and then click **Add Connection**.

3. Type **(local)\NetSDK** in the server name text box.

4. Click the radio button labeled **Use Windows NT Integrated security** to select it. (*Note*: If your server uses SQL Server authentication, in the User name text box type **sa**. Leave the password text box blank. Click the **Blank password** check box to select it.)

5. In the "Select the database on the server" drop-down list box, click **Northwind**.

6. Click the **Test Connection** button. Click **OK** in the alert message. Click **OK** to close the dialog box.

7. Look at the database contents within the Data Connections tool and answer the questions in the following list. Type your answers on the Ch6Proj2.aspx page.

   ❐ What are the names of the tables in the Northwind database?

   ❐ How many records are in the customers table? (*Hint:* You can count them manually or create a stored procedure that will return to you the number of records.)

   ❐ What is the primary key column for the customers table?

   ❐ Which datatypes are used in the customers table?

   ❐ Which columns are required to have a value?

   ❐ Which field(s) must contain unique values within the column?

8. Look at the **Products by Category** view. Type your answers to the questions in the following list on the Ch6Proj2.aspx page.

   ❐ What are the two tables that are joined together in the query?

   ❐ What is the relationship between the tables?

   ❐ What field is used to establish a relationship between the tables? How many records are displayed in the view?

9. Look at the **Ten Most Expensive Products** stored procedure. Type your answers to the questions in the following list on the Ch6Proj2.aspx page.

   ❐ What is the name of the table being used?

   ❐ What is the purpose of the ROWCOUNT property?

   ❐ What are the keywords used to sort the data?

10. Look at the **CustOrderHist** stored procedure. Type your answers to the questions in the following list on the Ch6Proj2.aspx page.

    ❐ What is the name of the table being used?

    ❐ What is the name of the parameter?

    ❐ What symbol is used to identify the parameter?

    ❐ What is the datatype of the parameter? Is the parameter an input or output parameter?

    ❐ Why does the stored procedure say ALTER PROCEDURE instead of CREATE PROCEDURE?

11. Save the Ch6Proj2.aspx page in your Chapter6 solution. Print the Web page.

Project 6-3

In this project, you will create a customer database using Visual Studio .NET.

1. Start **Visual Studio .NET** and open your **Chapter6** solution if necessary.

2. In Visual Studio .NET, create a database named **Ch6Proj3**. (See your instructor for information on extracting and/or placing the Ch6Proj3.mdf file.)

3. Use the information in Table 6-4 to determine the column names, datatypes, lengths, and properties.

Table 6-4   Customer database information

Column Name	DataType	Length	Allow Nulls
CustomerID	int	4	No
CustomerName	nvarchar	50	Yes
EmailAddress	nvarchar	50	Yes
Password	nvarchar	50	Yes
MembershipLevel	int	4	Yes

6

4. In the properties at the bottom half of the window, change the Identity for the CustomerID column from No to **Yes** using the drop-down list arrow. The Identity Seed should be set to **1**, and the Identity Increment should be set to **1**. This creates a new value for each new record entered in the database.

5. Right-click the **CustomerID** column name and select **Set Primary Key**. A yellow key appears at the side of the column name to indicate that this column is the primary key column.

6. Click the **Save All** button and save the table as **Customers**.

7. Enter the data listed in Table 6-5. Let the MSDE assign the values for the CustomerID column.

Table 6-5   Customer data

Column Name	Row1	Row2	Row3	Row4
CustomerID				
CustomerName	June Mayzer	Ralph Waldon	Joseph Reno	Kevin Marx
EmailAddress	JM@ tarastore.com	RW@ tarastore.com	JR@ tarastore.com	KM@ tarastore.com
Password	Franklin	Bears	Crypto	Loyola
MembershipLevel	2	1	2	3

8. Print the table and the schema. (*Note:* You can print the screen by pressing the **PrntScrn** key. You can also copy the screen shot by pressing the **Shift** key and the **PrntScrn** key at the same time. Then, you can paste this into a word processor.)

Project 6-4

In this project, you will create an orders database table using Visual Studio .NET.

1. Start **Visual Studio .NET** and open your **Chapter6** solution if necessary.

2. In Visual Studio .NET, create a database named **Ch6Proj4**.

3. Use the information in Table 6-6 to determine the column names, datatypes, lengths, and properties.

Table 6-6 Customer order information

Column Name	DataType	Length	Allow Nulls
OrderID	int	4	No
CustomerID	int	4	No
ProductName	nvarchar	50	Yes
ProductDescription	nvarchar	50	Yes
ShippingMethod	int	4	Yes

4. In the properties at the bottom half of the window, change the Identity for the OrderID column from No to **Yes** using the drop-down list arrow. The Identity Seed should be set to **1**, and the Identity Increment should be set to **1**. This creates a new value for each new record entered in the database.

5. Right-click the **OrderID** column name and select **Set Primary Key**. A yellow key appears at the side of the column name to indicate that this column is the primary key column.

6. Click the **Save All** button and save the table as **Orders**.

7. Enter the data listed in Table 6-7. Let the MSDE assign the values for the OrderID column.

Table 6-7 Additional product information

Column Name	Row1	Row2	Row3	Row4
OrderID				
CustomerID	1	1	3	4
ProductName	Letter Opener	Business Card Holder	Cat Bowl	Shamrock Paperweight
ProductDescription	Letter Opener by Waterford.	Business Card Holder by Waterford	Cat Bowl by Belinda Bradshaw	Shamrock Paperweight by Waterford
ShippingMethod	1	2	3	1

8. Print the table and the schema. (*Note:* You can print the screen by pressing the **PrntScrn** key. You can also copy the screen shot by pressing the **Shift** key and the **PrntScrn** key at the same time. Then, you can paste this into a word processor.)

Project 6-5

In this project, you will create a stored procedure in the GrocerToGo database using Visual Studio .NET.

1. Start **Visual Studio .NET** and open your **Chapter6** solution if necessary.

2. Create a new stored procedure named **sp_DisplayProducts** in the GrocerToGo database.

3. The stored procedure should display the ProductID, CategoryID, ProductName, and Manufacturer columns from the Products table, as shown in the code that follows this paragraph. All records should be displayed.

```
SELECT ProductID, CategoryID,
ProductName, Manufacturer
FROM Products
```

4. Run the stored procedure. Print the results displayed in the Output window. Save the results as **Ch6Proj5.txt** in the C:\Inetpub\wwwroot\Chapter6 directory.

Project 6-6

In this project, you will create a stored procedure in the GrocerToGo database using Visual Studio .NET.

6

1. Start **Visual Studio .NET** and open your **Chapter6** solution if necessary.

2. Create a stored procedure named **sp_ProductDetails**.

3. The stored procedure should display all of the columns. It should display only the records that match the ProductID that is provided when the stored procedure is called.

4. Add an input parameter named **@param_ProductID** that has a datatype of **int**. (*Note:* You do not specify the size of this input variable.)

5. Add the **SQL SELECT** statement to retrieve the values from the database. Select all products from the Products table where the ProductID equals the input parameter named **@param_ProductID**.

6. Run the stored procedure. Use the ProductID **3002** when you are asked for an input parameter.

7. Save the stored procedure. Print the results displayed in the Output window. Save the results as **Ch6Proj6.txt** in the C:\Inetpub\wwwroot\Chapter6 directory.

CASE PROJECTS

Tara Store — The ADO.NET Data Model

Your customer has requested that your company support the .NET Framework. Their application requires access to an SQL Server database. Research the use of ADO.NET in enterprise applications. Use the Help menu in Visual Studio .NET, the *www.asp.net* Web site, the *www.msdn.microsoft.com/library* Web site, the QuickStart Web site (*localhost/quickstart*), and the *www.GotDotNet.com* Web site to locate more information. Write up a chart that compares the ADO.NET object model to the ADO object model. Save the page as Ch6Case1.aspx. Save the page in your Chapter6 solution. Print the Web page.

Tara Store — Creating a Database Using Visual Studio .NET

Your boss has asked you to create a demonstration shopping cart application. Your first step is to set up a sample database. Create a database named Ch6Case2 using your local SQL Server. Create a Product table and a Categories table. Each table must have a primary key. Create the database diagram. Establish a relationship between the tables using the primary keys. Save the diagram as Categories. Enter sample data into the tables. Print the database diagram, the table schema, and the data for the two tables.

Tara Store — Creating Stored Procedures with Visual Studio .NET

Your boss has heard that it's more efficient to use a stored procedure than an SQL query. He would like you to create and run several queries using stored procedures. Using the Northwind database, create a new stored procedure named sp_USCustomers. Retrieve the records for all customers in the USA. Sort the results based on the Region and CompanyName columns. Run the stored procedure and print out the results. Save the results as Ch6Case3.txt in your c:\Inetpub\wwwroot\Chapter6 directory.

I Buy Spy — Creating a Database for a Shopping Cart with Visual Studio .NET

You are developing a sample Web database shopping cart to teach new Web developers how to create tables in Visual Studio .NET. Recreate the I Buy Spy online store located at *www.ibuyspy.com/IBS_Store/*. Visit the I Buy Spy store online. Read the documentation at *www.ibuyspy.com/ibuyspy/IBuySpy%20Store%20Whitepaper.doc*. Reconstruct the database and the tables in the shopping cart. Name the database Ch6Case4. Create a data diagram using the Database Designer. Name the data diagram Ch6Case4Diagram as shown in Figure 6-21. Print each of the table schemas and the data.

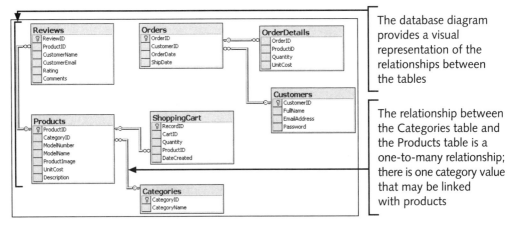

Figure 6-21   Database diagram

7

BUILDING DATA-DRIVEN ASP.NET APPLICATIONS

In this chapter, you will:

♦ Learn about the various methods used to bind data to Web Server controls
♦ Bind an array to various Web Server controls
♦ Bind a hash table to a DataGrid and Repeater control
♦ Populate a DropDownList control from an array
♦ Populate a DataGrid control from a hash table
♦ Modify the appearance of a DataGrid control using templates
♦ Modify the appearance of a Repeater control using templates
♦ Modify the appearance of a DataList control using templates

---

One of the challenges that Web developers face is the variety of data sources and the variety of ways in which data can be displayed in Web applications. For example, a data source can be a simple hash table, an array, or a database. Data can be displayed as a simple list, a drop-down list, or a table. A Web developer must be able to use various techniques to build data-driven Web applications. Using ASP.NET, you can separate the data source from the presentation of the data. In the previous chapter, you learned how to connect to and manage a database. In this chapter, you will learn how to work with various controls to display data in your Web applications.

DATA BINDING TECHNIQUES

In Chapter 6 you learned to create a SQL Server database using Visual Studio .NET. Data can be stored in many forms, not just databases. **Data source** is a term that represents the data. Data can be in the form of a single item, such as the name of an image, or it can be in the form of multiple items, for example a list or an array containing the names of many images. Lists of data can be stored in various formats such as array lists and hash tables. In ASP.NET, array lists are stored in ArrayList objects, and hash tables are stored in HashTable objects.

The data from the data source can be retrieved and used by a Web Server control. The process of assigning the data source to a Web control is called **data binding**. For example, a single expression data source may be an image name such as "home.gif". The Image Web Server control can assign this data source as the value for the ImageUrl property. When the page is requested the browser would display the home.gif image. As shown in Figure 7-1, the data source can be single expressions or repeated expressions. Repeated expressions include hash tables, array lists, and databases. Data binding usually occurs when the page is first loaded, or when the data has changed.

The two types of data binding are single-value binding and repeat-value binding. When a single piece of data or a single expression is bound to a control, it is called **single-value binding**. Single-value binding is sometimes used to store single values such as constants and read-only properties. **Repeat-value binding** allows you to bind your control to multiple items. Examples of repeat-value binding include databases, hash tables, and array lists.

Although it is possible to bind data to HTML Server controls, in this chapter you will work with Web Server controls.

Some Web controls, such as RadioButtonLists and CheckBoxLists controls, can display multiple values. These values can be obtained from various types of data sources, such as array lists, hash tables, and databases. In Chapter 3, you created Web pages that bound an ArrayList object to a RadioButtonList control, and a HashTable object to a CheckBoxList control. There are several Web Server controls such as DropDownList controls that are designed to be bound to repeated expressions and databases.

There are many advantages to binding data to controls. If the data changes, the data control automatically reflects the change. Data binding allows you to get records synchronously—the ability to retrieve records is not tied to the page loading process. As a result the whole page is more responsive and loads more quickly. Data binding results in fewer trips to the server, since you normally won't need to interact with the server once the requested data has been downloaded. Any interaction with the database requires a round trip to the server to refresh the page, which ensures total browser compatibility. However, you can improve performance when interacting with database by caching the pages on the server. You will learn more about caching databases in the next chapter.

In this chapter you will learn how to bind different types of data to many different types of ASP.NET controls. In this chapter, you will bind an ArrayList object and a HashTable object to a DropDownList control, a ListBox control, a RadioButtonList control, and a CheckBoxList control. Then, you will bind a HashTable object to a DataGrid control, a DataList control, and then a Repeater control. After learning basic data binding techniques, you will then change the data source to a database. You will use the .NET DataAdapter, DataSet, and DataView objects to retrieve data from a database. You will bind a DataSet object to a DataGrid control. Next, you will create a Web page to modify the data displayed by the DataGrid control. You will then use templates to modify the appearance of the DataGrid, Repeater, and DataList controls. By the end of this chapter, you will have learned a variety of databinding techniques.

7

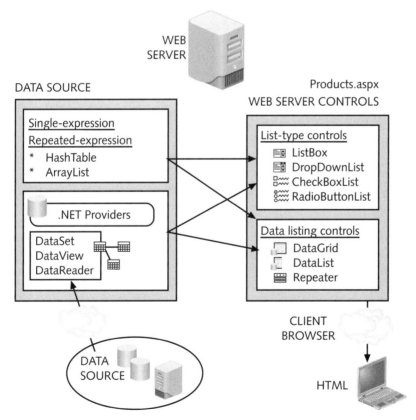

Figure 7-1 Binding data sources to a variety of Web Server controls

Single-Expression Binding

Single-expression binding is used to bind a single value or expression to a control. To bind a single expression to an ASP.NET control, you use the pound sign (#) before the expression's name. The expression is enclosed within inline server tags (<% %>). No other code can be placed inside the tags, as shown in the code following this paragraph. The ImageURL variable stores the location of the image. Later in the page, the image location can be retrieved and used to display the image.

```
<% Dim ImageURL As String = "logo.gif" %>
<img name="Logo" src="<%# ImageURL %>" alt="Logo" />
```

In the previous example, you retrieved the value from a variable. The data that is being bound can also be in the form of a property, procedure, or expression. You can use the bound expression to display the value in a Web page, to store a value, or to use the value in another expression.

The data is not bound until the **DataBind method** is called from the page, or from the control. This is important because the data is stored separately from the control. The data is integrated into the control only when the control is created in the Web server's memory. If the data has changed before the data is bound to the control, the most recent data will be used. The DataBind method for the page is called using Page.DataBind(). The Page.DataBind procedure is often called within the Page_Load event handler so that the data is bound before the page is displayed. You can also bind the expression to a single control by calling the DataBind method of an individual control, such as Logo.DataBind().

In this chapter, you will insert code both manually and using the wizards. There is a greater chance for programming errors to occur when Web developers type in the code. Make sure to double-check the spelling and syntax when you enter your code, especially for connection strings and while working in HTML view. Using the wizards when possible will also decrease the chance of making typographical errors.

In previous examples, you assigned the value of the function to a property of a control. For example, you would write `txtImageURL.Text = GetImageURL()`. In the following exercise, you will create a Web page that contains a read-only property and a function. You will bind all the page Data controls using Page.DataBind, then display the bound Data controls in the Web page. The Label Web Server and Text Box Web Server controls are bound to the value from the ImageURL property. The Image Button control is bound to the value returned by the GetImageURL function. When the page is rendered, the controls are bound to the values, and displayed in the Web page.

1. Start Visual Studio .NET.

2. Click **File** on the menu bar, point to **New**, and then click **Project**. This opens the New Project window.

3. Click the **Visual Basic Projects** folder icon, and then click the **ASP.NET Web Application** icon under Templates. Type **Chapter7** in the Location text box in place of WebApplication1. Click **OK** to create the solution, project, and default files.

4. Open **Windows Explorer**. Navigate to your **Chapter07data** folder. Select the **images** folder and the **data** folder. Go to the **Edit** menu and select **Copy**. Go back to Visual Studio .NET 2003. Right-click the **Chapter7** project and select **Paste**. The image folder and data folder will be copied into your project.

5. Right-click the **Chapter7** project, point to **Add**, and then click **Add Existing Item**. Change the Files of type drop-down list from VB Code Files to **All Files**. Browse to locate the **Chapter07Data** folder. Select all files from the Chapter07Data folder except the data and images folders. Click the **Open** button to import the files into your project. Messages will appear that ask you to create a class for several of the .aspx files. When prompted, click **Yes** in each instance to create new class files. (*Note*: You can close the Start Page and the default WebForm1.aspx in the main code window. You will not be modifying these pages in this chapter. You can click the minus sign next to the images folder to collapse the folder.)

6. Double-click **SingleBind.aspx** in the Solution Explorer window to open the page. Double-click on the page to open the code behind the page, which is named SingleBind.aspx.vb. Add the code below directly above the Page_Load event procedure. This code creates a new property named ImageURL that contains a string. The property is read-only, which means that it cannot be changed. When the property is called, the string "logo.gif" is returned.

```
ReadOnly Property ImageURL() As String
    Get
        Return "logo.gif"
    End Get
End Property
```

7. Below the code you just added, add the code following this paragraph, which creates a function named GetImageURL. The function returns "images/logo.gif" when the function is called.

```
Function GetImageURL() As String
    Return "images/logo.gif"
End Function
```

8. In the Page_Load event procedure, after the comment, add the code following this paragraph. This code binds all of the data controls in the page to the data sources identified in their properties, as shown in Figure 7-2.

```
Page.DataBind()
```

7

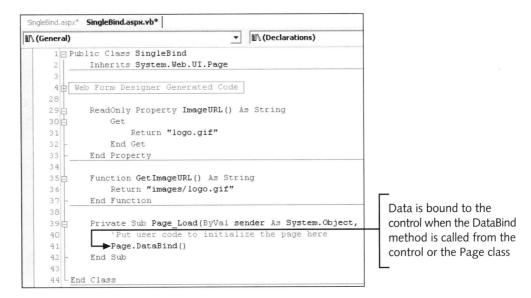

Figure 7-2   Return an expression from a property or function

9. Click the **Save All** button and close the SingleBind.aspx.vb page. Click the **SingleBind.aspx** tab to edit the SingleBind.aspx page, if necessary.

10. To select the first control, open the Properties window if needed, click the drop-down list arrow at the top, and select the control '**lblImageURL**'. (*Note*: This drop-down list contains all of the controls within the page. This is an alternative way to select controls.) Verify that the ID of the control is lblImageURL. In the Text property, add the code **<%# ImageURL %>**. This code will insert the image name into the label control when the page is rendered.

11. Click the second control, which is the a TextBox Web Server control, to select it. The control is below the first control. Verify that the ID of the control is txtImageURL. You can set the Text property using the DataBindings dialog box. Click the **(DataBindings)** property. Click the **Build** button. Click **Text** in the Bindable Properties list. Click the **Custom binding expression:** radio button. In the text box below, type **ImageURL**, as shown in Figure 7-3, and click **OK**. This will place a database icon next to the Text property in the Properties Window and insert code into HTML view. (*Note*: The binding expression method is an alternative to setting the Text property to "<%# ImageURL%>" in HTML view.)

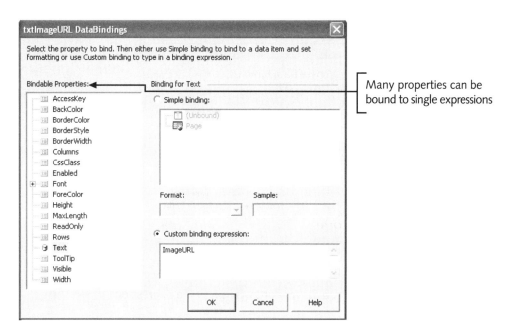

Figure 7-3   DataBindings dialog box

12. Click on the last control, which is below the second, to select it. Verify that the ID of the Image Web Server control is imgImageURL. Change the ImageUrl property to **<%# GetImageURL %>**. This will create the binding expression for the imgImageURL control. (*Note*: If you add the image path here, instead of in the function, the binding expression is returned. Therefore, it is better to have the path included in the function or property, and not in the ASP.NET control.)

13. Click the **Save All** button. Click **Build** on the menu bar, and then click **Build Solution**.

14. Right-click on the page, and then click **View in Browser**. Your page should look like the one in Figure 7-4.

15. Close any open pages.

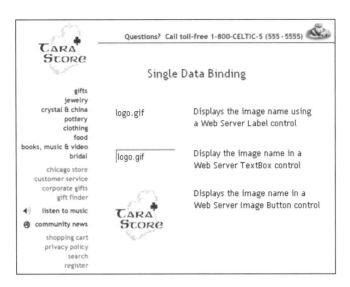

Figure 7-4   Binding Web Server controls to a single expression

Repeated-Expression Binding

Binding a set of data to an ASP.NET control is called repeated-value binding. There are several Web Server controls that you can use to bind to repeated expressions, as shown in Figure 7-5. All of these controls are members of the WebControls class (System.Web.UI.WebControls). These controls inherit from classes that can be bound to data. The ListControl class and BaseDataList class contain members that can be bound to repeated expressions. Both of these classes inherit from the WebControls class (System.Web.UI.WebControls). The DropDownList, ListBox, CheckBoxList, and RadioButtonList controls inherit from the ListControl class. The DataList and DataGrid controls inherit from the BaseDataList class. The Repeater control inherits directly from the System.Web.UI.Control class. Because these controls inherit from different base classes, some properties are not available in all controls. However, all controls use the same technique to bind to data expressions and data sources. All of these controls contain a DataSource property that can be set to a data expression. When the DataBind method of the page is called, the control is bound to the data in the DataSource property.

The repeated expression, which is bound to the data control, can be a collection, such as a hash table, or an array list. You can also bind the data to a DataSet, DataView, or DataReader object.

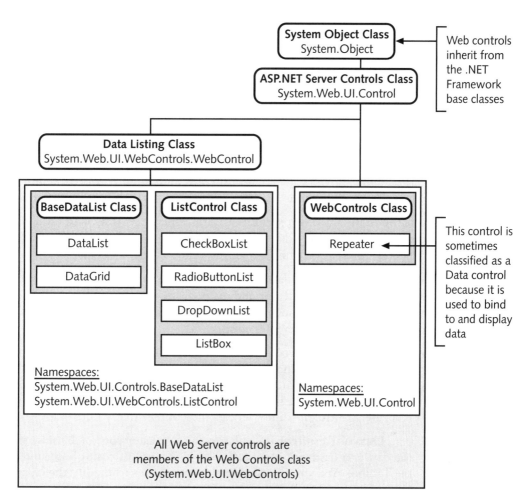

Figure 7-5   Web Server controls inherit from different classes

- The **DataSet object** is a cached set of records retrieved from the database. DataSet works like a virtual data store because it is disconnected from the original database source. The DataSet object can contain one or more DataTable objects. Because of this, you must identify the table members with the DataMember property of the DataSet. The **DataMember property** is the control that binds to one or more tables within a DataSet object.

- A **DataView object** contains a subset of rows of data from a DataTable object.

- A **DataReader object** is a read-only, forward-only stream of data from the database. A DataReader object is similar to the DataView object because it returns one or more rows of data. However, the DataReader object is a not a disconnected source of data. The data connection remains open while the

DataReader object reads the data. The DataReader object provides better performance than the DataView or DataSet objects. If you use the DataReader object, you can only read the rows once. As a result, you cannot create multiple controls with the data returned from the DataReader object.

DATA CONTROLS

ASP.NET supports several types of Web Server controls that can be bound to data sources. These **data-binding controls** are used to bind to the data sources, and then display the data in the Web page. The most commonly used repeated-binding data controls include the DropDownList, ListBox, Repeater, DataList, and DataGrid controls.

The DropDownList and ListBox controls both display the data using the HTML select tag. However, the DropDownList control usually only displays one value at a time, while the ListBox control generally displays all the values at the same time.

The Repeater, DataList, and DataGrid controls share a common programming model because they all inherit directly or indirectly from the System.Web.UI.Control class. However, the DataList and DataGrid controls both inherit WebControl class functionality, such as the Style and Appearance properties.

- The **Repeater control** is a small, lightweight control. It inherits only the basic Control class functionality, such as the ID property and a child Controls collection. The Repeater control displays the data using HTML controls that you can define. There is no visible interface or formatting available with the Repeater control; it simply repeats the content that you define.

- The **DataList control** is similar to the Repeater control, because it displays the data as a basic list. However, there is a DataList control user interface in the Toolbox. You can use the DataList properties to modify the layout of the horizontal or vertical columns.

- The **DataGrid control** allows you to use DataView, DataSet, or DataReader objects as the data source. The DataGrid control repeats content you define once for each data row. When the control is rendered, the page places the data in a table.

Binding Data to a DropDownList Control

In the following exercise, you will create a Web page that contains an array list and hash table, binds all the page Data controls, and then displays the bound DropDownList controls in the Web page. The code to create a DropDownList control is as follows.

```
<asp:dropdownlist id="MyDDL1" runat="server">
</asp:dropdownlist>
```

This example uses the IsPostBack property of the page class to determine if this page has been resubmitted to the server. If the page has not been posted back to the server, then the array list and hash table are populated with values, and are bound to the Web Server controls. If the page has been posted back to the server, then the values of what was selected from the drop-down lists are displayed in the Web page. This example demonstrates that the DropDownList control can be bound to a variety of data sources. (*Note*: In the next chapter, you will learn to bind the DropDownList control to a DataSet, DataView, and DataReader object.)

In this example, the data source is identified with the **DataSource property** of the DropDownList control. You must specify which item is displayed in the Web page using the **DataTextField property**. You use the **DataValueField property** to specify the value property of the DropDownList items, which is displayed only in the HTML source view of the rendered Web page. The DataValueField property corresponds to the value property of the HTML <option> control. The value can be formatted using the **DataTextFormatString property** of the DropDownList control. The expression {0:C} will format the value as currency. (*Note*: The 0 in 0:C is the number zero, not a letter.)

> You can use the DataTextFormatString property of a control to format the output as currency. For example, you can use the format: MyDataList.DataTextFormatString = "{0:C}". You can also use the Eval expression to format the value as currency, or another data type. Other regular expression formats, such as percentage, are also available. (*Note*: Several of these exercises use the same data for the HashTable and ArrayList objects. You will uncomment the code that declares these objects.)

In the following exercise, you will bind the array list and hash table to the DropDownList controls.

1. Open the **Chapter7** project in Visual Studio .NET if it is not already open.

2. If the page is not open, double-click the **DropDownList.aspx** page icon in the Solution Explorer window to open it. Then double-click on the whitespace area of the page to open the code behind the page, which is named DropDownList.aspx.vb.

3. Immediately after the comment ' Insert the code here, add the code to bind the DropDownList control named **MyDD1** to the array named arr1:

   ```
   MyDD1.DataSource = arr1
   ```

4. Immediately after the preceding code, add the code to bind the DropDownList control named **MyDD2** to the hash table. In this instance, the key item in the hash table is assigned to the DataTextField property, and therefore is displayed on the Web page.

   ```
   MyDD2.DataSource = MyHash
   MyDD2.DataTextField = "Key"
   MyDD2.DataValueField = "Value"
   ```

5. Immediately after the preceding code, add the code to bind the DropDownList control to the hash table. In this case, the value items of the hash table are assigned to the DataTextField property of the DropDownList control, and are therefore displayed on the Web page. The value contains the price of the items. The price is formatted as currency, using the DataTextFormatString property.

```
MyDD3.DataSource = MyHash
MyDD3.DataTextField = "Value"
MyDD3.DataValueField = "Key"
MyDD3.DataTextFormatString = "{0:C}"
```

6. Immediately after the preceding code, bind the data expressions to the DataSource property of the DropDownList controls:

```
Page.DataBind()
```

7. Click the **Save All** button. Click **Build** on the menu bar, and then click **Build Solution**.

8. Click the **DropDownList.aspx** tab at the top of the main window. Right-click on the page, and then click **View in Browser**. Select **Shamrock Paperweight** from the first drop-down list. Your page should look like the one shown in Figure 7-6. (*Note*: The second and third drop-down lists were created from the same HashTable object as the DataSource property. However, these drop-down lists were created with different DropDownList controls. Different values were assigned to the DataTextField properties for each of the DropDownList controls. Therefore, the two drop-down lists appear different in the browser window.) Click **Submit**.

9. Select **Belleek Colleen Vase** and **$22.00** from the last two drop-down lists. Click **Submit**.

10. The values selected are displayed in the Web page.

11. Close any open pages.

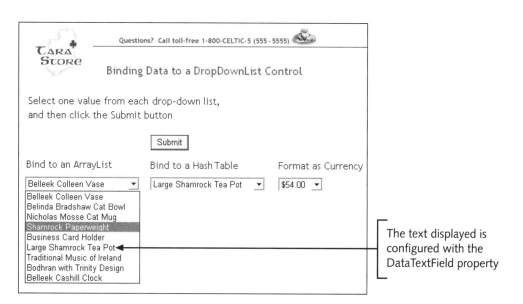

Figure 7-6   Binding data to a DropDownList control

Binding Data to a ListBox Control

The ListBox control can be bound to data. In the following exercise, you will create an array list and hash table, bind all the page Web Server controls, and then display the bound data ListBox controls in the Web page. The code used to create a ListBox control is as follows:

```
<asp:listbox id="MyLB1" runat="server">
</asp:listbox>
```

The ListBox control generates an HTML <select> tag. The property is set to display more than one value in the list. The ListBox control is often used when the user may select more than one value in the control. The data source in the ListBox control is identified with the **DataSource property**. Each item in the DataSource property will correspond to an <option> in the <select> tag. The text that is displayed for each option is identified with the **DataTextField property**. The **DataValueField property** is used to specify the value property of the ListBox items, which is displayed only in the HTML source view of the rendered Web page. The DataValueField property corresponds to the value property of the HTML <option> control. The value can be formatted using the **DataTextFormatString property** of the ListBox control.

In the following example, the code creates the same ArrayList and HashTable objects that were in the last exercise. However, in this case, these objects are bound to several ListBox controls named MyLB1, MyLB2, and MyLB3. You will bind the ListBox controls to the array list and hash table.

1. Open the **Chapter7** project in Visual Studio .NET if it is not already open. Double-click the **ListBox.aspx page** in the Solution Explorer window. Double-click on the whitespace area to open the code behind the page.

2. Immediately after the comment ' Insert the code here, add the code to bind the ListBox control named MyLB1 to the array:

```
MyLB1.DataSource = arr1
```

3. Immediately after the preceding code, add the code to bind the ListBox control named **MyLB2** to the hash table:

```
MyLB2.DataSource = MyHash
MyLB2.DataTextField = "Key"
MyLB2.DataValueField = "Value"
```

4. Immediately after the preceding code, add the code to bind the ListBox control named **MyLB3** to the hash table:

```
MyLB3.DataSource = MyHash
MyLB3.DataValueField = "Key"
MyLB3.DataTextField = "Value"
MyLB3.DataTextFormatString = "{0:C}"
```

5. Immediately after the preceding code, bind the data expressions to the DataSource property of the ListBox controls:

```
Page.DataBind()
```

6. Click the **Save All** button. Click **Build** on the menu bar, and then click **Build Solution**.

7. Close the Output box, and then click the **ListBox.aspx** tab. Right-click on the page, and then select **View in Browser**.

8. Select **Belinda Bradshaw Cat Bowl** from the first ListBox. Select **Business Card Holder** from the second ListBox. Select **$54.00** from the third ListBox. Click the **Submit** button. The values selected are displayed in the Web page, as shown in Figure 7-7.

9. Close any open pages.

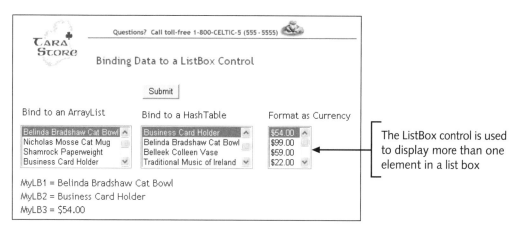

Figure 7-7   Binding data to a ListBox control

Binding Data to a RadioButtonList and CheckBoxList Control

Both the RadioButtonList and CheckBoxList controls can be bound to data. In the following exercise, you will create an array list and hash table, bind all the page data controls, and then display the bound data using the RadioButtonList and CheckBoxList controls in the Web page. The code to insert a RadioButtonList and a CheckBoxList control is as follows:

```
<asp:checkboxlist id="MyCBL1" runat="server">
</asp:checkboxlist>
<asp:radiobuttonlist id="MyRBL1" runat="server">
</asp:radiobuttonlist>
```

Each item in the DataSource property will correspond to an <input> tag where the type is listed as radio or checkbox. The text that is displayed for each HTML <input> control is identified with the **DataTextField property**. The **DataValueField property** is used to specify the Value property of the items, which is displayed only in the HTML source view of the rendered Web page. The DataValueField property corresponds to the Value property of the HTML <input> control.

In this exercise, you will bind a hash table and array list to both a CheckBoxList control and a RadioButtonList control. (*Note*: The btnSubmit_Click event procedure will retrieve the values of the CheckBoxList control and the RadioButtonList control and display the results.)

1. Open the **Chapter7** project in Visual Studio .NET if it is not already open. Double-click the **CheckBoxRadio.aspx** page in the Solution Explorer window to open the page in the main code window.

2. Double-click in the whitespace on the page to open the code behind the page, which is named CheckBoxRadio.aspx.vb.

3. Immediately after the comment ' Insert the code here, add the code to bind the RadioButtonList and CheckBoxList controls to the array list object:

```
CheckBoxList1.DataSource = arr1
RadioButtonList1.DataSource = arr1
```

4. Immediately after the preceding code above, add the code to bind the RadioButtonList and CheckBoxList controls to the hash table:

```
CheckBoxList2.DataSource = MyHash
CheckBoxList2.DataTextField = "Key"
CheckBoxList2.DataValueField = "Value"
RadioButtonList2.DataSource = MyHash
RadioButtonList2.DataValueField = "Key"
RadioButtonList2.DataTextField = "Value"
RadioButtonList2.DataTextFormatString = "{0:C}"
```

5. Immediately after the preceding code, add the code to bind the data expressions to the DataSource property of the ListBox controls:

```
Page.DataBind()
```

> The btnSubmit_Click procedure runs when the button is clicked. Because the user can select more than one check box, variables are used to store the values that the user selected. The code stores the values from the CheckBoxList controls in the variables named strResult1 and strResult2. Then, the code will assign the values selected in both CheckBoxList controls to the Text property of the lblCBL control. This will display the values selected in both CheckBoxList controls. Then the code stores the values from the first and second RadioButtonList controls in the variables RadioButtonList1 and RadioButtonList2. Next, the code assigns the values selected in both RadioButtonList controls to the Text property of the lblRBL control. This will display the values selected in both RadioButtonList controls.

6. Click the **Save All** button. Click **Build** on the menu bar, and then click **Build Solution**.

7. Click the **CheckBoxRadio.aspx** tab. Right-click on the page, and then select **View in Browser**.

8. Select **Shamrock Paperweight** from the first RadioButtonList control. Select **$34.00** from the second RadioButtonList control. Select **Belleek Colleen Vase** from the first CheckBoxList control. Select **Shamrock Paperweight** and **Business Card Holder** from the second CheckBoxList control. Click the **Submit** button. The values selected are displayed in the Web page, as shown in Figure 7-8.

9. Close any open pages.

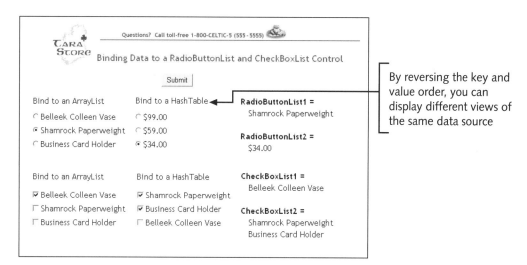

Figure 7-8   Binding data to CheckBoxList and RadioButtonList controls

Binding Data to a DataGrid Control

The DataGrid control can be bound to various data sources. In this example, you will bind the DataGrid control to a hash table. You will insert columns that will be bound to the key and value items in the hash table, and you will change the heading text property. (*Note*: In the next chapter, you will bind the DataGrid control to a DataSet object.) The code to insert a DataGrid control is as follows:

```
<asp:DataGrid id="MyDG1" runat="server">
</asp:DataGrid>
```

The DataGrid control contains many properties to help format the bound data. The **AutoGenerateColumns property** does not allow you to specify the columns that you want to bind to your data source. (*Note*: You do not have to bind all of the data columns in your data source to the DataGrid control.) The **HeaderText property** allows you to change the string displayed at the top of the column headings. (*Note*: You can include HTML tags in the headings.) The DataFormatString property is used to display currency and is applied to the values displayed within the DataGrid control. The {0:C} will format the value as currency.

In the following exercise, you will bind a DataGrid control to a hash table.

1. Open the **Chapter7** project in Visual Studio .NET if it is not already open.

2. Double-click **DataGridSimple.aspx** in the Solution Explorer window to open the page. In the Web Forms tab in the Toolbox, click and drag the **DataGrid** control to the page and place the control below the Label control. In the Properties window, change the (ID) property to **MyDG**. Change the AutoGenerateColumns property to **False**.

3. Right-click the **MyDG** control and select **Auto Format**. The left pane in the Auto Format dialog box contains preformatted schemes, and the right pane allows you to preview individual schemes. In the left pane, select **Simple 3** and click **OK.** The format scheme is applied to the MyDG control.

4. Right-click on the page, and then click **View HTML Source**. Locate the code where the DataGrid control is inserted. After the opening <asp:DataGrid ... > tag, insert a blank line.

5. In the blank line you just entered, type the following code, which binds the key and value items to the columns within the DataGrid control, and formats the value as currency. Your code should look like the code in Figure 7-9. (*Note*: The code in the figure has been modified so that you can view the entire code window.)

```
<Columns>
    <asp:BoundColumn DataField="Key"
HeaderText="Products">
    </asp:BoundColumn>
    <asp:BoundColumn DataField="Value">
HeaderText="Price"
DataFormatString="{0:C}">
    </asp:BoundColumn>
</Columns>
```

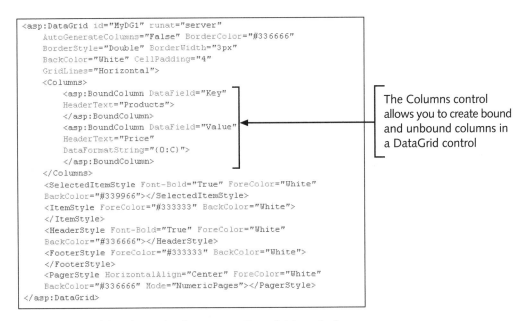

```
<asp:DataGrid id="MyDG1" runat="server"
    AutoGenerateColumns="False" BorderColor="#336666"
    BorderStyle="Double" BorderWidth="3px"
    BackColor="White" CellPadding="4"
    GridLines="Horizontal">
    <Columns>
        <asp:BoundColumn DataField="Key"
        HeaderText="Products">
        </asp:BoundColumn>
        <asp:BoundColumn DataField="Value"
        HeaderText="Price"
        DataFormatString="{0:C}">
        </asp:BoundColumn>
    </Columns>
    <SelectedItemStyle Font-Bold="True" ForeColor="White"
    BackColor="#339966"></SelectedItemStyle>
    <ItemStyle ForeColor="#333333" BackColor="White">
    </ItemStyle>
    <HeaderStyle Font-Bold="True" ForeColor="White"
    BackColor="#336666"></HeaderStyle>
    <FooterStyle ForeColor="#333333" BackColor="White">
    </FooterStyle>
    <PagerStyle HorizontalAlign="Center" ForeColor="White"
    BackColor="#336666" Mode="NumericPages"></PagerStyle>
</asp:DataGrid>
```

The Columns control allows you to create bound and unbound columns in a DataGrid control

Figure 7-9 Adding bound columns to a DataGrid control

6. Right-click the page, and then click **View Design**. Double-click the page to open the code behind the page, which is named DataGridSimple.aspx.vb. The Page_Load event handler contains the code that creates a hash table.

7. Immediately after the comment ' Insert the code here, add the code to bind the DataGrid control named **MyDG** to the hash table:

```
MyDG.DataSource = MyHash
```

8. Immediately below the preceding code, add the code to bind the data expressions to the DataSource property of the DataGrid control. Notice that here the DataBind method is called specifically for the DataGrid control.

```
MyDG.DataBind()
```

9. Click the **Save All** button. Click **Build** on the menu bar, and then click **Build Solution**.

10. Click the **DataGridSimple.aspx** tab at the top of the main window. Right-click on the page, and then click **View in Browser**. Your page should look like the one shown in Figure 7-10.

11. Close any open pages.

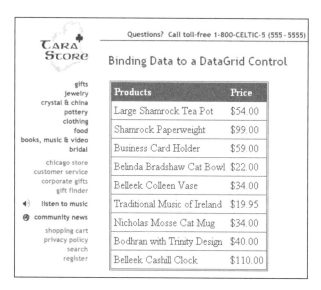

Figure 7-10   Binding data to a DataGrid control

Binding Data to a DataList Control

The DataList control allows you to display values as a simple list. When you add the DataList controls, you need to identify the columns to bind to the data. In the following example, the DataList control is bound to the key and value items of the hash table.

DataList and DataGrid controls support templates to configure the appearance of the control and the values bound to the controls. The code to insert a DataList control is as follows:

```
<asp:DataList id="MyDL1" runat="server">
</asp:DataList>
```

The data-binding instructions are stored within the templates. The DataList control requires you to configure an **ItemTemplate** within the control in order to display the data. Within the ItemTemplate is the **DataItem** property. (*Note*: This same DataItem property is also applied to the DataGrid control.) The **DataRow** property is referenced as a DataItem object within the container control and the field.

The **DataBinder.Eval function** is used to bind data along with formatting instructions. For example, if a product cost 25 U.S. dollars, but you wanted to display the data as $25.00, you could format the data using HTML after the data is bound. Another method is to apply a formatting rule to the data that is being bound so that the formatting is applied at run time before the data is sent to the HTML code. Usually there are three arguments passed for Web Server controls that display lists of data. The DataList, DataGrid, and Repeater controls use templates and therefore must use a naming container named **Container.DataItem** to store the results. The second parameter is usually the name of the data element, which is passed within quotation marks. The third parameter passed is the formatting instructions, which are also passed within quotation marks. For example, with "{0:c}", the 0 represents the data element and the c represents currency. Both C and c represent currency. P or p represents percent. In the latter case, the value is converted to a percent value and the percent sign is appended to the data.

Additional information such as the formatting rules for the DataBinder.Eval function are located within the Visual Studio .NET help files and the MSDN online library at *http://msdn.microsoft.com/ library/en-us/cpgenref/html/cpconDataBindingExpressionSyntax.asp* and at *http://msdn.microsoft.com/library/en-us/cpguide/html/ cpconstandardnumericformatstrings.asp.*

In the following exercise, you will bind a DataList control to a hash table.

1. Double-click **DataList.aspx** in the Solution Explorer window to open the page. In the Web Forms tab in the Toolbox, click and drag the **DataList** control to the page and place the control below the Label1 control that reads "Binding Data to a DataList control." In the Properties window, change the (ID) property to **MyDL**.

2. Right-click the page, and then click **View HTML_source**. Locate the code where the DataList control is inserted. After the opening <asp:DataList ... > control, insert a blank line. In the blank line, insert the code following this paragraph to create the ItemTemplate. The <b></b> tags format the name of

the product as bold. The parentheses surround the value that is bound to the items in the hash table. The parameter to format the data as currency can be passed to the DataItem property. Notice that the DataBinder.Eval function evaluates the entire expression with the parameters that are passed in the following code:

```
<ItemTemplate>
 <b>
 <%# Container.DataItem.Key %></b>
 (<%# DataBinder.Eval(Container.DataItem,"Value", ⤶
 "{0:C}")%>)
</ItemTemplate>
```

3. Switch to Design view. Double-click on the page to open the code behind the page, which is named DataList.aspx.vb.

4. Immediately after the comment ' Insert the code here, add the code to bind the DataList control named **MyDL** to the hash table:

MyDL.DataSource = MyHash

5. Immediately below the previous code, add the code to bind the data expressions to the Data Source property of the DataList control.

MyDL.DataBind( )

6. Click the **Save All** button. Click **Build** on the menu bar, and then click **Build Solution**.

7. Click the **DataList.aspx** tab. Right-click on the page, and then click **View in Browser**. The page should appear as shown in Figure 7-11.

8. Close any open pages.

You can apply the same Auto Format schemes to the DataGrid and the DataList controls. Simply right-click the DataList control and select Auto Format. In the left pane of the Auto Format dialog box, select your scheme and click OK. The format scheme is applied to the DataList control. It is possible to expand the Visual Studio .NET project to create your own schemes for enteprise applications using additional tools with the Enterprise version of Visual Studio .NET.

In a later exercise, you will learn to use templates to modify the appearance of the data controls. They allow you another way to customize the appearance of your data controls.

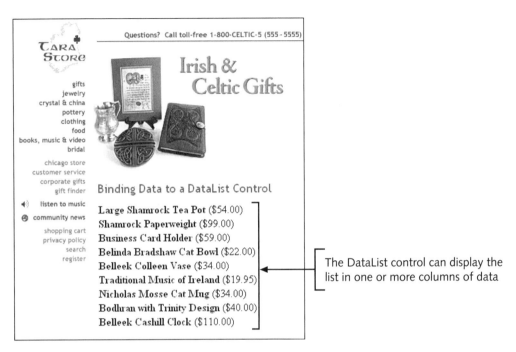

The DataList control can display the list in one or more columns of data

Figure 7-11 Binding data to a DataList control

Binding Data to a Repeater Control

The Repeater control allows you to bind data to a list. Because the Repeater control has no default appearance, you must use the HTML view of the Web Form to modify the control. You can modify the layout of the list or table using templates. The templates available to the Repeater control include the header, footer, alternating, item, and separator templates. Therefore, the Repeater can be used to create tables, comma-delimited lists, bulleted lists, and numbered lists. The Repeater control is similar to the DataList control, but renders additional HTML elements and properties to allow you more control over the data output.

In order to position the Repeater control, you must use additional controls such as the HTML <div> tag or Panel control.

You need to add control code to display the values from the Repeater control. The sample code following this paragraph inserts a Repeater control into the page. The data is inserted into the Repeater control with an ItemTemplate. The Key property is used to indicate the key from the data source. The Value property is used to pass the value from the data source. The Container.DataItem represents each item within the data source. You can add HTML tags to format the ItemTemplate of the Repeater control. (*Note*: The ItemTemplate is used with all of the data controls to display the data.)

```
<asp:Repeater id="Repeater1" runat="server">
  <ItemTemplate>
    <b><%# Container.DataItem.Key %></b>
    (<%# Container.DataItem.Value %>)<br />
  </ItemTemplate>
</asp:Repeater>
```

You can format the value of the Repeater control as currency using the same format as the DataList control, as shown in the following sample:

```
<b><%# Container.DataItem.Key %></b>
(<%# DataBinder.Eval(Container.DataItem, ⤸
"Value","{0:C}") %>)
<br />
```

The following example shows you how to insert a simple Repeater control into a Web page. The Repeater control is bound to a hash table.

1. Open the **Chapter7** project in Visual Studio .NET if it is not already open.

2. Double-click the file **Repeater.aspx** in the Solution Explorer window to open the page. In the Web Forms tab in the Toolbox, click and drag the **Repeater** control to the page and place the control inside the Panel control named Panel1.

3. Right-click on the page, and then click **View HTML Source**. Between the opening and closing Repeater tags (<asp:Repeater ... ></aspRepeater>), insert the code following this paragraph to create the ItemTemplate within the Repeater control tags. The bold tags format the name of the product. (*Note*: In this example, the product price is formatted as currency.)

```
<ItemTemplate>
    <b><%# Container.DataItem.Key %></b>
    (<%# DataBinder.Eval(Container.DataItem,"Value", ⤸
      "{0:C}") %>)
    <br />
</ItemTemplate>
```

4. Click the **Design** tab to return to Design view. Double-click on the page to open the code behind the page, which is named Repeater.aspx.vb.

5. Immediately after the comment ' Insert code here, add the following code to bind the Repeater control named **Repeater1** to the hash table:

```
Repeater1.DataSource = MyHash
```

6. Bind the data expressions to the data source property of the Repeater control. Notice that here the DataBind method is called specifically for the Repeater control.

```
Repeater1.DataBind()
```

7. Click the **Save All** button. Click **Build** on the menu bar, and then click **Build Solution**.

8. Click the **Repeater.aspx** tab. Right-click on the page, and then select **View in browser**. Your page will look like Figure 7-12.

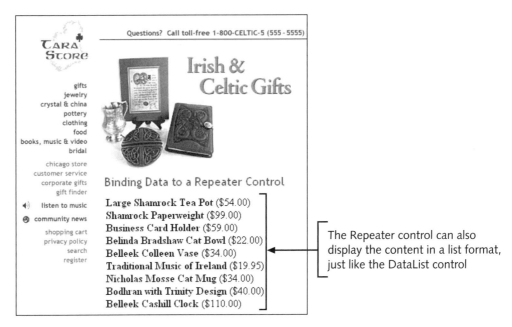

Figure 7-12   Binding data to a Repeater control

9. Close any open pages.

BINDING A DATAVIEW OBJECT TO A DATAGRID CONTROL

You can use the DataGrid control to format the data from a variety of data sources such as a hash table, array list, or database. You can bind a DataGrid control to a different data source using the DataSource property. There are two main ways to connect to the database. You can use the DataReader object to create a connection to the database and receive records individually, or you can use the DataAdapter object to return a DataSet object. The DataSet object is a set of records disconnected from the database.

Building Connections to a Database

When you create a connection to a database, you must use the .NET Connection object, which locates the database using a **ConnectionString property**. You can create the connection string and all of the data objects manually within the code, or use the graphical user interface provided within the Server Explorer and Toolbox windows. The sample code following this paragraph shows how to create a connection string and a database, and a Connection object. You need to pass the connection string to the Connection object so that the Connection object knows which database to connect to. The ConnectionString (CS) property contains data to locate and connect to the database. The CS property includes any authentication requirements such as the user ID and password. The syntax for the CS varies with the type of database used and the provider chosen, as discussed in Chapter 6. (*Note*: It is important not to break the string across multiple lines of text.) The connection string is stored in a variable CS. The CS can also be a global object in the Web configuration or in a User control. (*Note*: If you use the tools in Visual Studio .NET to build your connection, you use a graphical interface to achieve the same results.) Because the Connection object is used to connect to an Access database, the OleDb.OleDbConnection class is used to create the Connection object.

```
Dim CS as String =
  "Provider=Microsoft.Jet.OLEDB.4.0;DataSource="& _
  "C:\Inetpub\wwwroot\Chapter7\data\TaraStore.mdb"
Dim objCS As New System.Data.OleDb.OleDbConnection(CS)
```

To decrease typing errors, you can create the connection strings using the DataAdapter Wizard. Then, you can copy and paste the connection string from the code behind the page into your new code. Some developers have found it useful to create a connection string text file using Notepad. They store connection strings that were repeatedly used across projects. By using this method, they cut down on typographical errors.

The sample code following this paragraph shows how to create a SQL Select statement that will retrieve all of the records for the first category. The DataAdapter object will be created using the System.Data.OleDb.OleDbDataAdapter class and will create a Connection object using the connection string and SQL statement. The DataAdapter object is used to manage the connection and create a DataSet object named objDS. The Connection object and SQL variable are passed as parameters when the object is created. The DataAdapter object is used to get the data from the database and populate the DataSet object. Unless you are using a SQL Server database, use System.Data.OleDb.OleDbDataAdapter as the Data Provider. (*Note*: You will need to import the `System.Data.OleDb` namespace into your page using the code `<%@Import Namespace="System.Data.OleDb"%>` or import `System.Data.OleDb` at the first line in the code behind the page. You can also add the namespace reference to your Web References; you don't have to use the fully qualified name.) It is not until the Fill method of the DataAdapter object is called that the DataSet object is filled with data from the Products table.

```
Dim SQL As String = _
  "SELECT * FROM Products where SubCategoryID=1"
```

```
Dim objDA As New _
   System.Data.OleDb.OleDbDataAdapter(SQL, objCS)
Dim objDS As New DataSet()
objDA.Fill(objDS, "Products")
```

The last part of the code is used to define the DataView object. The DataView object is created from the default view of the first table in the DataSource object. The DefaultView property will return all of the columns for all of the rows in the table. The table listed is 0, which is the first table in the DataSet object. Then, the DataSource property of the DataGrid object is set to the DataView object, and the DataGrid control is bound to the DataSource object when the Page.DataBind method is called.

```
Dim objDV As DataView
objDV = objDS.Tables(0).DefaultView
MyDG1.DataSource = objDV
Page.DataBind()
```

Binding a DataGrid Control to the TaraStore Access Database

Although you can enter the code manually, you can also use the graphical user interface to create the .NET Data Provider objects and Web Server controls. In the following exercise, you will use the graphical user interface to bind the DataSource property to a database table named Products, which is stored in the TaraStore.mdb database file. The two tables within the TaraStore.mdb database file are Products and Categories. You will use the DataAdapter object to manage the connection with the database and return the DataSet object. The DataSet object will contain a single table named Products, with a single DataView object. The page uses the default DataView object to retrieve the data and displays the default DataGrid control. The default DataGrid control shows all of the columns—even if they are empty.

1. Open the **Chapter7** project in Visual Studio .NET if it is not already open.

2. Open the Server Explorer window from the View window, if necessary. In the Server Explorer window, create a data connection to the TaraStore database. Right-click **Data Connections**, and then select **Add Connection**. In the Data Link Properties box, click the **Provider** tab. Select **Microsoft Jet 4.0 OLE DB Provider**. This is the OLE DB Data Provider for the Access database engine. Click the **Next** button, and the Connection tab will open with a different connection form. Click the **Build** button labeled with three dots (**...**) and browse to locate your TaraStore database. The default location for the TaraStore database is C:\Inetpub\wwwroot\Chapter7\data\TaraStore.mdb. Click **Open**. By default the username and password is entered. Click the **Test Connection** button. If the Test connection succeeded message is displayed in the alert box, click the **OK** button, then click **OK** to close the Data Link

Properties dialog box. If any other message is displayed, verify your database name and user information and create the connection again.

3. Double-click the file **DataGridDisplay.aspx** in the Solution Explorer window to select it, and then click the **DataGrid** control. The properties for the DataGrid control should appear in the Properties window. Verify that the ID property is **MyDG**.

4. Close the Server Explorer window, and then click the **Data** tab in the Toolbox. Click and drag the **OleDbDataAdapter** control to the Web page. The DataAdapter Configuration Wizard opens. Click the **Next** button. In the Data Connection drop-down list box, select the **Access.C:\Inetpub\wwwroot\Chapter7\ data\TaraStore.mdb.Admin** data connection, and then click the **Next** button.

5. In the Choose a Query Type pane, only the Use SQL statements radio button is selected because Access does not support stored procedures. Click the **Next** button.

6. In the Generate the SQL statements form, click the **Query Builder** button. The Add Table window opens. Select the **Products** table, and then click the **Add** button. Click the **Close** button to close the window. The Query Builder that opens is the same wizard that you used in the previous chapter to create your SQL statements.

7. Click the **ModelName**, **ProductID**, **SubCategoryID** and **UnitCost** check boxes in the Products column list. In the Criteria box for the SubCategoryID column, enter **=2**. Uncheck the **Output** check box for the SubCategoryID, as shown in figure 7-13. Then, the SubCategoryID will not be shown in the DataGrid. Click **OK**. The SQL code created is displayed in the Generate the SQL statements form. Click **Next** to continue. (*Note*: View Wizard Results will show that several SQL statements and a table mapping were created. These are used by the OleDbDataAdapter object to manage the data updates to the database.)

7

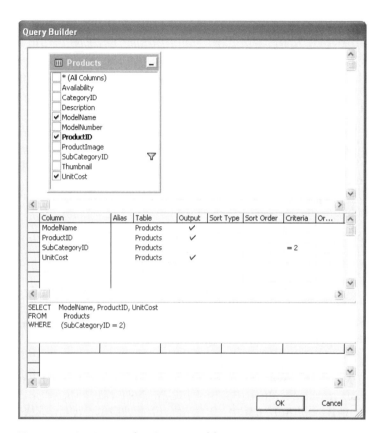

Figure 7-13   Using the Query Builder

8. Click **Finish**. A dialog box appears asking if you want to include the password in the connection string. The dialog box displays a message that says "The password is saved as clear text and is readable in the source codes and the compiled assembly." Click the **Include Password** button.

The DataAdapter object named OleDbDataAdapter1 and the connection object named OleDbConnection1 are added to a tray located at the bottom of your Web Form in Design view. (*Note*: Objects that do not contain a visual component are shown in the tray. You can modify the properties of these components using the Properties window. Therefore, if you click OleDbConnection1, the Properties window will display the DataSource, Data Provider, and ConnectionString property information.)

 If your database is not located on the same physical computer as the Web server, the database password may be sent in clear text across the network or Internet. Additional information about Web database security is located in Chapter 8 and Appendix B.

9. Now you need to create a DataSet object. Click **Data** on the menu bar, and then click **Generate Dataset**. In the Generate Dataset window select the radio button labeled **New**. In the text box, delete **DataSet1** and type **MyDS**. The Products table that is managed by OleDbDataAdapter1 has already been selected. Leave the Add this dataset to the designer check box checked. Click **OK**.

10. Select the Dataset labeled **MyDS1** in Design view. Click **Data** on the menu bar, and then click **Preview Data.** The data adapter Preview window opens. Because the fill method of the DataAdapter has not yet been called, the data is not populated in the DataSet.

11. Select **OleDbDataAdapter1** from the data adapters drop-down list. If needed, select **Chapter7.MyDS** from the target drop-down list. Click the **Fill Dataset** button, which will call the Fill method of the DataAdapter. Your data should be displayed in the window, as shown in figure 7-14. (*Note*: You can click the field names to sort the dataset. The size of the dataset is displayed above the data table. You can change the width of the columns by clicking and dragging the line between the columns. You can also change the size of the window by clicking and dragging the lower-right corner of the window.)

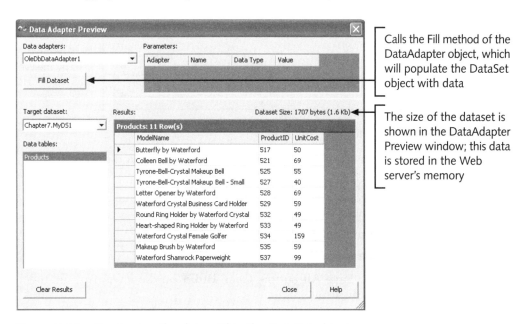

Figure 7-14   Previewing the data within the DataSet object

12. Click the **Close** button.

13. Drag and drop the **DataView** control from the Data tab in the Toolbox to the Web page.

14. You need to assign a table to the DataView object. With the **DataView** object selected, go to the Properties window, and then click the drop-down list arrow for the **Table** property. Click the **plus sign** next to MyDS1, and then click **Products**. The Table property is listed as MyDS1.Products.

15. Click the **DataGrid** control. You need to set the DataSource property of the DataGrid to the DataView object. Click the drop-down **list arrow** for the DataSource property, and then select **DataView1**. The DataAdapter, Connection, DataSet, and DataView objects are not displayed on the Web page, but in the tray at the bottom of the Web form in Design view, as shown in Figure 7-15. You can access the properties for these objects using the Properties window. If you use the Data tab to create your data objects, do not edit the automatically generated code in the section labled "Web Form Designer Generated Code" in the code behind the page.

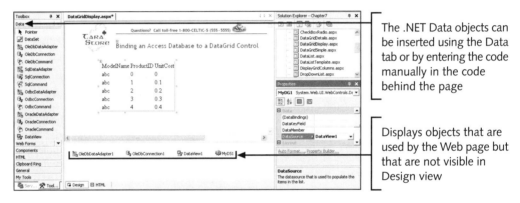

The .NET Data objects can be inserted using the Data tab or by entering the code manually in the code behind the page

Displays objects that are used by the Web page but that are not visible in Design view

Figure 7-15   Using .NET Data objects

16. Double-click on the page to open the code behind the page.

17. In the Page_Load handler, add the following code to fill the DataAdapter object and to bind the data control to the data source listed in the DataSource property:

```
OleDbDataAdapter1.Fill(MyDS1)

Page.DataBind()
```

18. Click the **Save All** button. Click **Build** on the menu bar, and then click **Build Solution**.

19. Click the **DataGridDisplay.aspx** tab. Right-click on the page, and then click **View in Browser**. Your page should look like the one in Figure 7-16. The page displays the product information in a basic table. You can use templates later to format the appearance of the table and the data. If you received an error message when you viewed the Web page, you will need to reset your NTFS permissions and then refresh the Web page. Information on resetting the Web permissions can be found in the next section of this chapter.

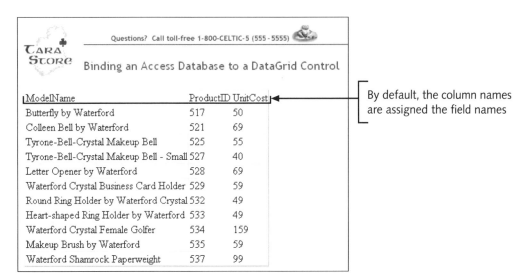

Figure 7-16   Binding a DataGrid to a database

20. Click on the **DataGridDisplay.aspx.vb** page. Click the **plus sign** next to the Web Form Designer Generated Code. The code displayed is the code that is used by the page to create the connection string, Connection object, Command object, DataAdapter object, DataSet object, DataTable object, and DataView object.

21. Close any open pages.

Common Database Error Messages

Most types of errors in Web database applications are related to database connections. If you see the error message displayed in Figure 7-17, that means that you will have to configure the permissions for the ASP.NET Machine account to manage the file. The **ASP.NET Machine accoun**t is used by the Web server to run ASP.NET pages and allow them to interact with the Web server. By default, the user cannot modify a file-based database because the ASP.NET Machine user does not have NTFS permissions to manage the database.

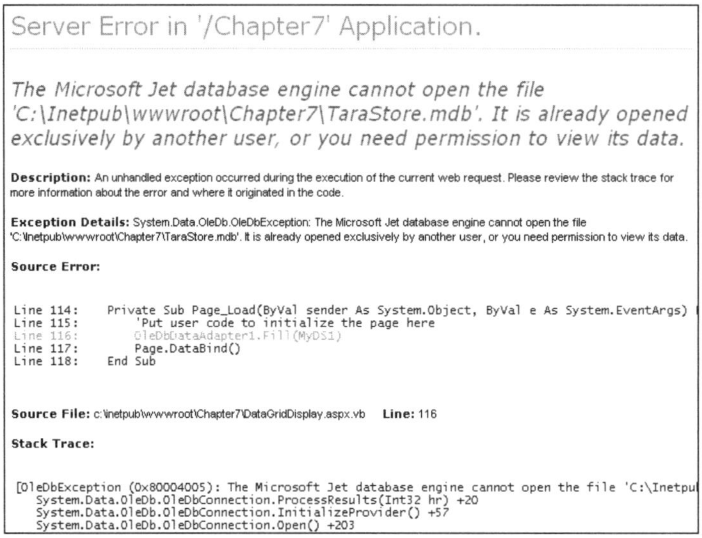

Figure 7-17   Database permission error message

The following steps will allow you to set the permissions for the ASP.NET Machine user account. (*Note*: These steps are similar to the steps in Chapter 4 when you set the permissions for the Uploads folder.) This will allow the user to read and write to the database.

1. Click the **Start** menu and then click **Run**. Type **%SystemRoot%\explorer.exe C:\inetpub\wwwroot\chapter7\data** in the text box and click **OK** to open the Chapter7\data\ directory in Windows Explorer. (*Note*: By default, it's located at C:\Inetpub\wwwroot\Chapter7\data.)

2. Right-click the **TaraStore** database and select **Properties**. (*Note*: There may be two database icons labeled TaraStore. One is the database and the other is the Microsoft Office Access Record-Locking Information. This file appears only if the Access database is opened by another user.)

3. Click the **Security** tab. This tab allows you to add Windows user accounts and set the NTFS permissions for each user. (*Note*: A message may appear that says "The permissions on Uploads are incorrectly ordered, which may cause some entries to be ineffective. Press **OK** to continue and sort the permissions correctly, or Cancel to reset the permissions." Click **OK**. If you click Cancel, the permissions will be reset to allow the Everyone account to have full access to the folder, which is a security risk.)

4. Click the **Add** button. In the lower text box, enter the full name for the ASP.NET Machine user account, which is called **MACHINENAME\ ASPNET**. *MACHINENAME* is the name of your computer. Click the **OK** button.

5. Then, click the Apply check boxes labeled **Modify**, **Read & Execute**, **Read**, and **Write** in the permissions panel.

6. Click the **OK** button. Close Windows Explorer.

7. In the Chapter7 project, open the **DataGridDisplay.aspx** page if needed. Right-click the page and select **View in Browser**.

Microsoft Access Database Connection Error Messages

After you change permissions, you may still receive other error messages. You may receive an error message like the one shown in Figure 7-18 that says "Could not lock file." Although the error points to the OleDbDataAdapter1 object, the problem is the ability for the object to open a connection to the database. There are several reasons that this may occur. First, this often happens if the file has been opened in Microsoft Access and the file was not closed properly.

Another possibility is that the locking mode permissions have been set to restrict editing the record. The TaraStore.mdb database was created in Microsoft Access XP 2003. The Open Mode property has been set to shared by default. The Record Locking property has been set to no locks. Databases are opened with record-level locking. The TaraStore.mdb database properties are displayed in Figure 7-19. (*Note:* To view the Open Mode and Database Record Locking properties in Microsoft Access, open the database in Microsoft Access XP 2003. Select the Tools menu, and then select Options. In the Options window, select the Advanced tab.) You can locate additional information about database locking mode permissions in the MSDN Online Library at *http://msdn.microsoft.com/library* or in the Visual Studio .NET Help files.

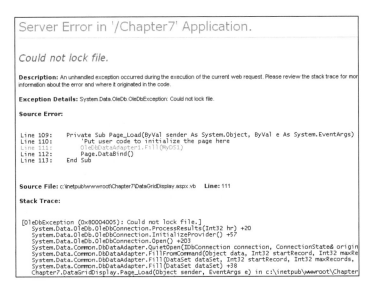

Figure 7-18   Database record locking and folder permissions error message

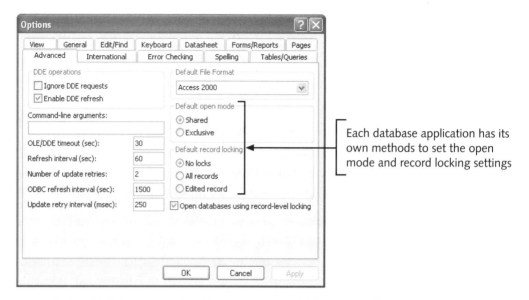

The most likely cause for the error message in Figure 7-18 is that you have to reset your NTFS directory permissions. You should make sure the account that runs your ASP.NET Web application has write permissions to the directory that contains the database. The ASP.NET Machine account must be able to create a Microsoft Access LDB lock file in the directory. The Microsoft Access LDB lock file is named after the database (databasename. ldb). Change the user permissions to allow the user to have permissions to that directory. Then, Access can create the Microsoft Access LDB lock file when the file is opened. (*Note*: If you have further data connection errors, you can visit *www.dbforums.com* and search for additional information on connection errors.) If you set the permissions at the folder level, the permissions will be inherited by the files within the folder. Usually, it's better to place the databases into a separate folder so that the permissions can be set for the databases separately from the permissions for the Web pages.

If you received either error message when you completed the last activity, reset your NTFS permissions according to the steps in the following step sequence, and then refresh the Web page.

1. Click the **Start** menu and select **Run**. Type **%SystemRoot%\explorer.exe C:\Inetpub\wwwroot\Chapter7** in the text box and click **OK** to open the Chapter7 directory in Windows Explorer. (*Note*: By default, it's located at C:\Inetpub\wwwroot\Chapter7\.)

2. Right-click the **data** folder and select **Properties**.

3. Click the **Security** tab.

4. Click the **Add** button. In the lower text box, enter the full name for the ASP.NET Machine user account, which is called *MACHINENAME* **ASPNET**. MACHINENAME is the name of your computer. Click the **OK** button.

5. Then, click the Apply check boxes labeled **Modify**, **Read & Execute**, **List Folder Contents**, **Read**, and **Write** in the permissions panel.

6. Click the **OK** button. Close Windows Explorer.

7. In the Chapter7 project, open the **DataGridDisplay.aspx** page if needed. Right-click on the page and select **View in Browser**.

If you are still having difficulty with binding a database to a Web control, refer to Appendix B for more information on database configurations and troubleshooting tips.

By default, all of the columns are displayed. AutoGenerateColumns is used to indicate that all of the columns will be generated by the DataGrid control. You can turn this feature off by setting the **AutoGenerateColumns property** to False. Then, you have to use the Columns template to build your columns manually. The **Columns template** contains all of the bound and unbound columns. A **bound column** is a table column that contains data bound to a field in the database. You specify the data from the database column by using the DataField property. Bound columns are identified with the ASP.NET BoundColumn tag within the Columns template. **Unbound columns** do not automatically contain data from the database.

Modifying Data Columns in the DataGrid Control

The appearance of the DataGrid control can be modified using the Auto Format schemes, using a Property Builder, or using templates. In the next section, you will learn to apply templates to the DataGrid control. In this section you will modify the appearance of the DataGrid control using the Property Builder. You can modify the appearance of the individual columns, and display only selected columns. By default, the header text of the column displays the column name in the database. The **HeaderText property** allows you to modify the text message at the top of the column. The DataGrid and DataList controls both support templates. You can build the templates manually or use the tools within Visual Studio .NET.

Each column contains a **header**, **footer**, and **item** section. There are two ways to format the styles for these sections. You can insert the style information within the <asp:bound> opening tag or use a separate tag. For example, to format the font color and text color for the item section within the CategoryID column, you could use the following code:

```
<asp:BoundColumn HeaderText="Category ID"
        DataField="CategoryID"
        ItemStyle-Font-Name="Trebuchet MS"
        ItemStyle-ForeColor="DarkSlateGray">
</asp:BoundColumn>
```

You could also use the **ItemStyle tag**, as shown in the following code snippet:

```
<asp:BoundColumn HeaderText="Category ID"
  DataField="CategoryID">
      <ItemStyle Font-Names="Trebuchet MS"
         ForeColor="DarkSlateGray">
      </ItemStyle>
</asp:BoundColumn>
```

You can format the footer using the **FooterStyle tag** and the header using the **HeaderStyle tag**. A listing of available styles is located in the Properties window when you place the cursor within the <asp:BoundColumn> tag. When these styles are formatted using tags, such as the ItemStyle tag, they are called **style templates**. They allow you to format the style using tags or the properties of the control. You will learn how to set the style properties using the Properties window in a later exercise.

In the following exercise, you will bind a database to a DataGrid control. Then, you will build and format each of the columns manually.

1. Open the **Chapter7** project in Visual Studio .NET if it is not already open.

2. Double-click the file **DisplayGridColumns.aspx** in the Solution Explorer window to open the page.

3. Click the **Data** tab in the Toolbox. Click and drag the **OleDbDataAdapter** control to the Web page. The DataAdapter Configuration Wizard opens. Click the **Next** button. In the Data Connection drop-down list box, select the **Access.C:\Inetpub\wwwroot\Chapter7\data\TaraStore.mdb. Admin** data connection, and then click the **Next** button. Click the **Next** button again.

4. In the Generate the SQL statements form, type **SELECT * FROM Categories**, click the **Next** button, then click **Finish**. The DataAdapter object named OleDbDataAdapter1 and the Connection object named OleDbConnection1 are added to your Design view. When the dialog box opens requesting whether you want the password to be saved in the connection string, click **Include Password**.

5. To create the DataSet, click **Data** on the menu bar, and then click **Generate Dataset**. In the Generate Dataset window, select the radio button labeled **New**. In the text box, type **MyCatDS**. The Categories table, which is managed by OleDbDataAdapter1, has already been selected. Leave the Add this dataset to the designer check box checked. Click **OK**.

6. Drag and drop the **DataView** control from the Data tab in the Toolbox to the Web page.

7. You need to assign a table to the DataView control. With the **DataView** control selected, go to the Properties window, and then click the **drop-down list arrow** for the Table property. Click the **plus sign** next to MyCatDS1

and then click **Categories**. The Table property is listed as MyCatDS1.Categories.

8. Click the **DataGrid** control. You need to set the DataSource property of the DataGrid control to the DataView object. Click the drop-down **list arrow** for the DataSource property, and then select **DataView1**. You can see the headings for the columns that are displayed by default. These columns include CategoryID, CategoryName, CatImage, Description, Thumbnail, and TinyThumb.

9. Double-click on the page to open the code behind the page.

10. In the Page_Load handler, add the following code to fill the DataAdapter object and to bind the Data control to the data source listed in the DataSource property:

```
OleDbDataAdapter1.Fill(MyCatDS1)
Page.DataBind()
```

11. Click the **DisplayGridColumns.aspx** tab. Click the **DataGrid** control, and then change the AutoGenerateColumns property to **False**. In the Properties window, change the CellPadding property to **5**.

12. Click the **HTML** tab to edit the page in HTML view. Locate the <asp:DataGrid> and </asp:DataGrid> tags. Between the DataGrid tags, insert the following code to add a bound column:

```
<Columns>
    <asp:BoundColumn HeaderText="ID"
      DataField="CategoryID">
    </asp:BoundColumn>
    <asp:BoundColumn HeaderText="Name"
      DataField="CategoryName">
    </asp:BoundColumn>
</Columns>
```

Although you are entering the code manually, you could also use the Property Builder to format the properties, as shown in Figure 7-20.

13. Modify the styles of the columns. Add the code following this paragraph between each of the <asp:BoundColumn></asp:BoundColumn>tags for both the CategoryID and the CategoryName columns. Notice how IntelliSense helps display the choices for the property names and values. You can use the Color Picker dialog box to select the color, or enter it manually, as shown in the sample code following this paragraph. (*Note*: You can also use the Property Builder to format the properties of the individual columns.) Below are the two code snippets for the first and second columns. Place the first snippet within the bound column control for the CategoryID field and the second snippet within the bound column control for the CategoryName field.

7

```
<ItemStyle Font-Names="Trebuchet MS" HorizontalAlign=
"Center" ForeColor="DarkSlateGray"></ItemStyle>
<ItemStyle Font-Names="Trebuchet MS" ForeColor=
"DarkSlateGray"></ItemStyle>
```

14. Click the **Design** tab to return to Design view.

15. Right-click the **DataGrid** control, and then click **Property Builder**. Notice that the DataSource listed in the Property Builder is DataView1.

16. Click the **Columns** tab. Click **ID** in the Selected columns list. Change the HeaderText property of the CategoryID field from ID to **Category ID**.

17. Click the **Format** tab. Click **Header** in the Objects list box. In the Forecolor drop-down list box, select **White**, and in the Back Color drop-down list box, type **DarkSlateGray**. In the Font name drop-down list box, select **Trebuchet MS**. Check the **Bold** check box. Change the Horizontal alignment drop-down list box to **Center**.

18. Click the **plus sign** next to Columns[0] - Category ID to expand the selection. Click **Items** from the Objects box to display the properties available. Change the Font size property to **X-Small**.

19. Click the **plus sign** next to Columns[1] - Name to expand the selection. Click **Items** from the Objects box to display the properties available. Change the Font size property to **X-Small**. Click **OK**. Your screen should resemble Figure 7-20.

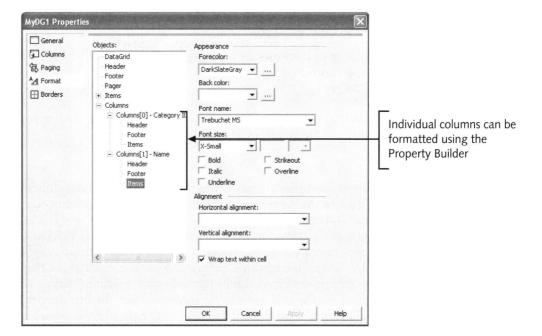

Figure 7-20   The Property Builder

20. Click the **Save All** button. Click **Build** on the menu bar, and then click **Build Solution**.

21. Right-click on the page, and then click **View in Browser**. The page displays the category information in a basic table, as shown in Figure 7-21.

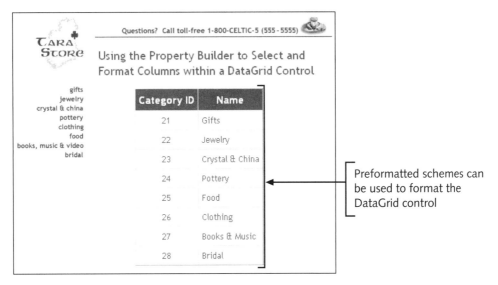

Figure 7-21   Displaying the DataGrid control

22. Close any open pages.

WORKING WITH DATA COLUMNS, TEMPLATES, AND COLUMN STYLES

In this section, you will learn to use different types of columns, templates, and column style properties in order to modify the content and appearance of the data within the DataGrid control. Many of the techniques can also be applied to the other controls because they inherit the same class. You will learn how to apply templates to the Repeater control and the DataList control.

Data Columns

There are several types of columns that are used to display and edit data. **Edit mode** allows you to modify data. An **EditCommandColumn** is a type of column that contains three predefined buttons which allow you to change the mode of the row from display to edit. You will learn more about the EditCommandColumn and edit mode in the next chapter.

In the previous exercise, you used BoundColumns to display the data in display mode. **Display mode** is a state where you are only displaying the data. As you saw in the last exercise, BoundColumns can be used to retrieve and display the data. Some limited formatting with styles can be applied to the data within a BoundColumn. You can modify the text, font, and color of the column header and footer, the column width, and format the data. The data in the column can be set to read-only so that the data cannot be modified within the DataGrid object.

In the next exercise in this chapter, you will use ButtonColumns, HyperlinkColumns, and TemplateColumns to display data with additional content. **ButtonColumns** are used to insert a button that can activate row-specific procedures. You can modify the button's text and type using the **LinkButton** or **Button property**. You can use the **CommandName property** to identify a procedure that is called when the button is clicked. The **ItemCommand event** is raised when any button is clicked within a DataGrid control. (*Note*: You will learn more about the ButtonColumn object in the next chapter.) A **HyperlinkColumn** displays a hyperlink that you can customize. You can hard-code the text displayed and the URL of the hyperlink or set these properties with values from the data. **TemplateColumn** allows you to customize the columns in both display and edit modes. You will learn to use TemplateColumns to edit data in the next chapter.

Templates

Templates are used to bind data to individual areas within the control and to format the areas within the control. These special areas include the header, footer, and item sections. The appearance of these templates can be modified manually or by using the Property Builder. (*Note*: If you create columns manually, you should turn the AutoGenerateColumns property to False or duplicate columns will appear in the DataGrid control.)

TemplateColumns are customized using the HeaderTemplate, FooterTemplate, ItemTemplate, and EditItemTemplate templates. (*Note*: Columns bound directly to data cannot make use of the templates because the data for the columns is retrieved directly from the DataSource property. Only unbound TemplateColumn objects can be modified using the templates.) Details of these templates are as follows:

- **HeaderTemplate** is used to configure the data contained within the header section. Instead of using the HeaderText property for the column control, you will use HeaderTemplate to modify contents of the header cell. Therefore, you can use these templates to display images as well as textual content.

- **FooterTemplate** is used to configure the data contained within the footer section.

- **ItemTemplate** is used to configure how the row will appear in display mode. Instead of inserting the name of a graphic, you can insert an image control and set the src property to the name of the graphic. Then, the image would be displayed in the row in display mode.

- **EditItemTemplate** allows you to configure the columns in edit mode. Instead of editing the data using text boxes, you can use other types of controls such as check boxes and drop-down lists to edit the data.

Column Styles

The DataGrid control contains a Property Builder Wizard that helps you configure the appearance of the header, footer, and item templates. The following is a list of the style objects that can be used to modify the header, footer, and item templates.

- **HeaderStyle** is used to format the HeaderTemplate object. You can use the Properties window to modify the styles, or add the style information manually in the Web page.

- **FooterStyle** is used to format the FooterTemplate object.

- **ItemStyle** is used to format the rows of data.

- **AlternatingItemStyle** is used to format every other row of data.

- **SelectedItemStyle** is used to format the currently selected row.

- **EditItemStyle** is used to format the row when you are in edit mode and will be making changes to values in the columns.

- **PagerStyle** is used to format the page navigation controls. These controls are used when the number of rows exceeds the number of rows that can be displayed on the Web page. The number of rows that are displayed on the Web page are configured using the PageSize property of the DataGrid control.

Using ButtonColumn, HyperlinkColumn, and TemplateColumn to Modify the DataGrid Control

In this example, the categories and products data are displayed using two different DataGrid objects. Each DataGrid is bound to a different DataView object that was derived from the same DataSet object. The DataSet object is created by two different DataAdapter objects, which allow you to create two separate queries with two separate sets of results. You will configure these two separate adapters to query the Products table and the Categories table, and combine the results into a single DataSet object. (*Note:* The SQL Join command is often used to combine tables within a single SQL query. You can combine tables within a single DataSet object without using the SQL Join command.) You will create a DataView object, which will display the results from each table.

In this example, you will view the code that created the Column and Template objects. The Categories DataGrid object uses the ItemTemplate object within the TemplateColumn object to display the categories as a hyperlink. The hyperlink is created using the <asp:HyperLink> <asp:HyperLink> tags. The hyperlink will refresh the current page, and pass a parameter in the QueryString object, which will change the graphic and filter the data in the Products DataGrid object using the **RowFilter property**. The header section and the border are not displayed.

The Products DataGrid object uses HyperlinkColumn to create the hyperlink to the Products.aspx page. The hyperlink contains a QueryString object that contains the Product ID number, which is used by the Products.aspx page to display the individual product information. The zoom image and hyperlink were inserted using the TemplateColumn object. The BoundColumn object is used to display the price of the product. The **Count property** of the DataView1 object is used to display the total number of records displayed in the FooterTemplate object.

1. Open the **Chapter7** project in Visual Studio .NET if it is not already open.

2. Double-click the file **DataGridDetails.aspx** in the Solution Explorer window to open the page.

3. Click the **Data** tab in the Toolbox window. Click and drag the **OleDbDataAdapter** control to the Web page. The DataAdapter Configuration Wizard opens. Click the **Next** button. In the Data Connection drop-down list box, select the **Access.C:\Inetpub\wwwroot\Chapter7\ data\TaraStore.mdb.Admin** data connection, and then click the **Next** button. Click the **Next** button again.

4. In the Generate the SQL statements form, type **SELECT * FROM Products**. When the dialog box opens and requests whether you want the password to be saved in the connection string, click **Include Password**. Click the **Next** button, then click **Finish**. The DataAdapter object named OleDbDataAdapter1 and the Connection object named OleDbConnection1 are added to your Design view.

5. Drag and drop another **OleDbDataAdapter** object to the Web page from the Data tab. OleDbDataAdapter2 is added to your Design view in the tray. The DataAdapter Wizard opens. Click the **Next** button. In the Data Connection drop-down list box, select **Access.C:\Inetpub\wwwroot\Chapter7\ data\TaraStore.mdb. Admin** data connection, and then click the **Next** button. Click the **Next** button again. In the Generate SQL statements form, type **SELECT * FROM Categories**, click the **Next** button, and then click **Finish**. The OleDbDataAdapter2 object uses the OleDbConnection1 object to create the connection to the database. To create the DataSet, click **Data** on the menu bar, and then click **Generate Dataset**. In the Generate Dataset window, select the radio button labeled **New**. In the text box, type **DS_MyProducts**. The Products and Categories tables, which are managed by OleDbDataAdapter1 and OleDbDataAdapter2, have already been selected. Leave the Add this dataset to the designer check box checked. Click **OK**.

6. Drag and drop the **DataView** control from the Data tab in the Toolbox to the Web page. You need to assign a table to the DataView1 object. Select the **DataView1** object, go to the Properties window, and then click the **drop-down list arrow** for the Table property. Click the **plus sign** next to DS_MyProducts1, and then click **Products**. The Table property is listed as DS_MyProducts1.Products.

7. Drag and drop the **DataView** control from the Data tab in the Toolbox to the Web page. You need to assign a table to the DataView2 object. Select the **DataView2** object, go to the Properties window, and then click the **drop-down list arrow** for the Table property. Click the **plus sign** next to DS_MyProducts1, and then click **Categories**. The Table property is listed as DS_MyProducts1.Categories.

8. You need to set the DataSource property of the two DataGrid objects to the DataView1 and DataView2 objects. Click the **Products** DataGrid control. Click the **drop-down list arrow** for the DataSource property, and then select **DataView1**. Click the **Categories** DataGrid control. Click the **drop-down list arrow** for the DataSource property, and then select **DataView2**. The Data view and tray should look like the one in Figure 7-22.

9. Double-click in the whitespace on the page to open the code behind the page. In the first section in the Page_Load procedure, locate the comment 'Insert the code here. Type the code that follows this paragraph. The code creates a filter string named MySearch that is used to filter the products listed within the DataView1 object.

```
DataView1.RowFilter = MySearch
```

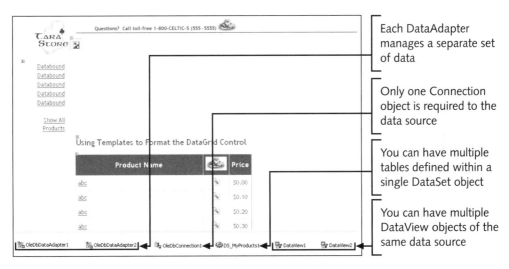

Figure 7-22   Using multiple tables within a DataSet object

10. After the comment 'Insert the data binding code here, insert the code following this paragraph to fill the DataSet using the commands provided by the DataAdapter objects and to bind the DataGrid controls to the DataView objects. The code behind the page should look like Figure 7-23.

```
OleDbDataAdapter1.Fill(DS_MyProducts1)
OleDbDataAdapter2.Fill(DS_MyProducts1)
Page.DataBind()
```

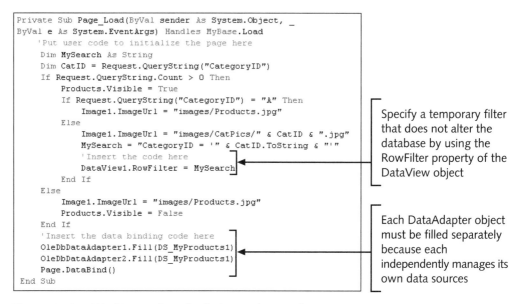

```
Private Sub Page_Load(ByVal sender As System.Object, _
ByVal e As System.EventArgs) Handles MyBase.Load
    'Put user code to initialize the page here
    Dim MySearch As String
    Dim CatID = Request.QueryString("CategoryID")
    If Request.QueryString.Count > 0 Then
        Products.Visible = True
        If Request.QueryString("CategoryID") = "A" Then
            Image1.ImageUrl = "images/Products.jpg"
        Else
            Image1.ImageUrl = "images/CatPics/" & CatID & ".jpg"
            MySearch = "CategoryID = '" & CatID.ToString & "'"
            'Insert the code here
            DataView1.RowFilter = MySearch
        End If
    Else
        Image1.ImageUrl = "images/Products.jpg"
        Products.Visible = False
    End If
    'Insert the data binding code here
    OleDbDataAdapter1.Fill(DS_MyProducts1)
    OleDbDataAdapter2.Fill(DS_MyProducts1)
    Page.DataBind()
End Sub
```

Specify a temporary filter that does not alter the database by using the RowFilter property of the DataView object

Each DataAdapter object must be filled separately because each independently manages its own data sources

Figure 7-23 Working with multiple DataAdapter objects

11. Click the **DataGridDetails.aspx** tab. Click the **HTML** tab. Locate the **Categories** DataGrid object. The DataGrid style properties, and the ItemStyle and FooterStyle tags, are used to format the data. The properties in the style tags are set using classes defined within the Styles.css cascading style sheet. ItemTemplate is used to display the data as a hyperlink. FooterTemplate is used to create a hyperlink, which will be used to select all of the products from DataView1. ShowHeader is set to False and ShowFooter to True in order to show the FooterTemplate template, but not the HeaderTemplate template. The source code for the Categories DataGrid object should look like the one in Figure 7-24. (Note: The properties may appear in a different order than the figure in order to display all of them within a single figure.)

```
<asp:datagrid id=Categories runat="server" Width="99px" Height="118px"
DataSource="<%# DataView2 %>" AutoGenerateColumns="False"
GridLines="None" ShowHeader="False" ShowFooter="True"
style="Z-INDEX: 105; LEFT: 21px; POSITION: absolute; TOP: 101px" >
    <ItemStyle CssClass=MyStyle></ItemStyle>
    <FooterStyle CssClass=MyStyle></FooterStyle>
    <Columns>
        <asp:TemplateColumn>
            <ItemTemplate>
                <asp:HyperLink Target="_self" id="Hyperlink4" runat="server"
                NavigateUrl='<%# "DataGridDetails.aspx?CategoryID=" & _
                DataBinder.Eval(Container, "DataItem.CategoryID") %>'>
                        <%# DataBinder.Eval(Container, "DataItem.CategoryName") %>
                </asp:HyperLink>
            </ItemTemplate>
            <FooterTemplate>
                <asp:HyperLink Target="_self" id="Hyperlink2" runat="server"
                NavigateUrl='DataGridDetails.aspx?CategoryID=A'>
                    <br />Show All Products
                </asp:HyperLink>
            </FooterTemplate>
        </asp:TemplateColumn>
    </Columns>
</asp:datagrid>
```

ItemTemplate will repeat for a single column for each row of data

FooterTemplate will format the footer cell only if the ShowFooter property is set to True

Figure 7-24   Using templates to format the DataGrid object

12. Locate the **Products** DataGrid object. The DataGrid style properties, and the HeaderStyle, ItemStyle, AlternatingItemStyle, and FooterStyle tags, format the data using classes defined within the cascading style sheet. HeaderItem is used to display a header section. ItemTemplate is used to display the data using three columns. FooterTemplate is used to to display a bottom border. The three columns were created using the HyperLinkColumn, TemplateColumn, and BoundColumn objects. Additional ItemStyle and FooterStyle properties are set for only the HyperLinkColumn object. The Count property of the DataView1 object is used to display the total number of records displayed.

13. Click the **Design** tab. Click the **Save All** button. Click **Build** on the menu bar, and then click **Build Solution**.

14. Right-click on the page, and then click **View in Browser**. Click the **Clothing** link. A list of 36 items will appear, as shown in Figure 7-25 (only five items are shown in the figure). Click the second magnifying glass. A window opens with the product thumbnail image. Close the window. Click the **Dark Blue Donegal Tweed cap** link. The Products.aspx page opens, which retrieves the QueryString object and displays the product image and product ID.

15. Close any open pages.

The tutorials that are installed with Visual Studio .NET are known as walkthroughs. The walkthrough named Adding DataGrid Web Server Controls to a Web Forms Page will walk you through how to format a DataGrid control using the Property Builder. When you view Dynamic Help, the help resources are divided into Help, Samples, and Getting Started. A link to the Web Walkthroughs and the Visual Studio Walkthroughs is located in the Getting Started section.

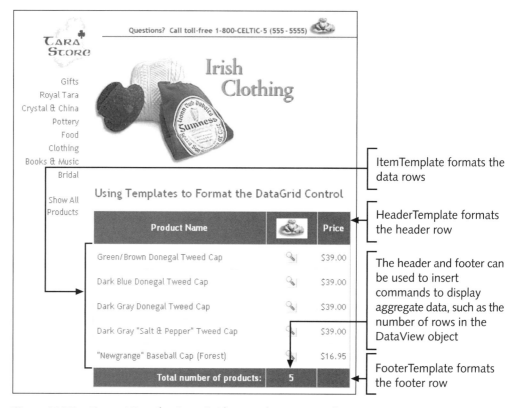

Figure 7-25   Formatting the DataGrid control using templates

Using Templates to Modify the Repeater Control

You can use templates to modify the Repeater control. Remember that the Repeater control repeats only once. In the following example, you will create a header template that contains the heading graphics. You will use a footer template to create an area that contains a company logo and links to the home page. In the body of the Web page, you will use an ItemTemplate object, which is bound to the data in the database. You will use the product image names to display the product images, and create hyperlinks. Within the ItemTemplate object, you can retrieve the values of the data columns using `<%# Container.DataItem("ColumnName") %>`, where ColumnName is the name of the column in the database. You can format the output using any of the standard HTML tags.

1. Open the **Chapter7** project in Visual Studio .NET if it is not already open.

2. Double-click the file **RepeaterTemplate.aspx** in the Solution Explorer window to open the page.

3. Click the **Data** tab in the Toolbox. Click and drag the **OleDbDataAdapter** control to the Web page. The DataAdapter Configuration Wizard opens. Click the **Next** button. In the Data Connection drop-down list box, select the **Access.C:\Inetpub\wwwroot\Chapter7\data\TaraStore.mdb. Admin** data connection, and then click the **Next** button. Click the **Next** button again.

4. In the Generate the SQL statements form, type **SELECT * FROM Products WHERE (SubCategoryID = 2)**, click the **Next** button, and then click **Finish**. The DataAdapter object named OleDbDataAdapter1 and the Connection object named OleDbConnection1 are added to your Design view. When the dialog box opens requesting if you want the password to be saved in the connection string, click **Include Password**.

5. To create the DataSet, click **Data** on the menu bar, and then click **Generate Dataset**. In the Generate Dataset window, select the radio button labeled **New**. In the text box, type **DS_WFProducts**. The Products table, which is managed by OleDbDataAdapter1, has already been selected. Leave the Add this DataSet to the designer check box checked. Click **OK**.

6. Drag and drop the **DataView** control from the Data tab in the Toolbox to the Web page.

7. You need to assign a table to the DataView control. With the **DataView** control selected, go to the **Properties** window, and click the drop-down list arrow for the **Table** property. Click the **plus sign** next to DS_WFProducts, and then click **Products**. The Table property is listed as DS_WFProducts.Products.

8. Click the **Repeater** control. You need to set the DataSource property of the Repeater to the DataView object. Click the drop-down **list arrow** for the DataSource property, and then select **DataView1**.

9. Double-click on the page to open the code behind the page. In the Page_Load handler, add the following code to fill the DataAdapter object and to bind the Data control to the data source listed in the DataSource property:

```
OleDbDataAdapter1.Fill(DS_WFProducts1)
Page.DataBind()
```

10. Click the **RepeaterTemplate.aspx** tab to return to the page. Click the **HTML** tab. Within the <asp:Repeater></asp:Repeater> tags, add the code following code to create the HeaderTemplate template:

```
<HeaderTemplate>
  <div>
      <img src="images/CatPics/1.jpg"><br />
      <img src="images/560green.gif">
  </div>
</HeaderTemplate>
```

7

11. Immediately after the preceding code, add the following code to create the FooterTemplate template:

```
<FooterTemplate>
    <img src="images/560green.gif">
    <div align="center">
        <img src="images/logo.gif" align="left">
        <br />
        For more information visit <b>
        <a href="http://www.TaraStore.com">
                http://www.TaraStore.com
        </a></b>
        <br />
        1-800-555-5555
    </div>
</FooterTemplate>
```

12. Immediately after the preceding code, add the code following this paragraph to create the SeparatorTemplate template. This separates each row visually for the end user. (*Note*: This is not as useful with multiple column displays.)

```
<SeparatorTemplate>
    <img src="images/560green.gif">
</SeparatorTemplate>
```

13. Immediately after the preceding code, add the code following this paragraph to create the ItemTemplate template. Use a table to make the layout clearer for the viewer. (*Note*: You might want to lay out your table tags first before inserting data, to verify your HTML tags.)

```
<ItemTemplate>
  <table width="500"><tr><td width="170" align="center">
  </td><td width="330">
  </td></tr></table>
</ItemTemplate>
```

14. Within the first table cell tags (`<td width="170"align="center"></td>`), enter the code following this paragraph to display the product image as a hyperlinked image. Notice that the thumbnail is displayed in the Web page. When the visitor clicks on the thumbnail image, the product image is displayed. (*Note*: Make sure to type the strings on one line with no spaces.)

```
<a href ="images/ProductPics/ ↵
    <%# Container.DataItem("ProductImage") %>">
    <img src="images/ProductThumbnails/ ↵
    <%# Container.DataItem("Thumbnail") %>"
    hspace="2" border="0">
</a>
```

15. Within the second table cell tags (<td width="330"></td>), enter the code following this paragraph to display the product image as a text hyperlink. When you click the product name, the product image is displayed. This cell also displays the price formatted as currency and the model number. Notice how the HTML tags are used to format the labels as bold and italic. (*Note*: Do not split strings across two lines of code.)

```
<b><a href="images/ProductPics/ ⤶
<%# Container.DataItem("ProductImage") %>">
</a></b><br/>
<i>Description: </i>
<%# Container.DataItem("Description") %><br />
<i>Price: </i>
<%# DataBinder.Eval(Container.DataItem, _
"UnitCost", "{0:C}") %><br />
<i>Item #: </i>
<%# Container.DataItem("ModelNumber") %>
```

16. Click the **Save All** button. Click **Build** on the menu bar, and then click **Build Solution**. (*Note*: Do not click the Design View tab. ItemTemplate is no longer editable within Design view because of the string that was split within the href property.)

17. Right-click on the page, and then click **View in Browser**. The page should appear as shown in Figure 7-26.

18. Close any open pages.

7

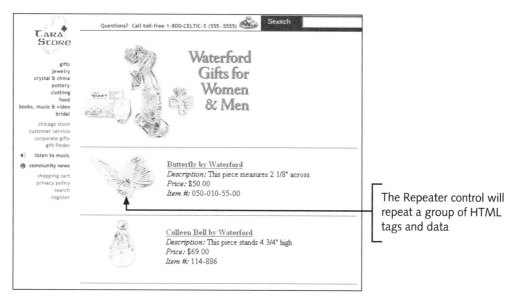

Figure 7-26   Using templates to format the Repeater control

Using Templates to Modify the DataList Control

In the previous exercise, you had to add table tags within the ItemTemplate to format the output of the Repeater control. One of the advantages of using the DataList control rather than the Repeater control is that the DataList control can be used to create multiple columns of data without using the table tags in the ItemTemplate. You can alter the number of columns displayed and the direction or layout. The number of columns is the number of columns of data displayed across the Web page. The number of columns repeated is formatted using the **RepeatColumns property**. The RepeatColumns property must be an integer. The **RepeatDirections property** stores the direction of the columns. If the columns repeat horizontally, then the value is RepeatColumns.Horizontal. If they repeat vertically, then the value is RepeatColumns.Vertical. These properties are properties of the DataList control, and not the template.

You can use templates to modify the DataList control. In the following exercise, you will display the data using the DataList control formatted as multiple columns. Within the DataList control, you can use the table tags to format the output more precisely. You need to make sure that the width of the tables is specified in order to ensure that the entire output is visible. In this example, you are going to create the data objects manually in the code behind the page.

 You can reuse the DataSets once they are created within the Web application. When you generated the DataSet, a file with the extension .xsd was created. This file contains the DataSet schema and a reference to a Visual Basic file that contains the code to generate the data. If you show all the files in the Solution Explorer window, you can expand the .xsd file to view the code behind the page.

1. Open the **Chapter7** project in Visual Studio .NET if it is not already open.

2. Double-click on the page to open the code behind the page, which is named **DataListTemplate.aspx.vb**. Within the Page_Load event handler, add the following code to create a connection to your database, create the SQL select query, and create the Connection object:

```
If Not Page.IsPostBack() Then
Dim CS As String = _
  "Provider=Microsoft.Jet.OLEDB.4.0;Data " & _
  "Source=C:\Inetpub\wwwroot\Chapter7\data\TaraStore.mdb"
Dim SQL As String = _
  "SELECT * FROM Products WHERE SubCategoryID=2"
Dim objCS As New System.Data.OleDb.OleDbConnection(CS)
```

3. Immediately after the preceding code, add the following code to create the DataAdapter object, the DataSet object, and the DataView object:

```
Dim objDA As New _
  System.Data.OleDb.OleDbDataAdapter(SQL, objCS)
```

```
Dim objDS As New DataSet
objDA.Fill(objDS, "Products")
Dim objDV As DataView
objDV = objDS.Tables(0).DefaultView
```

4. Add the following code to set the DataSource property of the DataList control to the DataView object and bind the Data controls to the data source using the DataBind method of the Page object:

```
MyDL1.DataSource = objDV
```

```
Page.DataBind()
```

```
Else
```

```
End If
```

5. Click the **DataListTemplate.aspx** tab, then click the **DataList** control. Change the RepeatColumns property in the Properties window to **2**.

6. Click the **HTML** tab to edit the DataList control. Locate the <asp:DataList></asp:DataList> controls. Between the DataList controls add the following code to create the HeaderTemplate and the FooterTemplate templates:

```
<HeaderTemplate>
  <div>
      <img src="images/CatPics/1.jpg"><br />
      <img src="images/560green.gif" width="800">
  </div>
</HeaderTemplate>
<FooterTemplate>
    <img src="images/560green.gif" width="800">
    <div align="center">
        <img src="images/logo.gif" align="left">
        <br>
        For more information visit <b>
        <a href="http://www.TaraStore.com">
                http://www.TaraStore.com
        </a></b>
        <br>
        1-800-555-5555
    </div>
</FooterTemplate>
```

7. Add the code following this paragraph to create the ItemTemplate. Use a table to make the layout clearer for the viewer. (*Note*: You might want to lay out your table tags first before inserting data, to verify your HTML tags.) The same method used in the previous exercise, called DataItem, returns the value for the database column specified in the parentheses. You can also use DataBinder.Eval to evaluate the results as an expression and apply formatting arguments such as currency.

```
<ItemTemplate>
  <table><tr><td width="200" align="center">
    <a href= "images/ProductPics/<%# ¬
      Container.DataItem("ProductImage") %>">
      <img src=
      "images/ProductThumbnails/<%# Container.DataItem("
thumbnail") %>"
      hspace="2" border="0">
    </a>
    </td>
    <td width="200">
    <b>
    <a href= "images/ProductPics/<%# ¬
      Container.DataItem("ProductImage") %>">
      <%# Container.DataItem("ModelName")%>
    </a></b>
  <br />
    <i>Description: </i>
    <%# Container.DataItem("Description") %>
    <br />
    <i>Price: </i>
    <%# DataBinder.Eval(Container.DataItem, _
      "UnitCost", "{0:C}") %>
    <br>
    <i>Item #: </i>
    <%# Container.DataItem("ModelNumber") %>
  </td></tr></table>
</ItemTemplate>
```

8. Click the **Save All** button. Click **Build** on the menu bar, and then click **Build Solution**. (*Note*: Once you have entered the ItemTemplate code, you cannot go back to Design view because Design view cannot interpret the quotation marks correctly.)

9. Right-click on the page, and then click **View in Browser**. (*Note*: Do not view the page in HTML view.) Figure 7-27 shows how the page appears in the browser.

10. Close any open pages.

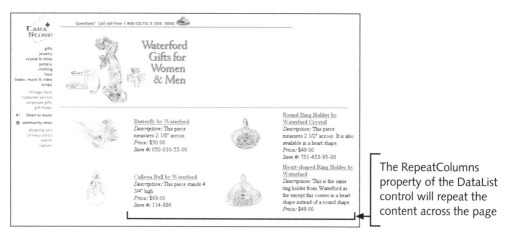

The RepeatColumns property of the DataList control will repeat the content across the page

Figure 7-27   Using templates to format the DataList control

CHAPTER SUMMARY

❐ Data can be displayed using Web Server controls. The DropDownList, ListBox, CheckBoxList, and RadioButtonList controls inherit from a ListControls class. DropDownList usually only displays one value at a time, while ListBox generally displays all the values at the same time.

❐ The DataList and DataGrid controls inherit from the BaseDataList class. The DataList control uses an ItemTemplate to display the values. The DataGrid control allows you to create bound and unbound columns. Bound columns contain a value that is bound to a value in the database. The DataList and DataGrid controls use templates to create the header, footer, and item sections of the data control. You can format these controls using the graphical Style Builder tool or manually.

❐ The Repeater control inherits directly from the System.Web.UI.Control class. The Repeater control must be edited manually in HTML view. There is no graphical tool to edit the Repeater control.

❐ Data that consists of a repeated expression can be bound to the Web Server controls. Web Server controls can be bound to many types of data such as a hash table, array list, DataSet, DataView, or DataReader object.

❐ A DataAdapter object creates and manages the connection to the database. The Connection uses the connection string to locate the database. The DataAdapter object uses the SQL statement and the connection object. The DataAdapter object uses the Fill method to populate the DataSet object with the table specified in the parameter for the Fill command.

❐ The DataSet object can contain one or more DataTable objects. A DataView object contains a subset of rows of data from a DataTable object. A DataReader object is a read-only, forward-only stream of data from the database. The data connection remains open while the DataReader object reads the data. The DataReader object provides better performance than the DataView or DataSet objects.

❐ You can create the .NET objects and Web controls manually, or you can use Visual Studio .NET graphical controls to generate the code to create the objects and controls.

REVIEW QUESTIONS

1. Which of the following controls cannot be used to display data in a Web page?

   a. DataList

   b. DataView

   c. DataGrid

   d. Repeater

2. What method can be used to bind the DG1 control to a hash table?

   a. DG1.Bind()

   b. Page.Bind()

   c. DG1.DataBind()

   d. Bind.Page()

3. Which technique can be used to store values that can later be retrieved?

   a. Property

   b. Method

   c. Function

   d. a or b

4. What keyword is used to identify the value returned from a function?

   a. Provider

   b. Return

   c. Function

   d. Else

5. Which Data control is inherited from the BaseDataList class?

   a. CheckBoxList

   b. DropDownList

   c. DataList

   d. RadioButton

 6. Which Data control is inherited from the ListControls class?

   a. CheckBoxList

   b. DropDownList

   c. ListBox

   d. all of the above

 7. Which object provides a read-only, forward-only stream of data from the database?

   a. DataReader

   b. DataSet

   c. DataView

   d. ArrayList

 8. Which data control displays one value at a time?

   a. ListBox

   b. DropDownList

   c. DataList

   d. DataGrid

 9. Which control does not have a visual interface in the Visual Studio .NET Toolbox?

   a. DataGrid

   b. DataList

   c. CheckBoxList

   d. Repeater

10. Which method is used to insert a new item into an ArrayList?

   a. Insert

   b. Add

   c. Fill

   d. InsertCommand

11. Which property of the Data controls identifies where to get its data?

   a. DataView

   b. DataSource

   c. DataTable

   d. DataTextField

12. What property allows you to format a value as currency?

   a. FormatCurrency

   b. Format $C

   c. DataTextFormatString

   d. DataTextField

13. Which property is used to identify the column to be displayed in a DropDownList control?

    a. DataValueField

    b. DataTextFormat

    c. DataTextFormatString

    d. DataTextField

14. What is the fully qualified name of the Connection object for a non-SQL Database?

    a. System.Data.OleDb.OleDbConnection

    b. System.Data.OleDb.OleDbConnection(CS)

    c. System.Data.OleDb

    d. System.Data.OleDbConnection

15. What object is used to get the data from the database and populate the DataSet object?

    a. DataAdapter

    b. DataSet

    c. DataConnection

    d. DataView

16. Which method is used to get the data from the database and populate the DataSet object?

    a. Fill

    b. Get

    c. Select

    d. InsertCommand

17. Which property must be set to False before you can change the displayed DataGrid columns?

    a. AutoFormatColumns

    b. FormatColumns

    c. AutoDataColumns

    d. AutoGenerateColumns

18. What ASP.NET tag is used to format a bound column in a DataGrid control?

    a. <asp:BoundColumn>

    b. <Columns>

    c. <ASP:Columns>

    d. a and b

19. Which template includes the values from the database?

    a. HeaderTemplate

    b. FooterTemplate

    c. AlternatingTemplate

    d. ItemTemplate

20. In the template that contains the value, which expression returns a value from a column named "thumbnail"?

    a. <%# Container.DataItem("thumbnail") %>

    b. <%# Columns.DataItem("thumbnail") %>

    c. <%# Columns ("thumbnail") %>

    d. <%# Columns.thumbnail %>

7

HANDS-ON PROJECTS

Project 7-1

In this project, you will create a Web page that binds an array to a DropDownList control.

1. Start **Visual Studio .NET** and open your **Chapter7** solution if it is not already open.

2. Add a Web page named **Ch7Proj1.aspx** that displays an array using a DropDownList control.

3. Create an array named **arr1**, which has five items.

4. Insert the following values into the array: **Paper**, **Pencils**, **Glue**, **Notepads**, **Pens**.

5. Insert the DropDownList control named **MyDD1**.

6. When the page loads, populate the MyDD1 control with the values in the array, and bind the values to the control.

7. Add an **ASP.NET Label** control to the page. When the user clicks the Submit button, display the value in the Label control.

8. Add headings, graphics, fonts, and colors to enhance the appearance of the page. (*Note:* The additional office-specific images included on the disk are bookshelf.gif, colorednotecardspink.gif, computer.gif, gluepinkpaper.gif, pencilsfan.gif, ringnotecards.gif, and yellownotepad.gif.)

9. View your Web page in the browser. Print the Web page, the source code within Visual Studio .NET, and the source code from the browser.

Project 7-2

In this project, you will create a Web page that binds a hash table to a DropDownList control.

1. Start **Visual Studio .NET** and open your **Chapter7** solution if it is not already open.

2. Add a Web page called **Ch7Proj2.aspx** that will display a hash table using a DropDownList control.

3. Create a hash table named **MyHash**, which has five items.

4. Insert the following items into the hash table as the keys: **Yellow Notepads**, **Pencils**, **School Glue**, **Colored Index Cards**, **Ring Index Cards**. The values are yellownotepad.gif, pencilsfan.gif, gluepinkpaper.gif, colorednotecardspink.gif, and ringnotecards.gif, respectively.

5. Insert the DropDownList control named **MyDD1**.

6. When the page loads, populate the MyDD1 control with the values in the hash table, and bind the values to the control.

7. Insert an Image control named **IMG1**. The first image should be pencilsfan.gif.

8. Add an **ASP.NET Label** control to the page. When the user clicks the Submit button, display the value in the Label control.

9. Add headings, graphics, fonts, and colors to enhance the appearance of the page. (*Note*: The additional office specific images included on the disk are bookshelf.gif and computer.gif.)

10. Save your page and build your solution.

11. View your Web page in the browser. Print the Web page, the source code within Visual Studio .NET, and the source code from the browser.

Project 7-3

In this project, you will create a Web page that binds a HashTable object to a DataGrid control.

1. Start **Visual Studio .NET** and open your **Chapter7** solution if necessary.

2. Add a Web page named **Ch7Proj3.aspx** that will display a hash table using a DropDownList control.

3. Create a hash table named **MyHash**, which has five items.

4. Insert the following items into the hash table as the keys: **Yellow Notepads**, **Pencils**, **School Glue**, **Colored Index Cards**, **Ring Index Cards**. The values are 3.5, 2.75, 3.5, 4.5, and 5.3, respectively.

5. Insert the DataGrid control named **MyDG1**.

6. Change the AutoGenerateColumns property to **False**.

7. Type the code following this paragraph to add the Columns collection to the DataGrid control to insert the items in the hash table. Format the HeaderText to reflect the contents of the column.

```
<Columns>
<ASP:BoundColumn HeaderText="Product Name"
  DataField="Key" />
<ASP:BoundColumn HeaderText="Product Price"
  DataField="Value"
DataFormatString="{0:C}" />
</Columns>
```

8. When the page loads, populate the MyDG1 control with the values in the hash table, and bind the values to the control.

9. Add headings, graphics, fonts, and colors to enhance the appearance of the page and the templates. (*Note*: The additional office specific images included on the disk are bookshelf.gif, colorednotecardspink.gif, computer.gif, gluepinkpaper.gif, pencilsfan.gif, ringnotecards.gif, and yellownotepad.gif.)

10. Save your page and build your solution.

11. View your Web page in the browser. Print the Web page, the source code within Visual Studio .NET, and the source code from the browser.

Project 7-4

In this project, you will create a Web page that binds a database to a Repeater control. You will manually add the code to create the data objects. You will modify the Repeater control. The page will display all the columns in the products table for all of the products.

1. Start **Visual Studio .NET** and open your **Chapter7** solution if necessary.

2. Add a Web page named **Ch7Proj4.aspx** that displays a table from a database using a DataGrid control.

3. Add the DataGrid control to the page. The ID should be **MyDG1**.

4. In the code behind the page, add the code following this paragraph to create the data connection to the TaraStore database. Make sure to change the SQL Select statement to choose all the products in the database. Make sure to assign the DataView control to the DataSource property of the DataGrid control.

```
If Not Page.IsPostBack() Then
  Dim CS As String = _
  "Provider=Microsoft.Jet.OLEDB.4.0;Data " _
  & "Source=C:\Inetpub\wwwroot\Chapter7\data\ ↲
TaraStore.mdb"
  Dim SQL As String = "SELECT * FROM Products"
  Dim objCS As New System.Data.OleDb.OleDbConnection(CS)
  Dim objDA As New System.Data.OleDb.OleDbDataAdapter ↲
  (SQL, objCS)
```

```
    Dim objDS As New DataSet
    objDA.Fill(objDS, "Products")
    Dim objDV As DataView
    objDV = objDS.Tables(0).DefaultView
    MyDG1.DataSource = objDV
    Page.DataBind()
  Else
  End If
```

5. Use the Property Builder to modify the DataGrid control. Change the heading color, font name, font size, and background color. Change the background color of the alternating rows to something other than white. Change the heading text properties for all of the columns in the table. Change the font size of the item template to **X-Small** so you can see more of the table on one screen.

6. Add headings, graphics, fonts, and colors to enhance the appearance of the page.

7. Save your page and build your solution.

8. View your Web page in the browser. Print the Web page, the source code within Visual Studio .NET, and the source code from the browser.

Project 7-5

In this project, you will create a Web page that binds a database to a Repeater control. You will modify the Repeater control using templates.

1. Start **Visual Studio .NET** and open your **Chapter7** solution if necessary.

2. Add a Web page named **Ch7Proj5.aspx** that displays a database using a Repeater control.

3. In the code behind the page, add the code following this paragraph to create the data connection to the TaraStore database. Make sure to change the SQL Select statement to choose all the products in the database. Make sure to assign the DataView control to the DataSource property of the Repeater control.

```
If Not Page.IsPostBack() Then
  Dim CS As String = _
  "Provider=Microsoft.Jet.OLEDB.4.0;Data " _
  & "Source=C:\Inetpub\wwwroot\Chapter7\data\ ↵
TaraStore.mdb"
  Dim SQL As String = _
    "SELECT * FROM Products where SubCategoryID=2"
  Dim objCS As New System.Data.OleDb.OleDbConnection(CS)
  Dim objDA As _
  New System.Data.OleDb.OleDbDataAdapter(SQL, objCS)
  Dim objDS As New DataSet
  objDA.Fill(objDS, "Products")
  Dim objDV As DataView
  objDV = objDS.Tables(0).DefaultView
  MyRP1.DataSource = objDV
  Page.DataBind()
Else
End If
```

4. In Design view of the Web page, add a Panel control to the page. Delete the text within the Panel control.

5. Add the Repeater control inside the Panel control. The ID should be **MyRP1**.

6. Within the Repeater control tags, add the code following this paragraph to add a HeaderTemplate to display the category image. (*Hint*: You will have to do this in HTML view.)

```
<HeaderTemplate>
  <div>
      <img src="images/CatPics/1.jpg"><br />
      <img src="images/560green.gif">
  </div>
</HeaderTemplate>
```

7. Within the Repeater control tags, add the following code to add a FooterTemplate to display the footer:

```
<FooterTemplate>
    <img src="images/560green.gif">
    <div align="center">
        <img src="images/logo.gif" align="left">
        <br />
        For more information visit <b>
        <a href="http://www.TaraStore.com">
              http://www.TaraStore.com
        </a></b>
        <br />
        1-800-555-5555
    </div>
</FooterTemplate>
```

8. Add the following code to add the ItemTemplate:

```
<ItemTemplate>
  <b><%# Container.DataItem("ModelName")%></b>
  <br />
  <i>Description: </i>
  <%# Container.DataItem("Description") %>
  <br />
  <i>Price: </i>
  <%# DataBinder.Eval(Container.DataItem, _
    "UnitCost", "{0:C}") %>
  <br />
  <i>Item #: </i>
  <%# Container.DataItem("ModelNumber") %>
  <br /><br />
</ItemTemplate>
```

9. Add headings, graphics, fonts, and colors to enhance the appearance of the page.

10. Save your page and build your solution.

11. View your Web page in the browser. Print the Web page, the source code within Visual Studio .NET, and the source code from the browser.

7

CASE PROJECTS

Tara Store — Web Server Controls

Your manager has asked you to provide information about the various Web Server controls that can be bound to data sources. Go to the Help menu within Visual Studio .NET and search for the Web Server controls listed in this chapter. If you do not have Visual Studio .NET Help installed, you can search for the information at *http://msdn.microsoft.com*. Create a Web page that describes at least five Web Server controls. Provide an example of the syntax used to insert each control into the Web page. Add headings, graphics, fonts, and colors to enhance the appearance of the page. Save the page as Ch7Case1.aspx. Print the Web page.

Tara Store — Retrieving the UserID Using a Hash Table

Your boss would like you to create a listing of UserIDs and passwords in a hash table. You are to use the hash table to create a Web page that displays the users in the table. When the user clicks the Submit button, his or her password should be displayed in a Web Server Label control and all of the users and passwords should be displayed in a DataList control. Add headings, graphics, fonts, and colors to enhance the appearance of the page. Save the page as Ch7Case2.aspx. Print the Web page.

Tara Store — Displaying a Product Listing Page with the DataGrid Control

Your boss has asked you to create a shopping cart application. In the first phase, you must create a database that contains the product information. Place the database in your project data directory. You can use SQL Server, Access, or another database application to create the database. Include the name of the product, price, description, product ID, and product image name. Insert some sample data. Create a Web page that displays the data using a DataGrid control. Format the DataGrid control using the Property Builder. Change the font color, background color, cell alignment, font name, and font size for HeaderTemplate and ItemTemplate for each of the columns. Change the background color of the alternating rows. Add headings, graphics, fonts, and colors to enhance the appearance of the page. Save the page as Ch7Case3.aspx. Print the Web page and the source code.

Tara Store — Displaying a Product Listing Page with the DataList Control

Your boss has asked you to create a shopping cart application. In the first phase, you must create a database that contains the product information. Place the database in your project data directory. You can use SQL Server, Access, or another database application to create the database. Include the name of the product, price, description, product ID, and product image name. (*Note*: If you created the database in the previous case, you can reuse that database.) Insert some sample data. Create a Web page that displays the data using a DataList control. Format the DataList using the DataList templates. Change the font color, background color, cell alignment, font name, and font size for the HeaderTemplate and the ItemTemplate for each of the columns. Change the background color of the alternating rows. Change the display so that there are always two columns of data displayed on one page. Add headings, graphics, fonts, and colors to enhance the appearance of the page. Save the page as Ch7Case4.aspx. Print the Web page and the source code.

Tara Store — Displaying a Product Listing Page with the Repeater Control

7

Your boss has asked you to create a shopping cart application. In the first phase, you must create a database that contains the product information. Place the database in your project data directory. You can use SQL Server, Access, or another database application to create the database. (*Note*: If you created the database in one of the earlier cases, you can reuse that database.) Include the name of the product, price, description, product ID, and product image name. Insert some sample data. Create a Web page that displays the data using a DataGrid control. Format the Repeater using the templates. Change the font color, background color, cell alignment, font name, and font size for the HeaderTemplate and the ItemTemplate for each of the columns. Change the background color of the alternating rows. Add headings, graphics, fonts, and colors to enhance the appearance of the page. Save the page as Ch7Case5.aspx. Print the Web page and the source code.

8

BUILDING DATA-DRIVEN
WEB APPLICATIONS

In this chapter, you will:

♦ Learn how to use data sources in Visual Studio .NET

♦ Build search queries using SQL

♦ Page, sort, and filter data using the DataGrid control

♦ Insert, modify, and delete records using the DataGrid control

♦ Build a reusable Visual Basic .NET component that retrieves a DataSet

---

Web data management is an ever-evolving component of Web development. Businesses must quickly create Web data-driven applications that display data, allow the user to customize the data displayed, and allow the administrator to manage the data remotely. Visual Studio .NET provides new data objects that you can use to manage your data connections, and new Data controls that you can use to manage your data within the Web page. These new ASP.NET Data controls can also be used to allow the end user to manipulate the data from the Web page.

In this chapter, you will learn how to retrieve data using the DataReader and DataSet controls. Using the DataReader, you will learn how to use SQL statements and stored procedures to retrieve data. Then, you will learn how to modify the appearance of the data using the built-in templates and properties of the DataGrid control. You will also learn how to add, delete, and modify records using the DataGrid control.

USING DATA SOURCES IN VISUAL STUDIO .NET

Web developers must create Web applications that can coexist with evolving data structures. Using Visual Studio .NET, you can create stored procedures to collect data from the database. Then you can create Data controls in the Web page, which are bound to the data source defined within the Data component. When a database administrator decides to change a field name, the administrator can also make the change in the stored procedure. No changes need be made to the application, because the data application tier is separate from the business and presentation tiers. If the Web store owner decides to change the appearance of the Web page, the Web developer can make the change in the Web page, without affecting the data application layer. In previous versions of ASP, you could change the Web page without changing the data application layer. However, the code was intermixed with HTML and was more difficult and costly to maintain.

Visual Studio .NET allows you to create connections to various data sources, such as arrays, hash tables, and databases. The process of binding the data is the same regardless of the data source. To bind the data source to the control, you must assign the data source to the DataSource property of the Data control, and then call either the DataBind method of the control or the DataBind method of the page. It is simpler to access data from a HashTable or ArrayList than from a database because you are only accessing one object, the HashTable or ArrayList.

You can retrieve the data using a DataReader object. The DataReader object provides a read-only, direct connection to the data source. You might choose to use the DataReader when you want to retrieve data that does not change with the client. The DataBind method is used to bind the DataReader to the Data control.

When accessing data from a database, you can access the data from multiple tables. These tables are received as a DataSet object. A **DataSet** contains a DataTables collection. Individual **DataTables** within the DataTables collection can have relationships defined between the DataTable objects. You can use the DataTable to specify the subset of tables and records that you want to access. The DataView object is used to retrieve a subset of one of the tables within the DataSet. However, the results were always received by the Recordset object as a single table. With a DataSet object, the data can be received as a group of one or more related tables. The DataBind method is used to bind the DataSet or DataView to the Data control.

The DataReader Object

The **DataReader object** is used to retrieve a read-only, non-buffered stream of data from a database. **Non-buffered** means only one record at any one time is stored in memory. When the new record is read, the old record is first removed from memory. Because the information read is a stream of data, it is retrieved sequentially and is read-only. The DataReader can retrieve the records faster than the DataSet. The DataReader cannot be used to retrieve a disconnected set of data, because the DataReader is directly connected to the database and reads each row individually. The DataReader can retrieve a forward-only set of data, which means that you cannot move backwards through the rows of data. Therefore, the data retrieved by the DataReader can only be bound to a single control.

There are two special types of DataReader objects, which are used for the SqlClient, OleDb, Odbc, and OracleClient classes. You execute the same steps to implement the DataReader, but the objects have different names. There is only a small difference in code between the DataReader objects. However, there is a substantial difference in performance between them. The **SqlDataReader** object is used with SQL Server databases, while the **OleDbDataReader** object is used with all other OleDb-accessible databases, such as older versions of Oracle, and Microsoft Access. New versions of Oracle use the **OracleDataReader** object, and old versions of legacy databases can use the **OdbcDataReader** object. The DataReader can significantly improve the performance of your application.

In the current version of Visual Studio .NET, there are no tools in the Toolbox for creating the DataReader object. Therefore, you have to write code to instantiate the DataReader object, and read the data from the code behind the page. (*Note:* There are visual tools on the Data tab within the Toolbox that can be used to create the Command and Connection objects.)

The sample code that follows this paragraph creates a SQL string and a Connection object. The Command object is created using the active connection and SQL statement. The ExecuteReader method of the Command object returns the OleDbDataReader object. (*Note:* The ↵ symbol is used to show that the code continues on the next line. When you enter the code, type the code on a single line.)

```
Dim CS As String = "Provider=Microsoft.Jet.OLEDB.4.0; ↵
Data Source=C:\Inetpub\wwwroot\Chapter8\data\TaraStore.mdb;"
Dim objCN As New OleDb.OleDbConnection(CS)
objCN.Open()
Dim mySQL As String = "SELECT * FROM Categories"
Dim objCM As New OleDb.OleDbCommand(mySQL, objCN)
Dim objDR As OleDb.OleDbDataReader
objDR = objCM.ExecuteReader()
```

You can also use the ConnectionString property of the Connection object, as shown in the sample code that follows this paragraph. The first connection string uses a user ID to connect to an Access database.

```
SqlConnection1.ConnectionString = _
    "Provider=Microsoft.Jet.OLEDB.4.0; ↵
Data Source=C:\Inetpub\wwwroot\Chapter8\data\TaraStore.mdb;"
```

You can also use Visual Studio .NET to create the Data Connection object. You can drag the Data Connection object to the Design view of a Web page. Using the Data Link dialog box you can set up a connection to a specific database. You can also drag the database from an existing data connection listed in the Data Connections in the Server Explorer window. These methods will create the connection string to the database. The second connection string is created by Visual Studio .NET and uses Windows NT trusted security to connect to a SQL Server database.

```
SqlConnection2.ConnectionString = _
"data source=(local)\NetSDK; initial catalogue=Chapter6; ↵
integrated  security=SSPI;workstation id=COURSE; ↵
packet size=4096";
```

After you have created the DataReader object, you can access the Read method to retrieve the data stream. The **Read method** of the DataReader reads records in a forward-only direction. Each record is read, and then displayed on the Web page, because only one record is stored in memory at a time. Once you have read the record, you can access the value of a column using the name of the column within quotations, or the index number. The index number is the number of the column in the order in which it is retrieved. The index number for the first column is 0. The sample code that follows this paragraph reads the data from the DataReader and returns the value in the CategoryName column for each row. The CategoryName column could have been retrieved using `objDR(0)`.

```
While objDR.Read()
Response.Write(objDR("CategoryName"))
End While
```

Because you have an open connection to the data stream, you must always call the **Close method** of the DataReader object when you have finished reading the data. You can also pass the CloseConnection property as a parameter when you call the Execute method of the Command object. This causes the Command object to close the connection to the DataReader for you. The following code illustrates how to close the DataReader object using the Command object:

```
objCM.ExecuteReader(CommandBehavior.CloseConnection)
```

 You can use stored procedures in combination with the DataReader object. If you run a command that contains any output parameters or return values, these values are not available until you close the DataReader object.

USING A DATAREADER OBJECT WITH AN ACCESS DATABASE

The steps for implementing a DataReader object with an Access database are in the following numbered list. Read these steps carefully before attempting the exercises in the next section.

1. Create a connection string. The connection string contains the database provider name, the data location, and the username and password, which are required to connect to the database. The syntax of the connection string varies with the type of database used. In this example, the name of the provider for the Access database is "Microsoft.Jet.OLEDB.4.0". The code following this paragraph shows

the sample connection string. (*Note*: Because the connection string is a string, it should not be split across multiple lines, unless you concatenate it.)

```
Dim CS As String = "Provider=Microsoft.Jet.OLEDB.4.0; ↵
Data Source=C:\Inetpub\wwwroot\Chapter8\data\ ↵
TaraStore.mdb"
```

2. Create a Connection object, as shown in the following code:

```
Dim objCN As New OleDb.OleDbConnection(CS)
```

3. Open the connection, as shown in the code that follows this paragraph. (*Note*: If you are using Visual Studio .NET, the Open method appears on the IntelliSense menu.)

```
objCN.Open()
```

4. Create a variable that contains a SQL command or stored procedure, as shown in the code sample that follows this paragraph. (*Note*: Do not split the string across multiple lines of code.) Retrieve the columns from the Categories table.

```
Dim mySQL As String = "SELECT * FROM Categories"
```

5. Create the Command object using the SQL variable and the Connection object, as shown in the following code sample:

```
Dim objCM As New OleDb.OleDbCommand(mySQL, objCN)
```

6. Declare the variable, which contains the DataReader object, as shown in the following code sample:

```
Dim objDR As OleDb.OleDbDataReader
```

7. Use the ExecuteReader method of the Command object to retrieve the data and place the data in the DataReader object, as shown in the following code sample:

```
objDR = objCM.ExecuteReader()
```

8. Read the data from the DataReader object, and write the column values to the Web page, as shown in the code sample that follows this paragraph. (*Note*: You are not limited to writing only the values; you can write out other content, HTML code, and expressions.)

```
While objDR.Read()
Response.Write(objDR("CategoryName"))
End While
```

9. Close the DataReader object, as shown in the following code sample:

```
objDR.Close()
```

10. Close the data connection, as shown in the code sample that follows this paragraph. (*Note*: You don't have to release the variables because the garbage collector will reclaim the variables when they are no longer referenced.)

```
objCN.Close()
```

You can access the data as a string or in its native data type. For example, you can use the GetDateTime method to retrieve the data as a Date object. You can also retrieve the schema information about the current data returned set by using the GetSchemaTable method. This method returns a DataTable object that contains the schema information as a table. Each column maps to a property of the column returned in the result set, where ColumnName is the name of the property and the value of the column is the value of the property.

Using the DataReader to Retrieve Data from a Database

In the following exercise, you will first set up the project and import the data files. Then you will use the DataReader object to retrieve data and display a listing of categories in the TaraStore database. The Label control at the left of the main image is named lblCat. You will display the values of the categories from the TaraStore database using the DataReader object.

1. Start **Visual Studio .NET**.

2. Click **File** on the menu bar, point to **New**, and then click **Project**. This opens the New Project window.

3. Click the **Visual Basic Projects** icon, then click the **ASP.NET Web Application** icon under Templates. Type **Chapter8** in the Location text box in place of WebApplication1. Click **OK** to create the solution, project, and default files.

4. Open Windows Exporer. (*Note:* You can go to the **Start** menu, click **Run**, type **%SystemRoot%\explorer.exe** in the text box, and click **OK**.) Navigate to your **Chapter08Data** folder. Select both the **data** folder and the **images** folder, click the **Edit** menu, and then click **Copy**. Go back to Visual Studio .NET 2003. Right-click the **Chapter8** project and select **Paste**. The data folder, images folder, subfolders, and the images will be copied into your project.

5. Right-click **Chapter8** in the Solution Explorer window, point to **Add**, and then click **Add Existing Item**. Navigate to your Chapter08Data directory. Change the Files of type drop-down list from VB Code Files to **All Files**. Select all files from the Chapter08Data folder except the data and images folders. Click the **Open** button to import the files into your project. When prompted, click **Yes** in the dialog box to create the new class files.

6. Double-click the **DataReader.aspx** page icon in the Solution Explorer window to open the page. Double-click the page to open the code behind the page, which is named **DataReader.aspx.vb**.

7. Within the Page_Load procedure, add the code that follows this paragraph. (*Note:* The location of your database may be different, depending on where your Web site is installed on the Web server. Your system administrator can provide you with the physical path to your files.) This code creates the connection

string and the Connection object, and opens the connection. The connection string should be on a single line. (*Note*: Do not split the connection string across two lines of code. You cannot split a string across multiple lines of code unless you concatenate the string.)

```
Dim CS As String = ↵
  "Provider=Microsoft.Jet.OLEDG.4.0; ↵
  Data Source=C:\Inetpub\wwwroot\ ↵
  Chapter8\data\TaraStore.mdb;" ↵
Dim objCN As New OleDb.OleConnection(CS)
objCN.Open()
```

8. Below this, add the following code to create the variable to store the SQL command:

```
Dim mySQL As String = _
  "SELECT CategoryName FROM Categories"
```

9. Below this, add the following code to create the Command object using the SQL command and the Connection object:

```
Dim objCM As New OleDb.OleDbCommand(mySQL, objCN)
```

10. Below this, add the code following this paragraph to create the variable that stores the DataReader object. (*Note*: It is more useful to name the DataReader object something like objDR. In most samples installed with Visual Studio .NET the DataReader object is named result.)

```
Dim objDR As OleDb.OleDbDataReader
objDR = objCM.ExecuteReader()
```

11. Below this, add the following code to declare a variable named **MyCat** to store the data from the DataReader object:

```
Dim MyCat As String
```

12. Below this, add the code following this paragraph to read the record from the DataReader. Concatenate the CategoryName field with the MyCat variable and a line break tag. Store the results from the concatenation in the MyCat variable. This ensures that all records are stored in the MyCat variable.

```
While objDR.Read()
MyCat = MyCat + (objDR("CategoryName") & "<br />")
End While
```

13. Below this, add the following code to close the DataReader and Connection objects:

```
objDR.Close()
objCN.Close()
```

14. Below this, add the code that follows this paragraph to assign the contents of the MyCat variable to the Text property of the label named lblCat. The label displays the results from the DataReader in the Web page.

```
lblCat.Text = MyCat
```

15. Click the **Save All** button. Click **Build** on the menu bar, then click **Build Solution**.

16. Click the **DataReader.aspx** tab to return to the Web page. Right-click on the page, and then click **View in Browser**. Your page should look like the one in Figure 8-1. The lblCat Label control displays the category menu on the left side of the page.

17. Close any open pages.

Figure 8-1   Displaying data from a Microsoft Access database with the DataReader object

BUILDING ADVANCED QUERIES USING SQL

You can modify the SQL commands to retrieve a select group of records. In the previous exercise, you evaluated a single SQL statement within a single SELECT statement. You can add SQL conditions to retrieve a subset of records from the database. The SQL statement is the **search condition**, which identifies the criterion that is used to filter the records. A search condition evaluates to either true or false. The search condition uses the WHERE keyword to identify the search condition.

The search condition is also referred to as the WHERE condition in SQL. The discussion in this section is focused on building a search condition. You can learn more about how to build SQL statements in *A Guide to SQL, Sixth Edition* by Pratt (© 2002, Course Technology).

The SQL statement **"WHERE username='John'"** would evaluate to true or false. For records in which the username is John, the record is returned in the data set. In Access and SQL, you can create more complex queries using multiple search conditions within the same statement. When the keyword "AND" is used to separate conditions, both search conditions must be resolved to true. If the keyword "OR" is used to separate conditions, only one of the search conditions needs to be resolved to true.

The search condition consists of an expression, followed by a comparison operator, and another expression. An expression can be simple, such as the name of a field, or it can be a string, a number, or a value passed from a form. If the expression is a string, the string must be enclosed within quotation marks. Strings are case sensitive when used as expressions. So, "product" and "PRODUCT" are not evaluated as equal expressions. An expression that contains a date must append the pound sign (#) before and after the date. The keyword NULL can be used to search for empty fields. An empty string is not the same as a NULL field, because NULL fields do not contain any data. The word NULL is used as the expression. A comparison operator is used to evaluate the expression. Valid comparison operators include +, <, >, <>, IS, and ISNOT. The syntax to create search criteria in a SQL statement is as follows:

```
WHERE [expression1][comparisonoperator][expression2]
```

You can use a static value as the comparative expression or use a variable that contains a value. If the value is a string, single quotes are used around the value. If the value passed is a number, you do not need the single quotes. The sample code that follows this paragraph contains valid expressions that use multiple search criteria and data types. (*Note*: While strings use quotes, the dates use pound signs, and the numbers, variables, and constants do not use quotes.)

```
WHERE user='katie' AND pwd='pass'
WHERE state='IL' OR state='IN' AND people>=10000
WHERE lastVisit>#11/12/2003# OR member='new'
WHERE member='staff' AND salary>35000
WHERE birth=IS NULL OR email=IS NULL
```

By using the keywords "AND" and "OR", you can combine multiple search criteria within the same SQL statement. For example, you can create a query that lists the product names of any product where the number of items is less than five. This information could be provided to the person in charge of ordering new supplies. However, you don't need to order discontinued products. By using combination queries, you can combine all of these search criteria into one SQL statement.

8

The ORDER BY statement allows you to sort the results based on one or more columns. You can separate multiple sort columns with a comma. When there are multiple sort columns, the rows will be sorted by the first sort column, then the second, and so forth. You can specify the sort order as ascending with ASC or descending with DESC. The sample SQL statement that follows this paragraph displays a list of category names, where the CategoryName is Jewelry or the CategoryID is greater than three. The rows returned are sorted by CategoryName in ascending order.

```
SELECT CategoryName, CategoryID, CatImage, ↵
       Thumbnail, Description
FROM Categories
WHERE (CategoryName='Jewelry') OR (CategoryID>3)
ORDER BY CategoryName ASC;
```

Building SQL Queries to Insert, Modify, and Delete Data

You can use the following SQL statements to insert, update, and delete records:

- INSERT to add a new record

- DELETE to delete one or more rows of data

- UPDATE to modify one or more rows of data

In SQL, you must create an INSERT query in order to create a new record. Insert queries can only be performed on one table at a time, and only one record at a time can be inserted. Furthermore you must specify a value for every field. If no value is available, you can substitute the word "NULL" for the value. You must enter strings using quotation marks. If you enter the fields without specifying the field names, you must enter them in the order that the fields appear in the database structure. If you have used an autonumber field in Access or an identity field in SQL Server, you can't enter a value in that field. The database automatically inserts a value when the record is added. The syntax for inserting a new record into a table that has only five fields using SQL is as follows. The values are entered sequentially in the table. In the following example, the string 'chair' is placed in the first column and 153.00 is placed in the second column:

```
INSERT INTO Products
VALUES ('chair',153.00,#12/1/2000#,NULL,'furniture')
```

 Databases use slightly different versions of SQL. Some databases will not allow you to use double quotation marks. When you need to enter a string, use quotation marks. For example, `SELECT * FROM customers WHERE lastname='Kalata'` would be rewritten as `SELECT * FROM customers WHERE lastname = 'Kalata;`. If the value of the string contains a literal single quotation mark, you will have to modify your SQL statement to use one of the escape characters. If the string contains a single quotation mark, insert an additional single quotation mark in front of the initial quotation mark. As an example of this, `SELECT * FROM customers`

WHERE `lastname = 'O'Malley'` would be rewritten as `SELECT *`
`FROM customers WHERE lastname = 'O"Malley'`. (Note that
you also cannot enter any of the SQL keywords in your code. Information on the
the keywords can be found at *http://msdn.microsoft.com/library/en-us/*
tsqlref/ts_ra-rz_9oj7.asp.)

Another method of entering information is to modify the QuotedIdentifier
property witin SQL Server 2000. The QuotedIdentifier property controls how
literal strings are identified in SQL statements. Additional information on
using quotation marks and strings within SQL statements can be located at
http://msdn.microsoft.com/library/en-us/tsqlref/ts_set-set_9jxu.asp and
http://msdn.microsoft.com/library/en-us/sqldmo/dmoref_p_q_6cc9.asp.

You can specify the field names in parentheses after the table if you plan to enter values
for only a subset of fields. The sample code that follows this paragraph demonstrates how
to enter only the product name and price. It is better to specify the field names because
if the order of the columns is changed, then the SQL query will have to be changed.

```
INSERT INTO Products(name, price)
VALUES('chair',153.00)
```

The SQL statement uses the UPDATE command instead of the SELECT or INSERT
commands to modify a record. The UPDATE command needs to know which table to
update as well as which fields and values. The keyword SET is used to assign the values
to the field names. The properties of the Command object are set, and the Execute
method is called to perform the update. If you do not specify a search condition using
the WHERE clause, the value is updated for all records in the database. The code snippet following this paragraph assigns the entire SQL statement to a variable named SQL.
Note that the SQL statement is stored as a string and therefore must be enclosed within
double quotation marks. If you write the code across multiple lines, you will have to
concatenate the SQL statement using multiple strings. It is easier to read the code by
concatenating in a pattern for each line, such as name=value. Note that this is a common place in which inattentive developers make typographical errors.

```
SQL = "UPDATE Products SET " & _
" ProductName='Claddagh Ring'," & _
" UnitCost=25.45 WHERE ProductID=353"
```

To use the SQL statement with variables, you can replace the static values with variables
that contain values, as shown in the sample code that follows this paragraph. (*Note:* It is
important to make sure the single quotation marks are included for strings, and the
pound sign for dates. You will have to concatenate the variable between the set of strings
such as SQL = `"FieldName='" & VariableName & "'," .`)

```
SQL = "UPDATE Products SET " & _
" ProductName='" & MyProduct & "'," & _
" UnitCost=" & MyCost & _
" WHERE ProductID=" & MyProductID
```

The SQL DELETE command is used to delete records within the database. When you use the DELETE command, you must specify which records to delete and the name of the table. If you do not specify a specific record or set of records using the WHERE clause, the entire set of records is deleted. The following sample code passes a value to the SQL DELETE command so that only a single record is deleted.

```
SQL = "DELETE FROM Products " & _
" WHERE ProductID=" & MyProductID
```

 Before you run an UPDATE, INSERT, or DELETE command, you should first run the SQL statement as a SELECT query to ensure that you are operating on the correct data source. It's useful to display the data to the user and confirm his or her intent to modify the database before the SQL statement is executed.

Securing SQL Databases

In Chapter 6, you learned how to create SQL queries and stored procedures with Visual Studio .NET. **Stored procedures** are SQL programming statements that can be reused. They can contain SQL commands and can be as simple as a select statement. You can also pass values as parameters to the stored procedures. Stored procedures are queries that reside on the database server, and because they are compiled by the database server they are more efficient. Once you create the stored procedure, you can call it from an ASP.NET page and cause it to operate.

Popular databases such as Oracle and Microsoft SQL Server support stored procedures. In Microsoft Access, a stored procedure is called a **parameter query**. For example, you can develop a SQL statement that selects all records where the state field contains a value that matches a variable called strState. This SQL statement can be saved as a stored procedure and executed at a later time. When the stored procedure is called, you can then pass the value of the state, such as "IL," to the state variable strState. Not all databases support the concept of stored procedures.

Hackers are people who intrude into another person's software. Their intentions may be to expose the data, modify the data, or delete the data. Therefore, it's important to prevent them from gaining access to the SQL Server database. One of the main reasons for implementing stored procedures is to prevent SQL injection. **SQL injection** is a technique that is used by hackers to attach SQL statements to an existing SQL query in order to run additional commands. When a user enters data within a text box that is combined with an SQL statement, the hacker can insert additional SQL statements within that text box. This action injects the hacker's own SQL commands. To prevent SQL injection, always use stored procedures with sensitive data. You can read more about SQL injection at *http://msdn.microsoft.com/library/en-us/dnsqlmag04/html/InjectionProtection.asp*. Additional information on how to build secure SQL Server Web database applications can be found at *http://msdn.microsoft.com/data/sqlsolutions/sqlsecurity/default.aspx* and *http://msdn.microsoft.com./SQL/sqlsecurity/default.aspx*. Additional information about security of Web applications is covered in Chapter 10.

You can secure your SQL Server database by not leaving your password blank and by also using a strong password. A **strong password** uses a combination of numbers and special characters to make it more difficult to guess. Your system administrator, Web administrator, or database administrator will provide you with the user ID and password required to connect to a database.

 You can use Query Analyzer to manage your database, create stored procedures and SQL scripts, and run ad hoc SQL queries. SQL scripts are a series of SQL statements stored in a plain text file that can be run within Query Analyzer. They are often used when building the database, populating the database with data, and backing up the database. In the Enterprise version of SQL Server, the software comes with an administration tool called Enterprise Manager. This tool allows you to add user roles to a database, change user passwords, and manage databases. There is an HTML version of Enterprise Manager available for download free from Microsoft. You should ask your system administrator which SQL Server tools are available to you to manage your SQL Server databases. In many large companies, a database administrator is responsible for creation, maintenance, and deletion of databases, stored procedures, and SQL scripts.

8

Using the DataReader Object with a SQL Server Database

In the sample code that follows this paragraph, the connection string DataSource property identifies the name of the SQL Server. The Initial Catalog identifies the name of the database. The names of the Connection, Command, and DataReader objects are SqlConnection, SqlCommand, and SqlDataReader. The steps required to retrieve the data using the DataReader object are the same for both the OleDb and SqlClient databases. The following code is the code from the preceding exercise, rewritten to support a SQL Server database using the SqlDataReader object:

```
Dim CS As String = "Data Source=localhost;Initial ↵
  Catalog=TaraStoreSQL;User Id=sa;password=;"
Dim objCN As New SqlClient.SqlConnection(CS)
objCN.Open()
Dim mySQL As String = _
  "SELECT CategoryName FROM Categories"
Dim objCM As New SqlClient.SqlCommand(mySQL, objCN)
Dim objDR As SqlClient.SqlDataReader
objDR = objCM.ExecuteReader()
Dim MyCat As String
While objDR.Read()
MyCat = MyCat + (objDR("CategoryName") & "<br />")
End While
objDR.Close()
objCN.Close()
lblCat.Text = MyCat
```

Localhost is the keyword used to represent the local instance of the server. Therefore, the keyword localhost will only work if the SQL Server is on the same physical computer as the Web server. You can also specify the fully qualified name or IP address of the SQL Server. If you have multiple instances of SQL Servers installed on the same machine, you may want to use MachineName\SQLServerName to reference your SQL Server or MSDE database server.

Upsizing an Access Database to SQL Server

Sometimes you might be hired to work on a Web site that uses an existing database created in Access. Access does not provide the same level of robustness and security as a SQL Server database. You can connect many users simultaneously with SQL Server, but not with Access. Although Access can in theory support up to 20 simultaneous connections to an Access database via the Web, in practice this is not usually the case. You will have more control over security with a SQL Server database. Because Access is file based, the data can be downloaded by merely typing the URL of the database in the browser, if it's stored within the Web directory structure. The Internet Guest Account (IUSR_*MACHINENAME*) on the Web server needs to have **read permission** to the database in order to retrieve the data and display the data in the Web page. Because the file has read permission, the end user can download the Access database. (Some users use the password feature within Access to protect the database. Then, when the user downloads the file, they need to enter an additional password to retrieve the data.) With SQL Server, the database is stored by SQL Server and is not downloadable from the browser. Therefore, you can use SQL Server for secure transactions, such as shopping carts.

You can use the Upsizing Wizard to upgrade to SQL Server. The Upsizing Wizard is available in Access 97, Access 2000, Access XP, and Access 2003. After you have upsized the database, Access provides a report that contains information about the new database. In the following exercise, you will upsize an Access database to SQL Server. Your user account needs **write** permission to the Access database in order to upsize the database.

1. Start **Microsoft Access**. (On most computers you click **Start**, point to **All Programs**, click **Microsoft Office**, and then click **Microsoft Office Access 2003**.)

2. Click **File** on the menu bar, then click **Open**. In the Open dialog box, navigate to C:\Inetpub\wwwroot\Chapter8\data, select the file **TaraStore.mdb**, and then click **Open**.

3. Click **Tools** on the menu bar, point to **Database Utilities**, then click **Upsizing Wizard**.

4. Verify that the radio button labeled Create new database is selected, and then click **Next**.

5. In the drop-down list box, select **(local)\NetSDK** for the name of the SQL Server database. (*Note:* You can also use the keywords (local) or localhost, or the name of your SQL Server, IP address, or Fully Qualified Domain Name (FQDN), to identify the database server.)

6. Choose the authentication method for your SQL Server that you used in Chapters 6 and 7. You will use these permissions throughout the entire chapter.

   a. If you use SQL Server authentication, type **sa** in the Login ID text box, and type **password** in the the Password text box. (*Note:* You must use an account with CREATE DATABASE privileges.)

   b. If you use Windows authentication, check the **Use Trusted Connection** check box.

7. In the last text box, delete the text, and then type **Ch8TaraStoreSQL** as the name of the new SQL Server database, and then click **Next**. Figure 8-2 shows the connection settings for a SQL Server that is known as (local)\NetSDK; the sa user account's password is set to password.

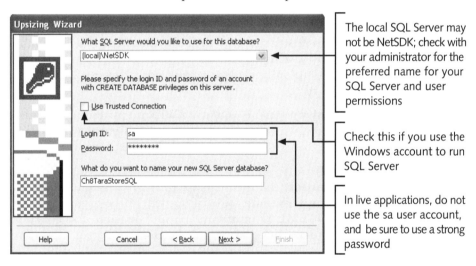

Figure 8-2   Setting connection properties to a SQL Server database

8. In the Upsizing Wizard dialog box, click the **>>** button to select all the tables in the database to be exported to SQL Server. Click the **Next** button to advance to the next step. Figure 8-3 shows that the Categories, Products, and SubCategories tables will be exported to the new SQL Server database. The next window allows you to modify how the table attributes are exported. Do not make any changes to this window. Click the **Next** button to advance to the next step.

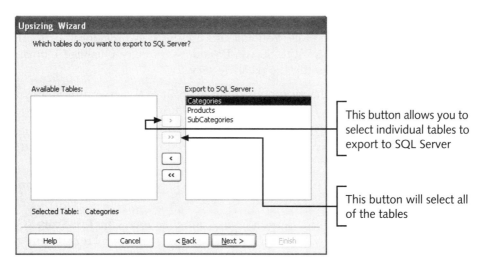

Figure 8-3   Exporting tables to SQL Server

9. The next window allows you to export an Access application. There is no application with this database, so the radio button No application changes is already selected for you. (*Note*: If this option has not been selected for you, select the radio button labeled No application changes.) Click the **Next** button to advance to the next step.

10. Click the **Finish** button. The Upsizing Wizard upsizes the database, and then produces a report, which contains information about the tables and objects upsized to SQL Server. (*Note*: You can print or export the report to another application.)

11. Click the **File** menu, and then select **Export**. Navigate to your **c:\Inetpub\wwwroot\Chapter8\data** folder if needed. In the Save as type drop-down list box, select **HTML Documents**. In the File name text box, type **TSUpsizeReport**. Click **Export**. In the HTML Output Options window, click **OK**.

12. Open a browser and view the report at **http://localhost/chapter8/data/TSUpsizeReport.html**. At the top of the page is the name of the SQL Server database and the original Access database. You can view the data types that were changed when the data fields were updated to SQL Server.

13. Click the **Next** hyperlink at the bottom of the page. In the Categories table, the CategoryID field data type was changed from Number to int; and the CategoryName field data type was changed from Text to nvarchar.

14. Click the **Next** hyperlink at the bottom of the page. As shown in Figure 8-4, the UnitCost field data type in the Products table was changed from Currency to money.

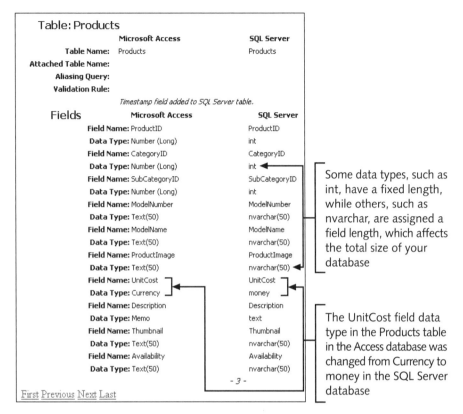

Figure 8-4   Upsize Report in HTML format

15. Click the **Next** hyperlink at the bottom of the page. In the SubCategories table, the Description field data type was changed from Memo to text. Close the browser window.

16. Close the Upsizing Wizard Report window by clicking the **Close Window** button.

17. Close the database and Microsoft Access.

When you upsize the database, a field named upsize_ts is added to each of the tables with a date and time stamp. You can use this information to determine which data was updated.

Using the DataReader Object to Display Data

In the following exercise, you will use the upsized database to create a page to display the category list using the DataReader object. You will use the Connection object to store the connection string.

1. Open the **Chapter8** solution in Visual Studio .NET. (*Note:* Your browser must always be online when you are opening a solution. You do not have to be connected to the Internet, but the browser must be configured to be online.)

2. Right-click **Data Connections** in the Server Explorer window, and then click **Add Connection**.

3. In the Connection tab of the Data Link Properties dialog box, type **(local)\NetSDK** in the server name text box. If your application uses SQL Server authentication, select the **Use a specific user name and password** radio button, type **sa** in the User name text box, and then enter **password** in the Password text box. Check the **Allow saving password** check box. If your SQL Server uses Windows authentication check the **Use Windows NT Integrated security** radio button.

4. In the drop-down list box select the database named **Ch8TaraStoreSQL**, and then click the **OK** button.

5. In the Server Explorer window, expand the Ch8TaraStoreSQL data connection by clicking the **plus sign** (+).

6. Double-click **DataReaderSQL.aspx** in the Solution Explorer window to open the page. Click **(MachineName)\NetSDK.Ch8TaraStoreSQL.dbo** under Data Connections in the Server Explorer window and drag it to the Web page. If prompted, click **Include password** in the window. An SQL Connection object named SqlConnection1 is added to the page.

7. Double-click on the whitespace on the page to open the code behind the page, which is named **DataReaderSQL.aspx.vb**.

8. Within the Page_Load procedure, add the following code to create the objects and retrieve the data using the DataReader object:

```
SqlConnection1.Open()
Dim mySQL As String = _
  "SELECT CategoryName FROM Categories"
Dim objCM As New _
  SqlClient.SqlCommand(mySQL, SqlConnection1)
Dim objDR As SqlClient.SqlDataReader
objDR = objCM.ExecuteReader()
Dim MyCat As String
While objDR.Read()
  MyCat = MyCat + (objDR("CategoryName") & "<br />")
End While
```

```
objDR.Close()
SqlConnection1.Close()
lblCat.Text = MyCat
```

9. Click the **Save All** button. Click **Build** on the menu bar, then click **Build Solution**. Click the **DataReaderSQL.aspx** tab to select the Web page.

10. Right-click on the page, and then click **View in Browser**. The page should look the same as the page shown in Figure 8-1. The DataReader.aspx and DataReaderSQL.aspx files have the same HTML template. The code behind the page is the same, except the reference to the connection to the database is changed from the Access database to the SQL Server database, and the data object names are changed. Therefore, the output from both pages in the Web page is identical.

11. Close any open pages.

Using the DataReader Object with Stored Procedures

8

You can use the DataReader object in combination with the Command object in order to work with stored procedures. Stored procedures are useful for running queries in which input and output parameters are required. When you use a stored procedure, the **CommandType procedure** is set to CommandType.StoredProcedure to indicate that the SQL command is a stored procedure and not a SQL query. When the command is configured, you must specify the stored procedure and the CommandType, as shown in the following sample code:

```
Dim objCM As SqlClient.SqlCommand
objCM = New _
SqlClient.SqlCommand("ProductCategoryList", objCN)
objCM.CommandType = CommandType.StoredProcedure
```

In this example, you create a stored procedure to display all of the product categories. The category list is bound to a Hyperlink control. When the user clicks the link, the DataReaderProducts page opens. The CategoryID field is passed with the hyperlink as a query string to the DataReaderProducts page. Then, you create a stored procedure that displays only the products of the category that was clicked. In this first section, you create the stored procedure to retrieve the categories, retrieve them with the DataReader object, and display them with the DataList object and ASP.NET Hyperlink controls.

1. Open the **Chapter8** project if it is not already open.

2. In the Server Explorer window, under the MACHINENAME\ NetSDK.Ch8TaraStoreSQL.dbo data connection, right-click **Stored Procedures**, and then click **New Stored Procedure**. The stored procedure document opens with the default text for creating the stored procedure.

3. To delete the default text, click **Edit** on the menu bar, then click **Select All**. Click **Edit** on the menu bar again, then click **Delete**.

4. Type the code that follows this paragraph. The code creates a stored procedure named **CategoryList**. When this stored procedure is run, it returns a list
of the product categories.

```
CREATE PROCEDURE dbo.CategoryList
    AS
SELECT *
    FROM Categories
    ORDER BY CategoryID ASC
RETURN
```

5. Click the **Save All** button. Close the CategoryList stored procedure window.

6. Double-click **DataReaderStoredProc.aspx** in the Solution Explorer window
to open the page. Click the **HTML** tab. The data can't be bound directly to a
Label control because the Label control is not a member of the data controls
and therefore does not have a DataSource property. Therefore, the HTML
template uses a DataList control named MyList to bind the DataReader object
and display the data. The DataList control displays the lblCat Label control with
the data value for each row returned from the DataReader object. The following
code snippet shows the basic format for displaying the category list using the
DataList object. (*Note*: The DataList formatting properties are not shown in the
code.) Do not make any changes to the HTML template. Click the **Design** tab
to return to Design view.

```
<asp:datalist id="MyList" runat="server" EnableViewState=
  "false">
<ItemTemplate>
<asp:Label id="lblCat"
  Text='<%#DataBinder.Eval(Container.DataItem, "Category
  Name") %>'
  runat="server"/>
</ItemTemplate>
</asp:datalist>
```

7. Click **(MachineName)\NetSDK.Ch8TaraStoreSQL.dbo** under Data
Connections in the Server Explorer window and drag it to the Web page. If
prompted, click **Include password** in the window. An SQL Connection
object named SqlConnection1 is added to the page.

8. Double-click on the whitespace on the page to open the code behind the
page, which is named **DataReaderStoredProc.aspx.vb**.

9. Within the Page_Load procedure, add the code that follows this paragraph to
open the connection. (*Note*: You can also create the connection string manually.)

```
SqlConnection1.Open()
```

10. Below this, add the sample code that follow this paragraph to create the
Command object. When you create the new command, instead of passing a
SQL command or the name of the table, pass the name of the stored procedure,

CategoryList. Then, you must specify the CommandType as StoredProcedure. (*Note*: By default the CommandType is Text, which means that you are passing a SQL command. CommandType Table means that you are passing the table name as the command.)

```
Dim objCM As SqlClient.SqlCommand
objCM = New_
SqlClient.SqlCommand("CategoryList", _
SqlConnection1)
objCM.CommandType = CommandType.StoredProcedure
```

11. Below this, add the code following this paragraph to create the DataReader object named **objDR**. Use the Command object with the DataReader to retrieve the data. Assign the DataReader object to the DataSource DataList control named MyList and bind the data to the control.

```
Dim objDR As SqlClient.SqlDataReader
objDR= _
objCM.ExecuteReader(CommandBehavior.CloseConnection)
MyList.DataSource = objDR
MyList.DataBind()
```

12. Figure 8-5 shows the entire Page_Load procedure. Click the **Save All** button. Click **Build** on the menu bar, then click **Build Solution**.

13. Click the **DataReaderStoredProc.aspx** tab to view the Web page. Right-click on the page, and then click **View in Browser**. The page should look identical to the one in Figure 8-1 because the HTML template is the same as the first two exercises. Only the data source and the reference to the data objects are changed.

14. Close any open pages.

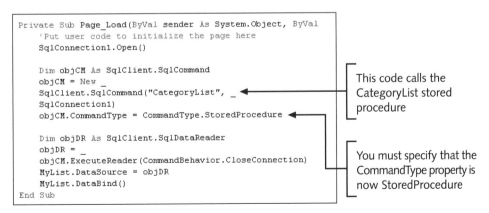

Figure 8-5   Using stored procedures to display data with the DataReader object

Using the DataReader Object with Parameters

In the following exercise, you will work with two pages. The DataReaderDisplay.aspx page displays data using SQL statements, and the DataReaderDisplay.aspx page displays the same data using stored procedures. You will view the DataReaderDisplay.aspx page. Then, you will create several stored procedures and modify the DataReaderProducts.aspx page to display data using stored procedures. The DataReaderProducts.aspx page is the same as the DataReaderDisplay.aspx page except that it will use stored procedures to retrieve the data.

1. Open the **Chapter8** project if it is not already open. Double-click **DataReaderDisplay.aspx** in the Solution Explorer window. There are several DataList controls in this page: MyCatList to display the categories in the main menu, MySubCatList to display the subcategories, MyProdList to display the products within a category, and MyProduct to display a single product.

2. In the tray, delete the **SQLConnection1** object. This connection object connects to the (MachineName)\NetSDK server. You must change the object to connect to your SQL Server. You can do this graphically or edit the SqlConnection1.ConnectionString property in the Web Form Designer Generated Code region manually. This is not recommended unless you are proficient at creating connection strings. The following is the code for the SqlConnection1.ConnectionString property. (*Note*: The SqlConnection1. ConnectionString property is a single string and will be concatenated into two lines in the code behind the page.)

```
Me.SqlConnection1.ConnectionString = _
  "workstation id=(MachineName);
  packet size=4096;
  user id=sa;
  data source=""(MachineName)\NetSDK"";
  persist security info=True;
  initial catalog=Ch8TaraStoreSQL;
  password=password"
```

3. Inserting a new Connection object will change SqlConnection1.Connection String property to locate your SQL Server. Click **(MachineName)\NetSDK. Ch8TaraStoreSQL.dbo** under Data Connections in the Server Explorer window and drag it to the Web page. If prompted, select **Include password** in the window. A SQL Connection object named SqlConnection1 is added to the page. This page will demonstrate how the code uses SQL statements to retrieve the data instead of stored procedures.

4. Double-click the whitespace of the **DataReaderDisplay.aspx** page to open the code behind the page. Notice that the four functions defined are GetCat(), GetSubCats(), GetProducts(), and GetProduct(). These functions display the categories, subcategories, product lists, and individual products using SQL statements instead of stored procedures. The querystring in the hyperlink

varies depending on which function will be called. The QueryString stores the value of the CategoryID, SubCategoryID, and ProductID, the selected item index, and the name of the DataList object that should be displayed. Close any open windows.

5. Click the **Save All** button. Click **Build** on the menu bar, and then click **Build Solution**. Open a browser window and go to **http://localhost/Chapter8/ DataReader Display.aspx**. Select **Gifts**, then **Waterford Gifts for Men**, and then **Letter Opener by Waterford**. Close the browser window. (*Note:* A detailed explanation of how the links were created will follow in the next exercise. This display page is to show you what the page would look like if simple SQL statements were used instead of stored procedures.)

In the previous exercise you created the CategoryList stored procedure. In the following steps, you will create stored procedures in the Server Explorer window.

1. Open the **Server Explorer** window.

Recall that to create a stored procedure, open the Server Explorer window, expand the Ch8TaraStoreSQL data connection by clicking the plus sign, right-click Stored Procedures, and then click New Stored Procedure. Delete all of the existing code in the stored procedure. Then type the new stored procedure, and click the Save All button.

2. Create the SubCategoryByCategory stored procedure by using the following code:

```
CREATE PROCEDURE dbo.SubCategoryByCategory
    @CategoryID int
AS
SELECT *
    FROM SubCategories
    WHERE CategoryID = @CategoryID
    ORDER BY SubCategoryID
RETURN
```

3. Create the ProductsBySubCategory stored procedure by using the following code:

```
CREATE PROCEDURE dbo.ProductsBySubCategory
    @SubCategoryID int
AS
SELECT *
    FROM Products
    WHERE SubCategoryID = @SubCategoryID
    ORDER BY ModelName
RETURN
```

4. Create the SingleProductByProductID stored procedure by using the following code:

```
CREATE PROCEDURE dbo.SingleProductByProductID
    @ProductID int
AS
SELECT *
    FROM Products
    WHERE ProductID = @ProductID
    ORDER BY ModelName
RETURN
```

How the QueryString Passes Data from the Database

When a visitor displays the page for the first time, the main categories are displayed using the MyCatList DataList control. This data for this control was retrieved by the GetCat function. The DataReader in the GetCat function calls the CategoryList stored procedure. No parameter is passed because all of the main categories are to be displayed. The home page image is displayed using the LargeImage Web Image control. The Visible property is set to False for the other DataList controls so that they do not appear on the page.

When the user clicks a main category, a hyperlink is sent to the server requesting the same page (DataReaderProducts.aspx?CatID=21&selItem=0&Show=cat). The code behind the page processes the QueryString, and it retrieves the CatID, selItem, and Show values and stores them in variables. Because the value of Show is cat, the LargeImage Web Image control ImageUrl property is set to "images/CatPics/" & CatID & ".jpg" so that it displays the main category image. This is done using concatenation because the data has not been retrieved from the database. The GetSubCats procedure is called and passed the CatID argument. The GetSubCats procedure will use the DataReader object and a Parameter object to pass the CatID to the SubCategoryByCategory stored procedure. This procedure will return a list of the SubCategories, which is then bound to the MySubCatList DataList control.

When the user clicks a subcategory, a hyperlink is sent to the server requesting the same page (DataReaderProducts.aspx?CatID=21&SubCatID=1&selItem=0&Show=prodlist). The code behind the page processes the QueryString, and it retrieves the CatID, SubCatID, selItem, and Show values and stores them in variables. Because the value of Show is prodlist, the LargeImage Web Image control ImageUrl property is set to "images/SubCatPics/" & SubCatID & ".jpg" so that it displays the subcategory image. This is done using concatenation because the data has not been retrieved from the database. The GetProducts procedure is called and passed the SubCatID argument. The GetProducts procedure will use the DataReader object and a Parameter object to pass the SubCatID to the ProductsBySubCategory stored procedure. This procedure will return a list of the products, which is then bound to the MyProdList DataList control.

When the user clicks a product, a hyperlink is sent to the server requesting the same page (DataReaderProducts.aspx?ProdID=548&CatID=21&SubCatID=1&selItem=0&Show

=prod). The code behind the page processes the QueryString, and it retrieves the ProdID, CatID, SubCatID, selItem, and Show values and stores them in variables. Because the value of Show is prod, the LargeImage Web Image control ImageUrl property is set to "images/ProductPics/" & ProdID & ".jpg" so that it displays the product image. This is done using concatenation because the data has not been retrieved from the database. The GetProduct procedure is called and passed the ProdID argument. The GetProduct procedure will use the DataReader object and a Parameter object to pass the ProdID to the SingleProductByProductID stored procedure. This procedure will return a single product, which is then bound to the MyProduct DataList control. The MyProduct DataList control displays the Cost, Model Number, Availability, and Description values for that specific product.

Now you will use stored procedures you just created to retrieve the data that is bound to the DataList controls in the Web page. You will modify the page to use stored procedures instead of SQL statements to retrieve the data.

1. Double-click **DataReaderProducts.aspx** in the Solution Explorer window. In the tray, delete the **SQLConnection1** object. This connection object connects to the (MachineName)\NetSDK server. You must change the object to connect to your SQL Server.

2. Click **(MachineName)\NetSDK.Ch8TaraStoreSQL.dbo** under Data Connections in the Server Explorer window and drag it to the Web page. If necessary, select **Include password** in the window. A SQL Connection object named SqlConnection1 is added to the page.

3. Double-click the **DataReaderProducts.aspx** page to display the code behind the page. Locate the comment 'Insert code snippet here. After the comment, type the code shown after this paragraph. This code will create the parameter named paramCatID, which stores the CategoryID. This code will create and add the Parameter object to the Parameters Collection of the Command object. There is no change in the DataReader code that executes the command. (*Note:* The other parameters have been entered for you. Refer to Chapter 6 for more information on parameter queries and Parameter objects.)

```
Dim paramCatID As SqlParameter
paramCatID = New SqlParameter("@CategoryID",
SqlDbType.Int, 4)
paramCatID.Value = CatID
objCM2.Parameters.Add(paramCatID)
```

4. Click the **Save All** button. Click **Build** on the menu bar, and then click **Build Solution**.

5. Click the **DataReaderProducts.aspx** tab to view the Web page. Right-click on the page, and then click **View in Browser**. The Page_Load event procedure code will call the GetCat function, which runs the CategoryList stored procedure. The main category list is returned and bound to the MyCatList DataList control.

8

6. Click **Gifts**. The querystring is ?CatID=21&selItem=0&Show=cat. In the code behind the page, the GetSubCats(CatID) code will call the function, which then uses the CatID when it runs the SubCategoryByCategory stored procedure. The category list is returned. Your page should look like the one in Figure 8-6.

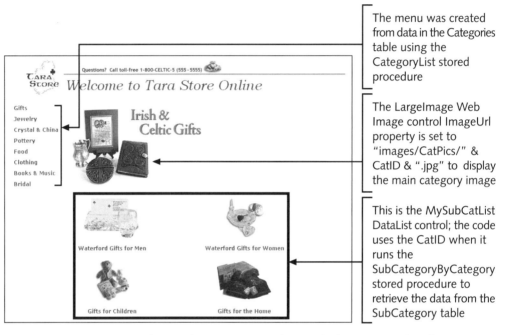

The menu was created from data in the Categories table using the CategoryList stored procedure

The LargeImage Web Image control ImageUrl property is set to "images/CatPics/" & CatID & ".jpg" to display the main category image

This is the MySubCatList DataList control; the code uses the CatID when it runs the SubCategoryByCategory stored procedure to retrieve the data from the SubCategory table

Figure 8-6   Using a stored procedure to retrieve data with the DataReader object

7. Click **Waterford Gifts for Men**. The querystring is ?CatID=21&SubCatID=1&selItem=0&Show=prodlist. In the code behind the page, the GetProducts (SubCatID) code will call the GetProducts function, which then uses the SubCatID when it runs the ProductsBySubCategory stored procedure. The product list is returned. Your page should look like the one in Figure 8-7.

8. Click **Letter Opener by Waterford**. The querystring is ?ProdID=548&CatID=21&SubCatID=1&selItem=4&Show=prod. In the code behind the page, the GetProduct(ProdID) code will call the GetProduct function, which then uses the ProdID when it runs the SingleProductByProductID stored procedure. The single product is returned. Your page should look like the one in Figure 8-8.

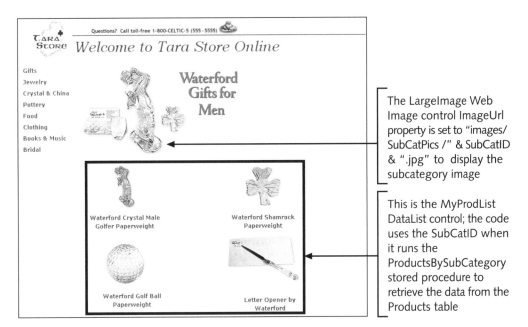

The LargeImage Web Image control ImageUrl property is set to "images/ SubCatPics /" & SubCatID & ".jpg" to display the subcategory image

This is the MyProdList DataList control; the code uses the SubCatID when it runs the ProductsBySubCategory stored procedure to retrieve the data from the Products table

Figure 8-7   Displaying a list of products using a stored procedure

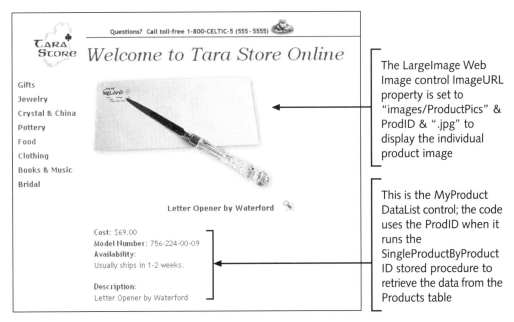

The LargeImage Web Image control ImageURL property is set to "images/ProductPics" & ProdID & ".jpg" to display the individual product image

This is the MyProduct DataList control; the code uses the ProdID when it runs the SingleProductByProduct ID stored procedure to retrieve the data from the Products table

Figure 8-8   Displaying a single product using a stored procedure

9. Close the browser. In Visual Studio .NET, close any open pages.

The DataAdapter, DataSet, and DataView Objects

Usually, the DataAdapter, DataSet, and DataView objects are used together to retrieve data from the database. The DataSet does not know the source of the data. Only the DataAdapter knows where the data is located. The DataAdapter represents a database connection and a set of commands used to manage the data within the DataSet object. The DataAdapter contains a Fill method and an Update method. The **Update method** is used to update the records in the original database on the values changed in the DataSet. The **Fill method** of the DataAdapter object is used to get the data from the database and populate the DataSet object. The DataView object is a collection of data from the DataSet. The default DataView for the DataSet for a specific table is the collection of all the records in the table. There can be many DataViews retrieved from a DataSet. The ASP.NET Data controls, for example the DataGrid control, are bound to the DataView object. Visual Studio .NET contains visual controls to create the DataAdapter, DataSet, and DataView objects. The following list describes one method for inserting a DataAdapter object, creating the DataSet and DataView objects, then displaying the data:

1. Create the Web Form in Visual Studio .NET.
2. Add a DataAdapter from the Data tab in the Toolbox.
3. Select your database connection in the DataAdapter Wizard.
4. Use the Query Builder to build a SQL statement.
5. Add a DataSet object from the Data tab in the Toolbox.
6. Use Generate DataSet Methods from the Data menu. You can preview your data before you insert the data into the Web page.
7. Create a DataView object.
8. Assign a table to the DataView object.
9. Assign the DataSource property of an ASP.NET Data control such as the DataGrid to the DataView object.
10. In the code behind the Web page, call the Fill method of the DataAdapter.
11. Bind the controls to the data source.
12. Save and build the solution, and view the Web page in a browser.

There are many ways to work with the DataAdapter and DataSet objects. For example, you could access the tables directly from the DataSet without explicitly creating a DataView object. You would then assign the DataSource property to one of the tables within the DataSet object. It's recommended for beginners to first learn how to work with the DataAdapter, DataSet, and DataView, and then learn to work with DataTables.

The DataAdapter is used to populate the DataSet. The DataSet can consist of multiple related tables. When you create the DataAdapter using the DataAdapter Wizard, you are creating a SQL command and identifying the Connection object. Then, you must manually identify the DataSet object to be filled with data when the Fill method is called. After you fill the DataSet, you use a DataView to identify which subset of the DataSet you want to access. If there is only one table involved, then you can simply use the default DataView object, or you can identify the table or SQL statement to use to retrieve a table for the DataView.

The code sample following the paragraph shows how you can fill the DataSet with data using the Fill method of the DataAdapter. Then, you can create a DataView from the DataSet, which is a subset of one of the tables within the DataSet. In this example, the default DataView contains all of the rows from the Categories table. Then, the DataGrid control is bound to the DataView object using the DataBind method of the DataGrid control.

```
SqlDataAdapter1.Fill(MyDS)
Dim MyDV As DataView = New DataView(MyDS, "Categories")
MyDG.DataSource = MyDV
MyDG.DataBind()
```

You can refer to the DataTable in the DataView by the table name or by its index position within the Tables collection. The DataTables collection is a series of tables within the DataSet. When you create the DataView, you are referring to one of the tables within the Tables collection. DefaultView returns all of the data within the DataTable. But you must identify which table to retrieve. The index position is the number that represents that DataTable within the Tables collection. The sample code that follows this paragraph shows how to retrieve all of the data within the first table of the Tables collection from the MyDS DataSet object. The DataView is then bound to the MyDG DataGrid control.

```
Dim objDV As New DataView()
objDV = MyDS.Tables(0).DefaultView
MyDG.DataSource = objDV
MyDG.DataBind()
```

The DataAdapter also has other methods and properties. The **SelectCommand method** allows you to identify the command used to retrieve the records. When the Fill method is called, the DataAdapter uses the SQL command identified by the SelectCommand property, to determine which records to retrieve. In the following sample code, the DataAdapter is used to fill a dataset using the Categories DataTable object:

```
Dim CN As New SqlConnection(CS)
Dim MySQL As String = "Select * From Categories"
MyDS = New DataSet()
MyDA = New SqlDataAdapter(MySQL, CN)
MyDA.Fill(MyDS, "Categories")
```

The DataAdapter contains a Command Builder method to automatically generate commands to insert, modify, and delete data. The database tables must have primary keys defined in order to use the Command Builder. Although you can write the code to access the Command Builder manually, it is much simpler to use the DataAdapter Wizard to activate the Command Builder. The Command Builder creates the SelectCommand, InsertCommand, and DeleteCommand.

Using the DataView to Retrieve Data from a Database

Once you create the DataAdapter object and fill the DataSet object, you define a DataView which will be bound to your Data control. In the following exercise, you use Visual Studio .NET to create a DataAdapter, add a DataSet object, generate the DataSet methods, and create a DataView. You will bind the DataView object to an ASP.NET Data control to display the data.

1. Open the **Chapter8** project in Visual Studio .NET.

2. Double-click the **DataViewProducts.aspx** page icon in the Solution Explorer window.

3. Open the Toolbox if it is not already open, click the **Data** tab, then drag and drop **SqlDataAdapter** from the Data tab to Web page. The DataAdapter Configuration Wizard opens. Click the **Next** button.

4. In the drop-down list, select the connection to your Ch8TaraStoreSQL database. (*Note*: The connection should be *MachineName*.Ch8TaraStoreSQL.dbo, where MachineName is the name of your SQL Server.) Click the **Next** button.

5. In the Query Type window, you can design your own query with a SQL Builder, create a new stored procedure, or use an existing stored procedure. Leave the default radio button labeled **Use SQL statements** selected and click the **Next** button.

6. Click the **Query Builder** button to open the Query Builder. Select the **Products** table from the Add Table window, click **Add**, and then click the **Close** button.

7. In the Field List box, select the **ProductID**, **SubCategoryID**, **ModelName**, **ProductImage**, **UnitCost**, and **Thumbnail** fields. Click the **OK** button. Click the **Next** button. The SQL SELECT, INSERT, UPDATE, and DELETE statements are generated for you, along with table mappings and a command object. The table mappings contain information about the column names within each table. Click the **Finish** button. If prompted, select **Include password** in the window. The DataAdapter and DataConnection objects are added to the page.

8. Now you need to create a DataSet object. Click **Data** on the menu bar, and then click **Generate Dataset**. In the Generate Dataset window, select the radio button labeled **New**. In the text box, type **DS_DataViewProducts**. The Products table has already been selected. Click **OK**.

9. Select the DataSet icon in Design view. Click **Data** on the menu bar, then click **Preview Data**. Click the **Fill Dataset** button. Your data should be displayed in the window. Click the **Close** button.

10. Drag and drop the **DataView** control from the **Data** tab in the Toolbox to the Web page.

11. You need to assign a table to the DataView. With the **DataView** selected, go to the Properties window, and click the drop-down **list arrow** for the Table property. Click the **plus sign** next to DS_DataViewProducts1, and then click **Products**. In the Properties window, locate the Row Filter property and enter the value **SubCategoryID=19**.

12. You need to assign a data source to the DataGrid object. Select the **DataGrid** object. In the Properties window, set the DataSource property to **DataView1**. (*Note*: This may already be selected for you.)

13. Double-click the whitespace on the DataViewProducts.aspx page to open the code behind the page.

14. Within the Page_Load procedure, add the code that follows this paragraph. This code calls the Fill method of the DataAdapter to add the data to the DataSet. You must pass the name of the DataSet, DS_DataViewProducts1, as a parameter to the DataAdapter. You then have to bind the controls to the DataSource property using the Bind method of the Data control for the page. In this example, the Bind method of the Page object is used.

```
SqlDataAdapter1.Fill(DS_DataViewProducts1)
Page.DataBind()
```

15. Click the **Save All** button. Click **Build** on the menu bar, and then click **Build Solution**.

16. Click the **DataViewProducts.aspx** tab to return to the Web page. Right-click on the page, and then click **View in Browser**. Your page should look like the one in Figure 8-9.

17. Close any open pages.

8

The entire DataSet object contains 444 products; however, because the RowFilter property was used, the page displays only 11 products; the DataView object was bound to the DataGrid control; the first three products are shown here

Figure 8-9 Retrieving data with the DataSet and DataView objects

You can dynamically modify the properties of the Web controls using the code behind the page. For example, if you use a DataReader to bind to a DataGrid control, the DataSource property is set in the code behind the page. The syntax for calling the column and HeaderText property is `DataGrid.Columns(i).HeaderText`. For a DataGrid control named MyDG, you can change the heading of the first column to Last Name by inserting the code statement `MyDG.Columns(0).HeaderText="Last Name"`. You are accessing the columns using the Columns collection, which starts with the number 0. This same principle can be applied to other Web properties.

CUSTOMIZING THE DATAGRID CONTROL

The DataGrid control allows you to customize the appearance of the control and the data contained within the columns. In the previous chapter you learned how to modify the appearance of the DataGrid using the Properties window. You learned that you can display bound columns that contain data that is bound to a column in the database. You can display the data or use the data in an expression, such as the source of an image tag. You can also display unbound columns. Unbound columns often contain buttons and other form fields. Some additional features that the DataGrid includes are sorting and filtering. The DataGrid filter allows you to temporarily select a subset of records from the DataGrid. The filter does not remove the data from the database, but only removes the records from the Web page. When the filter is removed, the records are redisplayed within the Web page.

Paging and Sorting Data with the DataGrid Control

Sorting can be performed in the code behind the page, or by using the Visual Studio .NET tools. The default sorting creates a **Link Button control** for the column name, at the top of the column. When the user clicks the Link Button control, the DataGrid is sorted by that column. The DataGrid does not actually sort the rows. Instead, it raises a **SortCommand event**, which causes the data to be rebound to the DataSource. You must add the code to perform the sorting when the event occurs. The sort expression is passed as an argument, which is represented as **e.SortExpression**. You have to get the value that is selected as the sort key, and then rebind the DataGrid to the DataView. You can also create your own custom sorting rules, whereby you determine which bound or unbound template columns are sorted. If you create your own custom sorting, you can use an image or an image button for the sort link at the top of the column headings.

Paging is turned off by default. When paging is turned on, you can display a subset of records on a page. A navigation bar at the bottom of the page allows you to page through the data across Web pages. Sometimes the content cannot be displayed on one page. By default, the > and < codes are used to display < and > when there are additional pages used to display data. You can format the navigation bar with your own custom text. You can also modify the navigation bar to include the number of pages, with links to each page. This allows the visitor to jump to a specific group of records. The default number of records displayed is 10. The paging property of the DataGrid also raises a **PageIndexChanged event** when the user clicks the Link button. Therefore, you also have to add the code to handle the event. The event handler retrieves the **NewPageIndex property**, which is the page the user wants to browse to. This property is retrieved when the user clicks the link button. Then, you can set the **CurrentPageIndex property** to the NewPageIndex and rebind the data to the DataGrid control.

In this exercise, you learn how to turn paging on. You will modify the DataGrid control from the previous exercise to support sorting.

1. Open the **Chapter8** project in Visual Studio .NET if necessary. Open the **DataSetProducts.aspx** Web page, if it is not already open.

2. Double-click the **PageSortProducts.aspx** page in the Solution Explorer window.

3. Click the **Data** tab in the Toolbox. Drag the **SqlDataAdapter** from the Data tab to the Web page. Click **Next** to continue. In the drop-down list box, select the connection to your **Ch8TaraStoreSQL** database. Click **Next**.

4. In the Query Type window, leave the Use SQL statements selected and click the **Next** button. In the window, type **SELECT * FROM Products;**, click **Next**, and then click **Finish**. If prompted, select **Include password** in the window.

5. Click **Data** on the menu bar, and then click **Generate DataSet**. In the Generate DataSet window, select the radio button labeled **New**. In the text box, type **DS_PageSortProducts**. The Products table has already been selected. Click **OK**.

6. Drag and drop the **DataView** control from the Data tab in the Toolbox to the Web page. With the DataView selected, go to the Properties window, and click the drop-down **list arrow** for the Table property. Click the **plus sign** next to DS_PageSortProducts1, and then click **Products**. With the DataView selected, go to the Properties window, and enter **SubCategoryID=19** for the RowFilter property.

7. Select the **DataGrid** object. In the Properties window, set the DataSource property to **DataView1**.

Now you will modify the properties of the DataGrid control to show the footer and header, configure the PageSize property, and modify the text used to create hyperlinks for the next and previous pages. Then, you will modify the code behind the page to fill the DataSet object and bind the DataGrid control to the DataView object. You will insert the code to sort the page and allow paging of the DataGrid control.

1. Click the **DataGrid** control, and then go to the Properties window and make the following changes:

   a. Change the ShowFooter property to **True**.

   b. Change the ShowHeader property to **True**.

   c. Change the AllowSorting property to **True**.

   d. Change the AllowPaging propery to **True**.

   e. Change the PageSize property from 10 to **3**.

   f. Click the **plus** sign next to the PageStyle property.

   g. Change the ForeColor property to **red**.

   h. In the NextPageText property, replace the > with **Next**.

   i. Change the PrevPageText property from < to **Previous**.

   j. Change the Position property to **TopAndBottom**.

2. Double-click the whitespace on the page to view the code behind the page. In the Page_Load event procedure, add the following code to fill the DataAdapter object and bind the data to the DataGrid control:

```
SqlDataAdapter1.Fill(DS_PageSortProducts1)
Page.DataBind()
```

3. Select **MyDG** from the Class List drop-down list box. Select **SortCommand** from the Method Name list box. The code to create the MyDG_SortCommand event procedure is inserted for you. Within this procedure, type the code that handles the SortCommand event and assigns a value to the **Sort** property of the DataView object, as follows:

```
DataView1.Sort = e.SortExpression
MyDG.DataBind()
```

4. Select **PageIndexChanged** from the Method Name list box. The code to create the MyDG_PageIndexChanged event procedure is inserted for you. Within this procedure, type the code that handles the PageIndexChanged event and assigns a value to the CurrentPageIndex property of the DataGrid object, as follows:

```
MyDG.CurrentPageIndex = e.NewPageIndex
MyDG.DataBind()
```

5. Click the **Save All** button. Click **Build** on the menu bar, and then click **Build Solution**.

6. Click the **PageSortProducts.aspx** tab. Right-click on the page, and then click **View in Browser**. Click the **Product Name** link button. Your page should look like the one in Figure 8-10. (*Note*: If you click on the image, you will link to the image file.)

7. Click the **Next** hyperlink. St. Andrews Golf Club Covers is the first product on the new list. Click the **St. Andrews Golf Club Covers** image. The image opens in the browser window.

8. Close any open pages.

Figure 8-10   Sorting and paging data in a DataGrid control

Filtering Data with the DataGrid Control

You can use the graphical tools and wizards that are located on the Data Tab in the Toolbox and in the Data menu to create your data objects, or you can create the data objects manually in the code behind the page. When you use the graphical tools and wizards, Visual Studio .NET inserts the code to create the data objects in the grayed out region within the code behind the page. For example, when you drag a DataAdapter object from the Data tab to the Web page, Visual Studio .NET inserts the code to create a DataAdapter object and a Connection object; it also sets values for the SelectCommand as well as the InsertCommand, UpdateCommand, and DeleteCommand properties. Much of this code is unnecessary if all you want to do is display the data. It is not recommended to remove this unnecessary code manually. A better option is to manually insert the code in the code behind the page to create the data objects and set their properties.

Filtering data is the process of selecting a subset of data. Filtering data can be performed in the code behind the page or by using the Visual Studio .NET tools. To filter the data in a DataView object, set the RowFilter property of the DataView object to the SQL filter command that queries the DataView object. This SQL filter command is the value of the WHERE clause. For example, to select all of the products that belong to Category 19, the SQL statement would be "SELECT * FROM Products WHERE CategoryID = 19". The SQL filter command would be "CategoryID = 19". The RowFilter property can be set in the Properties window, or in the code behind the page using DataView.RowFilter = "SQL filter command".

In this exercise, the code to create the ConnectionString property, and the DataConnection, DataAdapter, DataSet and DataView objects, has been inserted for you into the code behind the page. The page will display only the products form the Products table. You will modify the code to support filtering. You retrieve the Category ID from a form field named txtSearch, which is used to filter the data.

1. Open the **Chapter 8** project in Visual Studio .NET, if necessary. Open the **DataSetSearch.aspx** Web page.

2. Double-click the whitespace on the page to open the code behind the page. The code to import the System, System.Data, and System.Data.SqlClient namespaces has already been inserted for you at the top of the page. Above the Page_Load event handler, add the code following this paragraph to create the two variables. MySearch will be used to store the phrase that the user types in the text box. (*Note*: the RecNum variable, which has already been declared for you, is used to store the number of records in the database where the model-name field matches the MySearch value.)

```
Dim MySearch As String
```

3. After the comment that says ' insert the Page_Load code snippet here, type the code that follows this paragraph. When the user first views the page, the code sets the default value for the TextBox control named txtSearch and hides the DataGrid control named MyDG.

```
If Not Page.IsPostBack Then
    txtSearch.Text = ""
    MyDG.Visible = False
Else
    BindMyDG()
End If
```

4. The .NET data objects have already been added to the page, as shown in Figure 8-11. Locate the data controls in the code behind the page. Notice that the command passed when the SqlDataAdapter was created is the SQL statement "Select * from Products". If this statement were executed, 144 records would be returned.

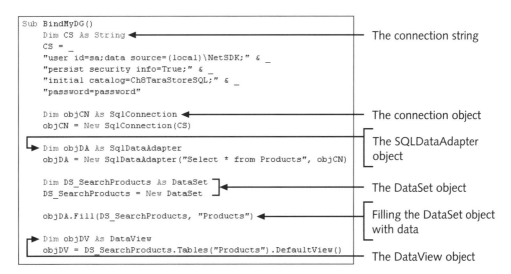

Figure 8-11   Creating the .NET data objects manually

5. After the comment that says ' insert the RowFilter code snippet here, insert the code that follows this paragraph. The code resets the RowFilter property for the DataView object to the value that was entered in the text box. This value is represented by the MySearch variable. The asterisk is used so that the user does not have to enter an exact match. If the user enters "him", then products such as Thimble by Royal Tara and the Himself Coffee Mug will be displayed. Then, the page will retrieve the number of records returned by the DataView object using the Count property and assigning it to the RecNum

variable. (*Note:* The wildcard characters, such as the * and ?, represent different input. The * represents any number of characters while ? represents a single alphanumeric character.)

```
MySearch = "ModelName LIKE '*" & txtSearch.Text & "*'"
objDV.RowFilter = MySearch
RecNum = objDV.Count.ToString
```

6. Click the **Save All** button. Click **Build** on the menu bar, then click **Build Solution**. The code to display a message with the total number of records has been added for you as shown in Figure 8-12. Locate the data controls in the code behind the page. The Select Case statement compares the objDV.Count property to values. If there are no records, the DataGrid object is not displayed. If there are one to three records, the DataGrid object is displayed, but the AllowPaging property is turned off so that the Previous and Next hyperlinks are not displayed. (*Note:* Additional ways to customize the paging controls are described in the Visual Studio .NET documentation.) If there are more than three records, the AllowPaging property is turned on.

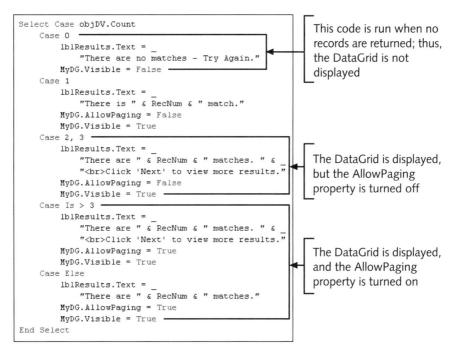

```
Select Case objDV.Count
    Case 0
        lblResults.Text = _
            "There are no matches - Try Again."
        MyDG.Visible = False
    Case 1
        lblResults.Text = _
            "There is " & RecNum & " match."
        MyDG.AllowPaging = False
        MyDG.Visible = True
    Case 2, 3
        lblResults.Text = _
            "There are " & RecNum & " matches. " & _
            "<br>Click 'Next' to view more results."
        MyDG.AllowPaging = False
        MyDG.Visible = True
    Case Is > 3
        lblResults.Text = _
            "There are " & RecNum & " matches. " & _
            "<br>Click 'Next' to view more results."
        MyDG.AllowPaging = True
        MyDG.Visible = True
    Case Else
        lblResults.Text = _
            "There are " & RecNum & " matches."
        MyDG.AllowPaging = True
        MyDG.Visible = True
End Select
```

This code is run when no records are returned; thus, the DataGrid is not displayed

The DataGrid is displayed, but the AllowPaging property is turned off

The DataGrid is displayed, and the AllowPaging property is turned on

Figure 8-12   Customizing the results displayed in the Web page

7. After the comment that says 'Insert the data binding code snippet here, type the code that follows this paragraph. This sets the DataSource property of the DataGrid control to the **DataView** object, and it rebinds the DataView object to the DataGrid control.

```
MyDG.DataSource = objDV
Page.DataBind()
```

8. Click the **Save All** button. Click **Build** on the menu bar, and then click **Build Solution**. Click the **DataSetSearch.aspx** tab to view the Web page. Right-click on the page, and then click **View in Browser**. Type **Towel** in the search text box, and then click **Go**. Your page should look like the one in Figure 8-13.

9. Close any open pages.

Figure 8-13   Building a search tool using Visual Studio .NET

Create a Search Feature Using a Stored Procedure

To avoid SQL injections, you can use stored procedures to prevent hackers from inserting code into a concatenated SQL statement. The following exercise produces the same output as the last exercise. However, in this exercise, you will create the stored procedure that will run the command.

1. Open the Server Explorer window, and create a new stored procedure named **FilterDataGrid** with the code following this paragraph. When you are finished entering the code, click the **Save All** button, and then close the stored procedure page.

```
CREATE PROCEDURE dbo.FilterDataGrid
  @MySearchTerm nvarchar(20)
AS
SELECT *
FROM Products
WHERE (ModelName LIKE @MySearchTerm )
ORDER BY ModelName
RETURN
```

2. Double-click the **DataSetSearchSP.aspx** page in the Solution Explorer window. Double-click on the whitespace on the page to open the code behind the page. The .NET data objects have already been added to the page, as shown in Figure 8-14. Locate the data controls in the code behind the page. Notice that the Command.CommandText property is set to the FilterDataGrid stored procedure. The @MySearchTerm parameter is created. The DataAdapter uses both the Connection and the Command objects to obtain the data from the database. The MySearch variable, which stores the value that the user entered in the text box, is used to set the value for the @MySearchTerm parameter. When the command is executed, the parameter will be passed to the stored procedure. (*Note*: You may have to change the connection string properties to match your database security permissions.)

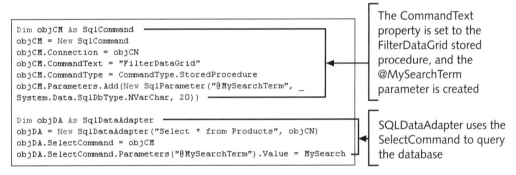

```
Dim objCM As SqlCommand
objCM = New SqlCommand
objCM.Connection = objCN
objCM.CommandText = "FilterDataGrid"
objCM.CommandType = CommandType.StoredProcedure
objCM.Parameters.Add(New SqlParameter("@MySearchTerm", _
System.Data.SqlDbType.NVarChar, 20))

Dim objDA As SqlDataAdapter
objDA = New SqlDataAdapter("Select * from Products", objCN)
objDA.SelectCommand = objCM
objDA.SelectCommand.Parameters("@MySearchTerm").Value = MySearch
```

The CommandText property is set to the FilterDataGrid stored procedure, and the @MySearchTerm parameter is created

SQLDataAdapter uses the SelectCommand to query the database

Figure 8-14   Using stored procedures to perform a search query

3. Click the **Save All** button. Click **Build** on the menu bar, and then click **Build Solution**.

4. Click the **DataSetSearchSP.aspx** tab to view the Web page. Right-click the page, and then click **View in Browser**. Type **Towel** in the search text box, and then click **Go**. Your page should look like the one in Figure 8-13 because the HTML template is identical—the only difference is the search command technique used in the code behind the page.

5. Close any open pages.

INSERTING, MODIFYING, AND DELETING RECORDS

To maintain a database you must be able to create new records, modify existing records, and delete records. You can accomplish this by using SQL commands or by using the methods built into the Data controls. You can use the Command Builder method built into the DataGrid, DataList, and Repeater controls to help you build methods and procedures to maintain the database.

Using the DataGrid Control to Maintain a Database

The DataGrid control allows you to bind data to the columns. You can use the DataGrid control to insert, modify, and delete data. In previous exercises you learned that the DataGrid control allows you to create a bound column. You learned that all columns support style properties, as follows:

- *AlternatingItemStyle*—Identifies the style for alternating rows
- *EditItemStyle*—Identifies the style for a row being edited
- *FooterStyle*—Identifies the style for the footer row
- *HeaderStyle*—Identifies the style for the header row
- *ItemStyle*—Identifies the style for individual items within the list or control
- *PagerStyle*—Identifies the style for the page selection controls
- *SelectedItemStyle*—Identifies the style for the currently selected item

All columns within the DataGrid control allow you to configure the appearance of the column, along with the **HeaderText**, **HeaderImageURL**, and **FooterText properties**. You can also set the **Visible property** for a column, which allows you to show or hide the column. The **SortExpression property** can be used to identify the column from the data source that is used when sorting the column.

BoundColumn objects are used by the DataGrid control to bind data to a column in the DataGrid control. All BoundColumn objects also allow you to specify the **DataField** property, which identifies the column from the data source bound to the column, and a **DataFormatString property**, which identifies the formatting rules for the contents of the BoundColumn object. The **ReadOnly property** is used with BoundColumn objects to stop the user from editing a column when the DataGrid control is in edit mode.

When you pass a request to retrieve the contents of a cell in a bound column, the request is passed as an argument. When you update a BoundColumn object, the columns are sent using **DataGridCommandEventArgs**, which are represented with the variable *e*. When you want to access a specific cell within a DataGrid object, you must use the **Item property** of the e object. The e.Item property contains an indexed Cells collection that contains one Cell object for each column in the DataGrid control. For a bound control, the data is found in the first control in the Controls collection of the cell. The following sample code retrieves the contents as a string from the TextBox control that is displayed in the second column:

```
Sub UpdateItem(ByVal sender As Object, ↲
    ByVal e As DataGridCommandEventArgs)
  Dim MyData As String
  Dim MyTB As TextBox
  MyTB = CType(e.Item.Cells(1).Controls(0), TextBox)
  MyData = MyTB.Text
End Sub
```

The **TemplateColumn object** is used to provide additional content, such as HTML. The column can contain bound data as well as unbound data. You can configure the **EditItemTemplate property** to be used when the DataGrid is in edit mode. The **HeaderTemplate** and **FooterTemplate objects** appear at the top and bottom of the TemplateColumn, respectively, and may contain HTML elements and controls. The **ItemTemplate column** contains HTML elements and controls within the column.

When you pass a request to retrieve the contents of a cell in a TemplateColumn object, the request is passed as an argument. The e.Item property in the TemplateColumn object also contains an indexed Cells collection that contains one cell for each column in the DataGrid control. However, the data is contained within the controls you created within the template. You can use the FindControl method and the control's name to retrieve the data within the cell. The sample code that follows this paragraph retrieves the data from the TextBox control by using the Name property of the control. The name of the control requested is "ProductName," which is found in the second column of the DataGrid control.

```
Sub UpdateItem(ByVal sender As Object, ↲
    ByVal e As DataGridCommandEventArgs)
Dim MyData As String
Dim box As TextBox
MyTB = CType(e.Item.Cells(1).FindControl("FirstName"), ↲
  TextBox)
MyData = MyTB.text
End Sub
```

A **HyperLinkColumn object** is used by the DataGrid control to bind a hyperlink to data. It is often used to select a value, such as the CategoryID from a DataGrid control that displays the category list, and open a related set of data such as the list of products for a particular category. The **Text property** identifies the text of the hyperlink, which is formatted with the **DataNavigateURLFormatString property**. The **DataTextField property** is the value of the data source that is displayed as text, and is formatted by the **DataTextFormatString property**. The **NavigateURL property** and the **DataNavigateURL property** both identify a URL the client is redirected to when the hyperlink is clicked. If both properties are set, NavigateURL takes precedence. The **Target property** identifies which window to open the Web page in. The value of Target can be _Top, _New, _Parent, or _Blank.

A **ButtonColumn object** is used by the DataGrid control to insert a user-defined button. You can use the buttons for adding and deleting records, and to execute other commands. By default the buttons created for you in a ButtonColumn or EditCommandColumn object are **LinkButtons**. They appear as hyperlink buttons, but have additional functionality similar to a button. You can also specify that the ButtonType property for the ButtonColumn object be **PushButton**, which means that the appearance of the button would be similar to a physical button.

Inserting a New Record with the DataReader Control and with Stored Procedures and Parameters

You can write code to insert or delete records, or you can use the methods built into the data controls. In the following exercise, you build a stored procedure to insert a new record, then create the Web page to call the stored procedure and insert the new record.

1. Open the **Chapter8** project in Visual Studio .NET if necessary.

2. In the Server Explorer window, under the Data Connections, click the **plus sign** next to the Ch8TaraStoreSQL database, click the **plus sign** next to Tables, then click **Categories**. Right-click **Categories**, and then click **Design Table**. In the Properties pane for the CategoryID field, change the Identity to **Yes**. Click the **Save All** button and close the window.

3. In the Server Explorer window, right-click **Stored Procedure** under the Ch8TaraStoreSQL database, and then click **New Stored Procedure**. Select and delete all of the text in the stored procedure. Type the code that follows this paragraph. The code inserts a new record. The stored procedure takes four parameters, @CatName, @CatImage, @CatThumb, and @CatDesc. @CatID is also a parameter, but it's an output parameter, so the value is returned when the procedure is called.

```
CREATE Procedure AddCatSQL
  (
  @CatName nvarchar(50),
  @CatImage nvarchar(50),
  @CatThumb nvarchar(50),
  @CatDesc ntext,
  @CatID int OUTPUT
)
AS
INSERT INTO Categories
  (CategoryName, CatImage, Thumbnail, Description)
  VALUES (@CatName, @CatImage, @CatThumb, @CatDesc)
SELECT
  @CatID = @@Identity
RETURN
```

8

4. Click the **Save All** button. (*Note:* There is an additional field, TinyThumb, in the Categories table. When you insert data, you do not have to include all of the fields. However, any primary and secondary keys and the required fields must be inserted when the record is created.)

5. Double-click the **InsertCat.aspx** page icon in the Solution Explorer window.

6. Double-click the whitespace on the page to open the code behind the page.

7. In the onClick event handler for the btnAdd button, the code to create the connection string and Connection object has been entered for you. The code to retrieve the values from the text boxes also has been entered for you. Type the following code below the first comment to retrieve the values from the description text box on the form:

```
Dim CatDesc As String = tCatDesc.Text
```

8. The code to create the Command object and assign AddCatSQL has been entered for you. Insert the following code to retrieve the CatID of the new record below the second comment:

```
Dim pCatID As SqlClient.SqlParameter
pCatID = New SqlClient.SqlParameter("@CatID", ↩
SqlDbType.Int, 4)
pCatID.Direction = ParameterDirection.Output
oCM.Parameters.Add(pCatID)
```

9. The code to create the other parameters and assign the values from the text boxes has been entered for you. The data type and length of the parameters can be found in the stored procedure. Insert the code following this paragraph to create the pCatDesc parameter. Type the code below the third comment.

```
Dim pCatDesc As SqlClient.SqlParameter
pCatDesc = New SqlClient.SqlParameter("@CatDesc", ↩
    SqlDbType.NText)
pCatDesc.Value = CatDesc
oCM.Parameters.Add(pCatID)
```

10. After the fourth comment in the existing code on your screen, add the code following this paragraph to open the connection and execute the command using the **ExecuteNonQuery**. (*Note:* The ExecuteNonQuery does not return the records, only the output parameter.)

```
SqlConnection1.Open()
oCM.ExecuteNonQuery()
SqlConnection1.Close()
```

11. Click the **Save All** button. Click **Build** on the menu bar, then click **Build Solution**.

12. Click on the **InsertCat.aspx** tab. Right-click on the page, and then click **View in Browser**. Your page should look like the one in Figure 8-15.

13. Enter the category name **Waterford**. The description is **Waterford Crystal**. The category image name is **29.jpg**, and the thumbnail image name is **29.gif**. When you are finished, add the new record by clicking the **Add** button. (*Note*: When the record has been added, the Web page uses a button that redirects the user to the DataReaderSQL.aspx page, which displays the category list from the Categories table. At that point, the new record has been added. If the user remains on the page, the text boxes are emptied by setting the Text property to an empty string. In a Web application, you will likely want to display some feedback to the user indicating that the record was added successfully. Some developers display the record to the end user, or provide a hyperlink to display the set of records that includes the newly added record.)

14. Double-click the **Categories** table in the Server Explorer window. You should see your new row added to the bottom of the table.

15. Close any open pages.

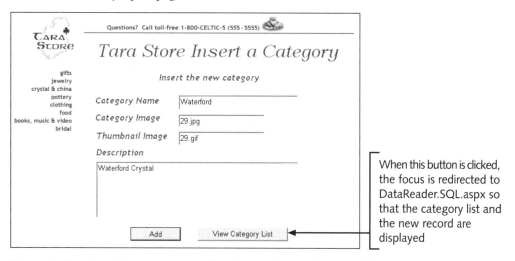

Figure 8-15   Inserting a new record with stored procedures and the DataReader object

Deleting a Record with the DataGrid Control

You can use the DataGrid control to add records to and delete them from the DataSet object. You can use a ButtonColumn object to trigger the Add and Delete record function, or you can use a TemplateColumn object. The table uses the **ItemCommand property** to insert Add and Delete command functions. In the following exercise, you create a Web page that contains a DataGrid control that allows you to delete the record from a table.

1. Open the **Chapter8** project in Visual Studio .NET if necessary.

2. Double-click the **DeleteCat.aspx** page icon in the Solution Explorer window.

3. In the Toolbox, click the **Data** tab and drag and drop the **SqlDataAdapter** control to the Web page. The DataAdapter Configuration Wizard opens. Click the **Next** button.

4. In the drop-down list box, select the connection to your Ch8TaraStoreSQL database. Click the **Next** button. In the Query Type window, leave the default radio button labeled **Use SQL statements** selected and click the **Next** button.

5. Click the **Query Builder** button to open the Query Builder. Select the **Categories** table from the Add Table window, click **Add**, then click the **Close** button.

6. In the Field List box, select the **CategoryID**, **CategoryName**, **CatImage**, **Thumbnail**, and **Description** fields. Click the **OK** button, then click the **Next** button to generate the SQL SELECT, INSERT, UPDATE, and DELETE statements, along with a Command object. Then, click the **Finish** button. If prompted, select **Include password** in the window. The DataAdapter and Connection objects are added to the page.

7. To create a DataSet object, click **Data** on the menu bar, and then click **Generate Dataset**. In the Generate Dataset window, select the radio button labeled **New**. In the text box, type **DS_Cat**. The Categories table has already been selected. Click the **OK** button.

8. Select the DataSet, click **Data** on the menu bar, then click **Preview Data**. Click the **Fill Dataset** button. Your data should be displayed in the window. Click the **Close** button.

9. Drag and drop the **DataView** control from the **Data** tab in the Toolbox to the Web page.

10. You need to assign a table to the DataView. With the **DataView** selected, go to the Properties window, and click the **Table property** drop-down list. Click the **plus sign** next to the DataSet named DS_Cat1, and then select the table named **Categories**.

11. To assign a data source to the DataGrid object, select the **DataGrid** object. In the Properties window, set the DataSource property to **DataView1**.

12. Double-click on the page to open the code behind the page, which is named DeleteCat.aspx.vb.

13. Within the Page_Load procedure, add the code that follows this paragraph to call the Fill method of the DataAdapter to add the data to the DataSet. You must pass the name of the DataSet, DS_Cat1, as a parameter to the DataAdapter. You then bind the controls to the data sources using the DataBind method.

```
SqlDataAdapter1.Fill(DS_Cat1)
Page.DataBind()
```

14. Click the **Save All** button. Click **Build** on the menu bar, then click **Build Solution**.

15. Click the **DeleteCat.aspx** tab to view the page. Right-click on the **DeleteCat.aspx** page, and then click **View in Browser**.

16. Close the browser window and any open pages.

Using the ItemCommand Property of the DataGrid Control to Delete Data

The Web page you just created simply displays the records. Now you need to modify the DataGrid control and add the event handlers to the code behind the page. The DataGrid control can contain objects such as cells, rows, and other data controls that can initiate events. In order to determine which event sent the command, the events are bubbled up to the DataGrid control. There are several approaches to deleting records from a DataGrid control. You can insert your code into the ItemCommand event handler of the DataGrid object, or you can use the DeleteCommand event handler of the DataGrid control.

You can use the onItemCommand property of the DataGrid control to assign a function or event handler to the ItemCommand event. For example, when the user clicks the Delete hyperlink, the **CommandName** is passed to the DataGrid control, which initiates the event. In your code, you can detect which control triggered the event by comparing the CommandName value.

In the following exercise, you modify the DataGrid control to delete the record. When the user clicks the Delete hyperlink, The CommandName is assigned to "RemoveFromCat". RemoveFromCat is passed to the "Grid_CatCommand" event handler that is triggered when an event is bubbled up to the DataGrid control.

1. Open the **Chapter8** project in Visual Studio .NET if necessary. Open the **DeleteCat.aspx** page in Design view.

2. Right-click the DataGrid, then click **Property Builder**. In the General tab, change the Data key field property in the drop-down list to **CategoryID**.

3. In the MyDG Properties window, click the **Columns** tab. Deselect the **Create columns automatically at runtime** check box. You will add the bound and template columns manually.

4. Select the **CategoryID**, **CategoryName**, **CatImage**, **Thumbnail**, and **Description** fields in the Available columns list. Click the **>** sign to move the fields to the Selected columns list. For the CategoryID field, change the header text to **Category ID**. Change the CategoryName header text to **Category Name**. Change the CatImage header text to **Image**.

5. In the Available Columns list, scroll down to and click the **Template Column** and click the **>** button to copy the entry to the Selected columns list. Move the Template Column to the top of the list by clicking the **up arrow** five times. In the Header text box type **Select a Task**, then click **OK**.

8

6. Switch to HTML view by clicking the **HTML** tab. In the DataGrid tag, locate the <asp:TemplateColumn> </asp:TemplateColumn> tags. Inside the tags, add the code that follows this paragraph. The code creates an ItemTemplate within the TemplateColumn. The template contains an Add and Delete Link button.

```
<ItemTemplate>
    <asp:LinkButton ID="RemoveButton"
    CommandName="RemoveFromCat"
    Text="Delete" ForeColor="blue" runat="server" />
</ItemTemplate>
```

7. Click the **Design** tab to return to Design view. Right-click on the page, and then click **View Code** to open the code behind the page.

8. Select MyDG from the Class Name drop-down list, then select ItemCommand from the Method Name drop-down list. This code handles the Grid_CatCommand event. If the user clicks the Delete button, then the command name that is passed to the DataGrid is RemoveFromCat. Insert the following code into the MyDG_ItemCommand event procedure:

```
If e.CommandSource.CommandName = "RemoveFromCat" Then
  Else
End If
  Page.DataBind()
```

9. Insert a line above the Else statement. Insert the following code to get the value from the second column, which contains the CategoryID, and assign it to the variable CatID:

```
Dim CatIDCell As TableCell = e.Item.Cells(1)
Dim CatID As String = CatIDCell.Text
```

10. Below this, add the code that follows this paragraph to create the SQL command and the Command object. Notice that the SQL command uses the DELETE SQL command and deletes only the record where the CategoryID matches the value passed in the CatID variable. The CatID variable contains an integer, and therefore you do not need single quotation marks within the SQL command.

```
Dim objCM As SqlClient.SqlCommand
Dim MySQL As String
MySQL = "DELETE FROM Categories WHERE CategoryID =" ↵
  & CatID
objCM = New SqlClient.SqlCommand(MySQL, SqlConnection1)
```

11. Next, add the code that follows this paragraph. The code will open the connection and execute the SQL command using the ExecuteNonQuery method of the Command object, so no records will be returned. It then rebinds the

controls to the DataSource to show the changes, and reloads the page using the Response.Redirect method.

```
SqlConnection1.Open()
objCM.ExecuteNonQuery()
SqlConnection1.Close()
Page.DataBind()
Response.Redirect("DeleteCat.aspx")
```

12. Click the **Save All** button. Click **Build** on the menu bar, and then click **Build Solution**.

13. Right-click on the **DeleteCat.aspx** page, and then click **View in Browser**. The page should look like the one in Figure 8-16. (*Note:* The Web page does not provide any feedback. In a Web application you will likely want to display some feedback to the user indicating that the record was deleted successfully.)

14. Click the last **delete** hyperlink in the first column to delete the record in which the category name was Waterford.

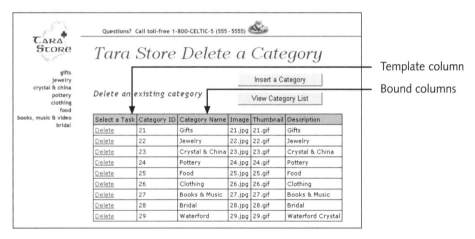

Figure 8-16   Deleting an existing record with the DataGrid control

Using the DeleteCommand Property of the DataGrid Control to Delete Data

You can use the **DeleteCommand property** to delete data from the DataGrid control. The DeleteCommand property, which is labeled as onDeleteCommand, allows you to set the code that deletes the record. DeleteCatDelCmd.aspx uses the onDeleteCommand property. In the HTML template, the onDeleteCommand property for the MyDG DataGrid control is set to MyDG_DeleteCommand. The DataKeyField property is set to CategoryID, which is the field used to locate records. The ButtonColumn object is used to insert a column with text messages that say Delete. The CommandName property for this column is Delete.

In the code behind the page, objCN and CS are declared module variables to store the SqlConnection object and the connection string. In the Page_Load event procedure, CS is assigned to the connection string and the Connection object is created. If the page is first loaded, the BindGrid function is called. This calling displays the initial set of data.

The BindGrid function creates the SqlDataAdapter, DataSet, and DataView objects and populates the DataSet object. The DataSource property of the DataGrid control is set to the DataView object. The data is bound to the DataGrid control.

The MyDG_DeleteCommand event procedure executes when the MyDG.DeleteCommand is called. The Command object is created, along with a connection string and a Parameter object. @CatID represents the category ID of the row that was clicked. e.Item.ItemIndex represents the current selected row. After the Connection object is opened, the Try-Catch-Finally statements are used to determine if there was an error deleting the record. (You will learn more about these statements later in this chapter.) After the Command object executes the command using the ExecuteNonQuery method, the Connection object closes the connection to the database, and the BindGrid function is called to rebind the data to the DataGrid control.

 This example demonstrates the use of the DeleteCommand property. You will not be entering code in this example.

1. Double-click the **InsertCat.aspx** page in the Solution Explorer window. Right-click the page and click **View in Browser**. Enter the category name **Belleek**. The description is **Belleek China**. The category image name is **30.jpg**, and the Thumbnail image name is **30**.gif. When you are finished, add the new record by clicking the **Add** button.

2. Double-click **DeleteCatDelCmd.aspx** in the Solution Explorer window. Right-click the page and click **View in Browser**. Click the last **delete** hyperlink in the first column to delete the record where the category name was Belleek.

3. Close any open pages.

Updating the Database Using the DataGrid Control

The DataGrid control uses the EditCommandColumn object to help add interactivity to your DataGrid object. The **EditCommandColumn object** helps you edit and update your data in the DataGrid control. You can update a single row of data, or enable all rows to be edited within the DataGrid control by using the **EditCommand** in combination with the TemplateColumn. The **EditCommandColumn object** is a button column that contains **LinkButtons** labeled Edit, Update, and Cancel. These LinkButtons are used to edit a single row of data within the DataGrid control. (*Note:* You can also create a Delete LinkButton to delete a record from within the DataGrid control.) The EditCommandColumn object also allows you to change the text of the Edit, Update, and Cancel buttons with the **EditText**, **UpdateText**, and **CancelText properties**. You define these properties when you create the EditCommandColumn object.

When you click the Edit button the EditCommand event is thrown. You can intercept this event using the **onEditCommand** event handler that is assigned within the DataGrid properties. The **EditItemIndex property** is set by the DataGrid object to the selected row, and then the table cells for the single row are displayed as text boxes. After the user enters the new data and clicks the Update LinkButton, the **UpdateCommand event** is triggered. **CancelCommand** is triggered when the user clicks the Cancel LinkButton. You must also include code to handle the **onCancelCommand** and **onUpdateCommand** events.

Many of the built-in Visual Studio .NET examples demonstrate how to edit data with a DataGrid control by deleting the row, then adding a new row with the data, instead of updating the current row. You should consider the consequences of deleting and recreating rows of data, especially when you are assigning unique IDs.

In the following exercise, you will create a Web page that uses a DataGrid control to display the Categories table. Then, you will modify the DataGrid to edit a record.

1. Open the **Chapter8** project in Visual Studio .NET if necessary.

2. Double-click **EditCat.aspx** in the Solution Explorer window. In the Toolbox, click the **Data** tab, then drag and drop the **SqlDataAdapter** to the Web page. The DataAdapter Configuration Wizard opens. Click the **Next** button.

3. In the drop-down list box, select the connection to your Ch8TaraStoreSQL database. Click the **Next** button.

4. In the Query Type window, leave the default radio button selected and click the **Next** button.

5. Click the **Query Builder** button to open the Query Builder. Select the **Categories** table from the Add Table window, and then click **Add**. Click the **Close** button.

6. In the Field list box, select the **CategoryID**, **CategoryName**, **CatImage**, **Thumbnail**, and **Description** fields. Click **OK**, then click **Next** to generate the SQL SELECT, INSERT, UPDATE, and DELETE statements, along with a command object. Then, click the **Finish** button. If prompted, select **Include password** in the window. The DataAdapter and DataConnection objects are added to the page.

7. To create a DataSet object, click **Data** on the menu bar, and then click **Generate Dataset**. In the Generate Dataset window, select the radio button labeled **New**. In the text box, type **DS_EditCat**. The Categories table has already been selected. Click the **OK** button.

8

8. Select the DataSet, click **Data** on the menu bar, and then click **Preview Data**. Click the **Fill Dataset** button. Your data should be displayed in the window. Click the **Close** button.

9. Drag and drop the **DataView** control from the Data tab in the Toolbox onto the Web page.

10. You need to assign a table to the DataView. With the **DataView** selected, go to the Properties window, and click the **Table** property drop-down list. Click the **plus sign** next to the DataSet named DS_EditCat1, and then select the table named **Categories**.

11. To assign a data source to the DataGrid object, select the **DataGrid** object. In the Properties window, set the DataSource property to **DataView1**.

12. Double-click the page to open the code behind the page, which is named EditCat.aspx.vb.

13. Within the Page_Load procedure, add the code that follows this paragraph. The code will call the Fill method of the DataAdapter, which adds the data to the DataSet. You must pass the name of the DataSet, DS_EditCat1, as a parameter to the DataAdapter. The code then binds the controls to the data sources using the DataBind method.

```
SqlDataAdapter1.Fill(DS_EditCat1)
If Not Page.IsPostBack Then
  Page.DataBind()
End If
```

14. Click the **Save All** button. Click **Build** on the menu bar, and then click **Build Solution**.

15. Click the **EditCat.aspx** tab to view the page. Right-click on the page **EditCat.aspx**, and then click **View in Browser**.

16. Close the browser window and any open pages.

Creating Custom Command Procedures to Modify the Database

You can use Visual Studio .NET to create your code to manage the data within the DataGrid, or build your own code to manage the data. The following sample code would be added to the <asp:DataGrid> tag to indicate which procedures would manage the data:

```
OnCancelCommand="MyCancelEdit"
OnEditCommand="MyEditItem"
OnUpdateCommand="MyUpdateItem"
```

Then, you have to create the code to manage the data for each procedure. In the sample code that follows this paragraph, you would cancel the command, or allow the DataGrid to edit the data. You must always bind the data either directly or through a function after the command.

```
Sub MyCancelEdit(ByVal sender As Object, ⤶
    ByVal e As DataGridCommandEventArgs)
    MyDG.EditItemIndex = -1
    BindGrid()
End Sub
Sub MyEditItem(ByVal sender As Object, ⤶
    ByVal e As DataGridCommandEventArgs)
    MyDG.EditItemIndex = e.Item.ItemIndex
    BindGrid()
End Sub
```

Then, for each of the DataGrid text boxes, retrieve the values from the DataGrid text boxes. This code is added within the UpdateItem procedure. (*Note:* You can assign the value to a variable, and then assign the variable to the parameter, or you can assign the value to the parameter directly.)

```
Sub MyUpdateItem(ByVal sender As Object, ⤶
  ByVal e As DataGridCommandEventArgs)
Dim CatNameT As TextBox
CatNameT = e.Item.Cells(2).Controls(0)
Dim CatImageT As TextBox
CatImageT = e.Item.Cells(3).Controls(0)
End Sub
```

You can create the SQL command using parameters instead of variables. Use the UPDATE SQL command to perform an update query, and then add the code to create the Command object using the SQL command.

```
Dim MySQL As String = "UPDATE Categories SET " _
& " CategoryName=@CatName, " _
& " CatImage=@CatImage," _
& " Thumbnail=@CatThumb," _
& " Description=@CatDesc" _
& " WHERE (CategoryID=@CatID); "
Dim objCM As SqlCommand
objCM = New SqlCommand(MySQL, SqlConnection1)
```

You would then need to create the parameters and add them to the Parameters collection of the Command object.

```
objCM.Parameters.Add(New SqlParameter("@CatName", ⤶
  SqlDbType.NVarChar, 50))
objCM.Parameters.Add(New SqlParameter("@CatImage", ⤶
  SqlDbType.NVarChar, 50))
```

8

Next, you need to create the parameter for the CatID. Because the CatID is not being edited in the DataGrid form, you need to retrieve the value from the ItemIndex property, and then assign the values from the text box to the Parameter objects.

```
objCM.Parameters.Add(New SqlParameter("@CatID", ↵
  SqlDbType.Int))
objCM.Parameters("@CatID").Value = _
  MyDG.DataKeys.Item(e.Item.ItemIndex)
objCM.Parameters("@CatName").Value = _
  CType(CatNameT.Text, String)
```

Detecting Database Connection Errors

When you edit a record, you should try to determine if the record was added success-fully, or if there was an error. If the record is not added successfully, and an exception is triggered, the Web page can catch the exception, which contains information about the error such as the exception number, which helps you determine the type of error that occurred. For example, if you try to add a record and the primary key already exists, the exception number returned is 2627. If you are updating a record and do not correctly form the SQL command, the exception number returned might be 137. In order to determine if an exception occurred, you can enclose the code within a Try-Catch con-struct. The Try-Catch construct allows you to place code in the Try section that you want to execute. If an exception is thrown within this code, the code within the Catch section runs. The exception can be caught and stored as an object in a variable. You can access the exception number using the Number property of the Exception object. In the fol-lowing exercise, you will modify the DataGrid to edit a record and use the Try-Catch construct to detect if there was an error when you attempted to update the database.

The sample code that follows this paragraph shows how to add the Try-Catch construct. In the Try section, you add the code to open the connection, execute the SQL update command, rebind the data to the DataGrid, close the connection, and reset the EditItemIndex to -1. Also, you change the Text property of the label to indicate that the record was successfully updated. If its exception number is 2627, the code displays a mes-sage indicating that the record was not added because the primary key cannot have a duplicate value in the table. Otherwise, the code displays a general error message. (*Note:* You can use this technique to send e-mail to the database administrator, run a program, or perform other functions.)

```
Try
  SqlConnection1.Open()
  objCM.ExecuteNonQuery()
  SqlConnection1.Close()
  MyDG.EditItemIndex = -1
  BindGrid()
  MyLabel.Text = _
  "<b>The record was updated successfully.</b><br>"
End Try
```

```
Catch ex As SqlException
   If ex.Number = 2627 Then
      MyLabel.Text = "ERROR: A record already exists" _
      & " with the same primary key"
   Else
      ' Dim Msg As String = ex.Number.GetType.Name
      MyLabel.Text = ex.Number & _
      "ERROR: Could not update record," _
      & " please review the values you entered." '& Msg
      MyLabel.Style("color") = "red"
   End If
End If
```

 You can write the MySQL variable out in the Catch section. It is useful to write out the SQL command statement and any variables when you are trying to determine why an error occurred. You will learn more about error detection in Chapter 10.

Updating Data with the DataGrid Control

At the top of the Code View window in Visual Studio .NET, there are two drop-down lists. The drop-down list on the left, called Class Name, lists the class names that exist within the page. These classes are used to instantiate the objects in the page. The drop-down list on the right, called Method Name, lists the events of the objects. You can use these features to help you build your code to edit the DataGrid.

In the following exercise, you will use the built-in features of Visual Studio .NET to edit data using a DataGrid control. This exercise will show you how to use significantly less code than if you had created the code manually, as shown in the preceding code example.

1. Open the **Chapter8** project in Visual Studio .NET if necessary. Open the **EditCat.aspx** page in Design view.

2. Right-click on the DataGrid, and then click **Property Builder**. In the General tab, change the DataSource to **DS_EditCat1**, change the Data key field property in the drop-down list to **CategoryID**, and change the DataMember to **Categories**. (*Note*: The DataKeyField is used to specify the field that is used to identify the record when changes are requested. The DataMember identifies the table within the DataSet.)

3. In the MyDG Properties window, click the **Columns** tab. In the Available columns list, scroll down to Button Column and click the **plus sign** to expand the list. Click **Edit**, **Update**, **Cancel**, and then click the **>** button to copy the entry to the Selected columns list. (*Note*: Notice that the HeaderText, FooterText, HeaderImage, SortExpression, EditText, UpdateText, CancelText, ButtonType, and Visible properties can be defined for this column.) Click **OK**.

4. Right-click the page and select **View Code** to open the code behind the page. At the top of the page above the Public Class EditCat statement, insert the following code to import the SqlClient class:

```
Imports System.Data.SqlClient
```

5. Reset the Class Name drop-down list to **MyDG**, if necessary. In the Method Name drop-down list box, select **CancelCommand**, which inserts the MyDG_CancelCommand procedure block into the code. Within the MyDG_CancelCommand procedure block, enter the code that follows this paragraph. The code cancels the edit.

```
MyDG.EditItemIndex = -1
MyDG.DataBind()
```

6. Select **MyDG** from the Class Name drop-down list box. Select **EditCommand** from the Method Name drop-down list box, which inserts the MyDG_EditCommand procedure block into the code. Within the MyDG_EditCommand procedure block enter the following code:

```
MyDG.EditItemIndex = e.Item.ItemIndex
MyDG.DataBind()
```

7. Select **MyDG** from the Class Name drop-down list box. Select **Update command** from the Method name drop-down list box. This selection inserts the MyDG_Update command procedure block into the code. Within the MyDG_Update command procedure block, enter the following code:

```
Dim key As String = _
  MyDG.DataKeys(e.Item.ItemIndex).ToString()
Dim CatName, CatImage, CatThumb, CatDesc As String
Dim tb As TextBox
tb = CType(e.Item.Cells(2).Controls(0), TextBox)
CatName = tb.Text
tb = CType(e.Item.Cells(3).Controls(0), TextBox)
CatImage = tb.Text
tb = CType(e.Item.Cells(4).Controls(0), TextBox)
CatThumb = tb.Text
tb = CType(e.Item.Cells(5).Controls(0), TextBox)
CatDesc = tb.Text
```

8. Below this, add the code following this paragraph. The code uses the FindByCategory method and the key value to locate the row in the DataSet that is being updated. The letter *r* represents the row. Then, the code provides the values for each of the columns using the variables from the previous step.

```
Dim r As DS_EditCat.CategoriesRow
r = DS_EditCat1.Categories.FindByCategoryID(key)
r.CategoryName = CatName
r.CatImage = CatImage
r.Thumbnail = CatThumb
r.Description = CatDesc
```

9. Below this, add the code following this paragraph. The code calls the Update method of the DataAdapter object, which will update the DataSet. It then resets the command to display mode and rebinds the data to the DataGrid.

```
SqlDataAdapter1.Update(DS_EditCat1)
MyDG.EditItemIndex = -1
MyDG.DataBind()
```

10. Click the **Save All** button. Click **Build** on the menu bar, then click **Build Solution**.

11. Click the **EditCat.aspx** tab, right-click the page, and select **View in Browser**.

12. Click the **Edit** hyperlink for the Food category. In the Category name column, change the name of the category from Food to **Food and Snacks**. The page should look like the one in Figure 8-17. Click the **Update** hyperlink.

13. Click the **Edit** hyperlink for the Food category. Change the category name back to **Food**. Click the **Update** hyperlink.

14. Close any open pages.

8

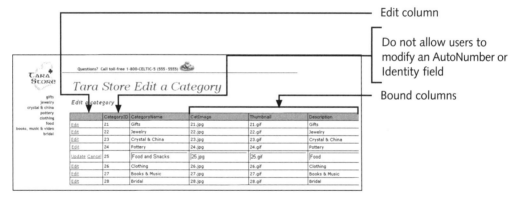

Figure 8-17   Using the DataGrid control to update a database

A great way to learn more about data and databinding is by using the walk-throughs within Visual Studio .NET. These walkthroughs are tutorials that help you learn the more complex tasks within the program. A walkthrough on editing the DataGrid control is available at *http://msdn.microsoft.com/library/en-us/vbcon/html/vbwlkwalkthroughusingdatagridwebcontroltoreadwritedata.asp*.

Building Reusable Visual Basic .NET Database Components

In the previous exercises, your code to access the database resided in the code behind the page. If you needed to access the stored procedure again in another page, you had to recreate all of the same code. Instead, you can store the code in a central area so that it can be reused in multiple pages. You have already learned how to create a User control to centralize code. However, you can also create a Visual Basic component to store code that is reused across the application. Visual Basic .NET allows you to create components that create objects, access stored procedures, and return data. Because the code is compiled with the application in the namespace, you do not have to register the component in each page as you would a User control.

In this section, you will create a reusable variable and a reusable component. Then you will retrieve the variable and create the component from the Web page. The Web page displays a menu, a home page image, and a list of products. When the user first views the page, the category list is displayed as a menu using a DataList control, along with a home page image. When the user clicks a category, the index number of the selected item and the category ID are passed in the querystring to the same page. When the page is reloaded, the querystring is read, and the values from the selected item and CategoryID are retrieved and stored in variables. These variables are used to retrieve the list of products in the category that was selected. Then, the list of products is bound to a DataList control in the Web page.

Creating a Global Variable in the Web Configuration File

In this section, you will create a global variable, which will contain the connection string. By default, Visual Studio .NET creates a configuration file named Web.config. The Web.config file, which is stored at the root level of the Web site, is a global configuration file. You can create a variable in this file and make it available to the entire application. Web.config is an XML-based text file that is editable using a simple text editor such as Notepad. Because this is an XML-based file, the first line of the file indicates the version of XML that the file is compatible with. The configuration tag is the root node for the configuration file. All tags must be nested within the configuration node. You can include comments within the file using the HTML comment tags. The appSettings tag indicates the global application settings for the Web site.

You use the add tag to create global application variables. The variables are stored as key and value pairs. The key represents the name of the variable, which you use later to retrieve the value. You can add many pairs of keys and values within the appSettings node. In the sample that follows this paragraph, the name of the application, Tara Store, is stored as StoreName. CSTS is the name of the key that retrieves the connection string to the database. You can include many connection strings within the Web.config file. You can also include connection strings within Web.config files that are stored in subdirectories. (*Note:* The connection string in the code that follows this paragraph is a long string of text and should not be broken across multiple lines in the actual Web.config file.)

```
<?xml version="1.0" encoding="utf-8" ?>
<configuration>
  <!-- application specific settings -->
  <appSettings>
     <add key = "StoreName" value = "Tara Store" />
     <add key = "CSTS" value = ↵
     "server=(local)\NetSDK; uid=sa;
        pwd=password;=;database=Ch8TaraStoreSQL" />
  </appSettings>
</configuration>
```

To access the key and value pairs, you can assign the values to a variable or access them directly. The sample code that follows this paragraph assigns the values from the StoreName and CS keys, and stores them in variables named MyStoreName and MyCS, respectively. Later in the code, you can use the variables to access the values.

```
Dim MyStoreName as String
MyStoreName = ↵
  ConfigurationSettings.AppSettings("StoreName")
Response.write(MyStoreName)
Dim CS as String
MyCS = ConfigurationSettings.AppSettings("CS")
Response.write(MyCS)
```

In the following exercise, you will modify the configuration file to create a new global variable named CSTS. The CSTS variable contains the connection string to your database.

1. Open the **Chapter8** project in Visual Studio .NET if necessary.

2. Double-click the **Web.config** file in the Solution Explorer window. The configuration node and some additional tags are already added for you. Add the code following this paragraph to create the global connection string. The global connection string is stored in the CSTS key. (*Note*: Do not reenter the XML declaration and configuration nodes. Make sure to enter the connection string all on one line.) The code should be placed immediately below the opening configuration tag.

```
<appSettings>
<add key="CSTS" value="server=(local)\NetSDK; ↵
      uid=sa;pwd=password;database=Ch8TaraStoreSQL" />
</appSettings>
```

Tip — If you only have one instance of SQL Server installed, you can refer to the server using localhost, (local) \NetSDK, *MACHINENAME*\NetSDK, or *MACHINENAME*. It's useful to store the connection strings in a central location because they can be used across Web pages and components.

3. Click the **Save All** button. Click **Build** on the menu bar, then click **Build Solution**.

Creating a Visual Basic .NET Component

The component is a Visual Basic .NET file that contains a visual template and the code behind the component page. This means that you can use the graphical tools to add items to your class. You can drag and drop data objects onto the component designer, or you can add them manually in the code behind the component page.

The component contains a class definition named after the component. It's best not to name the component with the same name as the project because when you are finished you will build the solution. The class will be compiled into the same application namespace as your project. (*Note*: It is possible to create additional namespaces within a project.)

When you plan to use the class, you must instantiate an instance of the class. Then, public functions that are created within the class can be referenced by *ClassName.FunctionName()*. You can pass parameters to the function. Using this method allows you to store global functions within public classes that can be accessed throughout your application. By having these functions defined in an external file, the functions can be more easily shared and managed within an application.

In the following exercise, you will create a component and add a Connection object. You will import the System and System.Data namespaces. Then, you will add four functions that will be used to retrieve the category list, subcategory list, product list, and product information.

The page that will call these four functions is CatMenu.aspx. The CatMenu.aspx HTML template and these four functions are identical to the ones you saw previously in the DataReaderDisplay.aspx and DataReaderProducts.aspx pages. The only modification made to the HTML template was to change the reference in the hyperlinks to the CatMenu.aspx page instead of the DataReaderDisplay.aspx page. In the next exercise, you will call the four functions from the CatMenu.aspx page. In this exercise, however, you will only add the functions to the Ch8Products component.

1. Open the **Chapter8** project in Visual Studio .NET if necessary.

2. Right-click **Chapter8** in the Solution Explorer window, point to **Add**, then click **Add Component**. In the Name text box type **Ch8Products.vb** to name the component, and then click **Open**. The page opens in Design view.

3. Click **(*MachineName*)\NetSDK.Ch8TaraStoreSQL.dbo** under Data Connections in the Server Explorer window and drag it to the Web page. If prompted, select **Include password** in the window. An SQL Connection object named SqlConnection1 is added to the page.

4. Right-click on the page, and then click **View Code**. The name of the file Ch8Products is used to create a new class named Ch8Products within the Chapter8 namespace.

5. Add the code to import the system, configuration, and data-related namespaces. (*Note*: If you are working with Oracle or Access, you import the System.Data.OleDb instead of System.Data.SqlClient namespace.) In order to add the namespace, you must add the code above the Public Class Ch8Products statement. Click immediately before the first word, **Public**, then press **Enter** to create a new line. Then, add the code to import the SqlClient and Configuration namespaces.

```
Imports System.Data.SQLClient
Imports System.Configuration
```

6. In the Solution Explorer window, double-click the **DataReaderDisplay.aspx** page. When the page opens, double-click on the whitespace area to open the code behind the page. Locate and select the entire four functions beginning with the line "**Public Function GetCat() As SqlDataReader**" and ending with the line "**End Function**" in the fourth function. Click the **Edit** menu and then click **Copy**.

7. Click the **Ch8Products.vb** page tab, click the line below "Component Designer generated code," click the **Edit** menu, and then click **Paste**. The four functions should appear in the component code behind the page, as shown in Figure 8-18.

8

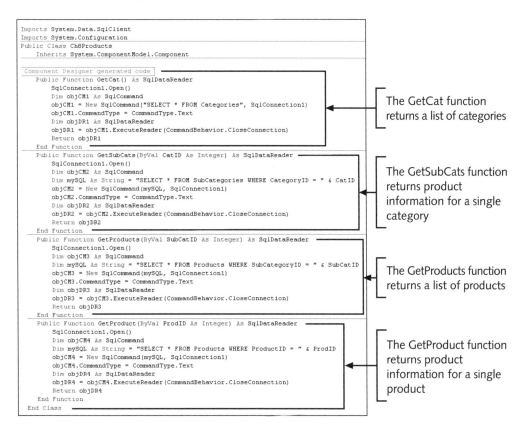

```
Imports System.Data.SqlClient
Imports System.Configuration
Public Class Ch8Products
    Inherits System.ComponentModel.Component

Component Designer generated code
    Public Function GetCat() As SqlDataReader
        SqlConnection1.Open()
        Dim objCM1 As SqlCommand
        objCM1 = New SqlCommand("SELECT * FROM Categories", SqlConnection1)
        objCM1.CommandType = CommandType.Text
        Dim objDR1 As SqlDataReader
        objDR1 = objCM1.ExecuteReader(CommandBehavior.CloseConnection)
        Return objDR1
    End Function
    Public Function GetSubCats(ByVal CatID As Integer) As SqlDataReader
        SqlConnection1.Open()
        Dim objCM2 As SqlCommand
        Dim mySQL As String = "SELECT * FROM SubCategories WHERE CategoryID = " & CatID
        objCM2 = New SqlCommand(mySQL, SqlConnection1)
        objCM2.CommandType = CommandType.Text
        Dim objDR2 As SqlDataReader
        objDR2 = objCM2.ExecuteReader(CommandBehavior.CloseConnection)
        Return objDR2
    End Function
    Public Function GetProducts(ByVal SubCatID As Integer) As SqlDataReader
        SqlConnection1.Open()
        Dim objCM3 As SqlCommand
        Dim mySQL As String = "SELECT * FROM Products WHERE SubCategoryID = " & SubCatID
        objCM3 = New SqlCommand(mySQL, SqlConnection1)
        objCM3.CommandType = CommandType.Text
        Dim objDR3 As SqlDataReader
        objDR3 = objCM3.ExecuteReader(CommandBehavior.CloseConnection)
        Return objDR3
    End Function
    Public Function GetProduct(ByVal ProdID As Integer) As SqlDataReader
        SqlConnection1.Open()
        Dim objCM4 As SqlCommand
        Dim mySQL As String = "SELECT * FROM Products WHERE ProductID = " & ProdID
        objCM4 = New SqlCommand(mySQL, SqlConnection1)
        objCM4.CommandType = CommandType.Text
        Dim objDR4 As SqlDataReader
        objDR4 = objCM4.ExecuteReader(CommandBehavior.CloseConnection)
        Return objDR4
    End Function
End Class
```

The GetCat function returns a list of categories

The GetSubCats function returns product information for a single category

The GetProducts function returns a list of products

The GetProduct function returns product information for a single product

Figure 8-18   Creating resuasble Visual Basic .NET components

8. Click the **Save All** button. Click **Build** on the menu bar, then click **Build Solution**. Close the component files.

Calling the Component from the Web Page

After you have created the component, your Web page can access the data by simply instantiating the Ch8Products class as a new object from the Ch8Products class, and then calling the function using the new class.

Although it will look like you are adding more code than in the original DataReaderDisplay.aspx page, this method is better for Web applications. The benefit of storing the functions in an external class is that the entire set of functions does not have to be stored within each Web page. In addition, you can select which functions to call from your Web page. If the stored procedure changes, you need only change the function within one page, instead of throughout all the pages on your site. Therefore, using components to store your functions is more efficient than storing them in individual pages.

In this exercise, the code to call two of the functions has already been inserted for you. You will insert the code to call the GetCat and GetSubCats functions, which will retrieve the category and subcategory data and bind the data to the DataList controls. You will pass a parameter to the GetSubCats function that is used by the stored procedure to retrieve only those subcategories that match the CatID parameter. In other words, only the subcategories that belong to the main category will be listed.

1. Open the **Chapter8** project in Visual Studio .NET if necessary.

2. Double-click the **CatMenu.aspx** page in the Solution Explorer window. Then double-click on the whitespace area to open the code behind the page. Under the comment that says 'Retrieve the category list, type the code following this paragraph. The code creates the new class called CatList based on the Ch8Products class. It then calls the GetCat function to retrieve the category list and binds the list to the MyCatList control.

```
Dim CatList As Chapter8.Ch8Products
CatList = New Chapter8.Ch8Products
MyCatList.DataSource = CatList.GetCat()
MyCatList.DataBind()
```

3. Under the comment that says 'Retrieve the subcategory list, type the code following this paragraph. The code creates the new class called SubCatList based on the Ch8Products class; it then calls the GetSubCats function to retrieve the subcategory list, passes the CatID parameter to the function, and binds the list to the MySubCatList control.

```
Dim SubCatList As Chapter8.Ch8Products
SubCatList = New Chapter8.Ch8Products
MySubCatList.DataSource = SubCatList.GetSubCats(CatID)
MySubCatList.DataBind()
```

4. Under the comment that says 'Retrieve the product list, insert the code that follows this paragraph. The code creates the new class called ProductList based on the Ch8Products class, calls the GetProducts function to retrieve the product list and passes the function the SubCatID parameter, and binds the list to the MyProdList control.

```
Dim ProductList As Chapter8.Ch8Products
ProductList = New Chapter8.Ch8Products
MyProdList.DataSource = ProductList.GetProducts(SubCatID)
MyProdList.DataBind()
```

5. Under the comment that says 'Retrieve the individual product information, insert the code that follows this paragraph. The code creates the new class called Product based on the Ch8Products class, calls the GetProduct function to retrieve the product list, passes the function the ProdID parameter, and binds the list to the MyProduct control.

```
Dim Product As Chapter8.Ch8Products
Product = New Chapter8.Ch8Products
MyProduct.DataSource = Product.GetProduct(ProdID)
MyProduct.DataBind()
```

6. Click the **Save All** button. Click **Build** on the menu bar, then click **Build Solution**.

7. Click the **CatMenu.aspx** tab to view the page. Right-click on the page, and then click **View in Browser**. Click the **Jewelry** hyperlink. Click the **Women's Jewelry** hyperlink, and then click the **Pendant with Celtic Knot** hyperlink. Your page should look like the one in Figure 8-19.

8. Close any open pages.

Figure 8-19   Creating Web pages from reusable Visual Basic .NET components

CHAPTER SUMMARY

❑ ADO.NET provides a variety of data objects that can be accessed from a Web page. By using the Web controls, you can bind the ADO.NET objects dynamically.

❑ The DataSet is used to store the data from the various data sources. The Fill method of the DataAdapter object populates the DataSet object using a SQL command or stored procedure.

❑ The DataSet object consists of a DataTables collection. The DataTables collection consists of one or more DataTable objects.

❑ The DataView object is used to retrieve a subset of data from the DataSet object. The DataView object can combine data from a single table, or a SQL command, but will result in a single DataTable object. The default DataView object is the first table in the DataTables collection.

❑ You can refer to the DataTable object using the name or the position of the DataTable object within the DataTables collection. You can bind your Web controls to a DataView object. You can dynamically display the data by controlling when the BindData method is called, and for which Web controls. You can bind all of the controls at once or do so individually.

- The DataGrid control contains several style templates that you can use to format the appearance of the control. The DataGrid control contains different column types such as EditColumn, HyperlinkColumn, ButtonColumn, and TemplateColumn. You can customize the Column properties using the Style properties for each column.

- EditColumn is typically used to insert LinkButtons that enable you to update data in a database.

- ButtonColumn is typically used to insert Add and Delete buttons, which are used to insert and delete records in the database.

- Both BoundColumns and TemplateColumns are used to display data from a data source.

- When you use Visual Studio .NET, the DataGrid control creates objects that allow you to insert, modify, and delete data in the database. However, you still need to identify the command to run when the event is triggered. For example, when the user clicks the Delete button, you need to identify the event handler to delete the record.

- Components allow you to separate business logic from presentation. The Visual Basic .NET component contains classes that are used to create objects within the application. Within the classes, you can define properties and functions. You can create functions that return data from a database. The compiled component is stored in the bin directory in the namespace defined for the application. Therefore, you can access the component from any page within your application.

- You can create global variables using the Web.config application configuration file, which is located in the root of the Web site. You can create additional Web.config configuration files within subdirectories within the same site. However, all of the key and value pairs defined in the global Web.config file are available from any Web page in the application.

8

REVIEW QUESTIONS

1. Which object is not used to retrieve data from a database?

   a. DataView

   b. DataReader

   c. DataSet

   d. DataGrid

2. What method is used to insert the data into a DataSet?

   a. Fill

   b. GenerateData

   c. FillAdaptor

   d. FillData

3. Which menu is used to create the DataSet?

   a. DataSet

   b. Data

   c. Build

   d. Generate

4. Which object is a read-only stream of data?

   a. DataAdapter

   b. DataRepeater

   c. DataReader

   d. ADOReader

5. Which feature(s) does the DataGrid control support?

   a. Automatic paging

   b. Filtering records

   c. Sorting records

   d. all of the above

6. Which event is raised by the DataGrid control when the user clicks the Page Next button?

   a. PageIndexChanged

   b. NewPageIndex

   c. CurrentPageIndex

   d. GetDataSetPage2

7. Which event handler in the DataGrid control is responsible for intercepting a sort request?

   a. SortCommand

   b. PagePrevText

   c. DataGridPageChangedEventArgs

   d. SortExpression

8. Which property is used to identify the window to open the page when you click the link in a HyperLinkColumn?

   a. DataTextFormatString

   b. Target

   c. DataNavigateURL

   d. DataTextField

9. Which button(s) can be used with the DataGrid EditCommandColumn?

   a. LinkButton

   b. PushButton

   c. ImageButton

   d. all of the above

10. Which window(s) is/are used to configure the DataGrid control?

    a. Properties window

    b. Property Builder

    c. DataGrid Wizard

    d. a and b

11. Which command(s) appear in the DataGrid EditCommandColumn?

    a. CancelCommand

    b. UpdateCommand

    c. DeleteCommand

    d. a and b

12. Which property allows you to change the LinkButton type in a DataGrid control?

    a. ButtonType

    b. LinkButton

    c. Button

    d. GridButton

13. Which property allows you to specify the column that identifies the unique record in a DataGrid control?

    a. DataKeyField

    b. UpdateCommand

    c. EditItemIndex

    d. ItemIndex

14. Which is not a feature of the DataGrid control?

    a. HeaderText

    b. HeaderImage

    c. SortExpression

    d. AcceptButton

15. What is the name of the namespace for the OLE DB .NET managed provider?

    a. `System.Data.SqlClient`

    b. `System.Data`

    c. `System.Data.OleDb`

    d. `System.Data.ODBC`

16. Which SQL command is used to create a new record in the database?

    a. Update

    b. Insert

    c. AddNew

    d. Add

17. What is/are stored in the field when there is no value?

    a. NULL

    b. Nothing

    c. " "

    d. all of the above

18. Where can you store the connection string so that it is available to all pages within your application?

    a. Global.ASP

    b. Web.config

    c. Config.Web

    d. Default.asp

19. What is the value assigned to the CommandType parameter of the Command object when the page requests a stored procedure?

    a. CommandType.StoredProcedure

    b. StoredProcedure

    c. Command.StoredProcedure

    d. objCM.StoredProc

20. Which of the following statements would retrieve a value from the selItem key in the querystring?

    a. `Dim SelID As String = Request.Params("selItem")`

    b. `SelID = Request ("selItem")`

    c. `Dim SelID As String = Response.Querystring("selItem")`

    d. `Set SelID As String = Request.Params("selItem")`

HANDS-ON PROJECTS

Project 8-1

In this project, you use the DataReader object to display data from the Pubs database using the Label control.

1. Start **Visual Studio .NET** and open your **Chapter8** solution if necessary.
2. Create a new page named **Ch8Proj1.aspx**. Add a Label control named **MyLabel**.
3. Add a Connection object and open the connection. (*Note:* Add a Data Connection to the Pubs database. Refer to the chapter material for how to create Data Connections. Then, you can drag the database onto the page from the Server Explorer window to create the Connection object.)

 You can use localhost or choose your servername from the drop-down list. You should choose the authentication method provided by your system administrator. If you do not have a username or password, try selecting Windows NT integrated security to establish a connection to the database.

4. In the Page_Load procedure, add the following code to open the connection to the Connection object and create the variable to store the SQL SELECT command, which will retrieve the list of authors:

```
SqlConnection1.Open()
Dim mySQL As String = _
    "SELECT au_fname, au_lname FROM Authors"
```

5. Below this, add the following code to create the Command object using the SQL command:

```
Dim objCM As New SqlClient.SqlCommand(mySQL, ↵
    SqlConnection1)
```

6. Below this, add the following code to create the DataReader object by calling the ExecuteReader method of the Command object and storing the object in a variable named objDR:

```
Dim objDR As SqlClient.SqlDataReader
objDR = objCM.ExecuteReader()
```

7. Below this, add the following code to declare a variable named MyAuthor to store the data from the DataReader object:

```
Dim MyAuthor As String
```

8. Below this, add the code following this paragraph to read the record from the DataReader and store the value with a line break tag in the variable. Make sure to concatenate the data with the MyAuthor variable. This ensures that all records are stored in the MyAuthor variable.

```
While objDR.Read()
  MyAuthor += (objDR("au_fname") & _
  ""&_
(objDR("au_lname") & "<br />"))
End While
```

9. Below this, add the following code to close the DataReader and the Connection objects:

```
objDR.Close()
SqlConnection1.Close()
```

10. Below this, add the code following this paragraph to assign the contents of the MyAuthor variable to the text property of the label named **lblAuthor**. The label displays the results from the DataReader in the Web page.

```
MyLabel.Text = MyAuthor
```

11. Add a stylesheet, images, and other controls to enhance the page. You can use the stylesheet Ch8Proj1 in your project folder and the images from the images\pubs folder in your project folder, or you can use your own stylesheet and images. You can insert additional content such as a page heading and description. Change the values of the controls using the code behind the page.

12. Click the **Save All** button. Click **Build** on the menu bar, then click **Build Solution**. (*Note:* You can add graphics and text to enhance the appearance of your Web page.)

13. View the **Ch8Proj1.aspx** file in a browser. Print the Web page, the source code, and the configuration file, then close all of the files. A sample of what the page should look like is in Figure 8-20.

Pubs Bookstore

Our Featured Authors

This is a list of the authors who we stock regularly.

Abraham Bennet
Reginald Blotchet-Halls
Cheryl Carson
Michel DeFrance
Innes del Castillo
Ann Dull
Marjorie Green
Morningstar Greene
Burt Gringlesby
Sheryl Hunter
Livia Karsen
Charlene Locksley
Stearns MacFeather
Heather McBadden
Michael O'Leary
Sylvia Panteley
Albert Ringer
Anne Ringer
Meander Smith
Dean Straight
Dirk Stringer
Johnson White
Akiko Yokomoto

We provide a variety of books for all ages.

Figure 8-20 Working with the DataReader object

Project 8-2

In this project, you use the DataReader object to display data from a SQL Server database. This project requires you to have the Northwind database installed on your SQL Server.

1. Start **Visual Studio .NET** and open your **Chapter8** solution if necessary. Create a new page named **Ch8Proj2.aspx**. Add a Label control named **MyLabel**.

2. Add a Connection object and open the connection. (*Note:* You can drag the database onto the page from the Server Explorer window to create the Connection object.) Open the code behind the page, and in the Page_Load event procedure, open the connection using the following code:

   ```
   SqlConnection1.Open()
   ```

3. Below this, add the code to create the variable to store the SQL command.

   ```
   Dim mySQL As String = "SELECT * FROM Employees ↵
       WHERE (Country=N'USA') ORDER BY LastName"
   ```

4. Below this, add the code to create the Command object using the SQL command.

```
Dim objCM As New SqlClient.SqlCommand(mySQL,
SqlConnection1)
```

5. Below this, add the code to create the DataReader object by calling the ExecuteReader method of the Command object and storing the object in a variable named objDR.

```
Dim objDR As SqlClient.SqlDataReader
objDR = objCM.ExecuteReader()
```

6. Below this, add the code to declare a variable named **MyEmployee** to store the data from the DataReader object. Read the record from the DataReader and store the value with a line break tag in the variable. Make sure to concatenate the data with the MyEmployee variable. This ensures that all records are stored in the MyEmployee variable.

```
Dim MyEmployee As String
While objDR.Read()
   MyEmployee += "(" & objDR("EmployeeID") & _
   ")  Ext. "  & _
   objDR("Extension") & "   " & _
   objDR("LastName") & ", " & _
   objDR("FirstName") & "<br /><br />"
End While
```

7. Below this, add the code to close the DataReader and the Connection objects. Assign the contents of the MyEmployee variable to the Text property of the label named MyLabel. The label displays the results from the DataReader in the Web page.

```
objDR.Close()
SqlConnection1.Close()
MyLabel.Text = MyEmployee
```

8. Add a stylesheet, images, and other controls to enhance the page. You can use the stylesheet Ch8Proj2 in your project folder and the images from the images\Northwind folder in your project folder, or you can use your own stylesheet and images. You can insert additional content such as a page heading and description. Change the values of the controls using the code behind the page.

9. Click the **Save All** button. Click **Build** on the menu bar, then click **Build Solution**. (*Note:* You can add graphics and text to enhance the appearance of your Web page.)

10. View the **Ch8Proj2.aspx** file in a browser. Print the Web page, the source code, and the configuration file, then close all of the files. A sample of what the page should look like is in Figure 8-21.

Figure 8-21   Displaying data with the DataReader object

Project 8-3

In this project, you create a Web page that uses stored procedures from the Pubs database using Visual Studio .NET. You will need to create the DisplayStates stored procedure that displays as hyperlinks the list of states where authors live. Then, you will add the DisplayAuthors stored procedure, which will list the authors in the selected state.

1. Start **Visual Studio .NET** and open your **Chapter8** solution if necessary.

2. In the Server Explorer window, expand the Pubs data connection by clicking the **plus sign** (+). Right-click **Stored Procedures**, and then select **New Stored Procedure**. Click **Edit** on the menu bar, then click **Select All**. Click **Edit** on the menu bar, and then click **Delete**. Type the code that follows this paragraph. The code creates a stored procedure named **DisplayStates**. This returns an alphabetical list of the states. The DISTINCT command will return only one value for each possible value. In other words, if five authors live in Wisconsin, WI would only be returned once.

```
CREATE PROCEDURE dbo.DisplayStates
    AS
SELECT DISTINCT State FROM Authors
    ORDER BY State ASC
RETURN
```

3. Right-click **Stored Procedures**, and then click **New Stored Procedure**. Click **Edit** on the menu bar, and then click **Select All**. Next, click **Edit** on the menu bar, and then click **Delete**. Type the code that follows this paragraph to create a stored procedure named **DisplayAuthors**. This returns a list of the states where the authors live when the state parameter is passed to the stored procedure.

```
CREATE PROCEDURE dbo.DisplayAuthors
    @State nchar(2)
AS
SELECT au_lname, au_fname, phone FROM Authors
    WHERE State = @State
    ORDER BY au_lname ASC
RETURN
```

4. Click the **Save All** button. Close the stored procedure windows.

5. Add a new Web page named **Ch8Proj3.aspx**. Drag a Connection object to the page from the Pubs database. In the Web page, add a Label control named **MyLabel** that displays the list of states from the DataReader.

6. Drag a **DataGrid** control from the Toolbox and change the ID property to **MyDG**. Format the DataGrid using the Property window, AutoFormat, or Property Builder.

7. Add a stylesheet, images, and other controls to enhance the page. You can use the stylesheet Ch8Proj3 in your project folder and the images\Pubs folder in your project folder, or you can use your own stylesheet and images. You can insert additional content such as a page heading and description. Change the values or the controls using the code behind the page.

8. Open the code behind the page. Within the Page_Load procedure, add the code that follows this paragaph. This creates the objects and retrieves the data using the DataReader object.

```
SqlConnection1.Open()
Dim objCM As SqlClient.SqlCommand
objCM = New SqlClient.SqlCommand("DisplayStates", ↵
  SqlConnection1)
objCM.CommandType = CommandType.StoredProcedure
Dim objDR As SqlClient.SqlDataReader
objDR = objCM.ExecuteReader()
Dim MyStateList As String
MyStateList = "Select a state: <br /><br />"
While objDR.Read()
    MyStateList += _
    " <a href='Ch8Proj3.aspx?MyState=" & _
    objDR("State") & "'>" & _
    objDR("State") & "</a><br />"
End While
objDR.Close()
```

```
SqlConnection1.Close()
MyLabel.Text = MyStateList
```

9. Immediately after the code that you added in the preceding step, add the code to retrieve the value from the querystring and assign it to a variable. If there is a value, make the DataGrid visible and open the data connection.

```
Dim State As String = Request.Params("MyState")
If Not State Is Nothing Then
  MyDG.Visible = True
  SqlConnection1.Open()
```

10. Below this, add the code that follows this paragraph. The code uses the Command object you created earlier. Pass the name of the stored procedure, DisplayAuthors. Specify the CommandType as **StoredProcedure**. Add a parameter for the State column.

```
objCM = New SqlClient.SqlCommand("DisplayAuthors", ↵
  SqlConnection1)
objCM.CommandType = CommandType.StoredProcedure
Dim pState As SqlClient.SqlParameter
pState = New SqlClient.SqlParameter("@State", ↵
  SqlDbType.NChar, 2)
pState.Value = State
objCM.Parameters.Add(pState)
```

11. Below this, add the code that follows this paragraph. The code returns a DataReader object when the Command object executes the stored procedure. Assign the DataReader object to the DataSource property of the DataGrid control named MyDG and bind the data to the control.

```
objDR = _
objCM.ExecuteReader(CommandBehavior.CloseConnection)
MyDG.DataSource = objDR
MyDG.DataBind()
```

12. Below this, add the following code so that if there is no value for the state from the querystring, HomeImage is displayed and the DataGrid control is hidden:

```
Else
    MyDG.Visible = False
End If
```

13. Save the page and view it in the browser. Click a state, and the list of authors should appear in the window. Print the results displayed in the Output window. A sample of what the page should look like is in Figure 8-22.

8

Figure 8-22 Working with a parameter query

Project 8-4

In this project, you will use the Northwind database. You will retrieve a list of company names that supply products to Northwind Traders and display them using a DataList control. The company names are listed as hyperlinks. When the user clicks a company name, a list of products that they supply are listed as hyperlinks in a DataList control. When the user clicks a product, a list of information about the product is displayed in a DataList control.

1. Start **Visual Studio .NET** and open your **Chapter8** solution if necessary. Double-click the **Ch8Proj4.aspx** page. This contains the HTML template with three DataList controls named SupplierList, ProductList, and Product.

2. Open the **Web.config** file, and add an entry to create a key that will store an application variable named **CSNW**. Assign a connection string to the Northwind database to the CSNW variable. A sample connection string is shown in the code

that follows this paragraph. Check with your system administrator if you cannot connect to the database using this connection string.

```
"server=(local)\NetSDK;uid=sa;pwd=password;database=
Northwind"
```

3. Double-click the whitespace to open the code behind the page. At the top of the code behind the page, above the page class definition, insert the code to import the System.Configuration and System.Data namespaces.

4. Below the Web Form Designer Generated Code region, declare a variable **objCN** to store the Connection object, and create a string variable named **CS** to store the connection string. (*Note:* Remember that your Connection object is connecting to a SQL Server database, so you need to use the SqlConnection object as your Connection object. In this exercise, you will have to make sure you use the objects that refer to the SQL Server versions of the .NET providers.)

5. Create three functions. The first function is named GetSupplierList, which will return a DataReader object when the function is called. In the function, open the Connection object. Declare a variable named mySQL to store the SQL statement. The SQL statement is "SELECT * FROM Suppliers ORDER BY CompanyName ASC". Declare a variable named objCM1 to store the Command object and assign the mySQL and the Connection object to the Command object. Declare a variable ObjDR1 to store the DataReader object. Use the ExecuteReader method to run the SQL statement and insert the data into the DataReader object. Use the CommandBehavior.CloseConnection method to close the DataReader object. Then, add the code to return the DataReader object. *Note:* The code for the first function is as follows:

```
Public Function GetSupplierList() As SqlDataReader
  objCN.Open()
  Dim mySQL As String = _
  "SELECT * FROM Suppliers ORDER BY CompanyName ASC"
  Dim objCM1 As SQLCommand
  objCM1 = New SqlCommand(mySQL, objCN)
  objCM1.CommandType = CommandType.Text
  Dim objDR1 As SqlDataReader
  objDR1 =
  objCM1.ExecuteReader(CommandBehavior.CloseConnection)
  Return objDR1
End Function
```

6. The second function is named **GetProductList**, which will return a DataReader object when the function is called. An integer named **CategoryID** must be included as an input parameter when the function is called. In the function, open the Connection object. Declare a variable named **mySQL** to store the SQL statement. The SQL statement is **Dim mySQL As String = "SELECT * FROM Products WHERE SupplierID = " & SupplierID**. Declare a variable named **objCM2** to store the Command object and assign the mySQL and the Connection object to the Command object. Declare a variable **ObjDR2** to store

the DataReader object. Use the ExecuteReader method to run the SQL statement and insert the data into the DataReader object. Use the CommandBehavior.CloseConnection method to close the DataReader object. Then, return the DataReader object.

7. The third function is named **GetProduct**, which will return a DataReader object when the function is called. An integer named **ProductID** must be included as an input parameter when the function is called. In the function, open the Connection object. Declare a variable named **mySQL** to store the SQL statement. The SQL statement is **"SELECT * FROM Products WHERE ProductID = " & ProductID**. Declare a variable named **objCM3** to store the Command object and assign the mySQL and the Connection object to the Command object. Declare a variable **ObjDR3** to store the DataReader object. Use the ExecuteReader method to run the SQL statement and insert the data into the DataReader object. Use the **CommandBehavior.CloseConnection** method to close the DataReader object. Then, return the DataReader object.

8. In the Page_Load procedure, insert the code to assign values to the Text properties for the Label controls. The lblCompanyName Label control should say **"Northwind Traders"**. The lblDescription Label control should say **"We import and export specialty foods from around the world."**. The lblHeading Label control should say **"Our Product Catalog"**. The first time the page is shown, the lblDirectionsLabel control should say **"Click on the company name to see a list of products."**.

9. Assign the connection string from the **CSNW** application variable to the **CS** variable. Then, create the new **objCN** variable using the new connection string.

10. Retrieve the parameters from the QueryString and assign them to variables. Assign the string variable SelID to the parameter selItem using the statement **Dim SelID As String = Request.Params("selItem")**. Assign the string variable **SupplierID** to the parameter SupplierID. Assign the string variable **ProductID** to the parameter ProductID.

11. Assign the DataReader object returned from the GetSupplierList function to the DataSource property of the SupplierList DataList control. Then, bind the data to the control.

12. Use a Case Select statement, as discussed in the following lettered list, to determine which hyperlink was clicked:

    a. If the parameter Show is equal to "prodlist", then show only the **ProductList** DataList control and not the **Product** DataList control. Assign **SelID** to the SelectedIndex property of the SupplierList DataList control to keep the item selected. Assign the DataReader object returned from the GetProductList function to the DataSource property of the ProductList DataList control. Make sure to pass the **SupplierID** to the function as a parameter. Then, bind the data to the control. Change the Text property of the lblDirections Label control to **"Click the product for more product information."**.

    b. If the parameter Show is equal to "prod", then show both the ProductList and Product DataList controls. Assign the **SelID** to the SelectedIndex property of the

SupplierList DataList control to keep the item selected. Assign the DataReader object returned from the GetProductList function to the DataSource property of the ProductList DataList control. Make sure to pass the **SupplierID** to the function as a parameter. Then, bind the data to the control. Assign the DataReader object returned from the GetProduct function to the DataSource property of the Product DataList control. Make sure to pass the **ProductID** to the function as a parameter. Then, bind the data to the control.

13. Create a **Page_UnLoad** event procedure to close the Connection object.

14. Click the **Save All** button. Click **Build** on the menu bar, and then click **Build Solution**. In the **Ch8Proj4.aspx** page, right-click and select **View in Browser**. Click **Bigfoot Breweries** in the company name list, and then click **Laughing Lumberjack Lager** from the product list. The product information is displayed as shown in Figure 8-23. Close any open pages.

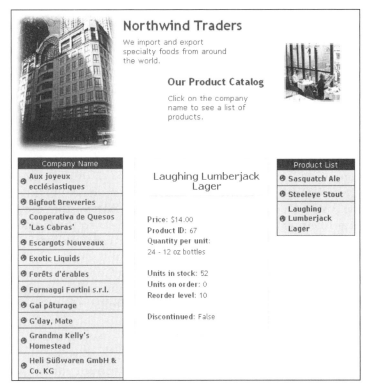

Figure 8-23   Working with functions and application configuration settings

Project 8-5

In this project, you will use the Northwind database. You will retrieve a list of product categories and display them using a DataList control. The products are listed as hyperlinks. When the user clicks a product, the products that the company supplies are listed as hyperlinks in a DataList control. When the user clicks a product, a list of information about the product is displayed in a DataList control.

1. Start Visual Studio .NET and open your **Chapter8** solution if necessary. Double-click the **Ch8Proj5.aspx** page. This contains the HTML template with three DataList controls: SupplierList, ProductList, and Product.

2. Open the **Web.config** file, and add an entry to create a key that will store an application variable named **CSNW**. Assign a connection string to the Northwind database to the CSNW variable. A sample connection string is shown in the code that follows this paragraph. Check with your system administrator if you cannot connect to the database using this connection string.

   ```
   "server=(local)\NetSDK;uid=sa;pwd=password;database= ↵
   Northwind"
   ```

3. Double-click the whitespace to open the code behind the page. At the top of the code behind the page, above the page class definition, insert the code to import the System.Configuration and System.Data namespaces.

4. Below the Web Form Designer Generated Code region, declare a variable **objCN** to store the Connection object, and create a string variable named **CS** to store the connection string. (*Tip*: Remember that your Connection object is connecting to a SQL Server database, so you need to use the SqlConnection object as your Connection object. In this exercise you will have to make sure you use the objects that refer to the SQL Server versions of the .NET providers.)

5. Create three functions. The first function is named GetCategoryList, which will return a DataReader object when the function is called. In the function, open the Connection object. Declare a variable named mySQL to store the SQL statement. The SQL statement is "SELECT * FROM Categories ORDER BY CategoryName ASC". Declare a variable named objCM1 to store the Command object and assign the mySQL and the Connection object to the Command object. Declare a variable ObjDR1 to store the DataReader object. Use the ExecuteReader method to run the SQL statement and insert the data into the DataReader object. Use the CommandBehavior.CloseConnection method to close the DataReader object. Then, add the code to return the DataReader object. Note that the code for the first function is as follows:

   ```
   objCN.Open()
   Dim objCM1 As SqlCommand
   Dim mySQL As String = _
   "SELECT * FROM Categories ORDER BY CategoryName ASC"
   objCM1 = New SqlCommand(mySQL,objCN)
   objCM1.CommandType = CommandType.Text
   Dim objDR1 As SqlDataReader
   objDR1 =
   objCM1.ExecuteReader(CommandBehavior.CloseConnection)
   Return objDR1
   ```

6. The second function is named **GetProductList**, which will return a DataReader object when the function is called. An integer named **SupplierID** must be included as an input parameter when the function is called. In the function, open the Connection object. Declare a variable named **mySQL** to store the SQL statement. The SQL statement is **"SELECT * FROM Products WHERE CategoryID = " & CategoryID**. Declare a variable named **objCM2** to store the Command object and assign the mySQL and the Connection object to the Command object. Declare a variable **ObjDR2** to store the DataReader object. Use the ExecuteReader method to run the SQL statement and insert the data into the DataReader object. Use the CommandBehavior.CloseConnection method to close the DataReader object. Then, return the DataReader object.

7. The third function is named **GetProduct**, which will return a DataReader object when the function is called. An integer named **ProductID** must be included as an input parameter when the function is called. In the function, open the Connection object. Declare a variable named **mySQL** to store the SQL statement. The SQL statement is **"SELECT * FROM Products WHERE ProductID = " & ProductID**. Declare a variable named **objCM3** to store the Command object and assign the mySQL and the Connection object to the Command object. Declare a variable **ObjDR3** to store the DataReader object. Use the ExecuteReader method to run the SQL statement and insert the data into the DataReader object. Use the **CommandBehavior.CloseConnection** method to close the DataReader object. Then, return the DataReader object.

8. In the Page_Load procedure, insert the code to assign values to the Text properties for the Label controls. The lblCompanyName Label control should say **"Northwind Traders"**. The lblDescription Label control should say **"We import and export specialty foods from around the world."**. The lblHeading Label control should say **"Our Product Catalog"**. The first time the page is shown, the lblDirectionsLabel control should say **"Click on the category name to see a list of products."**.

9. Assign the connection string from the CSNW application variable to the **CS** variable. Then, create the new **objCN** variable using the new connection string.

10. Retrieve the parameters from the QueryString and assign them to variables. Assign the string variable SelID to the parameter selItem using the statement **Dim SelID As String = Request.Params("selItem")**. Assign the string variable **CategoryID** to the parameter CategoryID. Assign the string variable **ProductID** to the parameter ProductID.

11. Assign the DataReader object returned from the GetCategoryList function to the DataSource property of the CategoryList DataList control. Then, bind the data to the control.

12. Use a **Case Select** statement, as discussed in the following lettered list, to determine which hyperlink was clicked:

 a. If the parameter Show is equal to "prodlist", then show only the ProductList DataList control and not the Product DataList control. Assign the **SelID** to the

SelectedIndex property of the CategoryList DataList control to keep the item selected. Assign the DataReader object returned from the GetProductList function to the DataSource property of the ProductList DataList control. Make sure to pass the CategoryID to the function as a parameter. Then, bind the data to the control. Change the Text property of the lblDirections Label control to **"Click the product for more product information."**.

b. If the parameter Show is equal to "prod", then show both the ProductList and Product DataList controls. Assign the **SelID** to the SelectedIndex property of the CategoryList DataList control to keep the item selected. Assign the DataReader object returned from the GetProductList function to the DataSource property of the ProductList DataList control. Make sure to pass the **CategoryID** to the function as a parameter. Then, bind the data to the control. Assign the DataReader object returned from the GetProduct function to the DataSource property of the Product DataList control. Make sure to pass the **ProductID** to the function as a parameter. Then, bind the data to the control.

13. Create a **Page_UnLoad** event procedure to close the Connection object.

14. Click the **Save All** button. Click **Build** on the menu bar, and then click **Build Solution**. In the **Ch8Proj5.aspx** page, right-click and select **View in Browser**. Click **Product** in the category list, and then click **Uncle Bob's Organic Dried Pears** from the product list. The product information is displayed as shown in Figure 8-24. Close any open pages.

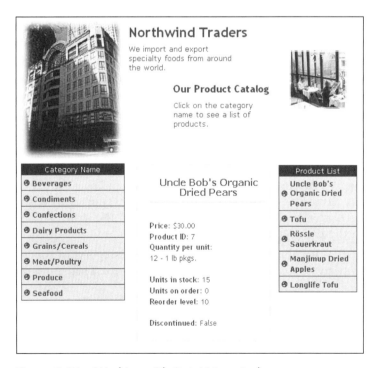

Figure 8-24   Working with DataList controls

CASE PROJECTS

Pubs Database — Displaying the Authors List Using a DataReader Object

Your boss would like to pick the name of the author from a drop-down list box, and then display the author's address information on the Web page. Using the Pubs database, create a stored procedure to retrieve the list of authors by last name (named ListAuthorsByLastNames), and the author's contact information (named AuthorsAddress) for a single author. (*Note:* You can also create a similar database if you do not have access to Pubs.) Create a page named Ch8Case1.aspx. Use a SQL DataAdapter, DataSet, and DataView to bind the results of the ListAuthorsByLastNames stored procedure to the drop-down list named DDAL.

When the page loads, display an image named HomeImage and the DDAL drop-down list that contains authors' last names, and a button named btnGo that says Go. The drop-down list will display the last names, but the value will store the author's ID. A Label control named MyLabel will not appear when the page loads. When you click the button, the page will reload, and the MyLabel control will appear, but not the HomeImage. When the user clicks the button, display the author's address information in the MyLabel control using the AuthorsAddress stored procedure. You will have to retrieve the value of the drop-down list. (*Hint:* You can use DDAL.SelectedItem.Value.ToString) Then, you will need to create the Command, Parameter, and DataReader objects. Use the Read method of the DataReader to display the data in the Label control. You may use the graphics located in the images/pubs folder in your project folder. A sample of how the page would look to the user after selecting an author is shown in Figure 8-25. Save the page as Ch8Case1.aspx in your data directory. Print the Web page, your source code, and the code behind the page.

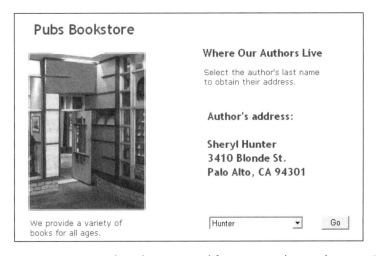

Figure 8-25   Binding data returned from a stored procedure to a DropDownList control

8

Grocer To Go — Displaying the Menu and Products List Using the DataReader Control

Add a data connection to the GrocerToGo database in the Server Explorer window. This is one of the sample databases that were installed with the QuickStart Web site. Create a key named CSGTG that will store a connection string to the GrocerToGo database in the Web.config file. Create a stored procedure named DisplayCats to display the category menu. Use the DataReader object to display the list. Bind the DataReader results to a DataList control. The menu should display hyperlinks. When you click a hyperlink, the CategoryID should be passed. Create a stored procedure named DisplayProducts that displays the list of products by category using the CategoryID as the input parameter. You must pass a parameter that contains the category ID to the stored procedure. Then, you need to display the products from the DisplayProducts stored procedure. You should retrieve the results from the DisplayProducts stored procedure using the DataReader object. Then, display the products using a DataList control. You can display the images by using the ImagePath column, which uses the/quickstart/aspplus/images/directory, or you can use the graphics located in the images/GrocerToGo folder in your projects directory. You would then have to change the data in the ImagePath field to your/images/GrocerToGo directory. Save the page as Ch8Case2.aspx in your data directory. Print the Web page, the source code, and the code behind the page.

Grocer To Go — Inserting and Deleting Records with the DataGrid Control

You are to create an administrative area to maintain the GrocerToGo database. You can modify the Categories table so that the CategoryID is an autonumber by changing the Identity property to Yes and making the column a primary key field. Create a page that allows you to add or delete records in the Categories table. Save the page as Ch8Case3_AddCat.aspx in your data directory. Create the stored procedure AddCatSQL that will be used to insert a new record. After the record is inserted, redirect the user to the Ch8Case3_Home.aspx page. Create a second page that allows you to delete a record in the Categories table. Save the page as Ch8Case3_DeleteCat.aspx in your data directory. After the record is deleted, redirect the user to the Ch8Case3_Home.aspx page. Create a third page that allows you to update a record in the Categories table. Save the page as Ch8Case3_EditCat.aspx in your data directory. After the record is updated, redirect the user to the Ch8Case3_Home.aspx page. Add graphics and content to enhance the appearance of your page. You can display the images by using the ImagePath column, which uses the /quickstart/aspplus/images/directory, or you can use the graphics located in the images/GrocerToGo folder in your projects directory. You would then have to change the data in the ImagePath field to your /images/GrocerToGo directory. A sample of what your Web pages might look like appears in Figure 8-26. Create a Web page that is used as the administrative tool home page with links to the other pages. Save the home page as Ch8Case3_Home.aspx in your data directory. Display the categories on the home page using the DataSet and DataView objects and a DataGrid. Print the Web pages, your source code, and the code behind the page for each of the pages.

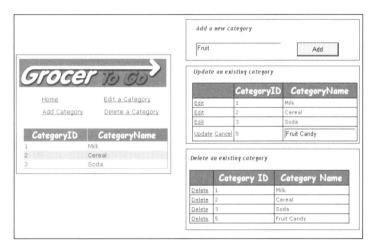

Figure 8-26   Managing data in the GrocerToGo database

8

9

CONFIGURING AN ASP.NET APPLICATION

> **In this chapter, you will:**
> ♦ Learn how to maintain state in an ASP.NET application
> ♦ Identify the configuration files used in an ASP.NET application
> ♦ Create a Web page that maintains state using an HTTP cookie
> ♦ Create a Web page that maintains state without using HTTP cookies
> ♦ Implement the security methods used in ASP.NET

In previous chapters of this book, you learned how to process forms and share data across Web pages using session variables. In a Web farm, load balancing servers will redistribute the clients based on the workload on the server. If one server crashes, the clients are redirected to a new server. In previous versions of ASP, session data could not be transferred across Web servers, which meant that when a Web server crashed, the session data no longer existed. As a result, a customer could place an order in his or her shopping basket, but if the server crashed, all of the items in the basket could be deleted. In this chapter, you will learn how to maintain session data and implement security using forms authentication. Forms authentication allows you to maintain form information and other data throughout an individual user's session, across the entire application, across multiple sessions, and across multiple servers. You will also learn how to create a Web application that does not rely on HTTP cookies to establish sessions.

WEB APPLICATIONS

A **Web application** is a group of files and folders (including virtual folders) located under the Web application's root directory. A Web application is defined by the Web server software. Internet Information Server (IIS) has the capacity to define multiple Web applications on the same computer. In IIS, the root directory of a Web application may be configured as a virtual web, or virtual directory.

A **virtual web** is a Web application that is stored outside of the C:\Inetpub\wwwroot folder. A **virtual directory** is a directory stored outside of the wwwroot folder. Configuring your Web sites as Web applications has many benefits. You can create application-level and session-level variables that are available to all pages within the Web application.

The Internet Information Services Management Tools

A series of Web pages or folders are configured as an application using the Web server's management tool that is a snap-in for the **Microsoft Management Console (MMC)**. Later in this chapter, you will learn to set the properties of Web applications using the MMC.

In the following exercise, you will create the Chapter9 project. Visual Studio .NET will configure the project as an application. Afterwards, you will view the application using the MMC.

1. Start **Visual Studio .NET**.

2. Click **File** on the menu bar, point to **New**, and then click **Project**. This opens the New Project window.

3. Under Project Types, click **Visual Basic Project**, and under Templates, click **ASP.NET Web Application**. Type **Chapter9** in place of WebApplication1 in the Location text box, and then click the **OK** button to create the solution, project, and default files.

4. Open Windows Explorer. (*Note:* To do so, click **Start**, click **Run**, type **%SystemRoot%\explorer.exe** in the text box, and then click **OK**.) Navigate to your **Chapter09Data** folder. Highlight all of the files and folders, right-click them, and then click **Copy**. Go back to Visual Studio .NET 2003. Right-click the **Chapter9** project and then click **Paste**. The data folder and the images folder will be copied into your project.

Next, you will view the Web applications installed on the Web server using the MMC. (*Note:* You can also open the MMC through the Administrative Tools folder located in the Control Panel. You can see this folder only in Classic View.)

1. Click **Start**, and then click **Run**. In the text box, type **%SystemRoot%\System32\inetsrv\iis.msc** and click **OK**.

2. Click the **plus** sign next to the computer name. Click the **plus** sign next to Web Sites. Click the **plus** sign next to Default Web Site. All of your Web applications,

folders, and virtual applications and directories are listed here, along with additional configuration folders, as shown in Figure 9-1. The package icon indicates that the directory is configured as an application.

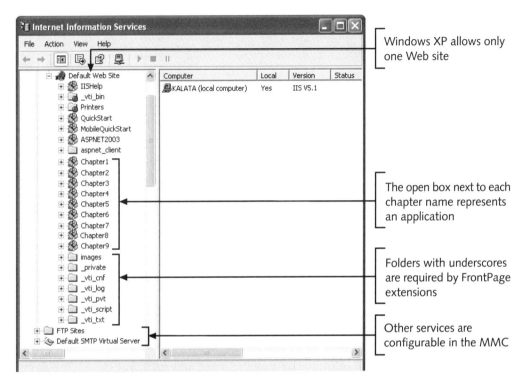

Figure 9-1   Configuring the Web server with the IIS MMC

3. Right-click the **Chapter9** icon and click **Properties**. The Web server property pages open to the Directory tab, as shown in Figure 9-2. Notice that the Local Path is set to \Chapter9, which means that the files are stores within C:\Inetpub\wwwroot\Chapter9. (*Note:* You can view the property pages for any of the Web applications that you have created with Visual Studio .NET.)

4. Close the Chapter9 Properties dialog box and Internet Information Services window.

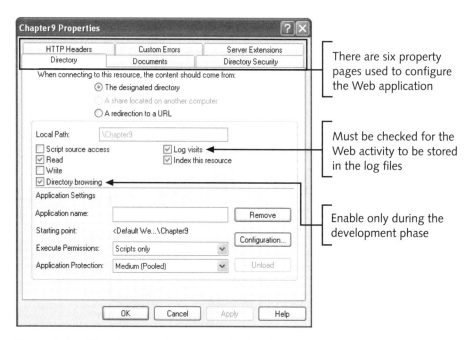

There are six property
pages used to configure
the Web application

Must be checked for the
Web activity to be stored
in the log files

Enable only during the
development phase

Figure 9-2   Chapter9 directory property sheet

The IIS Filters and Server Extensions property pages are available only at the
Web site level. You cannot configure these at the application level. Windows
XP Professional allows you to host only a single Web site. To host multiple
Web sites, you must use a network server copy of Internet Information
Services (IIS), which is available with Windows Server 2003.

When you created your chapter solutions using Visual Studio .NET, the program created the applications folder and configured the application. If you create your Web application using another editor, you may have to configure your application using the
MMC. Refer to Appendix E for more information on working with alternative editors.

Web Application Memory Models

Web applications need to run within a process that runs within an assigned memory space.
The **Internet Service Manager (ISM)** is used to configure the location of the process
that runs the application. The Application Protection property represents the type of
process memory allocation that is used for the application. The **Application Protection
property** can be set to Low (IIS Process), Medium (Pooled), or High (Isolated).

As shown in Figure 9-3, when the Application Protection property is set to Low (IIS
Process), the process runs within the Web server's memory. The applications run in this
model are called **IIS In-Process Applications** because they run within the Web

server's process. The default user assigned to manage the Web server's process is **IWAM_MACHINENAME**, where MACHINENAME represents the name of your computer. If the Web application crashes, the Web server will also crash, leaving all Web sites unavailable.

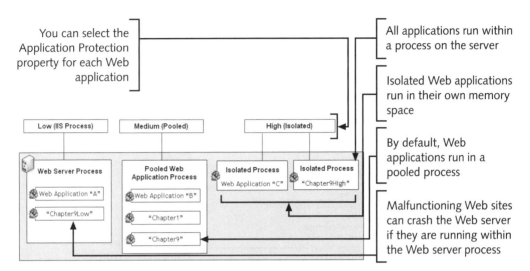

Figure 9-3   Web application memory models

By default, Visual Studio .NET configures the Application Protection property for Web applications to **Medium (Pooled)**, which means that the applications are pooled together to run in a single common process known as the **pooled Web application process** or the **IIS Out-of-Process Pooled Applications Process**. Then if one of the pooled Web applications crashes, the entire pooled Web application process crashes, but the Web server does not crash. As you can see in Figure 9-3, the Chapter1 and Chapter9 applications were configured to run within the pooled Web application process. Although the default user is IWAM_MACHINENAME, the application may be assigned to a separate user account.

If the Application Protection property is set to **High (Isolated)**, the application runs in its own **isolated process**. Then, if the application crashes, none of the other applications or the Web server will crash. As shown in Figure 9-3, the Chapter9High process is configured to run in an isolated process. Although the default use is IWAM_MACHINE NAME, the application may be assigned to a separate user account. Running an application in an isolated process has several implications. First, because it's assigned its own process, it is also assigned a unique identifier called the **Application ID** and a **Class Identifier (CLSID)**. These identifiers are used to identify the process associated with the application.

The **Component Services** management tool allows you to view how processes are organized. The Component Services uses the same management console interface as IIS.

Figure 9-4 shows the left side of the Component Services window. You can see that the W3SVC application is listed under the IIS In-Process Applications. The IIS Out-of-Process Pooled Applications part does not list every application that runs within the process. Rather, the Component Services configures only the single pooled process named **OutofProcessPool**.

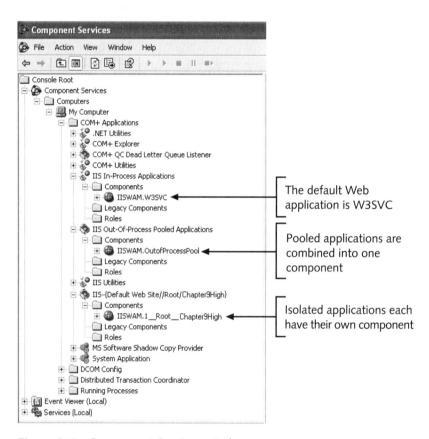

The default Web application is W3SVC

Pooled applications are combined into one component

Isolated applications each have their own component

Figure 9-4 Component Services window

For each Web application that is configured to run in an isolated process, the Component Services will contain a separate entry. If the application were named Chapter9High, the entry would be IIS—{Default Web Site/Root/Chapter9High}. You can use the Component Services to retrieve the Application ID and CLSID for applications that are run out-of-process.

In the following exercise, you will configure the Chapter9High application to run in an isolated process and locate the property pages used to configure the Chapter9High process.

1. Open a new instance of Visual Studio .NET, and create a new project named **Chapter9High**.

2. Click the **Save All** button. Click **Build** on the menu bar, and then click **Build Solution**.

3. Close the Chapter9High solution and then close Visual Studio .NET.

4. To open the IIS MMC, click **Start**, and then click **Run**. In the text box, type **%SystemRoot%\System32\inetsrv\iis.msc**. Click **OK**. The IIS MMC will open.

5. Double-click the computer name. Double-click **Web Sites**, and then double-click the **Default Web Site**.

6. Right-click **Chapter9High** and select **Properties**. The Chapter9High property pages open to the Directory tab.

7. In the drop-down list, change the Application Protection property from Medium (Pooled) to **High (Isolated)**, and click **OK**.

8. Close the IIS MMC window.

9. Click **Start**, and then click **Run**. Type **%systemroot%\system32\Com\ comexp.msc**, and then click **OK**.

10. Double-click **Component Services**, double-click **Computer**, double-click **My Computer**, and then double-click **Com+ Applications**. (*Note*: If you have installed Windows XP Service Pack 2, or a firewall, a message may appear indicating that the program is blocked. You need to unblock the connection for this exercise.)

11. Double-click **IIS—{Default Web Site/Root/Chapter9High}**, and then double-click **Components**.

12. Right-click **IISWAM.1_Root_Chapter9High** and click **Properties**. (*Note*: This is the Web Application Manager Object.) The General tab contains the Application ID and CLSID for the process, as shown in Figure 9-5.

13. Click **Cancel** and close the Component Services window.

Session Data

One of the biggest challenges in creating interactive Web pages is maintaining the state of the user. When you visit an interactive Web site, the site maintains information about your session, such as your IP address, what pages you clicked and when, when you visited the site, what browser you are using, and your preferences. User information can be tracked across user sessions and across the entire application. Some of this information is retrieved from the HTTP headers using the ServerVariables collection, which is exposed via the Request object, and some is retrieved from the properties of the Session object, such as the **SessionID**, a unique identifier that identifies each session. The SessionID is a number whose value is determined by several factors, including the current date, and the IP addresses of the client and server. You cannot change the value of the SessionID property. A special session cookie is used to maintain the session information. When the session ends, the cookie is discarded. If the user opens a new session, a new SessionID is issued. Therefore, a SessionID can be used to track a user across a single session, but not across multiple sessions. To track a user across multiple sessions, the SessionID can be stored in a client-side cookie or in a database that contains the identity of an individual. Some of the information Web sites track is retrieved from forms submitted by users. Once the user logs on with a user ID, the information collected can be correlated with past visits. The syntax for retrieving the SessionID property of the session object is `Session.SessionID`.

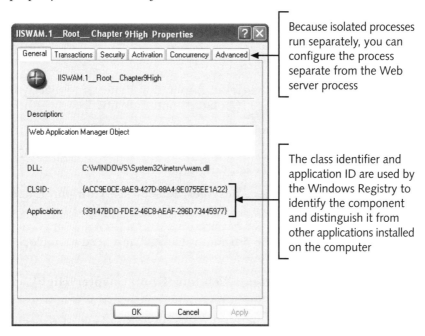

Because isolated processes run separately, you can configure the process separate from the Web server process

The class identifier and application ID are used by the Windows Registry to identify the component and distinguish it from other applications installed on the computer

Figure 9-5   Chapter9High component properties

The Application object allows you to maintain application state. You can maintain information across the entire Web application with the Application object. The Application object stores the application variables in the server's memory, and any user can access them from any page within the Web site.

The Session object is used to maintain session state. The session state maintains information across a single user's session. The session variables are also stored in the server's memory. However, session variables can only be accessed within the session that declared and assigned the session variables. When the session ends, the session variables are released from memory. The application variables are only released from memory when the Web application is stopped, when the Web server is stopped, or when the server is stopped.

The following code will store the Session ID in a session variable named SID. (*Note*: Later in this chapter, you will learn how to store session data using other methods including a State Server and a SQL Server.)

```
Dim SID As String = Session.SessionID
Session("SID") = SID
```

The following code will store a form field named username in a session variable named strName:

```
Dim strName As String = txtName.Text
Session("username") = strName
```

The following code will retrieve the UserAgent using the Request object and store the value in a session variable named UserAgent. Then, the SERVER_NAME server variable will be retrieved using the Request.ServerVariables collection and store the value in a session variable named SERVER_NAME.

```
Session("UserAgent") = Request.UserAgent.ToString
Session("SERVER_NAME") = _
    Request.ServerVariables("SERVER_NAME").ToString
```

The following code will display the SID, username, UserAgent, and SERVER_NAME session variables in a Label control:

```
Label1.Text = _
"SID = " &  Session("SID") & "<br />" & _
"username = " &  Session("username") & "<br />" & _
"UserAgent = " &  Session("UserAgent") & "<br />" & _
"SERVER_NAME = " &  Session("SERVER_NAME")
```

In this exercise, you will view the SessionGetVariables.aspx page, which shows the Session ID and all of the session variables and their values. At first, there will be no values assigned to the session variables. Then, you will view the SessionSetVariables.aspx page and log in. The session values will be assigned to the session variables. Then, you will view the SessionGetVariables.aspx page, which shows the Session ID and all of the session variables and their values. Then, you will delete the session variables. The Session ID will remain unchanged until you reopen the page in a separate browser window.

1. Right-click **SessionGetVariables.aspx** in the Solution Explorer window and select **View in Browser**. (*Note*: This exercise will not require you to open the file.) On a piece of paper, write down the Session ID displayed in the browser. Note that none of the values for the session variables are displayed, as shown in Figure 9-6.

Figure 9-6   Setting session variables

2. Click the **Set Session Variables** button. You are redirected to the SessionSetVariables.aspx page. Type your name and e-mail address in the Name and E-mail text boxes, as shown in Figure 9-7.

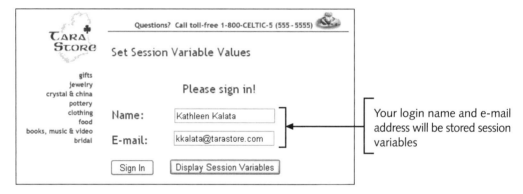

Figure 9-7   Retrieving session variables

3. Click the **Sign In** button. A message will be displayed that the session values are stored in the Session object and the values in the text boxes are set to nothing.

4. Click the **Display Session Variables** button. You are redirected to the SessionGetVariables.aspx page where the session variables are displayed with their values, as shown in Figure 9-8. The SID session variable will match the Session ID value you wrote down in Step 5.

5. Click the **Delete Session Variables** button, which will delete all of the values for the session variables and refresh the page. Notice that the Session ID does not change. You cannot change or delete the value of the Session ID.

6. Close any open Web pages.

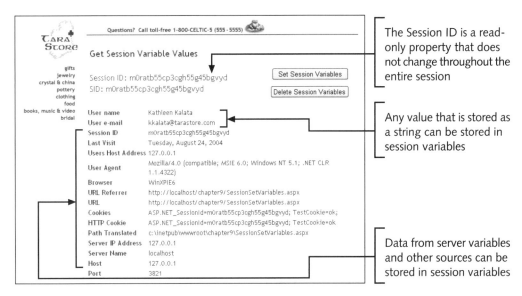

Figure 9-8   Resetting session variables

In the database diagram shown in Figure 9-9, you can set up a UsersTable with the UserID and Password fields. In a second table, named SessionData, you can store the information gathered from each session. This table would also have a field called UserID, which would be the link between the tables. (*Note*: UserID is a primary key in UsersTable, and a foreign key in SessionData.) When the user logs in, you can retrieve his or her SessionID and UserID, and write the information directly into the SessionData table. Then, in future visits, you can access the data obtained from past visits.

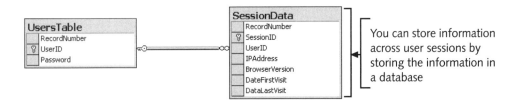

Figure 9-9   Storing session data from a Web application within a database

BUILDING INFORMATION MANAGEMENT SECURITY POLICIES

Web developers and system administrators who specialize in security are a hot commodity these days. The reality is that security has always been a problem, as there will always be individuals who try to circumvent the system for their own agendas. It has only been recently that the news media, and the common user, have become aware of the security issues with respect to the Internet and computer technologies. The problem that Web developers and system administrators face today is the existence of ever-evolving operating system software, applications, and business requirements. Software companies are constantly updating their software. Web applications have to build security protection into every level of their application.

Privacy and security are tied together. Security includes protecting resources, but also the information contained. The media has written many stories about private information collected about individuals that has been sold to companies. This has developed a lack of trust between consumers and companies. It's important to have a privacy policy that clearly demonstrates the company policy about how they handle customer information. Companies must also enforce this policy within their organization.

 Don't be surprised if individuals complete forms with fake data. Even validating the format of an e-mail address doesn't ensure that the e-mail is a real address. Many users have multiple e-mail addresses and may only provide a "junk" e-mail address to companies who require their e-mail address or for online contests.

Security Policies

Hackers today have multiple methods to attack Web sites. Hackers send malicious program code through e-mail by which they can obtain information from users such as their passwords, cookies, and other private information. One of the more recent methods is cross-site scripting. Cross-site scripting is where the hacker inserts malicious code through forms and querystrings. Forms allow the hacker to enter script code within input fields. ASP.NET contains an Encode method that can be used to force dangerous characters such as < and > to be encoded as < and >. The hacker cannot execute code from within the form fields using the browser without the < > characters. The following is sample code that uses the Encode utility to protect the contents entered in the Web page from being executed in the browser:

```
Dim strName As String
strName = txtName.ToString
message.Text = "Welcome " & HTTPUtility.Encode(strName)
```

You should provide information on your site to educate users to install virus checking programs and firewalls, and keep their virus data files up to date. You should educate them about cookies, privacy, and security issues, and have your privacy and security policies accessible from your home page. Third-party companies will provide security checks for your Web site. You can post your results on your home page for your customers, which will alleviate their concerns about transacting business with your site.

Security policies describe how the company is going to manage their Web applications. These policies include how to ensure that users enter valid data, how to ensure that the correct information is displayed to the authenticated user, and how to ensure that unauthorized users do not have access to resources. The Web developer must build security measures into his or her Web applications at every level. The bulleted list following this paragraph contains tasks that the Web developer can use to make a Web site more secure. In this chapter, you will learn how to implement many of these tasks.

- Use Web Forms to manage posting back data
- Use validation controls to validate user input and prevent cross-site scripting
- Use cookies only for non-private information
- Encrypt values stored within cookies
- Encrypt user data sent in a login form using SSL
- Encrypt user data stored in configuration files
- Develop a cookieless application for users who don't support cookies
- Use Web controls to develop login forms
- Use roles to assign permissions to resources
- Avoid using the guest account or anonymous user
- Not allow users to enter their Windows account information in a form that is unencrypted
- Avoid installing sample applications on live servers
- Avoid using default configuration on live servers
- Use virtual applications and folders to store protected data
- Move the Web root directory to a volume separate from the volume that contains the operating system files
- Back up the files regularly
- Log user activities
- Download the log files onto storage media
- Maintain documentation on configuration setup and any changes
- Monitor the network activity using log files and network utilities
- Maintain policies for when suspicious network activity occurs
- Store file-based databases such as Access outside of the Web root directory
- Use a server-based database instead of a file-based database
- Use stored procedures to interact with the databases

It's important to understand how the Web applications fit within the Windows security model. The Windows file system that allows you to protect files and folders is called Windows NTFS. Older operating systems may not use NTFS. When you installed your operating system, you should have selected NTFS as the file format. Information on installation of Windows XP Professional and NTFS is found in Appendix A. User accounts are assigned to individual users, groups, and services running on Windows such as ASP.NET. These accounts are assigned permission to resources using access control lists (ACTs). If a file is stored within a folder and the user has the ability to read the folder contents, they inherit the permission to read the file. This inherited permission can be overwritten at any time by changing the security permissions to the file.

When a user browses a Web site, the Web server determines if the user is permitted access to the Web page. If he or she is not, an access denied error message appears. The Web server uses configuration files to determine if the user has access to the Web page. In this chapter you will learn how to modify the configuration files to implement security policies. If they are permitted access, then Windows verifies that the user has permission to access the resource by checking their access control list. If they are permitted, the page is displayed; otherwise an error message appears. In this chapter you will learn how to modify the NTFS properties of resources. You will learn how to customize error messages in this chapter and in Chapter 10. Additional security measures may be in place for other resources. For example, a Web application that accesses a SQL server will need to send a connection string to the server which contains the user name and password. Even if the Web server and Windows allows access to the resource, they could still be denied access to the data by the SQL server.

Privacy Policies

It is important to understand the privacy needs of the user when you are designing your Web site. If you collect information about a user, you should inform the user. A **privacy policy** is often used to inform the user about the type of information that is being collected and about what is being done with that information.

Platform for Privacy Preferences (P3P) standards provides a way for browsers to obtain the privacy policy for Web sites. Currently only Internet Explorer version 6 can automatically display the privacy policy. (*Note*: To view the privacy policy, go to the View menu and click Privacy Report. Then, double-click the Web site that contains the privacy policy that you would like to view.)

Many users concerned about their privacy do not want Web sites to keep information about them. The following is a list of Web sites that discuss privacy issues and privacy policies:

- TRUSTe—*www.truste.org*
- Electronic Frontier Foundation—*www.eff.org*
- CDT - Center for Democracy & Technology—*www.cdt.org*
- ACP - Americans for Computer Privacy—*www.computerprivacy.org*
- Watchdog—*http://watchdog.cdt.org*

APPLICATION CONFIGURATION

In the past versions of ASP, the configuration of the Web site was contained primarily within a data structure called the **Metabase**, and some additional data was stored in the registry. The registry is where Windows applications typically store their configuration settings. The Web developer typically accessed the application settings via the Web server's snap-in application for the Microsoft Management Console (MMC) application, or by using the **Windows Scripting Host (WSH)** to create scripts to access the Metabase. The Web site could be configured locally using the MMC.

Today, you can configure the Web server using the ISM or ASP.NET. It is important to understand the Web server properties that can be configured using the MMC and ASP.NET.

Viewing the Web Server Property Pages

In the following exercise, you will view the IIS configuration from the MMC, and you will configure the Web site properties using the ISM.

9

1. Open the **Control Panel**.

2. Double-click the **Administrative Tools** icon. Double-click the **Internet Informaion Services** icon.

3. Double-click the computer name. Double-click **Web Sites**.

4. Right-click **Default Web Site**, and then click **Properties**. The IIS property pages open to the Web Site tab. The Web Site tab, as shown in Figure 9-10, contains configurations that identify the Web site, such as the IP address and TCP port. The number of simultaneous connections can be set along with the application timeout. The HTTP Keep-Alives Enabled property allows you to maintain state with newer browsers that support version 1.1 of HTTP.

5. Locate the Enable Logging check box on the Web Site tab, which is used to turn logging on. The W3C Extended Log File Format is the default log format and is already selected from the Actve log format drop-down list.

All of the applications created within the same Web site log connections within the same log file. However, you can disable logging for the log site by deselecting the Log visits check box on an application's Directory property sheet.

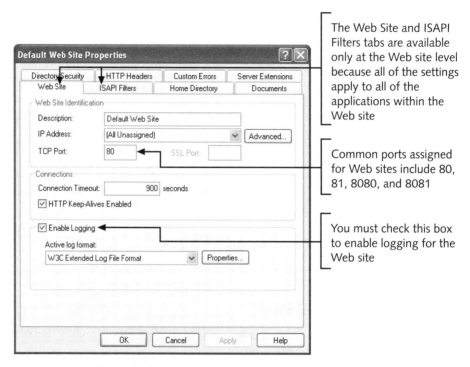

The Web Site and ISAPI Filters tabs are available only at the Web site level because all of the settings apply to all of the applications within the Web site

Common ports assigned for Web sites include 80, 81, 8080, and 8081

You must check this box to enable logging for the Web site

Figure 9-10 The default Web site property sheet

6. Click **Properties** to view the information that is logged. Each log format contains different information. The **W3C Extended Log File Format** contains extended properties that can be logged such as the Client IP Address, the User Name, the Method invoked, the HTTP Protocol Version, the User Agent, the Cookie, and the Referer. (*Note*: In this case Referer is spelled referer.) The default location for the Web server log files are %WinDir%\System32\LogFiles as shown in Figure 9-11. The default directory for the default Web site log files is W3SVC1. Each log filename is named after the date. The default naming scheme is *exyymmdd*.log, where *yymmdd* represents the last two digits of the year, the month, and the day. Single values, such as 2, are preceded by a 0. For example, the default log file name created on September 1, 2007, is ex070901. You can create new log files daily, or set a file size limit. (*Note*: It is recommended that you not allow the log files to increase in size without monitoring them closely. If the log files are on the C: drive and the hard drive disk space fills up, the system will crash.) Click **OK** to close the Extended Logging Properties dialog box.

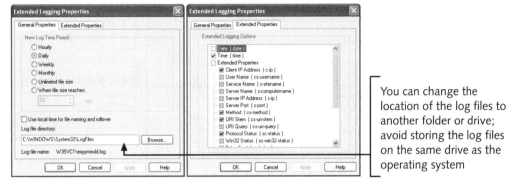

You can change the location of the log files to another folder or drive; avoid storing the log files on the same drive as the operating system

Figure 9-11   The default extended logging properties

If you set the New Log Time Period to "When file size reaches," the file will overwrite itself when it reaches the specified limit. These files may be required in an investigation or may need to be submitted to a court of law as evidence. Therefore, you should maintain copies of all of the log files on a backup device such as a CD disk or DVD.

The date and time logged in the file is based on the local time zone. If you leave the "Use local time for file naming and rollover" option unchecked, the log files will use the GMT time zone. This makes it easier to compare log files across a large organization that spans time zones.

The log file is a text file that can be opened in a text editor. Figure 9-12 shows the log file for the default Web site. The entries shown were made when the Chapter9High application was created by Visual Studio .NET, and then several of the Chapter8 samples were viewed. The three digit number next to each entry indicates an HTTP status message code. The 404 status message indicates that the resource could not be found. The 200 status message indicates that the request was successful. Some resources such as the images within a Web page are also logged when the page is downloaded. Resources such as the Visual Basic .NET files, schema definition files, and configuration files are not downloadable and are assigned a 403 status message, indicating access to the resource has been explicitly forbidden. You will learn more about status messages later in this chapter.

There are many applications that can be used to display the log file in a graphical format. You can also import the log file into a word processing document, a spreadsheet, or a database. You can also create your own application to display the log files in a graphical format. Commercial applications that include log file report writers include Analog (*www.analog.cx*), WebTrends (*www.netiq.com/webtrends/default.asp*), and Livestats (*www.deepmetrix.com*). These applications parse raw log files into visual and tabular reports that can be used to analyze your Web site traffic.

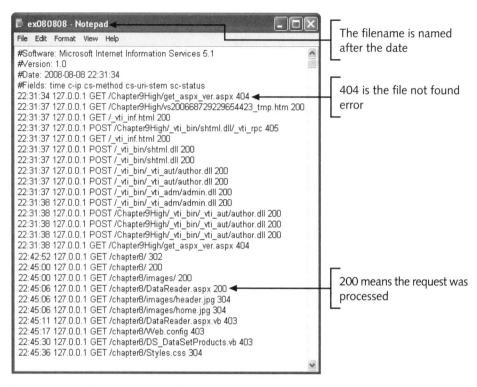

Figure 9-12   Raw data in a Web site log file

7. Click the **Documents** tab. The Documents tab allows you to select a different name for the default document. In ASP.NET, the default name is default.aspx. You can also enable a footer that will appear throughout your entire Web application using the IIS Document Footer property.

8. Click the **HTTP Headers** tab, which allows you to enable content expiration. You can force the Web application to have the page expire immediately after it is delivered, or configure a relative or absolute date and time for the page content to expire. (*Note:* The references on the HTTP Headers property page no longer is current. In 1999, the Recreational Software Advisory Council RSAC was incorporated into the Internet Content Rating Association (ICRA). The ICRA's goal is to preserve free speech on the Web, while portecting children from potentially hamful content.) Not all content is appropriate for all ages. It is useful to end users to place information about the Web site content in a conspicuous place on the home page.

9. Click the **Home Directory** tab. You can configure the Web site so it exists in another directory, hard drive, or Web server, or redirect the Web site to another URL, as shown in Figure 9-13. You can configure security properties using the Home Directory tab. The Read property allows visitors to read the Web page.

All Web pages must have the Read property enabled. The Directory browsing property allows you to see the contents of a folder if there is no default Web page in the folder. This is turned off by default. The Log visits property will allow the log file to log visits to the Web site. The Index this resource property will enable Index Server to include this Web resource in the Index Server search engine catalogues. The Write property allows FrontPage and Dreamweaver editors to publish to the Web site using the HTTP Put command that is built into the editor. Script source access allows visitors to access your script source code. Enabling this property is not recommended unless you are debugging your application. The Execute permissions are scripts only by default. The **Scripts only** permission allows you to read the resource and execute the scripts. The **Scripts and Executables** permission is reserved for the bin directory because it allows the user the ability to run programs on the server.

10. Press the **Configuration** button to get to the Application Configuration Settings. The first tab displays the application mappings. Application mappings are a listing of file extensions and the executable programs that were registered with the Web server to process files. For example, default.aspx, default.ascx, default,aspx.vb, and Web.config are all processed by aspnet_isapi.dll. Click the **Options** tab. The session timeout property, buffering, default language, and script timeout are configured here. Click the **Debugging** tab. You can configure your application to send a detailed ASP error message or a text error message to the client when a script error occurs, and you can also enable script debugging. Figure 9-14 shows the Options and Debugging tabs. Click **Cancel**.

11. Click the **Custom Errors** tab. You can configure your own custom error pages within IIS. The default error pages are located at %systemroot%\help\iisHelp\common. You will learn more about configuring custom error pages later in this chapter.

12. Click the **Directory Security** tab. You can enable anonymous access, basic authentication, or Windows authentication. You can enable IP address and domain name restrictions if you are running Windows Server. You can also configure client and server certificates within IIS. You will learn more about implementing security later in this chapter.

13. Click the **Cancel** button to close the property pages. Close the Internet Information Services window.

9

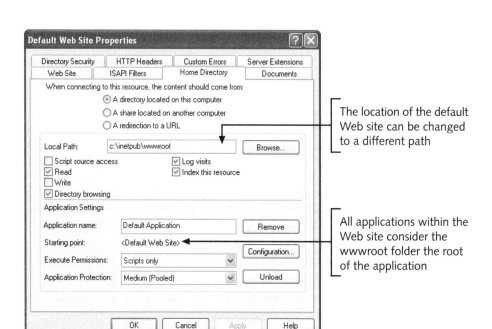

The location of the default
Web site can be changed
to a different path

All applications within the
Web site consider the
wwwroot folder the root
of the application

Figure 9-13   The default Home Directory tab

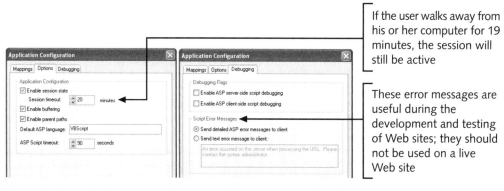

If the user walks away from
his or her computer for 19
minutes, the session will
still be active

These error messages are
useful during the
development and testing
of Web sites; they should
not be used on a live
Web site

Figure 9-14   Configuration choices on the Options and Debugging tabs

APPLICATION CONFIGURATION FILES

In addition to the IIS configuration settings, Web applications contain a series of XML-based configuration files that can be edited in a simple text editor such as Notepad. This text-based configuration file system allows Web server and ASP.NET application settings to be easily replicated across Web servers. This allows Web administrators to easily add a new Web server to the Web farm. Furthermore, Web developers can create their own applications to access the Web settings. They can access the Web settings remotely via the configuration files.

These application configuration files only pertain to ASP.NET resources. They do not provide authorization for other resources such as ASP, HTML, TXT, GIF, and JPEG files. These files are accessible by all users, and can be protected using other techniques, such as Windows NTFS permissions and IIS Web permissions.

Web applications can be configured in the global machine.config file or from within the application configuration files. The application configuration file is named Web.config. The application-level Web.config file is created by default when you create a Web application. Because this file is placed in the root directory of the application, the entire application inherits the settings configured in this file. It is possible to override these settings by placing a Web.config configuration file within a subdirectory, or by configuring the settings within the ASP.NET Web page.

Some settings can be configured only at the root level of the application, and some settings can be configured only at machine level. For example, the Compilation configuration contains a Debug property that is set to False in the default machine.config file and true in the Web.config file. In general, these configuration files are hierarchical. The settings in the Web.config file supercede the machine.config file. However, there are tools that ISPs can use to disable the capability for Web sites to overrule the machine.config settings. You can also modify the configuuration file to create your own configuration settings.

You can read more about configuration inheritence at *http://msdn. microsoft.com/library/en-us/cpguide/html/cpconfigurationinheritence.asp*. The IDP can alter the configuration settings so that they apply only to a specific resource. This is done by using the <location> tag. You can learn more about how to implement the <location> tag at *http://msdn.microsoft. com/library/en-us/cpguide/html/cpconfigurationlocationsettings.asp*.

The Web server contains a machine-level configuration file named machine.cfg. This configuration file is located in C:\WINNT\Microsoft.NET\Framework\v1.0.3705\ CONFIG\machine.config. This file contains configuration settings for the .NET Framework, Windows applications, and Web applications. (*Note*: The version of .NET you are running may vary. Also, in Windows XP this file is located in C:\WINDOWS\ Microsoft.NET\Framework\[version]\CONFIG\machine.config.) The version is the .NET Framework build version, such as **v1.1.4322**. The first line of the file is **<?xml version="1.0" encoding="UTF-8" ?>**. This line of code identifies the version of XML used to create the file. The root node of the file is <configuration>. All configuration settings are contained within this root node.

Because the file is XML compliant, the nodes, properties and values within the file are case sensitive.

9

The **configSections node** is used to identify the configuration sections and section groups. The Web configuration settings are delineated by the system.web section group. The system.web configuration section group is always nested within the system.web section group. There are approximately 30 configuration settings that can be changed within the system.web section group. Each of these settings is nested within the system.web section group. Each Web application configuration setting is configured as a node, and may include child nodes. The default machine.config file contains many preconfigured settings.

The code following this paragraph is the format of the machine.config configuration file. There may be many other nodes in addition to system.web. You can add comments to the file using the HTML comment tags. In this sample, WebConfigurationNodes represents a Web configuration node with a single child node named WebChildNode. Both types of nodes can contain one or more properties. (*Note*: These properties are also referred to as **attributes**.) Any node that does not contain any content can be written with a single tag. The closing tag is represented by the forward slash before the closing angle bracket in the node. The configuration file does not require any particular order for the nodes. However, the nodes must be nested according to XML rules. (*Note*: There are several other nodes not covered here.) In addition, the <location> tag allows you to specify a file or directory to which you can apply separate settings from the application settings.

```
<?xml version="1.0" encoding="UTF-8" ?>
<configuration>
  <configSections>
    <sectionGroup name="system.web">
    </sectionGroup>
  </configSections>
  <system.web>
    <!- - Comment goes here - ->
    <WebConfigurationNodes>
      <WebChildNode/>
    </WebConfigurationNodes>
  </system.web>
</configuration>
```

The following is a list of configuration nodes that are discussed in this chapter:

```
<configuration>
 <appSettings>
 <add/>
 </appsettings>
 <system.web>
 <pages/>
 <httpRuntime/>
 <globalization/>
 <compilation/>
 <trace/>
```

```
<customErrors>
 <error/>
</customErrors>
<sessionState/>
<processModel/>
<identity/>
<machineKey/>
<authentication>
 <forms>
  <credentials/>
 </forms>
 <passport/>
</authentication>
<authorization>
 <allow/>
 <deny/>
</authorization>
<system.web>
<configuration>
```

9

The AppSettings Configuration Node

You can use the **appSettings node** to configure custom key/value pairs known as **application variables**. This allows you to store data that can be used across the entire application. The key is used to retrieve the value at a later time.

In the sample code following this paragraph, a key named SN is created with a value of "Tara Store". A second key named CS is created. The value for CS is a string that stores the database connection string.

```
<appSettings>
  <add key="SN" value="Tara Store" />
  <add key="CS"
     value="Provider=Microsoft.Jet.OLEDB.4.0; ↵
     Password=''; ↵
     User ID=Admin; ↵
     Data Source= ↵
     C:\Inetpub\wwwroot\Chapter9\data\TaraStore.mdb;" />
</appSettings>
```

Within the Web page, you can easily retrieve the values of the application variables. In the following code below, the application variables SN and CS are written to the Web page:

```
Dim SN As String
Dim CS As String
SN = ConfigurationSettings.AppSettings("SN")
CS = ConfigurationSettings.AppSettings("CS")
Response.Write("Store Name: " & SN)
Response.Write("<BR />")
Response.Write("Connection String: " & CS)
```

You can assign values to be shared across all applications. The default appSettings node within the machine.config is as follows:

```
<appSettings>
   <add key="XML File Name" value="myXmlFileName.xml"/>
</appSettings>
```

The Pages Configuration Node

The **pages configuration node** allows you to configure settings that control how content is delivered to the Web page. Many of these settings are often configured at the page level. Using the pages configuration node, you can modify the buffer, enableSessionState, enableViewState, enableViewStateMac, and autoEventWireup properties.

The **buffer** is an area in memory on the server. As a request is processed, the data generated from the response is stored in the buffer. If the **Buffer property** is set to false, the end user sees content generated by the server faster. As a result, they perceive that the server has a faster response time. There is no increase in the actual performance of the Web server when you change the Buffer property to false. However, once content has been sent to the client, the header content is also sent. You cannot change the header content once content has been sent to the client. When you want to redirect the user to another page, the header content must be modified. Therefore, if you have code in your page that redirects the user to another page, you cannot set the buffer to false. Setting the Buffer property to true allows you to store the entire response from the request on the server, until the request has completed processing. If there is an error in your code, buffering the code will help prevent sending an incomplete page out to the browser.

As you learned earlier, the **enableSessionState** property allows you to use the Session capabilities of ASP.NET. You must enable sessions to have access to session variables, session IDs, and HTTP cookies. If you do not plan to use sessions, you can disable this property by setting it to false. You can also set the property to read-only so that you can use sessions, but cannot create new session data. The **enableViewStateMac** property is used to validate data. This property indicates that ASP.NET should run a machine authentication check (MAC) on the encrypted version of the view state to ensure that the data has not been altered on the client. The enableViewStateMac property is set to false by default because the validation method requires substantial server resources. The **enableViewState** property is used to store data in the _VIEWSTATE hidden form field in the Web page.

The code following this paragraph is the default configuration for the pages node in the machine.config file. Like many configuration properties, the pages configuration can also be set within the Web.config file and the within HTML view in the ASP.NET page.

(*Note:* You can configure the nodes using two tags such as `<pages></pages>` or use the single tag method `<pages/>`.)

```
<system.web>
   <pages
       buffer="true"
       enableSessionState="true"
       enableViewState="true"
       enableViewStateMac="true"
       autoEventWireup="true"
       validateRequest="true"
   />
</system.web>
```

Additonal properties can be set within the pages node. **SmartNavigation** allows the user to continue at the row where they left off when he or she refreshes the page. The smartNavigation property is set to false by default. The pageBaseType and userControlBaseType allows you to assign a typename to the property. The default for pageBaseType and userControlBaseType are System.Web.UI.Page and System.Web.UI.UserControl.

The httpRuntime Configuration Node

The **httpRuntime configuration node** sets the executionTimeout, maxRequestLength, and useFullyQualifiedRedirectURL properties. The **executionTimeout** is the time that a resource is allowed to execute before the request times out. The default executionTimeout value is 90 seconds. The **maxRequestLength** is the number of kilobytes that can be accepted from an HTTP request. The default maxRequestLength size is 4096 kilobytes (4 MB). Configuring this property will help you prevent users from uploading large files using HTTP.

Some hackers have been known to send a large number of requests to a Web server to keep the Web server busy. These attacks are called denial of service (DOS). By sending many requests, they stop the Web server from responding to legitimate requests. If you set the maxRequestLength to a smaller number, the hackers won't be able to send a large number of requests to the server.

The **useFullyQualifiedRedirectUrl property** is used to fully qualify the URL when the client has been redirected to a new page. For example, the code `Response.Redirect ("/login.aspx")` redirects the user to a login page using a relative address (/login.aspx). However, many clients, such as mobile phones, require fully qualified URLs when they are redirected. Therefore, if the **useFullyQualifiedRedirectUrl** property is set to true, when the client is redirected, the absolute URL is sent to the client, even if the code in the page identifies a relative address. The enableVersionHeader property sends a header value of X-AspNet-Version with each HTTP request. The code following this paragraph is a sample of the httpRuntime configuration node that would be found in the machine.config file.

Additional information about the default properties that are not discussed here can be found
in the comments within the machine.config file.

```
<httpRuntime
    executionTimeout="90"
    maxRequestLength="4096"
    useFullyQualifiedRedirectUrl="false"
    minFreeThreads="8"
    minLocalRequestFreeThreads="4"
    appRequestQueueLimit="100"
    enableVersionHeader="true"
/>
```

Globalization Configuration Node

Users can configure their computers to support a variety of languages. In U.S. English,
there are 26 alphabetical characters. But many languages use more than 26 alphabetical
characters. The characters on computers using such languages can be displayed in two
ways. You can display the text in a language-specific character set or in Unicode. In
Unicode, each unique character set has its own identity. Therefore, a Unicode-enabled
viewer, such as a browser, can view multiple languages at the same time. Internet
Explorer versions 4, 5, and 6 support the Unicode character set.

Unicode isn't the only possible method for encoding HTTP requests and responses. The
UTF8Encoding class is contained within the `System.Text` namespace. The default
value for encoding is UTF-8. **UTF-8** stands for UCS Transformation Format, 8-bit form,
which means that all Unicode character values are supported. (*Note*: The Code Page property also represents the encoding values. For UTF-8, the code page value is 65001.)

Using ASP.NET, you can configure the Web site to support the local culture and language. The **globalization node** is responsible for setting the encoding standard used for
incoming requests and outgoing responses. The **requestEncoding property** configures
the encoding of incoming requests, while the **responseEncoding property** configures
the encoding of outgoing responses. The **fileEncoding property** is used to identify the
encoding for ASP.NET resources. The following is the default configuration settings for
the globalization node for the machine.config and Web.config files:

```
<globalization
    requestEncoding="utf-8"
    responseEncoding="utf-8"
/>
```

The **Culture** and **uiCulture properties** are used to identify a language and culture
string. Possible values for these properties include en-US for United States English,
en-GB for British English, en-IE for Irish, and fr-FR for French. This property is used

to configure the local settings, such as the language and dates, for over 200 cultures. The following sample code shows the settings for the United States English culture:

```
<globalization
     requestEncoding="utf-8"
     responseEncoding="utf-8"
     culture="en-US"
     uiCulture="en-US"
/>
```

Setting the Culture Property

The globalization settings can also be modified in the Web page. In the Web page, you can display the date to see the effects of the Culture property. In the following exercise, you create a new project and modify the culture configuration properties within a Web page. (*Note*: Because these values are set as properties of the page, they can also be changed dynamically in the code behind the page. For example, when a user logs in, you can check his or her culture preferences and change the culture property to match their preference.)

1. Double-click **France.aspx** in the Solution Explorer window. In the Properties window, change the culture from en-US English (United States) to **fr-FR-French (France)**. Notice the large number of cultures that can be configured.

2. Double-click on the **France.aspx** page to edit the code behind the page. Add the following code to the Page_Load event procedure:

   `lblDT.Text = DateTime.Now.ToLongDateString`

3. Click the **Save All** button. Click **Build** on the menu bar, and then click **Build Solution**.

4. Switch back to the Web page. Right-click on the page, and then click **View in Browser**. Your page should look like the one in Figure 9-15.

5. Close any open pages.

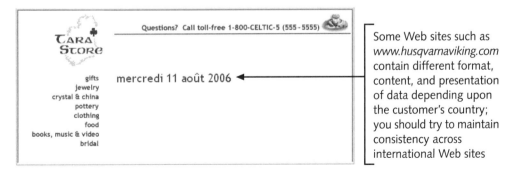

Figure 9-15   Changing the Culture property

Compilation Node Configuration

The **compilation node** contains configuration settings related to the language compilers use to build the application. By default, the compiler used in a Web application in Visual Studio .NET is Visual Basic .NET. However, you can change the default language for the compiler in the compilation node via the **DefaultLanguage property**. In the code following this paragraph, the language is set to Visual Basic .NET. The other language compilers that are installed by default with Visual Studio .NET include C#, J#, VBScript .NET, and Jscript .NET. (*Note*: Additional compilers such as Perl and Java are available.) The **Debug property** is used to configure the application to show the source code files when you are debugging the application. The Debug property is set to false by default in the machine.config file, but it's set to true by default in the Web.config file. Although the compiler builds the application in a .dll file, you still want to have access to the source code files during the debugging process.

By default, data types can be implicitly converted to less precise data types, even if data loss would occur. It would not be useful if the program converted 5.60 to 5 if 5.60 represented currency because .60 cents would be lost. You learned in Chapter 5 that you can use the Strict property in the HTML template or the code behind the page to turn the **Strict property** on, which would disallow implicit conversions. On the other hand, the **Explicit property** requires you to declare your variables before they are used.

You can set the Strict and Explicit properties within the Web.config and machine.config files. (*Note*: Other properties that can be configured within the computer node allow you to further customize how the compiler compiles the code behind the page.) The following is the default configuration for the compilation node within the Web.config file:

```
<compilation defaultLanguage="vb" debug="true" />
```

The Explicit property is turned on by default within the machine.config file. The following is a default configuration for the compilation node within the Web.config file:

```
<compilation debug="false" explicit="true" ↵
defaultLanguage ="vb">
```

You can change the compiler used in the Web page by modifying the language property in the @Page directive. You would need to use the file extension for the code behind the page that was configured for the new language. (*Note*: You would not do this with Web sites created with Visual Studio.NET. If you wanted to use another language, you would add a new project into the solution and select the new language in the template window. Then, the filename and the skeleton sample code in the code behind the page would already be set up for the new language. The location and names of the default languages provided with Visual Studio.NET are listed within the compilation node in the machine.config file.) The following is an example of how you would set the language property within the Web Form:

```
<%@ Page language="vb"%>
```

Trace Node Configuration

As you learned in Chapter 1, tracing is the ability to retrieve data to help identify the data that was communicated during the request or response. The Trace property can be turned on in the page, or in the configuration files in the **trace node**. In the page, you can turn tracing on by specifying `Trace="true"` in the @Page command. Figure 9-16 shows an example of trace results generated when tracing is turned on in a Web page.

Within the Web.config file, tracing can be customized. The **Enabled property** allows the application to turn tracing on. In the machine.config file, the enabled setting is set to false by default. On a production server, you do not want to display the trace results to the visitor. To avoid this, you can set the **localOnly property** to true, so that tracing results are only displayed to the localhost. To view the trace results, you access the Web site using the URL *http://localhost/*. The **traceMode property** allows you to sort trace results based on time using SortByTime or by category using SortByCategory.

The Trace property will append the trace information below the Web page when the page layout uses FlowLayout. If the page uses GridLayout and dynamic positioning, the trace information displayed is intermixed with the page content. In these cases, it's useful to use the trace utility program to obtain the trace information.

The **pageOutput property** allows you to display the trace results with the Web page. If the pageOutput property is set to false, then the output is not displayed with the page. Instead, you can access the tracing data using a trace utility program. The trace results are stored in memory and can later be accessed using the trace utility program. The number of trace results stored is configured using the **requestLimit property**. The default number of trace results stored in memory is 10. The following is the default trace settings for both the Web.config and the machine.config files:

```
<trace
    enabled="false"
    localOnly="true"
    pageOutput="false"
    requestLimit="10"
    traceMode="SortByTime"
/>
```

9

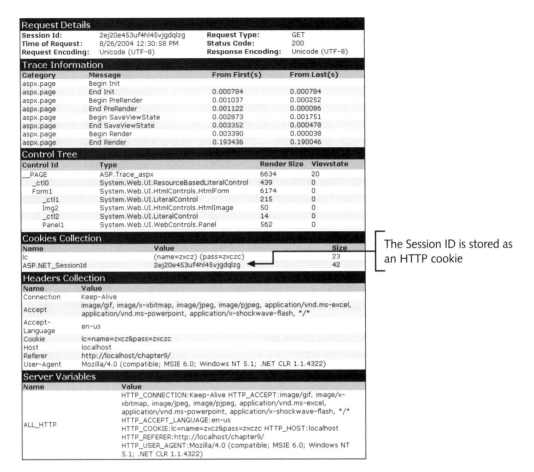

Request Details

Session Id:	2ej20e453uf4hl45vjgdqlzg	Request Type:	GET
Time of Request:	8/26/2004 12:30:58 PM	Status Code:	200
Request Encoding:	Unicode (UTF-8)	Response Encoding:	Unicode (UTF-8)

Trace Information

Category	Message	From First(s)	From Last(s)
aspx.page	Begin Init		
aspx.page	End Init	0.000784	0.000784
aspx.page	Begin PreRender	0.001037	0.000252
aspx.page	End PreRender	0.001122	0.000086
aspx.page	Begin SaveViewState	0.002873	0.001751
aspx.page	End SaveViewState	0.003352	0.000478
aspx.page	Begin Render	0.003390	0.000038
aspx.page	End Render	0.193436	0.190046

Control Tree

Control Id	Type	Render Size	Viewstate
__PAGE	ASP.Trace_aspx	6634	20
_ctl0	System.Web.UI.ResourceBasedLiteralControl	439	0
Form1	System.Web.UI.HtmlControls.HtmlForm	6174	0
_ctl1	System.Web.UI.LiteralControl	215	0
Img2	System.Web.UI.HtmlControls.HtmlImage	50	0
_ctl2	System.Web.UI.LiteralControl	14	0
Panel1	System.Web.UI.WebControls.Panel	562	0

Cookies Collection

Name	Value	Size
lc	(name=zxcz) (pass=zxczc)	23
ASP.NET_SessionId	2ej20e453uf4hl45vjgdqlzg	42

The Session ID is stored as an HTTP cookie

Headers Collection

Name	Value
Connection	Keep-Alive
Accept	image/gif, image/x-xbitmap, image/jpeg, image/pjpeg, application/vnd.ms-excel, application/vnd.ms-powerpoint, application/x-shockwave-flash, */*
Accept-Language	en-us
Cookie	lc=name=zxcz&pass=zxczc
Host	localhost
Referer	http://localhost/chapter9/
User-Agent	Mozilla/4.0 (compatible; MSIE 6.0; Windows NT 5.1; .NET CLR 1.1.4322)

Server Variables

Name	Value
ALL_HTTP	HTTP_CONNECTION:Keep-Alive HTTP_ACCEPT:image/gif, image/x-xbitmap, image/jpeg, image/pjpeg, application/vnd.ms-excel, application/vnd.ms-powerpoint, application/x-shockwave-flash, */* HTTP_ACCEPT_LANGUAGE:en-us HTTP_COOKIE:lc=name=zxcz&pass=zxczc HTTP_HOST:localhost HTTP_REFERER:http://localhost/chapter9/ HTTP_USER_AGENT:Mozilla/4.0 (compatible; MSIE 6.0; Windows NT 5.1; .NET CLR 1.1.4322)

Figure 9-16   A Web page with tracing enabled

The trace node will store the data in the **trace stack**, which can be read by the trace utility program. The .NET class that enables these tracing capabilities is the **TraceContext class**. You can configure your application to send additional data to the trace stack. The **Write method** is used to send information to the trace utility program. The syntax to use the Write method is `Trace.Write("CategoryName","Value")`. CategoryName argument is a string that contains the text label to be displayed in the trace output. The Value argument is a string that contains the value of CategoryName argument. You can use an expression to generate CategoryName or Value. The **Warn method** is used to send information to the trace utility program. The difference between the Write method and the Warn method is that the Warn method sends the output as red text. Therefore, the messages are easily viewed.

For example, in the code that follows this paragraph, the Web page calls a function named GetTotal. Each submit button function passes the price to the GetTotal function. The GetTotal function calculates the product of Price and Quantity and stores the results in a variable named Total. The variables Price, Quantity, and Total are all sent to the trace stack. The Web page then displays the results in the Label control named Order, like so:

```
Dim Total As Integer
Public Function GetTotal(Price as String) As String
    Total = CInt(Quantity.Text) * CInt(Price)
    Order.Text = "Total Cost: $ " & Total.ToString
    Trace.Write("Price: ", Price)
    Trace.Write("Quantity", Quantity.Text)
    Trace.Warn("Total: ", Total.ToString)
    Return Total
End Function
```

To view the trace data, you can use the Trace property, or use the trace utility program called **TraceTool**. You can open this program by going to *http://localhost/approot/ Trace.axd*. (*Note*: It is also available at *localhost/Configuration/Tracing/TraceTool/ trace.axd*.) The values that you add using Response.Write appear in the Category column, and their corresponding values appear in the Message column. The tool provides the trace stack information along with the physical directory of the page being traced. You can enable the Trace feature on any page in any directory even if the enabled property is turned off in the configuration file. It is usually recommended that you disable trace for production applications once the application has been deployed. If you have statements that use Trace.Write, you can leave the commands in the page without having an impact on performance. Later, you may want to use those statements again if you have to debug the application.

Using the Trace Utility Program

In the following exercise, you will set the trace feature for the entire application and then view a Web page that sends information to the trace stack. Then, you will view the trace stack using the TraceTool program.

1. Double-click **Web.config** in the Solution Explorer window.

2. Insert the following code under the comment `<!-- Insert trace settings here. -->`, as shown in Figure 9-17. (*Note*: Only the first part of the Web.config file is shown in the figure.)

```
<trace enabled="true"
    requestLimit="10"
    pageOutput="false"
    traceMode="SortByTime"
    localOnly="true" />
```

```
<?xml version="1.0" encoding="utf-8" ?>
<configuration>
<system.web>
    <globalization requestEncoding="utf-8"
        responseEncoding="utf-8" />
    <compilation defaultLanguage="vb"
        debug="true" />

    <!-- Insert trace settings here. -->
    <trace enabled="true"
        requestLimit="10"
        pageOutput="false"
        traceMode="SortByTime"
        localOnly="true"
    />
    <!-- Insert sessionState settings here. -->
```

You can enable tracing for the entire application or by a single page; set the localOnly property to true to prevent others from accessing the trace data from other locations

Figure 9-17   Setting the trace node in the Web.config file

3. Click the **Save All** button. Click **Build** on the menu bar, and then click **Build Solution**.

4. Double-click **Trace.aspx** in the Solution Explorer window.

5. Right-click the page and select **View in Browser**.

6. In the text box, type **2**. Click the **Add to My Cart** button in the Pendant with Celtic Knot column. The total is calculated and displayed as shown in Figure 9-18.

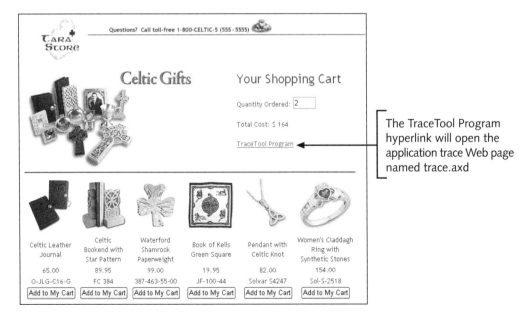

The TraceTool Program hyperlink will open the application trace Web page named trace.axd

Figure 9-18   Celtic Gifts Web page

7. Click the hyperlink labeled **TraceTool Program**. The TraceUtility program appears with two entries.

8. Click **View Details** for the first entry. This is the entry that was created when the Trace.aspx page was first viewed. No content appears in red because no trace messages have been written. Click the **back button** on the menu bar. (*Note*: The back button has a left-pointed blue arrow.)

Click **View Details** for the second entry, as shown in Figure 9-19. This entry was created when the user clicked on the button. The price, quantity, and total are all stored in the trace stack. However, the total is displayed in red text.

9. Close all open pages.

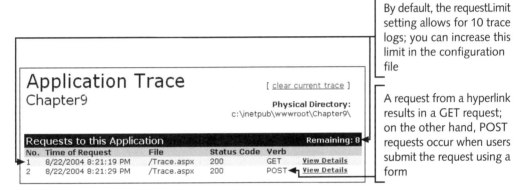

By default, the requestLimit setting allows for 10 trace logs; you can increase this limit in the configuration file

A request from a hyperlink results in a GET request; on the other hand, POST requests occur when users submit the request using a form

Figure 9-19   The TraceTool utility program

CustomErrors Node Configuration

When the user requests a page, the Web server provides the page, and an HTTP status message code indicates the status of the request. If the request is successfully met, the HTTP status code 200 is returned. An HTTP status code 404 indicates that the file requested could not be found. (*Note*: HTTP status codes in the 400s usually indicate a client-related error. HTTP status codes in the 500s usually indicate a server-related error.) The Web server and ASP.NET can be configured to send a Web page to the user indicating that an error has occurred.

Both ASP.NET and IIS provide error pages that describe the error, the error codes, and error messages. The IIS Web pages are located in the C:\winnt\Help\iisHelp\common\ directory. You can use Web Server MMC to configure custom error pages, as shown in Figure 9-20. However, because this tool is often not available to Web developers, custom error pages are seldom used. Furthermore, ASP.NET provides a variety of additional error messages that are not part of IIS. You can create a virtual directory named CustomErrors in which to store your default error pages, and then point the IIS custom error configuration and the ASP.NET configuration to this folder. Then, your application uses a common error message for both ASP.NET and IIS errors.

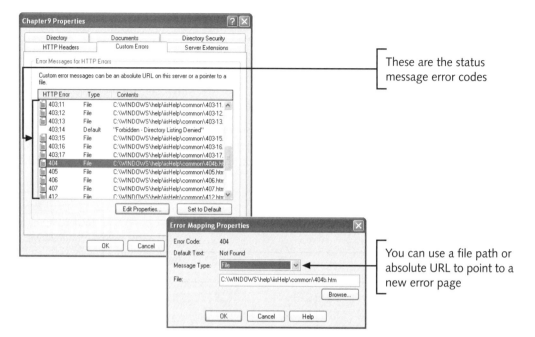

These are the status message error codes

You can use a file path or absolute URL to point to a new error page

Figure 9-20   Configuring custom error pages using the Custom Error property sheet

Instead of displaying static error messages, ASP.NET provides a rich error page. When an error occurs, the error page provides detailed information about stack traces and compilation errors. You can use this information to help determine where the error occurred, and how to correct the error. However, you may not want your visitors to see this information.

You can configure the **customErrors node** to set the mode to **RemoteOnly**, so that the rich error pages are only displayed locally. The RemoteOnly settings can be set to On or Off. If the RemoteOnly setting is **On**, then the application contains custom error pages. If the RemoteOnly setting is **Off**, then the ASP.NET error pages are displayed. The error messages can still be displayed when viewing the Web site using the localhost. But, if the user visits the Web site, and an error occurs, the user is redirected to a default error page or a custom error page. (*Note*: It is recommended that you set the RemoteOnly property to RemoteOnly or On in a production Web server.) You can also set the **defaultRedirect property**, which sets a default error page to be displayed if no applicable custom error page is configured. (*Note*: If an error occurs on the defaultRedirect page, the page does not continually redirect to itself.)

You may want to have access to multiple computers to test the custom error configuration techniques.

You can configure ASP.NET to use a custom error page for each HTTP status code by using the **error node**. The error node property **statusCode** indicates the status code of the error message. The **Redirect property** indicates the page to redirect the user to when the error is detected. The following sample code shows how to configure the default error page and a custom error page for the HTTP status code 404:

```
<customErrors
  mode="RemoteOnly"
  defaultRedirect="/defaultError.aspx"/>
  <error
     statusCode="404"
     redirect="/error404.aspx"/>
</customErrors>
```

 ASP.NET provides the ability to send messages to the Windows error logs. You can use the Application_OnError event handler to send the message to the Windows Event Log. Developers may want to send error messages to the Windows log files because it makes troubleshooting errors easier. You can see how the errors interact with other messages and services.

9

MAINTAINING STATE IN AN ASP.NET APPLICATION

There are several techniques that you can use to maintain state information in your ASP.NET Web applications. All three methods use a unique identifier to recognize the client across Web pages. A common method for maintaining state information in early Internet development was client-side cookies. Cookies are small files stored on the client's system. Another method was storing the identification information in a temporary object on the server. ASP.NET uses Application and Session objects to store data. The Session object allows you to store information on the server, but still requires the browser to support a cookie, called the HTTP cookie. However, this session information is volatile. If the Web server crashes, the session information is unrecoverable. Using ASP.NET you can create cookieless applications. Cookieless applications do not require the user to support client-side or server-side cookies. The identification data is passed with the URL. In this section, you will learn how to create Web applications that use client-side cookies, per session cookies, and cookieless Web applications.

Client-Side Cookies

Client-side cookies maintain information about an individual user across sessions. A **client-side cookie** is a small piece of information that is stored on a client's local computer. The **Cookies collection** is a group of cookies that are sent by the server through the header to the client. The browser application on the client receives the cookie and writes the cookie to the client's file system.

All Web servers have the ability to create a client-side cookie. If you are using Netscape Navigator, all cookies are stored in a single text file named cookies.txt, which is usually located in the root directory of the Netscape application. In Internet Explorer, each cookie is stored in a separate text file. In Windows XP, Internet Explorer stores cookies in C:\Documents and Settings\[UserID]\Cookies.

Because clients can delete their cookies at any time, your Web application should not depend upon the existence of a cookie. Always provide an alternate method for users who elect not to accept cookies, or who delete their cookies. Customers often misunderstand the purpose, value, structure, and security of cookies. You should always create a Web page on your site that informs the user of the privacy and security policies. In this page, you should provide a definition of cookies, inform the user whether the site uses cookies, and if so, indicate what information is stored in the cookie and what the cookie is used for. You should also inform the user that only the server that writes the cookie can read the cookie. TRUSTe (*www.etrust.com*) provides samples of what you might want to include in your privacy and security policy Web page. The following is a list of Web pages that contain more information about cookies, privacy issues, and links to more Web sites that discuss cookies:

- *www.microsoft.com/info/cookies.htm?RLD=291*

- *www.microsoft.com/info/*

- *msdn.microsoft.com/library/default.asp?url=/library/en-us/dninstj/html/cookies.asp*

Most users do not have an accurate understanding of what a cookie is. The cookie file, whether written by Netscape Navigator or Internet Explorer, stores the name of the cookie, the value, and the name of the server that wrote the cookie. Figure 9-21 shows the contents of a client-side cookie. The information stored in a cookie could easily be stored on the server. Storing the cookies with the client provides a means of automating client-side activities, such as the login process form's completion.

It's very useful to provide a sample of what a cookie looks like to the user on the security and privacy page. Cookies are limited in size to 4 KB. Most cookies are about 100–200 bytes in size. The maximum number of cookies allowed is currently 300. If the limit is reached, the oldest cookies are deleted. The maximum disk space for cookies is 1.2 MB, which is about the size of a floppy disk. Today, hard disk drives are available that can hold gigabytes of data. Therefore, cookies do not "eat up" a client's hard drive space. (*Note*: It's more likely that large amounts of hard drive space are used by the browser cache file, which contains all of the graphics and Web pages that the client has visited.)

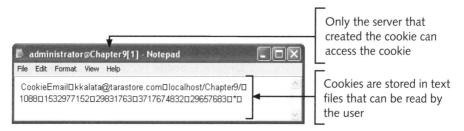

Only the server that created the cookie can access the cookie

Cookies are stored in text files that can be read by the user

Figure 9-21   A client-side cookie written by the Internet Explorer browser

Reading and Writing Client-Side Cookies Using JavaScript

The browser supports a Document object model with its own set of objects, properties, and methods. The Cookie property of the Document object allows you to store and read client-side cookies associated with the document. A cookie consists of the cookie name and a value, separated by an equals sign. For example, you can create a cookie named CookieEmail with the value of kkalata@tarastore.com by writing `document.cookie = "CookieEmail=kkalata@tarastore.com";`. You can assign the cookie an expiration date. The code following this paragraph sets a cookie named CookieEmail with a value of kkalata@tarastore.com, and an expiration date of January 7, 2007, and reads the cookie into a variable named ReadCookie. (*Note*: Each browser handles JavaScript, cookies, and dates differently. Netscape dates end with "GMT" and Internet Explorer dates end with"UTC".)

```
<script language="JavaScript">
document.cookie = "CookieEmail=kkalata@tarastore.com;
    expires =Monday, 07-Jan-07 12:00:00 GMT";
readCookie = document.cookie;
</script>
```

Each cookie name and value pair is separated by a semicolon. You need to separate each pair of cookies, and then separate the name and value.

In the following exercise, you will view a Web page that uses client-side cookies. When the user fills the form and clicks the Create Cookie button, the GetCookie function is called. This writes the cookie using the values passed in the form and then displays the cookie in an alert message box. When the user clicks the Delete Cookie button, the DeleteCookie function deletes the cookie by setting the expiration date to January 1, 2001.

1. Open the **Chapter9** application in Visual Studio .NET if necessary.

2. Double-click **ClientCookies.aspx** in the Solution Explorer window to open the page. Click the **HTML** tab to view the HTML code.

3. Click the **Save All** button. Click **Build** on the menu bar, and then click **Build Solution**.

4. Start your Web browser and enter the URL **http://localhost/chapter9/ ClientCookies.aspx**.

5. Fill in the form with your e-mail address, typing **password** in the password text box, and then click the **Create Cookie** button. An alert message box appears with the value of your cookie. Your page should look similar to the one in Figure 9-22. Your alert box will display the per session cookie known as the ASP.NET Session ID unless you have configured your browser to disallow session cookies. Click **OK** to close the alert message box.

6. To view the cookie, open Windows Explorer. (*Note*: Click **Start**, click **Run**, type **%SystemRoot%\explorer.exe** in the text box, and then click **OK**.) Navigate to your **C:\Documents and Settings\[*username*]\Cookies** folder. (*Note*: The path to your Cookies folder may be different.)

7. Right-click the **Name** column heading and select **Date Created**. A column named Date Created is added to the window. Click the **Date Created** column heading. The cookies will be resorted based on the date.

8. Find the cookie created today labeled [*username*]@Chapter9[1]. Right-click the **[*username*]@Chapter9[1]** file and select **Edit**. The file will open in Notepad. Notice that only the e-mail address was saved in the CookieEmail cookie, along with the application's root path. Because it is a text file, you may not want the user to be able to store the passwords in their cookie file in case other users log into the same computer and may have access to the other users' files.

9. Close the file and then close Windows Explorer.

10. Click the **Delete Cookie** button. The client cookie has been deleted.

11. Close any open pages.

HTTP Cookies

HTTP cookies are cookies created by the Web server rather than the browser. They are used to enable the Web server to identify the client. The SessionID is the value of the HTTP cookie that identifies the client's session. This **SessionID** is used to identify a Session object on the server. The Session object can be used to store session variables such as the user's e-mail address, contact information, purchasing habits, browser properties, and personal preferences. HTTP cookies are also known as **per session cookies** because they identify the session. HTTP cookies are only used during the client's session, and are deleted when the session ends.

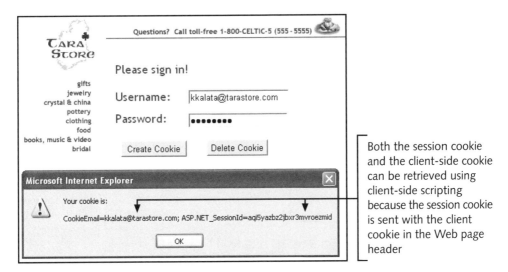

Figure 9-22 Creating a client-side cookie with Visual Studio .NET

By default, ASP and ASP.NET applications are configured to use HTTP cookies. The HTTP cookie is sent in the HTTP header, so it can be retrieved as an HTTP server variable called HTTP_COOKIE. You can view the value of the HTTP cookie and the client cookies when the trace property is turned on. The following is the syntax for retrieving a cookie from the HTTP header using the server variable HTTP_COOKIE from a Web page using the server variables:

```
<% Request.ServerVariables("HTTP_COOKIE") %>
```

Cookie Settings in the Internet Explorer Browser

In some browsers, users can disable client-side cookies, and still allow HTTP cookies. In Internet Explorer version 6.0 the cookie settings are stored in the Privacy Settings, as shown in Figure 9-23. You cannot assume that the client supports HTTP cookies or client-side cookies. Remember that the client can change these settings in the browser, but the programmer can't. (*Note*: If you are configuring an intranet Web site, your system administrator may have a policy about what types of cookies are allowed.)

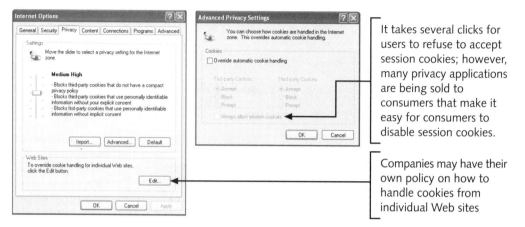

It takes several clicks for users to refuse to accept session cookies; however, many privacy applications are being sold to consumers that make it easy for consumers to disable session cookies.

Companies may have their own policy on how to handle cookies from individual Web sites

Figure 9-23 Changing the cookie setting in Internet Explorer 6

Figure 9-24 shows the various pre-configured cookie settings and the description that is provided to the end user. Notice that they do not include per session cookies. In order to disallow the per session cookies, the user has to access the advanced privacy settings.

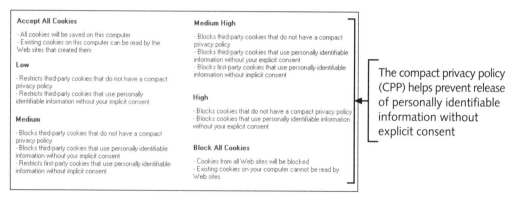

The compact privacy policy (CPP) helps prevent release of personally identifiable information without explicit consent

Figure 9-24 Privacy levels

Today, many Web sites track user information. Users want to allow many of their favorite Web sites to use cookies to provide them with capabilities such as automatic logons. However, after being bombarded with cookies and pop-up messages, they may decide simply to turn off their cookies. An alternative is to specify the domains that are allowed and denied the ability to read and write cookies. Figure 9-25 shows how the user can configure their cookie policy based on the domain name.

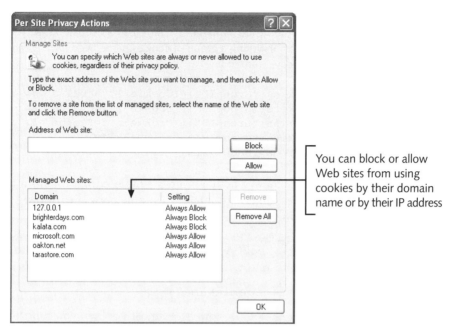

You can block or allow Web sites from using cookies by their domain name or by their IP address

Figure 9-25   Blocking and allowing cookies for individual Web sites

Creating Cookies with ASP.NET

The **HttpCookieCollection object** represents the cookie variables. There are two types of HTTP cookie collections within ASP.NET; both can be accessed via the Cookies object. The first type contains cookies that are passed by the client to the Web server from the Cookies header. The second contains cookies that have been generated on the server and transmitted to the client in the **Set-Cookie header**.

Following this paragraph is the syntax for writing a simple cookie using an absolute date. You can specify the number of days from the current date that you want the cookie to expire. If you expect your visitors to visit daily, then you can set the cookie to expire in "Date.Now.Today.AddDays(1)" days. If your visitors visit monthly, you can set the cookie to expire in "Date.Now.Today.AddDays(30)" days. If you want the browser to delete the cookie, you can specify a date in the past such as "Date.Now.Today.AddDays(-30)" or "July 4, 1776". The browser then deletes the cookie because the cookie has expired.

```
<% Response.Cookies("myCookie") = "value" %>
<% Response.Cookies("myCookie").Expires = "MM DD, YYYY" %>
```

Notice that the Response object, and not the Write method, writes the cookie. The Write method is used to write the value of a string to the Web page. The Response.Cookies method actually sends the cookie to the browser, which in turn writes the cookie to the client's file system.

The named group of cookies is also referred to as a dictionary cookie, and the individual cookies within it are sometimes referred to as cookie keys. The following is the syntax for writing a group of cookies named GroupID, where the cookie expires N days from today:

```
<% Response.Cookies("GroupID")("Cookie_1")="value" %>
<% Response.Cookies("GroupID")("Cookie_2")="value" %>
<% Response.Cookies("GroupID")("Cookie_n")="value" %>
<% Response.Cookies("GroupID").Expires =
      "Date.Now.Today.AddDays(N)" %>
```

You can retrieve a cookie's value—whether from a simple cookie or from a group of cookies—by using the Request object. To retrieve a simple cookie with one value, specify the name of the cookie. One of the benefits of using ASP.NET over client-side scripting is that the Request object parses out the cookie names and values for you. It is easy to retrieve the value of a cookie with one line of code. The following is the syntax for retrieving a simple cookie with one value:

```
<% Request.Cookies("CookieName") %>
```

To retrieve the value of a single cookie from a group of cookies, you must identify the name the cookie group as well as the name of the individual cookie. Below is the syntax for retrieving a single cookie from a group of cookies named GroupID. CookieName_n represents the name of the single cookie. A group cookie can contain multiple cookies, each with a different cookie name.

```
<% Request.Cookies("GroupID")("CookieName_n") %>
```

You can add additional cookies to the HTTP cookies. You can create an additional cookie with the Response object, read the value of the HTTP cookie using the Request object, and display it in a Web page.

In addition to the Request and Response objects, you can use the HttpCookie Collection to create and read cookies. The sample code that follows this paragraph shows how to write a cookie named CookieEmail with the value from a text box named txtEmail. MyCookie is then added to the Cookies Collection using the Add method of the Response object.

```
Dim MyCookie As New HttpCookie("CookieEmail")
MyCookie.Value = txtEmail.Value
Response.Cookies.Add(MyCookie)
```

Maintaining State with Cookies

In the following example, you will create a Web page that maintains state with HTTP cookies using the Response and Request objects. You will create a cookie named gc that contains the user's name, e-mail address, and SessionID. You will read the value of the cookie and write the value to the Web page. When the user clicks the Sign In button, the SignIn_ServerClick procedure will retrieve the values from the form, write out the cookie, display a message to the user, and reset the form values to nothing, as shown in Figure 9-26.

When the user clicks the Display Cookie button, the ShowCookie_ServerClick procedure is called, which will call the DisplayCookie function if there is a cookie named "gc" and which will display the cookie. If the user clicks the Sign Out button, the SignOut_ServerClick procedure will delete the cookie by changing the expiration date and will display a message to the user.

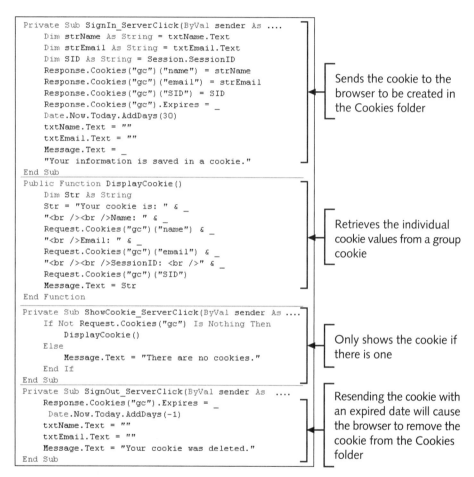

```
Private Sub SignIn_ServerClick(ByVal sender As ....
    Dim strName As String = txtName.Text
    Dim strEmail As String = txtEmail.Text
    Dim SID As String = Session.SessionID
    Response.Cookies("gc")("name") = strName
    Response.Cookies("gc")("email") = strEmail
    Response.Cookies("gc")("SID") = SID
    Response.Cookies("gc").Expires = _
    Date.Now.Today.AddDays(30)
    txtName.Text = ""
    txtEmail.Text = ""
    Message.Text = _
    "Your information is saved in a cookie."
End Sub
Public Function DisplayCookie()
    Dim Str As String
    Str = "Your cookie is: " & _
    "<br /><br />Name: " & _
    Request.Cookies("gc")("name") & _
    "<br />Email: " & _
    Request.Cookies("gc")("email") & _
    "<br /><br />SessionID: <br />" & _
    Request.Cookies("gc")("SID")
    Message.Text = Str
End Function
Private Sub ShowCookie_ServerClick(ByVal sender As ....
    If Not Request.Cookies("gc") Is Nothing Then
        DisplayCookie()
    Else
        Message.Text = "There are no cookies."
    End If
End Sub
Private Sub SignOut_ServerClick(ByVal sender As ....
    Response.Cookies("gc").Expires = _
     Date.Now.Today.AddDays(-1)
    txtName.Text = ""
    txtEmail.Text = ""
    Message.Text = "Your cookie was deleted."
End Sub
```

Sends the cookie to the browser to be created in the Cookies folder

Retrieves the individual cookie values from a group cookie

Only shows the cookie if there is one

Resending the cookie with an expired date will cause the browser to remove the cookie from the Cookies folder

Figure 9-26   Reading, writing, and displaying cookies

1. Open the **Chapter9** project in Visual Studio .NET, if necessary.

2. Double-click **Cookies.aspx** in the Solution Explorer window to open the page. Double-click the **Sign In** button to open the code behind the page.

3. In the SignIn_ServerClick event procedure, add the code that follows this paragraph to retrieve the values from the form. Add a variable to store the SessionID.

```
Dim strName As String = txtName.Text
Dim strEmail As String = txtEmail.Text
Dim SID As String = Session.SessionID
```

4. After the code that you have entered in the preceding step, add the code to write the values to a group of cookies named gc. The individual cookie keys are named name, email, and SID. Set the Expires property to specify when the cookie is deleted.

```
Response.Cookies("gc")("name") = strName
Response.Cookies("gc")("email") = strEmail
Response.Cookies("gc")("SID") = SID
Response.Cookies("gc").Expires = _
 Date.Now.Today.AddDays(30)
 txtName.Text = ""
 txtEmail.Text = ""
 Message.Text = _
 "Your information is saved in a cookie."
```

5. In the DisplayCookie function, add the code to read the cookies and store the results in a variable named Str. Display the value of Str in a text box named Message.

```
Dim Str As String
Str = "Your cookie is: " & _
"<br /><br />Name: " & _
Request.Cookies("gc")("name") & _
"<br />Email: " & _
Request.Cookies("gc")("email") & _
"<br /><br />SessionID: <br/>" & _
Request.Cookies("gc")("SID")
Message.Text = Str
```

6. The code should look as shown in Figure 9-26. Click the **Save All** button. Click **Build** on the menu bar, and then click **Build Solution**.

7. Open your Web browser and enter the URL **http://localhost/Chapter9/ Cookies.aspx**.

Figure 9-27   Using cookies

8. Fill in the form with your name and e-mail address, and click the **Sign In** button. Click the **Display Cookie** button. (*Note*: If a Windows dialog box asks if you want the system to remember the password for this page, click **Cancel**, or **No** in Windows XP.) The text box displays the value of your cookies.

9. Click the **Sign Out** button. Click the **Display Cookie** button. Your cookie has been deleted. Close any open pages.

Maintaining State Without HTTP Cookies

Previous versions of ASP required client support for HTTP cookies. These HTTP cookies were used to link the client's session to the Session object using the SessionID. The SessionID contains several properties. The **Timeout property** specifies when the session ends if no activity occurs. The default value for the session timeout is 20 minutes. The Session property data is stored as a HashTable of key and value pairs. If the Session ended, the session data contained within the session object was also lost. In ASP.NET, the Session object can be configured to store the data outside of the Web server, without requiring HTTP cookies. In ASP.NET, the session configuration is stored in the **sessionState node**, which is configured in the Web.config file. ASP.NET applications can maintain state without HTTP cookies, and can maintain the session data outside of the Web application. Therefore, more robust and reliable applications can be built with ASP.NET.

ASP.NET applications use the HTTP session cookie by default to maintain session data. The **Cookieless property** in the sessionState node in the Web.config file is used to determine if the session key should require cookies. The Cookieless property is set to false by default, which means that the default application requires cookies to maintain session state. Because users can refuse to accept HTTP cookies, the configuration can be set up to support session key management without requiring HTTP cookies. You can configure the application to use cookies or be cookieless, but you can't use both settings within the same application.

You can modify your application to support sessions without requiring HTTP session cookies. The process of creating a cookieless application is known as **cookie munging**. When the Cookieless property is set to true, the Web server appends the SessionID to any requested URL, as shown in Figure 9-28. The SessionID does not contain the session data. The session data is still maintained by the Web server, or outside the Web server. When the next page is requested, the Web server can use the SessionID, which is attached to the URL, to identify the client without requiring the client to have a cookie.

Creating a Cookieless Web Application

In the following example, you will modify your application to support visitors who do not accept HTTP cookies.

1. Open the **Chapter9** application in Visual Studio .NET, if necessary.

2. Double-click **Web.config** in the Solution Explorer window.

3. After the comment <!-- Insert sessionState settings here. -->, type the code that follows this paragraph to set the Cookieless property to true. The time-out property is set to two minutes. (*Note:* You may already have some properties, such as Cookieless and Timeout, set with sessionState. If you do, just modify the Cookies and Timeout properties. Do not create a second sessionState node.)

   ```
   <sessionState cookieless="true" timeout="2" />
   ```

4. Click the **Save All** button. Click **Build** on the menu bar, and then click **Build Solution**.

5. Open your Web browser and enter the URL **http://localhost/chapter9/ Cookieless.aspx**.

6. Fill in the form with your name and e-mail address and click the **Sign In** button. Click the **Display Cookie** button. Your page should look like the one in Figure 9-28. Notice that the SessionID appears within parentheses in the URL as the parent directory for the Web page.

7. In the file Web.config, reset the Cookieless property to false, and the Timeout property to 20.

8. Click the **Save All** button. Click **Build** on the menu bar, and then click **Build Solution**.

9. Close any open pages.

Storing Session Data

You can configure where the Web server stores the session data. In the machine.config and the Web.config files, the **sessionState node** allows you to configure the session management. Storing session data in the Web server memory results in the best perfor-mance. But if the Web server crashes, the data is lost. Therefore, you can configure the Web server to store your session data based on your information and performance needs. The **Mode property** is used to identify which storage method to use to store session data. The Mode property can be set to InProc, SQLServer, StateServer, or Off. Turning the mode to Off turns off session management. It's important to understand that the ses-sion data that is being stored is specific to the ASP.NET application. For example, ses-sion IDs and session variables are stored as session data. Browsers that don't accept HTTP cookies can't take advantage of session state. Therefore, if your visitors are likely to turn off HTTP cookies, you should build your application without using HTTP cookies. You can create your own custom session management application and store the data in the database.

Cookieless applications use cookie munging to combine the user session ID with the URL

Figure 9-28   Creating a cookieless Web application

A good resource that discusses the business application of state management is located at *http://msdn.microsoft.com/library/en-us/dnpag/html/diforwc.asp*.

Using the Web Server to Manage Session State

When the Mode is set to InProc, the data is stored in the Web server process. Because the data is not being sent out of process, this method provides the best performance. You should use this method if you are hosting your Web site on a single server, and if your session data is not critical. This method is not appropriate for a Web farm because the user's request can be redirected to another Web server if the Web server load values change, and the session data would not travel with the request. If you stop and restart the Web Server service, all session data from all sessions will be lost. (*Note*: The Web Server service can be stopped using the Services utility in the Administrative Tools. The Web Service is listed as World Wide Web Publishing. You can also stop and restart the service by using the iisreset command in the command prompt window. This will also stop any ASP.NET application.)

Furthermore, session data can be lost if the application domain or the aspnet_wp.exe process (or the w3wp.exe process for IIS version 6.0) has to restart. The application domain (known as AppDomain) is restarted when the configuration files or the bin directory are modified, when the memory limit setting listed in the processModel node in the configuration file has been reached, or if virus scanning software has modified the configuration files. The **processModel node** allows you to configure the idleTimeout, memoryLimit, and other server process related properties.

The following is a sample sessionState setting to run ASP.NET state management within the Web server process:

```
<sessionState mode="InProc"
    cookieless="true"
    timeout="20"
/>
```

Using State Server to Manage Session State

The **ASP.NET State Server** stores the session data from an ASP.NET application. The ASP.NET State Server is also known as the **State Server**. ASP.NET applications will run without starting the ASP.NET State Server. The ASP.NET program is located at %systemroot%\Microsoft.NET\Framework\[version]\aspnet_state.exe. You can set the Mode property to StateServer to store the data with a Windows service called **StateServer**. To use StateServer, the **aspnet_state service** needs to be running. You can start StateServer by using the DOS commands or the Windows Services utility program. The **stateNetwork Timeout** property is used to specify the number of seconds that the connection between the Web server and the State Server can be idle before the session is dropped. The default value for the stateNetworkTimeout property is 10 seconds. Because the service is run out of process from the Web server, the session data is reliably stored. Although the StateServer is reading the data out of process, generally it is located on the same server. Therefore, the performance is better than if the session data is sent to an external server. The StateServer service can be used across multiple Web servers.

If you select the mode as StateServer, you must also provide the **stateConnectionString**. The stateConnectionString identifies the TCP/IP connection to the State Server. Each network interface card (NIC) is assigned an IP address and up to five port numbers. The **TCP port number** is the connection where applications listen for messages sent to them. For example, the default port for the Web server is 80. So, the Web server listens on port 80 for http messages.

The stateConnectionString set to 127.0.0.1:42424 points to the local State Server. You can use the IP address or domain name to identify the State Server. The IP address 127.0.0.1 is often used to identify the local computer without having to specify the IP address of the NIC card. The IP address 127.0.0.1 is known as the **loopback** address because it always represents the local computer. The default port number for the State Server is 42424. However, any open port can be configured for state management. It is not recommended to use port numbers below 1024 because they are **well-known ports** that have been assigned to commonly used services by the Internet Assigned Numbers Authority (IANA). Ports 1024 through 49151 are registered to commonly used applications such as the State Server. If you assign a port in this range, you must ensure that the port assignment does not conflict with other applications running on the computer. It is recommended to use the default port number, or select a number between 49152 through 65535.

The following is a sample sessionState setting to run ASP.NET state management on a local State Server:

```
<sessionState
    mode="StateServer"
    stateConnectionString="tcpip=127.0.0.1:42424"
    stateNetworkTimeout="10"
    cookieless="false"
    timeout="20"
/>
```

 If you intend to use the same State Server for multiple Web servers, you must change the TCP/IP settings in the Web.config file so that each of the Web servers points to the same State Server. You cannot use the loopback IP address. You must also configure the machine key on each server. The machine key is used to encrypt the data going to the State Server. In order for the Web servers to be able to encrypt the session data, they must all have the same machine key.

 Because the port used by the State Server is the "well-known" port number, it is an easy target for attack by a hacker. You can change the port number by changing the TCP/IP settings. To change the TCP/IP settings you must edit the Windows registry keys. The registry key for the TCP/IP port setting is located in HKEY_LOCAL_MACHINE | System | CurrentControlSet | Services | aspnet_state | Parameters. In the Parameters node, you must click Port in the Name column. In the value data text box, you can enter a new value for the port and click the OK button.

To start the State Server using the command prompt window:

1. Open the command prompt window by clicking **Start**, then clicking **Run**.

2. Type **cmd** in the text box, and then press **Enter**. The command prompt window opens.

3. Type **net start aspnet_state**, and then press **Enter** to start the service. A message will be displayed when the service has been started successfully.

4. Type **net stop aspnet_state**, and then press **Enter** to stop the service. A message will be displayed when the service has been stopped successfully.

5. Close the command prompt window.

 The localhost is considered a trusted Web site by the browser. Therefore, Web pages will allow the localhost to save cookies, use session cookies, and perform other activities unless you specifically configure your browser (in the Internet Options window) not to trust the local computer.

State Server is a Windows service and can therefore be accessed via the Windows Services applet. In the following activity, you will start State Server using the Windows Services window:

1. Click **Start**, point to **Settings**, and then click **Control Panel**. Click **Classic View**, if necessary, to change your view to Classic View.

2. Double-click **Administrative Tools**.

3. Double-click **Services**.

4. In the Name column, double-click **ASP.NET State Service**.

5. To start the StateServer service, click the **Start** button. The keyword started in the Status column shows that the service has been started. (*Note:* You can also click the **Start** button on the Services toolbar. You can also open the ASP.NET State Service dialog box by right-clicking the **ASP.NET State** name and selecting **Properties**.)

6. You can set the service to start manually or automatically by selecting the value in the Startup type drop-down list, as shown in Figure 9-29. Automatic startup means that the service automatically starts whenever the server is restarted. Click **OK**, and then close the Services window.

7. Return to your ASP.NET application in Visual Studio .NET. Edit the **Web.config** file to support the session state parameters. Change the mode to **stateServer**. (*Note:* Use the sample code following this paragraph if you have set up the server using the default settings. The connection string may vary with your server. For example, it may include the port number 42424 to identify the service.)

```
<sessionState
  mode="StateServer"
  stateConnectString="tcpi=127.0.0.1:42424"
  stateNetworkTimeout="10"
  cookieless="false"
  timeout="20"
/>
```

8. Click the **Save All** button. Click **Build** on the menu bar, and then click **Build Solution**.

9. Change the mode in the Web.config file session state mode back to **InProc**.

10. Click the **Save All** button. Click **Build** on the menu bar, and then click **Build Solution**.

11. Close any open pages.

Tip You cannot store a built-in object in a Session object. Therefore, you should retrieve the information desired as a string and then assign it to a session variable.

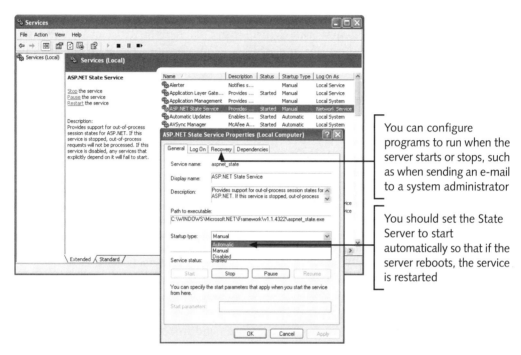

You can configure programs to run when the server starts or stops, such as when sending an e-mail to a system administrator

You should set the State Server to start automatically so that if the server reboots, the service is restarted

9

Figure 9-29   Starting the State Server to store session data

Using SQL Server to Manage Session State

If you set the mode to SQLServer, you can also use SQL Server to store your session data. SQL Server is run out of process, which means that the SQL Service runs outside of the Web Service, in its own memory space. Although using SQL Server to store session data does not provide the same performance as using the StateServer or InProc configuration, it does offer reliable storage of session data. SQL Server can be run on the same Windows server or another Windows server. You must identify the connection string used to connect to the SQL Server database. The connection string identifies the TCP/IP address and the authentication data required to connect to the database. The connection string must be a valid System.Data.SqlClient.SqlConnection string, minus the Initial Catalog.

 Tip Even if you use SQL Server or State Server to manage your session state, session data may be lost in a load balanced Web farm environment unless you configure the application path of the Web site to be the same for all of the Web servers in the Web farm. The application path is case sensitive.

To use SQLServer mode, you first must configure SQL Server to create the ASPState and tempdb databases. A SQL script file contains SQL commands to create, populate, and delete databases. The .NET Framework comes with a SQL script file, which is used to create the databases, tables, and several stored procedures required to store session data in SQL Server. The installation SQL script file is located by default in %systemroot%\ Microsoft.NET\Framework\[*version*]\InstallSqlState.sql. This script will also create the ASPStateTempApplications and ASPStateTempSessions tables in the tempdb database. Figure 9-30 shows Design view of the ASPStateTempSessions table. The table stores the Session ID in the SessionId column. The session data is stored in the SessionItemShort field. This field data type is varbinary, which means that you won't be able to view the data using the Data Connections in the Server Explorer window.

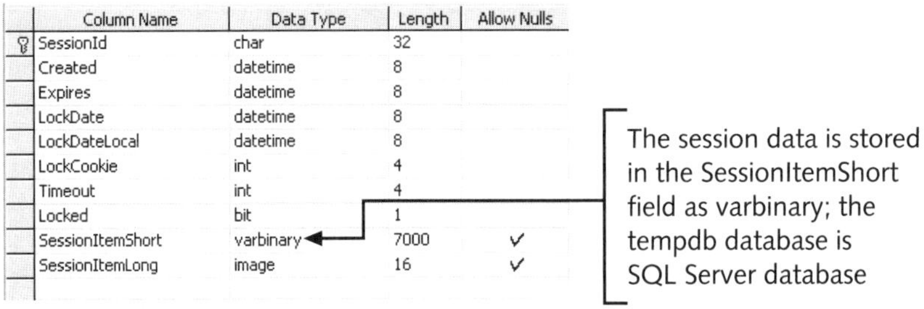

Column Name	Data Type	Length	Allow Nulls
SessionId	char	32	
Created	datetime	8	
Expires	datetime	8	
LockDate	datetime	8	
LockDateLocal	datetime	8	
LockCookie	int	4	
Timeout	int	4	
Locked	bit	1	
SessionItemShort	varbinary	7000	✓
SessionItemLong	image	16	✓

The session data is stored in the SessionItemShort field as varbinary; the tempdb database is SQL Server database

Figure 9-30

The following is the syntax for the command line statement that executes the installation SQL script. You can use the name localhost if the MSDE version of SQL Server is the only version installed on the server. Otherwise, you should use the full name of the server, *MACHINENAME*\NetSDK, or a fully qualified domain name.

```
OSQL -S [server name] -U [user] -P [password]
<InstallSqlState.sql
```

You must configure the sessionState configuration setting to run ASP.NET state management on a local SQL Server. The default TCP port number for SQL Server is 1433. If you have changed the SQL Server port number, you will have to insert the port number into the sqlConnectionString. You can pass the user ID and password, or you can use integrated Windows authentication by setting the sqlConnectionString property to "datasource=localhost;Integrated Security=SSPI;". The data source is the name of the SQL Server. You can pass the full name of the server or the IP address. If it is the only SQL Server on the local machine, you can pass the loopback address (127.0.0.1) or the keyword localhost. You can also use MACHINENAME\NetSDK to identify the SQL Server that is installed with the MSDE. The following is a sample sessionState configuration setting to run ASP.NET state management on a local SQL Server:

```
<sessionState
  mode="SQLServer"
  cookieless="false"
```

```
    timeout="20"
    sqlConnectionString="datasource=MACHINENAME\NetSDK;
    userid=sa;password=password"
/>
```

 Your path to OSQL.exe may be located in a different directory. If you installed the full version of SQL Server, the OSQL.exe file can be located in C:\Program Files\Microsoft SQL Server\80\Tools\Binn\.

The following exercise will use the command line tool that SQL Server provides to execute the SQL Server.

1. Log on to the server as the system administrator or as a user that belongs to the system administrators group. You must have administrative permissions to install the SQL Server service.

2. Go to the command prompt window by clicking **Start** then clicking **Run**. Type in **cmd** and press **Enter**.

3. Change directory to locate the installation scripts. The installation script is a script written in T-SQL, which installs SQL Server and sets up the session database. To change the directory, type **CD C:\WINNT\Microsoft.net \Framework\[Version]**. (*Note*: Version is the current version of .NET. You can have multiple versions of the .NET Framework on the same computer.)

4. On the command line prompt, type **OSQL -S localhost -U sa -P password <InstallSqlState.sql**. This is the command to start the service and send the output to the SQL Server. After the script runs, it will send output messages to the command prompt window. When the command line prompt is redisplayed, close the command prompt window.

To configure your Web server to use SQL Server to store the session state information, you must modify the configuration files. In general the application configuration files take precedence over the machine configuration files. You can assign localhost, the IP address, (local)\NetSDK, or MACHINENAME\NetSDK to the data source property. Check with your system administrator for the preferred method of connecting to your SQL Server database.

SQL Server can authenticate the user by verifying a user name and password or by using Windows integrated security. **Integrated security** represents that the SQL Server will use integrated Windows security to authenticate requests to access the database. Within the sqlConnectionString property, you must pass a user ID and password, or insert "Integrated Security=SSPI". The following is an example of using Windows integrated security as the authentication method for SQL Server:

```
<sessionState
    mode="SQLServer"
    sqlConnectionString="data source=localhost;
    Integrated Security=SSPI;"
```

```
        cookieless="false"
        timeout="20"
/>
```

Some system administrators may set up the computer so that only the settings within the machine.config file take precedence. The machine configuration file is located at %SystemRoot%\Microsoft.NET\Framework\[Version]\CONFIG\machine.config. The current version of the .NET Framework is v1.1.4322. The sessionState mode is set to InProc by default and must be changed to SQLServer. The **sqlConnectionString** property contains the connection string used to locate the SQL Server that contains the ASPState and tempdb databases. You can edit the machine.config file using a simple text editor such as Notepad. To open Notepad and edit the file, open a command prompt window and run the following command and then modify the sessionState property:

```
%SystemRoot%\NOTEPAD.EXE
%SystemRoot%\Microsoft.NET\Framework\
[Version]\CONFIG\machine.config
```

In the following exercise you will change the default configuration for the Chapter9 application. using the application configuration file.

1. Using Visual Studio .NET open the **Project9** solution if it is not already open.

2. Double-click the **Web.config** file in the Solution Explorer window to open the file, if it is not already open.

3. Delete the current <sessionState ... /> configuration node.

4. Type the following code below the comment that says <!-- Insert sessionState settings here. -->:

```
<!-- Insert sessionState settings here. -->
<sessionState
mode="SQLServer"
sqlConnectionString=
    "data source=MACHINENAME\NetSDK;
    user id=sa;password=password"
cookieless="false"
timeout="20"
/>
```

5. Click the **Save All** button. Go to the **Build** menu and select **Build Solution**.

In the next exercise, you will verify that the state information is being delivered to the SQL Server.

1. Right-click on **SessionSetVariables.aspx** in the Solution Explorer window and select **View in Browser**.

2. Fill in your name and e-mail address in the form and click the **Sign In** button.

3. Click the **Display Session Variables** button to view the session variables in the SessionGetVariables.aspx page.

4. In the Server Explorer window, right-click **Data Connections** and select **Add Connection**.

5. In the Data Link Properties window, enter the name of the SQL Server, such as *MACHINENAME*\NetSDK. Type **sa** and **password** in the User name and password text boxes. Check the **Allow saving password** check box. Select **tempdb** from the drop-down list and click the **OK** button. The connection appears in the Data Connections list.

6. Double-click *MACHINENAME***NetSDK.tempdb.dbo** in the Data Connections, and then double-click **Tables**.

7. Double-click **ASPStateTempSessions** to view the session data. The value of the SessionId in the table should match the Session ID in the SessionGetVariables.aspx page, as shown in Figure 9-31.

8. Close any open windows.

9

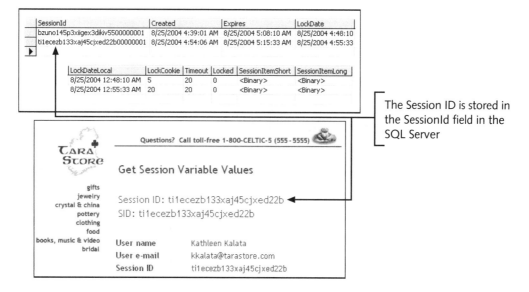

SessionId	Created	Expires	LockDate
bzuno145p3xiigex3dikiv5500000001	8/25/2004 4:39:01 AM	8/25/2004 5:08:10 AM	8/25/2004 4:48:10
ti1ecezb133xaj45cjxed22b00000001	8/25/2004 4:54:06 AM	8/25/2004 5:15:33 AM	8/25/2004 4:55:33

LockDateLocal	LockCookie	Timeout	Locked	SessionItemShort	SessionItemLong
8/25/2004 12:48:10 AM	5	20	0	<Binary>	<Binary>
8/25/2004 12:55:33 AM	20	20	0	<Binary>	<Binary>

The Session ID is stored in the SessionId field in the SQL Server

Questions? Call toll-free 1-800-CELTIC-5 (555 - 5555)

TARA Store

Get Session Variable Values

gifts
jewelry
crystal & china
pottery
clothing
food
books, music & video
bridal

Session ID: ti1ecezb133xaj45cjxed22b
SID: ti1ecezb133xaj45cjxed22b

User name   Kathleen Kalata
User e-mail   kkalata@tarastore.com
Session ID   ti1ecezb133xaj45cjxed22b

Figure 9-31   Storing session data using SQL Server

ASP.NET Security Methods

There are several ways to protect your ASP.NET Web applications. You can configure the application security settings in the machine.config and Web.config files. The two main principles of security are authentication and authorization. **Authentication** is the process of validating the identity of the request. (*Note:* Although the request is from a user, it is the request, not the user, that is authenticated. There are newer methods, such as biotechnological ones, that allow you to validate the user's identity. For example, some computer applications require users to submit their fingerprints or retinal images. However, this requires that additional hardware and software be installed on the client's workstation and the server.) The Authentication node's Mode property can be set to Windows, Passport, Forms, or None. The Authentication node includes the requireSSL and slidingExpiration properties. The requireSSL property is set to true to require the browser to send information using Secure Sockets Layer (SSL). The data, such as the value of cookies, is sent to the server and encrypted, the latter of which protects hackers from intercepting them and reading them over the Internet transport layers. The slidingExpiration property is set to true, which allows the authentication cookie to reset on each subsequent request so that the user would not have to be reauthenticated. The slidingExpiration property is set to false by default. The timeout would then be a sliding value, changing with each user request.

The Identity Node

The configuration files contain an **identity node** that can be used to impersonate a Windows user account. The **impersonate property** is used to indicate if impersonation is allowed. The impersonate property is set to false by default. Because the client does not have to log in with a separate account, this is considered a security risk The code following this paragraph is the default identity node in the machine configuration file. If you set impersonate to true, you will need to rely on Microsoft Internet Information Services (IIS) to authenticate the user. Impersonation is disabled by default in the machine.config file. You can pass a userName and password parameter in the identity node. If the userName is an empty string, it automatically implies that the application will use the IIS user account.

```
<identity impersonate="false" userName="" password=""/>
```

MachineKey Node Configuration

The **machineKey node** is used to identify a value and method to encrypt data on the server. The machineKey node allows you to set the values for encryption and decryption. The **validationKey** is used as part of the hash algorithm, so only ASP.NET applications that have the validationKey can use the data. Using the validationKey guarantees that the data is valid. The length of the validationKey must be between 40 and 128 hexadecimal characters. The validation property identifies what type of hash is to be created. Possible values for the validation type include MD5, SHA1, and 3DES. 3DES is the strongest algorithm for creating a hash value. The **decryptionKey** is used to guarantee that nontrusted sources can't read the text.

If you are using a single Web server, do not change the configuration file settings for the machineKey. You can use the AutoGenerate value for the validationKey and decryptionKey, like so:

```
<machineKey>
    validationKey= "D7564A7D6747E74CD4543636A544E643C3D36
    336C64"
    decryptionKey= "C2342B23C43E2D12124BA12366EF12312B123
    1CA23D"
    validation="SHA1"
    isolateApplications="false"
</machineKey>
```

The only time you need to specify the machineKey properties is when your Web server is part of a Web farm. The other Web servers in the Web farm need to access the data that the Web server generates. Therefore, all Web servers in a Web farm must have the same values set for the validationKeys and the decryptionKeys. (*Note:* They do not have to have the same value for both the validationKey and the decryptionKey, as long as the values are consistent across the Web farm.) Below are the default machineKey configuration settings.

```
<machineKey
    validationKey="AutoGenerate"
    decryptionKey="AutoGenerate"
    validation="SHA1"
/>
```

Authenticating Users with a Custom Authentication

To build your own custom authentication method, select None as the value for the Authentication node. You can build your own authentication methods such as validating the username and password with a hashed value.

Authenticating Users with Passport

The Authentication mode can also be set to Passport. **Passport** is a single sign-on passport identity system created by Microsoft. In a Web site, the browser collects the user's credentials and sends them to the Passport service. The Passport service authenticates the user and sends a cookie back. The benefit to the user is that he or she only has to log in once to access multiple resources and services. The benefit to the administrator is that he or she does not have to recreate the same account on every computer. The administrator can also use Active Directory to set up an account on a collection of Windows servers called a forest. You can learn more about Passport at *www.passport.com*. The sample code below shows the configuration settings for using the Passport service. When the Authentication mode is set to passport, the passport child node can be used. The redirectURL property of the passport node is used to provide an internal page or URL to redirect the user to when the request is not authenticated, or if the user has not logged in with the Passport service. The value of the redirectURL is typically the Passport login page. Passport requires that the Passport SDK be installed on the Web server. Although Passport is compatible with all browsers, it adds an external dependency for the authentication process. If any problems occur with the Passport server, it will adversely affect your Web site. You should build into your Web site procedures to use an alternative validation method if your Passport server is not working properly.

```
<authentication mode="passport">
    <passport redirectURL="gohere"/>
</authentication>
```

Authenticating Users with Windows Authentication

Windows authentication is best used for intranet Web sites where uses already have user accounts on the Windows server. The user must use the Microsoft Internet Explorer browser to view the Web site. Only this browser supports the Windows authentication mode. Users will view a login screen requesting their Windows account user name and password. There are several ways you can set the application to use Windows authentication:

- NTFS File and folder security properties using Windows Explorer
- Web site security properties using the Internet Information Services management tool
- Web application settings using the Web and machine configuration files

You can configure the server to disable the anonymous user so that all visitors must be authenticated by the server using their own valid Windows user accounts. If you use Windows authentication, the username and password are not sent over the Internet. Instead the information is used to generate a hash value that is sent over the Internet. The server knows the username and password and can therefore recreate the hash value. If the values are equal, the user is authenticated.

NTFS File and Folder Security Permissions

As you learned in Chapter 4, you can set the NTFS permissions to use only Windows authentication by setting the folder and file properties. You can add or delete users, or change their access permissions or group membership. If you are setting access permissions on a folder, the access permissions by default will apply to all of the items and subfolders. To set the folder and file permissions to use Windows authentication, you would do the following:

1. Open Windows Explorer.
2. Navigate to the individual folder or file.

3. Right-click the item, and then select Properties.

4. Click the Security tab.

5. Set the security permissions and click Apply.

NTFS permissions that can be assigned to users or groups are as follows:

- Full Control – modify, add, move, and delete files, and their properties, and directories; change permissions settings for all files and subdirectories

- Modify – view and modify files and file properties; add and delete files

- Read & Execute – run executable files, run scripts such as server-side VBScript and JavaScript

- List Folder Contents – view a listing of a folder

- Read Users – view files and file properties

- Write Users – write to a file; used to publish with FrontPage extensions

- No Access – no access to the resource

9

System administrators should maintain detailed documentation about the permissions assigned to users and groups.

When the user goes to the Web site from a remote computer, if Windows authentication is enabled, the Windows connect window opens. If they do not login with a valid user name and password, an access denied error message is displayed in the browser. You can customize the error message by modifying the default error page, by changing the default error page to a custom error page in the Custom Error tab in the Web site property pages, or by configuring the customErrors node in the configuration file to use a specific error message for error 401.2.

During development, if you are working on the local Web server, it is more difficult to test your Web site access security. If you change the setting in the MMC to Windows authentication, the login screen will not appear, because you are already logged in to the local computer with a valid Windows user account. Even if you log in as a different user, you will still be automatically authenticated because all user accounts belong to the Users group, and the Users group is authenticated for the Web site.

Web Server Permissions

You can set the authentication method to Windows and configure additional Web server permissions using the Internet Information Services (IIS) management tool, which is the Microsoft Management Console (MMC). The **Directory Security** tab in the Web site properties allows you to set the Web site access permissions, as shown in Figure 9-32. You can assign specific users access to the Web site using user names and passwords. (*Note*: If you use server software such as Windows Server 2003, you can set access based on a specific IP address, range of IP addresses, or domain name to IP addresses and domain names. This is useful for intranet Web applications where the IP addresses of the users are known.)

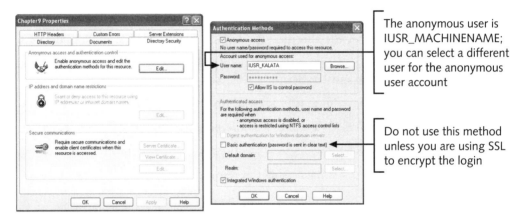

The anonymous user is IUSR_MACHINENAME; you can select a different user for the anonymous user account

Do not use this method unless you are using SSL to encrypt the login

Figure 9-32 Web site authentication methods

By default, browsers are assigned to the anonymous user account called the **Internet Guest Account** to verify the user. This account is named IUSR_*MACHINENAME*, where *MACHINENAME* is the name of the server.

If you change the Web server permissions to **basic authentication**, the user will need to enter their Windows username and password in the login window. However, their account information is sent as clear text over the Internet, which could be intercepted over the Internet by hackers using tools such as packet analyzers. Only set the permissions to basic authentication if you use SSL to encrypt the login page.

To set the folder and file permissions to use Windows authentication in the Web server property pages, do the following:

1. Open the **Internet Information Services (IIS)** management tool, which is the Microsoft Management Console (MMC).

2. Open the property pages for the Web application.

3. Click the **Security** tab.

4. Click **Edit** under Anonymous access and authentication control.

5. Deselect the **Anonymous access** check box. Only Integrated Windows authentication should be checked.

6. Click **OK**. Click **OK**, which applies the new settings.

Web Server Configuration Files

Sometimes Web programmers may not have local access to the server, and therefore cannot set the file and folder security properties using NTFS. The solution is to set these properties using the Web configuration files using the authentication and authorization nodes. When you set the Authentication mode to Windows, you are requiring that the application use Windows authentication, like so:

```
<authentication mode="Windows">
```

> If you set the permissions using Web server configuration files, the user will be allowed access to that resource. Windows is the default mode for the authentication node in both the application and machine configuration files.

In the following exercise, you will set the Chapter9 application to use Windows authentication and configure the users allowed to access the application.

1. Open your Chapter9 solution.

2. Double-click the **WindowsAuthentication.aspx** page in the Solution Explorer window.

3. Right-click the **WindowsAuthentication.aspx** page and select **View in Browser**. See Figure 9-33. The first welcome message does not recognize a user. The page uses the ASPNET account to process the page.

4. Double-click the **Web.config** file in the Solution Explorer window.

5. The authentication is set to Windows by default, and the authorization is set to <allow users="*" />, which means that the user is authenticated using the anonymous account and is a member of the Users group. Insert a blank line after the closing authentication node tag. On this blank line type **<identity impersonate="true" />**.

6. In the authorization node, replace the code <allow users="*" /> with the code that follows this paragraph. (*Note*: If you are not the administrator or member of the Administrators group, change the role and users to one that you have access to.)

```
<allow roles="BUILTIN\Administrators"
     users="BUILTIN\Administrator" />
<deny users="*" />
```

7. Click the **Save All** button. Go to the **Build** menu and select **Build** Solution.

8. Click the **Browse – WindowsAuthentication** tab. Right-click the page and select **Refresh Browser**. If you are a member of the Administrators group, your page will be displayed as shown in the second page in Figure 9-33. Notice that the welcome message now recognizes the user. Otherwise, a login page will appear.

9. Close all pages.

9

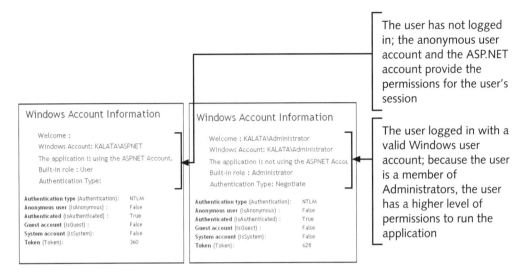

Figure 9-33   Retrieving information about Windows user accounts

 If you have another account that is not a member of the Administrators group, log into that account and view the WindowsAuthentication.aspx page in the browser. You will be prompted by the login window. If you attempt to log in with an invalid user, the Web browser will display the "Access is denied" error message.

 The Web.config file is saved in the solution files as WebWindows.config. The rest of this chapter will alter several of the same sections within the configuration file. The configuration files are saved so that you can refer to them at a later time. You cannot go back and do a previous exercise unless you use the correct Web.config file.

The code behind the page uses the WinID variable to store the WindowsIdentity object that will provide details about the user account. Therefore, at the top of the page the System.Security.Principal namespace that contains this object must be imported. The WindowsIdentity.GetCurrent method provides the current user account, as shown in the following code:

```
Dim WinID As WindowsIdentity
WinID = WindowsIdentity.GetCurrent
```

Various properties about the user can be retrieved, such as the authentication type, authenticated status, and name, as shown in the following code:

```
Label1.Text = WinID.AuthenticationType.ToString
Label2.Text = WinID.IsAuthenticated.ToString
Label3.Text = "Windows Account: " & WinID.Name
```

You can also use the Context object to obtain information about the user. The following code provides the user's name and authentication type:

```
Label4.Text = "Welcome : " & Context.User.Identity.Name
Label5.Text = "Authentication Type: " & _
    Context.User.Identity.AuthenticationType.ToString
```

The wp variable can be used to store the WindowsPrincipal object, using the current user account. The WindowsPrincipal provides access to methods that interact with the Windows security system, such as IsInRole. IsInRole will allow you to check if the user is a member of a specific role. You can determine if they are a member of a role using the role name or the numeric value that represents the role, as shown in the following code:

```
Dim wp As New WindowsPrincipal(WinID)
Label6.Text =  "Administrator"  & _
wp.IsInRole(WindowsBuiltInRole.Administrator
Label7.Text = "Backup Operator" & wp.IsInRole(551)
```

 If the user is logged on using Windows, you can also retrieve user information using the Request.ServerVariables("AUTH_USER") property.

Authorization Node Configuration

Authorization is the process of ensuring that you can only access the resources made available to you by the system administrators. The Windows NTFS file system allows you to set permissions on individual files and folders using an **access control list (ACL)**. The ACL determines who has the rights to read, write, modify, and delete resources. Each user who accesses a resource on the server is using a valid Windows account.

The authorization node is used to identify which resources can be accessed after the user is authenticated. The **allow node** is used to configure users that are allowed to access the application. The **deny node** is used to configure users that are not allowed to access the application. The **Users property** is used to identify the user. The wildcard * is used to identify all users. The wildcard ? is used to identify the anonymous user. A name may be provided to explicitly configure a user's access to the application's resources. The **Roles property** is used to identify a group of users. Groups of users are defined as a role in the Windows Active Directory. You can configure several users at the same time by separating the list of users with a comma, as shown in the code that follows this paragraph. If you set the authorization to deny for a user, and he or she attempts to access the resource, the application will return a 401 status code error message.

```
<authorization>
    <allow users="Joan, John"
    roles="Administrator, Customer"/>
    <deny users="?" roles="BlackList"/>
</authorization>
```

You can assign a verb to the allow and deny tags, which identifies the HTTP verbs to which the tag applies. Possible values for the verb property include GET, HEAD, and POST. The following code is a sample of the authorization node and how to insert the verb property. (*Note*: Don't forget that the configuration files are case sensitive. The verbs are typed in all uppercase characters.)

```
<authorization>
    <allow verb="GET" users="*"/>
    <allow verb="GET" users="kkalata"/>
    <allow verb="POST" roles="BUILTIN\Administrators"/>
    <deny verb="POST" users="*"/>
</authorization>
```

The users and roles configured in the authorization node are Windows accounts. Your applications will be more scalable if you use roles to assign access permissions. You can explicitly assign the user or group by specifying the [*domain name*]\[*user name*]. If you use a format called Active Directory to store your user data, you can display your user names and group names using the X.500 format, as shown in the following code:

```
<authorization>
  <deny users="jody@windsong.corp.tarastore.com" />
  <allow roles ="CN=Mulligan Storm,CN=FTE_northamerica,
  CN=Users, DC=windsong,DC=corp,
  DC=tarastore,DC=com" />
</authorization>
```

The two basic ways that developers implement authorization are role-based and resource-based. With **resource-based authorization**, individual resources are assigned specific permissions using the Windows NTFS permissions. For example, in an intranet application, a file named salary.aspx containing sensitive information would be explicitly assigned read access for the manager of a department. Each employee would then be assigned no access, so that they would not be able to read the data in the file. Resource-based authorization is not scalable and cannot take advantage of connection pooling, so it will use up more of the server memory resources.

Rather than assign permissions to the file for each user, you can use **role-based authorization**. Users are assigned to groups, which are then assigned permission to resources. Therefore the manager would be in one group, and all the employees would be in a second group. In addition to being a more scalable solution, this is also a better solution for managing users. In the case of, for example, a school, students enroll and drop classes throughout the semester. The application can assign students when they enroll to membership in the students group. Then, they would not have to change permission to the student resources each time a student enrolled.

The recommended strategy for role-based authorization is to authenticate the user in the front end of the Web application. Users, when they are entered into the system, are mapped to roles. These roles are assigned to operations such as accessing an application.

They are not usually assigned specific permissions to individual resource files. In this way, if files change within the application, you do not need to modify the permissions. The application would contain specific permission to access databases. You would not use a user account to access the database.

Authenticating Users with Forms Authentication

Forms authentication is a cookie-based authentication method. When you log in, using an ASP.NET form, the Web server checks the IP address and domain in the host header of the request.

 The Web server running on Windows Server 2003 can be configured to deny or allow user access to the Web server based on the client's IP address or domain name. Although this is one way to filter unwanted visitors, it does not prevent hackers from visiting your Web site. Unfortunately, experienced hackers can send a fake IP address in the header of the TCP/IP packet.

Once the Web server has validated the user's IP address, the Web server determines if the anonymous account is enabled. If the anonymous user account is enabled, then IIS passes the request to ASP.NET. ASP.NET determines if an authentication cookie is present in the TCP/IP header packet. If there is no cookie, the client is redirected to the login page. The user must submit credentials and be authenticated. Once the user has been authenticated, a cookie is added to the header packet. After a user has been authenticated, forms authentication uses an HTTP cookie to identify future requests. When ASP.NET has validated that there is a valid authentication cookie in the header, it checks to see if the user is authorized to access the resource. If the user has been authorized, the resource is sent to the client.

The user may be validated using the credential list within the configuration files, or the request may be validated against an XML file, a database, an in-memory structure, an LDAP directory, or even a Web service. A Web service is an application that is sent over HTTP using SOAP. The Web developer needs to know what login information to send to the Web service, and what information is returned, which indicates if the user is a valid account.

Forms Node Configuration

When the authentication mode is set to Forms, the child node forms may be configured. The **form child node** contains several properties that configure the HTTP cookie. The **Name property** is used to identify the cookie that contains the ID of the user. The default name is .ASPXAUTH. The **Path property** is the path that is valid for the cookie. The cookie is only visible to the path of the server that is identified in this property. The Default Path property is "/" because the server can access the cookie from any directory. The path value in the cookie is case sensitive. Timeout is the valid duration of the cookie. **Timeout** is a sliding value because each time a request is made, the value is reset. The default time-out value is 30 minutes. The **loginUrl** is the page to redirect the user to if he or she has not been authenticated or has been denied authentication. The default is "login.aspx". You have to create the login.aspx page, or change the loginUrl value to your login page.

The **Protection property** is used to protect the data in the HTTP cookie. The possible values for the Protection property are All, None, Encryption, and Validation. The first time the user sends a username and password, the cookie has not been created. Therefore, you must use SSL to encrypt the login information until the HTTP cookie is generated. There is no username or password stored in the HTTP cookie. The HTTP cookie merely identifies the client. If the Protection property is set to **None**, the HTTP cookie is stored as clear text. None is used only when the login is used for personalization purposes. When the Protection property is set to **Encryption**, the cookie is encrypted but the data is not validated. The application will encrypt the HTTP cookie. However, the encrypted cookie is simply an encrypted session ticket. When the Protection property is set to **Validation**, the data is validated but cookie is not encrypted. When the Protection property is set to **All**, both data validation and encryption are used. The default Protection property is all. The encryption of the data is performed using the machine key (*Note*: Triple Data Encryption Standard (TripleDES) is used if it's available and if the machine key is at least 48 bytes long. DES was developed by IBM in about 1974 and was adopted as a national standard in 1977. It is used to encrypt data. However, DES can be broken in less than 3.5 hours. Triple DES is a newer version of DES and is more secure than the original DES.) You must identify the encryption keys used to encrypt the HTTP cookie in the machine.config file.

Credentials Node Configuration

The **credentials node** is an optional child node of the forms node. The credentials node is used to provide the credentials for users that may access the application resources. The **PasswordFormat property** allows you to specify the encryption method used to encrypt the credentials. The possible values are Clear, SHA1, and MD5. SHA1 and MD5 store the password as a hash value.

The **user node** is a child node of the credentials node used to identify users. The **Name property** identifies the username. The **Password property** identifies the user's password. The method used to store the password is identified in the passwordFormat property.

```
<authentication>
    <forms
        name=".ASPXAUTH"
        loginUrl="login.aspx"
        protection="All"
        timeout="30"
        path="/" >
        <credentials passwordFormat="SHA1">
            <user name="User1" password="password1"/>
            <user name="User2" password="password2"/>
        </credentials>
    </forms>
</authentication>
```

The passwordFormat attribute is required. Using this simple forms authentication method is only recommended for small sites that do not have a high security requirement such as a small membership organization where financial or personal data is not stored. The user does not have to be a valid user account. You are creating the user information here. In the following exercise, you will use the CreateHashValue.aspx page to create a hash value for your password, as shown in Figure 9-34.

1. In the Solution Explorer window, right-click the **CreateHashValue.aspx** page and select **View in Browser**.

2. The SHA1 hashing algorithm is selected for you by default. In the password text box, type **pwd**, and click the **Create a Hash Value** button.

3. The hash value is displayed in the Label control. This is the value you would enter in the password property in the user node.

4. Close the window.

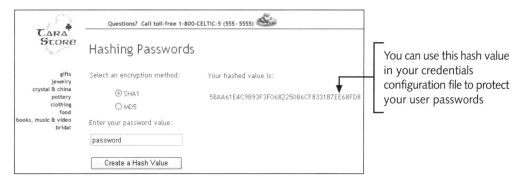

Figure 9-34   Hashing passwords

Once the user is validated, you can access that user's identity information. The sample code displays the user's name and the authentication method used in the Web page. (*Note:* This code could be placed in the Page_Load event handler or in a function.)

```
If User.identity.IsAuthenticated then
    Message.Text = "Welcome Member: " & _
    User.identity.name & _
    ". You were authenticated using: " & _
    User.identity.AuthenticationType & "."
Else
    Message.Text = "Welcome Stranger!"
End if
```

You should provide a method for users to log out, such as a logout button. You can create a click event handler that logs the user out of the application and destroys the temporary HTTP cookie. The sample code that follows this paragraph logs out the user when the user clicks a button named DoLogOut. (*Note*: You must import the System.Web.Security namespace into the application.)

```
Public Function DoLogOut(s as Object, e as EventArgs)
    FormsAuthentication.Signout()
    Response.Clear
    Response.Redirect("login.aspx")
End Function
```

Storing User Credentials in an XML File

The users credentials file is used to store user authentication data. You can create an XML file to store user information such as e-mail address and password, and later retrieve this information when the user is validated. The code that follows this paragraph is a sample of a users credentials file named XMLUserEmail.xml. You can validate the user credentials with static data, from the configuration file, from an XML file, or from a database.

```
<userlist>
  <user>
    <email>kkalata</email>
    <password>painter</password>
  </user>
  <user>
    <email>jdribben</email>
    <password>rosewood</password>
  </user>
</userlist>
```

To validate the user, in the code behind the page for the login Web Form, you must import the System.Web.Security, System.Data, System.Data.SqlClient, System.Xml, and System.IO namespaces. You must retrieve the values from the login form and assign them to a string variable. Then, you will create a DataSet object named ds which will be used to store the XML data file. Then, you will create a FileStream object named fs. FileStream objects are used to retrieve data from a file. You will learn more about this object in Chapter 12. You then pass the URL of the XML file as a parameter to a FileStream object. Then, use the ReadXml method of the DataSet object to retrieve the data and populate the DataSet with the data. After closing the FileStream object, you must use the DataTable object and DataRow object to search for the user. If the user e-mail is found, retrieve the password and compare it to the password that the user entered. If they do not match, redirect them to the form; otherwise, redirect them to the original Web page. Figure 9-35 shows a sample of how you could validate the user with an XML document.

```
Dim formpwd As String = UserPass.Value
Dim ue As String = UserEmail.Value
Dim email As String = "User='" & ue & "'"
Dim ds As DataSet = New DataSet
Dim fs As FileStream = New _
FileStream(Server.MapPath("XMLUserEmail.xml"), _
FileMode.Open, FileAccess.Read)
Dim reader As StreamReader = New StreamReader(fs)
ds.ReadXml(reader)
fs.Close()
Dim users As DataTable = ds.Tables(0)
Dim matches() As DataRow = users.Select(ue)
If (Not IsDBNull(matches)) And (matches.Length > 0) Then
    Dim row As DataRow = matches(0)
    Dim xmlpwd As String = CStr(row("Password"))
    If (0 <> String.Compare(xmlpwd, formpwd, False)) Then
        Message.Text = "We couldn't locate your login."
    Else
        FormsAuthentication.RedirectFromLoginPage _
        (ue, Persist.Checked)
    End If
End If
```

The FileStream object provides access to the StreamReader object; the ReadXML method of the DataSet object retrieves the data from the XML file and inserts it into a DataTable object

If there is a user, the code verifies that the passwords match

Figure 9-35   Building a login page using forms authentication with XML

9

You do not have to create the same names for the root, parent, or child nodes, but you do have to comply with the XML standards. Another method is to name the first node based on the user name, and the value would be the user password, as shown in the code that follows this paragraph. Your code to retrieve these values will be different than the code to retrieve the values in the previous code snippet.

```
<userlist>
    <kkalata>painter</kkalata>
    <jdribben>rosewood</jdribben>
</userlist>
```

Forms Authentication Using Credentials

In the following exercise, you will validate the user with the user account information in the credentials node. When the user requests a protected resource from the Web server such as SimpleFormsAuthentication.aspx and if there is no authorization cookie, the Web server redirects the request to a logon page, SimpleLogin.aspx. The URL for the redirection includes the querystring RETURNURL=/SimpleFormsAuthentication.aspx so that the logon page knows where the protected resource resides. For directories under the root, the character code %2f is used for representing forward slash in the URL. (*Note:* You can use SSL to protect the user's logon information from being sent as clear text.) After the user enters his or her user name and password and submits the form, the SimpleLogin.aspx page validates the user login information. If the user is validated, the browser is redirected to the original protected resource. An authentication ticket is issued as an authentication cookie so that the user will not have to return to the logon page. The http header sends "Set-Cookie: ASPXTICKET=*ABC123*;Path=/", where *ABC123* is the cookie ID, and

/ represents the root level of the Web server. (*Note:* The cookie is case sensitive. If you set the Path to a specific folder, the Path case must match the folder name.)

1. Double-click the **Web.config** file in the Solution Explorer window.

2. Delete the entire authentication node **<authentication mode= "Windows" />** and type the code following this paragraph. (*Note:* The Web.config file is case sensitive.) The password for kkalata is painter and the password for student is password.

```
<authentication mode="Forms" >
    <forms name=".SIMPLELOGIN"
        loginUrl="/Chapter9/SimpleLogin.aspx"
        path="/"
        protection="All"
        timeout="20">
      <credentials passwordFormat="SHA1" >
        <user name = "kkalata"
          password =
            "32562DB2022ABCC6384939403AA882ABB954
            2D04" />
        <user name = "student"
          password =
            "5BAA61E4C9B93F3F0682250B6CF8331B7EE6
            8FD8" />
      </credentials>
    </forms>
</authentication>
```

3. Delete the entire node **<identity impersonate="true" />**.

4. Locate the authorization node. Delete the entire **<allow ... />** tag. Change the deny tag to **<deny users="?" />**, which will deny the anonymous user account.

5. Click the **Save All** button.

6. Right-click the **SimpleFormsAuthentication.aspx** page and select **View in Browser**. You are redirected to the SimpleLogin.aspx page. Type **student** and **password** as the user name and password in the text boxes and then click the **Sign In** button. You will be validated against the credentials file and redirected to the originally requested page.

7. Close any open windows.

The Web.config file is saved in the solution files as WebFormsSimple.config. The rest of this chapter will alter several of the same sections within the configuration file. The configuration files are saved so that you can refer to them at a later time. You cannot go back and do a previous exercise unless you use the correct Web.config file.

Forms Authentication Using an XML File

In the following exercise, you create an XML file that retrieves the user's credentials. The general process is to retrieve the user login information, retrieve the XML data, and locate the user within the XML file. Then, if the user appears, validate the user. If the user is not validated, he or she is redirected by the Web configuration file to the login page. You will add a user to the XML file and change the configuration files to reflect the new user authentication model.

1. Double-click **XMLUsers.xml** in the Solution Explorer window to open the page, and then add a username and password to the list of users above the user named kkalata. The username and password is as follows:

```
<student>password</student>
```

2. Click the **Save All** button and close the file.

3. Double-click the **Web.config** file in the Solution Explorer window. Delete the entire **<authentication>...</authentication>** node and type the code shown after this paragraph. (*Note:* The Web.config file is case sensitive. Be sure to enter Forms, not forms, as the value.)

```
<authentication mode="Forms">
  <forms name=".XMLLOGIN"
  loginUrl="/Chapter9/XMLLogin.aspx"
  path="/"
  protection="All"
  timeout="20">
  </forms>
</authentication>
```

4. Click the **Save All** button and close the file.

In the next step, you will modify the login page to import the relevant namespaces, retrieve the values from the form, and compare the values to the XML file.

1. In the Solution Explorer window, double-click the **XMLLogin.aspx** page. On the page, double-click the button labeled **Sign In**. The code behind the page opens in the SignIn_ServerClick event procedure. In the first line of code at the top of the page, add the Imports statements to import the namespaces required to connect to XML files, as shown in the following code:

```
Imports System.Web.Security
Imports System.Xml
Imports System.IO
```

2. In the SignIn_ServerClick procedure, type the code to retrieve the values from the form and assign them to variables.

```
Dim pwd As String = Password.Value
Dim user As String = Username.Value
```

9

3. After the code from the previous step, type the code below that will create an XMLDocument object based on the XMLUsers.xml file. Then, use the GetElementsByTagName method to search for the username in the first nodes, like so:

```
Dim myFile As String = _
 Server.MapPath("XMLUsers.xml").ToString
Dim xmlDoc As New XmlDocument
 xmlDoc.Load(myFile)
Dim UserNode As XmlNodeList = _
 xmlDoc.GetElementsByTagName(user)
```

4. After the code from the previous step, type the code following this paragraph. The code will compare the password entered by the user with the password that is stored as the value of the node. If there is a match, then they are authenticated and redirected to the original page.

```
If Not Usernode Is Nothing Then
    If pwd = _
     UserNode(0).Firstchild().Value Then
FormsAuthentication.RedirectFromLoginPage _
(user, Persist.Checked)
    End If
End If
```

5. Click the **Save All** button and close the file.

The last step is to test forms authentication using an XML document with the XMLFormsAuthentication.aspx page.

1. Click the **Save All** button. Click **Build** on the menu bar, and then click **Build Solution**.

2. Open your Web browser and enter the URL **http://localhost/Chapter9/ XMLFormsAuthentication.aspx**. Because you are not yet authenticated, you are redirected to the XMLLogin.aspx page.

3. Fill in the login information that you entered in the XMLUsers.xml document, and click **Sign In**. A message welcomes you to the Web site. Click the **Log Off** button. You are redirected to the XMLLogin.aspx page. The Context.User.Identity.Name code causes the user name that the user entered to be displayed in the welcome message. If you had enter a fake name, no error message would appear. The login form will be redisplayed.

It's important to remember that you should always validate forms that are used to authenticate users or insert data into a database. You can use the Web Controls to validate the form controls.

4. Close any open pages.

Forms Authentication Using a Database

You can also authenticate your resources using a relational database. The process is similar to retrieving the values from the XML file. You must first retrieve the values from the Web page and store them in variables. Then, you must identify the connection string and the connection that is used to access the database. Then, retrieve the values from the database that match the values in the form. Set the Boolean variable to indicate that the user was authenticated. In the steps that follow, you will import the login database page, create the database, and configure the Web.config file.

1. Right-click **Data Connections** in Server Explorer, and then click **Create New SQL Server Database**. The Server text box should read *MachineName***NETSDK**. In the New Database Name text box, type **Webusers**. Click the **Use SQL Server Authentication** radio button. In the Login Name text box enter **sa**. Type **password** in the Password text box and click **OK**. A second window may open that prompts you for your password again. Enter **sa** in the Login ID text box and then enter **password** in the Password text box, and click **OK** again. (*Note:* Your system administrator can provide your login information for you. Some systems require Windows NT integrated security.)

2. Expand the **Webusers** database. Right-click **Tables**, and then select **New Table**.

3. In the Column Name column, enter **UserEmail** with the data type **varchar** and length **50**. Deselect the **Allow null** check box.

4. In the Column Name column, enter **UserPass** with the data type **varchar** and length **50**. Deselect the **Allow null** check box.

Your ASP.NET account must have permission to access every database you create. You may be prompted to re-enter your password because the password is not automatically stored with the data connection when you create the database using the Visual Studio.NET. You can disconnect the data connection, and then add the connection again, which would allow you to check the Allow saving password check box.

5. Click the **Save All** button. In the Choose Name window, enter **Users** as the name of the table, and then click **OK**. Close the table structure window.

6. In the Server Explorer window, under the WebUsers database connection, right-click **Stored Procedures**, and then click **New Stored Procedure**. Select all the text and press **Delete**. Then, enter the following:

```
Create PROCEDURE dbo.InsertData
AS
INSERT INTO users (UserEmail, UserPass )
    VALUES ('student', 'password')
INSERT INTO users (UserEmail, UserPass)
    VALUES ('kkalata', 'painter')
```

9

```
INSERT INTO users (UserEmail, UserPass)
    VALUES ('jdoherty', 'rosewood')
INSERT INTO users (UserEmail, UserPass)
    VALUES ('lshea', 'barley')
INSERT INTO users (UserEmail, UserPass)
    VALUES ('tgreen', 'grayslake')
INSERT INTO users (UserEmail, UserPass)
    VALUES ('mcavanagh', 'fisherman')
INSERT INTO users (UserEmail, UserPass)
    VALUES ('bmcintosh', 'candlelight')
RETURN
```

7. Click the **Save All** button. With the file open, right-click inside the stored procedure, and then click **Run Stored Procedure**. A window may open that prompts you for your password again. Enter **password** in the Password text box and click **OK** again. The data is inserted into the table. The Output Window opens and shows that seven records were affected by the stored procedure. There were 7 records added to the table.

8. Click the **Save All** button, and then close all the files. Click **Build** on the menu bar, and then click **Build Solution**.

9. Double-click **Web.config** in the Solution Explorer window to open the file. Delete the entire authentication node **<authentication>...</authentication>** node and type the following code:

```
<authentication mode="Forms">
  <forms name=".DBLOGIN"
  loginUrl="/Chapter9/DBLogin.aspx"
  path="/"
  protection="All"
  timeout="20">
  </forms>
</authentication>
```

10. Click the **Save All** button, and then close the file.

In the next set of steps, you will create the code in the login page to retrieve the form values and compare them with the data in the database.

1. In the Solution Explorer window, double-click **DBLogin.aspx** to open the page. On the page, double-click the button labeled **Sign In**. The code behind the page opens in the SignIn_ServerClick event procedure. In the first line of code in the page, add the Imports statements to import the Web.Security and Data namespaces.

```
Imports System.Web.Security
Imports System.Data
Imports System.Data.SqlClient
```

2. In the SignIn_ServerClick event procedure, enter the code that follows this
   paragraph to create a connection string to the database and to retrieve the values
   from the form. strUsr contains the username, and strPwd contains the user's
   password. Create a Boolean variable named blnIsAuth that stores the user's
   authentication status. The user is not authenticated by default. (*Note:* The
   connection string for SqlClient does not have to have the Provider identified.
   Your connection string will vary with the type of authentication that your SQL
   Server requires.)

```
Dim CS As String
CS = _
"user id=sa;password=password; " & _
"data source=(local)\NetSDK;" & _
"persist security info=True;" & _
"initial catalog=WebUsers;"
Dim strUsr As String = txtUsr.Value
Dim strPwd As String = txtPwd.Value
Dim blnIsAuth As Boolean = False
```

3. Create a SQL string to retrieve the user records as follows:

```
Dim strSQL As String
strSQL = "SELECT * FROM Users WHERE UserEmail='" _
    & strUsr & "' AND UserPass='" & strPwd & "'"
```

4. Enter the code that follows this paragraph. The code uses the Try-Catch
   procedure to create the database objects and retrieve the records. Create the
   Connection object and open the connection. Create the Command object and
   the DataReader object. Connect to the database with the DataReader object
   and read in the records. If there is a record, then set the Boolean value to True.

```
Try
        Dim objCN As New SqlClient.SqlConnection(CS)
        objCN.Open()
        Dim objCM As New SqlClient.SqlCommand(strSQL, objCN)
        Dim objDR As SqlClient.SqlDataReader
        objDR = objCM.ExecuteReader()
        If objDR.Read() Then
            blnIsAuth = True
        End If
        objDR.Close()
        objCN.Close()
```

5. Enter the code that follows this paragraph. The code displays an error message if an error occurs. This is helpful if there is a problem with connection
   to the database, column names, or other database related errors.

```
Catch objError As Exception
        Message.Text = "<b>* An Error occurred</b>.<br/>" _
        & objError.Message & "<br/>" & objError.Source
        Exit Sub
End Try
```

9

6. Enter the code that follows this paragraph. If the blnIsAuth variable is true, then redirect the user to the login page that is configured in the Forms child node in the authentication node in the Web configuration file. You must send a Boolean value to indicate if the user's authentication information should persist across browser sessions. If the user is not authenticated, display a custom error message inside the Message label in the Web page.

```
If blnIsAuth Then
 FormsAuthentication.RedirectFromLoginPage _
  (strUsr, Persist.Checked)
 Else
  Message.Text = _
  "We couldn't locate your login " & _
  "information.<br />" & _
  "Please try to log in again.<br />"
End If
```

7. Click the **Save All** button. Click **Build** on the menu bar, and then click **Build Solution**.

8. Open your Web browser and enter the URL **http://localhost/Chapter9/ DBFormsAuthentication.aspx**. The page displays a hyperlink back to the DBLogin.aspx page.

9. Fill in your login information, and then click the **Sign In** button. A message welcomes you to the Web site. Click the **Log Off** button. The page redirects back to the login page because you are no longer authenticated.

10. In the Web.config file, change the settings back to Windows authentication and allow all users, as shown in the following code:

```
<!--Insert authentication settings here. -->
<authentication mode="Windows"/>

<!--Insert authorization settings here. -->
<authorization>
    <allow users="*" />
</authorization>
```

11. Click the **Save All** button. Click **Build** on the menu bar, and then click **Build Solution**. Close any open pages.

Forms authentication is generally used for protecting the Web site and redirecting the user to the default.aspx page. Therefore, you may experience error messages that say the default.aspx page is not found. In a real application, you should name the default page default.aspx.

CHAPTER SUMMARY

❑ A Web application is a group of files and folders. The IIS Web server software configures the Web application using the Internet Services Manager, or you can configure it via the Web application configuration files.

❑ The machine.config file maintains information that is used across .NET applications. Within this file, the Web application is configured within the system.web node.

❑ The Web.config file configures the Web application. The Web.config file is an XML-compliant file that can be edited with a text editor. The configurations that are commonly configured in the Web.config file include state management, application timeout, application variables, globalization settings, default compiler language, trace mode, and custom error pages.

❑ The SessionID property is assigned by the server, and provides a way to identify the client during the user session. Sessions require the user to support HTTP cookies.

❑ A cookie can be used to maintain information across multiple sessions for a specific user. The cookie is a text file that is stored on the client's computer.

❑ Your Web sites should educate and inform users about the use of cookies, and about how the cookie affects their computer system. The cookie is passed in the HTTP header with the other HTTP server variables.

❑ Cookies can store single values, and multiple cookies can be stored in a named group of cookies. The cookie is written using the Response object, and retrieved using the Request object. The group of cookies is stored in the HTTPCookieCollection.

❑ You can store session data within the Web server process, within the State Server, or in a SQL Server database. State Server is a Windows service that must be turned on before session data can be stored in the State Server. If the Web server crashes, any session data within the State Server or SQL Server persists. The State Server and SQL Server can be used to store session data for a Web farm if the Web servers are configured to use the same server and machine key. The machine encrypts and decrypts data on the server.

❑ Authentication is the process of validating the identity of the request. Authorization is the process of validating the user access privileges to the resources.

❑ You can configure Web applications to support various types of authentication. Anonymous authentication means that the user does not have to log in with a special account. The Internet Guest Account represents the client. Basic authentication sends the login data as clear text. Windows authentication allows the user to log in without sending his or her login over the Internet. Forms authentication is a new technique in ASP.NET to protect the Web application. You can configure forms authentication in the Web.config file.

❑ Authorization within an ASP.NET application is conducted via the Web.config file or via the Windows NTFS permissions.

9

Review Questions

1. Which method of authentication is available with ASP.NET?

   a. forms authentication

   b. Windows authentication

   c. basic authentication

   d. all of the above

2. Which form of cookies is also known as HTTP cookies?

   a. response cookies

   b. ASP cookies

   c. per session cookies

   d. session cookies

3. A group of files and folders located under the Web applications root directory is called a _____.

   a. Web application

   b. Web directory

   c. Web folder

   d. none of the above

4. A(n) _____ is a unique identifier created by the Web server to maintain the identity of the client.

   a. Session GUID

   b. SessionID

   c. e-mail address

   d. CookieID

5. A(n) _____ is used to inform the user about the type of information that is being collected about the user, and to inform the user what is being done with that information.

   a. privacy policy

   b. security policy

   c. access policy

   d. all of the above

6. Which tool is used to configure IIS?

   a. Windows Scripting Host

   b. Internet Service Manager

   c. HTMLA

   d. all of the above

7. The _____ is used to store most of the IIS configuration data.

a. registry

b. metabase

c. database

d. Oracle

8. What log format provides extended properties?

a. W3C Extended Log File Format

b. ODBC

c. Microsoft IIS Format

d. all of the above

9. _____ is the default directory for the log files for the IIS Web server.

a. Window\LogFiles

b. Documents and Settings\LogFiles

c. Window\System32\LogFiles

d. WINNT\System32\LogFiles

10. Which permission is required to run ASP pages?

a. Write

b. Script

c. Execute

d. a and b

11. The _____ file is the configuration file for the Web server for ASP.NET applications.

a. machine.config

b. Web.config

c. global.asa

d. none of the above

12. The _____ is the root node in the Web application configuration file.

a. configuration node

b. System.Web node

c. Web node

d. WebConfigurationNodes node

9

13. The enableSessionState function is configured in the _____ node configuration.

    a. Pages

    b. HTTPRuntime

    c. AppSettings

    d. Globalization

14. The _____ function is used to store data in the _VIEWSTATE hidden form field.

    a. enableViewState

    b. enableViewStateMac

    c. enableSessionState

    d. autoEventWireUp

15. The default value for executionTimeout is _____.

    a. 20

    b. 90

    c. 404

    d. 4096

16. Which of the following would create a new application setting?

    a. <add key="StoreName" value="Tara Store"/>

    b. <add key.value="StoreName" text="Tara Store"/>

    c. <add field="StoreName" value="Tara Store"/>

    d. <add name="StoreName" text="Tara Store"/>

17. Which code sample retrieves an application setting named StoreName?

    a. ConfigurationSettings.AppSettings("StoreName")

    b. AppSettings("StoreName").Value

    c. ConfigurationSettings("StoreName").Text

    d. ConfigurationSettings("StoreName").Value

18. The _____ property is used to restrict trace results to the Web server console.

    a. localhost

    b. localOnly

    c. disabled

    d. pageOutput

19. The HTTP status message code _____ indicates the success of the HTTP request.

    a. 200

    b. 202

    c. 404

    d. 500

20. Your UserID is KALA9876. Client-side cookies are stored in the _____ directory.

    a. C:\Documents and Settings\KALA9876\Cookies

    b. C:\Windows\Cookies\KALA9876\

    c. C:\Program Files\Internet Explorer\KALA9876\Cookies

    d. C:\KALA9876\Cookies

21. The _____ object represents the client's cookie variables.

    a. HttpCollection

    b. ResponseCookieCollection

    c. CookiesCollections

    d. HttpCookieCollection

22. The Windows service used to store session data is called _____.

    a. SQL Server

    b. Oracle

    c. Session Server

    d. State Server

23. Your computer's name is DarkStar. The name of the Internet Guest Account is _____.

    a. IUSRDarkStar

    b. localhost

    c. IUSR_Guest

    d. IUSR_DarkStar

24. Which type of authentication sends the username and password as clear text over the Internet?

    a. anonymous authentication

    b. basic authentication

    c. Windows authentication

    d. all of the above

HANDS-ON PROJECTS

Project 9-1

In this project, you will create a page that educates the user about cookies.

1. Research the Internet to learn more about cookies. Visit five Web pages that discuss cookies.

2. Open your **Project9** in Visual Studio .NET and create a Web page called **Ch9Proj1.aspx**.

3. Add a heading that says **What You Should Know About Cookies**.

4. Write a paragraph that describes what a cookie is, what a cookie is used for, and what you will do with the information contained in the cookie. Describe the security information that relates to reading and writing cookies.

5. Add a heading that says **Cookie Resources**. Then, create a list of links to five or more Web pages on the Internet that discuss cookies. Format the list as a bulleted list.

6. Add a heading formatted as Heading 2, centered-aligned that says **Your Cookie**.

7. Use the code that follows this paragraph to display the cookies that have been written from your domain to the client's computer using the HTTP_COOKIE server variable. The ASP Session cookie is displayed to the user along with any other cookies that have been created by your domain.

```
Here is the cookie that has been written
to your computer from this domain: <br /><br />
<% = Request.ServerVariables("HTTP_COOKIE") %>
```

8. Modify the Web page's appearance with your favorite fonts, colors, and images. You can also modify the layout using a table, line breaks, blockquotes, or other HTML or ASP.NET tags.

9. Save the Web page as **Ch9Proj1.aspx**.

10. View the Web page in the browser. Print out the Web page and the HTML code.

Project 9-2

In this project, you will create a privacy policy.

1. Visit the TRUSTe Web site (*www.truste.com*). Visit Privacy Policies page at *www.truste.org/about/privacy_guidelines.php*. Click each link and read the document. Read the Model Privacy Policy Disclosures at *www.truste.org/docs/Model_Privacy_Policy_Disclosures.doc*. Read the Privacy Whitepaper at *www.truste.org/pdf/WriteAGreatPrivacyPolicy.pdf*.

2. Visit at least four Web sites that discuss privacy.

3. Locate at least three Web sites that contain privacy policies.

4. Open your **Project9** in Visual Studio .NET and create a Web page named **Ch9Proj2.aspx**.

5. Add a heading that says **Privacy Policy Resources**. List the sites you visited.

6. Add a heading that says **Sample Privacy Policy**. Then add a bulleted list of sample policies on the Internet.

7. Add a heading that says **Our Privacy Policy**. Then add at least one paragraph describing your Web site's privacy policy.

8. Modify the Web page's appearance with your favorite fonts, colors, and images. Use blockquote tags, line breaks, tables, or other HTML tags to format the layout of the page.

9. Save the Web page as **Ch9Proj2.aspx**.

10. View the Web page in the browser. Print out the Web page and the HTML code.

Project 9-3

In this project, you will create a page with a registration form. The page that processes the form writes the form field values to a cookie. The browser is redirected to a page that retrieves the cookie values, assigns them to session variables, and displays the session variables.

1. Open your **Project9** in Visual Studio .NET and create a Web page called **Ch9Proj3.aspx**.

2. Add a heading that says **Registration Form**.

3. Add two text box form fields named **name** and **pass**, with the labels named **username** and **password**.

4. Use the following code to add a hidden field named sid. The value of the field is the SessionID.

```
<INPUT type="hidden" id="sid"
value="<% = Session.SessionID %>" runat="server">
```

5. Add a label named **message**.

6. Add a button. In the button, display the text **Register Me!**

7. Double-click the button to edit the code behind the page. Use the code that follows this paragraph to retrieve the form values in the code behind the page and write them to cookies. The cookie group name should be **sc**. Assign the current date to a cookie named **mydate**. Assign the server variables HTTP_REFERER and REMOTE_ADDR to cookies named **referer** and **ip**.

```
<%
Response.Cookies("sc")("name") = Request.Form("name")
Response.Cookies("sc")("pass") = Request.Form("pass")
Response.Cookies("sc")("sid") = Request.Form("sid")
Response.Cookies("sc")("mydate") = _
   Now.Date.ToShortDateString
Response.Cookies("sc")("referer") = _
      Request.ServerVariables("HTTP_REFERER")
Response.Cookies("sc")("ip") = _
   Request.ServerVariables("REMOTE_ADDR")
```

9

8. Use the following code to display the cookie using the HTTP_COOKIE server variable:

```
message.Text = ↵
"Here is the cookie that has been written _
to your computer from this domain: <br /><br />" & _
Request.ServerVariables("HTTP_COOKIE")
```

9. Modify the Web page's appearance using your favorite fonts, colors, and images. Use line breaks, blockquotes, tables, or other HTML tags to format the page layout.

10. Save the page as **Ch9Proj3.aspx**.

11. View the **Ch9Proj3.aspx** Web page in the browser. Type **student** and **password** in the user name and password text boxes and click the **Register Me!** button. The HTTP cookie is displayed. Click the **Register Me!** button again, and the entire cookie is displayed. Print the Web page, the HTML source code, and the code behind the page.

Hands-on Project

Project 9-4

In this project, you will practice reading and writing cookies. You will create a Web page that collects the username and password. The form field values are saved as a cookie. When the user returns to the same Web page, the cookie is used to automatically log the user into the Web page.

1. Open your **Chapter9** project in Visual Studio .NET. Create a new Web page named **Ch9Proj4.aspx**

2. Add a login form with the form fields named **name** and **pass**, with labels that say **username** and **password**. Add a button named **btnLogin** that says **Login**.

3. Add the following code in the code behind the page to determine whether the user filled out the form when the user clicks on the btnLogin button:

```
If (name.Text<> "" And _
    pass.Text <> "") Then
```

4. Add the code that follows this paragraph. If the user filled out the form, retrieve the values from the form fields and assign them to the cookies. Name the group cookie **lc** and the cookies **name** and **pass**. The cookie should expire in seven days from the current date.

```
        Response.Cookies("lc")("name") = _
        Request.Form("name")
        Response.Cookies("lc")("pass") = _
        Request.Form("pass")
        Response.Cookies("lc").Expires = _
        Date.Now.Today.AddDays(7)
    Else
    End If
```

5. Next, add a script to detect whether a cookie is present, as in the code that follows this paragraph below. The cookie must have both a name and password stored in the cookie.

```
If (Request.Cookies("lc")("name") <> "") _
   And (Request.Cookies("lc")("pass") <> "") Then
```

6. Add the code that follows this paragraph. If there is a cookie, change the message label to **You were logged in with your cookie**. Retrieve the values from the cookie and display them in the browser.

```
message.Text = "You were logged in with your cookie."
message.Text += "<br />"
message.Text += Request.Cookies("lc")("name")
message.Text += "<br />"
message.Text += Request.Cookies("lc")("pass")
End If
```

7. Modify the Web page's appearance using your favorite fonts, colors, and images.

8. Save the Web page as **Ch9Proj4.aspx**.

9. View the Web page. Print your source code. Print out the Web page.

Project 9-5

In this project you will create a Web page that validates the user against a customer database using Visual Studio .NET.

1. Start **Visual Studio .NET** and open your **Chapter9** solution, if it is not already open.

2. In Visual Studio .NET create a database, using the MSDE named **Ch9Proj5**.

3. Use the the content from Table 9-1 to determine the column names, datatypes, lengths, and properties.

Table 9-1   Column information

Column Name	DataType	Length	Allow Nulls
CustomerID	Int	4	No
CustomerName	Nvarchar	50	No
EmailAddress	Nvarchar	50	Yes
Password	char	10	Yes
MembershipLevel	Int	4	Yes

4. In the properties at the bottom half of the window, change the Identity for the CustomerID column from No to **Yes** using the drop-down list arrow. The Identity Seed should be set to **1**, and Identity Increment should be set to **1**. This creates a new value for each new record entered in the database.

5. Right-click the **CustomerID** column name, and then click **Set Primary Key**. A yellow key appears at the side of the column name to indicate that this column is the primary key column.

6. Click the **Save All** button and save the table as **Customers**.

7. Enter the data listed in Table 9-2 in the database.

8. Create a Web page named **Ch9Proj5.aspx**. Add a login form with the txtEmail and textPWD text boxes to collect the user's login information.

9. Use the EmailAddress and Password fields from the database to validate the user.

10. Change the forms authentication in the Web.config file to point to the database.

11. Save the page, build the solution, and view the page in the browser. Test the validation by entering a name and a password from the Customers table. Print the Web page, the HTML code, the code behind the page, and the Web.config file.

12. Change the Web.config settings back to Windows authentication, and allow all users access to the Web site. Click the **Save All** button and build the solution.

Table 9-2   Additional column information

Column Name	Row1	Row2	Row3	Row4
CustomerID				
CustomerName	June Mayzer	Ralph Waldon	Joseph Reno	Kevin Marx
EmailAddress	JM@tarastore.com	RW@tarastore.com	JR@tarastore.com	KM@tarastore.com
Password	Franklin	Bears	Crypto	Loyola
MembershipLevel	2	1	2	3

Project 9-6

In this project you will create a Web page that validates the user against a customer XML file using Visual Studio .NET.

1. Start **Visual Studio .NET** and open your **Chapter9** solution if necessary.

2. Use the information in Table 9-3 to create an XML file that contains the username and password. Save the file as **Ch9Proj6.xml**.

The @ character has a hexidecimal value of 0 x 40 and cannot be included in a name of a node in an XML document.

Table 9-3   User information

Username	JM@ tarastore.com	RW@ tarastore.com	JR@ tarastore.com	KM@ tarastore.com
Password	Franklin	Bears	Crypto	Loyola

3. Create a Web page named **Ch9Proj6Login.aspx**. Add a login form with Username and Password text boxes.

4. Use the Username and Password fields from the XML file to validate the user.

5. Change the forms authentication in the Web.config file to point to the XML file.

6. Create a Web page named **Ch9Proj6.aspx**. Insert content to welcome the user. Enhance the appearance of the page with images and style sheets. Include a button that will allow the user to log out.

7. Save all of the pages, build the solution, and view the Ch9Proj6.aspx page in the browser. You will be redirected to the Ch9Proj6Login.aspx page. Test the validation by entering a name and password from the XML file and submit form. Print the Web page, the HTML code, the code behind the page, the XML file, and the Web.config file.

8. Change the Web.config settings back to Windows authentication, and allow all users access to the Web site. Click the **Save All** button and build the solution.

CASE PROJECTS

Tara Store — Creating an Individual Membership Login Page

The Tara Store membership has decided that they would like to log in using individual user IDs and passwords. Your task is to create the login page. The members were mailed the default password, TaraOnline, so they can log into the Web site. Create a page where they log in with their user ID and the password. When the user logs in, a message is displayed. You are to create the XML file named Ch9Case1.xml. Add graphics and content to enhance the Web page. Print out the Web page, the HTML code, and the code behind the page. Print out the Ch9Case1.xml file. When you are finished, change the authorization back to Windows and allow all users to access the site.

Tara Store — Testing the Home Page

You are in charge of revising the Tara Store home page. Your manager would like to know how quickly the objects in the page load compared to the current page. Create a new home page named Ch9Case2.aspx. (*Note:* You will want to turn on FlowLayout if you don't want the trace form to overlap your Web page.) Add content and graphics to enhance the page's layout. Use the trace command to access the trace results. Print the page with the trace results. Circle the value that indicates the total time the page took to load. Circle the control that took the longest time to load.

Tara Store — Configuring Custom Error Pages

You have had a number of complaints from customers about the error messages on your Web site. While working with the Web development team to correct the errors, you have been asked to design several custom error pages. Create a new Web page named Ch9Case3.aspx that contains two hyperlinks, one to Shamrock.aspx and one to Web.config. Add graphics and content to enhance the appearance of the page. Create a new Web page named Ch9Case3Error404.aspx, which is used when an HTTP status code 404 is sent. Indicate to the customer that the file he or she has entered has not been found. Provide a link to the Web site at Ch9Case3.aspx. Add graphics and content to enhance the appearance of the page. Create a second page named Ch9Case3Error.aspx that contains a general error message and a link to the Ch9Case3.aspx page. Add graphics and content to enhance the appearance of the page. Open the Web.config file. In the CustomErrors node, configure the application to use custom error pages. Configure the application to use the Ch9Case3Error404.aspx page when a file not found error occurs. For all other errors, redirect the browser to the Ch9Case3Error.aspx page. Print out all pages and the source code. Print out the configuration file. When you are finished, reset the CustomErrors Mode property to RemoteOnly, remove the error child node, save the file, and rebuild the application.

CHAPTER 10

TROUBLESHOOTING AND DEPLOYING AN ASP.NET APPLICATION

In this chapter, you will:

♦ Identify and handle ASP.NET errors

♦ Use the Visual Studio .NET Debugger tool to identify application errors

♦ Document the Web site using the Code Comment Report Wizard

♦ Use Page Output Caching to increase Web site performance

♦ Learn how to deploy an ASP.NET Web application

Today, customers demand that Web sites run without errors all of the time. Therefore, it is important to build Web applications that are error-free. When an error does occur, the Web developer tools should quickly allow you to detect, locate, and fix the error. One of the most difficult problems programmers faced was debugging their Web applications. With ASP.NET and Visual Studio .NET, the Web programmer has new error-handling and debugging tools. These tools help programmers catch and locate program errors faster, resulting in a more robust application.

ERROR HANDLING

Error handling is a collection of techniques that allow you to identify programming errors in your code, which are called bugs. Many errors are caused by incorrect syntax or spelling errors. These errors are easily identified using the Visual Studio .NET IntelliSense feature. However, some errors, such as programming logic errors, are more difficult to detect. To handle errors that arise during program execution, you can write code that interprets error messages and executes when an error is detected, even generating custom error messages and global error handlers.

All custom error pages should have a link to the home page and a link to the previous page. If no action occurs after 30 seconds, the page should be redirected back to the home page. You can redirect the user with Response.Redirect("[homepage.aspx]") or insert a meta tag into the HTML template that redirects the page on the client side. You should monitor the types of errors that occur. Some errors may be indicate that a hacker is attempting to attack your Web site or Web server. Activity resulting in HTTP or ASP.NET errors can be logged within the IIS log files and the Windows NT log files. You may want to configure custom error pages to alert the administrator when certain events, such as any failed attempts to access a protected resource, occur.

Creating a Custom Error Page Using the Web Configuration File

In the previous chapter, you learned how to use the Page directive to configure a Web page and Web application to display custom error pages when errors occur. The ErrorPage attribute of the Page property identifies the generic error page. When an error occurs, the client is redirected to this error page. The custom error page can also be set in the customErrors node in the Web.config file. When the Mode attribute is set to RemoteOnly, then only remote clients are redirected to the new page. The localhost still displays the default error message. When the application encounters an error, a status code is generated, and the application can be redirected to a new page. The resulting URL will be the URL of the error page, appended with a question mark and a QueryString. The QueryString consists of the name aspxerrorpath and the virtual path to the page that was requested. For example, if you were looking for a page named garden.aspx, and the name of the custom error page was nogarden.aspx, the resulting URL would be *http://localhost/Chapter10/nogarden.aspx?aspxerrorpath=/chapter10/garden.aspx*.

There is an excellent discussion in the help documentation on configuration of ASP.NET located at *http://msdn.microsoft.com/library/en-us/cpguide/html/cpconASPNETConfiguration.asp*.

You can locate the entire list of ASP.NET configuration schema at *http://msdn.microsoft.com/library/en-us/cpgenref/html/gngrfASPNETConfigurationSectionSchema.asp*.

Common Error Status Messages

Table 10-1 is a listing of the common status codes. These codes are exposed by the **HTTPStatusCode property** of the `System.NET` namespace.

Table 10-1   Common status codes

Status Code	Code Name	Description
200	OK	The request was received successfully.
301	Moved	The URL requested was moved to a new URL.
400	BadRequest	The server did not understand the request.
401	Unauthorized	The request required authentication.
403	Forbidden	Access to the resource was forbidden. This is usually because the ACL refused access to the resource.
404	NotFound	The server cannot locate the resource.
405	MethodNotAllowed	The method Post or Get is not allowed.
500	InternalServerError	A generic error occurred on the server.
503	ServiceUnavailable	The server is unavailable.

There is an excellent discussion of status codes in the help documentation at *http://msdn.microsoft.com/library/en-us/cpref/html/frlrfsystemwebhttpresponseclassstatustopic.asp* and at *http://msdn.microsoft.com/library/en-us/cpref/html/frlrfsystemnethttpstatuscodeclasstopic.asp*. The status code is also displayed in the trace page when the Trace property is turned on.

10

In the following exercise, you create a custom error message and enable your Web application configuration file to detect HTTP status errors. You will change the Web.config file to redirect the browser to a custom error page, when the page requested cannot be found.

1. Start **Visual Studio .NET**.

2. Click **File** on the menu bar, point to **New**, and then click **Project** to open the New Project window.

3. Under Project Types, click **Visual Basic Projects**, and under Templates, **click ASP.NET Web Application**. Type **Chapter10** in the Location text box in place of WebApplication1. Click **OK** to create the solution, project, and default files.

4. Right-click the **Chapter10** project, point to **Add**, and then click **Add Existing Item**. Change the Files of type drop-down list from VB Code Files to **All Files**. Browse to locate the **Chapter10Data** folder. Select all files from the Chapter10Data folder except the data and images folders. Click the **Open** button to import the files into your project. Messages will appear that ask you to create a class for several of the .aspx files. When prompted, click

Yes in each instance to create new class files. A message may appear that asks if you want to overwrite one or more of these files. Click **Yes** in each instance. (*Note:* You can close the Start Page and the default WebForm1.aspx in the main code window. You will not be modifying these pages in this chapter.)

5. Open **Windows Explorer**. (*Note*: Click **Start**, click **Run**, type **%SystemRoot%\explorer.exe** in the text box, and then click **OK**.) Navigate to your **Chapter10Data** folder. Highlight the **data** folder and the **images** folder, right-click, and select **Copy**. Go back to Visual Studio .NET 2003. Right-click the **Chapter10** project and select **Paste**. The data folder and the images folder will be copied into your project.

6. Double-click the **Web.config** file in the Solution Explorer window to open the file. Add the code following this paragraph to redirect the visitor to a custom error page when a file has not been found. Place this code on the line after the comment that says <!-- Insert customErrors settings here. -->. The code should appear as shown in Figure 10-1.

```
<customErrors defaultRedirect="CustomError.aspx" mode="On">
    <error statusCode="404" redirect="Error404.aspx" />
</customErrors>
```

```
<?xml version="1.0" encoding="utf-8" ?>
<configuration>
   <!-- Insert connection string settings here. -->

<system.web>
    <!-- Insert customErrors settings here. -->
        <customErrors defaultRedirect="CustomError.aspx" mode="On">
            <error statusCode="404" redirect="Error404.aspx" />
        </customErrors>

    <!-- Insert compilation settings here. -->


    <!-- Insert authentication settings here. -->
    <authentication mode="Windows" />

    <!-- Insert authorization settings here. -->
    <authorization>
            <allow users="*" />
    </authorization>
 </system.web>
</configuration>
```

The customErrors node can be used for any HTTP status error code; it cannot detect errors in your programming code

Figure 10-1 Modifying the Web.config file

7. Click the **Save All** button. Click **Build** on the menu bar, and then click **Build Solution**.

8. In the browser, go to **http://localhost/Chapter10/ Chapter10ErrorTest.aspx**. The page should be redirected to the custom errors page. Your page should look like the one in Figure 10-2. If you wait 30 seconds, the page will be redirected to the Ch10Home.aspx page.

9. Close any open pages.

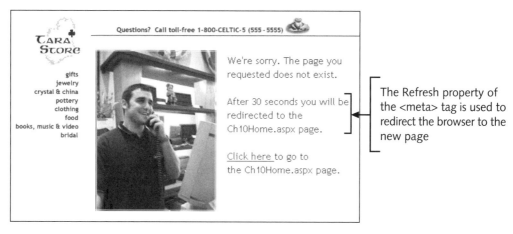

Figure 10-2   Using the Web.config file to configure custom error messages

 Within the MMC, the Web site properties contain a tab called Custom Errors. This lists the common errors and the default messages that are displayed by the Web server. You can use ASP.NET or IIS to manage custom errors. However, by using the Web.config file, the programmer does not need access to the MMC.

Using the Exception Classes to Identify Errors

The .NET System class contains an Exception class that acts as the base class for all exceptions. An exception is an object that is thrown when a predefined error occurs. For example, if the page cannot connect to the database, then an exception pointing to a problem with the database connection is thrown. Catching exceptions can help you quickly identify errors in your Web application. These predefined errors are categorized in the SystemException class and ApplicationException class. The **SystemException class** is the base class for all predefined exceptions. The **ApplicationException class** provides a base class to create user-defined exception objects. There are several predefined exceptions that are derived from the SystemException class. You can also use a general exception handler to catch general exceptions.

Common exceptions that are handled with the **Try-Catch-Finally block** include the SqlException, OleDbException, NullReferenceException, and IndexOutOfRangeException exceptions. The Try-Catch-Finally statement allows you to catch the specific error, and to read information about the exception.

SqlException is thrown when an error occurs from the SQL Server DataAdapter. This exception is often thrown when the database server does not exist. **OleDbException** is thrown when an error occurs from the OleDbDataAdapter. **NullReferenceException** is thrown when an error occurs when a null object is referenced. **IndexOutOfRangeException** is thrown when an Array object is improperly indexed. **ExternalException** class allows other classes to indirectly inherit from the SystemException class. Some objects, such as the OleDbException class, inherit from the ExternalException class, which is derived from the SystemException class.

When the exception object is created from the SystemException class, several properties and methods are exposed that can help identify the source of the error. The properties are exposed from the objects derived from the SystemException class.

- The **Message property** returns the error message.
- The **TargetSite property** returns the name of the method that threw the exception.
- The **HelpLink property** returns the Help file associated with the exception object.
- The **StackTrace property** returns the location where the exception occurred.
- The **InnerException property** returns the first exception within the error stack.
- The **ToString method** returns the fully qualified name of the object, and the other properties.
- The **HRESULT property** returns a coded numerical value that represents a specific exception.
- The **Source property** returns the name of the application or object that raised the exception.

Application-Level Error Handling

An ASP.NET application is a more than a collection of one or more ASP.NET pages. An ASP.NET application includes a Global Application File, called Global.asax, which allows you to tie the pages together so that information can be shared across pages. The **Global Application File** is a text file that contains scripts that are executed when the Web application starts and ends, and scripts that are executed when a browser session starts and ends. A Web application can have only one Global Application File, which must be located in the root directory of the Web application.

The Global Application File contains only server-side scripts. It does not contain any HTML or client-side scripts. The Web application executes the subroutines within the Global Application File before executing server code. The Global Application File defines four subroutines that run when the application starts and ends and when the session starts and ends. The four subroutines that are available in the Global Application File for both ASP and ASP.NET are:

- Application_OnStart

- Application_OnEnd

- Session_OnStart

- Session_OnEnd

 It is useful to keep all four subroutines listed in the Global Application File, even ones that are not used, since you might want to add code later to the subroutines.

By default, in ASP.NET, the Global.asax file includes the Application_BeginRequest, Application_AuthenticateRequest, and Application_Error event handlers. Application_BeginRequest occurs when an HTTP request is made. Application_AuthenticateRequest occurs when a client attempts to be authenticated.

You can retrieve information about an exception that was thrown from the **HttpContext class**. The **ToString method** provides the details of the exception object. To retrieve the last exception thrown by the application, you can use the **GetLastError method** from the **HttpServerUtility class**. (*Note:* You can also use the Error property of the HttpContext class to retrieve the last exception object thrown by the Web application.) You can clear all errors from the application using the **ClearError method** from the HttpContext class. You can redirect the client to a new URL when a general exception occurs by using the **Error property** of the HttpContext class.

Creating a Global Error Page Using the Global Application File

The following exercise, which consists of several stages, will help demonstrate how you can capture database errors by using the exception object. First, you will create the SQL Server database by upsizing an Access database. Then, you will retrieve the connection string for your database and insert the connection string as an application variable in the configuration file. Next, you will import a page to display the data. Finally, you will enable your Global Application File to detect a general error and redirect the client to a custom error message that displays the error properties of the exception object.

In the first part, you will upsize the Access database to SQL Server; then, you will create the stored procedures.

1. Start **Microsoft Access**. Open the **TaraStore.mdb** file within your Chapter10Data folder. Click **Tools** on the menu bar, point to **Database Utilities**, and then select **Upsizing Wizard**. The Create new database radio button is already selected. Click **Next** to continue.

2. In the drop-down list box select the name of your SQL Server, such as [*MACHINENAME*]\NetSDK. Select the authentication scheme for your SQL

Server. (*Note*: Some servers may require a trusted connection, and some servers may require you to provide a Login ID and password to connect. You can ask your system administrator for the correct authentication parameters.)

3. In the name text box, replace TaraStoreSQL with **Ch10TaraStoreSQL**. Click **Next** to continue. Click the **>>** button to select all available tables, and then click **Next** to continue. Click **Next** to continue twice, and then click **Finish**. Close the Upsizing Wizard report window, and then close Access.

4. Go to the **Start** menu and click **Run**. Browse to locate your **Chapter10Data** folder, select the **Ch10TaraStoreSQL.bat** file, and click **Open**. Click **OK**. The command prompt window will open, run a SQL script, and then close automatically. This command script will create the stored procedures for you. Open your **Chapter10** project in Visual Studio .NET if it is not already open.

5. In the Server Explorer window, right-click **Data Connections**, and then click **Add Connection**. In the server name drop-down list enter the name of your SQL Server, such as [*MACHINENAME*]\NetSDK. Select the appropriate authentication scheme to access the server. If you enter a user name and password, check the **Allow saving password** check box. (*Note*: This will depend upon how your SQL Server has been installed.) In the database drop-down list select **Ch10TaraStoreSQL**, and then click **OK**.

In this next stage, you will create the application variable that will contain the connection string. Your connection string will vary with the authentication used for your database and SQL Server.

1. In the Solution Explorer window, open **WebForm1.aspx** if it is not already open. Go to the Server Explorer window and drag the **Ch10TaraStoreSQL** database from the Data Connections to the Web page. Click **Include Password**.s The SqlConnection object named SqlConnection1 is added to the designer.

2. Click the **SqlConnection1** to select the Connection object. Then, in the Properties window, locate the ConnectionString property. Double-click the value of the connection string to select the entire connection string. Click **Edit** on the menu bar, and then click **Copy**.

3. Double-click **Web.config** in the Solution Explorer window to open the file. Add the code following this paragraph to create the global connection string, which is stored in the CS key. The code should be placed immediately below the opening configuration node tag, as shown in Figure 10-3. The value of the variable will be different for your connection, depending upon your database and SQL Server authentication. (*Note*: In Figure 10-3, the SQL Server uses the default authentication with the username sa and password as the password. The name of the local machine is listed as KALATA, and the server name is kalata\netsdk.) Remember that you will need to replace any double quotation marks in the connection string with single quotation marks. A single pair of double quotation marks encloses the entire connection string.

```
<appSettings>
   <add key="CS" value="[paste your connection here]" />
</appSettings>
```

```
<?xml version="1.0" encoding="utf-8" ?>
<configuration>
   <!-- Insert connection string settings here. -->
   <appSettings>
      <add key="CS" value="workstation id=KALATA;
      packet size=4096;user id=sa;
      data source='kalata\netsdk';
      persist security info=True;
      initial catalog=Ch10TaraStoreSQL;
      password=password"/>
   </appSettings>
</appSettings>
```

The name of your machine must match the value in the id property

The name of your SQL Server must match the name in the data source property

Figure 10-3   Adding an application variable to the Web.config file

4. Click the **Save All** button and close the Web.config file.

 In this next stage, you will create the component that will retrieve the data and import an existing page, which will be used to display the data.

When you created the project and imported the data files, you imported the CatMenu.aspx and Ch10Products.vb files. These are modified files that you created in Chapter 8. The Ch10Products.vb file contains the connection string to the (local)\NetSDK server and the Ch10TaraStoreSQL database using the sa user and password as the password. You may need to modify the Ch10Products.vb file if you use any other authorization methods.

5. Click **Build** on the menu bar, and then click **Build Solution**.

6. Open the browser and go to **http://localhost/Chapter10/CatMenu.aspx** to view the page. Click **Gifts**, and then click **Golf Gifts**. The page will appear as shown in Figure 10-4.

Your connection string will vary depending on whether your SQL Server authenticated the user with Windows integrated security or SQL Server security. If your server uses SQL Server security, your system administrator will provide you with the user ID, the password, the name of the database server, and the name of the database. If your server uses Windows authentication, your system administrator will provide you with the properties and values. The code following this paragraph is an example of a connection string for a database server that uses Windows authentication. (*Note*: Do not split the string across lines.)

```
value = "data source=[Machinename]\NetSDK;
initial catalog=Ch10TaraStoreSQL;
integrated security = SSPI;
persist security info= False;
workstation id = [Machinename];
packet size=4096"
```

10

Figure 10-4   Displaying the category list

In the next stage, you will add the code to check for general errors using the Global Application File.

1. Double-click the **Global.asax** file in the Solution Explorer window. Click the hyperlink labeled **Click here to switch to code view**. (*Note*: You can see that the event handlers have already added to the file the Application_BeginRequest, Application_AuthenticateRequest, and Application_Error event handlers.)

2. In the Application_Error event, add the code following this paragraph to redirect the user to a custom error page. Pass the error information in the QueryString. The **UrlEncode** method converts the error message to an HTTP-compatible message. (*Note*: Special characters such as blank spaces should be converted to HTTP-compatible codes before sending the request or an error may occur in processing the request.) The page should appear as shown in Figure 10-5.

```
Dim eMSG As String = Server.GetLastError.Message()
Dim eHL As String = Server.GetLastError.HelpLink()
Dim eST As String = Server.GetLastError.StackTrace()
Dim eTS As String = Server.GetLastError.ToString()

Context.ClearError()
Response.Redirect("CustomError.aspx?" & _
"eMSG=" & Server.UrlEncode(eMSG) & _
"&eHL=" & Server.UrlEncode(eHL) & _
"&eST=" & Server.UrlEncode(eST) & _
"&eTS=" & Server.UrlEncode(eTS))
```

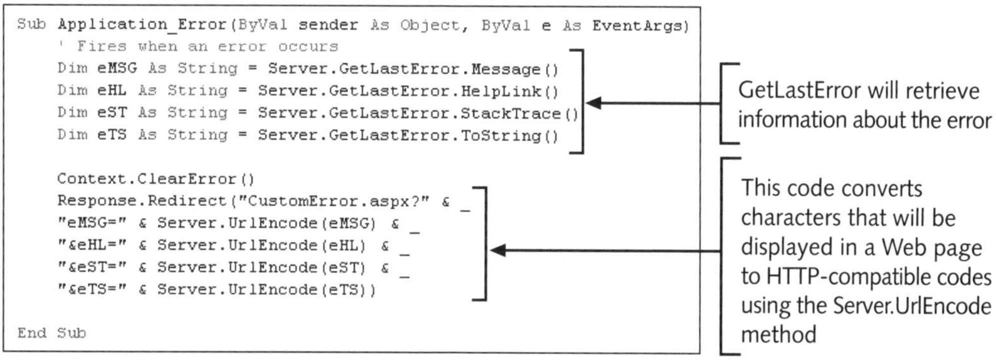

Figure 10-5   Modifying the Global.asax file

3. Click the **Save All** button. Close the Global.asax page.

4. Right-click the **Ch10Products.vb** file in the Solution Explorer window and select **View Code**. To generate an error, change the reference to the connection in the Ch10Products.vb page from ConfigurationSettings.AppSettings("CS") to **ConfigurationSettings.AppSettings("CS2")**.

5. Click the **Save All** button. Click **Build** on the menu bar, and then click **Build Solution**.

6. Right-click the **CustomError.aspx** page in the Solution Explorer window and select **View Code** to open the code behind the page. Modify the CustomError.aspx page to display the errors. After the comment that says 'Insert the code here, type the code that follows this paragraph, as shown in Figure 10-6. (*Note:* There is sometimes no HelpLink associated with the error, so you need to detect if the error object passed a HelpLink URL.)

```
lblEM.Text = Request.QueryString("eMSG")
Dim EHL As String = Request.QueryString("eHL")
If EHL <> "" Then
    lblEHL.Text = Request.QueryString("eHL")
```

```
Else
     lblEHL.Text = "There is no help link associated ⤸
with this error."
End If
lblAST.Text = Request.QueryString("eST")
lblETS.Text = Request.QueryString("eTS")
```

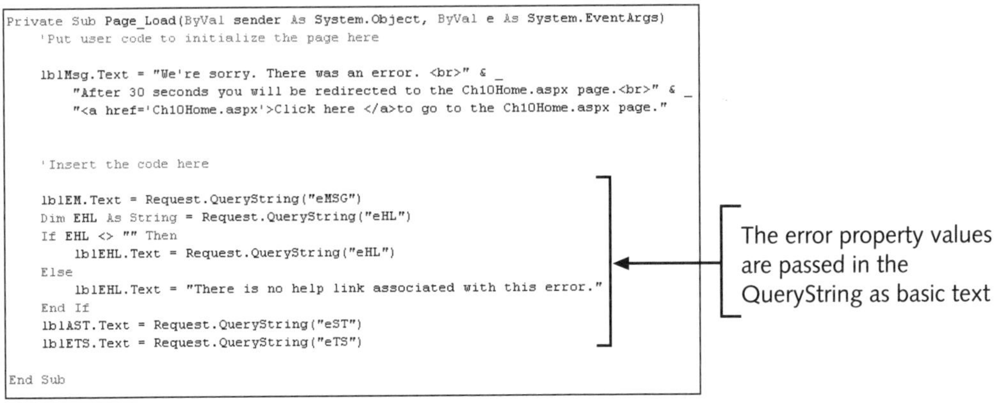

```
Private Sub Page_Load(ByVal sender As System.Object, ByVal e As System.EventArgs)
    'Put user code to initialize the page here

    lblMsg.Text = "We're sorry. There was an error. <br>" & _
        "After 30 seconds you will be redirected to the Ch10Home.aspx page.<br>" & _
        "<a href='Ch10Home.aspx'>Click here </a>to go to the Ch10Home.aspx page."


    'Insert the code here

    lblEM.Text = Request.QueryString("eMSG")
    Dim EHL As String = Request.QueryString("eHL")
    If EHL <> "" Then
        lblEHL.Text = Request.QueryString("eHL")
    Else
        lblEHL.Text = "There is no help link associated with this error."
    End If
    lblAST.Text = Request.QueryString("eST")
    lblETS.Text = Request.QueryString("eTS")

End Sub
```

The error property values are passed in the QueryString as basic text

Figure 10-6 Creating the custom error page

7. Click the **Save All** button. Click **Build** on the menu bar, and then click **Build Solution**.

8. In the browser, refresh the CatMenu.aspx page by clicking the **Refresh** button. The page should be redirected to the new custom errors page with the errors displayed. Your page should look like the one in Figure 10-7.

9. Double-click the **Global.asax** page in the Solution Explorer window. Click the **click here to switch to code view** hyperlink. Comment out the code in the Application_Error event handler. Do not delete the code.

10. To remove the error, click the **Ch10Products.vb tab**, and then change the CS2 application variable to **CS**.

11. Click the **Save All** button. Click **Build** on the menu bar, and then click **Build Solution**.

12. Close any open pages.

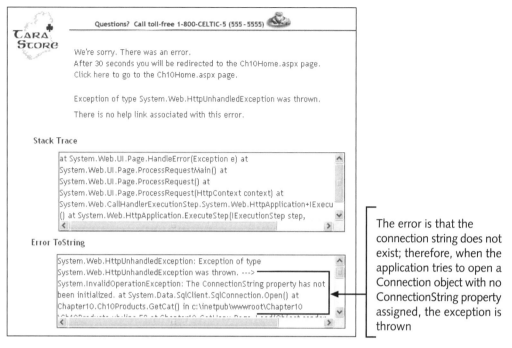

Figure 10-7   Viewing the custom error page

Using Try-Catch-Finally to Handle Specific Errors

You can take advantage of ASP.NET's language-independent, structured exception handling within your ASP.NET applications. The exception object forces you to deal with exceptions when they occur. If an exception is raised and you don't explicitly handle the exception, a general ASP.NET exception will occur, forcing the application to terminate without allowing the code to continue executing, resulting in an error page. Using the exception object makes finding errors much easier. To use the exception object, you can use a programming structure called Try-Catch-Finally. The **Try-Catch-Finally statement** allows you to attempt to run a block of code that detects when an error has occurred. The goal of the Try-Catch-Finally statement is to gracefully recover when an exception occurs. Rather than have an error message occur, you can customize the code that is executed. You can even log the error information captured from the error. The **Try statement** attempts to run a block of code. If there is an error, an exception object is created. The **Catch statement** catches the error as an exception object. You can use the Catch statement multiple times to catch multiple types of errors. The **Finally statement** allows you to execute a block of code.

In the following exercise, you will use the Try...Catch...Finally block to capture the SQL Server error and redirect the user to the custom error page, while passing the error object.

1. Open your **Chapter10** project in Visual Studio .NET if necessary. Open the **Web.config** file, if is not already open. Change the user account from sa to **sa2**. (*Note*: The name of your user account may vary.) Click the **Save All** button.

2. Double-click **CatMenuList.aspx** in the Solution Explorer window to open the file, and then double-click the page to open the code behind the page.

3. Beneath the comment ' Insert the Try statement here, type **Try**.

4. Beneath the comment 'Insert the Catch statement here, type the code that follows this paragraph. The code will catch the exception and redirect the client to the custom errors page. See Figure 10-8.

```
Catch Ex As SqlException
    Dim eMSG As String = Ex.Message
    Dim eHL As String = Ex.HelpLink
    Dim eST As String = Ex.StackTrace
    Dim eTS As String = Ex.ToString

    Response.Redirect("CustomErrorSQL.aspx?" & _
    "eMSG=" & System.Web.HttpUtility.UrlEncode(eMSG) & _
    "&eHL=" & System.Web.HttpUtility.UrlEncode(eHL) & _
    "&eST=" & System.Web.HttpUtility.UrlEncode(eST) & _
    "&eTS=" & System.Web.HttpUtility.UrlEncode(eTS))
End Try
```

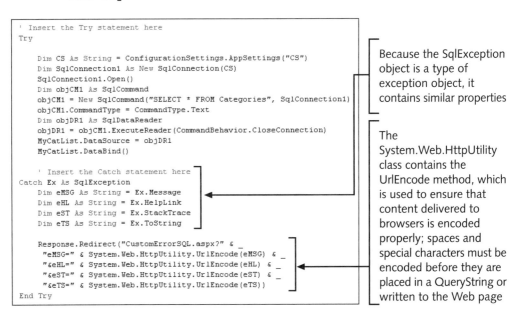

Because the SqlException object is a type of exception object, it contains similar properties

The System.Web.HttpUtility class contains the UrlEncode method, which is used to ensure that content delivered to browsers is encoded properly; spaces and special characters must be encoded before they are placed in a QueryString or written to the Web page

Figure 10-8 Using the Try-Catch-Finally handler to capture errors

5. Click the **Save All** button. Click **Build** on the menu bar, and then click **Build Solution**.

6. Open the browser and go to **http://localhost/Chapter10/CatMenuList.aspx** to view the page. You can see the exception information in the second text box, as shown in Figure 10-9. This error message indicates that the login failed for user sa2.

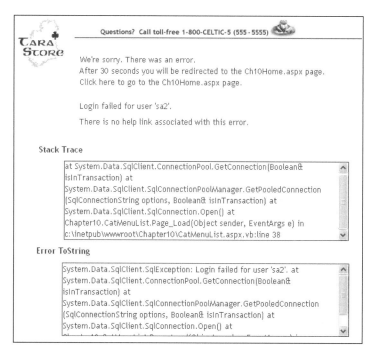

Figure 10-9   Viewing the exception information

7. Return to your Web application within Visual Studio .NET.

8. Change the user name in the connection string back to **sa** in the Web.config file.

9. Click the **Save All** button. Click **Build** on the menu bar, and then click **Build Solution**.

10. In the browser, refresh the CatMenuList.aspx page by clicking the **Refresh** button. The page should appear with the menu list and the home page image.

11. Close any open pages, and then close the browser window.

USING THE VISUAL STUDIO .NET DEBUGGER

Visual Studio .NET provides several debugging tools to debug .NET applications. A **debugger** allows you to step through the application at **breakpoints**, which are defined points in the program where processing stops so that you can view the variables, properties, and other application settings. This data can be helpful when trying to locate programming logic errors. (*Note*: You can use the debugger to debug your application across multiple languages.)

To debug your application, you must first enable the page to support debugging. The Page directive includes an attribute named Debug, which allows you to turn on support for debugging. The following sample code shows how to turn on debugging for a single page:

```
<%@ Page Debug="True" %>
```

You can also turn on debugging for the entire application by configuring debugging in the Web.config file. The following sample code shows how to turn on debugging for the entire Web application using the Web.config file:

```
<?xml version="1.0" encoding="UTF-8" ?>
<configuration>
    <system.web>
        <compilation
            debug="true" explicit="true"
            strict="true" defaultLanguage="vb">
        </compilation>
    </system.web>
</configuration>
```

 You can configure the debugger to open whenever an exception is thrown by the application. Then in your Catch block, you can write an exception handler. To enable debugging to handle exceptions, go to the Debug menu in Visual Studio .NET and select Exceptions. In the Exceptions dialog box, check both radio buttons labeled Break into the debugger.

After you have turned on debugging, you need to attach the ASP.NET service process to the debugger. Once the debugger is attached to the ASP.NET service, you do not have to repeat the steps. The debugger remembers the processes that have been attached.

Once the application is in debug mode, you can use the following Debug menu commands to configure how you want to step through the code:

- **Step Over** (F10) allows you to execute the current line of code. Use this command to step through the code line by line.

- **Step Into** (F11) allows you to step into a method that is being called on the current line.

- **Step Out** (Shift+F11) allows you to leave the method and return to the function call.

- **Run to Cursor** (Ctrl+F10) allows you to execute all the code between the current line and the current cursor position.

Once you have stepped into the application, you can view the variables, properties, and application data within Visual Studio .NET using one of the debugger windows. The following are some of the windows used within the debugger:

- The Locals window and the Auto window display the variables. Local variables are defined within the scope of the current method.

- The Me window displays the properties of the current object.

- The Watch window displays variables that you have specifically requested.

- The Call Stack window displays a hierarchical list of methods that have been called. The **Call Stack window** allows you to identify which statement called the method.

In the following example, you will attach the debugger, set the breakpoints, and step through an application.

1. Open the **Web.config** file, if necessary, and locate the comment that says <!-- Insert compilation settings here. -->. After that comment, insert the following code to turn on debugging for the application:

```
<compilation defaultLanguage="vb" debug="true" />
```

2. Right-click **CatMenuList.aspx** in the Solution Explorer window, and then click **Set as Start Page**.

3. Open the **CatMenuList.aspx** page, and then double-click on the page to open the code behind the page.

4. Insert a breakpoint by clicking the gray bar next to the code on line 34. (*Note:* This should be the line that contains the Try statement. Your line number may vary.) A red dot appears in the gray bar to mark the breakpoint. (*Note:* You can also insert a breakpoint by right-clicking on the line of code and selecting Insert Breakpoint from the pop-up menu.) Note that the color of the bar and dot may vary with your version of Windows as well as with the theme applied in the display properties.

5. Click **Debug** on the menu bar, and then click **Start**. The debugger stops the page in the Page_Load method on the breakpoint line, as shown in Figure 10-10. Note that the windows shown on your screen may vary with your user preferences.

10

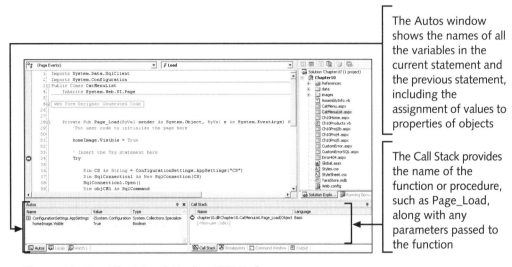

The Autos window shows the names of all the variables in the current statement and the previous statement, including the assignment of values to properties of objects

The Call Stack provides the name of the function or procedure, such as Page_Load, along with any parameters passed to the function

Figure 10-10 The Visual Studio .NET Debugger

6. Click **Debug** on the menu bar, and then click **Step Into**, as shown in Figure 10-11. The yellow arrow indicates the current line of code that the debugger is processing. The yellow arrow moves to the next line, as shown in Figure 10-12.

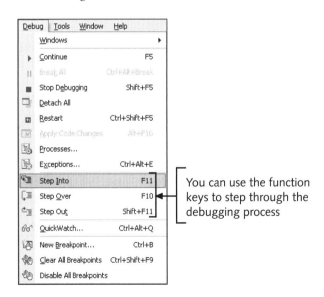

You can use the function keys to step through the debugging process

Figure 10-11 The Debug menu

7. Click **Debug** on the menu bar, and then click **Step Into**. The yellow arrow moves to the next block of code.

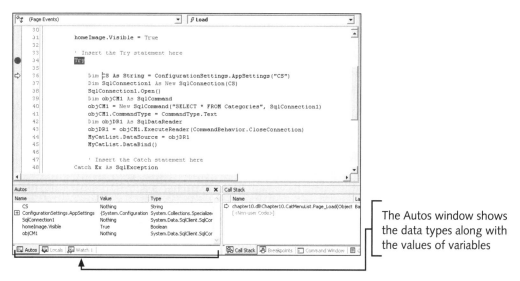

```
(Page Events)                              ▼  ƒ Load                              ▼
  30
  31        homeImage.Visible = True
  32
  33        ' Insert the Try statement here
● 34        Try
  35
⇨ 36            Dim CS As String = ConfigurationSettings.AppSettings("CS")
  37            Dim SqlConnection1 As New SqlConnection(CS)
  38            SqlConnection1.Open()
  39            Dim objCM1 As SqlCommand
  40            objCM1 = New SqlCommand("SELECT * FROM Categories", SqlConnection1)
  41            objCM1.CommandType = CommandType.Text
  42            Dim objDR1 As SqlDataReader
  43            objDR1 = objCM1.ExecuteReader(CommandBehavior.CloseConnection)
  44            MyCatList.DataSource = objDR1
  45            MyCatList.DataBind()
  46
  47            ' Insert the Catch statement here
  48        Catch Ex As SqlException
```

Autos			🔲 ✕	Call Stack
Name	Value	Type		Name
CS	Nothing	String		⇨ chapter10.dll!Chapter10.CatMenuList.Page_Load(Object Ba
⊞ ConfigurationSettings.AppSettings	{System.Configuration	System.Collections.Specialize		[<Non-user Code>]
SqlConnection1	Nothing	System.Data.SqlClient.SqlCor		
homeImage.Visible	True	Boolean		
objCM1	Nothing	System.Data.SqlClient.SqlCor		

🔲 Autos 🔲 Locals 🔍 Watch 1   🔲 Call Stack 🔲 Breakpoints 🔲 Command Window 🔲

The Autos window shows the data types along with the values of variables

Figure 10-12   The Autos window in the Debugger

8. Press **F11** slowly 7 more times. Each time you hit the F11 key, notice how the property names and values in the Autos window changes.

9. Click the **Locals** tab. The Locals window displays the variables that are within the scope of the current method. (*Note*: You can access the debugging commands from the menu, the keyboard, or the toolbars. If the Locals tab is not visible, go to the **Debug** menu, point to **Windows**, and then select **Locals**.)

10. To exit the debugger, click **Debug** on the menu bar, and then click **Stop Debugging**. The debugger windows will close automatically.

11. Click the **red dot** to remove the breakpoint.

12. Close any open windows.

Some programmers have difficulty using the debugger in a centralized server environment. The debugger can be used in a centralized server to debug applications across projects, even across multiple languages and servers. If you are interested in learning more about debugging in a large enterprise application, you should visit the MSDN Web Online Library Web site (*http://msdn.microsoft.com/library*) to read about the debugging tools, and visit the ASP.NET Web site (*http://www.asp.net*), which contains extensive links to user groups and forums that contain additional information on debugging complex and large applications.

DOCUMENTING THE WEB SITE

It's very important for developers to document their Web applications. If your application is well documented, then other programmers can read the documentation and quickly make the appropriate changes, without spending as much time analyzing the code. One of the features of ASP.NET is the automation of code documentation. You can create an automated Code Comment Web Report, which contains information about the objects, their inheritance, and their structure. You can view these pages offline using a browser and do not have to include them in the production version of your project.

 The report is stored by default in the Documents and Settings\Visual Studio Projects folder. Each project has a CodeCommentReport folder nested within the project folder. You can learn more about the Code Comment Web Report in the online documentation at *http://msdn.microsoft.com/library/en-us/ vsintro7/html/vxgrfCodeCommentWebReport.asp*.

Creating the Code Comment Web Report involves creating XML codes that document your application. These XML codes comply with the XML standards, which you learned about in Chapter 4. You can use XML codes to create additional documentation in your project. You can also use these XML codes to add comments that appear in the Web pages to document the code. However, the Code Comment Web Report feature is only available with C# in the current version of Visual Studio .NET. The C# compiler can be used directly to compile the project with the /doc parameter to process documentation comments to one or more files. The following is a listing of the XML codes that are supported within the Code Comment Web Report:

- <c>
- <para>
- <see>
- <code>
- <param>
- <seealso>
- <example>
- <paramref>
- <summary>
- <exception>
- <permission>
- <value>

- <include>

- <remarks>

- <list>

- <returns>

In the following exercise, you will document the Web page with comments and create the Code Comment Web Report. The report will list the pages and objects within the application, as well as the controls, and procedures within the page class. Note that the **REM** keyword or a single apostrophe can be used to comment your code.

1. In Visual Studio .NET, open your **Chapter10** project if necessary. Double-click **CatMenuComment.aspx** in the Solution Explorer window, and then double-click on the page to open the code behind the page.

2. Look at the comments within the code, as shown in Figure 10-13.

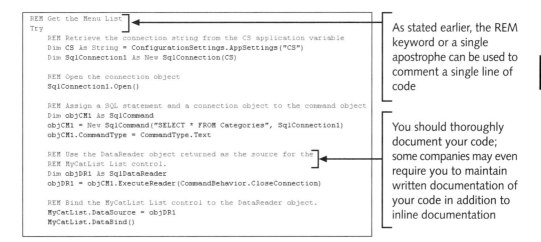

```
REM Get the Menu List
Try
    REM Retrieve the connection string from the CS application variable
    Dim CS As String = ConfigurationSettings.AppSettings("CS")
    Dim SqlConnection1 As New SqlConnection(CS)

    REM Open the connection object
    SqlConnection1.Open()

    REM Assign a SQL statement and a connection object to the command object
    Dim objCM1 As SqlCommand
    objCM1 = New SqlCommand("SELECT * FROM Categories", SqlConnection1)
    objCM1.CommandType = CommandType.Text

    REM Use the DataReader object returned as the source for the
    REM MyCatList List control.
    Dim objDR1 As SqlDataReader
    objDR1 = objCM1.ExecuteReader(CommandBehavior.CloseConnection)

    REM Bind the MyCatList List control to the DataReader object.
    MyCatList.DataSource = objDR1
    MyCatList.DataBind()
```

As stated earlier, the REM keyword or a single apostrophe can be used to comment a single line of code

You should thoroughly document your code; some companies may even require you to maintain written documentation of your code in addition to inline documentation

Figure 10-13 Adding comments to document the code

3. Click the **Save All** button. Click **Build** on the menu bar, and then click **Build Solution**.

4. Click **Tools** on the menu bar, and then click **Build Comment Web Pages**.

5. Click the radio button labeled **Build for selected Projects** to select it. Select **Chapter10**, as shown in Figure 10-14.

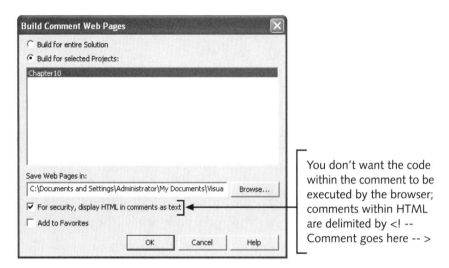

You don't want the code
within the comment to be
executed by the browser;
comments within HTML
are delimited by <! --
Comment goes here -- >

Figure 10-14   Saving the report

6. Click **Browse**. Navigate to the **Chapter10** project subfolder within the Visual Studio Projects folder. Over the Location window, right-click, point to **New**, and then select **Folder**. Type **CodeCommentReport** and press the **Enter** key. Click the **CodeCommentReport** folder. Click **Open**, and then click **OK**.

7. The Code Comment Web Report opens in Visual Studio .NET. Click the **Chapter10** hyperlink. (*Note*: If this page does not automatically open, you should open a browser window and then view the Web page named Solution_Chapter10.htm, which is located in the Chapter10\ CodeCommentReport\ folder.)

8. Click the **plus sign** next to Global in the window on the left side.

9. Click the hyperlink **CatMenuComment.aspx** in the window on the left side.

10. Click the hyperlink in the main window labeled **homeImage**. You can see the homeImage data type in the main window, as shown in Figure 10-15.

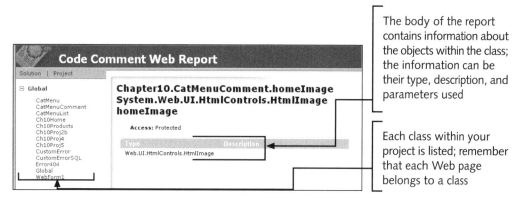

The body of the report contains information about the objects within the class; the information can be their type, description, and parameters used

Each class within your project is listed; remember that each Web page belongs to a class

Figure 10-15   Displaying the Code Comment Web Report

11. Close any open windows.

PAGE OUTPUT CACHING

Page Output Caching is the technique of caching ASP.NET pages on the Web server. When a Web page is compiled, the page is stored on the server in the cache. When another request is made for the same page, the page from the cache is returned to the client. Storing Web pages in the cache increases the performance of your Web application. When a change in the Web page is detected, a newer version of the page is recompiled and replaces the other version in the cache.

You can configure your Web application to use the Page Output Cache via two methods. The OutputCache directive is used to configure the cache for individual Web pages. The HTTPCachePolicy can be used to programmatically set the Page Output Cache. In this section, you will learn to enable the OutputCache directive.

You configure the Page Output Cache in the Web page by using the **OutputCache** directive. Parameters that configure the Page Output Cache include Duration and VaryByParam. The **Duration** identifies how long the document is left in cache. The duration is measured in seconds. After the duration expires, the page is removed from the cache. The next time the page is requested, it is recompiled and stored in the cache. The page is rendered from the version stored in the cache.

You use the **VaryByParam property** to cache any parameters passed with the page request. When a page is requested, a QueryString consisting of a series of parameter names and value pairs is attached to the URL. When the VaryByParam is set to the name of the parameter, the page is cached each time the page is requested using a different value. In other words, if the parameter name is LastName and the value is Kalata, the page is cached with the parameter Kalata. The next time the page is requested with the LastName equal to Kalata, the cached page is returned. However, if another user with the LastName equal to Shea requests the page, then the page is cached separately. The next time the page is requested with the LastName equal to Shea, the cached page for Shea is returned. Therefore, multiple versions of the same page can be cached to increase performance. You can separate multiple parameters with a comma, as shown in the following code sample:

```
<%@ OutputCache Duration="60"
    VaryByParam="LastName, Department" %>
```

There are different possible settings for VaryByParam. If you set VaryByParam to None, then regardless of the values of the parameters sent with the request, only the default page is cached. If the value is set to an asterisk (*), the page is cached for each possible key and value parameters for both Get and Post methods. You can set VaryByParam to Mode to a specific parameter key by using the key name. For example, to cache a page sent using the Get method that contains a form field named LastName and EmployeeID, the OutputCache directive is set to VaryByParam= "LastName;EmployeeID". The VaryByParam setting separates the key names using a semicolon.

There are several additional attributes that you can set with the OutputCache directive. The **Location** attribute determines where the cached versions are stored. The default value for the Location attribute is Any. If the value is set to Any, then any application caches the document for the duration specified. If the value is set to None, then caching is disabled for the page. If the Location attribute is set to Client, the document is cached on the browser. If the Location attribute is set to Downstream, a new document is generated and is eligible to be cached on the client. If the Location is set to Server, then only the server caches the document.

Web pages that access a data source often use the OutputCache directive, because parameters that are sent to query the database return different page results. When you use the OutputCache directive, each version of the page is cached in order to increase performance. The cached versions that are not actively used are removed from the cache when the duration expires.

There are additional techniques that allow you to control how the page is cached. The **VaryByCustom** attribute allows you to create custom strings to determine if a page should be cached. The **VaryByHeader** attribute allows you control the cached settings based on the HTTP header that is sent with the request. You can also use fragment caching to cache one or more user controls on the Web page with the **VaryByControl** attribute.

The HTTPCachePolicy uses the Cache property of the HTTPResponse class. Using the HTTPCachePolicy, you can configure the Web page to expire on a specific date and time. Using the Cache property of the HTTPResponse class, you can also cache pages that have invoked a Web service. You can find more information on the HTTPResponse class in the Visual Studio .NET SDK.

The following exercise demonstrates how to use the Page Output Cache to cache variations of the same Web page that display different data based on different parameters.

1. In Visual Studio .NET, open your **Chapter10** project if necessary. Double-click **CatMenuCache.aspx** in the Solution Explorer window.

2. Double-click on the page to open the code behind the page.

3. In the code behind the page, add the code in the Page_Load event handler to display the date and time. After the comment that says 'Insert the code here to display the date and time, type the following code:

```
lblMsg.Text = DateTime.Now.ToString("D") & _
"<br>" & DateTime.Now.ToString("D")
```

4. Close the code behind the page.

5. Click the **Save All** button. Click **Build** on the menu bar, and then click **Build Solution**.

6. Right-click on the page, and then click **View in Browser**. Click **Refresh** five times. The time continues to advance each time.

7. Return to the **CatMenuCache.aspx** page. Modify the HTML code to enable Page Output Caching. Insert the following code on the line after the @Page directive:

```
<%@ OutputCache Duration="60"
VaryByParam="CatID, selItem" %>
```

8. Click the **Save All** button. Click **Build** on the menu bar, and then click **Build Solution**.

9. Right-click on the page and select **View in Browser**. Your page should look like the one shown in Figure 10-16. Click the **Refresh Browser** button five times. The number of seconds will not change. If you click another hyperlink, the QueryString parameters displayed in the Web page will not change even though they are different in the URL string in the browser. After 60 seconds, if you refresh the page, the current time is displayed along with the QueryString values.

10. Close your browser and any open windows within your Visual Studio .NET application.

10

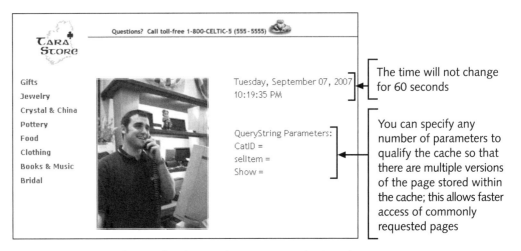

Figure 10-16 Displaying the date and time on a cached Web page

 Tip Because you may be altering the Web.config file within the hands-on projects and cases at the end of the chapter, the Web.config file is saved in the solution files for the chapter as WebCh10.config. The solution files are available from your instructor. If you want to keep your configuration file, you can create a new one with a different name by right-clicking on the project in the Solution Explorer window, selecting Add, selecting Add New Item, and then selecting Web Configuration. In the Name text box, type a new name, such as WebCh10.config, for the configuration file, and then click Open. This will create a blank configuration file. You can copy your old configuration file to this new one.

DEPLOYING AN ASP.NET WEB APPLICATION

In previous versions of ASP, before a component would work, you had to stop the Web service, log into the Web server locally, copy the component software to the server, register the component using the **RegServ32.exe application**, and then restart the Web service. Furthermore, once the component was installed, it was available to other installed applications on the server. It was very difficult to install multiple versions of the same application on the same server. In the current version of ASP.NET, deployment of Web applications is simpler and does not require registration of the component or stopping the Web service.

In ASP.NET, the DLL file contains the application logic, known as the assembly. The two locations for storing assemblies are the local application cache and the global assembly cache. The **local application cache** is the default location for the assemblies for the local application. The local application cache is the bin directory located under the root directory of the application. Only the local application can access the assembly in the local application cache.

To install a compiled DLL, simply copy the DLL file to the bin directory of the application. The **AppDomain class** manages the application process. The AppDomain controls the assemblies and threads, such as loading and unloading assemblies. When a new assembly is copied to the bin directory, the AppDomain class creates an in-memory shadow of the DLL file. The assembly that is loaded is the in-memory shadow. The DLL file is never locked. Therefore, any current connections with the in-memory shadow remain open. Any new connections are started with the new in-memory assembly. When there are no more connections with the current assembly, the assembly is removed. Any time the AppDomain detects a change in the DLL file, the in-memory shadow is replaced with the new version of the assembly.

The **global assembly cache** is the default location for assemblies that are available to the entire server. Therefore, the global assembly cache can be shared by multiple applications. A hosting service provider may install several versions of the same application in the global assembly cache. The DLL is stored on the server, but registered with the global assembly cache with the GacUtil.exe utility. Because there may be multiple versions of the same assembly, the GacUtil.exe utility registers the assembly and keeps track of the version of the assembly. The GacUtil.exe specifies the default version of the assembly. Applications are allowed to override the default settings.

10

CHAPTER SUMMARY

❑ Error handling is a collection of techniques that allow you to identify programming errors, called bugs, in your code.

❑ Status message codes are exposed by the HTTPStatusCode property.

❑ You can configure custom error pages within the Web page using the Page directive. You can configure custom errors for the application within the Web configuration file. The most common error message is the File Not Found (status 404) error message.

❑ The SystemException class is the base class for all predefined exceptions. The ApplicationException class provides a base class to create user-defined exception objects.

❑ SqlException is thrown when an error occurs from the SQL Server Data Adapter. This exception is often thrown when the database server does not exist. OleDbException is thrown when an error occurs from the OleDbDataAdapter.

❑ The Message property of the exception object returns the error message. The HelpLink property returns the Help file associated with the exception object. The StackTrace property returns the location where the exception occurred. The ToString method returns the fully qualified name of the object, and the other properties.

❐ The Global Application File is a text file that contains scripts that are executed when the Web application starts and ends, and scripts that are executed when a browser session starts and ends. A Web application can have only one Global Application File, which must reside in the root directory of the Web application.

❐ The Application_Error event occurs whenever an exception occurs in the Web application.

❐ The UrlEncode method converts the error message to an HTTP-compatible message.

❐ The Try-Catch-Finally statement allows you to attempt to run a block of code that detects when an error has occurred. The Try-Catch-Finally statement can help your applications gracefully recover when exceptions occur.

❐ A debugger allows you to step through the application at defined points, called breakpoints. The Step Into (F11) command allows you to step into a method that is being called on the current line. The Locals window displays the variables that are within the scope of the current method.

❐ The Code Comment Web Report contains information about the objects, including their inheritance and structure.

❐ You can cache Web pages using several techniques. Page Output Caching is the technique of caching ASP.NET pages on the Web server. The Page Output Cache is configured as a directive on the first line of the Web page. When a Web page is rendered, it is stored on the server in the cache. Parameters that are used to configure the Page Output Cache directive include Duration and VaryByParam. Duration identifies how long the document is left in cache. VaryByParam alters any parameters passed with the page request.

❐ The AppDomain class manages the application process, including controlling the assemblies and threads, and loading and unloading assemblies. The local application cache is the default location for the assemblies for the local application. The local application cache is the bin directory located under the root directory of the application. The global assembly cache is the default location for assemblies that are available to the entire server. The GacUtil.exe utility is used to register components in the global assembly cache.

REVIEW QUESTIONS

1. Error handling is a collection of techniques that allow you to identify programming errors in your code; these errors are called _____.

   a. viruses

   b. bugs

   c. worms

   d. parasites

2. Which type of error is not detected by Visual Studio .NET?

   a. spelling

   b. syntax

   c. programming logic

   d. grammatical

3. The Global Application File is located in:

   a. the root directory

   b. the include directory

   c. the cgi-bin directory

   d. the scripts directory

4. The name of the Global Application File in ASP.NET is:

   a. Global.inc

   b. Global.asa

   c. Global.aspx

   d. Global.asax

5. Which of the following subroutines is not contained in the Global Application File?

   a. Session_AuthenticateRequest

   b. Application_OnError

   c. Application_OnStart

   d. Application_OnEnd

6. Which attribute of the customErrors node in the Web.config file is used to configure error pages to be displayed only on the local server?

   a. RemoteOnly

   b. LocalOnly

   c. Remote

   d. all of the above

7. Which status error code is used to indicate that the method is not allowed?

   a. 301

   b. 403

   c. 405

   d. 501

8. Which status error code is used to indicate that the server is unavailable?

   a. 305

   b. 604

   c. 590

   d. 501

9. The _____ class is not derived directly from the SystemException class.

   a. SqlException

   b. OleDbException

   c. NullReferenceException

   d. IndexOutOfRangeException

10. The _____ property of the current exception object returns the fully qualified name of the object.

    a. TargetSite

    b. StackTrace

    c. InnerException

    d. ToString

11. The _____ method is used to convert the error message to an HTTP-compatible message.

    a. UrlEncode

    b. HTTPEncode

    c. ConvertMsg

    d. none of the above

12. The _____ statement captures the error as an exception object.

    a. Catch

    b. Try

    c. Finally

    d. Release

13. A _____ is a program used to locate errors.

    a. virus detection program

    b. debugger

    c. dewormer

    d. bug checker

14. You can step through the application at defined points called _____.

    a. breakpoints

    b. stops

    c. hops

    d. endpoints

15. To turn debugging on for the entire application, you must configure the _____ attribute in the compilation node of the Web.config file.

    a. debug

    b. Error

    c. customError

    d. system.web

16. The _____ command is used to execute the current line of code.

    a. Step Over

    b. Step Into

    c. Step Out

    d. Run to Cursor

17. The _____ key(s) allow(s) you to step into a method that is being called on the current line.

    a. F10

    b. F11

    c. F12

    d. Shift+F11

18. The _____ window is used to display variables that are within the scope of the current method.

    a. Locals

    b. Watch

    c. Call Stack

    d. a or b

19. When a Web page is compiled, the page is stored on the server in the _____.

    a. buffer

    b. cache

    c. global directory

    d. a and b

10

20. The statement Duration = "20" means that the page is recompiled in
_____ .

   a. 20 milliseconds

   b. 2 minutes

   c. 20 seconds

   d. 20 minutes

HANDS-ON PROJECTS

Project 10-1

In this project, you will create a custom error message, and enable your Web application configuration file to detect HTTP status errors.

1. Start **Visual Studio .NET** and open your **Chapter10** solution.

2. Open the code behind the page for the Web.config file. Locate the customErrors node and modify the code (as shown in the code following this paragraph) to redirect the visitor who has been denied access to a Web resource. (*Note*: Do not create a new customErrors node.)

```
<customErrors defaultRedirect=""customError.aspx" mode="On">
    <error statusCode="404" redirect="Ch10Proj1.aspx" />
</customErrors>
```

3. Create a new Web page named **Ch10Proj1.aspx**. Add graphics and content to indicate to the visitor that the resource has not been found. Provide the visitor with a link back to the Ch10Home.aspx page. (*Hint:* You can use the NavigateURL property of the Hyperlink control to configure the URL.)

4. Click the **Save All** button. Go to the Build menu and select **Build Solution**.

5. View the Web page in the browser at http://localhost/Chapter10/Ch10Proj1a.aspx. Since this page does not exist, you should be redirected to the Ch10Proj1.aspx page.

6. Print the Web page in the browser. Return to Visual Studio .NET and print your source code for the Ch10Proj1.aspx page, and the source code for the Web.config file.

7. Change the value of the redirect property in the customErrors node in the Web.config file back to **Error404.aspx**.

The Web.config file is saved as Ch10Proj1.config in the solution files.

Project 10-2

In this project you will use the Global Application File to detect a general error and redirect the client to a custom error message.

1. Open **Visual Studio .NET** and open your **Chapter10** solution if necessary.

2. Open the **Global.asax** file.

3. Modify the Application_Error event handler to redirect the user to a custom error page named Ch10Proj2a.aspx.

4. Create the custom error page named **Ch10Proj2a.aspx**. Display a message to the user indicating that an error occurred. Display a hyperlink to the Tara Store home page at Ch10Home.aspx. Modify the page with graphics and content to enhance the appearance of the Web page.

5. Right-click the **Ch10Proj2b.aspx** page in the Solution Explorer window and click **View Code**. In the code behind the page, use the code following this paragraph to bind the data to the DataReader returned from the GetCat( ) function in the Ch10Products class. Make sure that you type the code on the line after the comment 'Insert code here.

```
Dim CatList As Chapter10.Ch10Products
CatList = New Chapter10.Ch10Products
MyCatList.DataSource = CatList.GetCat()
MyCatList.DataBind()
```

6. Save your Web pages. Build the solution.

7. Open a browser and view the Ch10Proj2b.aspx page. The category list is displayed. When the user clicks a category, the category image is displayed.

8. Stop the SQL Server: the Taskbar contains an icon representing the SQL Server. Right-click on this icon, and then click **MSSQL Server - Stop**. Click **Yes** in the SQL Server Service Manager.

9. View the Ch10Proj2b.aspx Web page in the browser. Print the page that appears.

10. Start the SQL Server: right-click the **SQL Server** icon, and then click **MSSQL Server - Start**.

11. View the Ch10Proj2b.aspx Web page in the browser to make sure the database server has started.

12. Print the Web pages, the source code, and the Global.asax file.

13. Double-click the **Global.asax** page in the Solution Explorer window. Comment out the code in the Application_Error event handler. Do not delete the code.

14. Click the **Save All** button. Click **Build** on the menu bar, and then click **Build Solution**.

10

Project 10-3

In this project you will use the Try-Catch-Finally statement to attempt to run a block of code that detects when an error has occurred. The Web page shows the code that displays the list of products from the database using the DataSet object and the DataGrid control.

1. Start **Visual Studio .NET** and open your **Chapter10** solution if necessary.

2. In Visual Studio .NET create a new Web page named **Ch10Proj3.aspx**.

3. Add a SQL Server DataAdapter to connect to the Ch10TaraStoreSQL database.

4. Generate a DataSet object named **DS_Ch10Proj3** that retrieves the ProductID, ModelNumber, ModelName, and ProductImage fields from the Products table. (*Note*: Once you create the new DataSet object, it will be named DS_Ch10Proj31 by Visual Studio .NET, and then it will be visible within the Design window. Visual Studio .NET suggests the name for the DataSet object. However, you can change this when the DataSet object is generated.)

5. Add a DataView named **DataView1** to display the Products table in the DS_Ch10Proj31 dataset. (*Note*: You will need to set the Table property to the Products table in the Properties window.)

6. Add a DataGrid control named **MyDG**. Modify the DataGrid with colors and fonts to enhance the appearance.

7. In the code behind the page, add the following code to bind the DataView object to the DataGrid control in the Page_Load event handler:

   ```
   SqlDataAdapter1.Fill(DS_Ch10Proj31)
   Page.DataBind()
   ```

8. Save the page by clicking the **Save All** button. Build the project and view the page in the browser.

9. Go back to the Visual Studio .NET application and apply the Try-Catch-Finally statement to the code to catch SQL Server related errors. If an error occurs, redirect the user to the Ch10Home.aspx page. (*Hint*: Since the designer added the data access code behind the page, you can simply add the statement around the fill method, as shown in the code following this paragraph.)

   ```
   Try
       SqlDataAdapter1.Fill(DS_Ch10Proj31)
   Catch
       Response.Redirect("Ch10Home.aspx")
   Finally
   End Try
   Page.DataBind()
   ```

10. Stop the SQL Server: the Taskbar contains an icon representing the SQL Server. Right-click this icon, and then click **MSSQL Server – Stop**. Click **Yes**.

11. View the Ch10Proj3.aspx Web page in the browser. Print the page that appears.

12. Start the SQL Server: right-click the **SQL Server** icon, and then click **MSSQL Server – Start**.

13. View the Ch10Proj3.aspx Web page in the browser to make sure the database server has started.

14. Print the Web page, your source code for the Web page, and the code behind the page.

Project 10-4

In this project, you will document the Web page with comments and create the Code Comment Web Report.

1. Start **Visual Studio .NET** and open your Chapter10 solution if necessary.

2. Open **Ch10Proj4.aspx** from the Solution Explorer window. The page contains a form that includes text boxes for the user's name, e-mail address, and comments.

3. Click the **Save All** button. Build the solution.

4. Click **Tools** on the menu bar, and then click **Build Comment Web Pages**.

5. Click the radio button labeled **Build for selected Projects** to select it. Select **Chapter10**. Click **OK** twice to overwrite the existing Code Comment Web Report.

6. The report will open in Visual Studio .NET. (*Note*: If this page does not automatically open, you should open a browser window and then view the Web page named Solution_Chapter10.htm, which is located in the Chapter10\CodeCommentReport\ folder.)

7. Print the Code Comment Web Report. Print the report for the Ch10Proj4.aspx page.

Project 10-5

In this project, you will use the Page OutputCache feature to cache variations of the same Web page that display different data depending upon which parameters are given.

1. Start **Visual Studio .NET** and open your **Chapter10** solution if necessary.

2. Open the **Ch10Proj5.aspx** page from the Solution Explorer window. This page will display the list of categories from the Category table using a DataList control, and a list of products from the Products table using a DataGrid control.

3. Add the following code in the HTML template to cache the page for 60 seconds based on the CatID:

```
<%@ OutputCache Duration = "60"
VaryByParam = "CatID, SubCatID" %>
```

4. Click the **Save All** button. Build the solution.

5. Open the Web page in your browser. Print the Web page, the source code, and the code behind the page for the Ch10Proj5.aspx page.

6. Suppose there are a million visitors on your Web site today. If all of the pages are viewed within the next 60 minutes, count how many pages could be cached using this method.

10

CASE PROJECTS

Creating a Custom Error Message

You have been asked to create a custom error message that appears when the user does not find the file he or she requested or when the server is unavailable. When the file not found error occurs, redirect the user to the site map. Create a Web page named Ch10Case1a.aspx that contains a site map of all the pages you created in the chapter. Add graphics and content to enhance the appearance of the page. Add hyperlinks to each page in the Chapter10 Web application. Create a Web page named Ch10Case1b.aspx with a message that the Web server is currently unavailable. Add graphics and content to enhance the appearance of the page. Modify the configuration file to support the new error pages that are displayed when the client visits the Web site. (*Hint*: Status code 404 is means that the file is not found. Status code 500 indicates that there is an Internet server error.) Print the Web pages from the browser, the source code for each page, and the Web configuration file.

Creating a Custom Error Message for Database Server Errors

Your boss has asked you to modify the company's application to support custom errors that detect when a database error occurs. Create a new Web page named Ch10Case2a.aspx that explains to the visitor that a database error has occurred. Provide a link to the home page. Create a new page named Ch10Case2b.aspx that displays a listing of products in the Tara Store database only for products where the SubCategoryID is equal to 44. Preview the Web page in a browser. Print the Web page from the browser. Modify the Web page to support catching database errors. In the code behind the page, use Try-Catch-Finally to capture errors related to the SQL Server's Data Adapter. If an error occurs, redirect the user to a page named Ch10Case2a.aspx. Print the Web pages from the browser, and the source code for each page.

Working with the Visual Studio .NET Debugger

Your boss has heard of the new debugger available in Visual Studio .NET. Using the Visual Studio .NET SDK and help documents, read about how to use the debugger tool to identify programming logic errors. Visit five Web pages that describe how to use the debugger tool with ASP.NET and Web applications. You may use any of the Help windows within Visual Studio .NET to locate the help documents. Create a Web page named Ch10Case3.aspx that displays what each resource contains. List the name of the page as a hyperlink to the related help document. Print out the Web page, the source code, and the code behind the page.

Using Page Output Caching to Increase Performance

The Web page that displays the product list takes a long time to access the database and render the output. Your boss has asked you to increase the download performance. Using the Ch10TaraStore SQL Server database that you created earlier in the chapter, create a page named Ch10Case4.aspx to display a list of all of the products in the database where the CategoryID is equal to 24. Display the ProductID, SubCategoryID, ModelNumber, and ModelName. View the page in the browser. Modify the page to support Page Output Caching. The duration of time the page should remain cached is 5 minutes. Save the changes in the page and rebuild the solution. View the Web page in the browser. Print out the Web page, the source code, and the code behind the page.

10

11

CREATING XML WEB SERVICES

In this chapter, you will:

♦ Learn how to apply Web Services to business applications

♦ Identify the configuration files used in an ASP.NET application

♦ Identify Web Services standards and protocols

♦ Create a Web Service using Visual Studio .NET

♦ Create a Web page that consumes a Web Service using Visual Studio .NET

♦ Locate Web Services

♦ Explore the security methods used to protect a Web Service

Web Services are one of the two main applications that are built using ASP.NET technology. While Web Forms deliver Web content from a Web server to a Web-enabled client such as a Web browser, Web Services can deliver content to any device, application, or platform that supports XML Web Services.

One example of a Web Service is the business application developed between Dollar Rent-a-Car and Southwest Airlines. Many airlines share a common airline reservation system of which Southwest Airlines is not a part. Dollar Rent-a-Car created an application to provide reservations from within this airline reservation system. Without Web Services, Southwest would have had to join the airline reservation system in order to work with Dollar Rent-a-Car's system. Instead, Dollar Rent-a-Car and Southwest Airlines developed a Web Service using ASP.NET that allows their two systems to work together. By using Web Services, Southwest saved six months in development time, generated $10 million in incremental revenue, and saved $250,000 in middlemen's fees. They were able to recoup their initial investment. This is one example of how a company can save time and money by using Web Services to connect business systems. Web Services promise to bring information into applications from the Internet in much the same way that browsers have made information available to end users. In this chapter, you will learn to create and consume Web Services using Visual Studio .NET.

OVERVIEW OF WEB SERVICES

Web applications consist of a client, which is the browser application, and a Web server. The Web browser requests a Web page from the Web server. The Web server interacts with other applications, such as a SQL Server database. Then, the Web server delivers the Web page to the browser. But what if the owner of the Web site wants to share the Web site's data with another Web site? In the previous programming model, he or she would use a **Remote Procedure Call (RPC)** to call another application on the Web server. However, this is not useful when you need to create applications that work across platforms. Integrating systems across multiple platforms is time-consuming, costly, and often ineffective. The .NET Framework introduces Web Services as an integral part of the architecture, making it easy for you to create and consume these services with minimal amounts of code written.

With Visual Studio .NET and ASP.NET you can quickly build Web Services that expose parts of your Web application to other businesses and applications. The **Web Service** is part or all of a Web application that is publicly exposed so that other applications can interact with it. The program logic that is exposed via the Web Service is accessible through standard Web protocols such as HTTP, XML, and the Simple Object Access Protocol (SOAP). Therefore, the Web Service is platform independent. This means that any client can access the application using standard protocols.

 The SOAP calls are remote function calls that invoke method executions on Web Service components. The output is rendered as XML and passed back to the user.

Because Web Services are built using open standards, you can use them to develop applications that can be called from a variety of clients on a variety of platforms. As a result, Web Services combine the best aspects of component-based development and Web development. (*Note:* Web Services are like libraries that provide data and services to other applications. That is also why Web Services are sometimes referred to as the Application Programming Interface (API) for the Web application.) Web Services make it easier to build distributed Internet applications.

 Microsoft provides additional information about Web Services at *http://msdn.microsoft.com/webservices*. The .NET platform provides built-in support for invoking standards-based Web Services. Unlike other development platforms, you do not need additional tools or SDKs to build Web Services with .NET. All the necessary support is built into the .NET Framework itself.

Figure 11-1 shows how the Web Service client communicates with the Web server. The Web Service client can be a Web application, a mobile application, or even a Microsoft Web application. In Figure 11-1, the Web Service client is running a Web application. Therefore, in the figure, the Web Service client is a Web server and the content is delivered to a browser. (*Note:* The Web Service client does not have to be running on a Web server, unless it's running a Web application.) The browser is a client of the Web application. The browser does not know that the Web server is communicating with a Web Service. Additionally, the Web Service client does not know that the Web Service is communicating with any back-end applications or data sources.

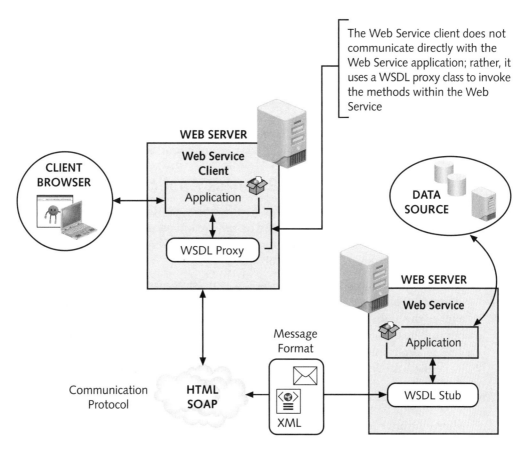

Figure 11-1   Web Services provide a mechanism for applications to communicate with each other

The Web Service client application does not communicate directly with the Web Service application. Rather, it creates a WSDL proxy. WSDL stands for **Web Service Description Language (WSDL)**. The **WSDL proxy** is a class that is used to invoke the Web Service. The WSDL proxy will communicate with the Web Service application through a WSDL stub. The **WSDL stub** is the code that communicates between the proxy class and the Web Service application. The purpose of the WSDL stub is to make the communication with the Web Service application simpler and transparent. The developer does not have to know about the inner workings of the Web Service application in order to invoke the Web Service. Rather, the WSDL stub knows what can be sent into and out of the Web Service application. The WSDL proxy and stub can be created manually using the WSDL command-line utility (wsdl.exe) or automatically when you use Visual Studio .NET to create and consume your Web Service.

The two applications need to be able to send messages and data back and forth across the a TCP/IP network such as the Internet. The messages and data are formatted using XML standards so that both applications can understand them. However, these messages and data need to be modified to be sent over the Internet using HTTP. They are packaged using **Simple Object Access Protocol (SOAP)** as an envelope for the messages and data. Later in this chapter, you will learn more about WSDL and SOAP.

Applying Web Services to Business Applications

There are dozens of ways in which Web Services can benefit businesses. One concept is to stream data, such as stock quotes or the weather forecast. The Web Service provides the data, and the client application connects to the Web Service to retrieve it. The client could be a browser or another Web site.

Another example of a Web Service is a real-estate database search application. Several companies list their homes with a multiple listing agent. A real estate company could expose the ability to search for a house in their real estate database. The real estate agents can use the browser to search for homes based on criteria such as the number of bedrooms. The multiple listing service company could allow other Web sites to connect to the real estate database Web Service. Then, they would be able to allow their customers to search for homes via their Web sites. For each sale that originated from the Web Service, the real estate company could pay the Web site a referral fee.

Microsoft offers documentation on several case studies where their enterprise customers create and consume Web Services. This documentation is at *http://msdn.microsoft.com/ webservices/understanding/casestudies/default.aspx*. (*Note*: You can manually search their case studies at *http://www.microsoft.com/resources/casestudies/FindCaseStudy.aspx*.)

Web Services focuses on business-to-business applications. However, a company can use Web Services to develop communication methods between applications within their own systems as well. This would be very useful to companies who must maintain back-end legacy systems. A Web Service can be created so that the back-end system can communicate with the newer applications. Because the Web Service can often be reused without additional programming, the Web Service can be reused across applications. For example, a human resource director in a hospital may desire to have an application that obtains information about a particular employee, but the human resources database may be stored within a mainframe application. The Web Service can be used to expose the data from the mainframe. If the human resource application sends the Web Service an employee ID, the Web Service will communicate with the mainframe and return the employee data. However, consider the additional situation in which the nursing administrator needs to be able to access employee data. Instead of building an additional application, the nursing administrator only needs to build his or her application and call the Web Service. He or she would not have to rebuild the Web Service.

Another recent trend on the Internet is for a Web site, for example an online magazine, to display books from an online bookstore. The Web site receives money, credit, or other bonuses for referring the user to the online bookstore to purchase the book. To create the link between the magazine and the online bookstore, you could hard-code the bookstore hyperlinks into your application. If the magazine is a significant business partner to the bookstore, you could create a custom distributed application to the bookstore's Web application.

A newer and controversial technique that has been used to retrieve product information is scraping. **Scraping** a Web site is the process of using a program to view a Web site and capture the source code. The programmer has to create an application that parses the HTML from the data. Then, the programmer has to create a program that integrates the new data into the Web site. This process would have to be repeated as often as the original Web site changed.

A better solution than any of these is for the bookstore to provide a Web Service to its catalogue application. Programmers could then use the Catalogue Web Service within their own Web applications. The bookstore could limit who has access to the Catalogue Web Service. They could expose the entire program as a Web Service, or only certain parts of the catalogue application. By making the catalogue application public, any programmer could use Visual Studio .NET tools to integrate his or her Web site with the bookstore application.

In addition to retrieving data, Web Services can also interact with the Web application. In the online bookstore Web Service, the programmer could expose the ordering functions as a Web Service. Then, your Web site could sell the books without the customer having to leave your site. You would provide the user interface for the order form. When the customer submitted the form, you would order the product via the Web Service. Thus, the Web Service allows your Web site to act as a distributor for other goods and services on the Internet.

There are many other uses of Web Services. For example, you could use a Web Service to deliver educational materials to schools around the country. Each school could integrate the Web Service into its own curriculum, instead of purchasing a prepackaged curriculum, or building a custom curriculum.

Web Services could also be used to build public service Web sites. For example, volunteer organizations share many common areas of interests and needs. A volunteer organization could build a Web Service that exposed their resources as a community service directory. The resources could be classified by type of service, such as fundraising, or they could be classified by the age of the targeted group. Then, any volunteer organization could use the same directory, or portions of the directory, within their Web site. For example, one organization might want to show only listings for services within its state, for children. Another organization might want to show only services for fundraising in the Midwestern states. By using Web Services, a variety of applications can access the data.

Web Services could be used to retrieve national statistical data such as the census, or government records. You could build the Web Service that contains information about all of the elected government positions. Although all counties in a state have their own governmental bodies, they all share the same state governmental body. Therefore, the counties would be able to access the state-specific data from the Web Service. Individual cities and villages could access the county governmental data and their own local governmental data.

Using Visual Studio .NET to Create and Consume Web Services

Web Services are at the core of the Microsoft .NET vision. Microsoft and IBM worked together to create the XML Web Services standards. However, Web Services can be created using a variety of developer tools and programming languages. The three main parts of building and consuming a Web Service are shown in Figure 11-2. As shown in this example, Tara Store has created a Web Service. They also created a contract that provides information about how to connect to the Web Service. Tara Store's new partner, MaryKate's Housewares, has contracted to use the Tara Store Web Service. They use the contract to learn how to connect to the Web Service. They create a proxy client, which connects to the Web Service. MaryKate's Housewares integrates the data into its own Web site. The end user could be using a variety of applications to access the Internet such as a mobile phone or Web browser. The client sees only the MaryKate's Housewares Web site. They are not aware of the involvement of Tara Store, or the source of the product listing. Although this is an example of a business-to-business-to-consumer application, some Web Services will be limited to business-to-business transactions.

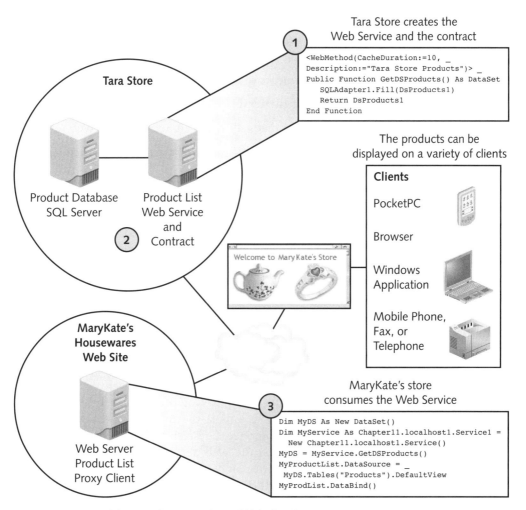

Figure 11-2 Building and consuming a Web Service

Building a Web Service

The easiest way to build a Web Service with .NET is to use Visual Studio .NET and create an ASP.NET Web Service project. Visual Studio .NET creates all the necessary files, including the Web Service files. The Web Service files are called service1.asmx and service1.asmx.vb by default. The service1.asmx.vb file is the code behind the page for the Web Service.

In order to create a Web Service, you must create a class method with standard input and output parameters and then mark those classes and the specific methods as exposable over the Internet by using the **<WebMethod>** keyword.

There are three major components that make up a Web Service:

- The Web Service on the server side

- The client application that calls the Web Service via a Web reference

- A WSDL Web Service description that describes the functionality of the Web Service

There are several resources for Web developers on using XML with Web Services. You can learn about using XML with Visual Studio .NET at *http://msdn.microsoft.com/library/en-us/vsintro7/html/vxorixmlinvisualstudio. asp*. You can locate sample business applications that contain and consume Web Services on the *www.IBuySpy.com* Web site or at *http://msdn.microsoft. com/webservices/building/livewebservices/default.aspx*.

The Web Service

The first part of the Web Service is the server application that is exposed. In ASP.NET, the name of the file for the Web Service must have the file extension .asmx. This Web Service file compiles into a class. So, a Web Service is a class that can be called over a TCP/IP network. As with a traditional Web page, you can create the source file of the Web Service by using a text editor such as Notepad, or a Web development tool such as Visual Studio .NET. You need to import the **System.Web.Services** namespace into the source code for the Web Service. The Web Service is compiled at runtime similarly to ASP.NET pages. Although the Web Service is typically created within a Web application in the same assembly, you can create a separate assembly for the Web Service. Web Services are part of the ASP.NET application model. Therefore, the Web Service must be accessible from a URL that is defined within the Web server. Because the Web Service was built within the ASP.NET Framework, it has access to the ASP.NET object model and all the ASP.NET objects such as Request, Session, and Application.

The Web Service page is also divided into Design view and the code behind the page. The code behind the page can be written in any of the .NET languages. You can specify which parts of the Web Service class should be exposed. The keyword <WebMethod> is used to identify the methods that are to be exposed. You can expose properties such as strings, integers, and expressions. Although you can expose objects such as the DataSet object, Web Services do not require you to create or expose programmable objects.

Locating Web Services

After the Web Service is created, developers must be able to locate a discovery file, known as the Web Service Description Language (WSDL) document. WSDL is a description language that contains the information on how to interact with the Web Service and how to format and send data to the Web Service. The WSDL document is an XML document that describes the methods, namespaces, and URL of the Web Service. When you use Visual Studio .NET to create your Web Service, it will automatically create the WSDL document for you. The WSDL schema is an open standard used to create the WSDL document.

As you can see in Figure 11-3, the Web Service client can locate the Web Service application several ways. The directory mechanism is the means to locate a Web Service through a **Web Service Discovery Directory**. Microsoft and IBM have teamed up to create the **Universal Description**, **Discovery**, **and Integration (UDDI)** specification, which can be used to create a third-party Web Service Discovery Directory. You can use these UDDI directories to locate Web Services and the WSDL document. You can learn more about the UDDI standards at *http://www.uddi.org*. Microsoft's UDDI server is located at UDDI.Microsoft.Com.

The second mechanism to locate the Web Service is known as discovery. The developer can visit the Web server and locate a Web Discovery Service file to locate the Web server. The **Web Discovery Service** file ends in the file extension .DISCO. The default DISCO file is named default.disco. This file points to all of the Web Services within your application and the location of the WSDL document. When you are using Visual Studio .NET, you can use the Server Explorer window to locate the Web Services on your server and network by reading the discovery files.

The third mechanism used to locate a Web Service is to request the URL of the WSDL document from the owner of the Web Service.

11

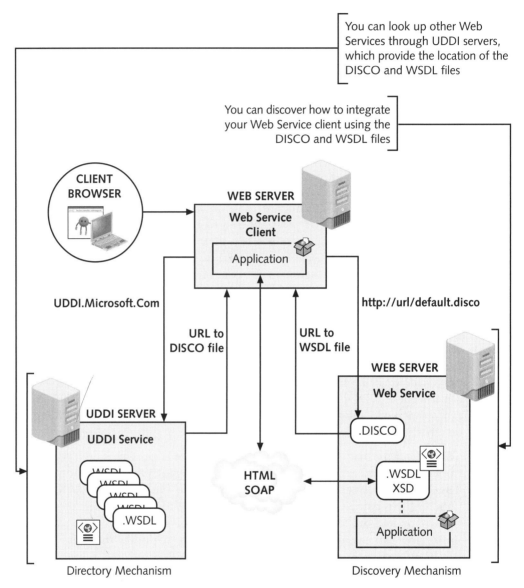

You can look up other Web
Services through UDDI servers,
which provide the location of the
DISCO and WSDL files

You can discover how to integrate
your Web Service client using the
DISCO and WSDL files

Figure 11-3   Locating Web Services

The Proxy Class

Web Services can be consumed programmatically or manually, and can be called from
within your Web or Windows application. Adding a **Web Reference** to your application allows you to treat the Web Service as a local application. Therefore, you can refer
to the Web Service class as if it were a local class.

Within Visual Studio .NET, the IntelliSense feature provides access to all of the properties and methods of the Web Service class. Even if the Web Service was created on a different platform with a different programming language, you can still call the Web Service class and create programs that interact with the Web Service properties and methods.

The Web Service client application does not call the Web Service class directly. The application uses the WSDL document to create a **proxy class**. The Web Service client application calls the proxy class to invoke the Web Service. The proxy class reads the WSDL document and verifies the delivery method. The XML-based request and response messages can be delivered using the HTTPGet method, the HTTPPost method, or SOAP. SOAP calls are remote function calls that invoke method executions on Web Service components. The output is rendered as XML and passed back to the Web Service client application. SOAP is an important part of creating and consuming Web Services—it's the protocol that's responsible for routing the RPC message from the client to the server and returning the result to the client application. SOAP is based on XML and follows a relatively simple design that's easy to implement. SOAP's simplicity has contributed to its widespread support on just about any platform and development environment. As long as a Web Service client client application has support for SOAP, it can call the remote Web Service and return data for it, assuming that the Web Service client application is authorized.

If you are sending the message using SOAP, the proxy class creates the **SOAP envelope**, and then passes the envelope to the Web Service. The SOAP envelope is used as a wrapper around the messages and provides information about the message format. After the Web server receives the SOAP request, it creates a new instance of the Web Service. After the Web Service has been executed the return value, indicated by the keyword **Return**, passes the output to the SOAP response. The SOAP response is sent over the HTTP connection to the proxy. The client converts the XML document into a format that is understandable by that client application.

If you think that the data within the Web Service will not change frequently, you may want to use the caching techniques you learned in the previous chapter to increase performance. Synchronous calls wait for a response from the Web server. Your Web Service client application performance degrades if you must wait a long time for the response from a Web Service. Asynchronous calls request the data from the Web Service, and then continue processing the Web Service client application. You can configure your application to send asynchronous calls to the Web Service to increase the performance of your application. In a production environment, you may not be involved in both creating and consuming the Web Service. You may only be creating the Web Service, and providing its description. Another company creates the Web Service client application that uses your Web Service Description document to create the interface to your Web Service application.

11

WEB SERVICES STANDARDS AND PROTOCOLS

The HTTP protocol was selected as the primary delivery protocol of Web Services because it can be used to deliver documents through proxy servers and firewalls. The three methods used to route the message over HTTP are HTTPGet, HTTPPost, and SOAP. When you create a Web Service page such as default.asmx, ASP.NET automatically creates the support for a test page also known as the Service Description page.

In addition to calling the Web Service, you can pass parameters to the Web Service page with a QueryString, using the HTTPGet method. The HTTPPost method passes the parameters as a URL-encoded string, which contains the form field variable names and values attached to the body of the message. The SOAP protocol is the default method by which ASP.NET internally calls a Web Service.

Programming Web Services with Visual Studio .NET

Web Services are fully integrated into the Visual Studio .NET development environment. When you use Visual Studio .NET to create your Web Service, the application generates the WSDL document, the DISCO document, and the test Web page. You can use the breakpoints within the debugger tool and the tracing features to debug your Web Service. When you use Visual Studio .NET to consume a Web Service, the application generates a client-side proxy class with both synchronous and asynchronous calls. Then, when you want to access an object, property, or function within the Web Service, the local Web application treats the Web Service as a local object. As a result, all the features of Visual Studio .NET, such as IntelliSense and debugging, are also supported.

The SOAP Contract

The SOAP protocol is an industry standard that is maintained by the WC3. **Simple Object Access Protocol (SOAP)** is an XML-based protocol used for messaging delivery. SOAP is language independent and platform independent. The SOAP message is a remote procedure call over HTTP using XML. Because it's an XML-based message format, it can easily be transmitted over HTTP through firewalls and proxy servers. Because SOAP can represent remote procedure calls and responses from another application, it allows the client application to call the Web Service over HTTP. The SOAP packet contains a SOAP envelope and the response in an XML document. The response may contain the XML data. And, because it serializes the calls and data in XML, SOAP provides a flexible way to express application defined data types. Once the application receives the XML data, the application can deserialize the data into an object such as the DataSet object. So, if you plan to create a Web Service that creates objects, you will likely want to call the Web Service by using SOAP.

SOAP is a simple protocol for publishing available services. The Soap contract is an XML-formatted document called the WSDL. The SOAP contract describes the interface to the Web Service. You can view the SOAP contract by opening a browser and typing the URL of the Web Service followed by "?WSDL". The WSDL file is an XML-formatted file that describes how to call the Web methods using the SOAP protocol. The WSDL document describes the message exchange contract. The WSDL document name has the file extension .sdl. So, the name of a SOAP contract for a Web Service named MyService would be MyService.sdl.

The SOAP contract uses the XML language to describe the location and interfaces that a particular service supports. The WSDL utility looks at the contract and generates the proxy class based on the contract. The WSDL utility is wsdl.exe. The utility requires you to pass the URL of the description. The parameter **?wsdl** is used to generate the proxy. The WSDL utility does not work with the Web Service directly, but through a proxy class. Because the default language used to generate the proxy class default is C#, you may want to use the /language or /l parameter to configure the language as Visual Basic .NET. The /protocol parameter is used for communication with the service. The /namespace parameter is used to configure the global namespace. The default namespace for the proxy class for all Web Services is http://tempuri.org. http://tempuri.org is a generic namespace used in WSDL documents. You can locate more information about the namespaces used in WSDL documents at the *http://tempuri.org* Web site. You should change the reference to the tempuri namespace to your namespace when you are ready to deploy your Web application. (*Note*: If you are using Visual Studio .NET to create and consume Web Services, you can change the Namespace attribute of the <WebMethod> tag.) After you create the proxy class, you need to compile it and place it inside the assembly cache. You can compile the application directly with the Visual Basic .NET or Visual C# compiler. The code following this paragraph is a sample of how you can use the WSDL command-line utility to look at the contract and generates the proxy class. wsdl is the command to call the WSDL utility, and /language:VB configures Visual Basic .NET as the language of the class. The URL provides the location of the contract to the Web Service.

```
wsdl /language:VB http://locahost/Service1.asmx?wsdl
```

The DISCO (discovery) document is not the SOAP contract. Rather, it's a pointer to the location of the Web Services within the Web project. The DISCO document is an XML document that examines the SOAP contract to describe the method and data formats within the Web Service. The DISCO document describes how the proxy class should make calls to the Web Service. Although in Visual Studio .NET you can use the tools to create and consume Web Services, you can also use command-line utilities without Visual Studio .NET. The wsdl.exe file is used to create the SOAP contract.

You will use the **Visual Basic .NET compiler (VBC.exe)** to create the discovery document. You use the VBC.exe compiler to create the proxy class for a Visual Basic .NET class. There are several parameters that can be passed when you use the utility. The /username and /password parameters are provided to authenticate the application to the Web server. The /domain parameter is the domain name that is needed to access the server. By default, the output from the discovery process is saved to a file in the current directory with the file extension .DISCO. You can specify an alternate directory with the /out parameter. You can suppress the output file entirely with the /nosave parameter. The /nologo parameter will suppress the Microsoft logo. The following sample code uses the Discovery tool to send the discovery information to a file in the temp directory:

```
Disco.exe /nologo /out:c:\temp\disco
http://localhost/websx/services.disco
```

The test page uses the HTTPGet method to test the Web Service. Therefore, the names and values are passed with the URL in the QueryString. Because the HTTPGet method was used, the data is returned in an XML format, and not in a SOAP message. However, this gives you the opportunity to verify that you can connect to the Web Service and retrieve data. Because Web Services use standard Web protocols, they follow typical Web rules. For example, Web Services are stateless, which means that, even though Web Services expose classes, they are more of a remote procedure call interface than a remote class interface. None of the major Web Service implementations support properties in any way. You can call methods with parameters rather than storing state in properties between method calls. To maintain state, you will have to use Web server-specific functionality, such as the ASP.NET Session object, to store the state and retrieve it on subsequent hits. Furthermore, since Web Services use the standard Web architecture, the same tools you have used for HTML-based browser applications can also be used in the Web Services code.

 A good article on how to consume a Web Service using SOAP and Perl is located at *http://msdn.microsoft.com/webservices/building/frameworkandstudio/ tipstricks/default.aspx?pull=/library/en-us/dnsoap/html/soapliteperl.asp.*

CREATING A WEB SERVICE

Web Services are fully integrated into the Visual Studio .NET development environment. When you use Visual Studio .NET to create your Web Service, the application generates the WSDL document, the DISCO document, and the test Web page. You can use the breakpoints within the debugger tool and the tracing features to debug your Web Service.

When you create a Web Service, there are two parts. When you create a Web Service in Visual Studio .NET, the file will automatically import the WebService namespace at the top of the file. Then, the page class is converted into a Web Service by the insertion of the **WebServiceAttribute**, which means that the **WebService** keyword is inserted before the class declaration. The use of the WebServiceAttribute is optional. However, as shown in the code that follows this paragraph, you can include several properties with the WebServiceAttribute, including Namespace and Description. The **Namespace property** identifies a unique URL that can distinguish your Web Service from other Web Services on the Internet. The default uses the domain tempuri.org. If you use tempuri.org as the namespace, your Web Service home page will display a message reminding you to change the namespace value. It is highly recommended to replace the tempuri.org namespace with your company's domain name. In the code that follows this paragraph, the default namespace was changed to tarastore.com. The **Description property** can be used to provide information about your Web Service. The Description attribute will appear on the Web Service home page. Therefore, you can use HTML commands to format the Description attribute. The **Name property** allows you to provide a name for the Web Service that will be displayed in the Web Service home page.

```
<System.Web.Services.WebService _
(Namespace:="http://tarastore.com/", _
Description:=
"<H2>Displaying Data from the Tara Store Database</H2>", _
Name:="Chapter 11 Web Service")> _
Public Class ServerVariables
    ...
End Class
```

Within the class defined within the Web Service, you will expose one or more methods or functions by using the **WebMethod attribute** as shown in the code that follows this paragraph. The WebMethod attribute provides several properties such as BufferResponse, CacheDuration, MessageName, and Description. The properties of the WebServiceAttribute are separated from the values using a semicolon and an equal sign. The **BufferResponse property** allows you to store the response on the server until the entire function is processed. Then, the data is returned to the client. By setting the BufferResponse property to true, you will improve your server performance by minimizing the communication required between the Web Server process and the ASP.NET worker process. The **CacheDuration property** is used to identify in seconds how long to cache results from the Web Service. The WebMethod will automatically cache the results for each unique parameter sent to the WebMethod. The MessageName property allows you to assign a name for the method that will be displayed within the Web Service home page. The **Description property** allows you to provide a description for the method that will be displayed within the Web Service home page. Because this is a string, you can format the description with HTML.

```
<WebMethod(CacheDuration:=10, _
Description:=
"GetCat() returns the category list
for the main menu.")> _
Public Function WS_GetCat() As DataSet
        Dim MySQL As String = "SELECT * FROM Categories"
        Dim objCM1 As New
        OleDbDataAdapter(MySQL, OleDbConnection1)
        Dim objDS1 As New DataSet
        objCM1.Fill(objDS1, "Categories")
        Return objDS1
End Function
```

11

In this exercise, you create a Web Service for Tara Store to allow other stores to display its merchandise. The Web Service returns data as a DataSet object. You will use the WebMethod in the declaration line to declare the function as a Web Service method. There are four functions that will be exposed; each corresponds to functions used in the CatMenu.aspx page from Chapter 10. You will insert the code manually instead of using the Visual Studio .NET DataAdapter wizard. The code creates the Connection String, DataAdapter object, Connection object, Command object, and DataSet object for each of the four functions. When a Web Service client application calls the Web Service, it will be able to access these four functions and receive a DataSet object with the results.

1. Start Visual Studio .NET.

2. Click **File** on the menu bar, point to **New**, and then click **Project**. This opens the New Project window.

3. Click the **Visual Basic Projects** folder icon, then click **ASP.NET Web Service** under Templates. Type **Chapter11WebService** in the Location text box in place of WebService1. (*Note*: The complete URL will be *http://localhost/Chapter11WebService*.) Click **OK** to create the solution, project, and default files. The default Web Service page, named Service1.asmx.vb, opens in Design view. Close the Service1.asmx.vb and Start pages. (*Note*: When you create the Web Service project, Visual Studio .NET automatically includes references to the System.Data, System.Drawing, System.Web, System.WebServices, and System.XML namespaces. Therefore, you do not have to import these namespaces into your projects.)

4. Open Windows Explorer. To do so, click **Start**, click **Run**, type **%SystemRoot%\explorer.exe** in the text box, and then click **OK**. Navigate to your **Chapter11Data\Chapter11WebService** folder. Select all of the files and folders, click the **Edit** menu, and select **Copy**. Go back to Visual Studio .NET 2003. Right-click the **Chapter11WebService** project and select **Paste**. The data folder, image folder, and data files will be copied into your project. Click **Yes** in the dialog box, if one appears, to create a class for the data file.

5. Right-click the **Ch11Products.vb** page in the Solution Explorer window and select **View Code**. The code creates a connection string variable, a Connection object and four functions. (*Note*: If you store the database in a different location, you must change the connection string to reflect the new location.)

6. Click the **Save All** button. Click **Build** on the menu bar, and then click **Build Solution**.

7. Open a browser window and go to **http://localhost/Chapter11WebService/CatMenu.aspx**. The list of categories and the home image should appear. (*Note*: If the page does not display the category list or the home image, you must verify the connection string and the permissions on the database and folder before proceeding to the next step.) Close the browser window.

8. In Visual Studio .NET, right-click the **Ch11WS_ProductsDS.asmx** page in the Solution Explorer window and select **View Code**. The Ch11WS_ProductsDS.asmx page is the Web Service home page.

9. Below the comment that says 'Insert the WS_GetCat()Method here, type the code that follows this paragraph. The code will configure the WS_GetCat() function as a WebMethod. You can refer to Figure 11-4 for the placement of the code.

```
<WebMethod(CacheDuration:=10, _
Description:= ⤶
"WS_GetCat() returns the category ⤶
list for the main menu.    ", _
BufferResponse:=True, _
MessageName:="GetCat() Method")> _
Public Function WS_GetCat() As DataSet
        Dim MySQL As String = "SELECT * FROM Categories"
        Dim objCM1 as New ⤶
        OleDbDataAdapter(MySQL, OleDbConnection1)
        Dim objDS1 As New DataSet
        objCM1.Fill(objDS1, "Categories")
        Return objDS1
End Function
```

11

```
Imports System.Data.OleDb
Imports System.Web.Services

<System.Web.Services.WebService _
(Namespace:="http://tarastore.com/", _
Description:="<H2>Displaying Data from the Tara Store Database</H2>", _
Name:="Chapter 11 Web Service")> _
Public Class Ch11WS_ProductsDS
    Inherits System.Web.Services.WebService

Web Services Designer Generated Code

    Dim CS As String = _
        "Data Source=" & _
        "C:\Inetpub\wwwroot\Chapter11WebService\data\TaraStore.mdb;" & _
        "Provider=Microsoft.Jet.OLEDB.4.0"
    Dim OleDbConnection1 As New OleDbConnection(CS)

    ' Insert the WS_GetCat() WebMethod here
    <WebMethod(CacheDuration:=10, _
    Description:="WS_GetCat() returns the category list for the main menu.", _
    BufferResponse:=True, _
    MessageName:="GetCat() Method")> _
    Public Function WS_GetCat() As DataSet
        Dim MySQL As String = "SELECT * FROM Categories"
        Dim objCM1 As New OleDbDataAdapter(MySQL, OleDbConnection1)
        Dim objDS1 As New DataSet
        objCM1.Fill(objDS1, "Categories")
        Return objDS1
    End Function
```

Import the Web Service and data namespaces

The Description and Name properties are displayed in the Web Service home page

Verify that the connection string is pointed to the location of your database

The WebMethod Description and MessageName properties are displayed in the Web Service home page

The Web Service will return a DataSet object

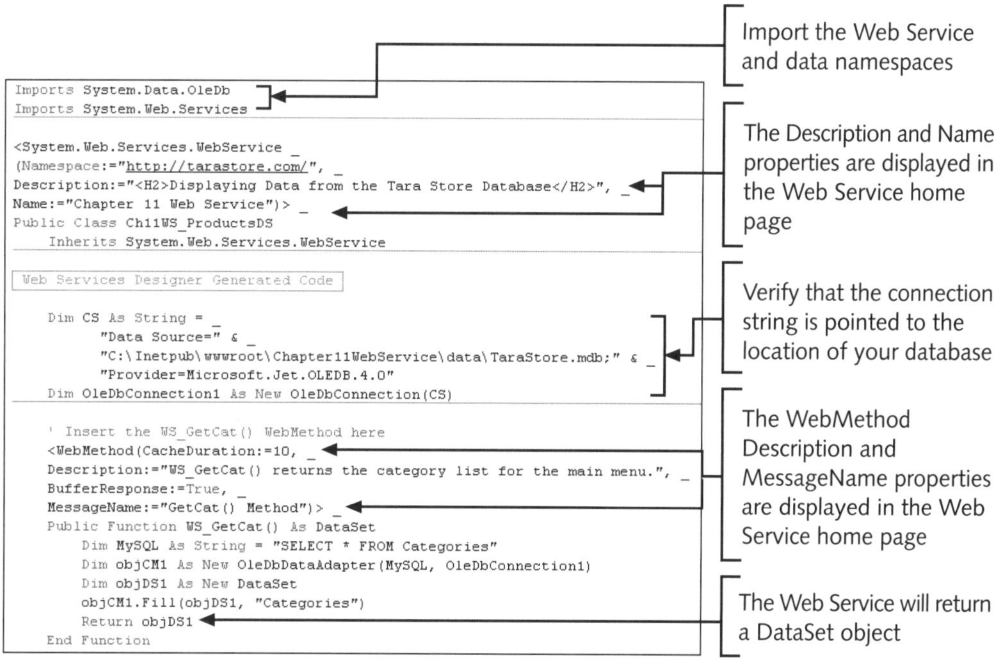

Figure 11-4   Creating a Web Service

10. Click the **Save All** button. Click **Build** on the menu bar, and then click **Build Solution**.

Previewing the Web Service Home Page

In the next part of the exercise, you will view the Web Service home page in a browser. This will provide you with a list of the functions and properties defined in the Web Service. In this example, there are four functions exposed. Clicking the hyperlinks will take you to the test page, where you can test each function. The test page shows sample code that illustrates the sample request and response that is used when communicating with the Web Service using SOAP, HTTPGet, or HTTPPost. From there you can test the Web Service by invoking the function and view the output in an XML–formatted document.

1. Open the browser. Go to the Web Service home page at *http://localhost/ Chapter11WebService/Ch11WS_ProductsDS.asmx*. Notice that the Web Service Description property is shown in the Web Service home page as <H2>Displaying Data from the Tara Store Database</H2>. Refer to Figure 11-5.

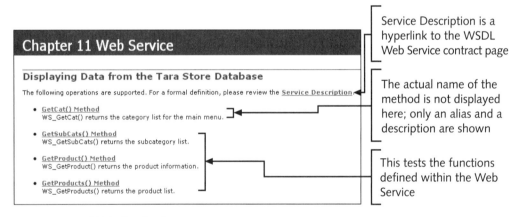

Figure 11-5   Web Service home page

2. Click the hyperlink named **GetCatMethod()**. This hyperlink is the method that was defined in the Web Service. (*Note:* The hyperlink takes you to a page with the URL *http://localhost/Chapter11WebService/Ch11WS_ProductsDS. asmx?op=GetCat()+Method.*) The plus sign (+) is used to represent a blank space in the URL. See Figure 11-6.

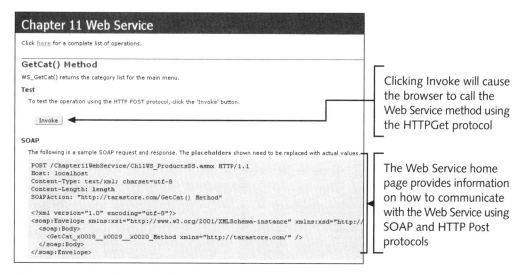

Figure 11-6   Invoking a Web Service method

3. Click the **Invoke** button to test the WS_GetCat() method displayed on the Web page as GetCat() method. An XML document is returned that describes the data and contains the data. The URL of the document is *http://localhost/ Chapter11WebService/Ch11WS_ProductsDS.asmx/GetCat()%20Method* as shown in Figure 11-7. The top portion of the document describes the data, and the lower portion contains the product data. There are no additional parameters passed with the QueryString in this example.

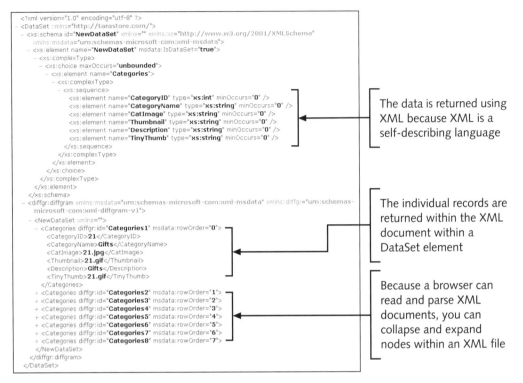

```
<?xml version="1.0" encoding="utf-8" ?>
- <DataSet xmlns="http://tarastore.com/">
  - <xs:schema id="NewDataSet" xmlns="" xmlns:xs="http://www.w3.org/2001/XMLSchema"
      xmlns:msdata="urn:schemas-microsoft-com:xml-msdata">
    - <xs:element name="NewDataSet" msdata:IsDataSet="true">
      - <xs:complexType>
        - <xs:choice maxOccurs="unbounded">
          - <xs:element name="Categories">
            - <xs:complexType>
              - <xs:sequence>
                  <xs:element name="CategoryID" type="xs:int" minOccurs="0" />
                  <xs:element name="CategoryName" type="xs:string" minOccurs="0" />
                  <xs:element name="CatImage" type="xs:string" minOccurs="0" />
                  <xs:element name="Thumbnail" type="xs:string" minOccurs="0" />
                  <xs:element name="Description" type="xs:string" minOccurs="0" />
                  <xs:element name="TinyThumb" type="xs:string" minOccurs="0" />
                </xs:sequence>
              </xs:complexType>
            </xs:element>
          </xs:choice>
        </xs:complexType>
      </xs:element>
    </xs:schema>
  - <diffgr:diffgram xmlns:msdata="urn:schemas-microsoft-com:xml-msdata" xmlns:diffgr="urn:schemas-
      microsoft-com:xml-diffgram-v1">
    - <NewDataSet xmlns="">
      - <Categories diffgr:id="Categories1" msdata:rowOrder="0">
          <CategoryID>21</CategoryID>
          <CategoryName>Gifts</CategoryName>
          <CatImage>21.jpg</CatImage>
          <Thumbnail>21.gif</Thumbnail>
          <Description>Gifts</Description>
          <TinyThumb>21.gif</TinyThumb>
        </Categories>
      + <Categories diffgr:id="Categories2" msdata:rowOrder="1">
      + <Categories diffgr:id="Categories3" msdata:rowOrder="2">
      + <Categories diffgr:id="Categories4" msdata:rowOrder="3">
      + <Categories diffgr:id="Categories5" msdata:rowOrder="4">
      + <Categories diffgr:id="Categories6" msdata:rowOrder="5">
      + <Categories diffgr:id="Categories7" msdata:rowOrder="6">
      + <Categories diffgr:id="Categories8" msdata:rowOrder="7">
      </NewDataSet>
    </diffgr:diffgram>
  </DataSet>
```

The data is returned using XML because XML is a self-describing language

The individual records are returned within the XML document within a DataSet element

Because a browser can read and parse XML documents, you can collapse and expand nodes within an XML file

Figure 11-7 Testing the Web Service

4. Close the browser window that contains the XML document.

5. Click the **Back** button in the browser to return to the Web Service home page.

6. Click the hyperlink labeled **Service Description** to view the service contract. The URL of the Service Description page is the same as that of the Web Service home page with ?WSDL appended. The Service Description page in the example is located at *http://localhost/Chapter11WebService/Ch11WS_ProductsDS. asmx?WSDL* as shown in Figure 11-8.

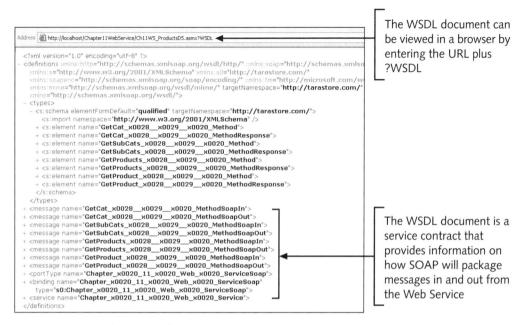

The WSDL document can be viewed in a browser by entering the URL plus ?WSDL

The WSDL document is a service contract that provides information on how SOAP will package messages in and out from the Web Service

Figure 11-8   Web Service description page

7. Close the browser window. Return to Visual Studio .NET. Click the **Save All** button. Click **Build** on the menu bar, then click **Build Solution**.

8. To close the solution, click **File** on the menu bar, and then click **Close Solution**.

You can turn the line numbering feature on or off. The line numbering feature is useful when you want to locate specific lines of code. To configure the line numbering feature, go to the Options command on the Tools menu. Click the Text Editor tab, select All Languages, then select General. Click the Line numbers check box to turn line numbering on, and then click OK.

USING A WEB SERVICE

You can call Web Services via the HTTPGet and HTTPPost methods, or via SOAP. Although the HTTPGet and HTTPPost methods are limited to sending only primitive data types such as integers, and strings, they can also send arrays of these primitive data types. The SOAP protocol allows you to send any structure, class, or enumerator over the Internet. For example, you can send an ADO object, such as a DataSet object, or an array of Data objects.

When you send the information over the Internet, the information is packaged in a format that can travel over a TCP/IP network. **Serialization** is the process of changing an object into a form that can be readily transported over the network. For example, you can serialize the output of a structure, such as a DataSet object, into a string. With Web Services, you use HTTPGet or HTTPPost to send an object; then the methods, properties, and values of the object can be rendered as elements of an XML document. The process of converting the object to an XML document is known as XML serialization. Once this has been done, you can use the HTTP Get and Post methods to retrieve the serialized object. You then change the string back into the original structure, which is known as **deserialization**. If the document is in XML format, you can also use LoadXML method of the XML Document Object Model (DOM) to retrieve the XML data. When you use Visual Studio .NET to create and consume Web Services, Visual Studio .NET will create the code necessary to serialize and deserialize your Web Services.

 You can learn more about XML serialization at *http://msdn.microsoft.com/ webservices/understanding/xmlfundamentals/default.aspx, http://msdn. microsoft.com/library/en-us/dnexxml/html/xml01202003.asp, http://msdn.microsoft.com/webservices/building/xmldevelopment/ xmlserialization/default.aspx*, and *http://msdn.microsoft.com/library/en-us/ cpguide/html/cpconintroducingxmlserialization.asp.*

When you use Visual Studio .NET to consume a Web Service, the application generates a client-side proxy class with both synchronous and asynchronous calls. Then, when you want to access an object, property, or function within the Web Service, the local Web application treats the Web Service as a local object. As a result, all the programming tools of Visual Studio .NET, such as IntelliSense and debugging, are also supported with Web Services.

The application that calls the Web Service is a Web Service client. You create a Web Service client from an ASP.NET page. The Web Service may be called by the HTTPGet and HTTPPost methods, or SOAP. The Server Explorer window allows you to see Web Services installed within your local Web server.

Consuming a Web Service from an ASP.NET Page

In the exercise following this paragraph, you create a Web page for a partner of Tara Store named MaryKate's Housewares, which wants to distribute Tara Store's products on its Web site. The owners hope to increase their market share by expanding their product line. However, they do not want their customers to know of their relationship with Tara Store. The Web page you create in the following step sequence consumes the Tara Store Web Service and displays Tara Store's products.

1. Start **Visual Studio .NET**.

2. Click **File** on the menu bar, point to **New**, and then click **Project**. This opens the New Project window.

3. Click **Visual Basic Projects** in the Project Types pane. Click **ASP.NET Web Application** in the Templates pane. Type **Chapter11** in the Location text box in place of WebApplication1. Click **OK** to create the solution, project, and default files.

4. Open Windows Explorer. (To do so, click **Start**, click **Run**, type **%SystemRoot%\explorer.exe** in the text box, and then click **OK**.) Navigate to your **Chapter11Data\Chapter11** folder. Select all of the files and folders, click the **Edit** menu, and select **Copy**. Go back to **Visual Studio .NET 2003**. Right-click the **Chapter11** project and select **Paste**. The images folder and data files will be copied into your project. Click **Yes** in the dialog box, if one appears, to create a class for the data file.

5. In the Solution Explorer window, right-click the **Chapter11** project, and then click **Add Web Reference**. The Add Web Reference dialog box opens. You can search for local or remote Web Services. See Figure 11-9.

6. In the address text box enter the URL of the home page of the Web Service, and then click **Go**. The URL is *http://localhost/Chapter11WebService/ Ch11WS_ProductsDS.asmx*. The home page appears in the left window, as shown in Figure 11-10. (*Note*: You can view the contract and definition within the dialog box.)

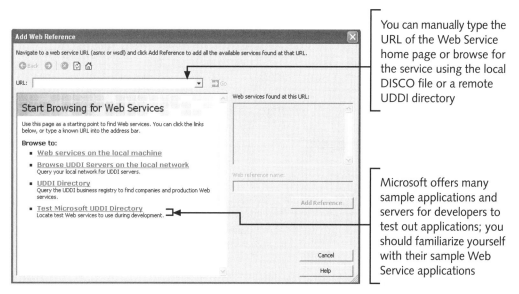

11

You can manually type the URL of the Web Service home page or browse for the service using the local DISCO file or a remote UDDI directory

Microsoft offers many sample applications and servers for developers to test out applications; you should familiarize yourself with their sample Web Service applications

Figure 11-9   Adding a Web reference

7. Click the **Add Reference** button to add the Web reference to the project. (*Note*: A folder named Web References is added to the project. The reference to the localhost is added to the project Web References folder. There can be more than one Web Service referred to. Therefore, the Web reference contains a map with the URL to the Web Services, and a copy of the service contract for each Web Service.) The System.Web.Service namespace is added to the list of project references in the Solution Explorer window, as shown in Figure 11-11.

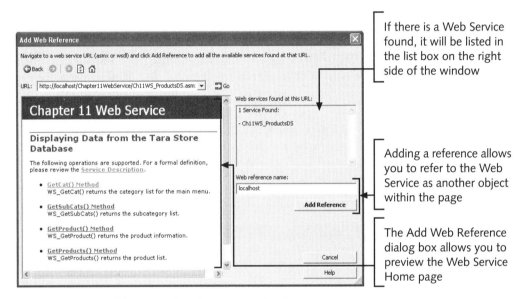

If there is a Web Service found, it will be listed in the list box on the right side of the window

Adding a reference allows you to refer to the Web Service as another object within the page

The Add Web Reference dialog box allows you to preview the Web Service Home page

Figure 11-10   Adding a Web reference to a Web project

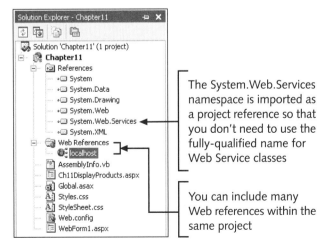

The System.Web.Services namespace is imported as a project reference so that you don't need to use the fully-qualified name for Web Service classes

You can include many Web references within the same project

Figure 11-11   Managing Web references using Solution Explorer

8. Double-click **Ch11DisplayProducts.aspx** in the Solution Explorer window to open the page in Design view. Double-click the page to open the code behind the page.

9. On the line below the comment that says 'Insert the code here, type the code that follows this paragraph. The code will create a new instance of the Web Service.

```
Dim MyDS As New DataSet
Dim MyService As
Chapter11.localhost.Chapter11WebService = _
New Chapter11.localhost.Chapter11WebService
MyDS = MyService.WS_GetProducts(ProdID)
MyProdList.DataSource = _
MyDS.Tables("Products").DefaultView
MyProdList.DataBind()
```

10. Click the **Save All** button. Click **Build** on the menu bar, and then click **Build Solution**.

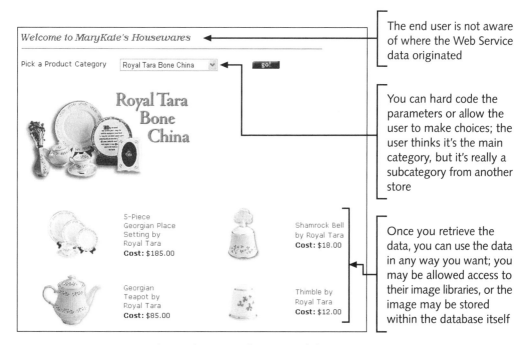

Figure 11-12   Viewing the Web Service from a Web browser

 The Web Services are included within the Web references in the Solution Explorer window. When you bring in a Web reference for the first time, local-host represents that Web Service. However, as you bring in additional Web References, the names of the Web Reference may vary with the namespace of the Web Service. Because you will be importing multiple Web references from the same server, localhost, Visual Studio .NET will append a number after localhost for each Web Service referenced. It's important to make sure that in your code you refer to the Web Service using the correct name in the Web reference list.

11. Click the **Ch11DisplayProducts.aspx** tab. Right-click the page, then click **View in Browser**. In the drop-down list box, select **Royal Tara Bone China** and click the **Go** button. A selection of products within the subcategory is displayed. Your page should look like the one in Figure 11-12.

12. Close any open pages.

Locating Web Services

There are many third-party Web Services available. The UDDI is a directory service that was initially created by Microsoft and IBM to provide businesses a method for registering and searching for Web Services. The UDDI allows you to search for third-party Web Services. The home page for UDDI is located at *www.uddi.org*. Additional information about UDDI can also be located on Microsoft's Web site at *uddi.microsoft.com/*. When you add a Web reference to your project, instead of typing the URL in the location text box, you can click on the UDDI hyperlink to locate Web Services.

In addition to the UDDI, you can find several third-party Web Services at *www.xmethods.net*, *www.coldrooster.com*, *www.asp.net*, and *www.gotdotnet.com*. In Figure 11-13, you can see that the XMethods Web site provides a listing of SOAP-based Web Services. Not all Web Services are created on Microsoft Windows platforms. However, you can easily integrate non-Windows Web Services into your application in the same way you would integrate Microsoft Windows Web Services.

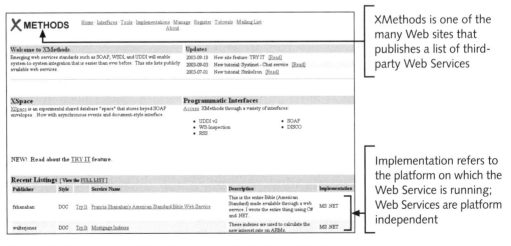

Figure 11-13 Sample Web Services available from XMethods

When you add a Web Service, you can locate additional Web Services on your local network or server. To locate local Web Services, add a Web Reference to your project. Instead of typing in the URL of the Web Service in the location text box, click the hyperlink Web References on Local Machine. The discovery document points you to where the Web Services are located. Notice in the image that the Web Service that you created earlier will be listed.

The following is a list of Web sites that discuss Web Services or provide Web Services:

- *directory.google.com/Top/Computers/Programming/Internet/Web_Services*
- *www.capescience.com/resources/webservices.shtml*
- *www.dmoz.org/Computers/Programming/Internet/Web_Services*
- *www.hitmill.com/webservices/direct.asp*
- *www.podb.com/webservice/webservdir.html*
- *www.prairietruckandtractor.com/webserdir.html*
- *www.programming-x.com/programming/uddi.html*
- *www.remotemethods.com*
- *www.soaprpc.com/webservice*
- *www.soapwebservices.com*
- *www.webservicelist.com*
- *www.webservice.us*
- *www.xmlwebservices.cc*

11

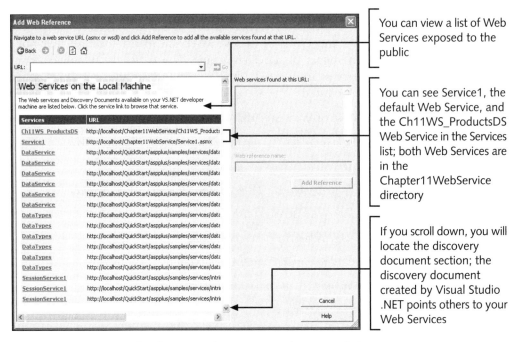

You can view a list of Web Services exposed to the public

You can see Service1, the default Web Service, and the Ch11WS_ProductsDS Web Service in the Services list; both Web Services are in the Chapter11WebService directory

If you scroll down, you will locate the discovery document section; the discovery document created by Visual Studio .NET points others to your Web Services

Figure 11-14   Using the discovery documents to locate Web Services

Microsoft provides additional Web Services for developers. You can locate the Microsoft Web Services at *http://msdn.microsoft.com/webservices/building/livewebservices/default.aspx*. Microsoft.com Web Services is an XML Web Service that will enable you to integrate information and services from MSDN, Technet, other Microsoft.com sites, and Microsoft Support. The Web Service provides information about top downloads from Microsoft. Microsoft MapPoint allows you to integrate high-quality maps and other location intelligence into your applications. Three additional Web Services that are useful for developers are as follows:

- *Amazon.Com Web Services - www.amazon.com/gp/browse.html/?node=3435361*

- *Google Web APIs Service - www.google.com/apis/*

- *TerraServer Web Service - terraserver-usa.com/webservices.aspx*

SECURING WEB SERVICES

In addition to configuring state management, you will want to make sure your Web Services are secure. You will want to limit access to your Web Services by using an authentication scheme. Although the Web Service architecture doesn't provide security for the developer, you can take advantage of the traditional security methods such as HTTP authentication services and SSL. Creating a secure Web Service is an important factor for business-to-business (B2B) and business-to-consumer (B2C) applications. You can secure a Web Service by using traditional methods such as IIS Web security, Windows authentication and Windows NTFS file permissions, and Passport authentication. Web Services also support the SSL protocol, which is used to encrypt data that is sent using the HTTP protocol. If you need to send the data securely over the Internet, you can also apply HTTPS instead of HTTP. The HTTPS protocol encrypts the message using Secure Sockets Layer (SSL) standards. You can identify when a Web site uses SSL because the HTTPS protocol is used as the protocol within the URL.

Microsoft provides the Web Services Enhancements (WSE) 2.0 Service Pack 1, which contains fixes to scalability and functionality; it also contains security tools that can be used to protect your Web Service. WSE simplifies the development and deployment of secure Web Services and allows developers and administrators to apply security policies on your Web Service more easily. You can download WES at *http://www.microsoft.com/downloads/details.aspx?familyid=fc5f06c5-821f-41d3-a4fe-6c7b56423841&displaylang=en.*

The Web Service is compiled with the application into an assembly that is stored in a dll file in the bin directory. The WebService.asmx file does not have to be deployed with the application. When the call is received for the Web Service, the dll contains the code to respond.

Access to the Web Service requires access to the Web Service page. As you recall, this page ends in .asmx. You can protect this file by using the Web Server authentication tools. In IIS, you can configure access to the Web site using the Directory Security tab. The Web server allows you to filter users by IP address or domain name. You can require a specific authentication method such as anonymous access, or a specific Windows user account. You can require the client to use a secure communications channel such as SSL. (*Note*: You can read more about IIS security at *http://msdn.microsoft.com/library/en-us/dnsecure/html/msdn_Websecurity.asp.* You can also learn more about IIS security at *http://support.microsoft.com/default.aspx?scid=kb;en-us;324964.*) In addition, you can protect your Web Service by using ASP.NET security methods. To learn more about these techniques, go to *http://msdn.microsoft.com/library/en-us/dnbda/html/authaspdotnet.asp.*

11

You can also apply Windows NTFS file or directory security to protect the Web Service page. Windows NTFS (Windows NT File System) allows you to protect the file by setting permission to the file for specific users and groups. The code following this paragraph configures the Web.config file to use Windows security to authenticate the user. Then, within Windows, you need to set the permissions on the file.

```
<authentication mode= "Windows">
</authentication>
```

 You can learn more about Windows security at *http://msdn.microsoft.com/ webservices/building/security/default.aspx*. You can also learn about the best practices for creating a secure server at *http://msdn.microsoft.com/library/ en-us/dnnetsec/html/ThreatCounter.asp*.

Although you used Visual Studio .NET to create your Web Service, there are some Web developers who will use other tools, such as the SOAP Toolkit, to create XML Web Services. There are several ways to protect Web Services using SOAP. SOAP can take advantage of HTTP authentication. You can also use SOAP headers with your own encryption algorithms to secure your Web Service. The SOAP header class is a class within the .NET Framework. You can inherit from this class, and then set the properties within the class. You can add data to the header and call methods. The SOAP packet contains a SOAP envelope and the response in an XML document. The response may contain the XML data.

CHAPTER SUMMARY

❏ Web Services are used to expose part or all of an application. In ASP.NET, the name of the file for the Web Service must end in the .asmx extension. The keyword <WebMethod> is used to identify the methods that are to be exposed.

❏ The Web Service Description Language (WSDL) schema is used to create a WSDL document that describes the functionality of the Web Service.

❏ Microsoft and IBM have teamed up to create the Universal Description, Discovery, and Integration (UDDI) specification, which is used to locate Web Services.

❏ Web Services may be called by the HTTPGet and HTTPPost methods, or by SOAP.

❏ In Visual Studio .NET, the Web application uses the WSDL document to create a proxy class. The Web application calls the proxy class to invoke the Web Service. The proxy class reads the WSDL document and verifies the delivery method.

❏ The SOAP contract is an XML-formatted document called the WSDL. The test page uses the HTTPGet method to test the Web Service.

❏ You can secure a Web Service by using the traditional methods such as IIS Web security, HTTPS with SSL, Windows authentication, and Passport authentication.

REVIEW QUESTIONS

1. Which method is used to call applications over a TCP/IP network?

    a. RPC

    b. ADO

    c. Web Service

    d. Web Form

2. What file extension is used to identify a Web Service?

    a. .asmx

    b. .aspx

    c. .asp

    d. .ascx

3. What format(s) is/are used to query the Web Service using the autogenerated test page?

    a. HTTPGet

    b. HTTPPost

    c. SOAP

    d. all of the above

4. The default namespace for all Web Services is _____.

    a. http://tempuri.org

    b. http://www.tempuri.com

    c. http://www.uddi.org

    d. http://www.uddi.net

5. The _____ keyword(s) is/are used to define a function as a Web Service.

    a. <Web Service>

    b. <WebService>

    c. <WebMethod>

    d. <Web Methods>

6. What keyword in the Web Service declaration is used to cache the results from the Web Service?

    a. CacheDuration

    b. Cache

    c. CacheAll

    d. WebCache

7. What keyword(s) in the Web Service declaration is/are used to describe the Web Service in the default test page?

   a. Description

   b. Name

   c. ID

   d. all of the above

8. Which URL would provide the Service Description Page?

   a. *http://localhost/WebService/Service1?WSDL*

   b. *http://localhost/WebService/WSDL?*

   c. *http://localhost/WebService/?WSDL*

   d. *http://localhost/WebService/Service1.asmx?WSDL*

9. Which method of the XML Document Object Model (DOM) is used to retrieve the XML data?

   a. GetXML

   b. LoadXML

   c. LoadXMLData

   d. ReadXMLData

10. Which object is used to call the Web Service?

    a. a Web Service Alias

    b. a Proxy Service

    c. a Proxy Class

    d. a Web Service Public Class

11. What does SOAP stand for?

    a. Simple Object Access Protocol

    b. Simple Object ASP Protocol

    c. Simple Object Access Pages

    d. Serialized Object Access Protocol

12. What method(s) should be used to call a Web Service that accesses a Data object?

    a. HTTPGet

    b. HTTPPost

    c. SOAP

    d. all of the above

13. What company(ies) initiated the UDDI standards?

    a. Microsoft

    b. IBM

    c. Sun

    d. a and b

14. The _____ is a directory service that provides businesses with a method to register and search for Web Services.

    a. UDDI

    b. ASP

    c. WebServices

    d. ASMX

15. What method(s) can be used to secure Web Services?

    a. IIS Web security

    b. Windows authentication

    c. SOAP headers

    d. all of the above

16. What third-party tool(s) from Microsoft provide(s) authentication services?

    a. NTFS

    b. Passport

    c. SSL

    d. all of the above

17. Which tool(s) within Visual Studio is/are used to add a Web Service to a Web project?

    a. Web reference

    b. Web Service

    c. XML Web Service

    d. all of the above

18. What is the file extension of the discovery document that is created when you create a Web Service in Visual Studio .NET?

    a. .DCO

    b. .ASMX

    c. .DISCO

    d. .DISC

11

19. If your company uses a firewall, when should you use Web Services?

    a. Never. You can't use Web Services with firewalls.

    b. Use them only if the company uses a proxy server.

    c. Anytime. Web Services can send files through a firewall.

    d. Use them only when the firewall supports the SOAP protocol.

20. What type(s) of applications can call a Web Service?

    a. Web applications

    b. Window applications

    c. Java applications

    d. all of the above

HANDS-ON PROJECTS

Project 11-1

In this project, you create a banner ad database that can be used with a banner ad Web Service.

1. Start **Visual Studio .NET** and open your **Chapter11** solution.

2. Right-click **Data Connections** in the Server Explorer window, and then click **Create New SQL Server Database**. Name the database Banners as shown in Figure 11-15. (*Note:* Your server name and authentication permissions may vary with your SQL server.)

You may have to reenter the user name and password if an additional dialog box appears. If it does, right-click the data connection in the Server Explorer window and select Modify Connection. Click the Allow saving password check box and click OK. Reenter the password and click OK.

3. Create a new table.

4. Add the fields to the table as shown in Figure 11-16. Make AdID an identity field and the primary key.

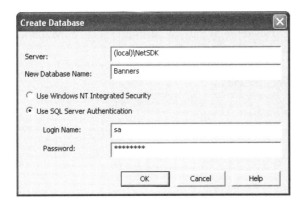

Figure 11-15   Creating the Banners database

Column Name	Data Type	Length	Allow Nulls
AdID	int	4	
CatID	int	4	✓
AdType	bit	1	✓
HTML	char	1000	✓
ImageURL	varchar	255	✓
LinkURL	varchar	255	✓
ALT	varchar	255	✓
Height	smallint	2	✓
Width	smallint	2	✓
Weight	smallint	2	✓
WeightScaled	smallint	2	✓
Active	bit	1	✓
Location	bit	1	✓

Columns	
Description	
Default Value	
Precision	10
Scale	0
Identity	Yes
Identity Seed	1
Identity Increment	1
Is RowGuid	No
Formula	
Collation	

Figure 11-16   Creating the Banners table

5. Save the table as **Banners**, and then add the data to the Banners table as shown in Figure 11-17.

AdID	CatID	AdType	HTML	ImageURL	LinkURL	ALT	Height	Width	Weight	WeightScaled	Active	Location
1	1	1	<NULL>	home.jpg	www.tarastore.com	Tara Store Home Page	50	500	10	10	1	0
2	2	1	<NULL>	waterford.jpg	www.tarastore.com	Waterford Products	50	500	10	20	1	0
3	3	1	<NULL>	china.jpg	www.tarastore.com	China Products	50	500	10	30	1	0
4	4	1	<NULL>	pottery.jpg	www.tarastore.com	Pottery Products	50	500	10	40	1	0
5	5	1	<NULL>	movies.jpg	www.tarastore.com	Movies About Ireland	50	500	10	50	1	0
6	6	1	<NULL>	books.jpg	www.tarastore.com	Books About Ireland	50	500	10	60	1	0
7	7	1	<NULL>	music.jpg	www.tarastore.com	Irish Music	50	500	10	70	1	0

Figure 11-17   Inserting the data for the Banners table

6. Create a new table named **Categories**.

7. Add the fields to the Categories table as shown in Figure 11-18. Make CatID an identity field and the primary key.

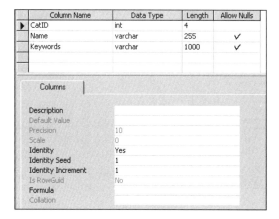

Column Name	Data Type	Length	Allow Nulls
CatID	int	4	
Name	varchar	255	✓
Keywords	varchar	1000	✓

Columns

Description	
Default Value	
Precision	10
Scale	0
Identity	Yes
Identity Seed	1
Identity Increment	1
Is RowGuid	No
Formula	
Collation	

Figure 11-18   Creating the Categories table

8. Add the data to the Categories table as shown in Figure 11-19.

CatID	Name	Keywords
1	TaraStore	Tara Home
2	Waterford	Waterford Crystal Glassware
3	China	China Royal Tara Plates
4	Pottery	Pottery Belinda Bradshaw Nicholas Mosse
5	Movies	Movies About Ireland
6	Books	Books About Ireland
7	Music	Irish Music

Figure 11-19   Inserting the data for the Categories table

9. Create a new table named **BannerHits**.

10. Add the fields to the BannerHits table as shown in Figure 11-20. Make HitID an identity field and the primary key.

Column Name	Data Type	Length	Allow Nulls
HitID	int	4	
AdID	int	4	✓
IP	varchar	50	✓
DateAndTime	datetime	8	✓
BrowserType	varchar	50	✓
BrowserVersion	varchar	10	✓

Columns

Description	
Default Value	
Precision	10
Scale	0
Identity	Yes
Identity Seed	1
Identity Increment	1
Is RowGuid	No
Formula	
Collation	

Figure 11-20   Creating the BannerHits table

11. Print the records in the Banners table in your database.

Project 11-2

11

In this project, you create a banner ad Web Service using a random number generator. You must have completed Project 11-1 in order to complete this project.

1. Start **Visual Studio .NET** and create a new Web Service project named **Chapter11Project2**. Use Windows Explorer to copy the Chapter11Data\ Chapter11Project2\images folder to import the banner images.

2. Double-click the **Service1.asmx.vb[Design]** page to edit the code behind the page. In Code view, add the code following this paragraph to create two properties, ImageURL and NavigateURL, which are both strings, as shown in Figure 11-21. You must add this after the Web Service class.

```
Public Class BannerAd
    Public ImageURL As String
    Public NavigateURL As String
End Class
```

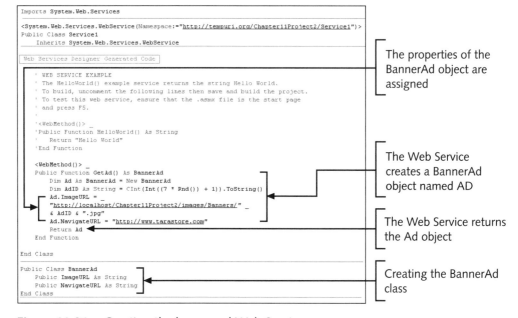

The properties of the BannerAd object are assigned

The Web Service creates a BannerAd object named AD

The Web Service returns the Ad object

Creating the BannerAd class

Figure 11-21   Creating the banner ad Web Service

3. Add the code following this paragraph to create the **WebMethod**, which displays the banner randomly. Then, add the GetAd function to generate a banner ad object with two properties, ImageURL and NavigateURL, which are both strings.

```
<WebMethod()> _
Public Function GetAd() As BannerAd
  Dim Ad As BannerAd = New BannerAd
  Dim AdID As String =
  CInt(Int((7 * Rnd()) + 1)).ToString()
  Ad.ImageURL = _
  "http://localhost/Chapter11Project2/
  images/Banners/" _
  & AdID & ".jpg"
  Ad.NavigateURL = "http://www.tarastore.com"
  Return Ad
End Function
```

4. Click the **Save All** button. Go to the **Build** menu and select **Build Solution**. Close the solution.

5. Open the **Chapter11** solution. Add a **Web Reference** to the new BannerAd Web Service at *http://localhost/Chapter11Project2/Service1.asmx*.

6. Create a new page named **Ch11Proj2DisplayBanner.aspx** that will retrieve one of the banner ads. Add a hyperlink object from the Web Forms tab. The hyperlink object's name is Hyperlink1 by default.

7. In Code view, add the code following this paragraph to call the Web Service and retrieve the image name and URL from the Web Service, as shown in Figure 11-22:

```
Dim MyService As Chapter11.localhost1.Service1 = _
New Chapter11.localhost1.Service1
HyperLink1.ImageUrl = MyService.GetAd.ImageURL
HyperLink1.NavigateUrl = MyService.GetAd.NavigateURL
```

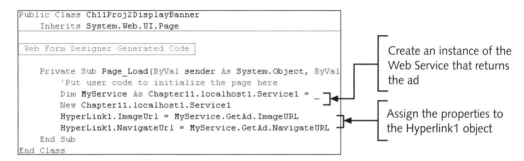

Figure 11-22   Retrieving the banner ad from the Web Service

8. Save the page and build the solution. View the page at *http://localhost/Chapter11/Ch11Proj2DisplayBanner.aspx* in the browser, as shown in Figure 11-23. Click the **Refresh** button several times to see the banner ad rotate images randomly. Print the Web page, your source code, and the source code for the Web Service.

Figure 11-23   Viewing the banner ad

Project 11-3

In this project, you create a banner ad Web Service using the values from the database. You must have completed Project 11-1 in order to complete this project.

1. Start **Visual Studio .NET**.

2. Create a new Web Service Solution named **Chapter11Project3**. Use Windows Explorer to copy the Chapter11Data\Chapter11Project3\images folder to import the banner images.

3. On the Service1.asmx page, use the SqlDataAdapter to connect to the **Banners** SQL Server database. Select all of the fields and all of the records within the Banners table. Then, generate a DataSet named **DS_Banners** based on the Banners table, and add the DataSet to the designer. Add a **DataView** and set the Table property to the **Banners** table.

4. Double-click the **Service1.asmx** page to edit the code behind the page. In Code view, add the code following this paragraph to create a function to generate a BannerAd object with properties for each of the properties in an image hyperlink such as **ImageURL**, **NavigateURL**, **ImageWidth**, **ImageHeight**, **AltText**. All of the properties are strings, as shown in the code following this paragraph. Make sure to add the class after the Web Service class.

```
Public Class BannerAd
     Public ImageURL As String
     Public NavigateURL As String
     Public ImageWidth As String
     Public ImageHeight As String
     Public AltText As String
End Class
```

5. Add the code following this paragraph to create the **WebMethod**, which displays the banner ads randomly. There are only seven banner ads in this example. So, in this instance, simply use the random function to generate a random number between 1 and 7, as shown in the following code:

```
<WebMethod()> _
Public Function GetAd() As BannerAd
Dim Ad As BannerAd = New BannerAd()
Dim AdID As String = CInt(Int((7 * Rnd()) + 1)).ToString()
Dim RecordPos As Integer = CInt(AdID)
```

```
<WebMethod()> _
Public Function GetAd() As BannerAd
    Dim Ad As BannerAd = New BannerAd
    Dim AdID As String = CInt(Int((7 * Rnd()) + 1)).ToString()
    Dim RecordPos As Integer = CInt(AdID)

    SqlConnection1.Open()
    Dim mySQL As String
    mySQL = "SELECT * FROM Banners WHERE AdID = " & RecordPos
    Dim objCM As New SqlClient.SqlCommand(mySQL, SqlConnection1)
    Dim objDR As SqlClient.SqlDataReader
    objDR = objCM.ExecuteReader()
    While objDR.Read()
        Ad.ImageURL = _
        "http://localhost/Chapter11Project3/images/Banners/" & _
         objDR("ImageURL").ToString
        Ad.NavigateURL = objDR("LinkURL").ToString
        Ad.ImageWidth = objDR("Width")
        Ad.ImageHeight = objDR("Height")
        Ad.AltText = objDR("ALT")
    End While
    objDR.Close()
    SqlConnection1.Close()
    Return Ad
End Function
```

Figure 11-24   Retrieving a single row of data from a DataView object

6. Add the code to retrieve the values from the database. Use the DataReader to retrieve only a single row based on the AdID property, as shown in Figure 11-24.

7. Click the **Save All** button. Click **Build** on the menu bar, and then click **Build Solution**. Close the solution.

8. Open the **Chapter11** solution and add a **Web Reference** to the new BannerAd Web Service at *http://localhost/Chapter11Project3/Service1.asmx*.

9. Create a new page named **Ch11Proj3DisplayBanner.aspx** that will retrieve one of the banner ads. Add a hyperlink object from the Web Forms tab. The hyperlink object's name is Hyperlink1 by default.

11

10. In Code view, add the code to call the Web Service and retrieve the image name and URL from the Web Service, as well as the ImageWidth, ImageHeight, and AltText properties, as shown in Figure 11-25. You must also create a shared function to handle the height and weight units, as shown in the code in Figure 11-25.

```
Private Sub Page_Load(ByVal sender As System.Object, ByVal e As
    'Put user code to initialize the page here
    Dim MyService As Chapter11.localhost2.Service1 = _
 New Chapter11.localhost2.Service1
    HyperLink1.ImageUrl = MyService.GetAd.ImageURL
    HyperLink1.NavigateUrl = "http://" & MyService.GetAd.NavigateURL
    HyperLink1.Width = Parse(MyService.GetAd.ImageWidth)
    HyperLink1.Height = Parse(MyService.GetAd.ImageHeight)
    HyperLink1.ToolTip = MyService.GetAd.AltText
End Sub

Public Overloads Shared Function Parse( _
    ByVal s As String _
) As Unit
End Function
```

Figure 11-25   Creating a banner ad from a Web Service

11. Save the page. Build the solution. View the page at *http://localhost/chapter11/ Ch11Proj3DisplayBanner.aspx* in the browser. Click the **Refresh** button several times to see the banner ad rotate images randomly. Print the Web page, your source code, and the source code for the Web Service.

Case Projects

Consuming Web Services

Your boss would like to use a third-party Web Service already established on the Internet. Your task is to implement a third-party Web Service. Visit a Web site such as *www.uddi.org, www.xmethods.net, www.asp.net*, or *www.gotdotnet.com*, or visit one of the Web Services mentioned in the chapter. Locate one Web Service that you would like to implement within your Web site. Create a Web page named Ch11Case1.aspx in the Chapter11 project that consumes the Web Service. In your Web page, document the information about the Web Service such as:

◻ Name of the Web Service

◻ URL where you found the Web Service

◻ Description of the Web Service

◻ Who owns the Web Service

❑ The costs required to use the Web Service

❑ The requirements to consume the Web Service

❑ The procedure for consuming the Web Service

View the Web page in the browser, print out the Web page and the source code.

Creating and Consuming a Membership Web Service

Your boss would like you to create a membership database that can be accessed by other companies. You decide to implement a membership Web Service named Chapter11Case2. Create a database named Ch11Members that contains member information. You can use Access or SQL Server to create your database. Then, create a Web Service named Chapter11Case2 that exposes the membership data. Create a new page named Ch11Case2.aspx that consumes the Web Service and displays the membership data. Print out your Web pages and the source code.

Creating a Banner Ad Web Service from a Database

Your store manager wants to provide a Web banner ad service that other companies can use to display one of your ten banner ads on their Web sites. Create a Web Service that allows another company to view your Web banner ads on their Web pages. Create at least 10 banner graphics. Create the Ch11Case3Banners database and the Banners table. Add the 10 graphics' data into the Banners table. Create the Web Service named Ch11Case3. Create a page to demonstrate how to implement your Web Service, as shown in Figure 11-26. Create a login page. If the company is validated, allow them to view all 10 banners ads. If they are not, only allow them to view one default banner ad. Show them the code to implement each of the banner ads using the Web Service. Print your Web page, the source code, and the Web Service source code.

11

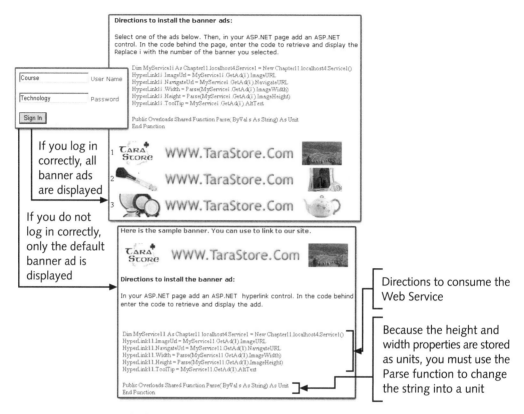

Figure 11-26 Sample banner ad Web Service

CHAPTER 12

EXTENDING ASP.NET
APPLICATIONS

In this chapter, you will:

♦ Send e-mail from the Web application
♦ Store and retrieve data from the Web server's file system
♦ Create and read files from an ASP.NET page
♦ Use Mobile controls to deliver content from a Web application

Businesses have learned through experience that they must provide additional services via their Web sites, rather than just delivering HTML content. In this chapter, you will learn how ASP.NET can work with other applications to increase the utility of a Web site. You will learn how to send e-mail from a Web page, so that when users complete a form, you can send them a customized e-mail message with their user information. You can also send the information to the administrator with a different custom message. You will also learn to save data to a file. Web sites often use databases and files to store user data, product information, or company data. In addition, you will learn to create Web applications that generate HTML Web pages on the fly, so that the Web content displayed can reflect user preferences. For example, you can create Web pages that store the users' favorite stock quotes, or display a list of newly published books by their favorite authors. Also, since a growing percentage of Internet customers use mobile devices to connect to the Internet, you will learn how to use Mobile controls to display your Web page content on a mobile device.

SENDING E-MAIL FROM THE WEB APPLICATION

In earlier chapters of this book, you learned how to process and validate form data. Often you will want to generate a customized automated e-mail reply that uses this form data, for example, to send an order confirmation to a customer. To send outbound e-mail from a Web page, you must use an e-mail server, along with an e-mail object or application to communicate with the e-mail server.

Security and Privacy Issues Related to E-Mail

E-mail is the process of sending messages through e-mail servers. These e-mail messages are primarily text-based, but may contain additional content such as HTML, images, and attached files. E-mail was widely used in universities prior to the World Wide Web, and has now become one of the primary functions of end users on the Internet.

Proliferation of viruses began to occur through e-mail as attachments. Anti-viral programs scan for viruses delivered through e-mail attachments and e-mail programs allow the end users to configure their program to disallow an e-mail attachment. These viruses may be programs that execute when the user opens the e-mail message. Some viruses are simple script programs that display annoying messages and steal information such as passwords. Others will cause programs or the operating system to become inoperable.

Recently, hackers have spread viruses that allow them to take over the end user's computer, allowing the hacker to use the computer to attack other computers. With the use of e-mail in the business community, Web developers must take precautions to ensure that their systems do not participate in delivering viruses through e-mail. In addition, system administrators must use virus protection programs to ensure that files are not infected on their systems. Moreover, Web developers must ensure that their Web applications do not allow unauthorized users to send e-mail through their Web application or e-mail server.

A major privacy issue related to e-mail is spam. **Spam** is unauthorized delivery of e-mail messages. The bulk of e-mail today on the Internet is spam. Because there is virtually no cost to deliver spam, it's commonly used as a marketing tool to attract customers. A vast amount of spam also consists of proliferation of pornographic and illicit material, such as advertisements of drugs. Some spam poses as legitimate e-mail and use hyperlinks to lure end users onto Web sites that download viruses and steal information such as passwords, bank account numbers, and credit card information. Web developers must ensure that their applications send only e-mail messages that are authorized by the organization.

There are other security and privacy issues related to e-mail. The Web developer must keep up-to-date with the latest threats and design their Web applications to protect against these threats. In this chapter, you will learn to configure the e-mail server. You will also learn to enhance your Web application by designing Web pages that can send out-bound e-mail from a Web page.

The E-Mail Server

The e-mail server, known as the SMTP server, is included when you install the IIS Web server. The **SMTP server** provides an easy way to transmit Internet mail. **Simple Mail Transfer Protocol (SMTP)** is a protocol, or set of rules, used to transfer mail between servers. The SMTP server contains several default folders, including Pickup, Queue, Badmail, Drop Route, Mailbox, and SortTemp. These folders are located by default in C:\Inetpub\MailRoot\. The Pickup folder is used to store outgoing mail messages. These messages are sent from the SMTP server to other servers. The default port for the SMTP server is 25. Mail messages can be placed in this directory by hand or by other software applications.

In the following exercise, you will verify that the e-mail server is installed and running. The property pages and configuration settings for the SMTP server will vary between Windows XP and other operating systems. E-mail servers are not available with all operating systems.

1. To verify that the SMTP services are running, click **Start**, and then click **Control Panel**. Click **Classic View** in Windows XP to show the Administrative Tools icon. Double-click the **Administrative Tools** icon. Double-click the **Services** icon. The Services window opens with the list of running and stopped services.

2. Scroll down the window until you locate the Simple Mail Transport Protocol (SMTP) service in the Name column, as shown in Figure 12-1. The Status column should say that the Simple Mail Transport Protocol (SMTP) has been Started. (*Note*: If it is stopped, you can right-click the Simple Mail Transport Protocol (SMTP) name and click Start.)

3. Close the Services window by clicking the **Close** button and then close the Administrative Tools folder.

Pausing a server will gracefully stop the server without interrupting active connections. You will prevent only new client connections; the server will continue to process existing connections and deliver queued messages.

12

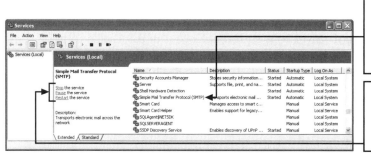

The SMTP service provides the ability for the server to send and receive e-mail messages; it does not send the e-mail message to the client

After you select the SMTP service, you can manually start, stop, or pause the server

Figure 12-1   Verifying that the SMTP service is running

You can right-click the Simple Mail Transport Protocol (SMTP) service to access the SMTP server properties. You can configure the service to automatically start when the server is booted by setting the startup type to Automatic. You can also identify what action you want to take if the service has failed. For example, you can run a file, restart the service, or reboot the computer. Your Webmaster or system administrator is usually the one responsible for configuring your e-mail server.

Configuring the E-Mail Server

The Microsoft Management Console (MMC) is the main interface to the administrative programs such as IIS and SMTP. You can access the SMTP server and IIS through the same Microsoft Management Console (MMC).(*Note*: You can open an MMC with no snap-ins using C:\WINDOWS\system32\mmc.exe. You would have to add the IIS and SMTP snap-ins to the console.) In the following exercise, you will view the SMTP settings through the MMC.

1. To open the ISM, click **Start**, and then click **Control Panel**. Double-click the **Administrative Tools** folder, and then double-click **Internet Information Services**. The Internet Information Services window opens.

2. Click the **plus sign** next to the computer icon to expand the list of FTP sites, Web sites, and SMTP servers available. (*Note*: You can also double-click the name of the computer or the computer icon to expand the menu.)

3. Click the name of the server. (*Note*: IIS places the Web sites and FTP sites in folders.)

4. Right-click the **Default SMTP Virtual Server** icon, and then click **Properties** to open the Default SMTP Virtual Server Properties window. You can configure the server properties on these property pages. Notice that on the General tab, you can enable logging. By default, if logging is enabled, the SMTP log files are stored in the C:\WINDOWS\System32\LogFiles\ SmtpSvc1 directory.

5. Click the check box labeled **Enable logging**. The default format is W3C Extended Log File Format. Click **Properties**. The Extended Logging Options window shows the same options are available for both the Web server and e-mail server. The default log file monitors the Time (time), Client IP Address (c-ip), Method (cs-method), URI Stem (cs-uri-stem), and Protocol Status (sc-status). Click **Cancel** to close the window.

The Microsoft IIS Log File Format and the National Center for Supercomputer Applications (NCSA) Common Log File Format are used to store fixed log information in an ASCII format. ASCII is a basic text format that can be read by most computers.

Server versions provide the ability to send IIS, FTP, and SMTP logging to an ODBC-compliant database. A SQL Server script located at C:\WINDOWS\ system32\inetsrv\logtemp.sql is provided to assist you in creating a compatible table named inetlog. This file contains a listing of the required fields and data types.

6. On the General tab, you can configure the number of connections and number of minutes per connection. To verify that the TCP port selected is 25, click **Advanced**. You can add additional IP addresses and modify the port settings here. Click **Cancel**. (*Note*: Services that do not explicitly assign an IP address use the default IP address and can be referred to as localhost. IP addresses are assigned to the network interface card. These addresses must be unique within the local network. If the server is connected to the Internet, the system administrator will configure the server to use a specific Internet address that is assigned to that organization.) See Figure 12-2.

12

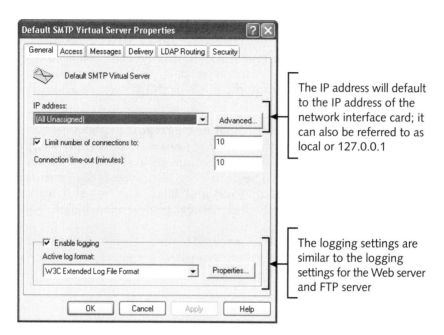

The IP address will default to the IP address of the network interface card; it can also be referred to as local or 127.0.0.1

The logging settings are similar to the logging settings for the Web server and FTP server

Figure 12-2 The General property page

7. Click the **Access** tab. The Access property page allows you to configure which accounts will be allowed to send e-mail through the Default SMTP Virtual Server.

8. Click the **Authentication button** to view the Authentication property page. You can allow the Internet anonymous user account to send e-mail, or restrict access using Basic or Windows authentication, as shown in Figure 12-3.

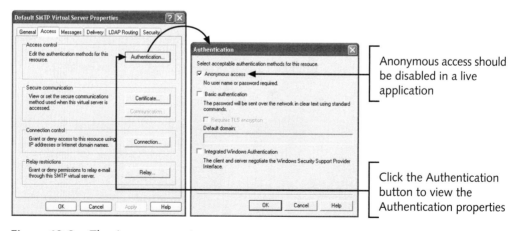

Anonymous access should be disabled in a live application

Click the Authentication button to view the Authentication properties

Figure 12-3 The Access property page

9. Click **Cancel** to return to the Access tab.

10. Click the **Messages** tab, as shown in Figure 12-4. The Messages property page allows you to configure the size of the message and the session size. The session size is the total size of all of the message body sections within a single connection. The Messages property page allows you to configure the number of messages per connection and the number of recipients per connection. For example, if there are 150 recipients on an e-mail list, the first 100 would be delivered using one connection, and then a new connection would open and deliver the remaining 50 messages. When an e-mail message is not sent, the message is deposited in the Badmail directory, which is located by default at C:\Inetpub\mailroot\Badmail. You can specify that a Non-Delivery report be e-mailed to you.

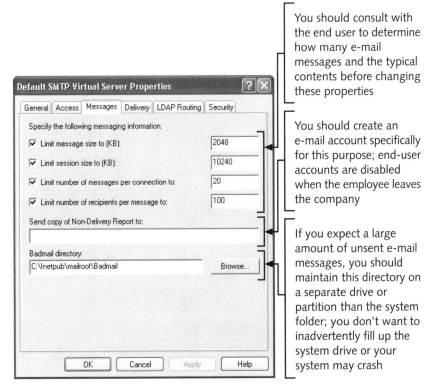

You should consult with the end user to determine how many e-mail messages and the typical contents before changing these properties

You should create an e-mail account specifically for this purpose; end-user accounts are disabled when the employee leaves the company

If you expect a large amount of unsent e-mail messages, you should maintain this directory on a separate drive or partition than the system folder; you don't want to inadvertently fill up the system drive or your system may crash

Figure 12-4   The Messages property page

11. Click the **Delivery** tab, as shown in Figure 12-5. The Delivery property page allows you to configure how the message is delivered. For example, if the e-mail cannot be sent, you can specify the number of minutes to wait before attempting to e-mail the message again.

The default settings are shown in Figure 12-5. The retry interval is the number of minutes the server waits before issuing a failed delivery status message for outbound e-mail messages. Networks can experience delays due to increased traffic. You can use delay notification to configure the server to wait before sending the failure notification. You can use different values for local or remote messages. Local settings would apply to the internal network, such as when you are configuring an intranet application.

12. Click **Outbound Security**. You can configure a different user account to send mail messages, as shown in Figure 12-6. You can use the anonymous account, or authenticate the user with basic authentication or Windows authentication. You can also require the authentication process to use a standard encryption protocol called Transport Layer Security (TLS). TLS is a more secure version of SSL and will encrypt the communication during the authentication process. Click **Cancel**.

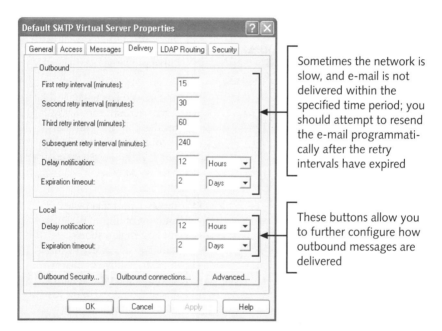

Figure 12-5   The Delivery property page

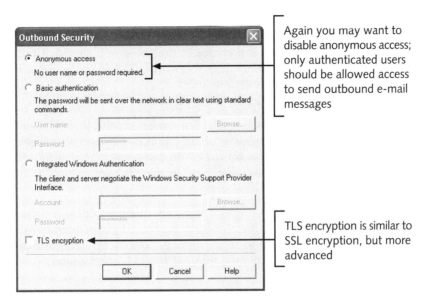

Again you may want to disable anonymous access; only authenticated users should be allowed access to send outbound e-mail messages

TLS encryption is similar to SSL encryption, but more advanced

Figure 12-6   The Outbound Security settings

13. Click **Outbound Connections**. You can limit the number of outbound messages, the time-out property, and the number of connections per domain, as shown in Figure 12-7. You can also change the port number for the mail server. The default port is 25. It is recommended not to use any of the well known port numbers. (*Note*: Refer to Chapter 9 for more information on port numbers.) Click **Cancel**.

12

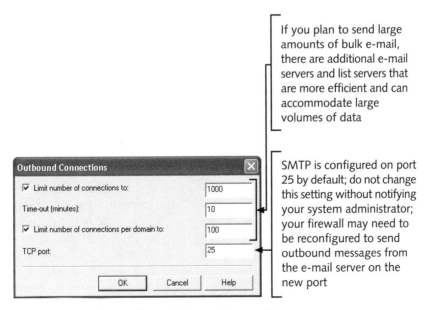

If you plan to send large amounts of bulk e-mail, there are additional e-mail servers and list servers that are more efficient and can accommodate large volumes of data

SMTP is configured on port 25 by default; do not change this setting without notifying your system administrator; your firewall may need to be reconfigured to send outbound messages from the e-mail server on the new port

Figure 12-7   The Outbound Connections settings

14. Click **Advanced**. You can configure which servers can access the Default SMTP Virtual Server to send or relay e-mail messages, as shown in Figure 12-8. Some e-mail servers reject the message if the Mail From line contains an invalid domain address. You can set the Masquerade domain field to a valid fully qualified domain name (FQDN). This will replace the local domain name listed in the Mail From line.

Messages can be routed to a number of servers on the Internet before it reaches its final destination server. Hop count is the number of servers the message is permitted to pass through. You can set the hop count property. If the hop count is more than what is set in the mail server configuration, the message is returned.

You can assign a smart host, which is a fully qualified domain name of a virtual server, instead of sending all of the e-mail messages directly to a domain. This configuration is used to route messages over a connection that may be more direct or less costly than a different route. Click **Cancel**.

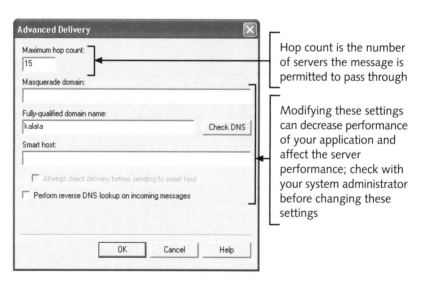

Figure 12-8 The Advanced delivery settings

15. Click the **LDAP Routing** tab to view the LDAP Routing properties, as shown in Figure 12-9. LDAP stands for Lightweight Directory Access Protocol. LDAP is the primary access protocol for Active Directory. Active Directory is a directory service that stores information about objects on a network. Users can access resources anywhere on the network using a single logon process.

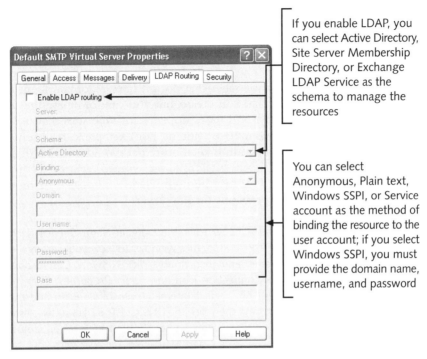

If you enable LDAP, you can select Active Directory, Site Server Membership Directory, or Exchange LDAP Service as the schema to manage the resources

You can select Anonymous, Plain text, Windows SSPI, or Service account as the method of binding the resource to the user account; if you select Windows SSPI, you must provide the domain name, username, and password

Figure 12-9   The LDAP Routing properties window

16. Click the last tab labeled **Security**. As shown in Figure 12-10, it allows you to configure who can access and change the SMTP settings. By default, only members of the administrators group can alter the SMTP settings. You should only allow trusted users to alter the SMTP settings. Click **Cancel**.

12

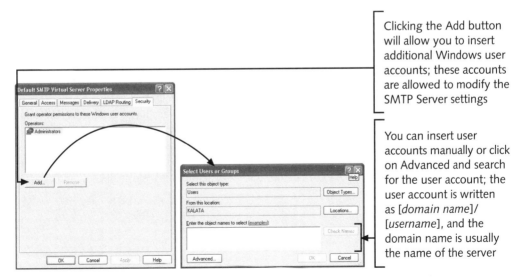

Clicking the Add button will allow you to insert additional Windows user accounts; these accounts are allowed to modify the SMTP Server settings

You can insert user accounts manually or click on Advanced and search for the user account; the user account is written as [*domain name*]/[*username*], and the domain name is usually the name of the server

Figure 12-10   The Security properties window

17. In the MMC, click the **plus sign** next to the envelope icon that represents the Default SMTP Virtual Server.

18. Click **Domains**. In the right window, your Web server is listed under the Domain Name column. The default domain is listed and cannot be deleted. The domain is used for messages that do not have a domain identified. You can delete any domain that you create, but you cannot delete the default domain. You may want to add more domains for Web sites that use multiple domain names for the same Web content. For example, e-mail sent to admin@tarastore.com and admin@tarastore.net would both be delivered to the same mail server. Current sessions allows you to terminate connections with the SMTP server. This may be used when a file that is being delivered is very large and causing problems on the server.

The default domain name is taken from the Domain Name Service (DNS) settings in the Advanced TCP/IP Properties window. To view your settings, go to Start, click Control Panel, and then double-click Network Connections. Right-click your network connection icon and select Properties. Click the Networking tab. In the list box, select Internet Protocol (TCP/IP) and click Properties. Click Advanced, and then click the DNS tab. The DNS suffixes listed are the domain names available. Domains configured as local or remote. Examples of domains are course.com and tarastore.net. Check with your system administrator before adding domains to your mail server.

19. Right-click the domain name in the Domain Name column, and then click **Properties**.

20. Click **Cancel** to close the window.

21. Click the **Close** button to close the Internet Information Services window.

22. Close the Administrative Tools window.

The configuration of the e-mail server and network affects how you can send outbound e-mail from your ASP.NET pages. If you have a firewall, or special routing, you must modify your code. For example, in some networks, if your e-mail address is john@yourschool.edu, you might have to explicitly state the domain of the e-mail server. If the e-mail server's name is darkstar, the e-mail address is john@darkstar.yourschool.edu.

You can read more about the SMTP server in the Help files. To open the Help files, go to Start, click Run, type %systemroot%\help\mail.chm, and click OK.

E-Mail Objects

An e-mail software application or component is used in order for the Web page to communicate with the e-mail server. A component known as CDONTS is provided with the SMTP server to allow third-party applications such as ASP.NET to communicate with the SMTP server. CDONTS is located in a server component called cdonts.dll, which is located in C:\WINDOWS\system32\ and is made available when you install the Microsoft SMTP server. The CDONTS component places your message in the Pickup folder. The CDONTS component is a scaled-down version of a collection of objects known as **Collaborative Data Objects (CDO)**. CDO is typically used to integrate your applications with active messaging systems such Microsoft Outlook and Microsoft Exchange Services. CDONTS is a collection of objects, properties, and methods that connect the SMTP service with the Web application. CDONTS and the SMTP service is available with Windows Server and Windows XP Professional. It is not available with Windows Millennium or Windows XP Home.

Figure 12-11 shows that the Web application can obtain the e-mail message information from a database or other data source. Then, the Web application will use an object known as CDONTS from the mail server to create the e-mail message and copy it in the Pickup folder on the SMTP server. The Web application accesses this mail object through the .NET Framework classes. The SMTP server places the e-mail message into the **Queue folder**. If the message recipient is a local account, it places the e-mail message into the **Drop folder**. If the message recipient is on a remote server, it sends the e-mail out to another server. The receiving mail server may accept or reject the e-mail message. The e-mail message is commonly rejected because the user's mailbox is full or the user is not a valid user account. Firewalls, anti-spam software, and virus detection software may also reject an e-mail message. The rejected message is returned to the SMTP server. The SMTP server responds by placing the message in the **Badmail folder** and creating a **Non-Delivery report (NDR)**.

12

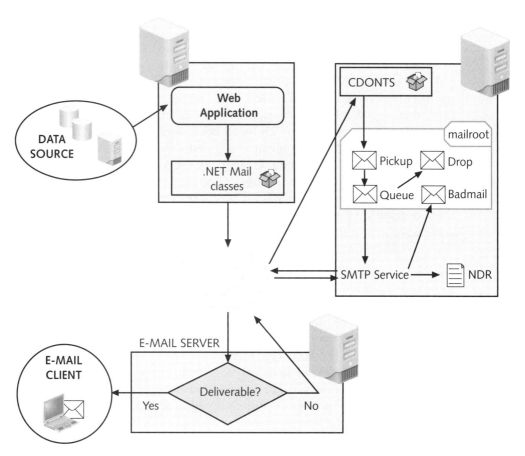

Figure 12-11   Sending outbound e-mail using CDONTS from a Web application

 You can find additional information on how to use CDONTS at *http://msdn.microsoft.com/library/en-us/exchanchor/htms/ msexchsvr_cdo_top.asp*

The .NET Mail Classes

You can access CDONTS by using three built-in classes within the .NET Framework. The `System.Web.Mail` **namespace** provides access to the MailMessage, MailAttachment, and SmtpMail classes. The **MailMessage class** provides access to the properties and methods used to construct an e-mail message. The **MailAttachment class** is used to identify a file that is to be sent with the e-mail message. These attached files are often called **attachments**. The **SmtpMail class** is used to send the e-mail message that is specified in the MailMessage class.

`System.Web.Mail` provides access to several classes that contain the properties and methods, as follows:

- MailAttachment class: Filename and Encoding properties

- MailEncoding class: UUEncode and Base64 properties

- MailFormat class: Text and HTML properties

- MailMessage class: To, From, Subject, Body, CC, and BCC properties

- MailPriority class: Normal, High, and Low properties

- SmtpMail class: Send method and SmtpServer property

Other properties that the MailMessage object created by the MailMessage class provides access to include BodyEncoding, BodyFormat, Fields, Headers, Priority, UrlContentBase, and UrlContentLocation. These properties can be set indirectly within the MailMessage object or directly by using the objects that contain the properties.

> To actually send e-mail, the Web server must be allowed to send outbound messages from the server, through the internal network, to the Internet. You should contact your system administrator to ensure that the routing permissions have been set up properly for your e-mail server. Some networks have policies against outbound e-mail messages due to the high prevalence of spam. You should provide your system administrator with your policy of how you will ensure that spam will not originate on your server.

The MailMessage Class Properties

The MailMessage class allows you to send the body of your message using different formats, such as basic text and HTML. The format of the e-mail message in the MailMessage class can be specified with the **MailFormat** enumeration. The possible enumerated values for e-mail format are MailFormat.Html and MailFormat.Text. The **MailFormat.Text** enumeration means that the format of the MailMessage is plain text. You should use Text when it is important that all e-mail applications be able to read the message. Some e-mail programs do not interpret HTML codes, and so these codes would be visible to the recipient. **MailFormat.Html** sends the output as HTML. E-mail programs that support the HTML format interpret the HTML commands in the same way that a browser interprets the HTML commands.

The priority of the e-mail message in the MailMessage class is configured with the **MailPriority** enumeration. You can use the MailPriority enumeration to indicate to the e-mail application the importance of the message. Some e-mail applications provide indicators, such as an exclamation point, to indicate that a message has been given a certain priority level. The MailPriority property does affect how quickly a message is sent. The three MailPriority property levels that you can set with the MailMessage class are **MailMessage.Normal**, **MailMessage.High**, and **MailMessage.Low**. The MailPriority is set to Normal by default.

The MailAttachment class provides properties and methods to construct an e-mail attachment. You need to specify the location of the attachment and the encoding format of the attachment. The location of the attachment is specified with the Filename property of the MailAttachment class. The **Filename property** is assigned a string value, which specifies the drive, path, and filename of the attachment. (*Note*: You can use the FileField text box to locate the filename of a local file within an ASP.NET page.) The encoding of the attachment is specified with the **MailEncoding enumerator**. **MailEncoding.UUEncode** is the default encoding format. Some files, such as graphics, must be encoded as binary before they are sent. You can specify binary encoding with the **MailEncoding.Base64** enumeration.

The MailMessage class consists of several properties that must be set before the message can be sent. These properties include the recipient, the sender, the subject, and the message body. The **MailMessage.To property** gets or sets the e-mail address of the recipient of the e-mail message. So, you can specify multiple recipients using the To property by separating each e-mail address with a semicolon.

The **MailMessage.From property** gets or sets the e-mail address of the sender of the message. The From property is used to identify the sender. Although it is possible to send anonymous e-mail by omitting the From property entirely, it is not recommended. You should specify a complete e-mail address for the sender. Some e-mail programs do not accept e-mail when the sender's address is not valid. It is useful to change the From property according to the message. For example, if the e-mail is being sent to customers, you might set the From property to "help@mydomain.com". That way, your customer can identify who is sending the e-mail. You cannot specify more than one address using the From property.

You must take precautions when sending e-mail from a Web application. A network administrator is usually the person who is responsible for the network security and for setting up the network servers. Because you can configure the To, From, Subject, Message, and attachments programmatically, it is important to configure your Web server so that it does not support e-mailing visitors without their permission. For example, you can configure the To property within the ASP.NET code so that the end user cannot change the e-mail address of the recipient. It's also important to configure your Web server and SMTP server to disable hackers from sending e-mail from your server. For example, you can configure the mail server not to relay messages from other servers.

The **MailMessage.Subject property** gets or sets the subject line of the e-mail message. You should not leave the subject blank. It is important to pick a meaningful phrase for the Subject property. Because many viruses are sent via e-mail, recipients often delete e-mail from unknown e-mail addresses, or with suspicious subject phrases like "Click here to win a car."

The **MailMessage.Body property** gets or sets the body of the e-mail message. You can create a variable to hold the entire message, or retrieve the value from a form field. Then, you can assign the contents of the variable or form field to the Body property.

The default encoding, format, and priority level are chosen from the default values of the MailEncoding, MailPriority, and MailFormat enumerations, unless you configure them using the MailMessage class. The MailMessage class also contains properties that you can use to configure the individual e-mail message with the **MailMessage.BodyEncoding**, **MailMessage.BodyFormat**, and **MailMessage.Priority properties**. (*Note*: Each of these properties uses the same values as their counterpart enumerations.)

There are several optional e-mail properties. The **MailMessage.Attachments property** is a list of attachments that is transmitted with the message that is identified with the MailAttachment class. The **Carbon Copy (MailMessage.Cc) property** gets or sets a semicolon-delimited list of e-mail addresses that receive a carbon copy of the e-mail message. You can separate multiple recipient addressees with semicolons (;).

The **Blind Carbon Copy (MailMessage.Bcc) property** sets a semicolon-delimited list of e-mail addresses that receive a blind carbon copy of the e-mail message. Blind carbon copies are used when you do not want the recipients to know that other individuals have been sent the same message. For example, you could send your customer an e-mail message, and send a blind carbon copy to your manager. The customer would not know that you sent a copy to your manager, and your manager's e-mail address would not be visible to the customer.

You can use the UrlContentBase and UrlContentLocation properties to insert content from another URL into the e-mail message. The **MailMessage.UrlContentBase property** gets or sets the URL base of all relative URLs used within the HTML-encoded body. The **MailMessage.UrlContentLocation property** is used to identify the location of content within the e-mail message. You can use the **MailMessage.Headers property** of the MailMessage class to specify custom headers that are sent with the e-mail message. Using the **MailMessage.Headers property**, you can add additional headers, such as a Reply-To header.

The SmtpMail class provides properties and methods to send an e-mail and attachments using the SMTP e-mail service built into Microsoft Windows operating systems. After the MailMessage class has been configured, you can call the Send method of the SmtpMail class to actually send the message. The Send method of the MailMessage object creates the message in the required format and writes it to the Queue folder; eventually the message is moved to the Pickup folder. Therefore, all e-mail is, by default, queued, ensuring that the calling program does not block network traffic. The SMTP server then delivers the message. (*Note*: After the message has been sent you should set the object to the keyword Nothing to release the object from memory.)

By default, the e-mail is sent using the default local SMTP server. However, you can change the SMTP server used to send the message with the **SmtpServer property** of the SmtpMail class. You can locate the name of the SmtpServer in the property pages of the Default SMTP Virtual Server within the Internet Services Manager console.

12

You can call also configure the MailMessage properties directly when you send the message with the SmtpMail class. You can pass the properties as parameters of the send method instead of defining each property individually. Each of these properties is passed as a string to the send method. The From property is placed first, followed by the To property, the Subject, and the MessageText. The following code illustrates how an e-mail message can be sent in one line of code:

```
SmtpMail.Send("sender@sender.com",
    "recipient@recipient.com", "Subject", "Message")
```

Sending an E-Mail Message from an ASP.NET Web Page

In the following exercise, you will create a Web page that sends a static message to a single recipient. You must have access to a directory on a computer with a SMTP server running and with CDONTS installed in order to complete this activity.

You should discuss with your system administrator how to connect your pages with your mail server. Some SMTP servers use the same Configuration object to define the configuration settings. Fields in the configuration object, such as sendusing, can be configured to specify where to place the message. You may be required to specify a username and password to authenticate the send message request.

1. Start **Visual Studio .NET**, then click **File** on the menu bar, point to **New**, and click **Project**. This opens the New Project window.

2. Click the **Visual Basic Projects** folder icon, then click **ASP.NET Web Application** under Templates. Type **Chapter12** in the Location text box in place of WebApplication1. Click the **OK** button to create the solution, project, and default files.

3. Open Windows Explorer. (*Note*: Click **Start**, click **Run**, type **%SystemRoot%\explorer.exe** in the text box, and then click **OK**.) Navigate to your **Chapter12Data** folder. Select all of the files and folders, click the **Edit** menu, and select **Copy**. Go back to Visual Studio .NET 2003. Right-click the **Chapter12** project and select **Paste**. The data folder, images folder, and data files will be copied into your project. Click **Yes** in the dialog box to create a class for the data file, if necessary. Close the Web Form1.aspx and the Start page.

4. Double-click the **Email_SendSingleMessage.aspx** page.

5. Double-click on the whitespace area on the page to view the code behind the page. On the first line of code, enter the following code to import the Mail classes from the `System.Web.Mail` namespace:

```
Imports System.Web.Mail
```

6. Enter the following code in the Page_Load handler to declare a variable MM to store the MailMessage objects:

```
Dim MM As New MailMessage()
```

7. Add the following code to configure the properties of the MailMessage object. Assign your e-mail address to the From and To properties. Don't type the brackets [ ].

```
MM.From = "[your_email@your_address.edu]"
MM.To = "[your_email@your_address.edu]"
MM.Subject = "CDONTS Exercise"
MM.Body = "I have completed the CDONTS exercise"
MM.BodyFormat = MailFormat.Text
MM.Priority = MailPriority.Normal
```

Tip

Depending on how your SMTP server is configured to route messages within your network, you may need to use a valid e-mail address for the To and From properties. If you are not allowed to send outbound e-mail messages, you can test the server by changing the second line of the code to MM.To = "student@[*Server name*]". This will route the message locally and place the message in the Drop folder.

8. Add the code following this paragraph. This will assign the server name and use the Send method of the SmtpMail object to send the message. Then, it will release the variables that are storing the Mail object.

```
SmtpMail.SmtpServer = "[Server name]"
SmtpMail.Send(MM)
MM = Nothing
```

9. Click the **Save All** button. Click **Build** on the menu bar, and then click **Build Solution**.

10. Right-click on the aspx page, and then click **View in Browser**. Your page should look like a blank page. The e-mail message has been created and placed in your Pickup folder and then into the Queue folder. If the e-mail was sent locally, it is delivered to the Drop directory. If the e-mail was sent remotely, the e-mail was forwarded to the other e-mail server.

11. Close the window.

12. On your desktop, double-click the **My Computer** icon, and then double-click the drive on which your Web server is installed. (By default the Web server is installed on drive C.) Double-click **Inetpub**, then **mailroot**, and then **Drop**.

13. Right-click the **envelope** icon, and then click **Open with**. In the window, scroll down until you see Notepad. Click **Notepad**, and then click **OK**. Your e-mail message should look similar to the one shown in Figure 12-12. (*Note*: If you select Open, the e-mail message opens in your default e-mail application.)

12

The e-mail message is copied to the Pickup folder and stored in the Queue folder for a short while, until it is either sent out to the remote server or placed in the Drop folder for a local user

Figure 12-12 Viewing an e-mail message

14. Close the file and close the Drop folder. (*Note:* When your e-mail server is ready, it places the e-mail message into the Pickup folder and sends it. Your e-mail server may not be configured to send the message. Some network settings prevent servers from sending mail via their networks. You should check with your system administrator for the e-mail server settings to send outbound mail through your network. If SMTP is enabled, you won't see the e-mail message. The e-mail will have been sent out for delivery.)

15. If you sent the e-mail to a valid e-mail account, you can now open your e-mail program and verify that you received the e-mail message.

Troubleshooting E-Mail messages

If you have a message in the browser that says "The SendUsing configuration value is invalid," as shown in Figure 12-13, then you must reconfigure the SMTP settings programmatically and assign a server name before the message is sent, like so:

```
SmtpMail.SmtpServer = "[Server Name]"
```

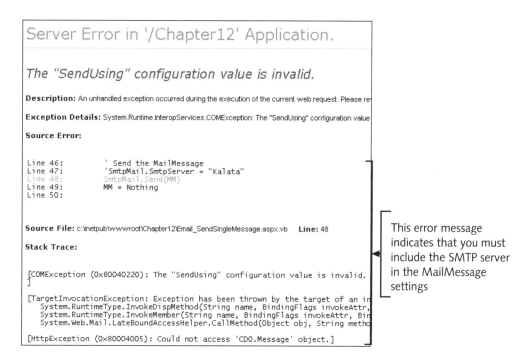

Figure 12-13   SMTP server configuration error

If you receive an error message that says, "The server rejected one or more recipient addresses," you know that the server response was 550 5.7.1 Unable to relay for [*your-email@your_address.edu*], and you have several options. One solution is to change the relay settings to allow your server to relay messages. To configure the server to allow relay messages from your local server, open the IIS MMC, right-click the SMTP server, select Properties, and click the Access tab. As shown in the Access property page on Figure 12-14, click the Relay button. Make sure to select the radio button labeled "Only the list below," and then click the Add button. Enter the IP address of the server in the Single computer IP address text box, and click OK. The IP address is listed in the Relay restrictions window as one of the computers that can relay messages. Click OK to close the window. Click OK to close the Access property page and close the MMC.

12

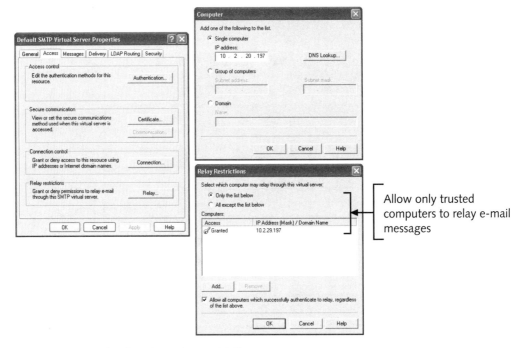

Allow only trusted
computers to relay e-mail
messages

Figure 12-14   Configuring relay restrictions

You can also use exception handling and error messages to help you determine the problem. For example, if you attempt to send an e-mail message to a non-valid e-mail address, the message will be returned with a Non-Delivery report (NDR). This NDR contains information about why the message was not delivered. For example, in Figure 12-15, the returned e-mail is shown in its raw text format, as it appears in Microsoft Outlook to the end user. The message was not delivered because the e-mail account did not exist.

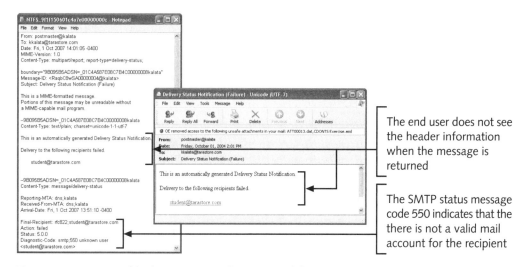

Figure 12-15   Troubleshooting e-mail message delivery

Hackers can still attempt to spam servers by spoofing e-mail addresses. Spoofing is where they trick the server into accepting the e-mail as a valid a-mail account. Current technology is being developed by Microsoft and other companies to validate the e-mail addresses using standards that prevent spoofing e-mail addresses.

Not all hosting service providers use the SMTP mail server as their e-mail server. You need to contact your HSP to determine what components interface with their e-mail server. Some hosting service providers may use the SMTP server, but require you to use a different e-mail component. For example, ServerObjects, Inc. (*www.serverobjects.com*) provides two mail components, named ASPMail and ASPQMail (*www.serverobjects.com/products.htm*), that are commonly used to enable an ASP page to send e-mail. Although the syntax is slightly different, the programming methods of CDONTS and ASPMail are very similar. You can view the documentation on ASPMail 3.0 at *www.serverobjects.com/comp/Aspmail3.htm* and on ASPQMail 2.x at *www.serverobjects.com/comp/AspQmail.htm*.

STORING AND RETRIEVING DATA IN THE WEB SERVER'S FILE SYSTEM

Another challenging task for Web developers is storing Web information in a file. There are several classes and objects within the `System.IO` namespace that allow you to interact with the Web servers' file system. The `System.IO` namespace allows synchronous and asynchronous reading and writing of data streams and files. In the following section, you will learn to access the directory structure, create and remove directories, and create, read, and delete files. There are several ways to create, read, and delete files and directories on the Web server. The `System.IO` namespace contains several classes, such as File, FileStream, and Directory, that allow you to create, read, and delete files. However, the newer classes, DirectoryInfo and FileInfo, allow more flexibility and easier access to the file system. In this section, you will learn to work with the DirectoryInfo and FileInfo class. The DirectoryInfo class allows you to obtain the properties of a directory and its subdirectories. The FileInfo class allows you access to the properties of a file, using the FileAttributes.

The FileSystemInfo class is the base class for both the FileInfo class and the DirectoryInfo class. Therefore, they share several methods and properties. If you have installed the QuickStart Web site, you can view the classes, methods, and properties associated with the System.IO namespace at *http://localhost/quickstart/aspplus/samples/classbrowser/vb/classbrowser.aspx?namespace=System.IO*, as shown in Figure 12-16.

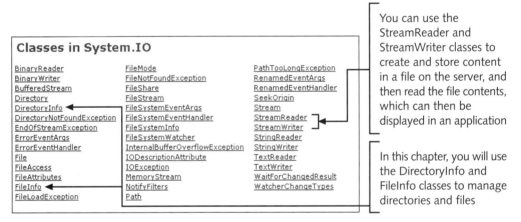

Classes in System.IO

BinaryReader	FileMode	PathTooLongException
BinaryWriter	FileNotFoundException	RenamedEventArgs
BufferedStream	FileShare	RenamedEventHandler
Directory	FileStream	SeekOrigin
DirectoryInfo	FileSystemEventArgs	Stream
DirectoryNotFoundException	FileSystemEventHandler	StreamReader
EndOfStreamException	FileSystemInfo	StreamWriter
ErrorEventArgs	FileSystemWatcher	StringReader
ErrorEventHandler	InternalBufferOverflowException	StringWriter
File	IODescriptionAttribute	TextReader
FileAccess	IOException	TextWriter
FileAttributes	MemoryStream	WaitForChangedResult
FileInfo	NotifyFilters	WatcherChangeTypes
FileLoadException	Path	

You can use the StreamReader and StreamWriter classes to create and store content in a file on the server, and then read the file contents, which can then be displayed in an application

In this chapter, you will use the DirectoryInfo and FileInfo classes to manage directories and files

Figure 12-16   Using the .NET Framework Class Browser Application to view the classes within the System.IO namespace

Working with Directories

The **DirectoryInfo** class provides several pieces of information about a directory. When you create a DirectoryInfo object based on the DirectoryInfo class, you must pass the complete path to a directory. The **Attributes property** of the DirectoryInfo class identifies whether the object is a directory. When the Attributes property is 16, the object is a directory. The **GetDirectories** method of the DirectoryInfo class is used to retrieve the collection of subdirectories. You can use a For-Each-Next loop to iterate through the collection to retrieve information about the subdirectories. Properties of the DirectoryInfo class include Attributes, CreationTime, CreationTimeUtc, Exists, Extension, FullName, LastAccessTime, LastAccessTimeUtc, LastWriteTime, LastWriteTimeUtc, Name, Parent, and Root. An example for creating a new

DirectoryInfo object named DD and retrieving the Name property is shown in the following code:

```
Dim DD As DirectoryInfo = _
    New DirectoryInfo("C:\Inetpub\wwwroot\Chapter12\")
Label1.Text = DD.FullName
```

You can iterate through the Directory Info object to retrieve the subdirectory list, as shown in the following code:

```
Dim MySubDirList As String
Dim SubDir As DirectoryInfo
For Each SubDir In DD.GetDirectories()
    MySubDir &= SubDir.Name & "<br />"
    Label2.Text = MySubDirList
Next
```

You can iterate through the FileInfo object to retrieve a list of files. You can use your knowledge of Visual Basic .NET to develop code to modify the display based on the file properties. FileInfo properties include Attributes, CreationTime, CreationTimeUtc, Directory, DirectoryName, Exists, Extension, FullName, LastAccessTime, LastAccessTimeUtc, LastWriteTime, LastWriteTimeUtc, Length, and Name. In the following code, the .aspx files are displayed as hyperlinks, the .vb and .resx files are not displayed, and all the rest of the files are listed as plain text:

```
Dim MyFileList, MyPath As String
MyPath = TextBox1.Text
Dim MyFile As FileInfo
For Each MyFile In DFL.GetFiles
    Select Case MyFile.Extension
        Case ".aspx"
            MyFileList &= _
            "<a href='" & MyFile.Name & "'>" & _
            MyFile.Name & "</a><br />"
        Case ".vb", ".resx"
        Case Else
            MyFileList &= MyFile.Name & "<br />"
    End Select
Next
Label3.Text = MyFileList
```

In the following example, you will retrieve the directory properties for C:\Inetpub\wwwroot\Chapter12, and the list of subdirectories within the Chapter12 directory.

1. In the Solution Explorer window, right-click the **DisplayChapter12Dir.aspx** page to view the code behind the page, and click **View Code**.

2. Enter the code following this paragraph in the DislayDirectoryInfo function. First, create the DirecroryInfo object.

```
Dim DD As DirectoryInfo = _
   New DirectoryInfo(MyPath)
```

3. Add the code following this paragraph to display data about the directory. Notice that the Date and Time properties must be formatted using the ToShortDateString or another date-to-string conversion method. The Name property is used to retrieve the values of the parent directory.

```
lbl1.Text = DD.FullName
lbl2.Text = DD.Name
lbl3.Text = DD.Attributes
lbl4.Text = DD.CreationTime.ToShortDateString
lbl5.Text = DD.LastAccessTime.ToShortDateString
lbl6.Text = DD.LastWriteTime.ToShortDateString
lbl7.Text = DD.Root.Name
lbl8.Text = DD.Parent.Name
lbl9.Text = DD.Exists
lbl10.Text = GetLength(DirSize(DD))
```

4. Click the **Save All** button. Click **Build** on the menu bar, and then click **Build Solution**.

5. In the Solution Explorer window, right-click **DisplayChapter12Dir.aspx** and select **View in Browser**. In the text box, type **c:\inetpub\wwwroot\Chapter12** and click **Go**. A listing of the subdirectories will appear. (*Note*: Because your Chapter12 folder may contain different directories your listing may appear different from the listing in Figure 12-17). The directory properties are shown along with a list of hyperlinks to the .aspx files within the directory.

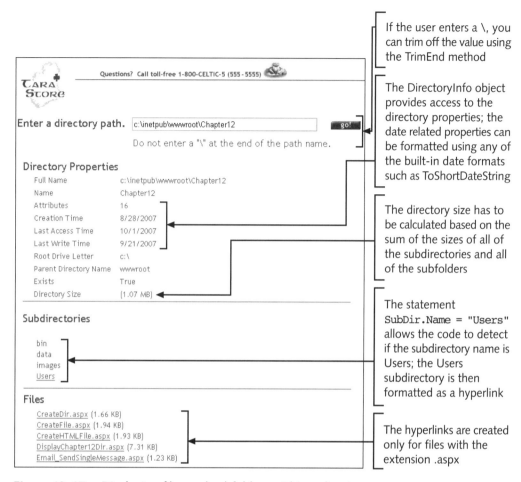

Figure 12-17   Displaying files and subfolders within a directory

6. In the text box, type **c:\inetpub\wwwroot\Chapter12\images\ ProductThumbs** and click **Go**. The images for the thumbnails are displayed as image hyperlinks, as shown in Figure 12-18.

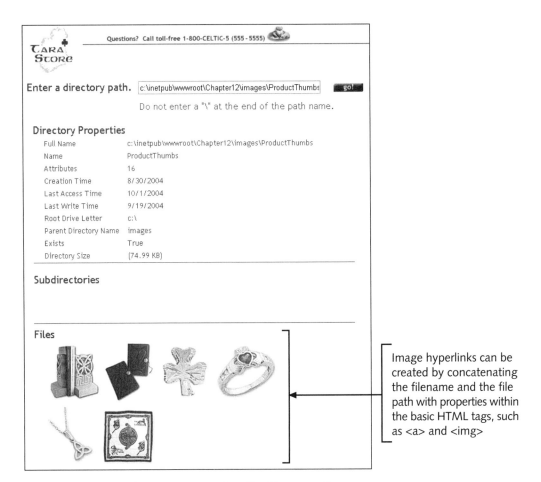

Figure 12-18   Displaying images using the file properties

7. In the text box, type **c:\Program Files** and click **Go**. An error message will appear, as shown in Figure 12-19. The ASP.NET user account does not have access to all files and folders on the server. (*Note*: If the user does not have access to all of the subdirectories, an error message may appear. This message is dependent upon the server security settings. Figure 12-18 shows the user did not have access to the C:\Program Files\MSSQL subdirectory.)

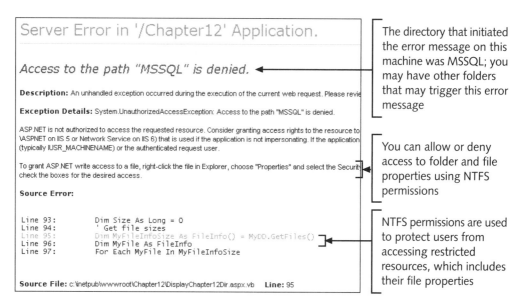

Figure 12-19   Using NTFS to protect files and folders

Creating and Deleting Directories

You can use the DirectoryInfo class to create and delete directories. You can use the **CreateSubdirectory method** to create a new directory. You must pass the name of the directory to the DirectoryInfo object. If the path to the directory is too long, or if the directory already exists, an exception may be thrown. You can catch these exceptions using the Try-Catch-End Try structure. The **ArgumentException** is used when you try to create a directory with invalid characters such as <>*?" or \\. If the directory already exists, the **IOException** is thrown. If the name of the path to the directory exceeds 248 characters, the **PathTooLongException** is thrown. If you don't have permission to create the folder, the **SecurityException** is thrown. When you delete the directory, you use the delete method of the DirectoryInfo object. If you attempt to delete a directory that does not exist, an IOException named **DirectoryNotFoundException** is thrown.

The **Delete method** is used to delete a directory with the DirectoryInfo class. You just have to call the Delete method. You can also use the Directory class directly to delete files. You must specify a file, and an optional Boolean value. With the Directory class you specify True or False as a parameter when you call the delete method. If you specify True, then all files and subdirectories are deleted. If you specify False, then if there are any files within the subdirectory, an exception is thrown. (*Note:* You can also use the Directory class within System.IO to create and delete directories.) In the following example, you will create and remove directories with the DirectoryInfo class. You will use a form to retrieve the name of the directory to create and delete.

Before completing the following exercise, you may need to modify the permissions in your Security tab. To do this, double-click My Computer, double-click the C: drive, double-click Inetpub, and then double-click the wwwroot directory. (In Windows XP, Inetpub is located on the C: drive by default.) Double-click the Chapter12 folder. Right-click the Users folder, and then click Properties. Click the Security tab. A warning message appears saying that the permissions on Users is incorrectly ordered. Click OK. (*Note*: If you click Cancel, the security permissions will default to the Everyone group with full control.) Click Add. The Select Users or Groups window opens. In the text box, enter [*MACHINENAME*]\ ASPNET. Click OK. With the ASPNET Machine Account selected in the Name column, click the Modify and Write check boxes to select them. Click Apply, and then click OK.

The Security tab is only visible on drives formatted with NTFS. The Security tab may not be visible on a Windows XP computer if simple file sharing is enabled. To disable simple file sharing, click Start, and then click My Computer. On the Tools menu, click Folder Options, and then click the View tab. In the Advanced settings section, clear the Use simple file sharing (Recommended) check box. Then click the OK button to close the window.

1. Right-click the **CreateDir.aspx** page in the Solution Explorer window to view the code behind the page, and then click **View Code**. Type the code that follows this paragraph in the DisplayDirectory function below the comment. This will retrieve the Users subdirectory list and bind it to a DropDownList control.

```
Dim DDL As DirectoryInfo = _
     New DirectoryInfo(MyPath)
Dim SubDir As DirectoryInfo
Dim MyHash As New Hashtable
For Each SubDir In DDL.GetDirectories()
    MyHash.Add(SubDir.Name, SubDir.Name)
Next
DropDownList1.DataTextField = "Key"
DropDownList1.DataValueField = "Value"
DropDownList1.DataSource = MyHash
DropDownList1.DataBind()
```

2. Type the code that follows this paragraph after the comment in the btnCreate_Click procedure. The MyPath variable contains the path to the c:\Inetpub\wwwroot\Chapter12\Users directory. This will create a new subdirectory in the Users directory. (*Note*: The rest of the procedure will redisplay the drop-down list with the new subdirectory added and a message in the Label control indicating that the subdirectory was created. Several Catch clauses are used to capture any exceptions thrown.)

```
Dim DD As DirectoryInfo = _
     New DirectoryInfo(MyPath)
DD.CreateSubdirectory(TextBox1.Text)
```

3. Type the code that follows this paragraph after the comment in the btnDelete_Click procedure. This will retrieve the subdirectory name from the DropDownList1 control, display a message in the Label control indicating the subdirectory was deleted, and delete the subdirectory. (*Note*: A Catch clause is used to capture an exception if the user tries to delete a subdirectory that does not exist.)

```
Dim DD2 As DirectoryInfo = _
New DirectoryInfo(MyPath & _
DropDownList1.SelectedItem.ToString)
Label1.Text = "The <b>" & _
DropDownList1.SelectedItem.ToString & _
" </b>directory was deleted."
DD2.Delete()
```

4. Click the **Save All** button. Click **Build** on the menu bar, and then click **Build Solution**.

5. In the Solution Explorer window, right-click **CreateDir.aspx**, and then click **View in Browser**.

6. Type **MyTest12** in the text box, and then click the **Create Directory** button, as shown in Figure 12-20. (*Note*: You can try to create an empty subdirectory, or a directory such as MyTest* that contains special characters, and a custom error message will be displayed.)

7. Click the **Delete Directory** button. The message that the MyTest12 directory was deleted is displayed. (*Note*: If you attempt to delete a subdirectory that does not exist, a custom error message will be displayed.)

12

8. Close any open files.

Figure 12-20 Managing the directory

Creating and Reading Files from an ASP.NET Page

You use the **FileInfo** class to create a file, read the contents of a file, and delete a file. The GetFiles method of the FileInfo object returns the files collection. You can retrieve the properties of a file with the FileInfo class. Some of the commonly used properties of the FileInfo class include **Attributes**, **CreationTime**, **LastAccessedTime**, **LastWriteTime**, **Name**, **FullName**, and **Exists**. The following is a list of additional properties that can be retrieved using the FileInfo class:

- The *Encrypted property* identifies that the object is encrypted.

- The *Hidden property* hides the file in the directory view.

- The *Compressed property* indicates whether or not a file is compressed.

- The *Archive property* indicates whether the file has been archived.

- The *NotContentIndexed property* identifies whether the Index Server will index the page.

- The *Offline property* identifies whether the file is to be available while the computer is offline.

- The *ReadOnly property* identifies whether the file is not to be modified by the user.

- The *System property* identifies whether the file is a system file. You can limit the directory view to avoid displaying system files. Then, the user can't accidentally modify or remove the system file.

- The *Temporary property* identifies whether the file is a temp file.

You can use the FileInfo class to create a basic text file or HTML file, copy a file to a new location, move a file to a new location, or delete a file. The **CopyTo** method copies a file from one path to another. The **MoveTo** method copies a file from one path to another, and then deletes the original file. The **Delete method** removes a file from the hard drive.

There are several objects that you can use to create, modify, read, and delete files. The File object contains methods for working with files. The File, Directory, and Path classes are derived from the System.Object class. However, the DirectoryInfo and FileInfo classes are derived from the System.IO.FileSystemInfo class. Both groups of classes allow you to interact with FileStream, BinaryReader, BinaryWriter, StreamReader, and StreamWriter classes, which allow you to read and write to files.

In the following exercise, you will create a new file, add material to the file from a form, display its properties using the FileInfo class, and delete the file. When you load the page, the default directions appear in the label. When you enter a filename and click the Create File button, the file is created using the name of the file and the CreateText method. The **CreateText method** returns a **StreamWriter object**. The **Create** and **CreateText methods** are used to create files. You can create a plain text file or an HTML file. You must pass the path of the new file to the CreateText method. The CreateText method returns the StreamWriter object and opens the file for editing. The Write method can be used to write HTML contents to the file. If you plan to create an HTML file, and want to display the contents at a later time, you should use the <XMP> tag to ignore the HTML tags in the file. Then, the HTML tags are displayed with the text and not interpreted by the browser. When you create the file, you can specify a relative path or a Universal Naming Convention (UNC) path for a server and share name. For example, the path to the file can be specified as "C:*MyDirectory**MyFileName*.txt", "C:*MyDirectory*", "*MyDirectory**MySubdirectory*", or "*MyServerName**MyShareName*".

Creating a Text File

The **Write method** of the StreamWriter object is used to write to the file. When you are finished, you need to use the **Close method** of the StreamWriter object to close the file. You can read the contents of the newly created file with the OpenText method of the FileInfo class. The **OpenText method** returns a **StreamReader object**, which can read through each line from the file. When you are finished, you need to use the Close method of the StreamReader object to close the file.

1. Double-click the **CreateFile.aspx** page in the Solution Explorer window.

2. Click the **CreateFile.aspx** tab. Then, double-click the button that says **Create File**. In the btnCreate_Click event procedure, after the comment, add the code following this paragraph to create the file using the value entered into the text box. This will store the path to the new file in the MyFile variable, create the

FileInfo object named MyFileInfo, create the StreamWriter object using the CreateText method in order to create the file, and open the file for writing.

```
Dim MyFile As String = MyPath & TextBox1.Text
Dim MyFileInfo As FileInfo = New FileInfo(MyFile)
Dim SW As StreamWriter = File.CreateText(MyFile)
```

3. Use the Write and WriteLine methods to send content to the file, as shown in the code that follows this paragraph. The WriteLine method places a return character at the end of the line. You can also use the Visual Basic .NET constant vbCrLf to represent a return character. You can assign the values using strings or content from the text box in the form. Replace [Your Name] with your own name.

```
SW.Write("This file was ")
SW.WriteLine("created by: ")
SW.Write("[Your Name] ")
SW.Write(vbCrLf)
SW.WriteLine("on " & Now.Date.ToShortDateString)
SW.WriteLine()
SW.WriteLine()
SW.Write(TextBox1.Text)
```

4. Add the following code, which closes the TextStream object when you are finished. Then, release the object by setting the variable to Nothing.

```
SW.Close()
MyFileInfo = Nothing
```

5. Click the **CreateFile.aspx** tab. Then, double-click the button that says **Delete File**. In the btnDelete_Click event procedure, after the comment, add the code following this paragraph to delete the file using the value entered into the text box. This will use the Delete method of the FileInfo object to delete the file. (*Note*: If the file is in use by another process, it cannot be deleted.)

```
Dim MyFileInfo As FileInfo = New FileInfo(MyFile)
Label1.Text = "The <b>" & _
DropDownList1.SelectedItem.ToString & _
" </b>file was deleted."
MyFileInfo.Delete()
MyFileInfo = Nothing
```

6. Click the **CreateFile.aspx** tab. Then, double-click the button that says **Display File Contents**.

7. In the btnDisplay_Click event procedure, after the comment, add the code following this paragraph to read the file using the filename selected from the drop-down list. The code uses the StreamReader object to retrieve the file from the File object and open the file with the OpenText method. The ReadToEnd method reads the entire file line by line until it reaches the end

of the file. The contents of the file are assigned to the Text property of the Label control in the Web page.

```
Dim MyFileInfo As FileInfo = New FileInfo(MyFile)
Dim SR As StreamReader = MyFileInfo.OpenText()
Label3.Text = SR.ReadToEnd
SR.Close()
SR = Nothing
```

8. Click the **Save All** button. Click **Build** on the menu bar, and then click **Build Solution**.

9. Click the **CreateFile.aspx** tab. Right-click on the page, and then click **View in Browser**.

10. Type **MyChapter12.txt** in the text box, and then click the **Create File** button.

11. Select the **MyChapter12.txt** file in the drop-down list. Click the **Display File Contents** button. The contents of the file are displayed, as shown in Figure 12-21.

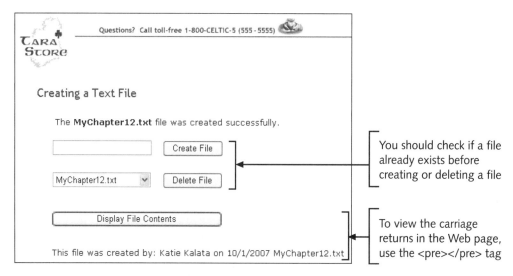

Figure 12-21   Creating a text file

12. Click the **Delete File** button. Your file is deleted.

13. Close the file.

Notice that the carriage returns are not recognized in the browser. HTML ignores carriage returns and white space such as tabs. You must use HTML tags to ensure that the contents are placed on the correct line.

Creating an HTML Page

In the following exercise, you will create a file named CreateHTMLFile.aspx, which includes HTML commands.

1. Right-click the **CreateHTMLFile.aspx** page in the Solution Explorer window, and then click **View Code**.

2. Enter the following code in the Page_Load handler, after the comment, to display the default message:

```
If Not Page.IsPostBack Then
    HyperLink1.Text = ""
    Label3.Text = _
    "Enter the name of the HTML file to create."
End If
```

3. Click the **CreateHTMLFile.aspx** tab. Then, double-click the button that says **Create File**. In the btnCreate_Click event procedure, after the comment, add the code following this paragraph. This will create the file using the value entered into the text box, and set the hyperlink to an empty string so that it is not displayed.

```
Dim MyFile As String = MyPath & TextBox1.Text
Dim MyFileInfo As FileInfo = New FileInfo(MyFile)
HyperLink1.Text = ""
Label1.Text = "<b>The file was created!</b>"
Dim SW As StreamWriter = File.CreateText(MyFile)
```

4. Add the code following this paragraph. The code enters the basic HTML tags. The body of the page content comes from the TextBox2 control.

```
SW.WriteLine("<html><head>")
SW.WriteLine("<title>Creating an HTML File: ")
SW.WriteLine(TextBox1.Text)
SW.WriteLine("</title></head>")
SW.WriteLine("<body>")
SW.WriteLine(TextBox2.Text)
SW.WriteLine("<hr /><br /><br />Created on ")
SW.WriteLine(Now.Date.ToShortDateString)
SW.WriteLine("</body></html>")
SW.Close()
MyFileInfo = Nothing
```

5. Add the following code to set the properties of the hyperlink and display the hyperlink:

```
HyperLink1.Text = "Click here to read the HTML file!"
HyperLink1.NavigateUrl = _
"http://localhost/Chapter12/Users/" & TextBox1.Text
Label1.Text = ""
```

6. Click the **CreateHTMLFile.aspx** tab. Then, double-click the button that says **Delete File**. In the btnDelete_Click event procedure, after the comment, add the following code to delete the file:

```
Dim MyFile As String = MyPath & TextBox1.Text
Dim MyFileInfo As FileInfo = New FileInfo(MyFile)
HyperLink1.Text = ""
Label1.Text = "<b>The File was deleted!</b>"
MyFileInfo.Delete()
MyFileInfo = Nothing
```

7. Click the **Save All** button. Click **Build** on the menu bar, and then click **Build Solution**.

8. Click the **CreateHTMLFile.aspx** tab. Then, right-click on the page and click **View in Browser**.

9. Type **MyChapter12.htm** in the first text box. In the second text box, type **Welcome to my Web site**.

10. Click the **Create File** button. The file is created and the new hyperlink is displayed, as shown in Figure 12-22.

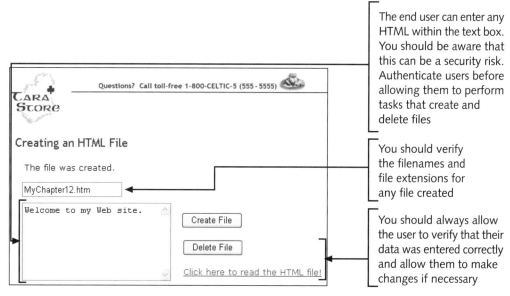

The end user can enter any HTML within the text box. You should be aware that this can be a security risk. Authenticate users before allowing them to perform tasks that create and delete files

You should verify the filenames and file extensions for any file created

You should always allow the user to verify that their data was entered correctly and allow them to make changes if necessary

Figure 12-22   Creating an HTML file

11. Click the hyperlink to open the page in the browser. The contents of the file are displayed in the browser.

12. Click the **Back** button in the browser.

13. Click the **Delete File** button. Your file is deleted. (*Note*: If you were to refresh the page, the File Not Found error message would appear.)

14. Close the file. To close the solution, go to the **File** menu and select **Close Solution**.

Security Issues

Security is not a linear concept. Security today involves securing not only the operating system and files, but also the applications that run on the server. You've already learned about NTFS and how to set the permissions for users and groups for specific files and folders. You've also learned about how services such as ASP.NET, IIS, and SQL Server run using a user account such as the local system account, IUSR_MACHINENAME, and ASPNET.

Of course, some programs provide additional security measures. SQL Server provides the ability to create its own set of usernames and passwords, such as the sa user. You can create a login form processed by ASP.NET for Web applications. The hierarchy of files and folders can be modified in IIS using virtual applications and virtual directories. That way, potential hackers would not know the physical paths to files. You can turn off FTP access to your company Web site so that potential hackers cannot upload files using FTP. Newer security methods such as firewalls allow you to restrict or allow traffic to specific applications or ports that the applications are listening on. The Web server can be placed outside of the company network, but protected by a firewall. This area is called the demilitarized zone (DMZ).

Some Web developers have created Web security programs using JavaScripts. JavaScripts run on the client and are not adequate for securing a Web site. As an example of such a situation, consider a not-for-profit company with over 4,000 members in Chicago, Illinois that created online courses for their membership. They hired two programmers who made two major mistakes with respect to their Web site. First, they used Microsoft FrontPage forms to store the end-user data, including credit card numbers and personal information. Microsoft FrontPage extensions allow you to process forms quickly, and store the information in a text file or database. However, it is up to the Web developer to secure these files, by using methods built into Microsoft FrontPage or by configuring NTFS. While it is possible to secure a Web site using Microsoft FrontPage, they didn't have the knowledge to implement it. Second, they used JavaScripts to process the login form. All JavaScripts are client-based, so all Web sites that use them must allow the browser to read the client-program. If the end-user clicks the escape button quickly, and they have a slower connection to the Internet, it is possible to stop the processing of the redirection scripts, view the JavaScript code, and hack into the Web site.

In earlier chapters, you learned to create a login script using ASP.NET. If the user were validated, he or she was redirected to a new page; otherwise, he or she was redirected back to the login page. This method needs to be combined with other security methods. Hackers can search the Web site and guess at the names of files in an attempt to hack into the site. To counteract this threat, you must use methods such as Forms Authentication presented in Chapter 9 to validate the user. This way, the user must be validated for each ASP.NET resource.

You also learned that Access is a file and can be downloaded by the end user. This file can be protected using passwords within the file. Again, hackers can use password detection programs to hack into the file. A better alternative is to use a server-based database program such as Microsoft SQL Server or Oracle.

Similarly, an end user can right-click a graphic and save the image locally. Companies that try to protect their graphics by using JavaScript are wasting their time. Copies of these Web pages, including the graphics, are stored locally in the browser's cache directory. End users can browse and copy files from this folder. In addition, they can either save the entire page to another location or view the location of the image in the source code and go to the image file directly by typing the URL in the browser location text box.

All of these examples show that security is not a simple topic, and it not just related to processing a login page. Your company should determine what their policy is with regards to uploading, storing, and retrieving files from a Web program. Other methods can be used to prevent theft of intellectual property. For example, Adobe's PhotoShop (*www.adobe.com*) and other graphics programs allow the graphics designer to embed a watermark in the image. This provides the company with some protections if the case is taken to court. Content that is textual can be presented in PDF format, preventing the ability to quickly cut and paste content into another piece of work.

Web site management tools that include the ability to upload files are usually provided for employees within the company. Your company can restrict the user of the Web site management tools to be within the company's network and firewall. Your company may also want to restrict which type of files can be uploaded and their maximum file size. You can configure a specific folder where only one user can upload files. The Midwest Alliance for Nursing Informatics (MANI) is a not-for-profit group based in Illinois. (*Note*: MANI is now assimilated within the Chicago-based Healthcare Information Management Systems Society called HIMSS.) The MANI board members were allowed to upload certain types of files to their Web site. When they tried to upload the membership directory, the program made a copy of the old directory and then copied the new directory with the same filename as the old directory. This prevented errors when board members modified the file name of the database. In addition, board members were allowed to upload newsletters. However, the newsletters were contained within a separate directory with different NTFS permissions.

You should identify the needs for your Web site before you start creating the application. Building a secure and robust Web application takes time and costs more money than a simple one-level HTML Web site. You will need management approval for allocating costs to the project. Many times, company employees don't know the possibilities or the implications of building Web sites. You may need to provide them with suggestions on how to use and how to secure the Web site. Inform them about the technical issues and challenges and then allow them to have input into the policy making decisions.

Be creative. By now you've learned many individual skill sets. You can start to combine them into robust applications.

WORKING WITH ALTERNATIVE PLATFORMS: PDAS AND MOBILE DEVICES

Today, a Web application is thought of as a series of Web pages viewed with a browser. However, each year more consumers are viewing Web content via alternative devices such as mobile phones. There are several major issues that affect the development of a Web application for mobile devices. First, because there is a wide range of hardware and software for these devices, not all of them have the same screen size, resolution, color, graphics, and multimedia capabilities. Some devices support a scaled-down version of a browser, and others only support text. Although some users connect directly via a network or wireless LAN, other users connect via modems or cellular phones. This means that Web developers have less control over the end-user interface than ever before. Therefore, you should focus on what you can control, which is the content you are providing to the end user.

The main platforms for portable devices are Palm, Windows Pocket PC, and Windows CE. Some platforms, such as the Pocket PC, use a browser to display Web pages, and some platforms use other HTML and XML interpreters. There are a wide range of mobile devices and platforms. Displaying Web pages is very difficult on a mobile device because of the limited screen size. However, new technologies, such as the Mobile Internet Toolkit, have made it easier for developers to create a single mobile application that can be displayed on a variety of mobile devices and platforms. As the telecommunications and network infrastructures are upgraded to newer technologies, more mobile and Internet capabilities will be built into mobile and portable devices. As a result, you will see a greater demand for Web applications to expand to these new markets.

The current Web site for Microsoft mobile solutions is *www.microsoft.com/windowsmobile/default.mspx*.

Frequently asked questions about developing applications for Windows Mobile applications are available at *http://msdn.microsoft.com/library/en-us/dnppcgen/html/devmobfaq.asp*. Because mobile phones have become more sophisticated and are offering capabilities similar to PDAs, they are often referred to as **Smartphones** or smart devices. PDAs, on the other hand, have additional capabilities, including phone and messaging.

There are several options for operating systems for these devices and several methods to program for these devices. Many of the new devices have the .NET Compact Framework installed. The .NET Compact Framework is a subset of the .NET Framework that is designed to run on portable and mobile devices. When you write the application using the .NET Compact Framework, the application is running on the client as a stand-alone application. When you use the ASP.NET Mobile controls built into Visual Studio .NET 2003, you are creating a server-based application, where the server runs the application.

You can use Visual Studio .NET to create .NET applications for the Pocket PC 2000, Pocket PC 2002, and Pocket PC 2003 devices. Some developers may choose to use eMbedded Visual Tools 3.0 to create their mobile applications. eMbedded Visual Tools 3.0 is a stand-alone development environment used to create mobile applications.

Mobile controls are built into the Microsoft .NET Framework version 1.1. You can learn more about developing ASP.NET Mobile Controls using Visual Studio .NET 2003 at *http://msdn.microsoft.com/vstudio/device/mobilecontrols/default.asp.*

 You can download the PocketPC emulators at *http://www.microsoft.com/ downloads/details.aspx?FamilyId=5C53E3B5-F2A2-47D7-A41D- 825FD68EBB6C&displaylang=en* and the Smartphone emulators at *http:// www.microsoft.com/downloads/details.aspx?FamilyId=791BAE52-B057- 4D72-B263-105534825CA5&displaylang=en.*

Creating a WML Document

The standard used to program on a mobile device is the **Wireless Application Protocol (WAP)**. WAP is an open standard that is available from the Open Mobile Alliance at *www.wapforum.com*. Within the WAP is the **Wireless S Protocol (WSP)**, which is a transport protocol that performs the same functions as HTTP for mobile devices. To work with Web content, the WAP standards use an application standard known as **Wireless Markup Language (WML)**. Files that use the WML end with the file extension .wml. These files can contain small programs written in a scripting language such as VBScript. If the file contains programming scripts, the file extension ends in .wmls. Wireless bitmap images end in .wbmp.

When you develop applications for wireless devices, you need to view the results on the device, or use a device simulator. Most mobile devices supply a simulator for developers. Device emulators simulate several devices and allow you to apply different templates, called skins, to the emulator. Each device has its own skin, which you can view on the device emulator. The simulator is installed on your desktop computer to test your applications. The Nokia 7110 phone device simulators are available at *http://www.forum.nokia.com*. You can also use the OpenWave device simulator to test several types of phones. The

12

OpenWave Simulator allows you to simulate phones from Ericsson, Mitsubishi, and Samsung. OpenWave can be found at *http://developer.openwave.com/dvl/*. A list of tested devices and emulators that are supported within Visual Studio .NET can be found at *http://msdn.microsoft.com/vstudio/device/mobilecontrols/devices.aspx*. There are over 265 devices tested for compatibility with Mobile controls. Tested Compaq devices are as shown in Figure 12-23.

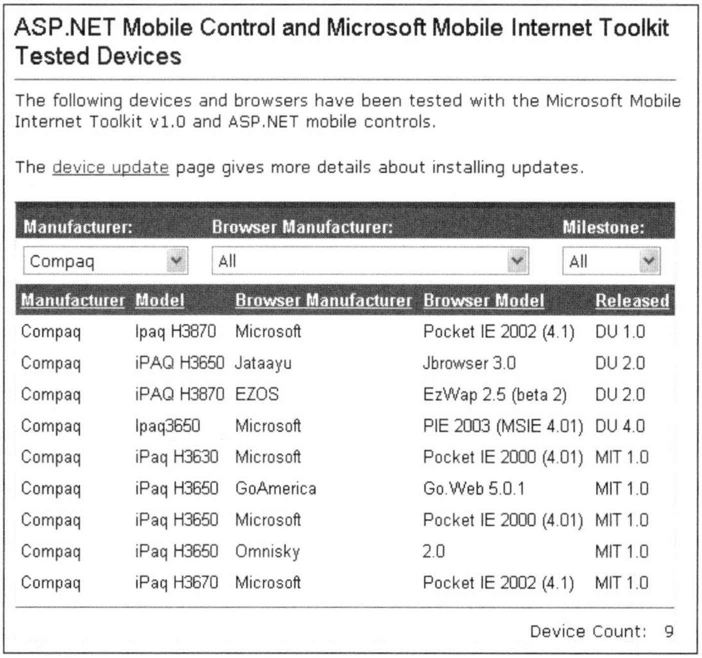

ASP.NET Mobile Control and Microsoft Mobile Internet Toolkit Tested Devices

The following devices and browsers have been tested with the Microsoft Mobile Internet Toolkit v1.0 and ASP.NET mobile controls.

The device update page gives more details about installing updates.

Manufacturer:	Browser Manufacturer:		Milestone:
Compaq	All		All

Manufacturer	Model	Browser Manufacturer	Browser Model	Released
Compaq	Ipaq H3870	Microsoft	Pocket IE 2002 (4.1)	DU 1.0
Compaq	iPAQ H3650	Jataayu	Jbrowser 3.0	DU 2.0
Compaq	iPAQ H3870	EZOS	EzWap 2.5 (beta 2)	DU 2.0
Compaq	Ipaq3650	Microsoft	PIE 2003 (MSIE 4.01)	DU 4.0
Compaq	iPaq H3630	Microsoft	Pocket IE 2000 (4.01)	MIT 1.0
Compaq	iPaq H3650	GoAmerica	Go.Web 5.0.1	MIT 1.0
Compaq	iPaq H3650	Microsoft	Pocket IE 2000 (4.01)	MIT 1.0
Compaq	iPaq H3650	Omnisky	2.0	MIT 1.0
Compaq	iPaq H3670	Microsoft	Pocket IE 2002 (4.1)	MIT 1.0

Device Count: 9

Figure 12-23   Compaq devices and browsers tested for compatibility with Mobile controls

You can configure your Web server to support WML files by adding a Mime Map for the file extension `.wml` with content type `text/vnd.wap.wml`.

WML is compliant with the XML protocols, and therefore is case sensitive. You must also close each tag, with a closing tag or by adding a forward slash to the end of the opening tag. All WML files contain the MIME type declared in the document type declaration:

```
<?xml version="1.0"?>
<!DOCTYPE wml PUBLIC =-//WAPFORUM??DTD WML 1.1//EN
"http:///www.wapforum.org/DTD/wml_1.1.xml">
```

The rest of the document is enclosed in a single pair of WML tags, which serve as the root element of the WML document. The WML card metaphor is used to organize content delivered to a mobile device. So, a WML file consists of a deck of cards. Each card is a screen of content. Although the entire file is sent to the device, only one screen is displayed at a time. Each card is identified with the card tag: <card>. The title attribute of the card is used to provide a description of the content within the card. You can link WML documents using a hyperlink created with an anchor tag <a>. The href property of the anchor tag is used to identify the target in the WML document. You can set the target to an internal target or to another URL. Additional tags, such as the line break, paragraph, and bold tags, are commonly used in mobile devices.

Building PDA and Mobile Applications in Visual Studio .NET

Older versions of Visual Studio .NET required the Web develoer to download the Mobile Internet Toolkit from Microsoft. The current Mobile controls available within Visual Studio .NET allow you to create mobile applications. These Mobile controls generate WML, compact HTML (cHTML) for Japanese i-mode phones, and HTML 3.2. The selection of what output is chosen is determined when the client connects to the Web application. In other words, two devices could connect to the same mobile application and the Mobile controls would generate a different set of code.

You can create ASP.NET pages that can be displayed on mobile devices. The ASP.NET Web pages that contain Mobile controls are known as **Mobile Forms**. The tool within Visual Studio .NET that allows you to create Mobile Forms using a GUI is called the **Mobile Internet Designer**. You do not have to create the WML code. ASP.NET will generate the code that is appropriate for the mobile device. So, if you use ASP.NET, the ASP.NET **Mobile controls** will generate the WML output for your Web application. Just as with Web Forms, you can also create Mobile Forms by using Visual Studio .NET or in a simple editor such as Notepad.

The Mobile QuickStart site, which is installed at *http://localhost/mobilequickstart/*, contains information on how to and create Mobile Forms, as shown in Figure 12-24.

The Mobile controls inherit from the `System.Web.Mobile` namespace. You can add Mobile Forms to an ASP.NET Web application, or create a mobile Web project and create the Mobile Forms within it. The Mobile Web Forms tab is shown in Figure 12-25.

12

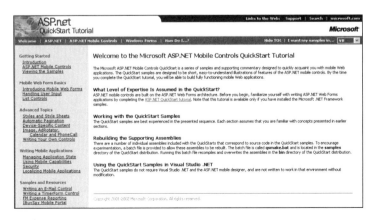

Figure 12-24   Mobile QuickStart Web site

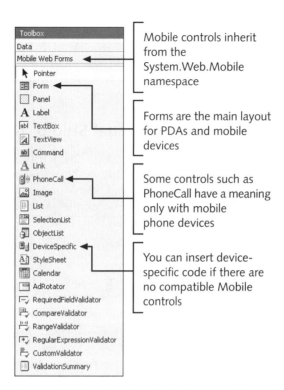

Mobile controls inherit from the System.Web.Mobile namespace

Forms are the main layout for PDAs and mobile devices

Some controls such as PhoneCall have a meaning only with mobile phone devices

You can insert device-specific code if there are no compatible Mobile controls

Figure 12-25   The Mobile Web Forms tab in the Toolbox

Using Mobile Controls in an ASP.NET Application

Mobile controls inherit a code behind the page named System.Web.UI. MobileControls.MobilePage. Each Web page contains a register directive that is used to register the mobile tag controls with the Mobile control namespace. So, on the first line of code in the Web page, you will see the code following this paragraph. This code is automatically placed on the Mobile Form by Visual Studio .NET when you create the mobile form.

```
<%@ Page Language="vb" AutoEventWireup="false"
Codebehind="MobileWebForm1.aspx.vb"
Inherits="Chapter12Mobile.MobileWebForm1" %>
<%@ Register TagPrefix="mobile"
Namespace="System.Web.UI.MobileControls"
Assembly="System.Web.Mobile" %>
```

Creating a Mobile Form

In the following exercise, you will create a basic Mobile Form using the Mobile Internet Designer. Because the WML is XML compliant, you can view the document in an XML reader such as Internet Explorer if you do not have a mobile device simulator installed.

1. Open your **Chapter12** solution if it is not already open. Right-click **Chapter12** in the Solution Explorer window, point to **Add**, and then click **Add New Item**. In the Templates pane, click **Mobile Web Form**. In the Name text box type **MFDisplayList.aspx**. Click the **Open** button. The Mobile Form appears smaller on the Web page. This is the default width of the form.

2. Add a Label control from the Mobile Forms tab.

3. With the Label control selected, view the properties in the Properties window. Change the (ID) of the label to **lblStoreName**.

4. Change the font to **Trebuchet MS,** the ForeColor property to **#004040**, the Alignment property to **Center**, and the Bold property to **True**.

5. Change the Text property to **Tara Store Home Page**.

6. Add a List control to the Mobile Form. For each item within the List control, the Text attribute assigns the value and the displayed text. The Decoration property identifies the type of list. By default, the List control Decoration property is set to none. The Decoration property may also be assigned to Numbered or Bulleted.

7. Change the List control properties for the font to **Trebuchet MS** and for the ForeColor to **#004040**.

8. Double-click on the page to view the code behind the page.

9. In the Page_Load event procedure, add the code following this paragraph. This will create an array named AR1 and populate the array with values. Then, it will bind the List control named List1 to the AR1 Array control.

```
Dim AR1 As New ArrayList(4)
AR1.Add("Irish History")
AR1.Add("Irish Music")
AR1.Add("Travel in Ireland")
AR1.Add("Sports in Ireland")
List1.DataSource=AR1
List1.DataBind()
```

10. Click the **Save All** button. Click **Build** on the menu bar, and then click **Build Solution**.

11. View the page in the browser at *http://localhost/Chapter12/MFDisplayList.aspx*. The page is displayed as shown in the Internet Explorer window in Figure 12-26. (*Note*: If you have a device emulator installed, you can also view the page in the device emulator.)

12

The Pocket PC 2003 Software Development Kit (SDK) includes an emulator that uses a virtual machine to run the full Pocket PC 2003 software. You can download the Pocket PC 2003 SDK from *http://microsoft.com/downloads/details.aspx?FamilyId=9996B314-0364-4623-9EDE-0B5FBB133652*. The entire installation package of the Pocket PC 2003 Software Development Kit (SDK) will require 214 MB of disk space. There are several prerequisites. After downloading and installing the application, you should read the installation documentation located at C:\Program Files\Windows CE Tools\wce420\POCKET PC 2003\readme.htm.

This is the Mobile Form in Design view within Visual Studio .NET

You can preview the application in the Internet Explorer browser

Figure 12-26   Viewing a Mobile Form

12. View the source code for the Web page in the browser. Notice that there is no sign of Mobile Forms or WML. The ASP.NET Web Application sent the code that was supported by the device.

13. In Visual Studio .NET, view the HTML source code for the Mobile Form by clicking the **HTML** tab. Notice that the form is tagged with the mobile prefix, and each of the form fields, Label and List, are tagged with the mobile prefix. Although these controls look similar to ASP.NET Web Form controls, they have additional properties to support Mobile Forms.

14. Close all the files and the solution.

In the preceding exercise, not all of the content is displayed on the screen. You must scroll down to view additional content. You can set the **Wrapping property** of the form to NoWrap to stop the control from wrapping. Wrapping allows content that extends over a long line to wrap to the next line. If wrapping is turned off, the user must scroll horizontally to view long lines. You can also set the **TextView property** to enable pagination for large amounts of text. You can set the **Paginate property** for the Mobile Form to true. Using pagination allows you to divide the list into multiple pages. When you create the list, you can display the default pagination properties, or set the values of the displayed text with the **PagerStyle properties**. In the sample code that follows this paragraph, the **PageLabel** property of the PagerStyle properties identifies the number of pages that are available. You can also add the **NextPageText** and **PreviousPageText** PagerStyle elements to your page and assign them a text value to display in the window, as shown in the following sample code:

```
PagerStyle -PageLabel="Page {0} of {1}"
PagerStyle -NextPageText="Continue"
PagerStyle -PreviousPageText="Back"
```

Each card can be represented by a separate Mobile Form within the WML document. You can then create a Link control to link to other cards within the same file, or to another WML file. The **NavigateURL** is used to identify links. The pound sign (#) is used to indicate an internal link.

With the WML file, you can easily insert scripts within the mobile form document. You can interact with page events, such as Page_Load. You can detect if the form has any mobile capabilities in the Page_Load event handler or in the Machine.config file. Within the Machine.config file, the <browserCaps> section identifies the support for mobile devices, which are exposed through the MobileCapabilities class. You can also use form templates to provide reusable content, such as the HeaderTemplate and FooterTemplate. Several Mobile Form controls can contain other controls such as the paragraph, line break, bold, italic, and anchor HTML tags.

Creating Multiple Web Forms

In the following activity, you will create additional Mobile Forms in the same document.

1. Open the **Chapter12** solution. Right-click **Chapter12** in the Solution Explorer window, point to **Add**, and then click **Add New Item**. In the Templates pane, select **Mobile Web Form**. In the Name text box type **MFHomePage.aspx**. Click the **Open** button. The Mobile Form appears smaller on the Web page. This is the default width of the form.

2. Add a Label control from the Mobile Forms tab. With the Label control selected, view the properties in the Properties window. Change the (ID) of the label to **lblStoreName**. Change the font to **Trebuchet MS**, the ForeColor property to **#004040**, the Alignment property to **Center**, and the Bold property to **True**. Change the Text property to **Tara Store Home Page**.

3. Add a List control to the Mobile Form. For each item within the List control, the Text attribute assigns the value and the displayed text. Change the Decoration property to **Numbered**. The Decoration property identifies the type of list such as bulleted or numbered lists. Change the List control properties for the font to **Trebuchet MS** and for the ForeColor to **#004040**. Change the ItemsAsLinks property for the list to **True**. The ItemsAsLinks property displays the items in the list as hyperlinks.

12

4. Drag a second form tag to the page from the Mobile Forms tab. Form2 is created. Change the (ID) property of Form2 to **Products**. Change the Title property to **Product Categories**. Add an **ObjectList** control to the form.

5. Drag a third form tag to the page from the Mobile Forms tab. Form2 is created. Change the (ID) property of Form2 to **ChicagoStore**. Change the Title property to **Chicago Store**.

6. Drag the **Image** tag to the ChicagoStore Mobile Form. You can specify the ImageURL property as **/Chapter12/images/ChicagoStore.jpg**. The ImageURL property is the location of the graphic file. Specify the Alternate Text property as **Chicago Store Image** so that if no images are supported, an alternate text message is displayed. (*Note*: On some devices, bitmapped graphics (BMP) are preferred over GIF files. You can use the **DeviceSpecific** filter property within the page or within the Web configuration file to identify the preferred format for the entire application. In general, browsers prefer the GIF format, whereas cellular devices prefer the BMP format.)

7. Drag a new form to the page from the Mobile Forms tab. Change the ID property to **CustomerService**. Change the Title property to **Customer Service**.

8. Drag the **PhoneCall** control to the form. (*Note*: In Internet Explorer 5.5 or earlier, a label with a link is displayed instead of placing the call.) Change the PhoneNumber property to **800-555-1212**. If the user's device is enabled, the control places the phone call. Change the AlternateURL to **#ChicagoStore** for devices that are not able to place calls. Change the Text property to **Call Tara Store**. Change the font to **Trebuchet MS** and the ForeColor property to **#004040**.

9. View the HTML source code by clicking the **HTML** tab, as shown in Figure 12-27. (*Note*: The text will not wrap the same as shown in the figure.)

10. Click the **Design** tab to return to Design view. Double-click the page to view the code behind the page.

```
<%@ Register TagPrefix="mobile" Namespace="System.Web.UI.MobileControls"
    Assembly="System.Web.Mobile" %>
<%@ Page Language="vb" AutoEventWireup="false"
    Codebehind="MFHomePage.aspx.vb" Inherits="Chapter12.MFHomePage" %>
<HEAD>
    <meta name="GENERATOR" content="Microsoft Visual Studio .NET 7.1">
    <meta name="CODE_LANGUAGE" content="Visual Basic .NET 7.1">
    <meta name="vs_targetSchema"
        content="http://schemas.microsoft.com/Mobile/Page">
</HEAD>
<body Xmlns:mobile="http://schemas.microsoft.com/Mobile/WebForm">
    <mobile:Form id="Form1" runat="server">
        <mobile:Label id="lblStoreName" runat="server"
            Alignment="Center" Font-Bold="True" ForeColor="#004040"
            Font-Name="Trebuchet MS">Tara Store Home Page</mobile:Label>
        <mobile:List id="List1" runat="server" ForeColor="#004040"
            Font-Name="Trebuchet MS" Decoration="Numbered"
            ItemsAsLinks="True"></mobile:List>
    </mobile:Form>
    <mobile:Form id="Products" title="Product Categories" runat="server">
        <mobile:ObjectList id="ObjectList1" runat="server"
            CommandStyle-StyleReference="subcommand"
            LabelStyle-StyleReference="title"></mobile:ObjectList>
    </mobile:Form>
    <mobile:Form id="ChicagoStore" title="Chicago Store" runat="server">
        <mobile:Image id="Image1" runat="server"
            ImageUrl="/Chapter12/images/ChicagoStore.jpg"></mobile:Image>
    </mobile:Form>
    <mobile:Form id="CustomerService" title="Customer Service" runat="server">
        <mobile:PhoneCall id="PhoneCall1" runat="server"
            ForeColor="#004040" Font-Name="Trebuchet MS"
            PhoneNumber="800-555-1212"
            AlternateUrl="#ChicagoStore">
            Call Tara Store </mobile:PhoneCall>
    </mobile:Form>
</body>
```

Figure 12-27   HTML code with Mobile Form controls

12

11. In the Page_Load event procedure, add the code following this paragraph. This will create a HashTable named AR1 and populate the array with values. Then, it will bind the List control named List1 to the AR1 structure. Notice that the Hash table was used to display a different value than what is sent when the user clicks on the link.

```
Dim AR1 As New Hashtable(8)
AR1.Add("#Products", "Products")
AR1.Add("#ChicagoStore", "Chicago Store")
AR1.Add("#CustomerService", "Customer Service")
List1.DataSource = AR1
List1.DataTextField = "Value"
List1.DataValueField = "Key"
List1.DataBind()
```

12. Add the following code to create the second array and bind the second array to the objects list:

```
Dim AR2 As New ArrayList(9)
AR2.Add("Gifts")
AR2.Add("China & Crystal")
AR2.Add("Pottery")
AR2.Add("Music, Books, Video")
AR2.Add("Bridal")
```

```
AR2.Add("Clothing")
AR2.Add("Food")
AR2.Add("Jewelry")
ObjectList1.DataSource = AR2
ObjectList1.DataBind()
```

13. Click the **Save All** button. Click **Build** on the menu bar, and then click **Build Solution**.

14. View the page in the browser at *http://localhost/Chapter12/MFHomePage.aspx*. The page is displayed as shown in Figure 12-28. (*Note*: If you have a device emulator installed, you can also view the page in the device emulator.)

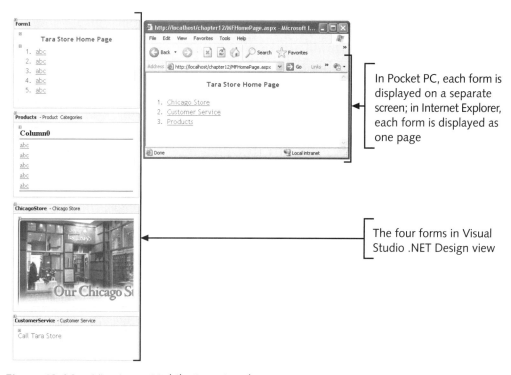

In Pocket PC, each form is displayed on a separate screen; in Internet Explorer, each form is displayed as one page

The four forms in Visual Studio .NET Design view

Figure 12-28 Viewing a Mobile Form in a browser

15. Click the **Products** link. Click the **Back** button in the browser.

16. Click the **Chicago Store** link. Click the **Back** button in the browser.

17. Click the **Customer Service** link.

18. Click the **Call** hyperlink. The browser is redirected to the Chicago Store page.

19. Close the browser.

20. Close all the files and the solution.

There are many other Mobile Form controls that you can insert into a Mobile Form. You can add AdRotator controls and Calendar controls to the Mobile Forms. You can also create a form with text boxes. However, the text fields can only exist on one line. Multiple-line text boxes are not supported. You can also use TextView control to insert long text blocks. TextView can support some formatting such as bold, italic, and hyperlinks. You can use the Numeric Text controls with WML devices only. The Password Text control displays an asterisk instead of the number in the screen window, but it does not hide the value from the code behind the page. You can use Validation controls to validate the form fields, similarly to how they are used with Web Forms. You cannot use client-side JavaScript to display error messages with the Validation controls. If you use a ValidationSummary control, you must keep the control on a separate form and use the formToValidate property to assign the control to a Mobile Form. The error messages are not displayed interactively as you move from control to control. Because the List object is created with a control, you can change the list items programmatically. You can insert command buttons that can be used to send a command with the OnItemCommand property for the ItemCommand event.

CHAPTER SUMMARY

- ❏ The SMTP server is the default mail service that is installed with the Internet Information Service Web server. The mail server's default root directory is C:\Inetpub\MailRoot\. The Pickup folder is used to store outgoing mail messages. Mail that cannot be delivered is sent to the BadMail directory. You can configure the SMTP server via the property sheets in the MMC application. The default port for the SMTP server is 25.

- ❏ The CDONTS object, from cdonts.dll, is installed with the SMTP server and enables you to send outbound e-mail from a Web page. The CDONTS component is only available if the SMTP mail server is installed. You can access the properties of the CDONTS object via the `System.Web.Mail` namespace. The MailMessage class provides the sender and recipient data, as well as the message content. The MailAttachment class is used to identify a file that is to be sent with the e-mail message. The SMTPMail class is used to send the e-mail message. E-mail can be sent as plain text or formatted with HTML. The Send method of the SmtpMail class creates the message in the required format and writes it to the Pickup folder, from where the SMTP server sends it.

- ❏ The `System.IO` namespace provides you with classes that interact with the Web server's file system. It contains several classes such as File, FileStream, and Directory, which allow you to create, read, and delete files. However, the newer classes, named DirectoryInfo and FileInfo, are more flexible and provide easier access to the file system.

- ❏ The DirectoryInfo class allows you to obtain the properties of a directory and its subdirectories.

12

❐ The GetDirectories method of the DirectoryInfo class is used to retrieve the collection of subdirectories. The CreateSubdirectory method is used to create a new directory. You can capture exceptions when creating directories and files with the Try-Catch-End Try structure.

❐ You can use the FileInfo class to copy a file to a new location, move a file to a new location, or delete a file. The FileInfo class allows you access to the properties of a file, using the FileAttributes. You can use the FileInfo class to create a basic text file or HTML file.

❐ The CreateText and Create methods of the FileInfo class return a StreamWriter object, which is used to create files. The open, OpenRead, OpenText, and OpenWrite methods allow you to open and read the file. The Write method of the StreamWriter object is used to write to the file. The OpenText method returns a StreamReader object, which can read through each line from the file.

❐ The Wireless Application Protocol (WAP) is an open standard used to create programs on a mobile device. Wireless Markup Language (WML) is the programming language used to create the code for the mobile applications. WML is compliant with the XML protocols. The WML files use cards to organize and divide the structure of the WML document. You can use additional HTML tags within the WML language, such as the anchor tag.

❐ Device emulators, such as the OpenWave Simulator, allow you to simulate phones from a variety of vendors. The Web server must be configured to recognize the mobile application file extensions, and to run the mobile applications. By using .NET developer applications, such as Visual Studio .NET and the Mobile Internet Toolkit, developers can create mobile applications, using ASP.NET Mobile server controls. A Web page that contains Mobile controls is called a Mobile Form. Mobile controls inherit a code behind the page named System.Web.UI.MobileControls.MobilePage. You can view the output of the WML file within a browser.

REVIEW QUESTIONS

1. Which service is used to deliver e-mail to another server?

   a. PopMail Server

   b. Web Publishing

   c. FTP Server

   d. SMTP Server

2. The CDONTS component creates the e-mail message and places the message in which folder?

   a. Pickup

   b. Queue

   c. Drop

   d. Badmail

3. Where is the e-mail message placed after all attempts to deliver the message have failed?

   a. Pickup

   b. Queue

   c. Drop

   d. Badmail

4. Where is the default main e-mail folder located?

   a. c:\Inetpub\Mail

   b. c:\Inetpub\MailRoot

   c. d:\Inetpub\Mail

   d. d:\Inetpub\mailroot

5. Which administrative tool is used to determine if the Simple Mail Transport Protocol (SMTP) has been started?

   a. Ftp Server

   b. Exchange Server

   c. Services

   d. SMTP Mail Manager

6. Which class provides access to the properties and methods to construct an e-mail message?

   a. MailMessage

   b. MailAttatchment

   c. SmtpMail

   d. System.Web.Mail

7. Which class is used to identify a file that is to be sent with the e-mail message?

   a. MailMessage

   b. MailAttatchment

   c. SmtpMail

   d. System.Web.Mail

8. Which property is used to indicate that the output of the message is HTML?

   a. MailFormat.Text

   b. MailFormat.HTML

   c. MailMessage.Normal

   d. MailEncoding.UUEncode

12

9. Which property is required when creating a MailMessage?

   a. MailMessage.UrlContentBase

   b. MailMessage.From

   c. MailMessage.CC

   d. MailMessage.BCC

10. Which character does not throw an ArgumentException when you create a directory?

    a. <

    b. z

    c. *

    d. ?

11. If you attempt to delete a directory that does not exist, an IOException named _____ is thrown.

    a. DirectoryNotFoundException

    b. SecurityException

    c. IOException

    d. PathTooLongException

12. Which of the following is not a property of the FileInfo class?

    a. CreationTime

    b. lastAccessedTime

    c. LastWriteTime

    d. DirectoryKey

13. What property is used to identify if the file is not to be modified by the user?

    a. ReadOnly

    b. Compressed

    c. NotContentIndexed

    d. Archive

14. If you want to copy a file to a new location, and delete the original file, which method of the FileInfo class should you use?

    a. CopyTo

    b. MoveTo

    c. Delete

    d. MakeFile

15. Which method returns a StreamWriter object?

    a. CreateText

    b. Create

    c. CreateFile

    d. a and b

16. Which tag causes the browser to ignore the HTML tags in the file?

    a. <XMP>

    b. <!-- -->

    c. <// >

    d. <Comment>

17. If you open a file using the OpenText method, you need to close the file with what method?

    a. Close

    b. EndFile

    c. CloseAll

    d. FreeObjects

18. From what namespace do Web Forms inherit?

    a. System.Web.Form.Mobile

    b. System.Web.MobileForm

    c. System.Data.Web

    d. System.IO.Web

19. What organization maintains the WAP standards?

    a. InterNIC

    b. Network Solutions

    c. World Wide Web Consortium

    d. WapForum.com

20. Which markup language is used to build WAP applications?

    a. WML

    b. ASP

    c. VB.BET

    d. ASP.NET

12

HANDS-ON PROJECTS

Project 12-1

In this project, you create a Web page that sends an e-mail message to a single recipient.

1. Start **Visual Studio .NET** and open your **Chapter12** solution.

2. Add a Web Form named **Ch12Proj1.aspx** to the project.

3. Double-click on the page to view the code behind the page. On the first line, enter the following code to import the Mail classes from the `System.Web.Mail` namespace:

   ```
   Imports System.Web.Mail
   ```

4. Enter the following code in the Page_Load handler to declare the variable MM to store the MailMessage object:

   ```
   Dim MM As New MailMessage()
   ```

5. Add the following code to configure the properties of the MailMessage object:

   ```
   MM.From = "yourname@yourdomain.com"
   MM.To = "yourname@yourdomain.com"
   MM.Subject = "Chapter 12 Project 1"
   MM.Body = "I have completed Chapter 12 Project 1"
   MM.BodyFormat = MailFormat.Text
   MM.Priority = MailPriority.High
   ```

6. Add the code following this paragraph. The code uses the Send method of the SmtpMail object to send the message. Then, it releases the variable that stores the Mail object.

   ```
   SmtpMail.Send(MM)
   MM = Nothing
   ```

7. Print your source code for the Ch12Proj1.aspx page.

8. Save the files and build the solution.

9. Right-click on the design page, and then click **View in Browser**. Your page should be blank. The e-mail message has been created and placed in your Pickup folder.

10. Open Windows Explorer. Click the **My Computer** icon, and then double-click the letter of the drive on which your Web server is installed. By default the Web server is installed on drive C. Double-click **Inetpub**, then **mailroot**, and then **Drop**.

11. Right-click the envelope icon, and then click **Open with**. In the window, scroll down until you see Notepad. Click **Notepad**, and then click the **OK** button.

12. Print the page in Notepad.

13. Close the file, close the Drop folder, and close the solution.

Project 12-2

In this project, you will create a Web page that sends an e-mail message to a single recipient. You will retrieve the values for the e-mail message properties from a form.

1. Start **Visual Studio .NET** and open your **Chapter12** solution.

2. Add a Web Form named **Ch12Proj2.aspx** to the project.

3. Add four TextBox controls to the page. The text boxes should be named **txtFrom**, **txtTo**, **txtSubject**, and **txtMsg**. Add a label for each control. Change the Text property of the labels to **From**, **To**, **Subject**, and **Message**.

4. Change the TextMode property of the txtMessage control to **MultiLine** and the Rows property to **10**.

5. Add a button to the page named **btnSend**. The label of the button should say **Send My E-mail Message**.

6. Double-click the **btnSend** button to view the code behind the page. On the first line of code on the entire page, enter the following code to import the Mail classes from the `System.Web.Mail` namespace:

   ```
   Imports System.Web.Mail
   ```

7. Enter the code following this paragraph in the **btnSend_Click event** handler to declare the variable MM to store the MailMessage object:

   ```
   Dim MM As New MailMessage()
   ```

8. Add the following code to retrieve the values from the variables and assign them to the MailMessage object properties:

   ```
   MM.From = txtFrom.Text
   MM.To = txtTo.Text
   MM.Subject = txtSubject.Text
   MM.Body = txtMsg.Text
   ```

9. Add the following code to configure the additional properties of the MailMessage object:

   ```
   MM.BodyFormat = MailFormat.Text
   MM.Priority = MailPriority.High
   ```

10. Add the code following this paragraph. The code uses the Send method of the SmtpMail object to send the message. Then, it releases the variable that is storing the mail object.

    ```
    SmtpMail.Send(MM)
    MM = Nothing
    ```

11. Print your source code for the Ch12Proj2.aspx page.

12. Save the files and build the solution.

13. Right-click on the page, and then click **View in Browser**. Fill out the Web Form with your e-mail in the To and From text boxes. In the Subject text box, enter **Chapter 12 Project 2** and in the Message text box enter **I have completed project 2**. Click the **Send My E-mail Message** button.

12

14. Locate your Pickup file, right-click on the **envelope** icon, and then select **Open with**. In the window, scroll down until you see Notepad. Click on **Notepad**, and then click the **OK** button.

15. Print the Pickup page in Notepad. Close the file, close the Pickup folder, and close the solution.

Project 12-3

In this project, you display the directory properties. The visitor provides the directory URL in a form.

1. Open **Visual Studio .NET** and open your **Chapter12** solution.

2. Add a Web Form named **Ch12Proj3.aspx** to the project.

3. Add a text box named **txtDirectoryName** and a button named **btnGetDirInfo**. Change the Text property of the button to **Submit**.

4. Add an ASP.NET Label control named **lblDirInfo**.

5. Double-click on the page to view the code behind the page. On the first line of code, enter the following code to import the Mail classes from the `System.IO` namespace:

```
Imports System.IO
```

6. Enter the code following this paragraph in the Page_Load handler. If the page has been loaded before, then you can retrieve a value from the text box, and create the DirectoryInfo object.

```
If Page.IsPostBack Then
```

7. Add the following code to display data about the directory in the Label control:

```
Dim myPath As String = txtDirectoryName.Text
Dim DD As DirectoryInfo = _
New DirectoryInfo("c:\inetpub\wwwroot\Chapter12\Users\")"
lblDirInfo.Text = _
"<b>Directory Properties for " & myPath _
& "</b><br /><br/>" & _
"<b>The Parent Directory " & _
"</b><br /><br/>" & _
"The full name of the parent directory was " _
& DD.FullName & "<br />"
DD.CreateSubdirectory(txtDirectoryName.Text)
```

8. Add the code following this paragraph to display information about the subdirectories of the directory. You must create a variable named SD, which represents each subdirectory, and use a For-Next loop to rotate through the subdirectories in the directory.

```
Dim SD As DirectoryInfo
lblDirInfo.Text = lblDirInfo.Text & _
"<br /><hr /><b>Subdirectories of " & _
myPath & "</b><br /><br />"
For Each SD In DD.GetDirectories()
```

```
      If SD.Name = txtDirectoryName.Text Then
            lblDirInfo.Text &= myPath & _
            " was created successfully. <br />"
      Else
      End If
   Next
```

9. Add the code following this paragraph to display a default message if the user has not visited the page before. (*Note:* The code for assigning the Text property of the Label control should be entered on one line.)

```
   Else
      lblDirInfo.Text = _
      "Enter the complete path to a" &_
      directory on the Web server."
   End If
```

10. Save the files and build the solution.

11. View the page in the browser at *http://localhost/Chapter12/Ch12Proj3.aspx*. Insert **Ch12Proj3** in the text box and click the button to submit the form.

12. Add graphics, color, fonts, and content to enhance the appearance of the form.

13. Print the Web page, the source code, and the code behind the page.

14. Close the file.

Project 12-4

In this project, you create a Web page from the contents of a form.

1. Open your **Chapter12** solution.

2. Add a Web Form named **Ch12Proj4.aspx** to the project.

3. Add a text box named **txtFileName**, which stores the name of the HTML file. Add a label that says **File Name** next to the text box.

4. Add a text box named **txtContents**, which will hold the new contents of the file. Add a label that says **Body** next to the text box.

5. Add a text box named **txtTitle**, which will hold the title of the new page. Add a label that says **Title** next to the text box.

6. Add a text box named **txtBGColor**, which will hold the background color of the new page. Add a label that says **Background Color** next to the text box.

7. Add a text box named **txtFGColor**, which will hold the foreground color of the new page. Add a label that says **Text Color** next to the text box.

8. Add a button named **btnCreateFile** that says **Create File**.

9. Add a Hyperlink control named **HLReadFile**, which will be used to store the URL to the new HTML page.

10. Add an ASP.NET Label control named **lblFileInfo**.

12

11. Double-click on the page to view the code behind the page. On the first line of code, enter the following code to import the FileInfo classes from the `System.IO` namespace:

```
Imports System.IO
```

12. Enter the following code in the Page_Load event handler to display the default message:

```
If Not Page.IsPostBack Then
  HLReadFile.Text = ""
  lblFileInfo.Text = _
    "Enter your data in each text box to create your Web
    page."
End If
```

13. In Design view, double-click **Create File** button. In the btnCreateFile_Click event procedure, add the code following this paragraph. This will create the file using the value entered into the text box. Then it will set the hyperlink to an empty string so that it is not displayed.

```
Dim FN As String = _
"c:\Inetpub\wwwroot\Chapter12\Users\" & txtFileName.Text
Dim NF As FileInfo = New FileInfo(FN)
lblFileInfo.Text = _
"<b>The File was created! " & "</b><br /><br />"
HLReadFile.Text = "Click here to read the HTML file!"
HLReadFile.NavigateUrl = _
"http://localhost/Chapter12/Users/" _
& txtFileName.Text
```

14. Add the code following this paragraph. This will create variables for the txtTitle, txtBGColor, and txtFGColor fields. It will also detect if the user has entered values for the txtTitle, txtBGColor, and txtFGColor fields. If no value was detected, it will insert a default value.

```
Dim BGC, FGC, MyTitle As String
If txtTitle.Text = "" Then
    MyTitle = "Creating a Web Page"
Else
    MyTitle = txtTitle.Text
End If
If txtBGColor.Text = "" Then
    BGC = "#ffffcc"
Else
    BGC = txtBGColor.Text
End If
If txtFGColor.Text = "" Then
    FGC = "#336600"
Else
    FGC = txtFGColor.Text
End If
```

15. Add the code following this paragraph to create the page and enter the basic HTML tags. The body of the page content comes from the text boxes.

```
Dim SW As StreamWriter = File.CreateText(FN)
SW.WriteLine("<html><head><title>")
SW.WriteLine(myTitle)
SW.WriteLine("</title></head><body BGColor=")
SW.Write(BGC)
SW.WriteLine(" Text=")
SW.Write(FGC)
SW.WriteLine(">")
SW.WriteLine(txtContents.Text)
SW.WriteLine("<hr /><br /><br />Created on ")
SW.WriteLine(Now.Date.ToShortDateString)
SW.WriteLine("</body></html>")
SW.Close()
FN = Nothing
```

16. Save the files and build the solution.

17. View the page in the browser at *http://localhost/Chapter12/Ch12Proj4.aspx*.

18. Enter **Ch12Proj4.htm** in the File Name text box. In the Title text box, enter **Community News**.

19. In the BackgroundColor text box, enter **#99CCCC**. In the Color text box, enter **#330099**.

20. In the Body text box, enter **Welcome to my Web site.**

21. Click the **Create File** button.

22. Click the hyperlink to open the page in the browser. The contents of the file are displayed in the browser.

23. Click the **Back** button in the browser.

24. Go back to Visual Studio .NET and close the file.

12

Project 12-5

In this project, you create a Microsoft Word document from the contents of a form on a Web page.

1. Open your **Chapter12** solution.

2. Add a Web Form named **Ch12Proj5.aspx** to the project.

3. Add a text box named **txtFileName**, which stores the name of the HTML file. Add a label that says **File Name** next to the text box.

4. Add a text box named **txtContents**, which will hold the new contents of the file. Add a label that says **Body** next to the text box.

5. Add a button named **btnCreateFile** that says **Create File**.

6. Add a Hyperlink control named **HLReadFile**, which will be used to store the URL to the new HTML page.

7. Add an ASP.NET Label control named **lblFileInfo**.

8. Double-click on the page to view the code behind the page. On the first line of code, enter the following code to import the FileInfo classes from the System.IO namespace:

```
Imports System.IO
```

9. Enter the following code in the Page_Load handler to display the default message:

```
If Not Page.IsPostBack Then
  HLReadFile.Text = ""
  lblFileInfo.Text = _
  "Create your own Word document."
End If
```

10. In Design view, double-click on the **Create File** button. In the btnCreateFile_Click event procedure, add the code following this paragraph. This will create the file using the value entered into the text box. It will then set the hyperlink to an empty string so that it is not displayed.

```
Dim FN As String = _
"c:\Inetpub\wwwroot\Chapter12\Users\" & txtFileName.Text
Dim NF As FileInfo = New FileInfo(FN)
lblFileInfo.Text = _
"<b>The File was created! " & "</b><br /><br />"
HLReadFile.Text = "Click here to read the doc file!"
HLReadFile.NavigateUrl = _
"http://localhost/Chapter12/Users/" _
& txtFileName.Text
```

11. Add the following code to create the page:

```
Dim SW As StreamWriter = File.CreateText(FN)
SW.WriteLine(txtContents.Text)
SW.Close()
NF = Nothing
```

12. Save the files and build the solution.

13. View the page in the browser at **http://localhost/Chapter12/ Ch12Proj5.aspx**.

14. Enter **Ch12Proj5.doc** in the File Name text box.

15. In the Body text box, enter **This is a test**.

16. Click the **Create File** button.

17. Click the hyperlink to open the page in the browser. The contents of the file are displayed in the browser. If the File Download dialog box appears, click **Open**. If you do not have Microsoft Word, the file opens in Microsoft Word Pad. (*Note:* If your browser does not open the file, open Microsoft Word directly, browse to your Chapter12\Users\ directory, and open the file from Microsoft Word.)

18. Close the browser.

19. Return to Visual Studio .NET and close the file.

Case Projects

E-Mailing a Feedback Form

Your manager at Tara Store has asked you to create a feedback form page. He wants the form to go to the support team. Create a Web page named Ch12Case1.aspx. Add a form with that collects the To, From, Subject, and Message data. The subject should be Customer Feedback. Make the To field have a value of your e-mail address and make the subject read-only so that the visitor cannot change the value of the field. Add a submit button that says Send My E-Mail Message. When the user clicks the button, configure the e-mail objects and send the e-mail message. Set the priority of the e-mail message to high. Enhance the appearance of the form with color, fonts, content, and graphics. Print the form, the source code, and the results from the e-mail message.

Configuring an E-Mail Message from a Database

Your manager would like to be able to send bulk e-mail messages to the store's customers. Create a database named Ch12Case2. (*Note*: You may use SQL Server or Microsoft Access to create your database.) Create a table named Members. Within the table, create a field named MemberID that is an identity field and a primary key field. Create an additional field named MemberEmail that contains the member e-mails. The MemberEmail field should be type varchar and 50 bytes long. Enter three new members with your e-mail address. Create a Web page named Ch12Case2.aspx. Add a form that will collect the From, Subject, and Message data. Make the From field have a value of your e-mail address and make it read only so that the visitor cannot change the value of the field. Add a submit button that says Send My E-Mail Message; the subject should be Announcement. Create a multiline ASP.NET List Box Server control named dlTo that will contain the list of member e-mail addresses. The dlTo field should be populated by the Ch12Case2 database. Then, the list should be sorted by MemberEmail address. (*Hint*: You can use the DataAdapter to create the Data Connection object. Then, create a dataset using the data from the DataAdapter. After this, create a DataView from the DataSet Members table. Then, if the page has not been posted back, fill the DataAdapter and bind the DataView to the list box control. When the page loads, retrieve the values of the member e-mails and place them in the txtTo drop-down list box.) Display the e-mail address in the list box, but the value of each option should be the MemberID field. When the user clicks the button, configure the e-mail objects and send the e-mail message to each member in the drop-down list box. (*Hint*: Because there are multiple items selected, you need to handle this in your code. You can use a For-Each-Next statement to loop through each of the items within the list box items collection. You can then retrieve the specific text value for the list box item that was selected.) Set the priority of the e-mail message to high. When the message has been sent, display a message to the user indicating that the e-mails have been sent. Enhance the appearance of the form with color, fonts, content, and graphics. Print the form, the source code, and the results from the e-mail messages. (*Note*: You can print the e-mail messages from the Drop folder if your e-mail server will not allow you to send mail out of your network.)

12

Creating a File Management System

Your manager has heard that it's more effective to manage files on the Web than to use a file transfer program (FTP) to create and upload files to the Web server. Create a simple Web-based file management system. Create the initial page as Ch12Case3.aspx. Allow the end user to enter the name of the file or directory. The path should be hard-coded as your Chapter12\Users\ directory. Add buttons that allow you to create and delete directories as well as files. The buttons should be named Create Directory, Delete Directory, Display Directory, Create File, Delete File, and Read File. Add a hyperlink to view the Web page in a browser. The directory information should be displayed in a Label control in the same page. When the Read File button is clicked, the file contents should be displayed in the Label control. Save your Web pages in your Chapter12 directory. Enhance the Web pages with graphics, color, and text. Print the page and the source code.

Creating a Mobile Web Application

Your customers are starting to use wireless and PDA devices to connect to the Web site. Create a series of five cards that display information about the online store. Save your Web application to your Chapter12\Users\ directory. The cards should be named Ch12Case4_1, Ch12Case4_2, Ch12Case4_3, Ch12Case4_4, and Ch12Case4_5. Enhance the Web pages with graphics, color, and text. Print the page and the source code.

A

VISUAL STUDIO .NET 2003 REQUIREMENTS, SETUP, AND CONFIGURATION

In this book, you will be using Visual Studio .NET 2003 to create your ASP.NET applications. To support your use of this book, this appendix will give you detailed information on the hardware, software, and software installation requirements that you will encounter throughout the chapters.

Note that this book was written using the default installation for Windows XP Professional SP1 and Visual Studio .NET 2003 Professional. Although this appendix provides additional information on installation, setup, and configuration, it cannot be used as a definitive guide. You should always read the installation manuals and readme guides that come with your software product. These documents contain the latest information related to software requirements, configuration, installation, and compatibility issues.

SOFTWARE REQUIREMENTS – IN BRIEF

The following is a short list of the software requirements for this book:

- *Operating system*: Windows XP Professional SP1
- *Web server*: Internet Information Server (Version 5 or higher)
- *Developer tools*: Visual Studio .NET 2003 Professional
- *Documentation*: Microsoft Developer Network Library (MSDN) or access to the online version of the MSDN at *http://msdn.microsoft.com*
- *Database server*: Microsoft Desktop Engine 2000 (MSDE) SP3 or later
- *Database application*: Microsoft Office XP (Access XP is the required application)

SOFTWARE REQUIREMENTS – IN DETAIL

This part of the appendix gives you detailed information on the software that you will use to work through the chapters of this book.

Operating System

You can install Visual Studio .NET 2003 on a variety of Windows operating systems. Because you are going to create Web applications, you need to have access to a local or a remote Web server. Versions that support local Web servers include the Windows XP Professional and Windows Server family of products. The samples in this book were created on a computer running Windows XP Professional.

There are three versions of the Windows XP Professional disks. The original version is called **Windows XP Professional**. The other versions are called Windows XP Professional SP1 and Windows Professional SP2. Your CD or DVD will identify which version you are installing. SP stands for service pack. **Service packs (SP)** are add-ons that provide updates to the operating system software. The service packs provide updates to the system that include security updates. Note that this book has not been fully tested with SP2.

Once your system is installed, you can identify which version you installed by going to the Start menu, selecting Control Panel, clicking the System icon, and reading the version under System. If you do not see the System icon, you need to change from Category View to Classic View by clicking on the hyperlink in the left pane labeled Switch to Classic View. **Classic View** is the default folder view available in Windows Professional 2000. Windows Professional XP can display the folders in Classic View or Category View. **Category View** displays the folder in a user friendly manner.

A

Windows XP Home edition does not come with a Web server. Therefore, you must use Windows XP Professional, or one of the server products such as Windows Server 2003. The Web server software is included with the same disk that you use to install Windows XP Professional. If you choose to install the software on one of the older server products such as Windows 2000 Server, you must first upgrade the Windows 2000 Server software to service pack 3 or later.

Web Server

Internet Information Server (IIS) version 5 is the Web server software available with Windows XP Professional. With Windows XP Professional SP1, version 5.1 is installed. Either of these versions of IIS will work with the examples in this book. There is also a version of IIS called 6.0 that is currently available. Although ASP.NET and Visual Studio .NET will work with this version of IIS, this book has not been tested with that version.

Visual Studio .NET 2003

There are different versions of Visual Studio .NET, as shown in Table A-1. The activities in this book will work with any of these versions except the Visual Studio .NET 2003 Standard Editions. This book is not compatible with any of the Visual Studio .NET 2003 Standard Editions.

Table A-1   Visual Studio .NET 2003 software versions

Version	Description and Features
Visual Studio .NET 2003 Enterprise	Most companies will be using **Visual Studio .NET 2003 Enterprise Architect**. Developers within these companies will likely be using the version known as **Visual Studio .NET 2003 Enterprise Developer**. These enterprise versions contain additional tools for creating and managing the application architecture and full versions of various server software programs for developing applications.
Visual Studio .NET 2003 Professional	**Visual Studio .NET 2003 Professional** includes the following programming languages: Visual Basic .NET, C#, J#, and C++. This version does not contain SQL Server, which is the database server. However, you can download for free the Microsoft SQL Developing Environment (MSDE), which is a personal version of SQL Server. Information on how to obtain and install the MSDE is provided in Appendix B.

Table A-1 Visual Studio .NET 2003 software versions (Continued)

Version	Description and Features
Visual Studio .NET 2003 Academic	This version is provided to schools as part of the Microsoft Academic Alliance. Schools are provided with the Visual Studio .NET 2003 Professional version, along with additional tools specifically designed for teachers and students. Faculty can distribute Visual Studio .NET 2003 to their students under limited conditions according to the MSDAA licensing agreement. Because the MSDAA program has been implemented successfully at many institutions and because of Microsoft's requirements, we are no longer able to bundle the software with the textbook. You can find out more information on participating in the MSDAA at *http://www.msdnaa.net*. Volume licensing is also available for Visual Studio .NET.
	The Visual Studio .NET 2003 academic tools include sample application, documentation, and detailed instructions for setting up Visual Studio .NET 2003 in a computer science lab setting. The academic tools also include an Assignment Manager, which provides the ability for students to submit their programs and for faculty to manage their students' progress.
Standard Editions	Students may be tempted to purchase the **Visual Studio .NET 2003 Standard Edition**. Students can purchase Visual Basic .NET, C#, and C++ separately. However, it is important to tell them not to purchase this version. Any of these standard versions of Visual Studio .NET 2003 will not allow them to create Web applications. Therefore, this version will not be compatible with any of the applications covered in this book.

A complete listing of the features, product information, and system requirements can be found through the Visual Studio .NET 2003 Web site at: *http://msdn.microsoft.com/vstudio/*. The following is a list of links to pages that contain more information about Visual Studio. NET.

- Features: *http://msdn.microsoft.com/vstudio/productinfo/overview/academic/features/comparison.aspx*.

- Product information: *http://msdn.microsoft.com/vstudio/productinfo/*.

- System requirements: *http://msdn.microsoft.com/vstudio/productinfo/sysreqs/default.aspx*

MSDN Library

The documentation for Visual Studio .NET Professional is provided in the MSDN Library. The **MSDN Library** contains help files, documentation, and other resources related to most of the Microsoft products, including Visual Studio .NET, the MSDE, SQL Server, Access XP, and IIS.

A

You can install the MSDN Library software using the disks provided with Visual Studio .NET Professional. You may also have access to more up to date versions of the library if you own a subscription to the library. If you have a subscription, Microsoft will send you an updated library disk about four to six times a year. Information about the subscriptions to the library is available at *http://msdn.microsoft.com/*.

The MSDN Library takes up a significant amount of hard drive disk space. If you install the optional MSDN Library documentation, you will need an additional 1.9 GB of hard drive space. Schools may install the MSDN Library in a shared location where all students would have access. You can choose to run the MSDN Library off of the disk media or a network drive. Note, of course, that students would not be able to access these files from an off-campus location.

You can also access much of the .NET documentation online at the MSDN Library at *http://msdn.microsoft.com/library/default.asp*. This book contains many references to online documentation at the MSDN Library. However, remember that online versions are subject to being removed, so having a local version is always a good idea.

Database Server

The **Microsoft Desktop Engine (MSDE)** is a single user version of the Microsoft SQL Server. It is available with several service packs. This book was tested with MSDE 2000 SP3. You can learn more about this version at *www.microsoft.com/sql/downloads/ 2000/sp3.asp*. Information on installation and configuration of the MSDE and troubleshooting data connectivity issues is covered in Appendix B. (*Note*: It is also possible to convert the database to Oracle, and use Oracle as the database server. None of the exercises in the book require Oracle. However, Chapter 6 covers connection strings and .NET Data Providers for the Oracle server.)

Database Application

Some of the exercises in Chapter 6 use Microsoft Access as the database application. The chapter demonstrates how to convert the Access databases to the MSDE server. The majority of the exercises are built with the MSDE server.

The activities with Access are provided to instruct the developer on the differences in writing applications with Access and SQL Server. Because there are minimal differences between the actual coding of Web applications that use Access and SQL Server, the reader can modify their code to use the database engine that they prefer. Chapter 6 will provide instruction on how to modify their code to use the database engine that they prefer.

Note that the exercises that are developed with the MSDE are not provided with differential instructions for Access users. There are some differences between the database engines such as the syntax of SQL instructions and ability to use stored procedures that will require the reader to reprogram some their Web application programming code. Although the reader can reconfigure the applications to work with either database engine, the author recommends using the database engine that is listed in the instructions of the exercises. (*Note*: You can open the file in Access XP, and then convert the file to an earlier version of Access. The upsizing wizard is available with Access 2000.)

Other Requirements for the Software

You will need a CD or DVD disk drive to install the software. The retail version comes with multiple CDs or a single DVD. You can also install the software from a network drive. The compressed version of the Visual Studio .NET 2003 Professional file is a very large file, about 575 MB. You would have to download the compressed version, extract the files into a temporary directory, and then run the setup installation files from the temporary directory. The location of the temporary directory is C:\Documents and Settings\[*USERNAME*]\Local Settings\Temp where *USERNAME* is the name of your user account or machine.

If you want to keep the setup installation files, you should extract these files to a different directory. This is too large of a file to realistically download through a dial-up connection. Most Internet hosting providers today limit the amount of data that you can download through the Internet. Therefore, it would be better to install the software from a network share, or distribute disks with the software. You will need a network connection to the Internet, or a modem and dialup account to register the operating system and programming software.

 It's best to install the software off of CD or DVD disk media.

HARDWARE REQUIREMENTS

Visual Studio .NET, Microsoft XP Professional, and Microsoft Office have specific hardware requirements. The information in this section is a listing of those minimal requirements.

The minimum memory required by Visual Studio .NET 2003 is 160 MB of RAM. This is also sufficient for installation of Windows XP Professional. However, it is recommended to have between 256 and 512 MB of RAM to complete the activities in this book and install all of the required software.

In all cases, Visual Studio .NET 2003 requires 900 MB of available space on the system drive, and an additional 3.3 GB of available space on the installation drive during the installation process. If you intend to install this on a single computer, using all of the default settings, it will take approximately 2 GB of free disk space.

The amount of hard drive space required for the OS varies with how you intend to install the product, which version you are using, and which features you install. First you need to have enough hard drive disk space to install the operating system. Microsoft recommends 1.5 GB of hard disk space for Windows XP Professional. If you plan to install the software over a network share, you will likely need additional space. The total amount that is required will vary with the features that you choose during installation.

If you install the complete Microsoft Office XP, it may take almost a gigabyte of hard drive disk space. Because you only need to be able to use Access XP with this book, you do not need to install the samples or documentation, but you do need to install the entire application, including the wizards. If the student completes every activity in the book, this would require about 60 MB of hard drive space, depending upon the graphics and databases the student includes within their Web pages.

Note that there are several ways you can modify the installation and configuration to reduce the hard drive space requirements. When installing Visual Studio .NET, you can uncheck the C++, C#, and J# languages. C++ takes about 493 MB of space, and C# takes about 475 MB of space. J# takes about 165 MB, and Visual Basic .NET takes about 422 MB of space. The .NET Framework SDK takes about 351 MB. Although Chapter 5 discusses C# and J#, you will not be required to use these languages. If you choose, you can later install these languages by rerunning the Visual Studio .NET setup program.

You can install the Microsoft MSDN Library using only the setup files and running the data files off the CD. You will want to install the wizards as you will be using the Upsizing Wizard to upgrade your database to the MSDE database engine.

Note that some of the book data files, such as the TaraStore.mdb database and graphics, are used across multiple chapters. By reusing these files, you can reduce the disk space requirement. You can create a single solution for the entire book, and then create a single project for each chapter. References to images would be to a central project directory.

It is recommended to have at least 256-512 MB RAM and 7 GB hard disk space to install the Windows XP Professional SP1, Visual Studio .NET 2003 Professional, MSDN Library, MSDE database software, and Internet Information Server (IIS) and to perform the activities in this book.

SOFTWARE INSTALLATION PROCESS

In this section, you will learn the nuances of the software installation process.

Operating System

This section is a summary of the steps required to install Windows XP Professional SP1 using the default installation procedure. Before starting the installation, you should always back up copies of your existing data files. Installing a new operating system will permanently delete all of your existing data files. The entire process of installing Windows XP Professional takes about an hour. There are different ways to install the software. You can install the operating system and replace the existing operating system files, or you can perform a clean, new installation.

 This section covers the general steps to install the operating system. Configuration, media, and connection variations can significantly change the installation sequence. Therefore, you should only use this section as a general reference. Always read your software installation documentation thoroughly before installing any product.

To start the process, do the following:

1. Make sure that your computer can start from the CD or DVD disk that contains the new Windows XP Professional software. You may have to change the Boot Sequence settings within your computer's BIOS settings. **BIOS settings** are the basic input and output settings required to turn on the computer and load the hardware devices. To do this for most computers, you need to turn on your computer and press the F2 function key as the computer starts.

2. In the BIOS menus will be a selection for changing the boot order. The **boot order** is the sequence the computer uses when looking for the software to start the computer. You must set the sequence to start looking first on the CD or DVD disk, then the hard drive.

3. Don't forget to save your settings before you leave the BIOS menu. Then restart the computer with the Windows XP Professional CD in the tray. The operating system will boot from the disk, install temporary files into memory, and then start the installation sequence.

4. You must determine if you are going to upgrade your existing operating system or completely install a new operating system. Choose the latter.

5. After reading through the licensing agreement, press the F8 key to continue. If you currently have an existing copy of Windows on your computer, the setup program will ask if you want to repair your system or install a new copy. You must press the Escape key to indicate that you do not want to repair your system; instead, you want to install a new copy of the software.

6. The setup program needs to know which drive to install the system. Hard drives can be split into sections called partitions. Always choose the first partition if you have no other operating systems on your computer. Although it is possible to install Windows XP Professional on a computer with multiple operating systems, in this book it is assumed that you have the system installed on the first partition, which is known as the C: drive.

7. The hard drive is formatted using a specific scheme. Make sure that your hard drive is formatted using NFTS and not FAT or FAT32. NTFS is the format that allows you to implement Windows security on files as well as directories.

8. After selecting the partition to install the software, and installing the system files, the system will ask about regional and language preferences, owner information, a computer name, and an administrator password. Leave the password text boxes empty for now. You can add a password at a later time through the user administrative tools that come with the operating system. You will then be asked to verify the correct date and time, and what time zone you are located in. The computer will install the rest of the Windows files. Then you will be asked about your networking settings. Typical is selected by default. Only select custom if your network administrator has instructed you to set up your network configuration manually. The computer can participate with a group of computers in a workgroup or domain. Workgroups and domains are logical groupings of computers that utilize different methods for networking and securing information. Leave the name of the group WORKGROUP and select Next.

 During the installation you will be asked for your product identification number. After your number is validated, the computer will restart. Make sure that you are using a valid number that you are legally authorized to use!

9. The system will reboot and start Windows XP Professional. Go through the introductory screens, which will set up your computer. You will be asked to use your network connection or dial-up modem to connect to the Internet and activate your copy of Windows XP Professional. If you don't have a connection, you can delay this for up to 30 days. Activation and Registration are two separate concepts. Activation means that your software has been acknowledged by Microsoft and can be used. Registration is where you provide user information such as your name and address. You do not need to register your copy of Windows in order to complete the activities in this book

10. You will be asked to set up your Internet configuration. You can do this if you have the settings from the Internet Service Provider. If you do not, you can skip this and do this at another time. You will be asked to provide a username for logging into the computer. Your user will be granted administrative privileges. After you have finished the setup procedure, the computer will reboot and you can log in and start Windows!

Web Server

You must modify your system before you can install Visual Studio .NET. First, you must install the Web server named Internet Information Server (IIS). IIS is also known as Internet Information Services. You must also make sure that your Web server is configured with the FrontPage server extensions.

Your Web server software will allow you to host one Web site and one FTP site. However, you can have many subwebs within your main Web site. **Subwebs** are Web applications that are located within the logical directory structure of default Web site. **Localhost** is the alias name for your default Web site and is mapped to your c:\Inetpub\wwwroot\ folder. The default Web site can also be called by the machine name or the loopback IP address, which is 127.0.0.1. The **loopback address** sends the signal back to the default IP address for the default network interface card (NIC). The **network interface card (NIC)** is the hardware that is used to connect to other computers. For example, if your machine name was Kalata, you could enter http://localhost, http://kalata/, or http://127.0.0.1.

In this book you will use Visual Studio .NET to create a subweb for each chapter. Visual Studio .NET 2003 refers to these subwebs as Web projects. You will refer to your main Web site as http://localhost/, and subwebs will be referred to as Web projects or Web applications.

Internet Information Server (IIS)

This section will provide you with a more detailed listing of activities required to install IIS. You will need your access to the Windows XP Professional CD during this activity.

1. Go to the **Start** menu, and then click **Control Panel**.

2. Click **Add or Remove Programs**.

3. Click **Add/Remove Windows Components**, which is located on the vertical menu on the left side of the window.

4. Check the **Internet Information Services (IIS)** check box. (See Figure A-1.) All of the server documentation, FrontPage 2000 Server Extensions, Internet Information Services Snap-In, Personal Web Manager, SMTP Service, and World Wide Web server are installed by default, along with other files. This requires about 20 MB. (*Note*: The FTP Service is not installed by default. You will have to install this manually.)

5. Click the **Details** button to open the Internet Information Services (IIS) dialog box.

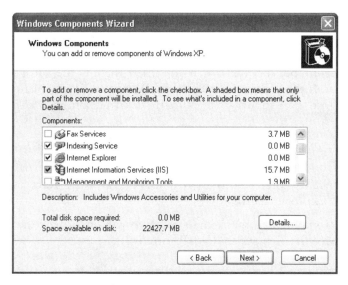

Figure A-1   Installing IIS from the Windows Components Wizard

6. To install the FTP Service, check the **File Transfer Protocol (FTP) Service** check box. (See Figure A-2.)

7. Verify that the FrontPage 2000 Server Extensions check box is checked. This means that the FrontPage 2000 server extensions will be installed by default and configured for the default Web site. If you do not have them installed and configured for the default Web site, you will not be able to publish to your server using Visual Studio .NET.

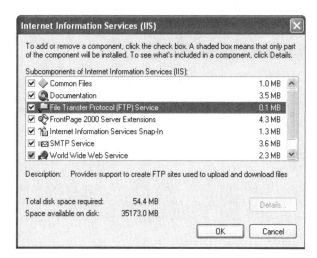

Figure A-2   Installing the File Transfer Protocol (FTP) Service

8. Click the **OK** button, and then click **Next** to continue.

9. You might be asked to insert the original Windows XP Professional CD. If so, insert it. Click the **OK** button, if necessary. The IIS components are installed. (*Note*: It's possible that when you insert the CD the autorun program will start. If the Welcome to Microsoft Windows XP installation window opens, close the window by clicking the **Exit** button.) Click **Finish** to continue.

10. Close the Add or Remove Programs window and then close the Control Panel window.

11. Launch Internet Explorer. (On most systems, you can click **Start** and click the **Internet Explorer** icon.)

12. Type **http://localhost** in the Address bar. Two windows open; they contain the help files for the Web server. (See Figure A-3.)

Figure A-3   Verifying that the Web server and ASP are running

13. Close both browser windows.

 If you want to access the IIS documentation, you will also need to install the Indexing Service. The Indexing Service requires an additional 54 MB of hard drive space. You can do this at the same time that you install IIS from the Add and Remove Components check box list.

A

The two help files that opened when you visited *http://localhost/* indicate that the Web server and FrontPage extensions are working. Note the following:

- The URL of the first page is *http://localhost/localstart.asp*. This page identifies that Windows XP Professional is running. If this page does not display, your Web server does not recognize ASP files. You need to read the directions in the next section of this appendix and reconfigure your extensions, or reinstall your Web server, or register the ASP file extensions with the Web server.

- The second page is located at *http://localhost/iishelp/iis/misc/default.asp*. This page is the Internet Information Services Getting Started page. If this page is not open, it may indicate that your FrontPage extensions are not installed correctly. In this case, you should uninstall the Web server, and reinstall it, making sure that the FrontPage extensions are installed.

FrontPage Extensions

FrontPage extensions are used by Visual Studio .NET to publish Web pages to the Web server. This section will help you verify that the FrontPage extensions are properly installed. If they are not installed correctly, you can use the steps listed in this section to reconfigure the extensions, or you will have to reinstall them using the Web server software.

If your system does not automatically configure the FrontPage extensions, you will need to manually add the extensions to the default Web site using the Internet Information Services management program. The name of the management program to configure the Web server is Internet Services Manager.

Verifying the Installation of FrontPage Extensions

To verify that the FrontPage extensions are installed, do the following:

1. Click **Start**, and then click **Run**.

2. In the Run window, type **%SystemRoot%\System32\inetsrv\iis.msc** in the text box, and click the **OK** button. (*Note:* You can also enter **C:\Windows\System32\inetsrv\iis.msc**, which is the absolute path to the iis.msc file.)

3. In the Internet Information Services window, click the **plus sign** next to the name of your local computer. Click the **plus sign** next to the Web Sites folder. (See Figure A-4.)

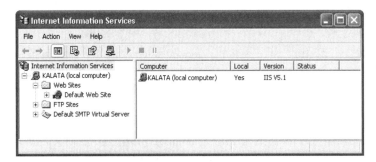

Figure A-4 Managing the default Web site with Internet Information Systems

4. Right-click **Default Web Site** and select **Properties**. The Default Web Site Properties dialog box opens.

5. Click **Server Extensions** tab. In the lower-left corner, verify that the server extensions is version 4.0.2.5322 or higher. If this is not present, then your extensions are not installed correctly. Please finish the steps listed here and then continue with the steps in the following section of this appendix. (See Figure A-5.)

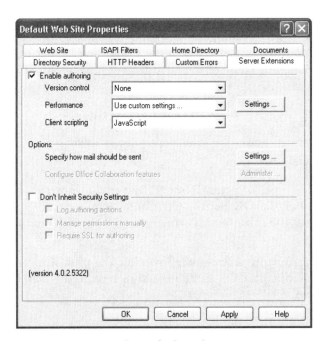

Figure A-5 Using the Default Web Site Properties to verify that FrontPage server extensions are installed

6. In the Default Web Site Properties dialog box, click the **Home Directory** tab. Notice that the default local path to the Web server root directory is c:\ inetpub\wwwroot\. It is important to note the location for the Web server root directory, as this will be the location of all of your Web applications. (See Figure A-6.)

Figure A-6   Using the Default Web Site Properties to identify the path to the Web site home directory

7. Click the **Configuration** button located in the Application Settings section. The Application Configuration window shows a listing of file extensions mapped to executable files. Verify that the file extensions .asa and .asp are in the extensions list. If they are not listed, then your Web server has not been correctly installed. You should uninstall and reinstall your Web server. (See Figure A-7.)

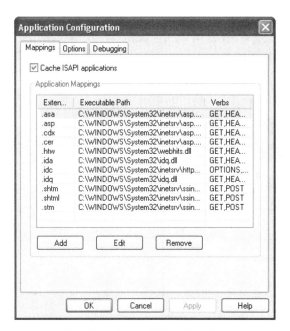

Figure A-7   Mapping of file extensions

8. Click **Cancel** to close the Application Configuration window.

9. Close the Default Web Site Properties dialog box.

10. Click **File** on the menu bar, and then click **Exit** to close the Internet Information Services window.

Configuring FrontPage Extensions

If your FrontPage extensions are not installed, you can try to install and configure them several ways, such as through the Internet Information Services using the Microsoft Management Console (MMC) window. Some applications such as Microsoft Office XP may install the FrontPage extensions. The steps in this section will help you configure the extensions through the Internet Information Services window. (*Note*: Do not complete these steps if your FrontPage extensions are installed correctly.)

It is better to reinstall the Web server with the FrontPage extensions than to try to configure them through the MMC. Configuring the FrontPage extension will modify existing projects such as creating new directories that Visual Studio .NET doesn't require.

1. Click **Start**, and then click **Run**.

2. In the Run window, type **%SystemRoot%\System32\inetsrv\iis.msc** in the text box, and click the **OK** button. (*Note*: You can also enter C:\Windows\ System32\inetsrv\iis.msc, which is the absolute path of this file on most computer systems.)

A

3. In the Internet Information Services window, click the **plus sign** next to the name of your local computer. Click the **plus sign** next to the Web Sites folder.

4. Right-click **Default Web Site**, point to **All Tasks**, and click **Configure Server Extensions**.

5. Complete the wizard by accepting the defaults.

6. Click **Finish** to complete your use of the wizard.

7. Click **File** on the menu bar, and then click **Exit** to close the Internet Information Services window.

If your FrontPage extensions are installed but not working correctly, there is a way to try to fix them without reinstalling the Web server, as shown in the following step sequence. (*Note*: Do not complete these steps if your FrontPage extensions are configured correctly.)

To fix the extensions:

1. Click **Start**, and then click **Run**.

2. In the Run window, type **C:\Windows\System32\inetsrv\iis.msc** in the text box, and click the **OK** button. (*Note*: You can also enter %SystemRoot%\ System32\inetsrv\iis.msc instead of the absolute path.)

3. In the Internet Information Services window, click the plus sign next to the name of your local computer. Click the **plus** sign next to the Web Sites folder.

4. Right-click **Default Web Site**, point to **All Tasks**, and then select **Check Server Extensions**. (See Figure A-8.)

Figure A-8   Checking FrontPage server extensions

5. A dialog box will ask "Do you want FrontPage to tighten up security as much as possible for all FrontPage webs?" Click **No**. The Check Web window lists the webs that were reviewed, if any problems were found, and any

corrective measures taken. For example, FrontPage will create a _private directory if one is not already configured in your Web site. (See Figure A-9.)

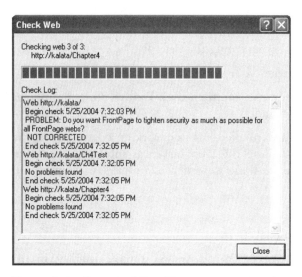

Figure A-9   Report of FrontPage server extensions

6. Click **Close**.

7. Click **File** on the menu bar, and then click **Exit** to close the Internet Information Services window.

 If none of these steps work, and your FrontPage extensions don't work correctly, or the Web server isn't configured correctly, do not install Visual Studio .NET. Rather, you should reinstall your operating system and reinstall the Web server. Make sure to back up all of your files before attempting to reinstall your system. All files are deleted when you perform a clean new installation of Windows XP Professional.

Visual Studio .NET Professional

In this section, you will learn about the basic choices for installing Visual Studio .NET Professional. Of course, the potential installation media include DVDs, multiple CDs, a network share, or the downloaded installation program. Therefore the steps to the installation of the program will vary with the type of medium, the version you are installing, and the configuration of your computer system.

Before the program installs, you may need to update your system with the Visual Studio .NET Prerequisites disk, which will update your system with the .NET components and install the .NET Framework. The prerequisites may be included with your installation disks. The entire process can take 1–2 hours, depending upon the speed of your

CD-ROM drive, the speed of your processor, memory, and the components that are selected during the installation process.

> If you do not require J#, C++, or C#, you can significantly decrease the installation time by choosing not to install those components. You can also choose not to install the MSDN documentation. The MSDN documentation contains information on the .NET Framework, including the classes and code samples. However, each time you attempt to view a help file, the computer would request you to insert the CD.

The following is a summary of the steps to a typical installation. Some steps will require you to insert a disk. Again, this step will vary with each type of installation media. You might be prompted to restart your computer after inserting the disk. If you receive the prompt, go ahead and restart the computer.

1. Insert the Visual Studio .NET CD Disk 1, or open the installation program. The Visual Studio .NET Setup window opens. This is the main window that will guide you through the installation process. (See Figure A-10.)

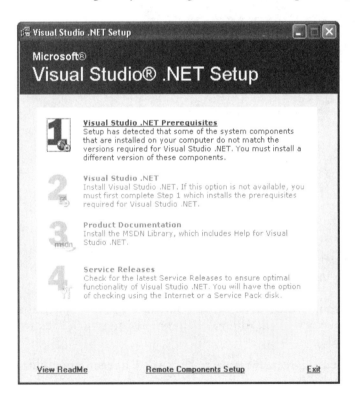

Figure A-10 Visual Studio .NET Setup window

2. Click **Visual Studio .NET Prerequisites**. (*Note:* You might be prompted to restart your computer at this point. If you receive the prompt, go ahead and restart the computer. You might also be prompted to change disks from the first installation disk to the Prerequisites disk. If prompted, change the disks, and click the **OK** button.)

3. Click the **I agree** option button, and then click the **Continue** link to continue.

4. Click the **Install Now!** link. (See Figure A-11.) Installation begins. Note that a reboot will be required after installing Microsoft Internet Explorer 6 Service Pack 1. After your system reboots, the installation program will continue.

5. Click the **Done** link. The installation of the Visual Studio .NET Prerequisites is complete. (See Figure A-12.) The Visual Studio .NET Setup window opens again.

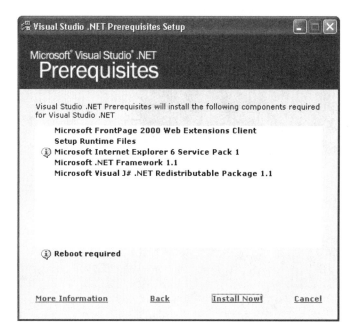

Figure A-11   Installing Visual Studio .NET prerequisites

6. Click the **Visual Studio .NET** link. Some files will be copied to a temporary directory. (*Note:* You may be prompted to switch back to the first installation disk.)

7. When the license agreement appears, click the **I agree** option button.

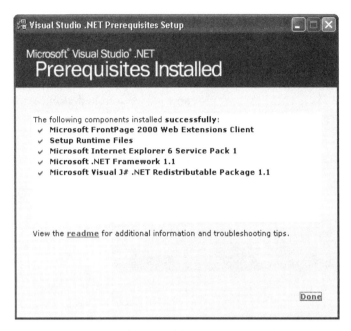

Figure A-12   Completion of the installation of Visual Studio .NET prerequisites

8. Enter the product key. (See Figure A-13.) (*Note*: If you are using a version from the MSDN or MSDNAA, a default product key will be entered and grayed out. You cannot change this product key value.)

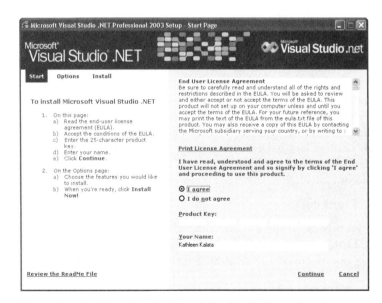

Figure A-13   Entering the Visual Studio .NET product key

9. Click the **Continue** link. The Options page opens. (See Figure A-14.) (*Note*: You can click the plus signs to expand the components to view which options are installed by default. On the right side of the window, you can view the name of the component, the default path to the component, and the space required. You can change the default path for some of the components. By default, Visual Basic .NET, C++, C#, and J# are installed along with the .NET Framework and its samples. The default installation requires 1.5 GB on the hard drive.)

10. Click the **Install Now!** link. (*Note*: During the installation, you may be requested to insert additional Visual Studio .NET disks depending upon your installation media. Respond to the prompts as required.)

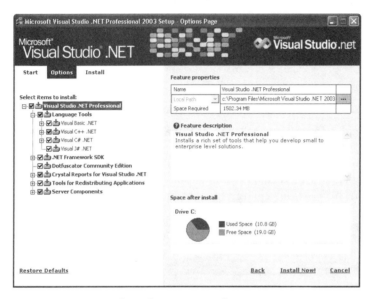

Figure A-14   Visual Studio .NET installation options

11. When the process is finished, you may be presented with a message and links to the installation log and error log files. (See Figure A-15.) (*Note*: If you have an installation error, you should view the file and print copies of the file for future reference.)

12. Click the **Done** link.

13. You are taken back to the Visual Studio .NET Setup window. Click the **Product Documentation** link to install the MSDN Library. The Insert Disk dialog box opens. Insert the requested CD, type the path to the CD, and then click **OK**.

14. The MSDN Setup Wizard will guide you through the installation. The exact steps may vary with the version of the MSDN Library you are installing. On the welcome screen, click **Next** to continue. Click the **I accept the terms in the license agreement** option button, and then click **Next** to continue.

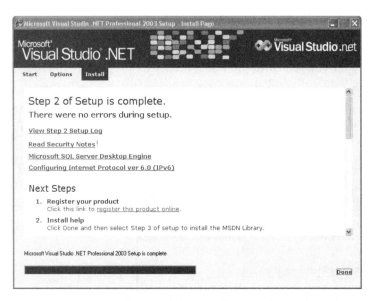

Figure A-15   Completion of the installation of Visual Studio .NET Professional

15. Enter your username and organization in the text boxes and click **Next** to continue.

16. Click the **Full** option button, click **Next**, click **Next**, and then click **Install** to continue. (See Figure A-16.) Insert additional disks as prompted. When the installation is complete, click the **Finish** button.

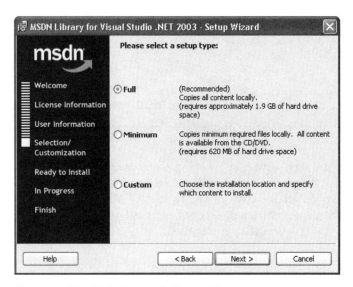

Figure A-16   MSDN installation options

17. You are taken back to the Visual Studio .NET Setup window. Click the **Service Releases** link. You can choose to install the service releases from the Internet or from a disk. Choose the option that works best for you and work through the prompts until you return to the Visual Studio .NET Setup window.

18. At the Visual Studio .NET Setup window, a message will say, "Steps 1 through 4 have been completed." You have completed the installation of Visual Studio .NET Professional. On the Visual Studio .NET Setup window, click the **Exit** button to leave the installation program. (See Figure A-17.)

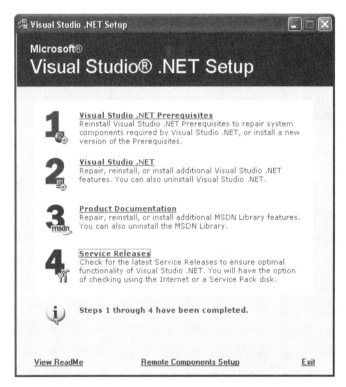

Figure A-17   Completion of the Visual Studio .NET setup program

 Note that you will likely want to install a virus protection program. These programs may alert the user when Visual Studio .NET creates new Web applications, or when you are installing Visual Studio .NET. You can disable your programs during the installation, or grant permission for the installation scripts to run during the installation process.

At this point, you don't need to do any more configuration of Visual Studio .NET. However, you should be made aware of the changes in your system configuration due to the installation of Visual Studio .NET, as follows:

- The setup program registered ASP.NET with the Web server so that the ASP.NET file extensions are recognized by the Web server. You can verify this by going to the IIS management console. (See Figure A-18.)

- Setup registered the file extensions with the ASP.NET engine located at C:\WINDOWS\Microsoft.NET\Framework\v1.1.4322\aspnet_isapi.dll. Notice that the previous version of ASP is still mapped to C:\WINDOWS\ System32\inetsrv\asp.dll, allowing previous applications to run concurrently with ASP.NET. Notice that the path for the ASP.NET dll file is within v1.14322, the version of the .NET Framework installed on your computer. Although you can install different versions of the .NET Framework on the same computer, it is not recommended for beginning students.

Figure A-18   Mapping of ASP.NET file extensions to the ASP.NET worker process

If your file mapping does not appear, you can remap the file extensions using the following steps. (*Note:* Do not complete these steps if your file extensions are mapped correctly.)

1. Go to the **Start** menu and click **Run**.

2. In the text box, type **cmd** and click **Open**.

3. In the command prompt window, type **C:\WINDOWS\Microsoft.NET\ Framework\[Version]** and press **Enter**. (*Note:* The [*Version*] represents the version that you are using such as v1.1.4322.)

4. Type **aspnet_regiis.exe –i** and press **Enter**.

5. Type **iisreset.exe** and press **Enter**.

6. Close the command prompt window.

7. Repeat the steps in the previous exercise to verify that the ASP.NET file extensions are mapped to the Web server.

In Windows XP Professional, all files, software applications and server applications require a Windows user account to be assigned to access and run the application and access the files. The following is a list of users that have been added by the Web server and Visual Studio .NET setup files:

- VS Developer Group

- Debugger Users Group

- SQLDebugger User

- ASP.NET_MachineName User

- IUSR_MachineName User

- IWAM_MachineName User

The VS Developer and Debugger Users groups, and the SQLDebugger user account, were added to this machine. The **VS Developer** group allows developers to create Web applications on the machine. The **Debugger Users** group and the **SQLDebugger** account allows Visual Studio .NET to debug applications locally and remotely. Add only trusted users to these accounts. **Trusted users** would be administrators and developers, but not anonymous users or guests. ASPNET is a user added by the .NET Framework. This user is known as the **ASP.NET Machine Account** because it is used to run the worker process located in aspnet_wp.dll, one of the processes that manage ASP.NET applications on the server. The ASP.NET machine account is the account that is used by ASP.NET Web pages when they access resources on the computer. For example, to create a new file in a folder on the Web server, or to upload a file to the Web server, you will need to give permissions to the ASP.NET machine account. Chapter 4 contains detailed instructions on setting permissions for the ASP.NET machine account.

Of course, IUSR_MachineName and IWAM_MachineName were added by the Web server software. If your machine name was Kalata, then these users would be named IUSR_Kalata and IWAM_Kalata. The **IUSR_MachineName** account is called the **Internet Guest Account** and is used for anonymous access to the Web server. For example, when a user browses a Web page, the connections are logged as occurring by IUSR_MachineName. The **IWAM_MachineName** account is called the **Launch IIS Process Account** and is used to launch applications out of the normal process.

To view the users and groups installed on your system, do the following:

1. Click **Start**, and then click **Run**.

2. In the Run window, type **%SystemRoot%\system32\compmgmt.msc /s**
   in the text box, and click the **OK** button. (*Note*: You can also enter the absolute
   path, C:\WINDOWS\system32\compmgmt.msc /s.)

3. In the left pane, click the **plus sign** next to Local Users and Groups.

4. Click **Users**, and the user accounts appear in the right pane. (See Figure A-19.)

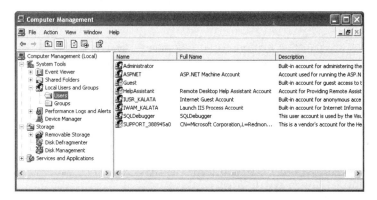

Figure A-19   User accounts added by the Web server and Visual Studio .NET

5. Click **Groups**, and the group accounts appear in the right pane. (See
   Figure A-20.)

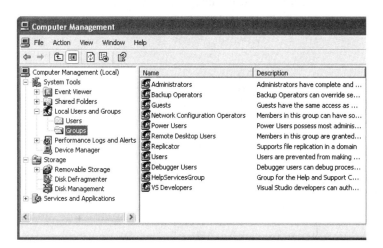

Figure A-20   Group accounts added by the Web server and Visual Studio .NET

6. Click **File** on the menu bar, and then click **Exit** to close the Internet Information Services window.

COMPATIBILITY ISSUES BETWEEN VISUAL STUDIO .NET 2002 AND 2003

One of the benefits of the .NET Framework is that you can install multiple instances of the same application. With Visual Studio .NET, you can even install multiple instances of the .NET Framework itself. ASP.NET and the previous version of ASP can also coexist on the same server.

 The asp.dll is the engine that processed ASP pages. As long as that file has not been removed, you can still process ASP pages with scripting languages such as VBScript.

Visual Studio .NET 2005 was still in beta testing at the time this book was written. This software version appears to have several major changes over the Visual Studio .NET 2003 version. The features within Visual Studio include enhancements in Web Services, XML, Web database, the development tools, and performance tools.

Of course, there are some compatibility issues with the QuickStart Web site and other samples. The QuickStart Web site contains the demonstration samples. The QuickStarts for the .NET Framework versions 1.0 and 1.1 share the same IIS Virtual Directory. Therefore, you cannot run both of them at the same time.

 Version 1.1 is installed with Visual Studio .NET 2003. You do not need version 1.0 to complete the exercises in this book.

B

TROUBLESHOOTING DATA CONNECTIVITY ISSUES

In Chapter 6, you learned how to download and install the MSDE server, the sample databases, and the QuickStart Web site. This appendix will provide you with additional information about the installation and configuration of the MSDE database server and how to troubleshoot database connectivity issues. (*Note*: You must install the MSDE before you can install and configure the samples that come with the .NET Framework.)

INSTALLING AND CONFIGURING THE DATABASE SERVER

It's important to understand that there are multiple ways to obtain the MSDE. The SQL Server 2000 Desktop Engine (MSDE) SP3 contains the desktop data engine, and the client connectivity components. These components include the OLE DB Provider for SQL Server, the SQL Server ODBC driver, and the client Net-Libraries. You can download these directly from Microsoft at *http://download.microsoft.com/download/8/7/5/875e38ea-e582-4ee2-9485-b459cd9c0082/sql2kdesksp3.exe*.

The database components contain the SQL Server Enterprise Manager, OSQL for SQL Server 2000, and the database client connectivity components. You can download the MSDE SP3 directly from Microsoft at *http://go.microsoft.com/fwlink/?linkid=13962* or at *http://download.microsoft.com/download/8/7/5/875e38ea-e582-4ee2-9485-b459cd9c0082/sql2ksp3.exe*. This file is approximately 56 MB. (*Note*: You can order a CD with the MSDE at *https://microsoft.order-5.com/trialstore/product.asp?catalog%5Fname=MSTrialandEval&category%5Fname=Windows+Server+System&product%5Fid=sqlsp3*.)

 More information on the MSDE can be found online at *http://www.microsoft.com/sql/msde/*.

The MSDE is available for free from Microsoft for developing and testing data-driven applications. This version will allow you to build applications for Web sites that serve up to 25 concurrent users. It is not meant for production applications. When you publish your application to a production server, you should upgrade your databases to a production server such as SQL Server or Oracle.

MSDE SP3 has networking protocols disabled so that the database won't connect to other servers. This is done as a security precaution. You can use a production version of SQL Server to complete any of the activities in this book. SQL Server will support more concurrent connections and comes with additional management tools such as Enterprise Manager. You must be logged in with Administrator privileges to install the MSDE and sample Web sites. (*Note*: You can read the details on the installation and configuration at C:\Program Files\Microsoft Visual Studio .NET 2003\SDK\v1.1\Samples\Setup\html\ConfigDetails.htm. You will need to have at least one network connection enabled.)

If you followed the MSDE installation directions in Chapter 6, the default name of the instance of the MSDE will be named NetSDK. So you will refer to the instance as (local)\NetSDK or [*Machine Name*]\NetSDK. The four sample databases installed with the QuickStart Web site are Pubs, Northwind, GrocerToGo, and Portal.

Table B-1 shows several of the setup switches used when installing the MSDE. SAPWD represents the system administrator password, which cannot be blank. For each database, a log file and a data file are created. The log file extension is .ldf and the data file extension is .mdf. These files are stored by default in c:\Program Files\Microsoft SQL

Server\MSSQL$NetSDK\data\. DATADIR is the default location for the log file and database files.

The MSDE supports a maximum of 16 named instances. That means that you can install the MSDE 16 times on one computer. You can change the instance name property known as INSTANCENAME, from NetSDK to a new name such as VSDOTNET. Do not use spaces or control characters in the instance name. You can name your instances or let the setup program number the instances. When the setup program runs, it installs your MSDE instance with a name—the default value for a named instance is C:\Program Files\ Microsoft SQL Server\MSSQL$<*instance_name*>\Binn\.

The setup program appends mssql$<*instance_name*>\binn\ to TARGETDIR. The file path must end with a backslash (\). If there are multiple instances with the same name, the setup program will number instances according to the numbering system the MSDE\Setup directory. When the setup program installs a default instance, it appends mssql\binn to the end of the path specified in the TARGETDIR parameter.

Table B-1   MSDE installation switches

Switch Parameter	Description and Default Values
SAPWD = "sa_password"	Assigns a strong password for the system administrator account (sa). Microsoft has changed the installation so that it's more difficult to set a blank or null password for the sa account.
BLANKSAPWD = 1	Overrides the default value and allows you to assign a blank password to the sa account. Assigning a null, blank, simple, or well-known password to the sa login can be a security risk because it allows unauthorized users to access your data.
INSTANCENAME = "instance_name"	Assigns a name for the instance. The default value for named instances is C:\Program Files\Microsoft SQL Server\ MSSQL$<*instance_name*>\Binn\.
DATADIR = "data_folder_path"	Assigns the folder where the SQL Server databases are stored. Setup program appends mssql\data to the end of the path specified in DATADIR. The default value is C:\Program Files\Microsoft SQL Server\MSSQL\Data\. The default value for named instances is C:\Program Files\Microsoft SQL Server\MSSQL$<*instance_name*>\ Data\. If you install a named instance, the setup program appends mssql$<*instance_name*>\data to the path. Setup builds two other folders at the same location as the Data folder: a Log folder for the database engine error logs, and an Install folder containing installation scripts.

Table B-1 MSDE installation switches (Continued)

Switch Parameter	Description and Default Values
TARGETDIR= "executable_folder_path"	Assigns the folder where the MSDE executable files are installed. The default value is C:\Program Files\Microsoft SQL Server\MSSQL\Binn\.
SECURITYMODE=SQL	Assigns mixed mode for authentication, so that the MSDE supports both SQL Server Authentication and Windows Authentication connections. If you plan to use Windows Authentication connections, you need to add the Windows local administrator's group to the SQL Server sysadmin role.
DISABLENETWORKPROTOCOLS=n	Network protocols are disabled by default. The MSDE can't directly communicate with other computers on the network. Net-Libraries and addresses are enabled if you set it to 0 or 1. The instance will use User Datagram Protocol (UDP) port 1434.

DATABASE CONNECTIVITY FOR WEB APPLICATIONS

There are two ways to have your Web applications authenticated by the MSDE database server. First, your Web application can be authenticated using Windows integrated authentication. This means that the Web application must connect to the MSDE server using a Windows account. The MSDE defaults to integrated authentication on Windows 2000 or XP computer. Web applications run using a Windows account called [*MachineName*]\ASPNET. This account needs to be given permission to access the MSDE server.

The second method that authenticates a Web database application is SQL Server authentication. SQL Server has the ability to manage users and permissions within the SQL Server software. Because MSDE is a version of SQL Server, you can also manage users for MSDE databases. You can assign a user ID and password that the Web application will use to connect to the MSDE server. SQL Server 2000 will use SQL Server authentication by default. You can modify the user permissions using SQL Server Client Tools or Enterprise Manager. Many Visual Studio .NET users may not have access to these tools. However, you can access the same database server commands by running the osql.exe program. The OSQL program can be accessed through the command line within DOS.

Configuring Windows Authentication for the MSDE Databases

In Chapter 6, the installation steps installed and configured the MSDE server to use SQL Server authentication. The switch named SECURITYMODE was set to SQL which changed the default login authentication mode from Windows NT authentication to

SQL authentication. However, if you used the MSDE setup program defaults to install the MSDE server, then the Web application will use Windows integrated authentication on a Windows XP computer.

If your Web application uses Windows authentication, you may need to change the permissions for the [*MachineName*]\ASPNET user account each time you create a database on the MSDE server. The ASP.NET process runs under the [*MachineName*]\ASPNET user account. In order for the account to access the MSDE database, this user must be granted rights to the MSDE databases. You will run several scripts to add the ASPNET account to have access to your database.

To manually grant access to the [*MachineName*]\ASPNET user account, replace *MachineName* with the name of your computer. First you must place the path to the osql.exe command in your PATH environment variable. The osql.exe program is used to execute SQL Server commands at the command level. The osql.exe program is located by default in the C:\Program Files\Microsoft SQL Server\80\Tools\Binn directory. The two types of environment variables are user and system variables. The environment variables are used to store information such as the location of applications, temporary files, libraries, and commonly used files.

The following steps will allow you to insert osql.exe into the PATH variable. (*Note*: Do not complete these steps if you have installed the MSDE using the installation instructions provided in Chapter 6.)

1. Go to the **Start** menu, and then select **Control Panel**.

2. Double-click the **System** icon and then click the **Advanced** tab. (*Note*: You may need to switch from Category to Classic view.)

3. Click the **Environment Variables** button.

4. In the Environment Variables window, scroll down the System variables pane and locate the Path variable.

5. Click the **Path** variable to select it, and then click the **Edit** button.

6. If the path to osql.exe is not listed in the Variable Value text box, scroll to the end of the text box, add a semicolon, and add the path **C:\sql2ksp3\x86\binn** to the Variable value. Be careful not to delete any of the other paths. Semicolons are used to delineate the path values. (*Note*: The drive letter and path to this program may vary on your system. If you do not know where the program was installed, you can search for the file. Click **Start**, click **Search**, and then click the **All files and folders** hyperlink. In the first text box, type **OSQL.EXE** and click the **Search** button. When the program is found, the path will be displayed in the Search Results window. Close the window.)

7. Click the **OK** button to accept the changes. (*Note*: If the value is there already, click **Cancel**.)

8. Click **OK** and then click **OK** again.

Each time you create a new database with the MSDE database server, you will have to run the following step sequence. (*Note:* Do not complete these steps if you have installed the MSDE using the installation instructions provided in Chapter 6.)

1. To open the command prompt window, go the **Start** menu and select **Run**.

2. Type **osql -E -S (local)\NetSDK -Q "sp_grantlogin '[MACHINENAME]\ASPNET'"** in the text box and click **OK**. A command prompt window will appear for a few seconds and close automatically.

3. Click **Start**, and then click **Run**. Type **osql -E -S (local)\NetSDK -d [mydatabasename] -Q "sp_grantdbaccess '[*MACHINENAME*]\ ASPNET'"** in the Open text box and click **OK**. Then, a command prompt window will appear for a few seconds and close automatically.

4. Click **Start**, and then click **Run**. Type **osql -E -S (local)\NetSDK -d [*mydatabasename*] -Q "sp_addrolemember 'db_owner', '[*MACHINENAME*]\ASPNET'"** in the Open text box and click **OK**. A command prompt window will appear for a few seconds and close automatically.

 If you need to run these commands frequently, it is useful to put these commands within a batch file. Then for each database you would run the batch file once, passing the username and database name as parameters.

There is another method that can be used to modify the database authentication configuration. The **Registry** stores information about your computer and the applications. You can modify the registration for the database server to change the authentication mode from Windows authentication to integrated SQL Server authentication. If you do this, then you do not have to run the osql.exe scripts each time you create a new database. Rather, you would change these settings once. Then, when you create a new database, you will assign a user ID and password to the database. You will be able to use the user ID and password in the database connection strings to authenticate the Web application.

Windows integrated authentication is the default setup for the SQL Server 2000 Server. To change the default authentication mode requires altering the Registry settings. It is very important to understand that if you modify the Registry incorrectly, you could alter the configuration settings for the application or computer that would make your computer inoperable. In other words, your computer may no longer work if you alter the Registry settings. The name of the Registry editor is known as RegEdit or Regedt32.

The following steps will allow you to change the MSDE to integrated authentication in Windows XP. (*Note*: Do not complete these steps if you have installed the MSDE using the installation instructions provided in Chapter 6.)

1. Stop SQL Server.

2. Open the Registry editor application by going to the **Start** menu, and then selecting **Run**.

3. Type **Regedit** in the Open text box and select **OK**. The Registry editor will open.

4. In the left pane, click the plus signs to expand **HKey_Local_Machine**, **Software**, **Microsoft**, **Microsoft SQL Server**, and then **[*Instance Name*]**. [Instance Name] represents the name of the MSDE. Then click **MSSQLServer** once.

5. In the right pane, double-click **LoginMode**. Change the value in the Value data text box default from 1, which represents integrated mode, to **0** for mixed mode.

For each named instance of the MSDE, you need only change the LoginMode value. That is, you need only change the LoginMode text box value from 1 to 2 and click OK. Mixed mode is identified using 0 or 2, and integrated mode uses 1.

Modifying the MSDE Registry settings is discussed in detail in the article named "INF: How to Change the Default Login Authentication Mode to SQL While Installing SQL Server 2000 Desktop Engine by Using Windows Installer," which can be located at *http://support.microsoft.com/default.aspx?scid=kb;EN-US; Q285097*. The article reference number is Q285097 INF.

C

WORKING WITH PROJECT AND SOLUTION FILES

In this book, you will be using Visual Studio .NET 2003 to create your ASP.NET applications. This appendix will provide you more detailed information working with projects and solution files and using the data and solution files.

MANAGING PROJECTS AND SOLUTIONS

The Web server available for Windows XP Professional can only accommodate one Web site. The default Web site is located in the c:\Inetpub\wwwroot folder. However, you can create multiple Web applications within the Web site using subwebs and virtual webs. **Subwebs** are folders beneath the wwwroot directory that are configured as a single Web application. **Virtual Webs** are folders outside of the wwwroot directory that are configured as a single Web application. **Virtual directories** are folders within a Web application that is not located in the same physical directory as the Web application. You can configure Web applications using the Microsoft Management Console (MMC) for Internet Information Server (IIS).

When you use Visual Studio .NET to create a Web application, project files and solution files are created. A **Visual Studio Projects folder** contains a folder for each solution that contains the solution files. By default, the Visual Studio Projects folder located within your user folder such as C:\Documents and Settings\[*Your Windows User Name*]\My Documents\Visual Studio Projects\[*SolutionName*]. Within Visual Studio .NET, you can change the location of this folder. (*Note*: To change the location of the Visual Studio Projects folder, go to the Tools menu, and select Options. In the left pane, double-click Environment, and then click Project and Solutions. The first text box is used to enter a new location for the Visual Studio Projects folder.) It is unlikely that you will need to access the solution files directly.

The solution files contain information about the location of the projects, and how these projects are managed and deployed. A solution can contain more than one project as well as additional solution files. The file extension for the solution file is .sln. Solution names cannot contain any of the following characters: %, %, $, *, |, \, :, ", <, >, ., ?, or /. They cannot contain leading or trailing spaces, or names reserved for Windows or DOS operating system files.

Note that it is useful to include the word "Solution," "soln," or "s" in the solution name, to help differentiate the solution name from the project file name. The solution file is often located with another file with the extension .suo. This is a binary file that contains the user options that are configured when you work with the solution. You can customize the development environment and save your settings within this file. The solution file is never stored within the Web server directory structure. The solution file can contain projects for Web applications that are local or remote, as well as other projects such as Windows applications and Web Services.

The solution file maintains information about the build versions. In Visual Studio .NET, when you right-click on the solution in the Solution Explorer Window, you can select Configuration Manager, which will open the Configuration Manager window. This window allows you to change the build options from debug to active or release. Debug is the default mode for building an application.

The following is a snippet from the WebProject1 Solution file. The long string within the parentheses is a unique Registry key for the WebProject1 class. The unique Registry key is associated with the path and name of the project, the URL, and a reference to a unique Windows Registry stored identifier.

```
Project("{F184B08F-C81C-45F6-A57F-5ABD9991F28F}") =
    "WebProject1",
    "http://localhost/WebProject1/WebProject1.vbproj",
    "{73B32626-C0D5-4D62-A552-0AC373B0A78F}"
EndProject
```

The Web project file contains information about the location of the project files, the referenced assemblies and imported namespaces, and a listing of files contained within the project. The project file extension varies with the programming language used to create the application. Web projects created using Visual Basic .NET contain the file extension .vbproj. These project files can be stored in the Web application's root directory. This file is XML compliant and can be viewed with a text editor such as Notepad. (*Note*: Do not make changes to the project or solution files outside of Visual Studio .NET.) The Web project file is located with an additional file named [*WebProject*].webinfo that keeps track of the location of the project's virtual root directory.

 Whether to use a single solution or not depends partly upon the size of the application. If you have changes to a single source file within a single project, you may have to rebuild one or more projects within the solution, due to project dependencies.

USING THE DATA FILES AND SOLUTION FILES

In each chapter, you will be creating one solution file. Your system may be set up to store the solution files within your user folder such as C:\Documents and Settings\[*Your Windows User Name*]\My Documents\Visual Studio Projects\Chapter*N*, where *N* is the chapter number. It is unlikely that you will need to access these files directly. The project files are stored by default with the Web application files.

You must have access to the data files to perform the activities within this book. The data files are available from the Course Technology Web site at *www.course.com* or through your instructor. The data files are compressed into several compressed files. You can uncompress them using a file compression utility, such as the following:

- WinZip 9.0: *www.tucows.com/preview/194294.html*
- Winace 2.5: *www.tucows.com/preview/194310.html*
- CoffeeCup Free Zip Wizard: *www.tucows.com/preview/194258.html*
- PKZip Standard Edition: *www.tucows.com/preview/308013.html*
- Zip 3.06.1: *www.tucows.com/preview/194312.html*

You can store these files on floppies, or on a hard drive. (*Note*: If you store the files on floppies, you will need to split some of the chapters into multiple floppy disks, a single zip disk, or a single CD. The data files will extract into a single folder with subfolders named Chapter01Data, Chapter02Data, and so on. You can store these folders within a single folder such as ASPNET2ED.) (See Figure C-1.) Within many of the chapters, there are subfolders named images and data. You should keep the same directory structure if you copy your files to floppy disks or burn a CD.

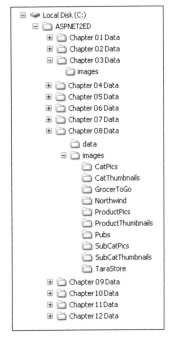

Figure C-1   Data folder structure

In each chapter, you will be asked once to import the data files. There are multiple ways to import files. In some chapters, you will import the files using Visual Studio .NET and in other chapters you will copy the data files into the project using Windows Explorer. If you import the data files using Visual Studio .NET, you will have to manually create any subfolders, and then separately import the files for each folder.

The solution files are provided to instructors only through the Course Technology Web site and with the Instructor's Resource Kit (IRK). The solution files are compressed into multiple zipped files to make downloading easier for instructors. The zipped solution files are extracted into single folders for each chapter. Within each chapter folder, there are several subfolders: Visual Studio Projects, wwwroot, and Microsoft SQL Server. (See Figure C-2.)

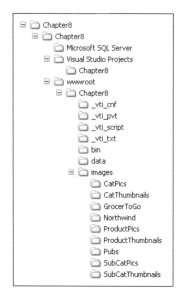

Figure C-2   The book's folder structure for solutions

The **Visual Studio Projects folder** in each of the chapter solution folders contains the solution files for that specific chapter. The **wwwroot folder** contains the Web application files, and the Web project files that are stored in the c:\Inetpub\wwwroot\ Chapter*N* directory, or wherever your Web server root directory is physically located.

Any of the Web pages, source code, style sheets, and configuration items can be opened within a basic text editor such as Notepad, or copied to Visual Studio .NET. You will find large snippets of code from the exercises within the instructor manual. You can copy and paste the code from there into your Web Form and the code behind the page to recreate the assignment.

When you create a database using the MSDE version of SQL Server, two files are created. The location of the log file and data files varies with how you installed the MSDE. If you followed the instructions in Chapter 6, the location is C:\Program Files\Microsoft SQL Server\MSSQL$NETSDK\Data. The **Microsoft SQL Server folder** contains both the log file and the data file. However, you cannot simply drag and drop these files into the MSDE data folder because the MSDE server needs to be configured to recognize these database files. Instructors can use several tools to install the chapter solution databases. Enterprise Manager can be used to create a new database and import the data, table structure, and stored procedures. Enterprise Manager is available with the full version or the Enterprise version of SQL Server. Another alternative is to use the Microsoft SQL Web Data Administrator. It is available for free download at *www.microsoft.com/downloads/details.aspx?FamilyID=C039A798-C57A-419E-ACBC-2A332CB7F959&displaylang=en.*

In most cases, you can recreate the chapter solutions by creating a new project and solution with the same name as the original project and solution, and then import all of the folders and files. You will have to rebuild the application.

If you decide to delete a project, you should first close Visual Studio .NET. Then, delete the entire folder within wwwroot and the solutions folder within the Visual Studio Project folder. You can then recreate the solution with the same name as the deleted solution. (*Note*: Always delete individual project files using Visual Studio .NET. If you delete them in Windows Explorer, the project may still contain references to the original file.)

Some solutions require additional files, such as components and data connections. You will want to recreate these connections to enable Visual Studio .NET to work directly with the chapter solution databases.

SETTING UP ALTERNATIVE CONFIGURATIONS FOR CLASSROOM INSTRUCTION

The student will need access to a server to post or FTP their ASP.NET Web pages. There are many ways to install and configure your Web development environment. You should plan your class hardware and software configuration, and you would likely benefit from consulting with your network administrator. This person will likely have additional information about the specifications of your network and lab, such as where students save files and preferences. If you are looking for additional information, the Visual Studio .NET MSDAA Academic Tools contain a significant amount of information about various configurations within a computer science lab setting.

The projects within this text book were created using the default installation and configuration. The Web projects were created on the local Web server, localhost. The database server used was the local MachineName\NetSDK, which is the MSDE version of SQL Server. This setup works well when students have access to the computer during class and outside of class. However, if the students save their project locally, they may not be able to access the project from another room, or outside of the school.

No matter what configuration is selected, the instructor will need administrative access to the server in order to view and grade homework assignments. The instructor needs to access the Visual Basic .NET code behind the page and the ASP.NET page.

There are different alternatives to publishing your Web projects on a local Web server. The following is a list of ways to handle the publishing of remote Web projects:

- Name Web projects after the student name: http://[*remoteserver*]/Student1_ Chapter2

- Create a virtual directory for each student: http://[*remoteserver*]/Student1/ Chapter1

- Create a virtual directory tree for each class: http://[*remoteserver*]/CIS220/ Section001/Fall2005/Student1/WebProject1

- Store project files on a floppy disk drive, a zip drive, or other removable media: http://localhost/Chapter1

C

Students can alter the names of the project to reflect their student identification or user name. For example, the projects would be named Student1_Chapter2, Student1_Chapter3, and so on. The student would create their application as http://[*remoteserver*]/Student1_Chapter2. The instructor would have to change each of the data files to reflect the change in the project name. For example, in the first line of each Web page is a reference to the project. This reference would have to be changed to the new project name. The other drawback to this option is that the Web directory will become very large.

The instructor can also create a virtual directory each of the students on the Web server. For instance, the instructor could name the folders after the student ID, such as Student1, Student2, etc. The student could create their projects in his or her own directory. When he or she creates a project such as WebProject1, he or she would type http://[*remoteserver*] /Student1/WebProject1 in the location text box in the New Project window. Therefore, the student would be publishing the Web applications in that central directory. The project files are stored in that directory by default. They must be able to access that central directory, and the directory where the solution files are located, from the other computers in your labs. The instructor can tell the students that the first time they create a project, their user directory would be created. (*Note*: The instructor may want to create user accounts and passwords for each student so that they cannot alter another students' files. Of course, the instructor would provide them with full control to their directories.)

The preceding option works well with a small number of students, or where the projects will be deleted each semester. Another option is to create a virtual directory tree where the Web project files would be identifiable based on the class, semester, student, and project. For example, http://[*remoteserver*]/CIS220/Section001/Fall2005/ Student1/Chapter1 could be used to reference a project for a student. Although it's a longer URL for the students to type, it would be easier for the instructors to manage the students' files. In addition, they would be able to remove files based on when they were taught.

Instructors can set up a virtual directory on the network that would reside on a student's floppy disk, which is accessed through a removable drive. Then, instructors would be able to collect the floppy disks and open the files using Notepad or Visual Studio .NET. The only problem here is that the students are limited to storing all of their files on a floppy disk drive, a zip drive, or other removable media. Students may want to store each chapter project on a separate floppy disk. If the instructor permits this, he or she will have to change the path in the Web server settings for each chapter and student.

In addition, some of the projects within the book contain more than a megabyte of data files and images. Storing these files on a single floppy disk is not an option. However, the instructor can store the images in a central location on the Web server, and change the data files to point to the central images directory. (*Note:* The MMC can be used to create and configure the virtual directory. Open the MMC and right click on the default Web site, select New, select Virtual Directory, and click Next. Enter an alias which will be used to reference the Virtual Directory and click Next. Enter the path to the Web project folder on the removable media and click Ok, click Next, and then click Finish. If you view the Virtual Directory property page using the MMC, the local path text box points to the folder on the removable media.)

In earlier chapters, instructors may want to have the student print out the browser view, the source code from the browser, the .vb file, and the .aspx file. Doing this helps show students that the server code generates the client code. It will also help them debug errors that may be related to client scripting and HTML. The instructor would have to manually check the code for errors. This would be useful in the early chapters where students are still learning how to publish to the class server.

Web Server Connection Methods Used to Publish Web Projects

There are issues regarding getting access to the Web server and allowing publishing of Web pages through Visual Studio .NET. Visual Studio .NET uses two methods to publish your Web pages to the Web server. This is the same whether you are publishing to the localhost Web server or remote Web server. The two methods to connect to the Web server and publish the Web projects are file share and FrontPage extensions. When students try to create a project, they will be asked which method they would like to use to connect to the Web server. The instructor can configure the method used to connect to the Web server in the Options menu, as shown in Figure C-3.

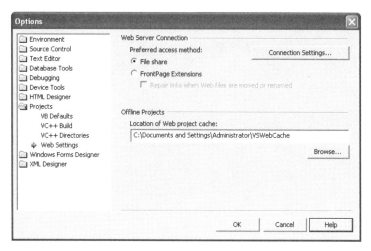

Figure C-3   Web server connection options

Selecting file share indicates that you want to directly access your project files on the Web server through a file share. In this case Visual Studio .NET does not require FrontPage server extensions to be installed on the server.

During installation of Visual Studio .NET, the **VS Developers** user group is created and assigned read/write permissions to the c:\Inetpub\wwwroot folder. Initially, the VS Developers group is created without any members. To create Web projects using file share on that computer, the Web developer needs to be manually added to the VS Developers user group. (*Note:* To modify group membership, go to Start, click Control Panel, in Classic View click Administrative Tools, and then click Computer Management. In the left pane, double-click Local Users and Groups, and then click Groups. In the right pane, right-click VS Developers, and then select Add to Group. Click Add. In the text box, enter the Web developer account name and click OK and then click OK. The Web developer user is added to the VS Developers group.)

Some networks store the project and solution files in a central repository, such as a UNIX server. The server can't run ASP.NET natively. Students' versions of Visual Studio .NET at home would not be configured to go out to the network at school and access the solution and project files. The project and solution files are not required on the Web server, but they are required to manipulate the Web project as an entity. In these cases, the instructor can change the location of the solution files to a removable drive media using the Options menu as described previously. Then, the student could take the disk home and open the solution file from home, even though the project files are stored remotely.

ASP.NET CONTROLS

In this book, you learned about many of the HTML Server controls and Web controls used within ASP.NET applications. This appendix will provide you with additional reference information about these controls and how they are related to each other.

CONTROL HIERARCHY

When you create a project in Visual Studio .NET, references to classes in the .NET Framework are added to the project in a folder called References. References to classes within external Web Services are added in a folder called Web References. For ASP.NET Web applications, the references added included System, System.Web, System.Drawing, System.Data, and System.XML. The System.Web class is required to create the Web Forms and several of the Web controls.

You can read about the class hierarchy and locate the classes, events, properties and methods by creating an ASP.NET Web application and using the Object Browser, as shown in Figure D-1.

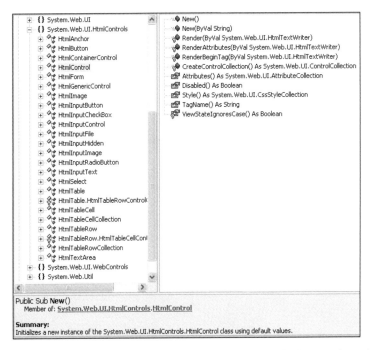

Figure D-1   Viewing the HTMLContainerControl Class in the Object Browser

You can also view the class hierarchy by using the Class Browser application at *http://localhost/quickstart/aspplus/doc/classbrowser.aspx*, as shown in Figure D-2. Additional properties that are inherited from other classes are also shown.

.NET Framework Class Browser

Namespaces

Class System.Web.UI.HtmlControls.HtmlContainerControl

Constructors

Visibility	Constructor	Parameters
public	HtmlContainerControl	( )
public	HtmlContainerControl	(String tag)

Events

Multicast	Type	Name
multicast	EventHandler	DataBinding
multicast	EventHandler	Disposed
multicast	EventHandler	Init
multicast	EventHandler	Load
multicast	EventHandler	PreRender
multicast	EventHandler	Unload

Properties

Visibility	Type	Name	Accessibility
public	AttributeCollection	Attributes	(Get)
public	Control	BindingContainer	(Get)
public	String	ClientID	(Get)
public	ControlCollection	Controls	(Get)
public	Boolean	Disabled	(Get , Set)
public	Boolean	EnableViewState	(Get , Set)
public	String	ID	(Get , Set)
public	String	InnerHtml	(Get , Set)
public	String	InnerText	(Get , Set)
public	Control	NamingContainer	(Get)
public	Page	Page	(Get , Set)
public	Control	Parent	(Get)
public	ISite	Site	(Get , Set)
public	CssStyleCollection	Style	(Get)
public	String	TagName	(Get)
public	String	TemplateSourceDirectory	(Get)
public	String	UniqueID	(Get)
public	Boolean	Visible	(Get , Set)

Hierarchy

System.Object ---> System.Web.UI.Control ---> System.Web.UI.HtmlControls.HtmlControl ---> System.Web.UI.HtmlControls.HtmlContainerControl

Implements

System.ComponentModel.IComponent , System.IDisposable , System.Web.UI.IParserAccessor , System.Web.UI.IDataBindingsAccessor , System.Web.UI.IAttributeAccessor

Subclassed By

System.Web.UI.HtmlControls.HtmlAnchor , System.Web.UI.HtmlControls.HtmlButton , System.Web.UI.HtmlControls.HtmlForm , System.Web.UI.HtmlControls.HtmlGenericControl , System.Web.UI.HtmlControls.HtmlSelect , System.Web.UI.HtmlControls.HtmlTable , System.Web.UI.HtmlControls.HtmlTableCell , System.Web.UI.HtmlControls.HtmlTableRow , System.Web.UI.HtmlControls.HtmlTextArea

Figure D-2   Viewing the HTMLContainerControl Class in the Class Browser

 You can also view more information about hierarchy of controls in the MSDN Library at *http://msdn.microsoft.com/linrary/*.

The following list contains the URLs to the documentation for the HTML Server and Web controls. These pages link to documentation of the classes, as well as the properties, methods, and events for each control within the class.

- System.Web.UI.HtmlControls Class: *http://msdn.microsoft.com/library/ en-us/cpref/html/frlrfsystemwebuihtmlcontrols.asp*

- System.Web.UI.WebControls Class: *http://msdn.microsoft.com/library/ en-us/cpref/html/frlrfSystemWebUIWebControls.asp*

HTML Server Controls

Throughout Chapters 1, 2, and 3, you learned about HTML Server controls, their properties, methods, and events. The HTML controls on the HTML tab in Visual Studio .NET are simple HTML controls. You must change their runat property in order to access the controls on the server. Then, they will be called HTML Server controls. These controls correspond to the basic HTML tags.

The HTML Server controls are created within the System.Web.UI.HTMLControls. HTMLControl class. That means that they inherit the System.Web.UI.Control class but they are also a member of the System.Web.UI.HTMLControls class. The three subclasses within the HTMLControl class are discussed in the list that follows this paragraph. Subclasses that create HTML Server controls will inherit the same events, methods, and properties. Some of these properties, such as ID, are inherited through other classes.

- HTMLImage control: The **HTMLImage** control contains the Align, Alt, Border, Height, Src, and Width properties.

- HtmlContainerControl control (HtmlAnchor, HtmlButton, HtmlForm, HtmlGenericControl, HtmlSelect, HtmlTable, HtmlTableCell, HtmlTableRow, and HtmlTextArea): The **HTMLContainerControl** class is used for HTML controls that implement beginning and ending tags. They share the properties InnerText and InnerHTML.

- HtmlInputControl control (HtmlInputButton, HtmlInputCheckBox, HtmlInputFile, HtmlInputHidden, HtmlInputImage, HtmlInputRadioButton, and HtmlInputText): The **HTMLInputControl** class shares the Name, Type, and Value properties.

You can reference each of these HTMLControl controls by its fully qualified name. For example, the HTMLAnchor, which is also called the Hyperlink HTML Server control, would be referenced as System.Web.UI.HTMLControls.HTMLAnchor.

Additional properties are available to Web controls through inheritance. The System.Web.UI.HTMLControls.HTMLControl class inherits from the System.Web.UI. Control class, and the System.Web.UI.Control class inherits from the Class control within the System.Object class. Therefore, these control properties are available to almost any .NET control, including Web controls and HTML Server controls.

Web Controls

You learned earlier that the tag name for user controls consisted of two parts, the class and the control name. Web controls are also known as ASP.NET controls because their tags are prefixed with "asp:" and followed by the control name. You have seen many of these controls on the Web Forms tab in the Toolbox. ASP.NET controls are commonly referred to as Web controls.

There are several logical groupings of Web controls. These are informal groupings of controls based on their function. They do not have any relationship to the control hierarchy.

However, in future editions of Visual Studio .NET, the number of controls will be increased and there will be a more structured grouping of controls to help facilitate understanding of how these controls are applied.

For example, a form may consist of text boxes and buttons. Therefore, the Form controls group includes the TextBox and Button controls. Data is displayed in a drop-down list or a data table. Therefore, the Data controls group includes the DropDownList and DataGrid control. Controls can enhance the Web site with non-traditional features such as calendars and rotating banners. Therefore, the Rich controls group includes the Calendar and AdRotator controls. The XML control is typically grouped with the Rich controls. However, the XML control and several other controls are not true Web controls because they exist within a different class hierarchy. LiteralControl, TemplateControl, PlaceHolder, Repeater, and Xml all inherit from the System.Web.UI. Control class. The following is a list of logical control groupings of Web controls:

- *Form controls*: Button, HyperLink, LinkButton, DataGridLinkButton, Image, ImageButton, TextBox, CheckBox, RadioButton, Label, Panel, Table, TableCell, TableRow, and DataGridTable

- *Validation controls*: BaseCompareValidator, CustomValidator, RegularExpressionValidator, RequiredFieldValidator, and ValidationSummary

- *Data controls*: CheckBoxList , RadioButtonList, DropDownList, ListBox, DataList, DataGrid, and Repeater

- *Rich controls*: AdRotator, Calendar, and XML

- *Non-traditional controls*: LiteralControl, TemplateControl, and PlaceHolder

The System.Web.UI.WebControls.WebControl Class Hierarchy

Throughout the book, you have learned about many Web controls and their properties, methods, and events. Web controls are created within the System.Web.UI.WebControls. WebControl class. That means that they inherit the System.Web.UI.Control class but are also members of the System.Web.UI.WebControls class.

The subclasses within the WebControl class are contained in the list that follows this paragraph. You can refer to all of these WebControl controls by their fully qualified names. For example, the AdRotator would be referenced as System.Web.UI.WebControls.AdRotator. Some of the classes, such as BaseDataList, do not appear on the Web Forms tab in the Toolbox. However, this abstract base class contains subclasses, such as DataGrid and DataList, that are controls listed on the Web Forms tab. This occurs because both controls require similar events, properties, and methods. Therefore a class was created to provide common events, properties, and methods.

- *AdRotator control*

- *BaseDataList class:* DataGrid, DataList

- *Button control*

- *Calendar control*

- *CheckBox control*: RadioButton

- *DataListItem class*

- *HyperLink control*

- *Image control*: ImageButton

- *Label control*: BaseValidator (BaseValidator contains subclasses BaseCompareValidator, CustomValidator, RegularExpressionValidator, RequiredFieldValidator)

- *LinkButton control*: DataGridLinkButton

- *ListControl class*: CheckBoxList, DropDownList, ListBox, RadioButtonList

- *Panel control*

- *Table control*: DataGridTable

- *TableCell class*: TableHeaderCell

- *TableRow class*: DataGridItem

- *TextBox control*

- *ValidationSummary control*

Properties, Events, and Methods of the System.Web.UI.WebControls.WebControl Class

Subclasses that create Web controls will inherit the same events, methods, and properties. Some of these properties, such as BackColor, can be set through the Properties window when the control is selected. Some of these properties, such as ID, are inherited through other classes. Properties such as ControlStyle are used by developers who work with creating custom controls. Properties such as TagKey are protected and not public. Table D-1 contains some properties available in the System.Web.UI. WebControls.WebControl class. (*Note*: "Get" and "Set" indicate whether you can retrieve or change the value of the property.)

Table D-1 System.Web.UI.WebControls.WebControl properties

Name Accessibility	Type	Description
AccessKey (Get, Set)	String	An underlined letter that allows you to quickly navigate the cursor to the Web control
Attributes (Get)	AttributeCollection	A collection of arbitrary attributes used only for rendering that do not correspond to properties on the Web control

Table D-1   System.Web.UI.WebControls.WebControl properties (Continued)

Name Accessibility	Type	Description
BackColor (Get, Set)	Color	Background color
BorderColor (Get, Set)	Color	Border color
BorderStyle (Get, Set)	BorderStyle	Border style
BorderWidth (Get, Set)	Unit	Border width
ControlStyle (Get)	Style	Style of the Web control
ControlStyleCreated (Get)	Boolean	Value indicates whether a Style object has been created for the ControlStyle property
CssClass (Get, Set)	String	Cascading Style Sheet (CSS) class rendered by the Web control on the client
Enabled (Get, Set)	Boolean	Value indicates whether the Web control is enabled
EnableViewState (Get, Set)	Boolean	Value indicates whether the control saves its state for round trips back to the server
Font (Get)	FontInfo	Font properties
ForeColor (Get, Set)	Color	Foreground color (typically the color of the text)
Height (Get, Set)	Unit	Height
Style (Get)	CssStyleCollection	A collection of text attributes that will be rendered as a style attribute on the outer tag of the Web control
TabIndex (Get, Set)	Int16	Tab index
TagKey	HtmlTextWriterTag	The System.Web.UI.HtmlTextWriterTag value that corresponds to this Web control
TagName	String	Name of the control tag
ToolTip (Get, Set)	String	Text displayed when the mouse pointer hovers over the Web control
Width (Get, Set)	Unit	Width

Additional properties are available to Web controls through inheritance. The properties listed in Table D-2 are available to Web controls because the System.Web.UI.WebControls.WebControl class inherits from the System.Web.UI.Control class, and the System.Web.UI.Control class inherits from the Class control within the System.Object class. Therefore, these control properties are available to almost any .NET control, including Web controls and HTML Server controls.

Table D-2   Inherited properties of a Web control

Name Accessibility	Type	Description	o
ClientID (Get)	String	The control identifier generated by ASP.NET	
ID (Get, Set)	String	Programmatic identifier for the control	
NamingContainer (Get)	Control	Gets a collection of text attributes that will be rendered as a style attribute on the outer tag of the control	
Page (Get, Set)	Page	A reference to the System.Web.UI.Page instance that contains the control	
Parent (Get)	Control	The control's parent control in the page control hierarchy	
TemplateSourceDirectory (Get)	String	The virtual directory of the System.Web.UI.Page or System.Web.UI.UserControl that contains the current control	
UniqueID (Get)	String	A unique, hierarchically-qualified identifier for the control	
Visible (Get, Set)	Boolean	Indicates if the control was rendered and therefore visible	

IMPLEMENTING THIRD-PARTY WEB CONTROLS

The ASP.NET Control Gallery at *www.asp.net/Default.aspx?tabindex=2&tabid=31* contains a myriad of third-party Web controls that you can include within your Web applications. The following is a list of Web sites that contain information on additional third-party Web controls:

- ASP.NET Resource Kit Released: *www.microsoft.com/downloads/details.aspx?FamilyID=aef6aa76-ab88-4264-87b4-8e946ef584d7&DisplayLang=en*

- Controls & Components: *http://msdn.microsoft.com/asp.net/downloads/components/default.aspx*

- Superexpert: Using Third Party Controls: *www.aspx.superexpert.com/default.aspx?id=156*

- The Future of Third-Party Controls: www.*fawcette.com/vsm/2002%5F01/online/online%5Feprods/asp%5Fjgoodyear01%5F24/*

ASP.NET 2.0 contains many more Web controls, which are built-into the developer software. The beta version of Visual Studio .NET 2005 will contain graphical tools to work with these Web controls. The following is a list of Web sites that discuss many of the new Web controls:

- ASP.NET 2.0 Internals: *http://msdn.microsoft.com/asp.net/default.aspx?pull=/library/en-us/dnvs05/html/Internals.asp*

- ASP.NET Home: ASP.NET Whidbey: *http://msdn.microsoft.com/asp.net/whidbey/ default.aspx*

- ASP.NET 2.0 QuickStart Beta: *http://beta.asp.net/quickstart/aspnet/*

BUILDING CUSTOM WEB CONTROLS

D

You can build custom controls and implement third-party Web controls. The following Web sites contain a vast amount of information on how to build controls:

- Authoring Custom Controls: *http://samples.gotdotnet.com/quickstart/aspplus/ doc/webctrlauthoring.aspx*

- Building ASP.NET User and Server Controls Part 1: *www.15seconds.com/issue/ 020319.htm*

- Building ASP.NET User and Server Controls Part 2: *www.15seconds.com/issue/ 020430.htm*

- Building DataBound Templated Custom ASP.NET Server Controls: *http://msdn.microsoft.com/asp.net/using/building/webcontrols/default.aspx?pull=/ library/en-us/dnaspp/html/databoundtemplatedcontrols.asp*

- Creating Custom Controls: *http://msdn.microsoft.com/library/en-us/cpguide/ html/cpcondevelopingwebformscontrols.asp*

- Controls and VS .NET: *www.swarren.net/CustomControls.doc*

- Developing ASP.NET Server Controls and Components: *www.microsoft.com/ mspress/books/5728.asp*

- Wiring-Up Event Handlers: *www.dotnetjunkies.com/tutorials.aspx?tutorialid=232*

E

USING ALTERNATIVE ASP.NET EDITORS

This book was tested using Visual Studio .NET. However, other editors may be used to create ASP.NET Web applications. This appendix gives you information about those editors.

EDITORS TO SUPPORT BUILDING APPLICATIONS

The following is a list of some popular editors that support building ASP.NET applications:

- ActiveSite Compiler 3.1 (Intorel): *www.intorel.com/sitecomp/*
- ASP Express (August Wind Software): *www.aspexpress.com/aspexpress.asp*
- ASP.NET Maker 1.0 (e.World Technology): *www.hkvstore.com/aspnetmaker/*
- ASPWizard 1.1D (ASPWizard): *www.aspwizard.co.uk/*
- BrightSword Designer (BrightSword Technologies): *www.brightsword.com/*
- CodeCharge Studio 2.3 (CodeCharge Studio): *www.yessoftware.com/index2.php*
- CuteEditor for .NET (Cutesoft): *http://cutesoft.net/ASP.NET+WYSIWYG+Editor/default.aspx*
- Demeanor for .NET (Wise Owl): *www.wiseowl.com/products/products.aspx*
- Developers Pad (Developers Pad): *www.developerspad.com/*
- Dreamweaver MX (Macromedia): *www.macromedia.com/software/studio/*
- eWebEditPro (Ektron): *www.ektron.com*
- ExcelEverywhere for ASP.NET (ExcelEverywhere): *www.exceleverywhere.com/article/articleview/37/*
- GXD_edit (GX-Design.NET): *www.gx-design.net*
- HandyHTML editor (SilverAge Software): *http://silveragesoftware.com/*
- Iron Speed Designer (Iron Speed): *www.ironspeed.com/download/*
- NeoScripter ASP Code Editor (NeoScript): *www.neoscripter.com/*
- Notepad (Microsoft): *C:\WINDOWS\Notepad.exe*
- PrimalCode 3.0 (SAPIEN Technologies): *www.sapien.com/primalcode.aspx*
- r.a.d.editor (telerik): *www.telerik.com/Default.aspx?PageId=1586*
- ScriptWorx .NET (SoftLite): *www.softlite.net/scriptworx/index.htm*
- SharpDevelop (IC#Code): *www.icsharpcode.net/*
- SPAW Editor (Solmetra): *www.solmetra.com/en/disp.php/en_products/en_spaw/en_spaw_about*
- TextPad (Helios Software Solutions): *www.textpad.com/*
- VBeXpress .NET (VBeXpress .NET): *www.vbexpress.com/vbexpressnet.asp*
- Visual Studio .NET 2003 (Microsoft): *http://msdn.microsoft.com/vstudio/*

- Visual Studio 2005 Home (Microsoft): *http://lab.msdn.microsoft.com/vs2005/default.aspx*

- Visual Web Developer 2005 Express Edition (Microsoft): *http://lab.msdn.microsoft.com/express/vwd*

- Web.config Editor (Hunter Stone): *www.hunterstone.com/wce*

- Webmatrix (Microsoft): *www.asp.net/webmatrix/default.aspx?tabindex=4&tabid=46*

- XPressDev Studio (Developer Express): *www.devexpress.com/?section=/Products/ActiveX/XDevStudio*

E

WEBMATRIX

WebMatrix is a community-supported, compact Web development tool. The home page for the application is *www.asp.net/webmatrix/default.aspx?tabIndex=4&tabId=46*. You can download the program at *www.asp.net/webmatrix/download.aspx?tabindex=4*. The WebMatrix program supports Web databases and is free. It is compatible with Windows XP Home Edition and does not require a Web server to create Web applications. That is, you can view them locally with the WebMatrix Web server or the IIS Web server. However, you will need to upload your pages to a Web server to deploy your Web pages. You can walk through a guided tour of WebMatrix at *www.asp.net/webmatrix/tour/getstarted/intro.aspx*.

The main difference between Visual Studio .NET and WebMatrix is that Web Forms in WebMatrix consist of one file, with the code behind the page being written at the top of the HTML template file.

Note that Microsoft is releasing a new scaled-down Web developer tool for ASP.NET 2.0. The tool is called the **Visual Web Developer Express Edition 2005**. The beta 1 version of this product was just released when this book went to press. The beta QuickStart site for ASP.NET 2.0 is available at *http://beta.asp.net/quickstart/aspnet/*. You can read more about this tool at *http://lab.msdn.microsoft.com/express/vwd/*.

SQL Server Express 2005 will replace the MSDE. It was available as a beta product when this book went to press. You can use this in conjunction with the Visual Web Developer Express Edition 2005 beta product. However, be careful as beta products have not been fully tested. They are often incompatible with other versions of the same product. In addition, they are not supported by Microsoft.

OTHER WEB DEVELOPER RESOURCES

In addition to the myriad of Web editors that support ASP.NET, there are many sample source projects, Web applications startup kits, and tutorials available from Microsoft and other companies. In addition, WebMatrix provides a connection within the application to the online component gallery known as the Control Gallery. This allows you to add in third-party server controls.

Note the following resources:

- ASP.NET Source Projects: *www.asp.net/Default.aspx?tabindex=6&tabid=41*

- ASP.NET Starter Kits: *www.asp.net/Default.aspx?tabindex=8&tabid=47*

- ASP.NET Control Gallery: *www.asp.net/Default.aspx?tabindex=2&tabid=31*

Index